Great War Stories

Great War Stories

The Colditz Story
P. R. Reid

The Bridge on the River Kwai
Pierre Boulle

The Battle of the River Plate
Dudley Pope

The Dam Busters
Paul Brickhill

Sundial

The Colditz Story
first published in Great Britain in 1952 by Hodder & Stoughton Ltd

The Bridge on the River Kwai
first published in Great Britain in 1954 by Secker & Warburg Ltd

The Battle of the River Plate
first published in Great Britain in 1956 by William Kimber and Co Ltd
Revised edition published 1974 by Pan Books Ltd

The Dam Busters
first published in Great Britain in 1951 by Evans Brothers Ltd

This edition first published in Great Britain in 1978 and reprinted in 1979 by

Sundial Publications Ltd, 59 Grosvenor Street, London W.1.

in collaboration with

William Heinemann Ltd, 15-16 Queen Street, London W.1.

and

Martin Secker & Warburg Ltd, 54 Poland Street, London W.1.

ISBN 0 904230 72 4

Printed in Great Britain by
William Clowes and Sons Ltd

Contents

The
Colditz Story

P.R.Reid
M.B.E.,M.C.

To My Wife Janey

APOLOGIA

Escape books are sometimes said to make escaping more difficult for the future, but the escape stories of the First World War made the majority of POWs in the Second World War escape-conscious. In the First World War escapers were an uncommon breed of men. A spirit was created by the early books which throve and bore fruit.

Minor escape techniques may have been made public by these early books, but they are never criticized for that by the escapers of the Second World War. Besides, much was left unsaid, and that applies even more to the stories of today – thanks to the authors who have deliberately omitted many details of enthralling interest. The different conditions of life in Germany were what our generation was really up against: the Gestapo, the Allied bombing and the Hitler Youth. Big Bertha cannot be compared to Allied air bombardment, nor can Allied air bombardment be compared to guided, stratospheric, atomic warhead rocket missiles. It will be the new conditions which will be the obstacles in the future, not escape books. The inspiration of escape books lives in men's memories and serves to keep alive the spirit of adventure.

ACKNOWLEDGMENTS

This book, written ten years after the events it portrays, would not have materialized without the help of many friends. They are, one and all, former Colditz POWs.

It has been necessary to omit from this edition the drawings by John Watton (who shared my captivity) with which the cloth-bound editions published by Hodder & Stoughton Ltd are illustrated.

Other officers, former Colditz inmates, who have helped me are: Flight Lieutenant H. D. Wardle, Lieutenant-Commander W. L. Stephens, Major P. Storie Pugh, Lieutenant-Colonel A. Neave, Captain K. Lockwood, Captain R. Howe, Colonel G. German, Major H. A. V. Elliott, Major R. R. F. T. Barry and Captain A. M. Allan. Major Elliott's many contributions and unstinted help have been of especial value, and I am grateful to Captain Allan for his correction of the German in the text.

I have been fortunate, too, in finding the whereabouts, on the Continent, of several ex-Colditz POWs of the Allied armies: Dutch, French, and Polish. Lieutenant-General C. Giebel, Major P. Mairesse Lebrun and Lieutenant F. Jablonowski (in the U.K.), in particular, have kindly given me their assistance.

Lastly, to my wife I owe much, for her comments and for her untiring help in the preparation of the material of the book.

P.R.R.

A plan of Colditz Castle is on pages 70–71

PROLOGUE

When I was a boy at school, I read with avidity three of the greatest escape books of the First World War. They were: *The Road to En-Dor* by E. H. Jones, *The Escape Club* by A. J. Evans, and *Within Four Walls* by H. A. Cartwright and M. C. C. Harrison. All of them, as exciting reading, are as fresh today as when they were first published. These three epics lived long in my memory, so that when the fortunes of war found me a prisoner in an enemy land the spirit enshrined in them urged me to follow the example of their authors.

A. J. Evans said that escaping is the greatest sport in the world. In my early twenties I thought that to ride in the Grand National Steeplechase at Aintree would be the epitome of sporting excitement – more so even than big-game hunting. I longed to do both. Since the war and my experiences as an escaper, my one-time ambitions have died a natural death. I feel I have quaffed deeply of the intoxicating cup of excitement and can retire to contemplate those 'unforgettable moments' of the past. I can think of no sport that is the peer of escape, where freedom, life, and loved ones are the prize of victory, and death the possible though by no means inevitable price of failure.

The Second World War had just come to a close when A. J. Evans wrote some further memoirs in a book he called *Escape and Liberation, 1940–1945*. In it he wrote:

> The whole story of Colditz will, no doubt, one day be told, and it will make an enthralling story; but it must be written by one of the men who was there.

This book is the story of Colditz. I was one of the men imprisoned there.

We called Colditz 'the bad boys' camp'; the Germans called it the *Straflager*. An officer had to pass an entrance exam before being admitted through its sacred – the French would say its *sacré* – portals. The qualifying or passing-out test was the performance of at least one escape from any one of the many 'Prep.-school' camps that were dotted all over Germany. Naturally, the qualifying escape exam was not set by the Germans, nor were 'full marks' a guarantee of entry – in fact, the contrary, for the hundred per cent candidate was never available to take up his vacancy. He was out of bounds and, happily for him, 'expelled' for good!

Unfortunately, the nearer the applicant's marking came to a hundred without actually attaining it, the more certain he was of finding a wooden trestle bed and straw palliasse awaiting him in Colditz.

The reader of this book, I feel, would also like to qualify before entering Colditz. He should run the gauntlet as hundreds of us did and pass the exam. So, in order to get him into training, he will, I hope, forgive me if he does not reach Colditz until Chapter IV. If he has read many escape books and is an old-timer, he may skip the early chapters. But at least in my qualifying exam I escaped as a woman – almost the only feminine interest in the book, I am sorry to say – so it might be worth while. . . .

When the reader eventually arrives at Colditz, I shall not waste his time with details that every escaper knows. All the other inhabitants are professionals, and professionals do not demean themselves with the lesser problems. In fact, there will not be time to go into all the details, for that was Colditz.

It was supposed to be impregnable and certainly looked like it for a long time. It was the German fortress from which there was no escape. It had been escape-proof in the 1914–18 War and was to be so again in this war, according to the Germans.

The garrison manning the camp outnumbered the prisoners at all times. The Castle was floodlit at night from every angle, in spite of the blackout. Notwithstanding the clear drops of a hundred feet or so on the outside from barred windows, there were sentries all round the camp within a palisade of barbed wire. Beyond the palisade were precipices of varying depth. A detailed description of the plan and elevations of the Castle is impossible, but the above outline gives an indication of what we were up against.

But the Germans overlooked the fact that successful escapes depend mostly on the accumulation of escape technique, and they gathered together in one place, in Colditz, all the escape technicians of the Allied forces from all over the world. Together with this, they concentrated in Colditz the highest morale it is possible to imagine.

To cite an example, let me mention 'Never-a-dull-moment' Paddon – Squadron Leader B. Paddon, RAF, in other words. He earned his title well, for he was never out of trouble. Time after time his escape preparations were discovered, or he was caught red-handed by the German 'snoops' wielding a contraband file or saw. He earned months of solitary confinement for himself and others, as well as the stopping of 'privileges' for the whole prisoner contingent. Colditz was proud of Paddon long before he escaped successfully. It was ironical that the opportunity for his last escape should have been provided by a court-martial charge earned by him in earlier days when he was busy qualifying for Colditz.

'Never a dull moment' might well have been the motto on the Castle's armorial bearings. If there were not three hundred and sixty-five escape attempts in a year at Colditz, there were not far short of that number in the four and a half years of its war history.

If the reader feels in a mood to launch into the feverish underground activity of a camp full of diehards, let him read on. But he should remember, as I said before, that a little preliminary training may be of advantage. It was at Laufen that not a few of the Colditz escapers began their studies, myself among them.

PART I: APPRENTICE

CHAPTER 1

ESCAPE RECONNAISSANCE

It was June 5th, 1940. We arrived at Laufen, about eighteen miles north-east of Salzburg, on the tenth day of my captivity. It was our final destination and we disembarked. My first impression was of a charming village on the banks of a murmuring river, the Salzach. The inhabitants lined the road and watched in silence as we marched by. The Salzach separates Bavaria from Austria at this point. We saw beside the river an enormous block-like building which looked a little like a medieval Schloss and a great deal like a huge asylum. It was the ancient palace of the Archbishop of Salzburg, sentimentally revered as the place where Mozart composed and played many of his works. To us, it was remarkable, on first inspection, only for the amazing number of windows it possessed; in one wall-face alone I counted over sixty. This was to be our permanent home.

We were the first arrivals. Everything was prepared for us in the way of barbed wire and guards falling over each other. We were paraded while the Commandant made an appearance, surrounded by his hierarchy, and delivered a speech. For the first time, we were searched individually and thoroughly. Our heads were shaven under riotous protest, and we were each given a small aluminium disc with a number on it. Our photos were taken and we were let loose into a small compound as fully recognized prisoners-of-war. Captain Patrick Reid RASC had become *Kriegsgefangen-ennummer* 257. The prison was Oflag VII C.

June 12th brought two hundred more arrivals, making our total four hundred. We were told that when the camp was full it would hold fifteen hundred officers. Many of the newcomers were allotted to our room, No. 66, and among them was Captain Rupert Barry of the 52nd Light Infantry. From the moment of our first meeting we talked escape.

He was sitting on a bench in front of a long kitchen-type table, playing patience with a pack of cards which he had made out of pieces of paper, when I came into the room.

I sat opposite him in silence for a long time, my chin in my hands. My mind wandered hundreds of miles away to a home in England.

The man in front of me continued his game, deliberately, carefully smoothing out and adjusting his pieces of paper. Occasionally he twirled his large guardee moustache with a slow controlled movement of his long fingers. My thoughts switched to him.

'Control. Yes, the man in front of me has certainly taught himself control. Maybe he has need of it. Still waters run deep,' I mused.

He looked up from his game. His dark eyes smouldered, but withal there was kindliness somewhere within and his smile was pleasant.

'I'm determined to get out of this place within three months,' I said, wondering in the next instant why I had confided in him.

'You're an optimist. Why the hurry?'

'I've got a date for Christmas which I don't want to miss. If I leave early in September, I could hope to get a sailing from Gibraltar or Lisbon in time.'

'I wouldn't mind joining you,' Rupert Barry said. 'My wife will never forgive me if I don't escape from here. She'll accuse me of not caring for her any more.'

'She sounds as if she's rather a strong personality.'

'That's one of the things I like about her,' he said, and added: 'You're obviously not married.'

'No, I'm a bachelor and what little eligibility I ever possessed is fading rapidly with every day that passes here.'

'How about a systematic reconnaissance of the premises?'

'Good, let's start.'

Rupert was twenty-nine, about five feet eleven inches tall, and well-proportioned. Considering the circumstances, he was dressed smartly and was an imposing personality with his handsome, rather sallow-complexioned face set off by the big dark guardee moustache and a large chin. Straight-nosed, brown-eyed, with dark-brown hair (after it had grown again!); a man who could play havoc with the female sex, but, in fact lived only for his wife 'Dodo' and his two children. He was a professional soldier and had been educated at King's School, Canterbury.

For several days we scoured the camp together on our reconnaissance tour. We examined all the possibilities of passing the barbed-wire entanglements in the compounds, discussed the pros and cons of rushing the gates, and argued over wall-climbs blatantly suicidal. When the floodlights were switched on at night, we judged the depths and positions of shadows, timed sentries on their beats, and stayed up for hours on end peering cautiously through windows to see if the guards became lazy or changed their habits in the early hours, giving us a possible opening. In the end we found ourselves concentrating on one particular corner of a tall building in the inner quadrangle, and our ideas filtered down to two opposing schemes.

The first, Rupert's idea, was simply a tunnel; the second, mine, involved a long roof-climb and a rope-descent. These were the embryos from which the first escape attempt from Laufen developed. Rupert's plan involved tedious work for months on end. Mine was a 'blitz'. We agreed it was worth making an experiment on my scheme before deciding what plan to adopt. We needed two helpers to act as observers while I did a trial run over the roofs. Sailor Nealy, a Lieutenant of the Fleet Air Arm, and Kenneth Lockwood, a Captain of the Queen's Royal Regiment, joined us. Both of them, without being over-curious, had expressed interest in our 'snooping' and had told us of their intention of making a break. We all four lived in room 66.

We held a meeting and I opened the proceedings. I told Nealy and Kenneth of the alternatives and of our intention to start with the roof. I went on:

'For the trial run we need a night with no moon – the darker the night the better.'

'Yes, but you don't want rain,' said Nealy. 'You'll career off the roof like a toboggan, and you'll have to wear gym shoes anyway.'

'A wind wouldn't matter. In fact it should help,' said Kenneth.

'You see the idea. We need all these conditions if possible. Rupert is the strongest of us, so I suggest he lets me down on the sheet-rope to the flat inter-connecting roof.'

'We'll need at least two sheets; better have three for the twelve-foot drop,' put in Kenneth.

'I'll drop and then carry on to the main roof. Kenneth, you'll have to watch my whole journey and check for visibility, shadows, and noise. Sailor, you'd better keep your eye on each sentry in turn as I come into his line of vision and area of responsibility, and watch for reactions.'

'The idea,' said Rupert, 'is that Pat will go to the far end of the long roof and see if it is practicable to make a sheet-descent outside the prison. There's a sentry in the roadway round the corner, but we don't know how much he can see. Pat can check on that too. A lot depends on the depth of shadow in which the descent will be made.'

'The moon will be nearly gone on June 30th. That's a Sunday,' I went on, 'and the guards should have drunk some beer and may be more sleepy than usual. I suggest we agree on that date, provided the weather is reasonable.'

The date was agreed and we discussed all the details of the climb. We were complete beginners – pioneers – and we had only enthusiasm and determination behind us. I suddenly had an idea:

'Wouldn't it make the climb a cakewalk if we could fuse all the lights? I believe I could do it.'

'How?'

'You know the wires run round the walls of the buildings on insulators, and they're only about eighteen inches apart. It's just a matter of shorting them.'

'And how do you think you can do that?'

I thought for a moment. 'I know. One of the windows in room 44 is only about four feet above the wires and is in pretty good shadow. If we can collect about forty razor-blades I'll attach these with drawing-pins to a piece of wood, forming a conductor and sharp knife at the same time. I can screw the piece of wood on to a broom-handle and there we are.'

'A good idea,' said Rupert, 'and if June 30th is our zero date, then the sooner the fusing is done the better.'

'I meant to fuse them on the 30th.'

'I don't think that's wise. It might create an uproar, and they might get the lights working again just when you were hanging somewhere in mid-air. It would be better to make the fusing a try-out too. Then we can see how long it takes them to repair the fuse.'

'All right,' I agreed, 'then I'll do the job, and while I'm fusing, you three had better take up positions around the buildings to note if any sections of the lighting do not go out with the rest.'

In due course the fusing was carried out. The razor-edged 'short-circuit' worked perfectly. I cut through the heavy insulation in a matter of a minute with a gentle sawing motion. There was a brilliant flash and all the floodlights I could see went out. There was some shouting and running about near the guard-house. In three minutes the lights went on again. This interval of time would not be enough for our purposes.

One of the main problems in escaping, which in course of time and through bitter experience we recognized, was that of deciding at a moment's notice whether all the conditions for an escape were right, or if not, which of them could be ignored. An opportunity once missed might not occur again for months or years, which made one keen to take it; yet if it were taken under adverse conditions, or if more important conditions were misjudged as being of less importance, then the escape was ruined. Another chance was gone and another gap in the enemy's defences closed for good.

There was a second problem. Whether a sentry would shoot or not on detection was entirely a matter for conjecture; probably he would. His orders were to shoot; this had been explicitly pointed out to us by the Camp Commandant at his memorable parade on our arrival. He had delivered a long harangue, and on the subject of escaping had said: 'It is useless to try to escape. Look around you at the impregnable barriers, the formidable array of machine-guns and rifles. To escape is impossible. Anyone attempting it will be shot.' He spoke English well and he spat out the word 'shot' with a malicious staccato that was no doubt intended to put escaping out of our minds for ever. 'These are my strict orders to the guards, who will carry out the command to the letter.' Awed silence was followed by roars of laughter as he added with Teutonic seriousness: 'If you escape a second time, you will be sent to a special camp.'

June 30th was a fine day. Evening approached and the stars came out – not a breath of wind, not a cloud! At 10.30 pm Rupert and I crept from our room and along the corridors, which were irregularly patrolled, to the room where the job was to begin. We looked carefully through the window, and listened. It was disconcertingly light outside, but the shadows were correspondingly dark and there was a new sound which we had not noticed before. The river, the pleasant gurgling stream rushing talkatively down from the mountains, made up for the silence reigning elsewhere. Yes, it was worth trying.

Rupert fetched Nealy and Lockwood, who took up positions at key windows. I estimated the trip would take about an hour and said I would not return earlier than that. Zero hour was 11.30 pm.

The drop was in full view of a sentry about fifty yards away, who could play a searchlight at will on any desired spot. I dropped quietly and quickly to the flat roof as the sentry's footbeats indicated his back was turned. I had stockings on my feet, old stockings cut out as mittens on my hands, and a borrowed balaclava helmet concealing the greater part of my face. All was well. Once on the flat roof I was hidden from view and I continued to the higher sloping roof which ran at right angles to the flat one. I had just succeeded, making a certain amount of noise, in climbing the five feet of the gutter in full view of a second sentry but helped by a shadow, when a commotion began among the guards, a running hither and thither with torches flashing and orders shouted. I lay like a dead thing, spread-eagled on the roof. The commotion increased, but it did not approach the quarter where I was. At midnight a continuous sound of murmuring voices broke out in the most distant of the four courtyards and, after listening for some time, I decided that the noise must be due to the arrival of another batch of prisoners. I continued with a lighter heart, for though the noise was far off, it would help me. As I moved, slates cracked like pistol shots, so it seemed to me, and broken pieces slid to the eaves with a long-drawn-out rattle. I had to cross over the ridge of the roof, because on the near side I was visible as soon as I left the gable end. On the far side I was out of sight and in deep shadow. I tried to spread my weight as evenly as possible and found the best way to move was to lie on my back with arms and legs stretched out and move slowly crabwise. The roof was forty yards long and the drop to the ground was sixty feet. One piece of luck that came my way on this long stretch of the journey was a roof walkway for chimney sweeps running about half the length, but even this made the most terrifying creaks and groans. It frightened the wits out of me, especially when a loose plank fell right off and slid, rattling loudly, down to the edge. I watched, transfixed with horror, waiting for the moment when it would topple over, and then it stopped, wedged in the gutter. I had to control my movements to such an extent that I was in continual danger of cramp. At the far end of the roof I could peer over the gable end and do my reconnaissance.

The end wall of the building descended to a narrow alley outside the prison. There was a sentry who marched to and fro along the street running parallel with the building. By studying his routine and timing his beat, we had previously established that a blind interval of some three minutes might be expected in the alley at each turn of the sentry's walk. We hoped to make use of this, provided there was sufficient deep shadow or other concealment in the alley. That was the purpose of the reconnaissance – a survey of the alley and of its precincts at the time of night when the escape was projected. There were other points to be established too; whether the climb was feasible, the speed at which we could move without making a noise loud enough to attract attention, and whether at the exposed points of the climb the darkness was sufficient.

Three and a half hours later I returned, having spent about half an hour at the prospective point of descent. I nearly failed at the twelve-foot climb back through the window. I was tired and a month's starvation diet had told on me. Rupert hauled me in. I made a most unholy row, but the sentry must have been only half-awake. It was 3 am. The next day we held a second meeting, and I gave my opinion.

'The proposed point of descent isn't good. The nearest anchor for a rope will mean carting along with us about twenty-five sheets or blankets. We would also have rucksacks and boots. The alley is a cul-de-sac, but I'm afraid the shadows are not helpful. The rope would be clearly visible in any position.'

'I heard you distinctly on several occasions,' reported Kenneth, to which Nealy added:

'Once I thought you had fallen off the roof. I couldn't see you because you were on the far side, but there was a long rumble and a crash against the gutter.'

'I think we may as well call it off,' said Rupert. 'If one man without luggage makes all that din, what are four going to do? Frankly, Pat, I think you were saved by the noise of the new arrivals. And, to clinch it, if the rope has got to dangle in the limelight, we shall never get away with it. I couldn't descend sixty feet on a home-made rope and give you time to heave it up again all within three minutes.'

We all agreed and decided to prospect further along the lines of Rupert's tunnel idea.

As for the new arrivals of the night, they turned out to be four hundred officers of the 51st Division who had been captured at St Valéry on the north coast of France on about June 12th. This meant crowding in the rooms, and our No. 66 finished up with fifty-seven occupants. The room was about fifteen yards by twelve yards by twelve feet high. In this space there were nineteen wooden three-tier bunks, half a dozen tables, a heating stove, and ten small wardrobe cupboards. Fifty-seven officers ate, slept and lived in this room, for at that time day-rooms were unheard of.

While I had been concentrating on my idea of escaping over the roofs, Rupert had been doing some quiet 'snooping' on his own. The word 'snooping' soon became recognized camp terminology. It meant touring the camp in a suspicious manner and was applied to both Germans and British. The Germans employed professional snoopers who became familiar figures in the camp. It was extraordinary how few people snooped effectively. Snoopers could usually be distinguished in a crowd a mile away, looking like habitual burglars searching for another safe to break.

Rupert was a good snooper chiefly because it was impossible for anyone to look at him without taking him for a man too honest and proud to demean himself. He noted a small locked room in the corner of the building backing against the alley (cul-de-sac) that I had examined from the roof-tops, and discovered that the room was a semi-basement. One day, while Kenneth kept watch for the German snoopers, Rupert, Nealy, and I undid the lock of the door and went in. We found some steps leading down to the floor, which was about five feet below the outside ground-level. Rupert proposed piercing the wall at floor-level, digging a tunnel across the street, and through or under the foundations of an old stone building at the other side. Nealy preferred crossing under the alley and coming up inside a small lean-to shed against a private house. The walls of the shed were made of vertical wooden slats with gaps in between. We could see piles of wooden logs inside. We adopted Nealy's suggestion because we thought we would have no heavy foundations to circumvent at the far end of our tunnel. As things turned out we were right, although even in this direction we did not know what form our exit would take.

We started to break through the wall on July 14th. I thought it was a propitious day – the anniversary of the storming of the Bastille!

We decided to work two shifts of two hours each per day, and in the afternoon, this being the quietest time from the point of view of internal camp disturbance, and at the same time the noisiest for external street sounds which would help to cover up the sound of our working. We kept the tunnel a complete secret except from one officer, Major Poole, who had been a prisoner-of-war in the 1914–18 War, and whose advice we sought. The routine was simple enough; one man worked at the wall-face, another man sat on a box inside the room with his eye glued to the keyhole of the door looking along the passage, a third man read a book, or otherwise behaved innocently, seated on the stone steps at the only entrance to the building a few yards away from the passage, a fourth man lounged, or exercised, in the farthest courtyard. After a couple of hours the two men outside and the two men inside would change places. Warning of the approach of any German was passed by noncommittal signals, such as the blowing of a nose, along the line, depending upon the direction from which he appeared. The man on the wall-face would immediately stop work on receipt of the signal.

The door of the room was opened by removing the screws holding the latch of the padlock. The latch was screwed up during each shift. The room contained lumber, including a large variety of rifle-range targets. There were painted French soldiers and English Tommies – lying, kneeling, and charging, as well as the usual bull's-eye type. If a German decided to come into the room, the only hope for the men inside was to hide amongst the lumber or in a small triangular space underneath the stone steps. The entrance to the tunnel was in the farthest corner of the room and was hidden in the darkness under an old table. For tools, we began with three stout six-inch nails. After some days we received an addition of a small hammer.

The hammer was the cause of one of the first major camp 'incidents', and gave us a 'friend in need' in a Royal Tank Regiment lieutenant called O'Hara, who as time went on became 'Scarlet O'Hara', one of the most notorious POWs in Germany. His face was so ruddy that the slightest excitement made it live up to the name.

On this particular day, a lorry came into one of the courtyards to deliver goods to the canteen, and although it was guarded by a sentry, O'Hara, with a confederate, 'Crash' Keeworth, secured the hammer and a very fine road-map of Germany from the tool-kit under the driver's seat. Keeworth pretended to steal something from the back of the lorry, distracting the sentry enough to ensure that Scarlet could perform his task with the utmost ease. The loss was, of course, soon discovered. The guard was called out and a special *Appell*, or parade, sounded. Incidentally, this *Appell* gave us some anxious moments, for we had to extract our two men from the room in double-quick time: a contingency for which we always had to be prepared, as we never knew what mischief the other prisoners might be up to.

The Commandant appeared at the parade foaming at the mouth. All his subordinates duly followed suit and shouted themselves into paroxysms of rage which were encouraged by derisive laughter from the British ranks. After interminable haranguing, both in English and German, we were given to understand that all privileges would be withdrawn until the hammer and map were returned. The parade then broke up with catcalls, hoots, and jeers. Scarlet had pulled off his job superbly, and we found a muffled hammer a much better tool than a roughly shaped stone!

After three weeks our tunnel had progressed three feet. We had pierced the stone and brick wall and found loose earth on the other side. Great was our rejoicing. Progress would be much faster now, but it was also obvious that shoring and timbering would be necessary to keep the roof of the tunnel from caving in. We found some lengths of three-inch timber in the target-room where we worked, and these, together with 'bed-boards', of which there was an unlimited supply, carried us the whole length of the tunnel.

Our wooden bunks supported the human body by means of about ten boards spanning the width of the bed. They were about three-quarters of an inch thick and two feet six inches long, and they became invaluable in innumerable ways as time went on. They were the escaper's most important raw material. Bed-boards could be used for roof timbers in a tunnel, carved into dummy pistols or German bayonets, and made into false doors and cupboards. Jumping ahead a little in time (in fact, about a year), a tunnel was built at Laufen under the direction of Captain Jim Rogers, R.E., in which no fewer than twelve hundred bedboards were used.

We learned by experience how best to carry these boards about, and eventually we were confident enough to meet and pass a German officer with a couple of them nursed tenderly under a negligently worn overcoat.

The tunnel now progressed more rapidly. So much so that it became impossible to get rid of the soil quickly enough by the method we employed at first, which was that of taking the rubble out in our pockets, especially elongated for the purpose to reach our knees, and emptying it surreptitiously as we lay on the grass in the compound. Rupert and I were one day carrying out this thankless task.

'At this rate, Pat,' protested Rupert, 'the tunnel will take us six months.'

'The only alternative is to pile up the soil in the target-room, and I don't like that,' I retorted.

'We can hide it in the corner under the steps.'

'Not all of it. The space isn't big enough.'

'We can cover what remains with old targets and rubbish.'

'If the Jerries take more than a glance at the room, they can't fail to notice it.'

'And if we plod on for six months, the Jerries will find the tunnel anyway,' rejoined Rupert.

'Why?'

'It's only a matter of time before we're caught. We take risks every day, and the longer we work the shorter the odds become against us. One day a Jerry will just be in the wrong place at the wrong time. The longer we work the more chance there is of that happening.'

'All right,' I concluded, 'then I agree. We'll make a "blitz" of it.'

In the week following our decision, we progressed three yards.

On the right of the tunnel we ran along the side of an old brick wall. Curiosity as to the purpose of this wall led to a lucky discovery and also to an unlucky incident. We made further measurements and found that we were not outside the main wall of the building as we had thought, but were running beside what was a completely sealed-up room under the lavatories on the first floor. By using a small mirror held out of the lavatory window we could see a manhole cover in the alleyway adjacent to the sealed chamber. We assumed that the chamber was an old sewage-pit, of which the manhole cover was the exit. If we could enter the sewage-pit and go out by the manhole cover, we would have a perfect exit to the tunnel which could be used over and over again. We decided to risk breaking through the wall on our right. It was lucky we made the measurements, for if we had proceeded with the tunnel, thinking we were outside the main wall, we would always have been three yards short in our calculation of the length of the tunnel.

But we nearly wrecked the whole scheme by breaking through the wall on our right! I was working away at the wall, which came away easily. As I removed a final brick, a flood of foul sewage rushed out at me, extinguishing the light. (Light was provided by German cooking-fat in a cigarette-tin with a pyjama-cord wick.) I lay prone in total darkness with a gushing torrent sweeping round me. I shouted to Rupert who was keeping guard:

'There's a flood coming in. I've got to stop it. The stench is asphyxiating. For God's sake, pull me out of the tunnel if I pass out.'

I heard Rupert say:

'I can smell it from here. I'll call you every half-minute and if you don't answer I'll come for you.'

I set about the hole as best I could with bricks and clay mud, in feverish anxiety. The tunnel was built downhill and the flood was mounting! Fortunately the pressure could not have been great on the other side, and after five minutes of frantic work I managed to reduce the torrent to a small trickle. I wormed my way back out of the tunnel. Rupert nearly fell off his box when he saw the appalling object which rose from the hole. Not much sewage had come into the room because of the downward slope of the tunnel made to provide ventilation at the working end. We knocked off for the day to let the flood settle. I cleaned myself up in the bathroom next door, and dry clothing was produced.

Next day I went in again with a light and made a proper dam of puddled clay, of which there was no lack, supported by boards driven into the floor of the tunnel. Needless to say, we abandoned the pit scheme and carried on in a forward direction. There always remained a small leak which necessitated our putting duck-boards along the whole length of the tunnel. As luck had it, the tunnel-level carried us just beneath the base of the main external wall. It would have been a heartbreaking job to tackle three feet of masonry in the confined space of the tunnel. Without further incident, towards the end of August we arrived under the lean-to woodshed at the other side of the alleyway.

Nealy had been given orders, in the middle of August, that he would move at short notice to a naval camp, as he belonged to the Fleet Air Arm. At the same time, with the lengthening of the tunnel we needed more workers. We sought Major Poole's advice. Finally, we asked 2nd Lieutenant 'Peter' Allan, Captain 'Dick' Howe, and Captain Barry O'Sullivan to join us, which they did with alacrity.

Our choice fell on Peter first because he could speak German fluently, and in fact was used as an interpreter with the Germans on many occasions. When the escape took place, it would be helpful to have a German speaker. The rest of us knew nothing of the language. Major Poole warned us to be careful to check up on his credentials: Where had he learnt German? The reply was – at school in Germany. Why was he at school in Germany? His father had business relations with Germany. These and other pointers as to his past were probed, mostly indirectly and unostentatiously through officers who said they knew him before the war.

All this goes to show how, from the start, in prisoner-of-war camps we were suspicious of the possibility of the planting of an 'agent provocateur' in our midst. Officers had read how these were placed in camps in the First World War to spy, and we certainly thought Nazi Germany would be capable of it in this war. Later these agents became known as 'stool pigeons'.

Peter passed the tests – we often laughed about it in later days – and he was as keen as mustard. A 2nd lieutenant of the Cameron Highlanders, standing only five feet six inches, he nevertheless swung his kilt as well as the tallest, and his tough legs showed he could walk long distances. He was fit in spite of the starvation. Educated at Tonbridge, he played both rugby and soccer well, and was an excellent bridge and chess player. He always managed to drive opponents into a frenzy by his unvarying stratagem of taking a pawn or two early in the game, and swopping like piece for like. He and Rupert were a match at bridge.

Dick Howe and Barry O'Sullivan were likewise tested. Neither proved difficult to check up on. Barry was the son of a British General and Dick had been known in England by a large number of the prisoners now at Laufen. Both belonged to the Royal Tank Regiment. Barry was of an effervescent nature and had been for some time in India. He was recommended by Poole for our acceptance on account of his keenness and determination to escape at all costs. The recommendation proved well founded.

Dick Howe was our own choice. He lived in room 66 with us and showed initiative combined with good sense, which made him the possible leader of a second group to escape via our tunnel. Already we had ideas of concealing our tunnel exit so that it could be used repeatedly.

Dick was a Londoner educated at Bedford Modern School and possessing a flair for mechanical engineering, and for wireless theory and practice. He had just been awarded the MC for his gallantry at Calais, where he had been landed with his group at a moment's notice to fight an action postponing the capture of that port by the Germans for several precious days.

He was good-looking and strongly built, if anything burly, and was about five feet ten inches tall. He laughed with a neigh like a horse, had a great sense of humour, and went about everything in a quiet manner with a slight grin as if he were looking for the funniest way of doing it.

Nealy left towards the end of August. I agreed to write to his parents if the escape was successful to let them know how he was faring.[1]

A few days later we had a bad scare. Barry O'Sullivan was digging at the face, I was hauling back the earth in improvised boxes – a tiring job crawling back and forth on one's tummy – and Peter Allan was doing 'keyhole' watch. From outside he received the signal – 'danger, cease work'. No sooner had he warned us than a German non-commissioned officer came down the corridor and, without hesitating, approached our door, unlocked the padlock, and pushed. The door did not open. We had devised a safety-catch on the inside – a rough-and-ready affair. It was our last defence for just such an event as this. The German swore, pulled the door with all his strength, tearing the latch off, then pushed again and peered through the narrow chink, to discover a rough piece of iron barring his way. This delaying action gave Peter Allan just sufficient time to jump down the steps and crawl behind the targets and into the tunnel. We all wore soft-soled shoes, otherwise Peter would have been heard.

A moment later the Jerry burst open the door. What he thought I do not

1 Nealy escaped from Stalag Luft III in the 'Great Escape' of March 1944, when fifty out of seventy-six officers were shot by the Gestapo. Nealy was a survivor.

know, but he must have been deceived by our safety-catch. This was made of rusty-looking material and fell downwards into position very easily so that the explanation might offer itself to a person finding an empty room barred on the inside, that it had fallen into position of its own accord on the last occasion when the door was shut. This we knew was about two or three months before. It was a long chance, but our only one, and it worked. Peter reported action at our end and later we heard the rest from our confederates. The Jerry came in, pushed the targets farther against our tunnel corner and went out again. After an interval Peter was sent out to inspect, but soon scuttled back saying, 'Jerries are returning!' This time several came in, carrying an assortment of targets which they piled up wherever there was room. They then nailed on the latch with some four-inch nails, turning them over on the inside, locked the padlock, and departed. Five minutes later a surreptitious knock on the door told us our own guard was outside. Peter and I went to the door and I whispered:

'We can't get out. They've driven in four-inch nails and turned them over on the inside. You'll never be able to remove the latch.'

'A prison within a prison,' mused Kenneth from outside. 'Can't you bend the nails?'

'Not a hope! The wood will split if we try. The nails are as thick as my little finger.'

'Well, what a pity! You'll just have to stay there until you've starved enough to crawl out under the door.'

'Shut up that nonsense, Kenneth! I've got an idea. Can you fetch me a file?'

'Why, certainly, old man! The ironmonger's shop is just around the corner,' and I heard him chuckling maddeningly on the other side of the door.

'It's not at all funny. You're on the right side of the door, but we're on the wrong side. I'm sure Scarlet O'Hara can produce a file. For heaven's sake, hurry!'

The file was produced in a very short time and passed under the door. I filed the nails through at the point where they were bent over. Kenneth on the outside levered the latch from the woodwork, drawing out the bitten-off nails. We left the room, replacing the nails quickly, and departed. The next day, in the interest of silence, we again shortened the nails and, rebending the filed-off ends, stuck them into their original positions, leaving no trace of the tampering.

The tunnel progressed. We were all interviewed and recommended to have a medical examination to see that we were fit enough for the arduous trek to the frontier. The examination included running up and down four flights of stairs at full speed, followed by a heart test. The result of the medical exam was reported, and unfortunately Barry O'Sullivan was asked to stand down in favour of someone else. His trouble was recurring malaria, contracted in the East. He was far too honest to conceal it from the doctor. The latter considered it a serious handicap and with reason.

We were very sorry to lose Barry. Although it consoled nobody at the time, it is pleasant to recall that Barry escaped shortly afterwards from another camp, and was about the first British escaper to reach Switzerland safely.

We chose Harry Elliott, a captain in the Irish Guards, to take his place. He passed all his tests, and his inclusion was agreed, so that the first escaping party still consisted of six officers. I hoped that others would be able to follow subsequently.

I had an important reason for limiting the first batch to six persons. Our sortie would be made from the woodshed and thence up the side street, for about thirty yards, to the main road. The side street was in full view of a permanent day-and-night sentry-post on a cat-walk about forty yards away from the woodshed alley. Although we would be walking away from him, the sentry would see each one of us. Six men appearing from a little-used cul-de-sac was quite a mouthful to swallow. So much so that I planned we should leave by ones and twos at intervals and, moreover, that at least two of us should dress up as women for the occasion. We also decided that after the escape we should separate for good into two parties of three each. Rupert and Peter Allan agreed to join me as one party, and the other three formed the second. My party made plans to go to Yugoslavia, while the other three were to head for Switzerland.

I asked that Scarlet O'Hara should be placed at the top of the list for any subsequent escape from the tunnel. He was already a man marked down by the Germans as dangerous, and wherever he was seen by a 'snoop', there suspicion followed. He was never long out of trouble and was quite irrepressible. Scarlet soon possessed a wide range of useful tools and implements, odd civilian attire, maps and other escape paraphernalia, which he concealed in various hide-outs all over the camp. He was a Canadian, small and wiry, and he loathed the Jerries so much that he was unable to pass one without muttering semi-audible curses and insults. He had a nature that craved excitement and intrigue; he was never so happy as when he was tinkering with some implement with a view to breaking out of the camp. He and 'Crash' Keeworth were the pet aversions of the Germans.

One day Scarlet was going through one of his hides. It was behind the cleaning-hatch of a chimney-flue. He had a square key to fit the hatch and used the large space within as an extra cupboard – mostly for contraband. The hatch was at the corner of a corridor, about nine feet from the ground.

The Camp Commandant had just declared that Army mess-tins were to be handed in as being illegal escape equipment. Any officer retaining a tin would be liable to heavy punishment. So Scarlet was busy hiding several mess-tins. His 'stooge', that is the officer keeping watch, passed him up the tins one after the other. As he handed the last one, a Goon (the senior Sergeant, or *Feldwebel* as it happened) surprised them. The stooge had only time to say, 'Goons', giving Scarlet's trousers a tug at the same time, and then walk away unconcerned as the Goon approached and stared up at Scarlet. Scarlet's head was inside the hatch and he did not hear the operative word. He shouted:

'What in hell's name do you think you're doing, trying to knock me off my stool?'

No answer.

'There's not enough room in this b—— hole. I reckon some of you guys'll have to find your own holes. I'm not a b—— storage contractor, anyway. B—— those b—— Huns. I'd like to wring their necks and knock their square heads together till their gold teeth fall out. Hey! hold this tin! I've got to make more space.'

Silence.

'Take the b—— tin, I said.'

The mess-tin was taken from his hand by the *Feldwebel*, who started pulling violently at the seat of his pants.

'For crying out loud! You'll have me over. What in hell's name do you want?'

At this juncture Scarlet's ruddy face appeared from the hatch and surveyed his mortal enemy beneath him holding one of his precious mess-tins.

It was obvious that Scarlet was not the right person to assist in building the tunnel. He was too conspicuous. So he was allotted the task of closing it up after our six had departed, with a view to his learning the job and going with the second batch.

Harry Elliott was introduced to tunnel work in a curious way. On his first shift he was given the post of keyhole stooge. Incidentally, this usually entailed suffering from a strained bloodshot eye for several days after the shift. No sooner had Harry taken up his position on this, his first day, than one of the camp's 'athletic types' approached the door. We had various 'athletic types'. Some ran round the compound for hours on end, others walked as if the devil were after them, others again did physical jerks and acrobatics, appearing to stand on their hands for more hours per day than their feet.

The particular 'athletic type' that approached the door was a boxer.

Harry told us the story afterwards:

'The man was obviously punch-drunk from his earliest childhood. His nose told his life-story. I thought he was heading for the bathroom next door. He certainly needed a shower – he was perspiring so much, as a matter of fact, that he looked as if he'd just come from one. He was shadow-boxing his way down the corridor with massive gloves on his fists. He started snorting vigorously as he passed out of my keyhole line of vision. The next thing I knew was a terrific crash against the door which sent me reeling backwards. I quickly put my eye to the keyhole again to see what was the matter. I was sent reeling again as the door shuddered under another blow. Another and another followed in quick succession. He was a formidable opponent even with a door beween us. I shouted at him through the keyhole, but between his loud snorts and the drum-like blows, a ship's siren couldn't have been heard. I just gave up and disappeared into the tunnel. I thought it the best place to be when the Jerries arrived.

'After ten minutes, when the door showed signs of decomposing, the ath-letic type retired – I suppose finally to cool himself off in the bathroom. The silence that followed made me feel I was in a tomb rather than a tunnel.'

Harry had an infectious laugh, almost a giggle, which was irresistible. When he told a story, listeners invariably started to laugh at the beginning and did not stop for a day or two. He was an Harrovian, older than most of us, and had several children. He loathed being a prisoner more than anyone else I knew in the camp, but he never showed it except when he took 'time off' to express his feelings for the German race, the *Herrenvolk*, with a picturesque invective difficult to equal. He was small and wiry, with darting blue eyes set in a sunburnt face. His voice was reminiscent of the 'Colonel Sahib' home from India after years of polo and pigsticking. He said he could always tell whether a man was an 'officer and a gentleman' by asking him to repeat one sentence, namely, 'I saw thousands and thousands of Boy Scouts routing around in their brown trousers.' He tested many officers, roaring with laughter at the result. No offence was ever taken or implied. It was Harry having his fun!

The tunnel grew towards completion and we were under the lean-to shed which I have mentioned before and which we now called the woodshed. We had to determine our exact position. The woodshed contained a pile of logs each about one yard long, and we dare not break cover under the passage of the shed immediately beyond the logs. I found a thin-steel rifle ramrod about three feet long in the target-room. While Rupert observed with a mirror the ground outside the shed from the lavatory window above, I made a small vertical hand-hole in the roof of the tunnel and slowly pushed the rod upwards. As soon as Rupert saw it he was to kick the lavatory wall once and make a mental note of its position. The alarm signal was two knocks in case of danger. The sound carried down the wall and was to be reported to me by a listener in the tunnel immediately beneath the wall foundations. I started at a point I estimated to be just outside the woodshed and pushed the rod upwards, digging away with the same hand until I began to think our tunnel was deeper underground than we had estimated. Suddenly the double knock was heard. I withdrew the rod like lightning and awaited a report. Some minutes later it came – whispered up the tunnel (noise carries like thunder in a tunnel). My rod had been waving about two feet above the roadway, but was so close to the shed that even Rupert had not noticed it for some time.

Now we continued with confidence, and after a few days I broke the surface under the wood-pile and first smelt wholesome fresh air. I was delighted, for whereas I had envisaged perilously removing logs to leave a natural archway, I found the logs were on a platform of wood raised some six inches above the earth. Furthermore, by inspection I found that a wainscot board had been placed along the shed passage against the platform, closing it off down to the ground.

The next thing to figure out was how to make a concealed exit. We were determined this tunnel should work for several escapes. Besides, the position of the exit and of the woodshed made it dangerous to attempt sending off a large number of officers at one time. Eventually I decided to dig away the ground just inside the wainscot and to support the earth of the passage-way with narrow wooden horizontal slats backed against two stakes driven vertically into the floor of the tunnel. Actually Dick did most of the work on his shift, and had to work very carefully and silently, hammering the stakes into the ground. The vertical wall of comparatively loose earth was thus held up by a little wooden dam. We christened it 'Shovewood'. The scheme of opening was simple. When all was ready, the slats would be removed and an opening quickly made at an angle of forty-five degrees upwards and out into the passage way, pulling the earth into the tunnel.

The escaping party having scrambled out, one person remaining behind would close up the tunnel again by replacing the slats one by one and filling the earth back behind them. Everything that would speed up this process was seized upon. Thus to save putting back earth that needed tamping, a couple of small strong wooden boxes were made ready which, placed behind the slats, would fill up much space and save valuable seconds. The final slat immediately beneath the wainscot was only two inches wide. In this way the last layer of earth outside could be spread, then tamped with a flat board and made to merge with the passage-way, the slat would be put in, and the earth backed up behind. It could not be a perfect job, but it was the best we could do, and we estimated that the owner of the woodshed would imagine that a chicken had been there and scratched about, or maybe that a rat had been at work.

The tunnel was ready on August 31st. It had taken just under seven weeks to build, and was eight yards long.

We were pleased with our work, especially when we thought of the slow progress made in the early days when we had stood a pint of beer to the one amongst us who had extracted the largest stone from the wall in each series of working shifts. I remember the first winner was Rupert, with a stone the size of an egg, then I won a pint with a half-brick. We closed the competition with two pints for Rupert when he cleared the wall by removing a piece of masonry twice the size of a man's head, which we could hardly lift.

The next decision ahead of us was the date and time of the escape. It was essential to be able to forecast the movements of the household which occupied the building beside the woodshed. From behind the wainscot in the tunnel, a watch was kept through a tiny peephole, which revealed a doorway into the house, a window and a washing-machine, but alas! not enough of a slatted door opening on to the roadway to allow us to ascertain what kind of a lock, if any, was on this door, which was to be our gateway to freedom. I made a mental note that, when we escaped, I would take a screwdriver with me. It might be useful!

The watch was maintained at first over the whole day, quickly shortening to concentrate on the more quiet periods. A graph was made of movements against the hours. A German woman spent much of her time in the shed.

We needed a definite 'all-quiet' period of at least half an hour, estimated thus: five minutes to open up, twelve minutes (two minutes per person) to sortie, and thirteen minutes to close up the tunnel again.

Two periods showed promise, but not the certainty, of half an hour's quiet. A sentry came on before dusk at the woodshed corner, and left after dawn. In fact, he spent most of the night leaning against the shed, and one fine morning had the audacity to relieve himself immediately over my head. The two periods were: one, immediately prior to the sentry's arrival, and the other immediately after his departure. He usually left at 6 am, and was followed by a patrol. These patrols had always to be reckoned with; some were at regular intervals, but most of them were irregular. They were always a nuisance, and much more so now in the final stage of arranging the getaway.

On the morning of September 4th, our watchers informed us that the woodshed sentry had departed at 5 am. This was good news and placed the early-morning escape in the most favourable light. The woman, according to the graph, could be relied upon not to enter the woodshed before

6.30 am, and usually she arrived a little later. Thus, at the best we would have an hour and a half, and at the worst half an hour. We decided to waste no further time, and to escape next morning. Our zero hour was 5 am on Thursday, September 5th.

CHAPTER 2

THE FIRST BID FOR FREEDOM

We ate well on September 4th and prepared our kit, putting the final touches to our clothing. Maps – good survey maps which had been found, and others carefully traced on thin lavatory paper – were distributed. Our staple diet of raw oatmeal mixed with sugar provided at the expense of the German kitchen, was packed. My portion of staple diet went into two small sacks of strongly sewn canvas which were to be hung round my neck so as to fall over my chest and form a buxom bust, for I was to escape as a woman. I still possessed a large brown canvas pouch, which I had found in a caserne at Charleville. This I could carry by hand when dressed as a woman, and later on my back as a man. There was no room for my boots, so I made a brown paper parcel of them.

My female attire consisted of a large red spotted handkerchief for my head, a white sports-shirt as a blouse, and a skirt made of an old grey window-curtain, which I had also picked up during the trek into Germany. My legs were shaved and 'sunburnt' with iodine, and I wore black plimsolls.

Once clear of the camp, I would change into a man again, wearing a green-grey Tyrolean hat, cleverly made and dyed from khaki by a British sergeant (a former tailor), a heavy pullover to go over my shirt, a small mackintosh groundsheet for wet weather (also picked up during the journey to Germany), a pair of dark-blue shorts cut from a Belgian airman's breeches (obtained by barter), white Bavarian woollen stockings of the pattern common to the country, purchased at a shocking price in the German canteen, and my brown army boots dyed black.

The others had similar clothing, with minor individual differences. The tailor had devised enough Tyrolean hats to go round and had fashioned an Austrian cloak for Harry Elliott. Lockwood was also to make his exit disguised as a woman, and his costume was more or less like mine. Rupert had an old grey blanket which he converted into a cloak. We were a motley crowd and hardly fit to pass close inspection by daylight, for we had not the experience required to produce really finished garments from scratch. But the idea was that we were young Austrian hikers, and we would only be seen at dusk or dawn.

That night our room-mates made dummies in our beds, good enough to pass the cursory glance of the German night patrol through the room. We all slept in different rooms in the same building as the tunnel, doubling up with other officers, and these arrangements were made as secretly as possible to avoid any hubbub or infectious atmosphere of excitement. The Senior Officers of the rooms in question, who had to declare nightly to the German Officer on the rounds the number of officers present, were not even aware of the additions to or subtractions from their flock.

We were to rise at 4 am. None of us slept much, though we took precautions against oversleeping by having a couple of 'knockers up' in reserve. I remember banging my head on the pillow four times – an old childhood habit which for some unaccountable reason usually worked. It was hardly necessary on this occasion. I passed a most unpleasant night with the cold sweat of nervous anticipation upon me, and with that peculiar nausea of the stomach which accompanies tense nerves and taut muscles. My mind turned over the pros and cons a hundred times; the chances of success, immediate and later, and the risks. If they shot, would they shoot to kill? If they caught us sooner or later, what were our chances – to be liquidated or to disappear into a Concentration Camp? At that period of the war, nobody knew the answers. It was the first escape from this prison, probably the first escape of British officers from any organized prison in Germany. We were the guinea-pigs.

We undertook the experiment with our eyes open, choosing between two alternatives: to attempt escape and risk the ultimate price, or face up to the sentence of indefinite imprisonment. There were many who resigned themselves from the beginning to the second of these alternatives. They were brave, but their natures differed from those of the men who escaped and failed, and escaped again; who having once made the choice between escape and resignation, could not give up, even if the war lasted the remainder of their lives. I am sure that the majority of the men who sought to escape did it for self-preservation. Instinctively, unconsciously, they felt that resignation meant not physical but mental death – maybe lunacy. My own case was not exceptional. One awful fit of depression sufficed to determine my future course as a prisoner. One dose of morbidity in which the vista of emptiness stretched beyond the horizon of my mind was quite enough.

At 4 am, in a grisly darkness, I fastened my bossom in place, and put on my blouse and skirt. We crept downstairs to our collecting-point in the washroom beside the tunnel-room. A tap was turned on quietly to fill a water-bottle. It went on dripping. The sound of the drops was loud and exasperating. A sentry stood only thirty yards away by the courtyard gate. I felt he must hear it. . . . It was nerves. Captain Gilliat, one of the assistants, wore a gas-cape. Why he chose this garment for the occasion I never knew. It crackled loudly with every movement and nearly drove us mad. A watcher was by now at the end of the tunnel, waiting to pass the signal when the sentry near the tunnel exit went off duty. Other stooges were posted at vantage-points to give the alarm in case a patrol suddenly appeared in the buildings. We waited.

At 5.15 am the sentry outside the tunnel still remained at his post. It was probable now he would not leave till 6 am. There was nothing to do but wait quietly while our hearts pounded through our ribs with suppressed excitement.

There was a thundering crash and a reverberating clang as if fifty dinner-gongs had been struck hard with hammers all at once. There was a second crash and a third, diminishing in intensity, and, finally, some strident squeaks. This must be the end – but no one was allowed to move. We had our stooges and we had time after a warning to disappear. The men in the tunnel-room were safely locked in and could hide in the tunnel. A panic would have been dangerous.

Dick Howe and Peter Allan, tired of the long wait, had leant against one of the twelve-foot-long, solid cast-iron troughs which were used as communal washbasins, and finally they had sat on the edge of it. The next instant the whole trough collapsed on to the concrete floor. If I had tried for weeks I doubt if I could have thought of a better way of making the loudest noise possible with the least effort. The succeeding crashes and squeaks which kept our hair standing on end were caused by Dick and Peter who, having made a frantic attempt to save the crash, were extricating themselves from the wreckage and bringing the trough to rest quietly on the floor.

We waited for the signal to return. A minute passed, five minutes passed, and then – we began to breathe again. No Germans appeared. I never found out why they did not come. The noise woke up most of the officers in the building, which was a large one, and the sentry thirty yards away near the courtyard must have jumped out of his skin. Yet for some unaccountable reason he did not act.

Six o'clock chimed out from a distant steeple. We waited more anxiously as every minute passed. At last, at 6.15 am, the signal came through: 'All clear!' In a moment the door was unlocked and we hustled into the tunnel. I crawled quickly to the end, listened for a second, and then set to work like a demon. Down went the slats and I shovelled earth and cinders to my right and below me as fast as I could. It was light outside. As the hole enlarged I could see the various shed details. All the usual household cleaning equipment, piles of cardboard boxes at one end, clothes drying on a line, and then the slatted door and its lock – a large and formidable-looking padlock on a hasp. Once I tried to get through, but the opening was still too small. I enlarged it further and then squirmed upwards and into the shed. I pulled Rupert and then Peter through after me, telling Dick, who was next, to wait below while we found the way out. We searched quickly. The padlock would not open to a piece of wire which I inserted as a key. I climbed the cardboard boxes to reach a large opening in the slats near the roof and slipped, nearly bringing the boxes down on top of me. Peter held them and we readjusted the pile. We tried the door into the house; it was locked. Then in a flash I thought of the screwdriver. (I had asked Scarlet to lend me one – just in case.) I looked more closely at the hasp on which the padlock was bolted. What a fool I was!

The way was clear. With hands fumbling nervously, I unscrewed three large screws securing the hasp to the wood and the door swung open. I looked at my watch.

'Dick!' I whispered hoarsely down into the tunnel. 'You'd better come up quick, it's 6.30.'

As he started to worm himself up through the hole, there came the sound of an approaching horse and cart.

'Hold everything, Dick!' I said, 'don't move,' and to the others: 'Flatten yourselves against the walls!'

A moment later the cart appeared. Dick remained rigid like a truncated man at floor-level! The driver did not look our way and the cart passed on. We pulled Dick out of the hole. I repeated to him what he already knew.

'We're late. Our safe half-hour is already over and the woman may come in at any moment. Someone's got to replace this.' I pointed at the hasp and padlock. 'It will take five minutes. Add to this twenty minutes to clear the six of us.'

'It will take Scarlet fifteen minutes to close and camouflage the hole,' said Dick. 'It's now 6.35. That means 7.15 before everything is clear.'

We looked at each other and I knew he read my thoughts. We had gone over the timetable so often together.

'I'm sorry, Dick! The graph has never shown the woman to be later than 7 o'clock, and she may arrive any minute. You'll have to lock up and follow tomorrow,' and I handed him the screwdriver.

'Make a good job of closing up our "Shovewood",' I added. 'Your escape depends on it.'

We quickly brushed each other down. I was worried about the back of my skirt, which had suffered in the exit as we had come out on our backs. I repeated nervously:

'Is my bottom clean? Is my bottom clean?'

For the sentry, about forty yards away on the trestle walkway, would see my back view and I did not want him to see a dirty skirt.

I tied my spotted handkerchief around my head, opened the door, and walked out into the sunlight. I turned the corner into the side street leading to the main road, and felt a gooseflesh sensation up my back and the sentry's stare burning through my shoulder-blades. I waited for the shot.

For thirty yards up the side street I walked with short steps imitating what I thought to be the gait of a middle-aged peasant woman, and thereby prolonging the agony of every yard. At last I reached the main road. There was no alarm and I turned the corner.

The road was almost deserted. A few people were cleaning their shop-windows, a restaurant manager was pinning up his menu, and a girl was brushing the pavement. A cyclist or two passed. The hush of dawn and of sleep still lay over the town. I received casual glances, but did not attract any stares.

After I had gone about two hundred yards I heard the heavy footsteps of two persons following me, marching in step. I turned into a square and crossed it diagonally towards the bridge over the river. The footsteps grew louder and nearer. I was being followed: a patrol had been sent after me by the suspicious sentry. They did not run for fear of making me run. I was finished – the game was up – but, I thought, I may as well play it to the end and I ambled along with my bundles across the bridge, not daring to turn round. How those footsteps echoed, first in the street, now on the bridge! The patrol came alongside and passed me without accosting me. I raised my head and to my relief saw two young hikers. They were Rupert and Peter, walking briskly away from me. I had never expected them so soon.

About a hundred yards past the bridge I turned right, following the other two. This route brought me alongside a local railway line and towards the outskirts of the town. We could see the line from the camp, and it had been arranged we should follow the path beside it and rendezvous in the woods about a quarter of a mile out of the town.

As I turned the corner, a little girl, playing with a toy, looked up at me and caught my eye. Astonishment was written all over her face. I might take in a casual adult observer, but I could not pass the keen observation of a child. She continued to look wide-eyed at me as I passed and when I was a few yards farther on I heard her running into a house – no doubt to tell her parents to come and look at the extraordinary man dressed up as a woman. Nobody came, so I presumed they just did not believe her. Grown-ups always know better than their children!

It was a misty morning heralding a hot day. I followed the railway into the woods, where it swept to the left in a big curve. I heard a train approaching and made for cover among the trees. It passed and I continued a short distance, expecting to see the other two waiting for me. There was no sign of them and I began to worry. I whistled, but there was no answer. I continued slowly, whistling 'We're going to hang out our washing on the Siegfried Line. . . .' They must be close by the woods. Still no answer. Then I heard shots in the distance and dogs barking. I immediately dashed into the woods and decided to hide and change rapidly. I could not go on in my makeshift skirt. Maybe the child's parents had phoned the camp or the police. They might search for someone with a skirt on!

I found myself close to the river and was soon in among high reeds, where I started to change. It was about 7.15 am. Shots continued spasmodically and the barking of dogs increased. I was at my wits' end and sure the 'hunt was up', and I had lost the other two. Rupert had the only compass – a good army one given him by a fellow-officer, who had managed to conceal it through all searches. I could not travel without one.

I suddenly heard people approaching along a wood path close to the reeds. I crouched and waited until I saw them. Thank God, it was my two hikers once more!

'I thought I'd lost you for good,' I said, quickly completing my change and hiding my skirt in the reeds. 'I was already bothering about how I was going to reach Yugoslavia without a compass.'

'What's all the shooting about?' said Peter.

'I haven't the foggiest idea. I don't like it. They've probably discovered something and are shooting up the camp. They'll be after us in no time. We'll have to hide up.'

'It sounds to me like rifle-range shooting,' said Rupert.

'Well, why have we never heard it before, then?' I questioned, 'and how do you account for the dogs?'

'Probably the village dogs barking at the gunfire.'

'The fact is, Rupert, we've never heard shooting like this before, and besides, it's still misty in places. I believe they're after us and we'd better hide up quickly.'

'I bet you five pounds it's range-shooting. Anyway, it's no use hiding here. We're much too close. Come on, let's make tracks!'

We made for the top of a high wooded hill which lay in our general direction southwards. From it we could see all the surrounding country. We crossed the railway, then a road and some open fields before entering the friendly cover of more woods. We simply scuttled across the fields, Rupert, who was the calmest, doing all he could to make us walk normally. In the woods we disturbed some chamois which fled away noisily, giving us the fright of our lives.

We had left tracks in the dew-laden grass of the fields and we were out of breath from the steep uphill going. We rested for a moment and smeared our boots with German mustard, which we had brought for the purpose of putting dogs off the scent, and then continued, climbing steeper and steeper. We heard woodcutters at work and kept clear of them. Eventually, at about 9 am, we reached the top of the hill.

The shooting and the barking of dogs had ceased. We gained confidence. Either the hunters had lost track of us or it had been a false alarm, as Rupert thought.

The camp *Appell*, that is, roll-call, was due and soon we should have an important matter decided. We had arranged that, from a window high up in the camp building, a sheet would be hung, as if to air; white for 'all clear', blue check if our absence had been discovered.

The Germans held two separate *Appells*, one for the Officers, and immediately afterwards one for the Other Ranks – in another courtyard. This gave us an opening of which we were not slow to avail ourselves. I had arranged with six 'good men and true' that they would stand in for the Officers' *Appell* and then do a rapid change in a lavatory into orderlies' attire and appear on the Other Ranks parade. Only three of them would be necessary today.

It was a glorious morning and I climbed a tree to look down into the valley, now clear of mist and bathed in luxurious sunshine. The view was beautiful, rich in September fruitfulness, with the river in the foreground rushing over its pebbly bed, a ribbon of sparkling light.

I could see our prison in the distance reflecting a warm golden colour from its walls. I had never thought that our Archbishop's Palace could be called beautiful, but from a distance it certainly was so. Then I realized why: I could not distinguish the windows in the walls. We were farther away than we had estimated, and the sunlight was at a bad angle. There was no hope of seeing a sheet of any colour. Later, when the sun had moved round, Peter climbed the tree, but he could scarcely distinguish the windows and, although his sight was keen, could see no sign of a sheet.

We hid the whole day in a copse of young fir-trees on the top of the hill. We were only disturbed once, by a woodman who passed close by but did not see us. We reconnoitred the southern slope of the hill along the route we were to take that night, but it was wooded for a long distance so we soon gave up, letting the darkness bring what it might. We were in very good hiding. I believe only dogs would ever have found us.

We lay in long grass in an open patch among the trees, dozing from time to time, scarcely ever talking. The sun shone in a cloudless sky. It was good to be alive, to breathe the air of freedom, the scent of pines and dry grass, to hear the murmur of flying insects around and the distant chopping of a woodman's axe, to listen to a lark above one's head – a fluttering speck against the infinity of the clear blue sky. We were free at last. A restful calm, a silent relish of this precious day spread over us. There was a hush on the sunbathed, pleasant countryside. We felt attuned to it. Our hearts were full of thanksgiving. Animals do not need to speak, I thought.

At meal-time we sat up and ate our meagre ration. We had worked it out to last us twelve days. We drank a mouthful of water each from a small bottle, exchanged a few remarks on the chances of Dick and the others the next day and then returned to our dreaming.

A beautiful autumnal evening set in, and with it came a chill in the air as the sun sank peacefully over the horizon. I have seldom in my life spent a happier day. The war did not seem to exist.

We clothed ourselves, put chalk in our socks and boots, and, as darkness approached, set off downhill through the woods – southwards to Yugoslavia. It was about one hundred and fifty miles away across the mountains of the Austrian Tyrol. We hoped to make it in ten days.

CHAPTER 3

THE PRICE OF FAILURE

We had a large-scale survey map which covered the first sixty miles of our journey. It showed all the contours, and even tiny villages and mountain paths. Its acquisition deserves an explanation.

Our camp was formerly the depot of the 100th Gebirgsjäger Regiment – mountain troops. At the top of one of our buildings was a staircase leading up to an attic. The former was entirely shut off by a wood partition and a door made of slats which was heavily chained and padlocked. We could not see far up the staircase, but its situation was intriguing and invited inspection.

One day Scarlet O'Hara solved the problem of how to by-pass the door. The stair passed diagonally across a window, the springer being about eight inches away from the glass. The sill of this window could be reached from the flight of stairs below by climbing on a man's shoulder. A thin man could worm himself up through the eight-inch gap on to the forbidden staircase, and thus the secrets of the attic were revealed. A few doors with very simple locks were no barrier to Scarlet, and an old storeroom was found in which there were many copies of survey maps of the district around Laufen. Other useful things, such as small hatchets, screws and nails, pens and coloured inks, were found, and even badges of the mountain regiment. We took away a small portion of everything, hoping the stock had never been accurately counted.

Before we escaped, someone a little too fat had tried the window route and split the glass. The Jerries realized what was happening and barred off the window completely. There was not much left in the attic by that time. The Germans created a big fuss and searched the camp and prisoners individually. The search lasted a day, but nothing seriously incriminating was found, and our tunnel, being behind German locks, was not troubled.

Rupert's compass had survived many such searches by employing the following simple ruse. Before being searched, the owner of the compass demanded urgently to go to the lavatory, meeting there by arrangement a friend who had been searched already. Although the owner was accompanied by a sentry while carrying out this simple duty, a moment always arrived when it was possible to slip the article to the friend unobserved. The method required good synchronization and deft handling of an opportunity, or even the making of an opportunity by diverting the attention of the sentry.

There was no moon and it soon became pitch-dark in the woods. We were in thick undergrowth and brambles and made slow progress, so much so that we altered our compass bearing and headed south-east, trying to find easier going. After about two hours we cleared the woods and were able to trek across country at a good speed, aiming at a chosen star which we checked by the compass as being in our line. It was then only necessary to look at the compass every hour or so and change our guiding star as the constellations moved in the sky.

Walking at night straight across country is an eerie experience. Only the actual ground for a few yards around is real, be it long grass, corn stubble, potato field, or moorland. Beyond this island lies an ocean composed entirely of shadows, unreal and mysterious. Into this outer world one gropes with the eyes, peering and straining all the time, seeking to solve its mysteries. Shadows of every shape, some grotesque, some frightening, varying infinitesimally and subtly in depth from the deepest black, through blues and greens to the patchy greys and whiteness of the ground mist. One walks into the unknown; one might be walking on the moon. Shadows are deceptive things. A little copse seems like an impenetrable forest. A field of hay may turn into a discouraging reedy marsh. A stook of corn suddenly takes on a fantastic resemblance to a silent listening man. A sheet-white ghost looms out of the mist. It moves – a stray cow shies off, as frightened as ourselves by the encounter. Stately mansions turn into derelict barns, and a distant hedge becomes a deep cutting with a railway line at the bottom. On this unreal planet one walks with every sense alert to the 'sticking-point.'

We went in single file spaced as far apart as possible, taking turns at leading with a white handkerchief draped over our backs. We would follow the leader, listening for the muttered warnings: 'ware wire, brambles, a ditch, marsh, and so on. We often stumbled. We avoided buildings, but even so, in the silence of the night, our progress would be heard by dogs and they would start barking as we hurried off into the shadows. We knew there was no big river in our path but we had to ford several streams, sometimes taking off boots and stockings and wading knee-deep to do so. We stopped to rest occasionally, and had a meal under a haystack at about 1 am.

As dawn approached, we searched for a hiding-place for the day and found one in a grove of trees far away from any buildings. We had done only thirteen miles, and were rather disappointed. We did not sleep much and were anxious to move on. The first part of our next night's march lay across a wide valley. Noting landmarks on our line, we set off a little before nightfall. Our feet were sore and blisters were appearing. Peter had borrowed a pair of suitable-looking boots which, however, did not fit him too well, and he developed enormous blisters on his heels. I had warned him what to expect. He stuck it well.

Later we found ourselves in mountainous country with occasional rushing torrents, waterfalls, and deep gorges, and mostly wooded. Farms, surrounded by small patches of cultivation cleared out of the woods, were few and far between.

The weather held fine. On our third day of freedom we considered making a start in daylight. By the early afternoon our impatience got the better of us and we set off.

After some steep climbing, we found a sparkling stream where in the clearer pools basked mountain trout.

'Rupert,' I said, 'I can't resist this. My clothes are wringing wet; I'm perspiring like a pig. I'm going to have a bathe.'

I started to undress. Rupert bent over a rock to feel the water.

'Ye gods!' he shouted, withdrawing his hand as if he had been scalded. 'This water comes straight from the North Pole.'

'Just what you need to freshen you up.' I thought of my long walking tours as a student, when I learnt the benefit of bathing my feet frequently in cold water.

'Peter,' I added, 'it'll do your blisters no end of good. I insist we all sit with our feet dangling in a pool for at least ten minutes.'

We all had a lightning dip, while our damp and sweaty clothes lay drying in the sun, and then we dangled our feet until we could not feel them any more. When we set off again, we were walking on air.

The going soon became so difficult that we took to paths and cattle tracks, and for the first time met another human being. Previously we had narrowly escaped being seen by some Hitler youths and girls whom we heard singing and laughing on our path close behind us. The new intruder was a woodman – we passed him with a casual 'Heil Hitler!' He took no notice of us.

Later we came upon a small farm and Peter made so bold as to ask the farmer the way. Although our survey map could hardly have been better, our route was strewn with deep narrow valleys and we became confused as to which one we were in.

As evening drew on we found another gurgling stream and, piling up some stones on its bank, we made a fire. We had hot soup from cubes and roasted some potatoes, which we had collected earlier from a potato patch. It was a heavenly meal. After a good rest and a doze, we pushed on again as night fell.

We tried to maintain our direction on the small mountain paths, but found ourselves more and more frequently consulting our map with the aid of matches. This was an unwelcome necessity, for we did not want a light to give us away, and, even in woods, shielded the matches with our capes. Eventually we found a minor road and embarked on it. Soon it started to wind downhill and in a general direction at right angles to ours. At the same time we became hemmed in with impenetrable-looking forest which we dared not enter. We did not want to go downhill; it was out of our way and, in any case, it is always an advantage when walking across country to keep high up; then, with a map, one's position can be checked by bearings taken on the surrounding country. At the rate we were going we would be in the main Salzburg (Salzach) valley by morning. Even from our map we could not be certain which road we were on. In fact, we were lost.

We decided to wait till dawn and retrace our steps until our position could be checked up. Penetrating about fifty yards into the woods, we lay down to sleep in a leafy hollow. It was bitterly cold and we huddled together for warmth, with our scanty coverings spread over all three of us. Our muscles ached and we spent a miserable few hours dozing fitfully. Just before daylight we could stand it no longer and were about to move off when Rupert suddenly declared in a horrified tone:

'The compass is gone, I can't find it!'

There was a long silence as we regarded each other. I broke the awkward spell.

'That's a nice kettle of fish! When do you last remember having it?'

'Miles away! Before we started coming downhill – the last time we lit those matches.'

We stared blankly at each other in the cold dawn, shivering miserably and depressed beyond description.

'Well! let's start searching,' I said. 'Be careful where we've been lying.

Start from one end of the hollow and let's work on our hands and knees in line. Feel first for lumps and don't turn over more leaves than you can possibly help.'

We searched, carefully patting the leaves and moss, advancing slowly yard by yard over the whole area of our bivouac.

'I've got it!' said Peter in triumph suddenly, holding it up like a trophy.

We sighed our relief. In this country, without a compass we could not keep a consistent course for five minutes.

After about two hours' walking, as the dawn came up, we were able to locate ourselves and once more set off in the right direction across meadows and along the edges of woods, following a mountain ridge while it ran more or less parallel with our course.

This was our fourth day of freedom and we had had no rain. We met nobody all day. By evening we had reached the main road which heads south-east from Golling to Radstadt and across the mountain hump by way of the Radstädter Tauern pass. From now on it was apparent we should have to follow the road, because the mountains were high and the valley was a gorge. We set off along the road in the cool of the evening. Within ten minutes several people passed us on foot or on bicycles, and a Jerry soldier ambled by with a 'Heil Hitler!' to which we replied with gusto. Although he had not appeared to see anything unusual in our now ragged and dirty clothing, we decided to retire into the woods and continue only after dark. This we did, and during the night we walked fast and with few stops, for the cold was becoming intense.

Our feet were at last becoming hardened. We made good going and by dawn had gone about twenty-four miles. There were two incidents during the night. At about 11 pm a girl on a bicycle caught us up and insisted on talking to us.

'*Guten Abend! wo gehen Sie hin?*' she volunteered, dismounting and walking along beside us.

'Forward hussy, what?' murmured Rupert under his breath.

'Peter, you're a lady-killer,' I whispered; 'go on, do your stuff.'

Peter took over.

'We're going to Abtenau. We've got army leave and are hiking. And where might you be going?'

Peter's German was correct even to the Austrian accent. The girl was pleased.

'I live at Voglau. It's only two miles from here on the main road. You come from Salzburg?'

'No, from Saalfelden,' replied Peter, naming a place as far away from Salzburg as possible.

'I'll walk with you to my house. Father may offer you beer.'

I understood enough to know that the conversation was taking an unhappy turn. I promptly sat down on a grass bank at the edge of the road and, pulling Rupert by his sleeve, said in an undertone, hoping my indifferent German accent would not be noticed, '*Hans! Kommen Sie hier. Ich gehe nicht weiter.*' Rupert took the hint and sat beside me. Peter and the girl were already some yards ahead. I heard her say: 'Your friends do not seem to like me. They will not speak. How rude they are.'

'They are not rude but very tired, *Fräulein*,' put in Peter. 'I am too tired to continue farther without a rest. *Auf Wiedersehen!* You must hurry home, for it is very late and your father will be worried. *Auf Wiedersehen!*'

With that Peter practically sat her on her bicycle and finally got rid of her. She left us a bit disgruntled and probably with some queer impressions. I doubt if she suspected us, though she was capable of talking to someone in a village who might. This was an added reason for our making good headway during the night and moving out of the district.

Occasionally a car passed with headlights blazing – no thought of blackout! – which gave us enough warning to take cover. We did not take cover for pedestrians who passed or for cyclists who, in any case, were liable to catch us up, unheard above the roar of a mountain river which the road now followed. We walked together, feeling that if we were accosted there was always one of us who could reply.

Approaching a small village beyond the junction town called Abtenau, we saw several lights and torches flickering. We hastily took to a field. The lights persisted for a long time – about two hours – and garrulous voices could be heard. Finally the episode wound up when a very drunken man passed down the road reeling from side to side, throwing and kicking his bicycle along in front of him. He was shouting and swearing and could be heard a mile away. Loud crashes punctuated his tirade, indicating that the bicycle was the victim of his rage and presumably the cause of it!

The lights were ominous. We continued when all was quiet and shortly afterwards encountered a small house with an army motor-cycle standing outside. Dogs barked as we passed, so we hurried on.

We were about three thousand feet above sea-level. The valley became narrower than ever and it was out of the question to travel other than on the road. In daylight we would be conspicuous walking through the small villages.

We rested during the fifth day (a Monday) on a promontory overlooking the road. Towards late afternoon a cold drizzle began to fall. We became restless and argued about going on. One by one we gave in and agreed to move. With our odd-looking capes and blankets over our shoulders, we trudged uphill along the now muddy road – passing a sawmill where a few men were working. They stared at us, and later a motor-lorry from the mill caught us up before we had time to take cover. As it passed, a youth leaned out and had a good stare at us.

This was disquieting. I insisted we should disappear again until nightfall. We found a resting-place beside the river among trees about fifteen yards from the road. The rain continued till nightfall and then ceased, leaving us cold, wet, and dispirited. I was nervous after the experience of the sawmill. We drank water copiously before starting. If a man drinks far more than he has the desire for, he can walk for eight hours without feeling unduly thirsty. We continued up the winding valley past straggling villages and small chalets. The night was pitch-dark and there were no stars. We were nearing the top of the pass and were only a few miles from Radstadt, which was the halfway point on our journey to Yugoslavia. We had walked about seventy-five miles.

We entered a small village at about 11.30 pm. It was called Lungötz. All was quiet. Suddenly the light of an electric torch was directed down at us from a window high above. After a few seconds it went out. Very suspicious! But there was nothing we could do about it in the middle of a village. We had been seen, so we had to bluff our way out. Coming to a fork in the road, we hesitated a moment while I peered at the signpost, and then took the left branch. After a couple of hundred yards we left the village behind and the road entered deep woods. We breathed more freely.

The next moment there was a loud crashing of branches and under-growth. Beams from powerful torches flashed on us and we saw the gleam of rifle barrels. Men shouted '*Halt! Halt! Wer da?*' We stopped, and Peter, a few steps ahead, answered '*Gut Freund.*' Three men jumped down to the road from the banks on either side and approached, with their rifles aimed at us from the hip. At a few yards' distance they began shouting at Peter all together. I could see they were very nervous.

'Who are you? What are you doing in the woods at this hour? Where are you going? Produce your papers!'

'One at a time! One at a time!' shouted Peter. 'What is all this fuss? We are innocent people. We are soldiers on leave and we go to Radstadt.'

'Where are your papers? We do not believe you. Show us your papers.'

'We do not carry papers. We are on leave.'

One of them approached Rupert and me and knocked the sticks which we held out of our hands with his rifle, jabbering hysterically at us. We could not have answered him if we had wanted to.

'So you have no papers. Why are your two companions silent? We think you are spies, enemies of the Reich!'

There was a moment when Rupert and I might have run for it – back down the road, zigzagging – leaving Peter. But the opportunity passed before we had time to pull our wits together. We might have got away with it if there were no patrols behind us.

Then the men were all shouting, '*Hände hoch! Hände hoch!*' and we put up our hands, Peter still protesting we were innocent and anxious to get on to Radstadt. It was no use. If Peter had been alone he might have deceived them, but we two were just so much dead weight and our dumbness or sullenness was the last straw.

We were marched back at bayonet point to a small inn in the village. Several windows in a house opposite were lit up. I recognized it as the house from which the torchlight had first been flashed at us. The owner of the torch had probably been in touch with the ambush party by signal. In the *Gaststube* (dining-room) of the inn, we were lined against a wall and ordered by one of the three policemen, more ferocious and nervous than the rest, to keep our arms stretched upwards. We were then left with two guards until about 1.30 am, when the third guard returned. We were marched out and put in the back of an open lorry, which I recognized as the one which had passed us, and were driven off down the road along which we had come. It was heartbreaking to see the landmarks we had passed only a few hours before as free men. The two guards sat facing us with their rifles at the ready. Since our capture there had not been the faintest chance of a getaway. The remainder of the night was spent at the police-station at Abtenau, then two hours' drive under armed guard, and we were back in the German *Kommandantur* at Oflag VII C, a depressed and sorry-looking trio.

A German under-officer approached us and we were 'for it'. He was the one who checked numbers at *Appells*, and he knew Peter well, since Peter had acted as camp interpreter on many occasions. He roared at us, forcing us to stand rigidly to attention while he tore off pieces of our clothing. He shook Peter wildly by the shoulders, spluttering into his face. It was a wonderful exhibition. He had obviously had a bad time since our absence was discovered.

After working off his revenge he led us to the German Camp Adjutant, who took us one by one into his office and questioned us. He began with me.

'It was useless to try to escape. You were warned. Now it is proved. You were fortunate not to have been shot. When did you leave?'

'I cannot say.'

'But what difference does it make? We know everything. Six of you escaped. You left on Saturday, did you not?'

'I don't know.'

'Herr Hauptmann, you are an officer and I understand your point of view, but when the whole matter is closed and finished, surely we can talk together freely?'

'Of course, Herr Oberst, I understand. I did not know you had recaptured three more officers.'

'That is a leading question. Please remember I am questioning you – and that you are not here to question me. You had money, of course?'

'Money? No.'

'Then how have you travelled so far in such a short time?'

'There are ways of travelling, Herr Oberst.'

'Ha! So you stole bicycles?'

I was becoming involved. My 'No' to the question concerning money was not a good answer. I fell back upon 'I cannot reply to your questions.'

'Unless you tell me the day you escaped, I shall have to assume you have stolen bicycles. This is a very serious charge.'

'I cannot help it.'

'You have concealed your absence at one *Appel*. How did you do it?'

'I did not do it.'

'You did not, but others did. You see, your absence was known at evening *Appell* on Saturday. Your escape was made at night. Therefore at the morning *Appell* your absence was concealed. You admit it was at night, do you not?'

'I admit nothing.'

'Do not be so silly. It was, of course, clever of you to hide in the grass compound. We are building a guard ring of barbed wire two yards from the fences now. You will not be able to repeat your escape. Did you hide near the river or high up?'

'I just concealed myself.'

'But where?'

'I cannot say.'

'I know that soldiers concealed your *Appell*. Unless you tell me their names, I shall be compelled to have them all punished. That is not fair, to punish all for the offence of six. What were their names?'

'I do not know.'

'You know well. If you do not give the names, it will be bad for all. You can save much hardship by a simple answer.'

'I am sorry, Herr Oberst.'

'Well then! You have either stolen bicycles or you have had assistance from outside the camp. For a prisoner to steal a bicycle is punishable with death. If you have received help, you can say so. I shall not ask the names and shall not charge you with theft of German private property. Come now, that is fair.'

'Your answer is so fair, Herr Oberst, that I know you will understand my inability to answer you.'

'You are a fool,' he answered, becoming angry. 'I have given you enough chances. You will suffer for your silence. Do you like concentration camps?

Do you like to starve? Do you like to die? I give you one more chance. Your obstinacy is madness – it has no reason. Did you receive any help?'

I did not answer.

'So you insult me. Very well. You will be punished for silent insolence as well. About turn! March!'

I left the room and the others were paraded in turn. The questioning and tactics were the same in each case, as I found out. Rupert and Peter gave nothing away. We had a pretty good idea by now of German bluff, and in our three months' imprisonment we were beginning to learn that even a POW had rights and that a document known as the 'Geneva Convention' existed.

I learnt in time to bless this International Convention for the treatment of Prisoners-of-War and must record here my gratitude to its authors. This product of the League of Nations stands as a testimony to our civilization. Its use in World War II demonstrated the force of that civilization amidst the threat of its ruin.

Our questioning ended, we were marched off to the town jail, which was close by, and each locked in a separate cell. For several days we languished in our dungeons like forgotten men. My cell was empty except for an unused heating stove, a bucket, and a jug of water. Wood floor, stone walls, and a tiny window just below a high ceiling made up my surroundings. There was no bed or bedding. At night the cold was intense, though it was only September.

During the day we walked our rooms or sat on the floor. We tried knocking to each other through the walls, which annoyed the guards, who cursed and threatened us if we continued. This depressing period was no doubt intended to demoralize us, for we were again taken individually and questioned, and when we refused to speak we were informed that we would be held for court martial.

When an officer is recaptured after an escape, the same principle holds good as when he is first taken prisoner – namely, that it is better to say nothing than tell lies. Lies may temporarily deceive the enemy in one direction, but they often lead him to unearth something which was never intended to be discovered. If I had replied to the question 'How did you escape?' by saying we escaped over the roofs, it was quite liable to upset a plan being prepared by other officers in the camp unknown to us.

If to the question 'When did you escape?' I gave a date several days before the actual event, I ran a good risk of being found out in a lie through a chance identification, or I might make the Germans so aghast at the length of my absence that the repercussion on future *Appell* precautions might be disastrous. If I named a date some time after the actual event, I immediately gave the Jerries false ideas as to how far I could travel in a given time and thereby enlarged the circumference of cordons for future escapers. I found also that Jerry quickly lost respect for an enemy who talked. He expects silence. It is in accord with his own rules.

We returned, to languish in our jail. Every second day we were thrown a slab of brown bread in the morning and given a bowl of soup at midday.

On the fourth day there was a loud commotion and we heard the voices of Dick Howe, Harry Elliott, and Kenneth Lockwood! They were locked in neighbouring cells. Their arrival was further cause for depression.

We soon made complaints about the bucket sanitation and were eventually allowed to use a lavatory at the end of the corridor. Then we complained of lack of exercise and were allowed to walk for half an hour daily in single file at twenty-five paces from each other in a circle in the Oflag courtyard, the other officers being temporarily shut off from the area.

We established communications with the camp and among ourselves. With the aid of pencil butts dropped in the courtyard where we walked, notes were later written on pieces of lavatory paper, and left to be picked up by officers. The first Red Cross parcels had just arrived. We asked for food in our notes and were soon receiving it: chocolate, sugar, Ovo-sport, cheese!

We would enter the courtyard carrying our towels as sweat-rags. After a turn or two we would notice an inconspicuous pile of swept-up dust. This was the food done up in a small round parcel. A towel would be dropped carelessly in the corner over the rubbish and left until the end of the half-hour's exercise. The towel and the parcel would then be recovered in one movement and nonchalantly carried back to the cells to be divided later and left in the lavatory.

Gradually we learnt each other's stories. We found out also that no one else had escaped, and were aghast at this and extremely disappointed. Men could have been escaping every other day or so. We could not understand it.

Dick Howe, Harry Elliott, and Kenneth Lockwood had been recaught about sixty-three miles away, on the road to Switzerland, after eight days of freedom. Their escape worked to plan. Scarlet O'Hara closed up the hole. After two days' march the three of them jumped a goods train near Golling which took them to a place called Saalfelden. Although they gained about four days' march by this, they had to retrace their steps for some two days to regain their correct route. They had some bad going and bad weather, and had to lie up for a day or two in deserted mountain huts. Walking along a river bank close to a village, they were accosted by two women who appeared to suspect them. Harry's German passed. The women were looking for a man who had burgled their house. Farther on they were trapped by a policeman who conducted them to the village to question them concerning the burglary. Only when they were searched did the local bobby realize he had strained at a gnat and had narrowly missed swallowing a camel.

After ten days in the cells we were told that there would not be a court martial after all, but we were to await our sentences. In due course these were meted out, and to our surprise varied considerably. Peter got off with a fortnight, Rupert and I were the longest with a month each, without retroactive effect from our first day in cell. The differences were explained by minor offences, such as carrying a cut-up German blanket or being in possession of a compass or a map and so on. The sentences were 'bread and water and solitary'; that is to say, bread and water only and a board bed for three days out of every four. On the fourth day the prisoner was given a mattress and two meals of thick potato soup or other gruel. As sentences finished we were allowed to live together in one cell; a large one with mattresses, blankets, and German prison ration food. Thus it came to pass, after forty days, that all six of us were together again. We wondered what would happen to us next. We knew that escaped prisoners were usually moved to new camps.

One day a camp padre was allowed to visit us and give us spiritual comfort. We had complained repeatedly that we were not allowed to read books, not even a Bible. Padre Wynne Price Rees gave us the first news as to what had happened to our tunnel.

For some inexplicable reason Scarlet O'Hara and others had postponed using the tunnel, at first for a week and then, upon our recapture, indefinitely. Finally, questions having been asked in the town as to whether any suspicious individuals had been seen between certain dates, a little girl was brought by her mother to the Camp Commandant. She reported having seen one morning, in a woodshed near the camp walls, a man in pyjamas whom she did not recognize as being anyone belonging to the household of the woodshed owner. A stranger in pyjamas in the woodshed of a house in the early morning – wonderful food for gossip in Laufen! This event occurred about three weeks after our escape. Little notice was taken of the child's story by anyone except an elderly *Feldwebel* who had been a POW in England during the First World War and who had helped German officers to build a tunnel. He went 'snooping' in the part of the camp near the woodshed, sounding the walls and floors. Eventually he arrived at the little locked room, where he came upon the hidden piles of earth and finally our tunnel entrance in the darkest corner under a table. It was camouflaged against casual observation by a large piece of painted cardboard made to fit the hole.

We could pride ourselves on the fact that the camouflage of the tunnel exit had held out. I felt a little ashamed that our entrance had not been better finished. My excuse was that I had never meant it to last three weeks and, moreover, we found from later experience that it was difficult under any circumstances to keep an escape-hole concealed for long after prisoners were known to have escaped.

The figure in pyjamas turned out to be Scarlet O'Hara, who was feverishly screwing up the woodshed door-bolt when he looked up to see the face and startled eyes of the little girl peering at him through the slats of the door. She bolted in terror, and Scarlet, equally frightened, disappeared backwards down our rabbit burrow at high speed. Scarlet's face was at no time beautiful, and I am sure the little girl had nightmares for weeks afterwards.

A few days after the padre's visit we were summoned and, to our utter astonishment, sent back to the camp. We became once more normal prisoners-of-war. It was not to be for long. A week later we were given an hour's notice to assemble for departure to an unknown destination.

The six of us had profited by our week to pass on what information and experience we had gained to the others, and we could not understand why the Germans had given us the opportunity. They had no microphones in Laufen, of that we were certain. Before we departed, our Senior British Officer (always known as the SBO) insisted on being told our destination. I believe he also insisted on this information being cabled to the International Red Cross. We packed our meagre belongings and, with a large five-gallon drum filled with cooked potatoes which we took it in turn to carry, two at a time, we set off on foot for the station under heavy guard. Our destination was Oflag IV C, Colditz, Saxony.

II: ESCAPE OFFICER

CHAPTER 4

THE FORTRESS PRISON

We left Laufen on November 7th, 1940, and arrived three days later in Colditz, Oflag IV C.

There was little or no chance of escape on the journey. Moreover, we had no escape material or reserve food (except potatoes!). The guards were watchful; we were always accompanied to the lavatory. We travelled sometimes in second class, sometimes in third, at all hours of the day and night. There were many changes and long waits, usually in the military waiting-rooms of stations. Passers-by eyed us curiously but without, I thought, great animosity. Those who made closer contact by speaking with our guards were concerned at our carrying potatoes with us. We, who had had three months of starvation diet, followed by many weeks of bread and water, were taking no risks and would have fought for those cold scraggy balls of starch with desperation!

We arrived at the small town of Colditz early one afternoon. Almost upon leaving the station we saw looming above us our future prison: beautiful, serene, majestic, and yet forbidding enough to make our hearts sink into our boots. It towered above us, dominating the whole village: a magnificent castle built on the edge of a cliff. It was the real fairy castle of childhood's story-books. What ogres there might live within! I thought of the dungeons and of all the stories I had ever heard of prisoners in chains, pining away their lives, of rats and tortures, and of unspeakable cruelties and abominations.

In such a castle, through the centuries, everything had happened and anything might happen again. To friendly peasants and tradespeople in the houses nestling beneath its shadows it may have signified protection and home, but to enemies from a distant country such a castle struck the note of doom and was a sight to make the bravest quail. Indeed, it was built with this end in view. Being about one thousand years old, although partly ruined, built over and altered many times, its inherent strength had preserved it from destruction through the stormy centuries.

It was built on the top of a high cliff promontory that jutted out over the River Mulde at a confluence with a tributary stream. The outside walls were on an average seven feet thick, and the inner courtyard of the Castle

was about two hundred and fifty feet above the river-level. The Castle
rooms in which we were to live were about another sixty feet above the
courtyard. The Castle was built by Augustus the Strong, King of Poland
and Elector of Saxony from 1694 to 1733, who was reputed to have had
three hundred and sixty-five children, one for every day of the year. He
built it upon ruins left by the Hussite wars of the fifteenth century. It had
seen many battles and sieges in a long history, and the present name,
Schloss Colditz, testified, not to its origin, but to a time when it was under
Polish domination. The 'itz' is a Slavonic not a Teutonic or Saxon ending.
The original spelling was Koldycze.

The River Mulde, we later learned, was a tributory of the Elbe, into
which it flowed forty miles to the north. Colditz was situated in the middle
of the triangle formed by the three great cities of Leipzig, Dresden, and
Chemnitz, in the heart of the German Reich and four hundred miles from
any frontier not directly under the Nazi heel. What a hope for would-be
escapers!

We marched slowly up the steep and narrow cobbled streets from the
station towards the Castle, eventually approaching it from the rear, that is
to say, from the mainland out of which the promontory protruded.
Entering the main arched gateway, we crossed a causeway astride what
had once been a deep, wide moat and passed under a second cavernous
archway whose oaken doors swung open and closed ominously behind us
with the clanging of heavy iron bars in true medieval fashion. We were then
in a courtyard about forty-five yards square, with some grass lawn and
flower-beds and surrounded on all four sides with buildings six stories high.
This was the *Kommandantur* or garrison area. We were escorted farther;
through a third cavernous archway with formidable doors, up an inclined
cobbled coach way for about fifty yards, then turning sharp right, through
a fourth and last archway with its normal complement of heavy oak and
iron work into the 'Sanctum Sanctorum', the inner courtyard. This was a
cobbled space about thirty yards by forty yards, surrounded on its four
sides by buildings whose roof ridges must have been ninety feet above the
cobbles. Little sun could ever penetrate here! It was an unspeakably grisly
place, made none the less so by the pallid faces which we noticed peering at
us through bars. There was not a sound in the courtyard. It was as if we
were entering some ghostly ruin. Footsteps echoed and the German words
of command seemed distorted out of reality. I had reached the stage of
commending my soul to the Almighty when the faces behind the bars
suddenly took on life; eyes shone, teeth flashed from behind unkempt
beards and words passed backwards into the inner depths:

'*Anglicy! Anglicy!*'

Heads crowded each other out behind tiny barred windows, and in less time than it took us to walk thirty yards there was a cheering mob at every window; not only at the small ones which we had first seen and which we were to come to know so well, but from every other window that we could see there were jostling heads, laughing and cheering. Welcome was written on every face. We breathed again as we realized we were among friends. They were Polish officers.

Relief was quickly followed by amazement as we heard the men behind the bars shout insults at the Germans in their own language, at the same time making violent gestures indicating throat-cutting of the unmistakable ear-to-ear variety. The Jerries were angry. They threatened reprisals, and quickly hustled us away to a building and up many flights of stairs into a couple of attic rooms, where they left us under lock and key behind a wooden grill.

We were not the first arrivals: three RAF officers were there to greet us! They were Flying Officers Howard D. Wardle, Keith Milne, and Donald Middleton.

Wardle, or 'Hank' as he was called, was a Canadian who had joined the RAF shortly before the war. He was dropping propaganda leaflets over Germany in April 1940, when his bomber was shot down. He parachuted and landed in trees as his parachute opened. He was one of the earliest British POWs of the war. He had escaped from the Schloss camp of Spangenburg, about twenty miles from Kassel, by climbing a high barricade on the way to a gymnasium just outside the camp precincts. The other two, also Canadians, had escaped dressed as painters complete with buckets of whitewash and a long ladder, which they carried between them. They had waited for a suitable moment when there appeared to be a particularly dumb Jerry on guard at the gate, marched up briskly, shouted the only words they knew in German and filed out. Having passed the gate, they continued jauntily until they were half-way down the hill on which the Schloss reposed. They then jettisoned ladder and buckets and made a bolt for the woods.

These escapes were in August 1940, and were probably the first escapes of the war from regular camps. None of the three travelled very far before recapture and it was, alas, only a matter of hours before they were back behind the bars. They suffered badly at the hands of their captors, being severely kicked and battered with rifle-butts. The local population were bitter and revengeful.

The three RAF officers had arrived a couple of days before us at night and had seen no one. They were told that sentences awaited them and that they would probably be shot. On the first morning at dawn they had been marched out to some woods in a deep valley flanking one side of the Castle and halted beside a high granite wall. . . . They had then been told to exercise themselves for half an hour! The Germans took a sadistic pleasure in putting the complete wind up the three of them. By the time they reached the high wall in the early half-light they had given up hope of ever seeing another sunrise. This joke over, the Jerries took them back to the rooms in which we found them.

Later that evening we made our first acquaintance with the Poles. There were hushed voices on the staircase, then four of them appeared beyond the grill. They unlocked the door with ease and advanced to greet us. We were the first English they had seen in the war, and the warmth of their welcome, coupled with their natural dignity of bearing, was touching. Each one of us might have been a hero, for to them we represented the friend who had come to their aid when in dire need, who had been prepared to fight in their cause. The Polish people are above all loyal, and they have long memories too – a capacity worth noting in our present times.

They brought food and some beer. Two of the four could speak English and the remainder French. They all spoke German. The meeting soon became noisy and there was much laughter, which the Poles love. Suddenly there was a warning signal from a Pole on the look-out by the stairs, and in less than no time they were all distributed under beds in the corners of our two rooms, where suppressed laughter continued up to the instant of the entry of a German officer with his *Feldwebel*.

The attic door, and others below, had, of course, been locked by the Poles, so that there was nothing to cause suspicion other than our laughter, which the Germans had overheard and had come to investigate. The officer was shocked that we, reviled prisoners, whose right to live depended on a word from him, should find occasion to laugh. It was like laughing in church, and he implied as much to us. He noticed we had shifted all the bunks to make more floor space and promptly made the *Feldwebel* move them back again into orderly rows. The Poles moved with the beds. No sooner had they departed than the Poles, like truant schoolboys, re-appeared, laughing louder than ever at the joke. They called the sergeant '*La Fouine*', the French for a marten, which has also a figurative meaning, namely 'a wily person', whose propensities have been translated into English as 'ferreting'. The merriment continued for a while, then they departed as they had come, leaving us to marvel at the facility with which they manipulated locks. In order to visit us they had unlocked no fewer than five doors with a couple of instruments that looked like a pair of button-hooks. Such was our introduction to Colditz, which was to be our prison house for several years.

There were about eighty Polish army officers in the camp when we arrived. They were among the cream of the Polish army and some had undoubtedly charged tanks at the head of their troop of horse. Although stripped of much of their military attire, they were always smartly turned out on parade. They wore black riding-boots which they kept in beautiful condition. Their Senior Officer was General Tadensz Piskor, and there was also an Admiral named Joseph Unrug.

The officers had all committed offences against the German Reich and the majority had escaped unsuccessfully at least once. They had been prisoners, of course, since the end of September 1939. So many of them had prison sentences outstanding against them that the half-dozen cells normally set apart for solitary confinement housed about six officers each. The cells were about three yards square and each had one small, heavily barred window. These were the windows we saw, crammed with grimy faces, immediately on entering the prison upon our arrival. Thus nearly half of their contingent was officially in solitary confinement!

Time passed more quickly in the new surroundings and in making new friends. The Germans, after a week or so, gave us permanent quarters: a dormitory with two-tier bunks, a washroom, a kitchen, and a day-room in a wing of the Castle separated from the Poles. The courtyard was the exercise area. At first we were given different hours to exercise, but the Jerries eventually gave up trying to keep us apart. To do so would have meant a sentry at every courtyard door, and there were half a dozen of these. Moreover, the Castle was a maze of staircases and intercommunicating doors, and the latter merely provided lock-picking practice for the Poles. We were so often found in each other's quarters that the Germans would have had to put the whole camp into 'solitary' to carry out their intentions, so they gave it up as a bad job.

A trickle of new arrivals increased the British contingent, until by Christmas we numbered sixteen officers. A few French and Belgian officers appeared. All the newcomers were offenders, mostly escapers, and it was impressed upon us that our Castle was 'the bad boys' camp', the 'Straflager' or 'Sonderlager' as the Germans called it. At the same time we also began to appreciate its impregnability from the escape point of view. This was to be the German fortress from which there was no escape, and it certainly looked for a long time as if it would live up to that reputation. As I said in my Prologue, the garrison manning the camp outnumbered the prisoners at all times; the Castle was floodlit at night from every angle despite the blackout, and notwithstanding the sheer drop of a hundred feet or so on the outside from barred windows, sentries surrounded the camp within a palisade of barbed wire. The enemy seemed to have everything in his favour. Escape would be a formidable proposition indeed.

The Poles entertained us magnificently over the Christmas period. They had food parcels from their homes in Poland. We had nothing until, lo and behold, on Christmas Eve Red Cross parcels arrived! The excitement had to be seen to be believed. They were bulk parcels; that is to say, they were not addressed individually, nor did each parcel contain an assortment of food. There were parcels of tinned meat, of tea, of cocoa, and so on. Apart from a bulk consignment which reached Laufen the previous August, these were our first parcels of food from England and we felt a surge of gratitude for this gift, without which our Christmas would have been a pathetic affair. We were also able to return, at least to a limited extent, the hospitality of the Poles, whose generosity was unbounded. We had to ration severely, for we could not count on a regular supply, and we made this first consignment, which we could have eaten in a few days, last for about two months. Our estimate was not far wrong.

Throughout the whole war, in fact, supplies of Red Cross parcels to Colditz were never regular and a reserve had always to be stocked. Parcels were despatched from England at the rate of one per week per person. In Colditz we received normally one, on rare occasions two, parcels per person in three weeks. The parcels both from the United Kingdom and from Canada were excellent in quality and variety. The 'individual' as opposed to the 'bulk' parcels weighed ten and a half pounds each and contained a selection of the following: tinned meat, vegetables, cheese, jam and butter, powdered egg, powdered milk, tea or cocoa, chocolate, sugar, and cooking-fat. These parcels were paid for to a large extent by a prisoner's relatives, but it became almost a universal rule at all camps that 'individual' parcels were put into a pool and everybody shared equally.

The Poles prepared a marionette show for Christmas. It was 'Snow-White and the Seven Dwarfs'. They had the full text of the story, and the characters were taken by persons behind the screen. It was a picturesque show, professionally produced both as to the acting and the décor. The marionettes were beautifully dressed and the frequently changing scenery was well painted. It lasted about two hours and was a great success. During the interval, sandwiches and beer were served and afterwards a feast was offered. The Poles had saved everything for months for this occasion. The beer was a ration, also saved. It was bottled lager which was handed out by the Jerries against prison money on spasmodic occasions. To begin with, in Colditz, it was not too scarce, but by the middle of 1941 it had disappeared completely.

CHAPTER 5

ROUTINE

Prisoners were not allowed so much as to look at a real Reichsmark; instead, the special paper money known as *Lagergeld* was issued. *Lagergeld* did not go far. The canteen offered for sale the usual razor-blades, toothpaste, shaving soap, and occasionally some turnip jam or beetroots in vinegar, and saccharine tablets. We could also buy musical instruments by order. They were very expensive – in fact, the prices were downright robbery – but they gave satisfaction to many amateur musicians.

During my sojourn in prison I bought two guitars, one for about £10 and the other for about £25, and a brass cornet for about £30. I must admit that the cornet was of good quality and the more expensive guitar was a beauty. The instruments came from a well-known firm in Leipzig. I studied the guitar for a year and a half, becoming fairly proficient. I could read music slowly and could play some classical pieces by heart. The cornet provided me with a means of letting off steam when I had nothing better to do. My colleagues limited the use of it to the washroom, with the door closed, in fine weather, at hours when they were normally out in the courtyard.

The German food was cooked in a large, well-equipped, and clean kitchen off the prison courtyard. Private cooking by the prisoners could also be done in our small kitchen provided with a cooking-stove and a hopelessly inadequate supply of coal. All loose and unessential items made of wood, together with large numbers of fixtures, partitions, floorboards, beds and the like, quickly disappeared into the greedy mouth of our grubby little pot-boiler and frying-pan heater. However, the smells which exuded from that murky room invariably outweighed any pangs of conscience, not to mention fears of reprisals, on account of the dubious origin of most of our fuel. My favourite meal was corned beef fried with dried currants or sultanas. Even today my mouth waters in grateful memory of the delectable dish which warded off many an incipient depression. Rupert Barry was the *chef par excellence* for this *specialité de la maison*. It was not an everyday meal – indeed, it was a rarity – which perhaps accounts for the poignant memories I still have of it.

The daily course of life, as may be expected, did not vary much. We awoke in the morning at 7.30 am to shouts of '*Aufstehen*' or 'get up' from a couple of German non-commissioned officers who passed through the dormitories. At 8 am, breakfast orderlies (our own troops), helped by officers, carried up from the German kitchen a large cauldron of 'ersatz' coffee (made from acorns), a certain number of loaves of bread, a small quantity of margarine, and on certain days a little sugar. At 8.30 am there was *Appell*. All ranks formed up in the courtyard, the Poles in one contingent, the British in another, with their respective senior officers in front. A German officer would appear. Everybody would salute everybody else and the German non-commissioned officers would go through a painstaking count of the bodies. When all was found correct there would be more saluting and the parade would break up. As time went on , the first of four daily *Appells* was sounded at 7 am by means of a factory hooter. By 9 am we were free to carry on any lawful pursuit such as reading, studying, language lessons, music lessons, or exercise. The Poles knew every language imaginable between them, and most Englishmen took up a foreign language with a Polish teacher in exchange for English lessons.

Teachers and pupils paired off and sought out quiet corners all over the Castle, where they would settle down to explain to each other the intricacies of the various European languages. Our living-room became a hive of industry and the low murmur of voices continued unabated throughout the morning hours. Those who sought more privacy chose to sit on the staircase or on blankets in the lobbies or out in the courtyard, if it was fine. Here, voices did not have to be hushed and temperament could be indulged in. I remember passing a couple once, deep in the throes of an English lesson, and I overheard the following instruction:

Teacher: 'Now we shall read. Start where we we left off yesterday.'
Pupil (*reading*): 'The leetle sheep——'
Teacher: 'Not "thee", say "the".'
Pupil: 'The leetle sheep——'
Teacher: 'No! "The little ship!"'
Pupil: 'The little sheep——'
Teacher: '*Not* "sheep", you ass, but "ship".'
Pupil: 'The leetle ship——'
Teacher: 'Damn it: Are you deaf? I've already said "little ship", not "leetle ship". Start all over again.'
Pupil: 'Thee little ship——' and so on.

When books started to arrive from the UK, study courses began. Later, a prison theatre was opened and plays, varieties, and concerts occupied much of the time of officers with any talent for amateur theatricals or musicals.

One variety concert, arranged by Lieutenant Teddy Barton, RASC, played to packed houses for several nights. It was called *Ballet Nonsense*. Costumes were made mostly out of crêpe paper, which served the purpose well. The orchestra was of surprisingly high quality and the airs and lyrics, composed by 'Jimmy' Yule (Lieutenant J. Yule, RCS) and Teddy Barton, gave the show a professional touch which savoured poignantly of Drury Lane and the Hippodrome. The orchestral talent was provided by a mixture of all the nationalities under the able band leadership of John Wilkins, a naval (submarine) Leading Telegraphist who had a fantastic aptitude for playing any wind instrument he chose to pick up, in a matter of days. The underlying theme of *Ballet Nonsense* was provided by a *corps de ballet* consisting of the toughest-looking, heaviest-moustached officers available, who performed miracles of energetic grace and unsophisticated elegance upon the resounding boards of the Colditz theatre stage attired in frilly crêpe paper ballet skirts and brassières.

Ballet Nonsense very nearly never came off! A grand piano was to be installed for the occasion. When it arrived in the courtyard, the workmen engaged in hauling it up the narrow stairs took off their jackets and waistcoats for the job. These, of course, quickly disappeared. The contents of pockets were left intact, but the civilian clothing was considered by the vast majority of the camp to be fair game!

The Commandant promptly closed the theatre and demanded the return of the clothing. Monetary compensation was offered by the POWs, but the return of the clothes – no! It was all very upsetting for the Management, who had gone to endless trouble over advertisements with decorative posters spread about the Castle. They, the Management, were in the throes of preparing postponement strips beginning with 'The Management regrets . . .' and were haggling over the phrases to follow, which were quite likely to put the author in 'solitary' for a month if he was not tactful as to their content, when their worries were dispelled in an unforeseen manner. The French, true to a Riviera tradition, solved the problem in their own way. When the morning after the piano incident dawned, a second poster had been superimposed over the *Ballet Nonsense* Folly Girls. It read:

FOR SUNSHINE HOLIDAYS
VISIT
SUNNY COLDITZ
HOLIDAY HOTEL
500 BEDS, ONE BATH
CUISINE
BY FRENCH CHEF
LARGE STAFF
ALWAYS ATTENTIVE AND VIGILANT
ONCE VISITED, NEVER LEFT

(The camp cook was a French chef, though he had no scope for his talent.)

After a month of futile searching for the clothes by the Jerries, the money was accepted and the theatre reopened. *Ballet Nonsense* was a far greater success, due to a month of extra rehearsals!

The midday meal at Colditz was sounded at 12.30 pm and consisted of thick barley gruel. Occasionally, pieces of hog's hide were cut up and put into the soup, which gave it a delicious odour of pork and that was about all. On such days the German menu on the blackboard outside the kitchen triumphantly announced '*Speck*' – in other words, bacon. It deceived nobody but the far-away 'Protecting Power' who read the menus, sent by the German *Kommandantur* in answer to questionaires. Nor did it deceive the 'Protecting Power' for long either; the latter was quickly disillusioned on its representatives' first visit to the camp. The 'Protecting Power' is a neutral Government which represents the interests of one belligerent

Day	Breakfast	Lunch	Dinner
Monday	Coffee-subst. 4 gr.	Potatoes 400 gr. Turnips 500 gr.	Jam-subst. 20 gr. Bread 300 gr.
Tuesday	Coffee-subst. 4 gr.	Potatoes 400 gr. Turnips 600 gr.	Jam-subst. 20 gr. Bread 300 gr.
Wednesday	Coffee-subst. 4 gr.	Potatoes 400 gr. Turnips 500 gr.	Jam-subst. 20 gr. Bread 300 gr.
Thursday	Coffee-subst. 4 gr.	Potatoes 400 gr. Turnips 600 gr.	Jam-subst. 20 gr. Bread 300 gr.
Friday	Coffee-subst. 4 gr.	Potatoes 400 gr. Turnips 600 gr.	Jam-subst. 20 gr. Bread 300 gr. Cheese 31.25 gr.
Saturday	Coffee-subst. 4 gr.	Potatoes 400 gr. Peas 112.5 gr. Millet 75 gr. Oats 62.5 gr. Cooking-fat 68 gr. Barley 37.5 gr.	Jam-subst. 20 gr. Sugar 175 gr. Jam 175 gr. Bread 300 gr.
Sunday	Coffee-subst. 3.5 gr.	Potatoes 350 gr. Fresh meat 250 gr. Turnips 600 gr.	Jam-subst. 30 gr. Bread 425 gr.

(*One English pound equals 454 grammes*)

Power in the territories of the other. In the case of the UK the Government was Switzerland's, and unstinted praise is due for its good work on behalf of British prisoners throughout the war.

The rations deteriorated as the war progressed. An idea of the German ration of food provided from about 1942 onwards is given by the table shown, which has been taken from a 'Protecting Power' report on Colditz.

It was inevitable that the camp should possess a cat. It arrived, of course, as a kitten and in time grew up into a fine brindled specimen through the undisputed and indulgent care of a rather fat Belgian officer. The two were inseparable, for the Belgian never stinted the cat's rations and the latter grew fat while the Belgian grew thin. One day the cat disappeared. His absence was mourned by all, while his master, though visibly moved, bore the loss with a smile. As the days passed it was assumed that the cat, tiring of monastic life, had gone a-roaming to find a mate, and the affair was forgotten. Then, a British orderly, while emptying the camp dustbins, came across a brown-paper parcel. Curiosity led him to open it and, as the layers of paper were unfolded, out fell an unmistakable brindled pelt. The cat was out of the bag; the smile had been on the face of the tiger.

In the afternoon, sport came to the fore. Foils made their appearance at one time and many took up fencing. The little courtyard only lent itself to games such as volley-ball; that is to say, a football pushed backwards and forwards over a high badminton net with about three players on each side. Boxing was another favourite pastime.

There was one game which deserves special mention. It was invented by the British and belonged to that category of local school game devised in almost every public school of England. The wall game at Eton is an example. The rules soon become a matter of tradition and depend on the surface and shape of the ground, the buildings round it, and various hazards such as jutting corners or stone steps. The Colditz variety, which we called 'stoolball', was played, of course, in the granite cobbled courtyard. It is the roughest game I have ever played, putting games like rugby football in the shade. The rules were simple. Two sides, consisting of any number of players and often as many as thirty a side, fought for possession of the football by any means. A player having the ball could run with it but could not hold it indefinitely; he had to bounce it occasionally while on the move. When tackled, he could do whatever he liked with it. A 'goalie' at each end of the yard sat on a stool – hence the name – and a goal was scored by touching the opponent's stool with the ball. Goal defence was by any means, including strangulation of the ball-holder, if necessary. There was a half-time when everybody was too tired to continue. There was no referee and there were, of course, no touchlines.

The game proceeded as a series of lightning dashes, appalling crashes, deafening shouts, formidable scrums – generally involving the whole side – rapid passing movements, as in a rugby three-quarter line, and with a cheering knot of spectators at every window. Nobody was ever seriously hurt, in spite of the fury and the pace at which the game was played. Clothing was ripped to pieces, while mass wrestling and throwing of bodies was the order of the day. To extract an opponent from a scrum it was recommendable to grab him by the scalp and one leg. I never saw any 'tripping'. This was probably due to the instinctive reaction of players to long schooling in our various ball games where tripping is forbidden. I realize now that this game was a manifestation of our suppressed desire for freedom. While the game was in action we were free. The surrounding walls were no longer a prison, but the confines of the game we played, and there were no constraining rules to curtail our freedom of action. I always felt much better after a game. Followed by a cold bath it put me on top of the world.

The Poles, and later the French when they arrived, were always interested spectators. Although we had no monopoly of the courtyard, they naturally took to their rooms and watched the game from windows. They eventually put up sides against the British and games were played against them, but these were not a success. Tempers were lost and the score became a matter of importance, which it never did in an 'all-British' game.

As time went on, the Jerries allowed us a couple of hours' exercise three times a week in a barbed-wire pen in the wooded grounds below the Castle, but within the external Castle walls. Here we played something resembling soccer – the hazards were the trees amongst which the game surged backwards and forwards. Our ball games amused the Jerries. Officers and NCOs were occasionally caught watching them surreptitiously – not because they were afraid of being seen as spectators, but because their vantage-points were supposed to be secret and were used for spying upon us.

Towards the afternoon musical instruments could be heard tuning up on all sides. As soon as they could be purchased, many officers started practising one type or another. In the late afternoon, too, we could usually rely upon a *Sondermeldung* – which was always a good diversion.

What happened was that the Germans, who had placed loudspeakers at strategic points throughout the Castle, would switch on the power when a German *Sondermeldung* or Special War Progress bulletin was announced. These were calculated to raise German morale through the Reich to incredible heights and correspondingly to demoralize Germany's enemies to the point of throwing in the sponge.

Anyway – in the camp – the power would suddenly be switched on with unmistakable crackling noises as the loudspeakers heated up. First a fanfare of trumpets sounded. Then, the strains of Listz's preludes would come over the air, followed after a few moments by the announcer's proclamation in solemn and sonorous tones:

> *Das Oberkommando der Wehrmacht gibt bekannt! In tagelangen schweren Kämpfen gegen einen stark gesicherten Geleitzug im Atlantik haben unsere Unterseeboote sechzehn Schiffe mit ingesamt hundertfünfzigtausend Bruttoregistertonnen versenkt. Ferner wurden zwei Zerstörer schwer beschädigt.*

As soon as the announcer had ceased, German brass bands would strike up *Wir fahren gegen Engeland*, and to the additional accompaniment of the whine of descending bombs, the crackle of machine-guns and the bursting of shells the act would attain a crescendo of power and then end with trumpets heralding victory.

The show was intended to make the bravest quail. It regularly produced pandemonium in the camp. No sooner had the ominous crackle of the loudspeakers started than windows all over the Castle would open, heads would reach out to the bars and every musical instrument that could be mustered was automatically requisitioned for the coming spectacle. As Liszt's preludes softened to give way to the announcer, this was the signal: drums, cymbals, clarinets, cornets, trombones and accordions, all gave voice at once in a cacophony that could be heard re-echoing from distant hills. The German *Kommandantur* shook with the reverberations.

But the Germans persevered and the war went on in earnest for several months, until eventually they gave in and the loudspeakers were for ever silenced.

Of course they tried all means at first to stop our counter-attack – but that was not easy. What broke the German morale, in the end, over the battle, was not so much the opposition we put up, as the insidious counter-propaganda we produced. For we recorded regularly the numbers of *Bruttoregistertonnen* involved, until we could show the Germans in the camp that there could not be a British ship left afloat, according to their figures.

In our less energetic moments, especially in the evenings, we played bridge and chess. Chess games, in a community where the passage of time was of no importance, went on for days. Players were known to sit up all night with a home-made, foul-smelling oil-lamp (for the electricity was turned off). The light had to be shaded so as not to show through the windows and bring the Jerries in.

There was also a card game for two players which we learnt from the Poles, called 'Gapin', which means, in Polish, 'a person who looks but does not see'! The term applied well to the game, for it was one in which many cards lay face upwards on the table. These cards could be made use of, provided a player held certain corresponding cards in his hand. The open cards were continually changing, so that concentration and quick thinking were necessary. The game was aggravating, for after finishing a turn an opponent could promptly make good use of a card overlooked. It was so exasperating a game that I have known friends not to be on speaking terms for days because of humiliation and wounded pride involved in the showing up of an opponent's obtuseness. Rupert Barry and I had a running 'Gapin Contest' with high stakes in *Lagergeld* which ended with the payment, after the war, of a fat cheque – to Rupert!

The last roll-call of the day occurred usually at 9 pm, after which soon came 'lights out'. At this 'witching hour' many of the nefarious escape activities of the camp started up. They were lumped together under the general heading of 'night shift'.

CHAPTER 6

THE SECOND TUNNEL

With Christmas fare inside us, optimism returned, and we began to wonder how the walls of our unbreachable fortress could be pierced. Tunnelling seemed to be the only solution, and we (the British) were such a small number, and so united in our resolution to escape, that we worked as one team. Lieutenant-Colonel Guy German (Royal Leicestershire Regiment), our senior officer, placed me in charge of operations, and kept aloof from them himself so as to be in a strong position *vis-à-vis* the Jerries. Nevertheless, he was keen to take part in any escape into which he could be fitted.

As at Laufen, we concentrated on parts of the Castle not used by ourselves. Our début was made early in January 1941 in a room on the ground floor under German lock and key. We were learning from the Poles their art of picking locks, and in this empty room, with our usual guards on the look-out for alarms, we started work. Loosening floor boards, we came on loose rubble and in a short time had a hole big enough for a man to work in, with the floorboards replaced over him.

I was dissatisfied with this tunnel entrance before long, because the boards were very old and one of them could be lifted easily; moreover, they sounded ominously hollow underfoot. I made a sliding trap-door out of bed boards, which fitted between the floor supporting-beams. The trap-door itself was a long, open-topped box which slid horizontally on wooden runners. The box was filled with the under-floor rubble. When the trap-door was closed, a German could lift the floorboards and see nothing suspicious; he could even stand on the trap-door. At the same time, the rubble filling damped out the hollow sound. Without any discussion, the trap-door became known as 'Shovewood II'!

The trap was soon tested in action. Hank Wardle and I were surprised one day when the Germans came to the room before we could disappear, but luckily not before we had closed the trap and replaced the floorboards.

I do not know why they came directly to this room. It was most unlikely they had then – as they had later – sound detectors around the Castle walls, which picked up noises of tunnelling. Their spies, set at various windows, may have remarked an unusual movement of British officers through certain doors in the buildings, not previously employed, or again some Polish orderlies (prisoners-of-war), whose rooms were close to where we worked may not have been trustworthy.

In any event, it was an awkward moment when the Germans unlocked the empty room and gazed upon two British officers doing physical jerks and press-ups, counting audibly, 'One – two – one – two –three and four – one – two——' with seraphic innocence written all over their faces. Luckily we spoke no German and had only to gesticulate in reply to their shouts. We were allowed to leave, but given to understand that the matter was not closed. The Germans searched the room after our departure, prising up floorboards, and then left.

The tunnel would never succeed now; that, at least, was plain. We promptly gave it up. The same afternoon, Hank and I, along with four others who had committed some minor offence, were called for, escorted to the room in which 'Shovewood II' reposed, and locked in.

Curiosity could not keep Kenneth away long, and almost as soon as the 'Goonery' had departed, he was at the door asking puckish questions.

'How do you like your new quarters?'

'I don't. Go and tell Colonel German what has happened. He'll kick up hell with the *Kommandant*. This is imprisonment without trial!'

'I shouldn't worry, Pat. They'll let you out in a month or so and it's a fine room for doing physical jerks in! You'll be so fit when you come out.'

'I'm fit enough now,' I answered, 'to knock your head off like a ninepin, if you don't do something quickly.'

'But there's the tunnel to get on with! No need to bother about shifts – you can just go on and on. Maybe you'll be out in a month by the tunnel instead of by the door!'

'Kenneth,' I shouted, exasperated, 'I'm getting out of this today. Go and fetch my "Universal".'

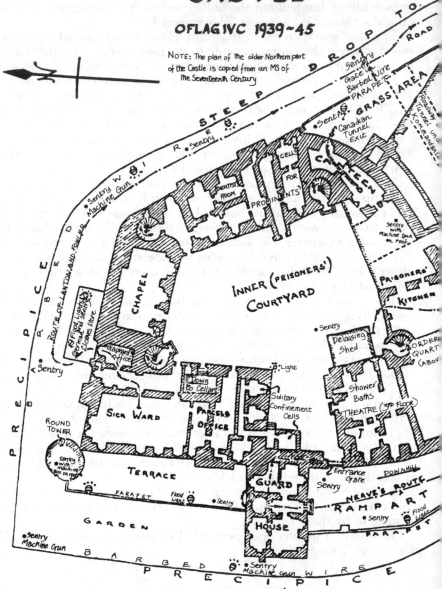

PLAN OF

COLDITZ CASTLE

OFLAG IVC 1939~45

NOTE: The plan of the older Northern part
of the Castle is copied from an MS of
the Seventeenth Century

ESCAPE ROUTES SHOWN THUS ▬▪▬▪▬

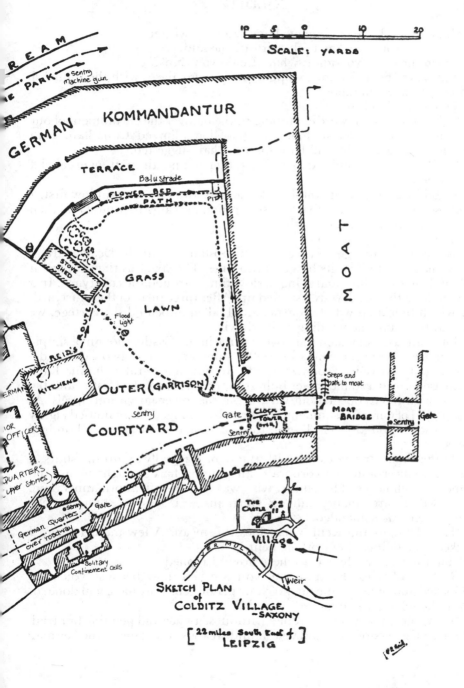

SCALE: YARDS

STREAM

E PARK • Sentry machine gun

GERMAN KOMMANDANTUR

TERRACE

Balustrade

FLOWER BED PATH

PIT

MOAT

STOVE SHED

GRASS LAWN

• Flood Light

REID'S ROUTE

GERMAN KITCHENS

OUTER (GARRISON)

Sentry

Gate

CLOCK TOWER (ONE)

MOAT BRIDGE

• Sentry

Gate

IOR OFFICERS

COURTYARD

Sentry

Steps and path to moat

QUARTERS (Upper Stories)

• Sentry

Gate

German Quarters over roadway

Solitary Confinement Cells

THE CASTLE

Village

RIVER MULDE

Weir

SKETCH PLAN
of
COLDITZ VILLAGE
— SAXONY

[22 miles South East of
LEIPZIG]

He went, and a few moments later returned with it.

'What do you want me to do with it?' he said.

'Open the door, you idiot; what else do you think?'

'But why? It's such a lovely opportunity to go ahead with the tunnel, I think I'll leave you there.'

'Open up!' I yelled.

Inside, the six of us were champing at the bit over the curtailment of our liberties. Hank, a tall six-foot length of loose-limbed Canadian, with freckles and curly hair, and handsome withal, suggested:

'Let's take the ruddy door off its hinges and drop it over a cliff somewhere.'

'Good idea,' I said, 'if you'll hack the bars away from a window first. I propose we carry the door in procession round the camp in protest and then dump it at the top of the Castle.'

Kenneth opened the door.

'Kenneth,' I said, 'go and get someone upstairs to play the Dead March!'

We had the door off its hinges in no time. The six of us then carried it solemnly like a coffin – marching in slow time – around the courtyard. In a few minutes the Dead March started up. After three turns of the courtyard, by which time a crowd of mourners had fallen in behind the cortège, we started to mount the winding stairs slowly.

The staircases, of which there were three in the Castle, though of simple design, were beautiful, consisting of flat stone steps about two yards wide, winding upwards in a perfect spiral around a central column. Each staircase formed a round tower built into the corners of the Castle, and the doors to all rooms opened outwards from the towers at various levels. At one period of our imprisonment, the British contingent were housed eighty steps above ground-level! To the top was a matter of about a hundred steps.

By the time our procession with the door was halfway up the stairs, a German officer and two corporals, all panting hard, caught us up and joined in behind us. The officer, who was known as Hauptmann Priem, possessed a rare quality among Germans – a sense of humour. An interpreter was demanded.

'Herr Hauptmann Reid, what does this mean? A few moments ago I locked you all into close confinement.'

'That is exactly why we are here now,' I replied.

'Not at all, Herr Hauptmann, you are here now because you have unlocked and removed the door of your prison cell. Why have you done so? – and how have you done so?'

'We protest at being imprisoned without sentence and pending fair trial. We are prisoners-of-war, and you should treat us according to the German

Army Code and the Geneva Convention.'

Priem smiled broadly and said:

'Very well! If you will return the door to its hinges, you shall go free, pending trial!'

I agreed, and the whole solemn procession wended its way downstairs again. The door was replaced ceremoniously with saluting and heel-clicking.

Priem was intrigued to know how we unhinged a locked door, so I gave him a short piece of twisted wire, which I had obtained specially for the eventuality of a search. This may seem an unwise thing to have done, but by now the Germans knew well that we could pass through a simply locked door. They had given up separating the different nationalities for that reason among others, and a piece of useless wire gave nothing away. We heard no more of the incident.

We continued our search for the weak spots in the Castle's armour. I was next attracted by the drains, and a trusted Polish orderly told me that once, when a certain manhole cover in the yard had been raised, he had seen small brick tunnels running in various directions. This sounded promising. There were two round manhole covers in the courtyard, but alas! they were in full view of spy windows and of the spyhole in the main courtyard gate.

I decided to make a reconnaissance by night. In the darkness we could unlock our staircase door into the courtyard – we were always locked into our quarters at night – and provided the guard outside the gate was not disturbed or tempted to switch on the courtyard lights, we could proceed with our examination. The moon was not up. It was February and bitterly cold. We knew the manhole covers were frozen solid to their bases, but we had prepared boiling water in our blackout kitchen. With Kenneth acting as doorkeeper with the key, Rupert made sorties at ten-minute intervals and poured the boiling contents of a kettle around the nearest cover. Then we both sortied, I with a stout piece of iron unscrewed from a door support, and together we managed to loosen and lift up the cover. The hole was not deep and there were the tunnels as the orderly had said. I jumped in and Rupert replaced the lid and disappeared. He was to return in half an hour.

My reconnaissance along the slimy tunnels, which were about three feet by two feet in section, arched and flat-bottomed, revealed one leading up to the camp building in which the canteen was housed. This was bricked up at the canteen entrance, but obviously continued inside. Another led to the kitchens, which accounted for the slime. A third was the outfall sewer and ran under the courtyard to another manhole. It looked promising and I followed it, but a couple of yards beyond the second manhole it, also, was bricked up with a small pipe at the bottom serving to drain the system. The pipe headed out under the courtyard gateway. I had my iron tool, a cigarette-lighter, and one of our home-made lamps. I tackled the brick; the joints were very tough indeed, and I made little impression. The wall had been recently built and obviously with special attention to strength.

Rupert returned on time and the two of us – myself pushing upwards from within – managed to remove the heavy cover. I was filthy and smelling badly, but there was hope in two directions!

During several nights following I took turns with Rupert and Dick Howe in attacking the brick wall in the tunnel with an assortment of steel bits and nails which we 'won' by various means.

The task proved hopeless, especially as we dare make very little noise. In the silence of the night, the sound of hammering could be plainly heard in the courtyard even from below ground. The tunnels and pipes echoed the sound and carried it a long way.

We thought of doing the job in daylight and I actually descended two days running in full view of those officers who happened to be exercising in the yard, but protected from the direction of the main gate by a small knot of Britishers while the manhole cover was being removed. Although I hammered loudly enough to wake the dead, I made little impression. The joints in the brickwork were made with '*ciment fondu*' – a specially tough cement.

We tried the second direction. Inside the canteen, where we bought our razor-blades and suchlike, in front of the counter on the buyers' side was a manhole cover. I had not far to seek for assistance in opening up this manhole, for Kenneth had already provided the solution. Some weeks before he had had himself appointed assistant manager and accountant of the canteen!

Kenneth was a London Stock Exchange man and the idea of keeping even the meagre canteen accounts evidently made him feel a little nearer home. He had been educated at Whitgift School and was by nature a tidy person, meticulous in his ways and in his speech. He made a point of buckling the nib of the pen used by the German *Feldwebel* (sergeant) in charge of the canteen so that that unfortunate man invariably started his day's accounts with a large blot at the top of his page. Kenneth explained to the *Feldwebel* on the first occasion that nibs made with poor wartime steel always buckled if used with bad wartime ink owing to the 'springiness' of the nib being affected by a film of corrosion. Thereafter he consoled the *Feldwebel* whenever the latter fell into his trap. He always added a titbit of demoralizing propaganda such as that the whole war was a shame and he was sure the Germans didn't want it any more than the English. Within a few months he had broken down the morale of the *Feldwebel* to such an extent that the latter was preaching sedition to his colleagues and had to be removed.

The table which Kenneth and the *Feldwebel* used for writing was situated under the only window in the room, at some distance from the counter. While a few people stood at the counter, and Kenneth distracted the German's attention with some accounting matter at the table, it was comparatively simple to tackle the manhole cover.

Incidentally, Kenneth in his position as canteen accountant had also to deal with the mail. This brought him into contact with the German camp interpreter, who was responsible for censoring our letters home. His name was Pfeiffer – in English 'Whistler' – and to suit his name his voice never descended below the treble clef.

Our group were leaning over the counter preparatory to dealing with the manhole when Pfeiffer entered the canteen and demanded to see Kenneth. I should say, in parenthesis, that we had been allowed, on rare occasions, to send home with our mail photographs taken by a German civilian photographer.

Pfeiffer addressed Kenneth:

'Herr Hauptmann, once again must I not tell you that officers on the backside of photographs to write forbidden are. Will you please foresee that my instructions be carried out?'

Before Kenneth had time to make any retort, a Polish officer, Felix Jablonowski, rushed into the canteen, beaming all over, and shouted:

'Have you heard the news? Benghazi has fallen down!' (It was early February 1941.)

We forgot the manhole and started cheering. Pfeiffer's brain must have been working at top pressure conjuring up a sarcastic retort to combat this exhibition of non-defeatist morale. There was a moment's lull in the cheering and he piped up shrilly:

'All that you too to the Marines can tell.'

The cheering redoubled in intensity.

When the excitement had died down, we continued our work. The manhole came away after some persuasion. Sure enough, there were tunnels leading in two directions, one connecting with the tunnel already noticed from the yard, and the other leading out under the window beside which Kenneth and the German worked. A second reconnaissance in more detail showed this latter to be about eighteen yards long and built on a curve. Under the window it was blocked up with large hewn stones and mortar. Outside the shop window and at the level of the canteen floor was a grass lawn, which also abutted the German section of the Castle. At the outer edge of this lawn was a stone balustrade, and then a forty-foot drop over a retaining wall to the level of the roadway which led down to the valley in which our football ground was situated. Maybe the tunnel led out to this wall. We had to find out.

A few days later we had made out of an iron bedpiece a key which opened the canteen door. Working at night as before, we would open our staircase entrance door and cross about ten yards of the courtyard to the canteen door. This opened, we would enter and lock it behind us. We then had to climb a high wooden partition in order to enter the canteen proper, as the door in this partition had a German-type Yale lock which foiled us. The partition separated the canteen from the camp office: a room in which all the haggling took place between our Commanding Officer and the German Camp Commandant on his periodic visits. The partition was surmounted with the aid of a couple of sheets used as ropes.

Entering our tunnel, we tackled the wall at the end. This time we were lucky. The mortar gave way easily and we were soon loosening huge stones which we removed to the other tunnel (the one leading back to the courtyard). Although the wall was four feet thick we were through it in a week of night shifts. Alas! the tunnel did not continue on the other side. Beyond the wall, under the grass, was sticky yellow clay.

My next idea was to make a vertical shaft which would bring the tunnel up to the grass. I would construct a trap-door which would be covered with grass and yet would open when required, thus repeating my Laufen idea of having the escape tunnel intact for further use. Escapes involved such an immense amount of labour, sometimes only to serve in the escape of one or two men, that it was always worth while attempting to leave the escape exit ready for future use.

Once out on the grass patch we could creep along under the Castle walls in the dark; descend the retaining wall with sheets; then continue past the guards' sleeping-quarters to the last defence – the twelve-foot wall of the Castle park surmounted for much of its length with barbed wire. This obstacle would not be difficult provided there was complete concealment, which was possible at night, and provided there was plenty of time to deal with the barbed wire. We had to pass in full view of a sentry at one point. He was only forty yards away, but as there were Germans who frequently passed the same point, this was not a serious difficulty.

I constructed out of bed-boards and stolen screws a trap which looked like a small table with collapsible legs – collapsible so as to enter the tunnel. The legs were also telescopic; that is to say, they could be extended by degrees to five feet in length. The table-top was a tray with vertical sides four inches deep. It sat in a frame and had shutters so that I could excavate upwards from below, removing half the table area at a time. As soon as the edge of the tray came to within an inch of the surface of the lawn I merely had to close both shutters and cut the last inch of earth around the tray with a sharp kinfe. Then, pushing the tray up I could lift it clear, still full of undisturbed grass. The last man out would replace the tray in the frame and patch up carefully any tell-tale marks around the edge. The frame, supported on its extended legs, set on stones at the bottom of the tunnel, would take the weight of a man standing on the tray. The tunnel floor (in the clay) was just five feet below the lawn surface. I need hardly mention that the contraption was christened 'Shovewood III'!

Before all this happened, our plans were temporarily upset. Two Polish officers got into the canteen one night when we were not working and tried to cut the bars outside the window which I have mentioned before. Cutting bars cannot be done silently. They did not take the precaution of having their own stooges either to distract the attention of the nearby sentry or to give warning of his approach. Throughout our work on the tunnel we had a signalling system from our rooms above which gave warning of this sentry's approach. He was normally out of sight from where our tunnel exit was to be, but he only had to extend his beat a few yards in order to come into view.

The Poles were caught red-handed and within a few days a huge floodlight was installed in such a position as to light up the whole lawn and all the prison windows opening on to it.

This was a good example of what was bound to happen in a camp holding none but officers bent on escape. We had already asked the Poles for liaison on escape projects so that we would not tread on each other's toes all the time, and now Colonel German called a meeting with their Senior Officers, at which an agreement was reached. The Senior Polish Officer was in a difficult position because he frankly could not control his officers; he knew that they might attempt to escape without telling him or anybody else. However, after this meeting the liaison improved, and when we offered some Poles places in our tunnel escape, mutual confidence was established.

Shortly after this incident about two hundred and fifty French officers, led by General Le Bleu, arrived at Colditz. All of them were not escapers by any means, but about one hundred of them were. Among the remainder were many French Jews who were segregated from the rest by the Germans and given their own quarters on the top floor of the Castle.

We had to come to an arrangement with the French Senior Officer over escape projects similar to that agreed with the Poles, but unfortunately the French liaison system was also found wanting – at the expense of our tunnel – before a workable understanding was reached.

To return to the thread of my story: we were not allowed to store any tinned food, expressly because it was potential escape rations. Over a period of time we had all stinted ourselves to collect a reserve for distribution when our tunnel would be ready. It amounted to three heavy sackloads. One night we were busy transporting the sacks into the tunnel from our quarters, where they were badly hidden. Rupert carried them one by one out of our courtyard door into the canteen. On the last trip all the courtyard lights were suddenly switched on from outside, and Rupert found himself between the doors, like Father Christmas caught *in flagrante delicto*! He made for the door of our quarters, which had to be unlocked again for him to re-enter. To our astonishment nothing further happened, so we completed our work for the night and returned to bed. Whether the Germans saw Rupert or not we shall never know, but since the Polish attempt they seemed to be more on the *qui vive*.

This incident was followed by a still more unfortunate one. Although the Germans often paid nocturnal visits to our quarters without warning, this did not seriously bother us. If we were in the tunnel, the doors were locked as usual, and pillows were placed in our beds to pass the casual inspection of a torch flashing along the rows of sleeping bodies.

One night, however, the Germans had been carousing – we could hear them. In fact, they kept our orderlies awake, and that was the start of the trouble. We had five staunch, 'game' orderlies, who had places reserved on our tunnel escape.

On this particular night, being unable to sleep for the Germans, one of the orderlies named Goldman, a Jew from Whitechapel, who had a sense of humour, started to barrack the German sentry outside the nearest window. Goldman had arrived at Colditz as Colonel German's orderly and was so voluble at their interrogation by the Camp Commandant that he was mistaken by him for our new SBO. The barracking must have been reported to the carousing Goons, for after some time, they arrived in the courtyard in force and headed for our quarters. Priem and another officer, the Regimental Sergeant-Major – Oberstabsfeldwebel Gephard – the corporal known as the *fouine* and half a dozen Goons entered and began shouting '*Aufstehen!*' They woke everyone up, poked the beds, and discovered that four officers were missing.

The Germans lost their heads. They had come upstairs drunk and disorderly, intent on having some fun at our expense, and had not expected this new turn of affairs. Gephard, who looked like the fat boy of Peckham, was wearing his dress parade uniform. He carried an enormous curved sword, which every now and then caught between his legs. He was despatched to count the orderlies.

'*Aufstehen! Aufstehen!*' he shouted. 'You English pig-dogs! I shall teach you——' Crash! – as he tripped up over his 'battle-axe'. Then, picking himself up he started again:

'You English pig-dogs! I shall teach you to laugh at German soldiers carrying out their duty! Tomorrow morning at dawn you shall be shot. All of you! I shall give the firing order myself.'

He strode up and down the room trying to increase his stature and to cope with his sword which clattered and jangled along behind him. 'Goldman!' he screamed, 'what are you doing with those playing-cards?'

Goldman had quietly given each orderly a card face downwards.

'We are about to draw for places in the order of shooting,' he replied.

Gephard spluttered and drew his sword.

'Swine! You dare to insult me personally!' – still struggling with his sword, which was too long for him to extract comfortably from the scabbard – 'Put down those cards at once. You will be the first and I shall not wait longer. I shall remove your head.'

Finally unsheathing the sword by holding the blade with both hands, he advanced on Goldman, waving it wildly around his head. The latter disappeared under a bed. Gephard's dignity prevented him from following. Instead, he performed a dance of rage around the bed, hacking at the wooden supports. Having let off steam, he sheathed the 'battle-axe' once more, quickly counted the orderlies, noting significantly the presence of Goldman still underneath the bed, departed with much jingling and tripped up once more as he slammed the door behind him.

The confusion in the officers' dormitory became indescribable. The officers were paraded along the middle of the room while Goons turned every bed inside out, and emptied the contents of cupboards all over the floor.

Priem, with his face glistening and his nose distinctly showing signs of the bottle, was torn between rage at having his carousal upset for longer than he had anticipated, and high spirits which were his more natural reaction to alcohol. He compromised between the two moods by seizing a pick-axe from one of his soldiers, and started to hack up the floor.

With mighty swings, accompanied by gleeful war-cries, he smote the floorboards, wrenching off large pieces of timber. With each blow he shouted a name: 'Benghazi'; 'Derna'; 'Tobruk' (Rommel was advancing in Africa at the time). As he shouted ' Tobruk', a huge length of flooring came away on the end of his axe and impaled to it under the board was a brand-new civilian felt hat! It had been very carefully hidden there by Lieutenant Alan Orr Ewing, Argyll and Sutherland Highlanders, nicknamed 'Scruffy', who had only the day before paid a large sum in *Lagermarks* to a French orderly to smuggle it into the camp.

This gave Priem an idea. He sent out orders for the dogs to be summoned. They arrived; were led to the beds of the missing officers; encouraged to sniff; and then unleashed. They left the dormitory and made for the foodbin in the kitchen where Goldman was already pottering. Priem followed them. Spying Goldman, he seized him by the collar and demanded:

'What direction have the missing officers taken?' to which Goldman answered:

'That's right! Hauptmann Priem, pick on me! Every time an officer wants to escape, he comes up to me and says: "Please, Goldman, may I go to Switzerland?"'

Priem saw the point, relaxed his grip, and shooed the dogs out of the food-bin. These promptly dashed out of the quarters and headed up the stairs, followed by Priem and Goldman's parting shot:

'That's right, Fido – they jumped off the bleedin' roof.'

When the dogs produced nothing, Priem sent out orders for the whole camp to be paraded. It was about 2 am by then. Suddenly, 'stooge' Wardle, a submarine officer lately arrived who was our look-out, shouted, 'They're heading for the canteen.' He had scarcely time to jump down into the tunnel, and I to pull the manhole cover over us, before the Jerries were in. They searched the canteen and tried hard to lift the manhole cover, but were unable to do so as I was hanging on to it for dear life from underneath, my fingers wedged in a protruding lip of the cover.

As soon as we noticed that a 'General *Appell*' had been called, I told Rupert and Dick (the others in the tunnel with me) to start at once building a false wall halfway up the tunnel, behind which they put our food store and other escape paraphernalia such as rucksacks, maps, compasses, and civilian clothing which we normally kept hidden there.

The hubbub continued in the courtyard for about an hour. The count was taken about half a dozen times amidst as much confusion as the prisoners could create without having themselves shot, and aided by the chaos caused by the Germans themselves, who were rushing all over the camp searching every room and turning all movable objects upside-down.

Rupert and Dick quietly continued their work and in a few hours had constructed a magnificent false wall with stones from the original wall which we had demolished, jointed with clay from under the lawn and coated with dust wherever the joints showed.

By 5 am all was quiet again. We departed as we had come and went to bed wondering how the Germans would react to our reappearance at morning *Appell*. We had apparently put them to a great deal of trouble, for we heard that, while the Jerries had had the whole camp on parade, they had carried out an individual identity check. Every officer paraded in front of a table where he was identified against his photograph and duly registered as present. We were recorded as having escaped, and messages, flashed to the OKW (*Oberkommando der Wehrmacht*), brought into action a network of precautions taken all over the country as a matter of routine for the recapture of prisoners.

At the morning *Appell*, when we were all found present again, confusion reigned once more. The Goons decided to hold a second identification parade which they completed after about two and a half hours. They then called out our four names, which they had managed to segregate at last, and we were paraded in front of everybody. They dismissed the parade and led us to the little interview room, in which most of our fights with the *Kommandantur* took place. We refused to explain our disappearance and were remanded for sentence for causing a disturbance and being absent from *Appell*. The OKW orders had to be countermanded and the Commandant, we heard, had a 'rap over the knuckles' for the incident.

The Goons were upset and watchful during the next few days. They again visited the canteen, and this time the manhole cover came away – too easily for our liking, of course! But they had done some scraping around the edges before trying it and were apparently satisfied it was the result of their own efforts. The dust and grit, inserted around the manhole cover, were placed there by us as a matter of routine after every working shift, so that the cover always looked as if it had not been touched for years. A Goon descended and, after an examination, declared 'nothing unusual' below. Kenneth, who was in the background of the shop, trying to appear occupied with his accounts, breathed an audible sigh of relief, which he quickly turned into a yawn for the benefit of his German colleague, busy at the same table.

The Germans were suspicious of this tunnel, either because they had seen Rupert doing Father Christmas in the courtyard or because they were warned by a spy in the camp. A third possibility would have been microphones, set to detect noises. Microphones were installed, to our knowledge, in many places later on, but it is doubtful whether the Jerries had them in Colditz at this period of the war. Microphones were installed in newly-built hutted camps for the RAF, but their installation in an old Schloss would have left telltale marks which we could have traced.

The spy – that is to say, a 'stooge' or prisoner in the camp – set by the Germans to report on us was a definite possibility, and our suspicions were later proved correct. Suffice it to say that we repeatedly found the Goons very quick on the trail of our activities. We tried hard to make our actions look normal when among other prisoners, but it was not easy, especially on escapes such as tunnels, which involved preparation over a long period of time. Incidentally, we employed the term 'stooge' very loosely! Our 'stooge' Wardle was certainly no spy.

The Goons concreted four heavy clasps into the floor around the canteen manhole cover. However, we dealt with these forthwith by loosening them before the concrete was set, in such a way that they could be turned aside. This was done in daylight while Kenneth as usual occupied the Goon, and a few officers acted as cover at the counter. In their normal position the clasps still held the cover firmly.

This done, we decided to give the tunnel a rest, as things were becoming too hot for our liking.

CHAPTER 7

THE COMMUNITY OF NATIONS

It was March 1941. The camp was slowly filling up; the British contingent had increased by a steady trickle of new arrivals, escapers all, except for a sprinkling of 'Saboteurs of the Reich' – we had three Padres who were classed in the second category. One day about sixty Dutch officers arrived. Curiously enough, their Senior Officer was Major English, ours being Colonel German! The Dutchmen were a fine company of men and a credit to their country. They were all Netherlands East Indies officers. At the outbreak of war, they had sailed home with their troops to Holland in order to help the Mother Country. When Holland was occupied, the German High Command offered an amnesty to all those Dutch officers who would sign a certain document; this, if treated honourably, precluded an officer from acting in any way contrary to the wishes of the German Reich; it also laid down conditions relative to the maintenance of law, order, and subservience within the country. It was apparently a cleverly worded document and most Dutch officers of the home forces signed it.

The Colonials, on the other hand, refused to sign it almost to a man and were promptly marched off to prison in Germany. After many vicissitudes, including unending wordy battles with the Germans and numerous escape attempts, they finally ended up lock, stock, and barrel in Colditz. Since they all spoke German fluently, were as obstinate as mules and as brave as lions, heartily despised the Germans and showed it, they presented special difficulties as prisoners!

They were always impeccably turned out on parade and maintained a high standard of discipline among themselves. I regret to say that the French and ourselves were the black sheep in matters of parade 'turn out'. The French officer is never tidy at the best of times. His uniform does not lend itself to smartness, and the French do not care about 'turn out' anyway.

The British were more unfortunate, and had an excuse for appearing a straggly-looking crowd. The British battledress is not particularly smart, and most of us had lost a part of it at our time of capture – a cap, or jacket, or gaiters – and many of us had to wear wooden-soled clogs, given us by the Germans. Occasionally a much-needed parcel came from home containing replacements for our worn-out kit, and the Red Cross once sent a bulk consignment of uniforms which were of great help. Still, we were a picturesque if not an unsightly company. The other nationalities had somehow succeeded in bringing much of their wardrobe with them, and, at any rate until time wore these out, they had a definite advantage over us. It was common for a Britisher to appear on parade, for instance, wearing a woollen balaclava or no cap at all, a khaki battledress blouse, blue RAF or red Czech trousers, home-knitted socks of any colour, and trailing a pair of clogs on his feet.

Speaking of the picturesque, colour was lent to our parades by two Yugoslav officers who had joined our happy throng. Their uniform, consisting of voluminous red trousers and sky-blue embroidered waistcoats, brought home to us what a Community of Nations we had become!

First, there was the Polish contingent. Then there were Englishmen, Irishmen, and Scotsmen. The Empire was represented by RAF officers from Canada, Australia, and New Zealand, and by an Army doctor, Captain Mazumdar, from India. The French included some officers from Algeria and the Jewish contingent. There were the two Yugoslavs and some Belgian officers. The Netherlands were represented by an aide-de-camp of Queen Wilhelmina and last, but not least, the Dutch East Indies Company completed this procession of nations.

Colditz was the only camp of this kind in Germany. The solidarity that existed among the various nationalities was always a matter of surprise to the Germans. The alliance amongst us was not fostered by any artificial means. It was natural, springing from something deep within us, and it withstood many tests. It was a sufficiently strong link to withstand any attempt by the Germans to alienate one nationality from another.

A favourite communal punishment meted out to any particular contingent was the curtailment of the hours of recreation allowed in the wooded park of the Castle. When this happened, the recreation parade was ostracized by all until the Germans withdrew the ban. If an officer of any one nationality was unfairly treated, the whole camp would go on strike without hesitation, the only condition agreed between us being the form of the strike! On one occasion, Captain Mazumdar, true to a noble tradition, went on hunger strike. I regret to say the whole camp did not follow suit! It was not easy to obtain unanimity and mutual sacrifice where such an elemental means of survival was concerned.

On another occasion the German camp doctor worked himself into a Polish 'hate' neurosis. He insisted that Poland no longer existed, and that in consequence every Polish officer, of whatever rank, should salute him smartly. He was a captain or *Stabsarzt*. When he tried to make the Polish General salute and went into a tantrum about it, this was too much for the Poles. The whole contingent went on hunger strike. The rest of the camp supported them in spirit! The SBOs of all the other nationalities sent parallel complaints concerning the doctor's attitude to the German commandant. After three days the commandant hauled his junior officer over the coals and the famished Polish officers, having registered a grudging salute from the *Stabsarzt*, took to their vittles again with ravenous ardour.

The German sentence upon the four of us who had disappeared for a night was a fortnight's solitary confinement. During this confinement a third unlucky incident occurred which piled up further difficulties in the way of our canteen tunnel escape. A Frenchman and a Pole managed to disappear one day, and were not missed until the evening *Appell*. The Goons suspected a getaway during the return of the prisoners from their recreation in the park, and searched all possible places of concealment in the proximity of the roadway leading down to it. The two officers were found, hiding up for nightfall, in the seldom-used basement of a house near the path (it was used as an air-raid shelter), into which they had slipped undetected. This operation was by no means easy. It had been done by split-second timing, with the assistance of officers who had successfully distracted the attention of the guards accompanying the parade on the march. The assisting officers placed themselves in the ranks so as to be near the guards who walked at intervals on either side. When the officers who were to escape reached a predetermined spot on the march, the others made gestures or remarks calculated to draw the attention of their nearby guards away from the scene of action. Three seconds after the pre-determined spot was reached, the escaping officers bolted. In five more seconds they were behind a concealing wall. During these five seconds some eight guards in view had to be made to 'look the other way'! The chances of success were very slight, but the trick worked. When the count was taken after the recreation period outside the courtyard gate, the assisting officers created confusion and a German-speaking officer browbeat the sergeant in charge into thinking he had made a wrong count to start with, and bluffed out the discrepancy in numbers.

It was a pity that in this case a brilliant beginning was not carried through to a successful end, and that the concealment of the count was not maintained at the later general *Appell*. The *Appell* normally called after dark in the lighted courtyard was, on this day, called in daylight, possibly due to the German sergeant's suspicions getting the better of him. *Appell* times were often changed without warning, especially to catch prisoners out, and this should not have been overlooked.

Be that as it may, the officers, when caught, made up a story concealing their real method of escape and leading the Germans to suspect a rope-descent from an attic skylight on the the grass lawn under which our tunnel exit lay hidden. A sentry was now placed with a beat which brought him in full view of our projected tunnel exit at intervals of one minute both day and night.

This incident led me to make a complaint through Colonel German and to request closer liaison and more co-operation among the various nationalities so that we did not continually trip over each other in our hurry to leave the camp! Common sense prevailed, and from this date I can record no further serious instances of overlapping in escape plans.

Our tunnel was, nevertheless, in 'Queer Street'. I disliked the idea of lengthening it and making a long-term job of it, as any prolonged lapse of time worked against the success of the venture. The Germans also started gradually to install new locks on certain doors at key-points throughout the camp. They began with the lock of the canteen, thereby foiling us temporarily in any attempt to spend long hours at work in the tunnel underneath.

We called the new locks 'cruciform' locks. The simplest description I can give of them is to compare them to four different Yale locks rolled into one. Kenneth Lockwood obtained an impression in candle-wax of the four arms of the cruciform key to the canteen. I worked for a long time on the manufacture of a false key. There was a dentist's room in the camp which was normally locked, as was also the dentist's cupboard of instruments, but these had presented little difficulty to budding burglars like ourselves. I wore out many of the bits of the dentist's electric drill in the process of making my key, but all my efforts were in vain. I am afraid the drills after I had finished with them were very blunt. Ever afterwards when I heard the agonizing shrieks of sufferers in the dentist's chair I felt a twinge of remorse that I should have been the cause of so much fruitless pain! I often wonder what would have been my fate if all the dentist's visitors had known my secret sin. Luckily for me, only one or two of my trusted confederates knew, and they kept the secret. The dentist, who was a French officer and fellow-prisoner, must have thought little of German tool-steel! He filled one of my teeth excellently before I had ruined his drills, using I do not know what kind of rubbish as filling. I cannot explain the existence of the up-to-date dentist's chair and equipment. The Poles said it was there when they arrived. Before the war the Castle had been used, among other things, as a lunatic asylum. Maybe it was thought too risky to allow lunatics to visit a dentist in the town!

At this unhappy stage, when we were casting around to decide what to do with our tunnel, Peter Allan and Howard Gee (a newcomer), both excellent German speakers, reported the existence of a helpful Goon sentry. He was a sympathetic type, and he started smuggling for us on a small scale; a fresh egg here and there in return for English chocolate, or a pound of real coffee in exchange for a tin of cocoa, and so on. He ran a terrific risk, but seemed to do it with equanimity – perhaps too much equanimity – and we decided also to take a risk and plunge. At several clandestine meetings, in doorways and behind angles in the courtyard walls, Peter and Howard Gee primed the sentry and eventually suggested that he might earn some 'big' money if he once 'looked the other way' for ten minutes while on sentry duty.

The sentry fell for the idea. He was told that we would have to arrange matters so that he did a tour of sentry duty for a given two-hour period, on a given day, on a certain beat, and that in the ten-minute interval, between two predetermined signals, he was to stand (which was permitted) at one particular end of his beat. He was to receive an advance of one hundred Reichmarks as his reward, which was settled at five hundred Reichmarks (about £34), and the remainder would be dropped out of a convenient window one hour after the ten-minute interval. The sentry was told also that no traces would be left which could lead to suspicion or involve him in accusations of neglect of duty. To all this he listened and finally agreed. The escape was on!

The first escape party consisted of twelve officers, including four Poles. The French and Dutch were as yet newcomers, whereas the Poles were by now old and trusted comrades, which accounted for their inclusion. Further, the participation of officers of another nationality was decided upon for reasons of language facilities offered, and for camp morale. The Poles had been most helpful since our arrival; the majority of them spoke German fluently, some of them knew Germany well, and those of us who thought of aiming for the North Sea or Poland took Poles as travelling companions. A few decided to travel alone.

My mind was occupied with another problem – how to arrange for the entry of thirteen officers, twelve escaping and one sealing up the entry, into the canteen? During opening hours I examined the cruciform lock closely and came to the conclusion that, from the inside, I could dismount the lock almost completely, allowing the door to open.

The escape would have to be done after the evening roll-call and in darkness.

The fateful day was decided upon – May 29th. I arranged to knock down the false wall the day before and extricate all our provisions and escape material. This was comparatively simple. During the two-hour lunch interval the canteen was locked. Before it was locked, however, I hid in a triangular recess which was used as a store cupboard and to which I had the key. When the canteen was locked up I had two clear hours to prepare everything. I removed the false wall, took out all our escape paraphernalia, hiding it in the cupboard, and prepared the tunnel exit so as to give the minimum amount of work for the final opening. After 2 o'clock, with a suitable screen of officers, I came out of the cupboard and all the stores were carried to our quarters.

The arrangements for the escape were as follows: Howard Gee, who was not in the first party, was to deal with the sentry. He would pass him the first signal on receipt of a sign from us in the tunnel. This was to be given by myself in the first instance at the opening end of the tunnel, passed to our thirteenth man on watch at the canteen window in the courtyard, who would then transmit it to our quarters by means of a shaded light. Gee could then signal to the sentry from an outside window. The 'all clear' was to be given in the same way, except that our thirteenth man had to come to the tunnel exit and receive the word from me when I had properly sealed up the exit after all were out. A piece of string pulled out through the earth served the purpose. I would be over the wall at the far end of the lawn before the signal would be transferred to the sentry.

May 29th loomed overcast and it soon began to rain. It rained all day in torrents, the heaviest rainfall we had ever had, but this would mean a dark night and it did not upset our plans. The sentry was told during the course of the afternoon what post he was to occupy. He was given his advance in cash and instructed to avoid the end of his beat nearest to the canteen on receipt of an agreed signal from a certain window, and to remain away from that end until another signal was given.

As the evening approached, the excitement grew. The lucky twelve dressed themselves in kit prepared during many months of patient work. From out of astonishing hiding-places came trousers and slouch caps made of grey German blankets, multi-coloured knitted pullovers, transformed and dyed army overcoats, windjackets and mackintoshes, dyed khaki shirts and home-knitted ties. These were donned and covered with army apparel. Maps and home-made compasses appeared, and subdued last-minute discussions took place concerning routes and escape instructions. As the time passed, impatience for the 'off' increased. I became alternately hot and cold, and my hands were clammy and my mouth was dry. We all felt the same, as I could tell by the forced laughs and the nervous jokes and banter which passed around.

I remained hidden in the canteen when it was locked up for the night, and dismounted the lock. When the evening *Appell* sounded, I slipped out of the door behind a well-placed crowd of officers. If a Goon pushed the door for any reason whatever we were finished. A wedge of paper alone held it. Sentries were posted for the *Appell* at all vantage-points, and one stood very close to the canteen. Immediately after the *Appell* we had to work fast, for all the prisoners then had to disperse to their rooms, the courtyard doors were locked, and every door tried by the German duty officer. All thirteen of us had to slip into the canteen behind the screen of assisting officers while German officers and NCOs were in the courtyard, and the lock had then to be remounted on the canteen door in double-quick time. The twelve escapers had to appear on parade dressed ready in their escape attire suitably covered with army overcoats and trousers. Assembled rucksacks had been placed in order in the tunnel during the lunch-time closing hours in the same way as before.

The *Appell* went off without a hitch. Colonel German, who had to stand alone in front, was looking remarkably fat, for he was escaping with us. He aroused no comment. Immediately after the 'dismiss' was given, and almost in front of the eyes of the sentry nearby, the thirteen chosen ones slipped silently through the door until all were in.

'Where do we go from here?' asked one of the Polish officers who had not worked on the tunnel.

'Over the palisades!' I replied, pointing to the high wooden partition, over which sheets had already been thrown.

He grabbed them and started to climb, making a noise like a bass drum on the partition door. A loud 'Sh! Sh!' as if a lavatory cistern was emptying greeted his effort.

'For God's sake!' I said, 'you're not in Paderewski's orchestra now.'

'No,' replied the Pole dramatically from the top of the partition, 'but his spirit is living with me, this night!'

Luckily the din in the courtyard covered any noise we made at this juncture.

While the lock was remounted on the door, I removed my army uniform and handed it to our thirteenth man. He was to collect all discarded clothes, conceal them in the cupboard, and remove them with assistance next day. I went straight away to the end of the tunnel, closely followed by Rupert Barry, for we were going together, and started work on the last few inches of earth beneath the surface of the opening. It was dark by now outside, and the rain was still pelting down. It began pouring through the earth covering the exit, and within five minutes I was drenched to the skin with muddy water. The lock-testing patrol tried the canteen door and passed. Soon all was quiet in the camp. Within an hour the sentry was reported by light flashes to be at his post. I gave the signal for him to keep away from the canteen window.

I worked frenziedly at the surface of grass, cutting out my square, and then slowly heaved the tray of the exit upwards. It came away, and as it did so a shaft of brilliant light shot down the tunnel. For a second I was bewildered and blinded. It was, of course, the light of the projector situated ten yards away from the opening, which lit up the whole of the wall-face on that particular side of the Castle. I lifted the tray clear. Streams of muddy water trickled into the tunnel around me. I pushed myself upwards, and with Rupert's assistance from behind, scrambled out.

Once out, I looked around. I was like an actor upon a stage. The floodlight made a huge grotesque image of my figure against the white wall. Row upon row of unfriendly windows, those of the German *Kommandantur*, frowned down upon me. The windows had no blackout curtains and a wandering inquisitive eye from within might easily turn my way. It was an unavoidable risk. Rupert began to climb out as I put the finishing touch to the tray for closing the hole. He was having some difficulty. He had handed up my rucksack and was levering himself upwards when I happened to look from my work at the wall in front of me, there to see a second giant shadow outlined beside my own crouching figure. The second shadow held a revolver in his hand.

'Get back! Get back!' I yelled to Rupert, as a guttural voice behind me shouted:

'*Hände hoch! Hände hoch!*'

I turned, to face a German officer levelling his pistol at my body, while another leaped for the hole. He was about to shoot down the opening.

'*Schiessen Sie nicht!*' I screamed several times.

A bullet or two down that stone- and brick-walled tunnel might have wrought considerable damage, filled as it was with human bodies. The officer at the hole did not shoot.

Germans suddenly appeared from everywhere, and all the officers were giving orders at once. I was led off to the *Kommandantur* and conducted to a bathroom where I was stripped completely and allowed to wash, and then to an office where I was confronted by Hauptmann Priem.

He was evidently pleased with his night's work and in high spirits.

'*Ah hah! Es ist Herr Hauptmann Reid. Das ist schön!*' he said as I walked in, and continued:

'Nobody could recognize who the nigger was until he was washed! And now that we have the nigger out of the woodpile, what has he got to say for himself?'

'I think the nigger in the woodpile was a certain German sentry, was he not?' I questioned in reply.

'Yes, indeed, Herr Hauptmann, German sentries know their duty. The whole matter has been reported to me from the start.'

'From before the start maybe?'

'Herr Hauptmann Reid, that is not the point. Where does your tunnel come from?'

'That is obvious,' I replied.

'From the canteen, then?'

'Yes.'

'But you have been locked in your quarters. You have a tunnel from your rooms to the canteen?'

'No!'

'But yes! You have just been counted on *Appell*. The canteen has been locked many hours ago. You have a tunnel?'

'No!'

'We shall see. How many of you are there?'

'So many I have never been able to count them properly!'

'Come now, Herr Hauptmann, the whole camp or just a few?'

'Just a few!'

'Good, then I hope our solitary confinement accommodation will not be too overcrowded!' said Priem, grinning broadly. He added:

'I was perturbed when first I saw you. I gave orders at once not to shoot. You see I had my men posted at all windows and beneath on the road. They were to shoot if any prisoners ran or struggled. I saw this figure which was you, writhing upon the ground. I thought you had fallen from the roof and that you were in great pain!'

While this was going on, hell had broken loose inside the prison. The courtyard was filled with troops, while posses dashed around wildly trying to locate the inside end of our rat-hole. In our quarters there was the usual parade in the day-room while the Goons prodded beds and unearthed the customary thirteen inert corpses made of coats and blankets. At first they were convinced the tunnel started in our quarters on the first floor and they uprooted floorboards accordingly. Slowly it dawned upon them that it might be worth while to try the canteen.

Once there, as body after body issued from the manhole amidst shouts along the tunnel of 'Goonery ahoy!' mingled with shouts from above of '*Hände hoch! Hände hoch!*' the Goons started hopping with excitement and revolvers were waving in all directions. The Jerry officer-in-charge was an elderly 2nd Lieutenant. He was white to the lips and shaking all over. It was a miracle the weapons did not go off, for the Jerries were out of control. They practically stripped all the escapers naked in their anxiety not to miss any escape booty.

The escapers, on the contrary, appeared reasonably calm. When one of them lit a cigarette, it was the signal for an outbreak. The Goons turned on him in a fury. The German 2nd Lieutenant was near him and the two of them were penned in a corner surrounded by an angry armed mob. A further uproar occurred when Colonel German's face appeared at the tunnel entrance. Consternation was followed by action and our Colonel could hardly rise out of the tunnel on account of the number of Germans who pressed around him. This was 'big-game' hunting, they must have thought.

Eventually some semblance of order was established and each officer in turn, after a thorough inspection, was escorted back to our quarters in his underclothes.

The next day the usual inquiry took place. The Germans had overhauled the tunnel, but what puzzled them was how thirteen men could be inside the canteen, which was locked with their unbreakable cruciform lock, so soon after an *Appell*, and after having been apparently closed up in their quarters for the night.

Special attention was paid to Kenneth Lockwood, of course, as canteen assistant. He was made to sit in front of a table on which a solitary object reposed – the official key of the canteen. Two German officers faced him and repeated ominously in German the question:

'How did you get into the canteen?'

Kenneth ignored the hypnotic key and asked them in return:

'Have you ever read *Alice in Wonderland*?'

This was duly interpreted.

'No,' they said. 'Why?'

'Because Alice got through small doors and keyholes by eating something to make her smaller.'

The interpreter had difficulty in getting this over, but suddenly they broke into roars of laughter and Kenneth was dismissed without further questioning.

For a long time they searched for a tunnel connecting with our quarters, but eventually gave it up. I imagine that, after some time, they worked out the method used – this was not difficult.

In due course we were all sentenced to a fortnight's 'solitary', but as usual, the solitary cells were all occupied and, instead, we carried out the sentence in two small communal rooms. Funnily enough, one of the rooms was that in which we had started our first tunnel, and in which Hank and I had been caught.

'Shovewood II' was still in good working order, and as we had previously concealed some food reserves there, it at last came into its own – we were not short of extra rations during our term of 'solitary'! The 'solitary', in this case, with thirteen officers jammed into two small rooms, was of the 'Black Hole of Calcutta' variety.

Needless to say, we never saw 'our' sentry again! He did not receive his four hundred Reichmarks, which was a good thing. It also puzzled the Jerries how we were getting supplies of German money.

CHAPTER 8

THE HEAVY PALLIASSE

No sooner were we all free again after our 'solitary', than a rare opportunity presented itself. One day, without warning, a large German lorry was driven into the courtyard under guard and stopped outside the door-way to our quarters. Some French troop prisoners descended. We knew a couple of them. They were not lodged in the camp but somewhere in the town where they worked, and they occasionally came into the camp to carry out odd jobs. We had naturally made contact to nose out particulars concerning the orientation of the village and the life of its inhabitants. Unfortunately, these Frenchmen appeared so rarely that they were useless as trafficking agents.

This time they had come to collect a large number of straw palliasses – the standard prison mattresses consisting of large canvas sacks filled with straw – which were stored on the floor above the Dutch quarters. The palliasses were needed for troops' quarters being prepared in the village to house, as it turned out afterwards, Russian prisoners-of-war. The French prisoners each collected a palliasse and, descending the winding staircase past our quarters, continued to the ground floor and then outside the main door swung the palliasses on to the lorry.

There was no time to waste. After hasty consultation, Peter Allan was selected for the attempt. He was small and light and could speak German fluently – so he was an ideal candidate for a one-man effort. We were prepared to try more, but Peter was to be the guinea-pig.

We rigged him out in what was left of our depleted stock of escape clothing, gave him money and packed him in one of our own palliasses, and then tackled the French.

On the stairway outside, I stopped our most likely Frenchman as he descended and pulled him into our quarters with his palliasse, saying:

'I want you to carry an officer downstairs inside a palliasse and load him on to the lorry.'

'*Mais c'est impossible,*' said the Frenchman.

'It is simple,' I assured him. 'It will be over in two minutes; nobody will notice it.'

'And if I am caught?'

'You will not be caught,' I argued, and pressed a tin of cigarettes into his hand.

'But the others?'

'They will not give you away. Give them some of the cigarettes.'

'I am not so sure,' was his reply. 'No! It is too dangerous. I shall be caught and flogged, or they may even shoot me.'

'You know you will not be shot. Courage! Would you not risk a flogging for the Allies, for France? We are all fighting this war together.'

'I would not risk much for many Frenchmen,' he said, cryptically, 'and France is no more!'

'Come now!' I cajoled, 'that is not a Frenchman speaking; that sounds like a collaborator. You are no collaborator. I know your reputation from Frenchmen in the camp who speak well of you. You have helped them. Can you not help us now?'

'Why should I suffer because a British officer wishes to be mad?'

'He is not mad. He is just like you and me. Remember, we officers are not able to move around like you. Why should he not want to escape?'

'*Eh bien!* I'll do it!' he consented, softening at last.

I breathed a sigh of relief and patted him on the shoulder. If he was caught, he was liable to suffer rough treatment.

Peter was already packed and waiting in another palliasse, which was propped over the Frenchman's shoulder. I never saw a bundle of canvas and straw looking less like a palliasse in my life, but the corners soon seemed to settle themselves out. By the time the Frenchman made his exit to the Courtyard, he was looking much more as if he were carrying ten pounds than ten stones.

Alas! he could not off-load the mattress on to the high floor of the lorry alone, so he did the sensible thing; he dropped his load on the ground and looked around, pretending to wipe his brow. An opportune moment arrived almost immediately, as a couple of our stooges on 'attention distracting' duty promptly started to tinker with the front of the car. The Jerries on guard moved to the front, and our Frenchman asked for help from a compatriot just relieved of his mattress. The two of them swung Peter as if he were a feather on top of the rapidly growing pile.

That was enough for the morning. We had no intention of risking another body on that lorry. In due course it departed and was ineffectually prodded by guards at the various gates before trundling off down to the town below.

Peter was duly off-loaded by his guardian, although some of the French were becoming 'windy' as to the enormity of their crime. The guardian was subjected to a good deal of barracking and some threats from his compatriots about the loss of privileges, food and such-like, which was the usual whine of all prisoners who preferred the *status quo* to doing anything that might hurt the feelings of their captors.

Peter understood French well, and heard it all from his recumbent position as he busily imitated an inert mattress in a hurry to be put on a nice board bed in an empty room somewhere in the town of Colditz. He was eventually so deposited and the lorry team disappeared for the lunch interval. All was silent.

Peter extricated himself and found that he was on the ground floor of a deserted house in the town. He opened the window and climbed into a small garden and from there to a road. Our bird had flown!

Peter reached Stuttgart and then Vienna. His greatest thrill was when he was picked up by a senior German SS officer travelling in style in a large car, and accompanied him for about a hundred miles on his way. Only a man like Peter Allan, who had spent six months at school in Germany, could have got away with the conversation involved in a cheek-by-jowl car journey of such a kind.

Meanwhile, in the afternoon, work was resumed by the French on a second load of mattresses and we resumed work on the preparation of a second 'heavy' mattress. Peter had been instructed to make his getaway quickly for the reason that if we failed in the second attempt we did not want the Germans to find Peter quietly lying in his mattress awaiting nightfall!

By now, however, the Frenchmen were frightened and even our staunch French orderly wilted under the weight of the second mattress, duly prepared by us with Lieutenant J. Hyde-Thompson, MC (Durham Light Infantry), resting inside. Unfortunately Hyde-Thompson weighed nearly twelve and a half stone and was sufficiently tall to give the lie to the desired impression of a well-stuffed palliasse. In the courtyard he was dumped on the ground next to the lorry and the Frenchmen refused to load him. Our distraction stooges worked overtime, but the French strike continued and eventually the Jerries became suspicious. The non-commissioned officer-in-charge called for an officer, and by the time the latter arrived the lorry was loaded and our 'heavy' mattress still lay leadenly on the ground.

The officer prodded and then ordered the non-commissioned officer to investigate, while he held his revolver cocked, expecting the worst. Hyde-Thompson duly appeared covered in straw, and was ignominiously led off for examination and a month's cooling off in the cells.

Fourteen days later we heard the sad and discouraging news that Peter Allan had been caught. His story was depressing.

He had reached Vienna and, having spent the last of his money, was looking around for ways and means to carry on to Poland. He thought of the American consulate – for the USA was still not at war. He went there and disclosed his identity. The Americans politely but firmly refused him any kind of help. After this he became despondent. He was worn out from long trekking, and the insidious loneliness of the solitary fleeing refugee in an enemy land descended on him. This curious sensation has to be lived through to be appreciated. It can lead a man to give himself up voluntarily, despite the consequences; to talk and mix with other human beings, be they even his jailers, means nothing to a hunted man, particularly in a city. He must have a strong inner fibre who can withstand the temptation for long. It was for this reason among others that escapers found it advisable to travel in pairs, where possible.

Peter Allan went into a park in Vienna and fell asleep on a bench. In the morning he awoke and found his legs paralysed with cramp. He crawled to the nearest habitation and was taken to hospital, where his resistance broke down. He was quite well looked after and was soon fit to be escorted back to Colditz, where the greater despondency of failure was to hold sway over him during a month's lonely imprisonment.

Two questions, at least, arise concerning this escape. First, why was a tall and heavy person selected for the second attempt? The answer is the same as that which accounts for pure strategy so frequently becoming modified by paramount policy, often, as in this case, resulting in the failure of the project. Hyde-Thompson had arrived in Colditz with a considerable amount of German money in his possession, following an abortive escape attempt. Although the money was not officially his own, he had had the wit to save it through many searches and he had a justifiable lien on it. Officers were searched on departure from one camp and again on arrival at a new one. This consisted of being stripped naked and having each piece of clothing carefully examined, while luggage was gone through with a toothcomb. Hyde-Thompson had given a large proportion of the money to me with alacrity for the canteen tunnel attempt, and some more had gone with Peter Allan. It was time he should be rewarded, and the mattress escape was offered.

Secondly, one may wonder at the attitude of the Americans in Vienna. The explanation is probably twofold. The official one is that the Americans, though neutral, were having a hard time holding on to their Vienna Consulate, and were continually in danger of being ordered out of the country at a moment's notice. They were doing important work and could not risk their position officially. The other explanation, which is quite plausible, is that Peter did not succeed in convincing the Consulate that he was not a German 'agent provocateur'. He had nothing to prove his case and he spoke German perfectly. His English might have been sufficient proof to an Englishman if tested *in extenso*. Yet I dare any Englishman to accept in a similar situation, but with the nationalities reversed, the voice and accent of an alleged American as being that of a genuine American.

CHAPTER 9

FRENCH DASH AND POLISH TEMPERAMENT

Lieutenant Mairesse Lebrun was a French cavalry officer, tall, handsome, and debonair, and a worthy compatriot of that famed cuirassier of Napoleon whose legendary escapades were so ably recounted by Conan Doyle in his book, *The Adventures of Brigadier Gerard.*

Lebrun had slipped the German leash from Colditz once already by what seems, in the telling, a simple ruse. In fact, it required quite expert handling. A very small Belgian officer was his confederate. On one of the 'Park' outings the Belgian officer concealed himself under the voluminous folds of a tall comrade's cloak at the outgoing 'numbering off' parade and was not counted. During the recreation period in the Park, Lebrun, with the aid of suitable diversions, climbed up among the rafters of an open-sided pavilion situated in the middle of the recreation pen. He was not missed because the Belgian provided the missing number, and the dogs did not get wind of him. Later he descended and, smartly dressed in a grey flannel suit sent by a friend from France, he walked to a local railway station and proffered a hundred-mark note at the booking-office in exchange for a ticket. Unfortunately, the note was an old one, no longer in circulation. The station-master became suspicious and finally locked Lebrun up in a cloakroom and telephoned the camp. The Camp Commandant replied that nothing was amiss and that his prisoner complement was complete. While he was phoning, Lebrun wrenched open a window and leaped out on top of an old woman, who naturally became upset and gave tongue. A chase ensued. He was finally cornered by the station personnel and recaptured. In due course he was returned to the Castle and handed over to the protesting Commandant.

This adventure lost Mairesse his fine suit and found him doing a month's 'solitary' confinement at the same time as Peter Allan.

One fine afternoon we heard many shots fired in the playground and rushed to the windows, but could see nothing because of the foliage. Terrific excitement followed in the German quarters and we saw posses of Goons with dogs descending at the double from the Castle and disappearing among the trees. Shouts and orders and the barking of dogs continued for some time and eventually faded away in the distance.

We heard by message from Peter Allan what had happened. The 'solitaries' – at the time a mere half a dozen – were having their daily exercise in the park, during which period they could mix freely. Being only a few, they were sparsely guarded, though confined to one end of the compound, where the prisoners played football among the trees. Lebrun was in the habit of doing exercises with two other Frenchmen, which included much leapfrogging. Now Lebrun was athletic. It was high summer and he was dressed in what remained to him of his former finery – shorts, a yellow cardigan, an open-necked shirt, and gym shoes – not good escaping clothes, but that was also what he reckoned the Germans would think. While a couple of the latter were lolling rather sleepily outside the wire and looking at anything but the prisoners, Lebrun innocently leapfrogged with the other Frenchmen.

It all happened in a flash. His French colleague stood near the wire and, forming with his two hands a stirrup into which Lebrun placed his foot, he catapulted him upwards. Acrobats can heave each other tremendous distances by this method. Precision of timing of muscular effort is its secret. Lebrun and his friend managed it, and the former sailed in a headlong dive over the nine-foot wire.

This was only half the battle. Lebrun ran twenty yards along the fence to the main wall of the park. He had to reclimb the wire, using it as a ladder, in order to hoist himself on to the top of the wall which was, at this point, about thirteen feet high. Rather than present a slowly moving target during this climb, Lebrun deliberately attracted the fire of the two nearest sentries by running backwards and forwards beside the wall. Their carbines once fired (and having missed), the reloading gave him the extra seconds he needed. He was on top of the wall by the time they fired again and dropped to the ground on the other side in a hail of bullets as the more distant sentries joined in the fusillade.

He disappeared and was never recaught. He certainly deserves the greatest credit for this escape, which was in the true French cavalry tradition and demanded the very quintessence of courage, remembering the effort was made in cold blood and with every opportunity for reflection on the consequences of a false step. A British officer, in a similar attempt a few years later, was shot dead. The escape savours of a generation of Frenchmen of whom the majority disappeared on the battlefields of the First World War and who, alas, never had the chance to sire and educate a generation like themselves to follow in their footsteps.

The loss, which was so deeply felt in the 'thirties and which found physical expression during the critical days of 1940, is happily in these days of the 'fifties fading like a bad dream. The young blood of France is quickening again and there is a new courage in the air.

I met Lebrun again long afterwards, when the war was over, and here is the end of his story.

Lebrun escaped on July 1st, 1941. Although he had the sleuth-hounds and a posse of Goons on his tail within ten minutes, he managed to hide in a field of wheat. (You must walk in backwards, rearranging the stalks as you go.) There he hid the whole afternoon with a search plane circling continuously above him. At 10 pm he set off. He had twenty German marks which were smuggled into his prison cell from the camp. He walked about fifty miles and then stole a bicycle and cycled between sixty and a hundred miles a day. He posed as an Italian officer and begged or bought food at lonely farmhouses, making sure, by a stealthy watch beforehand, that there were only women in the house. His bicycle 'sprang a leak', so he abandoned it and stole a second. On the journey to the Swiss frontier he was stopped twice by guards and ran for it each time. On the second occasion, about twenty-five miles from the frontier, he tripped the guard up with the aid of his bicycle and knocked him out with his bicycle pump. He took to the woods and crossed the frontier safely on July 8th.

Within a week he was in France. In December 1942 he crossed the Pyrenees and was taken prisoner by the Spaniards, who locked him up in a castle. He jumped from a window into the moat and broke his spine on some rocks at the bottom, was removed, laid down on a mattress, and left to die. A local French consul, however, who had previously been endeavouring to extricate the incarcerated Lebrun, heard of the accident and insisted on an immediate operation. Lebrun's life was saved. He eventually reached Algeria to carry on the war. Today, though permanently crippled by his fall, he is a pillar in his own country.

If any German had examined Lebrun's cell at Colditz when he left for his daily exercise on July 1st, he might have nipped Lebrun's escape in the bud. Lebrun had packed up his belongings and addressed them to himself in France. Months later they arrived – forwarded by Oberst-leutnant Prawitt, the Colditz Camp Commandant!

The most daredevil Polish officer at Colditz among a bunch of daredevils was 'Niki', 2nd Lieutenant (Ensign) N. Surmanowicz. He was a small weedy-looking young man with an untidy face made up of unequal-sided triangles. The fire that burnt in his soul showed only in his eyes, which glowed with fanatical ardour. He was a great friend of mine and we went on many marauding expeditions together through the forbidden parts of the camp. He taught me all I ever knew about lock-picking, at which he was an expert. It was Niki who had been one of our first visitors up in the loft on our arrival at Colditz. The manufacture of magnetic compasses was also a pastime of his. This he carried out with the aid of a home-made solenoid, employing the electric current of the main camp supply, which happened to be 'direct' current. The number of compasses fabricated by him alone, together with their pivots, compass cards, and glass-covered boxes, went into the fifties.

His schemes for escaping were, to my mind, mostly too wild to bear serious examination. He, on the other hand, thought my ideas were prosaic and I know he inwardly deprecated my painstaking way of setting about escape problems.

Like Lebrun, he relied on 'dash', to which he added a depth of cunning hardly to be equalled. In common with all the Poles, he despised the Germans, but, unfortunately also like many Poles, he underestimated his enemy; a form of conceit which, however, is not a monopoly of the Poles.

Niki spent as much time in solitary confinement as he spent with 'the common herd'. On one occasion, in the summer of 1941, he occupied a cell which had a small window, high up in the wall, opening on to our courtyard. Another Polish officer, Lieutenant Meitek Schmiel, a friend of Niki, occupied the cell next door. I received a message from him one day, saying that he and Schmiel were going to escape that night and would I join them!

I declined the invitation for two reasons; firstly, I thought Niki was crazy, and, secondly, I had given up the idea of escaping myself so long as I remained Escape Officer. With the British contingent on the increase rapidly, this latter course was the only one open to me if I wished to retain the confidence of our group as an impartial arbiter and helper.

I passed on Niki's invitation to a few of the most hare-brained among our company, but Niki's invitation was politely refused by all!

Nobody believed he was serious. Nobody believed he could ghost his way out of his heavily barred and padlocked cell, then open his friend's cell and then unlock the main door of the 'solitary' cell corridor which opened on to the courtyard. Having accomplished this feat he was inside the prison camp, the same as everyone else! Niki loved a challenge and he would chuckle with laughter for the rest of his life if he could show the Jerries once and for all that it took more than they could contrive to keep a Pole down.

He left the invitation open, giving a rendezvous in the courtyard outside the solitary confinement cells at 11 pm that night.

I was at my window watching as 11 pm struck, and on the minute I saw the door of the cells open slowly. All was dark and I could only faintly distinguish the two figures as they crept out. Then something dropped from a window high up in the Polish quarters. It was a rope made of sheets with a load strapped at the bottom – their escape kit, clothes and rucksacks. Next I saw the figures climb the rope one after the other to a ledge forty feet above the ground. What they were about to do was impossible, but they had achieved the impossible once already. I could no longer believe my eyes. The ledge they were on jutted four inches out from the sheer face of the wall of the building. They both held the rope, which was still suspended from the window above them. My heart pounded against my ribs as I saw them high above me with their backs against the wall moving along the ledge inch by inch a distance of ten yards before reaching the safety of a gutter on the eaves of the German guardhouse.

Once there, they were comparatively safe and out of sight if the courtyard lights were turned on. I then saw them climb up the roof to a skylight through which they disappeared, pulling the long rope of sheets, which was let loose by Polish confederates, after them.

Their next move, I knew, was to descend from a small window at the outer end of the attic of the German guardhouse. The drop was about one hundred and twenty feet, continuing down the face of the cliff upon which the Castle was built.

I retired to my bunk, weak at the knees and shaking, as if I had done the climb myself.

The next morning the two of them were back in their cells! I find it hard to tell the end of the story. Niki wore plimsolls for the climb, but his colleague, with Niki's agreement, preferred to wear boots of the moun-taineering type. As they both descended the long drop from the guard-house, the mountaineering boots made too much noise against the wall and awoke the German duty officer sleeping in the guardhouse. He opened the window, to see the rope dangling beside him and a body a few yards below him. He drew his revolver and, true to type, shouted '*Hände hoch!*' several times and called out the guard.

I spent a month in Niki's cell later on without being able to discover how he had opened the door!

After this episode the Germans placed a sentry in the courtyard. He remained all night with the lights full on, which was to prove a nuisance for later escape attempts.

CHAPTER 10

JUST TOO EASY

The summer months were passing – slowly enough for us – yet too fast for all our plans. Winter, relatively speaking, is the escapers' 'close season', though the Second World War was to see many time-hallowed rules of this nature broken.

There was a long curved room over the canteen where a batch of our British contingent slept and passed much of their time. Roughly speaking, two sides of this room backed on to the German section of the Castle, and these two walls always attracted our attention as holding out possibilities. A door in the end wall, in the very early days, had been opened by Niki, who had been beyond into a deserted attic. He could describe no more than that. The doorway had promptly been walled up. Although efforts were made to break through the wall, this had been constructed with such tough cement that noise gave us away and the Germans calmly replastered our puny efforts. This is possibly where they planted one of their microphones, which they later had everywhere.

The second wall, according to the officers who slept near it, backed on to German lavatories.

Tommy Elliot (Lieutenant, Durham County Light Infantry) and Ted Barton announced to me one day that they had started a fair-sized hole which was making good progress. In a matter of a couple of days they were practically through. Listening carefully, they established by sounds from the other side that the hole was near floor-level and appeared to be close to a lavatory bowl. A pinhole was made through the plaster face from the inside, and it was confirmed that the opening would be just off centre and below the seat of a porcelain water-closet.

No time could be lost – the Germans appeared unconscionably quiet and they might start a series of searches any day. The opening was not well concealed on our side and any search would have revealed it. I had my own misgivings, too, concerning the hole, but without evidence I could not withstand the enthusiasm of my fellow-officers for the venture.

The plan was simple. Towards late evening on the coming Sunday, when the German quarters would be at their quietest, the hole would be broken through and twelve officers at five-minute intervals between pairs or individuals would pass through in civilian attire and make their best way out. In effect, the entry into the German quarters would be only the beginning of their troubles, for they would still have to find their way to the exits of the German side of the Castle, then brave the various gates or, more probably, disappear into the wooded playground below the Castle and climb over the main wall under cover of trees.

Sunday arrived and the tension grew apace. The escapers appeared for a passing-out parade. Civilian attire was checked and in some cases altered or substituted by articles of civilian clothing supplied from the private hoards of willing helpers.

At this period of our captivity, escape equipment was becoming organized. Although every officer had not yet been equipped with identity papers, each had a home-made compass of one kind or another, a set of maps painfully traced over and over again from originals, and each was given some German money.

Every officer possessed his private escape kit, which he had ample time to devise during the long hours of enforced idleness – the devil indeed 'finds mischief still for idle hands to do' in a prison camp! And it was surprising what could be produced in the way of civilian clothing by dyeing and altering, by cutting up blankets, and by clever sewing and knitting. Many officers had their specialities and turned out articles in quantity.

I concentrated on the manufacture of 'gor blimey' caps and also rucksacks. My particular brand of cap, cut out of any suitably coloured blanket, having a peak stiffened with a piece of leather or other water-resisting stiffener and lined with a portion of coloured handkerchief and a soft-leather head-band, looked quite professional. My rucksacks were not always waterproof; they were made from dark-coloured or dyed, tough army material, with broad trouser braces adapted as straps, and the flaps and corners neatly edged with leather strips cut from boot tongues. They would pass in Germany as workmen's rucksacks.

Dyeing with 'ersatz' coffee or purple pencil lead became a fine art. The blue Royal Air Force uniform was readily adaptable and with skilful tailoring could become a passable civilian suit. Of course, real civilian clothing was what every officer ultimately aimed at possessing. This urgent desire accounts for the high premium set on the workmen's clothing which gave rise to the 'grand piano' incident.

A similar occasion arose once during one of the very rare visits of a German civilian dentist to supplement the work of our French army dentist. He was accompanied by two leech-like sentries, who kept so close to him that he hardly had room to wield his forceps.

The dentist's torture chamber was approached through a maze of small rooms and had two doors, one of which was supposed to be permanently locked but which we opened on our nefarious occasions with the aid of our universal keys. On the back of this door was a coat-hook, and on the hook our German dentist hung his Homburg hat and a fine fur-collared tweed overcoat.

This was indeed 'big game', and Dick Howe, with another British officer, 'Scorgie' Price, and a French officer named Jacques Prot were soon hot on the trail.

Dick arranged to pay an officer's dentist's bill. The dentist was paid in *Lagergeld* and Dick sought out an officer with a heavy bill – it came to a hundred marks. He collected the whole sum in one-mark notes. This would give him plenty of time. He arranged a signal with the other two. The operative word was 'Right'. When Dick said 'Right' loudly, Price was to open the locked door and remove the coat and hat.

Dick went to the dentist's room and insisted on interrupting the dentist's work to pay his brother-officer's bill. He drew him over to a table; the two sentries dutifully followed; and Dick started to count out laboriously his *Lagergeld*.

'*Eins, zwei, drei, . . .*' he started and carried on to *zehn*, at which point he looked up to see if he had the full attention of the dentist and his guards. 'Not quite', he thought, and he carried on painfully, '*elf, zwölf . . .*' By the time he reached *zwanzig* he had all their eyes riveted on the slowly rising pile of notes, so he said 'Right.' As he continued he sensed nothing had happened. At *dreiszig* he repeated 'Right' a little louder. Again nothing happened. At *vierzig* he filled his lungs and shouted 'Right' again. Still nothing happened. Doggedly he continued, holding the attention of all three, as his reserves of *Lagergeld* dwindled. As *fünfziz, sechzig, siebzig* passed, his 'Rights' crescendoed, to the amusement of his three spectators. Nothing happened. An operatic bass would have been proud of Dick's final rendering at *achtzig, neunzig*, and *hundert*. The scheme had failed, and the only persons laughing were the Germans at Dick's, by this time, comic act.

The dentist, still guffawing, collected all the notes together and before Dick's crestfallen gaze started recounting them. As he reached *zehn* he shouted 'R-r-reight', and Dick, to his own utter astonishment, felt rather than heard the door open behind them, and sensed an arm appearing around it. Before the dentist had reached *zwanzig* the door had closed again. Dick continued the pantomime and eventually, after assuring himself that the coat and hat had really disappeared, he retired from the scene with apologies – a shaken man.

The concealment of contraband material presented great difficulty, and many were the hours given up to devising ingenious ways of hiding our precious work. The common hiding-places and those at various times found out by the Germans were: behind false-backed cupboards and in trap-door hides, under floorboards, and sewn into mattresses and overcoat linings. Small items were often sealed in cigarette-tins, weighted and dropped into lavatory cisterns or concealed in stores of food. There were myriads of possibilities, and it is appropriate that the better ways remain undisclosed for the present. Men who may have nothing to think about for many a long, weary day in the years to come will rediscover them and sharpen their wits in the exercise.

To return to our twelve stalwarts perspiring with nervous anticipation, some even vomiting quietly in the seclusion of an *Abort*, waiting for the zero hour! At the appointed time, all was reported quiet on the other side of the wall. The hole was quickly broken out and the escapers started to squirm through in their correct order and at the appropriate intervals of time, while watchers at different vantage-points scanned the exits from the German quarters.

Soon reports began coming in: 'No exits'! and again 'No exits'! We persisted, however, for forty minutes by which time eight officers had passed through the hole. At this point I turned to the remaining four:

'I think it's too risky to continue without having a pause. What do you think?'

'It's suspicious that not one has poked his head out of the other end of the rabbit run yet!' said the next on the list to go.

'I don't think we can spoil anything by holding off and watching for results. If we go on pumping any more through as it is, they'll soon be bulging out of the *Kommandantur* windows.'

'Shall we stay on the field during half-time or go and have a drink?'

'Better stay here,' I advised. 'You may be wanted at a moment's notice, but have all your kit ready to hide too. Make a plan for a split-second hideaway in case the Jerries are on to the scheme and try to catch us in the rear.'

After fifteen minutes of inactivity the alarm was suddenly given. 'Jerries *en masse* entering courtyard, heading for our staircase!'

Well, that was the end of that! The Germans had laid a trap and we had walked into it, or eight of us had. The hole must have been marked during operations upon it, and a secret guard kept. As each of the eight escapers left the *Abort* and proceeded down a long corridor he was quietly shepherded into a room and put under guard!

Thus ended another depressing chapter for British morale in Colditz. The Germans had gained the upper hand and were playing with us. Our efforts were beginning to appear ridiculous.

CHAPTER 11

DUTCH PORCELAIN

British escaping reputation had reached rock bottom, and whatever conceit we had left was soon to receive a further blow, this time at the hands of the Dutch. From the beginning close relations were maintained with them, and, though at the start this did not involve revealing the full details of our respective plans, it soon developed into a very close co-operation, which was headed on the Dutch side by a Captain Van den Heuvel.

The Dutch were not very long at Colditz before Van den Heuvel warned me of an impending attempt. 'Vandy', as he was inevitably called, was a fairly tall, big-chested man with a round face, florid complexion, and an almost permanent broad grin. His mouth was large enough in repose, but when he smiled it was from ear to ear. He had hidden depths of pride and a terrific temper, revealed on very rare occasions. He spoke English well, but with a droll Dutch accent.

'How are you, Vandy?' I would ask him, to which his unvarying reply was: 'Rather vell, thank you,' with emphasis on the 'rather.'

'Patt,' he said to me one day, ''ve are about to trry our virst vlight vrom Golditz. I can only zay it is vrom the direczion ov the park and it vill take place on Zunday.'

Sunday passed calmly and in the evening I went to see Vandy.

'Well, Vandy, there's been no excitement. What have you got up your sleeve?' I asked.

'Aah! Patt,' he replied, with a mischievous twinkle in his eye, 'I haf two more op my sleeve vor next Zunday, two haf gone today!'

He was grinning as usual and was like a dog with two tails. His pleasure was infectious and I could not help laughing.

At the morning *Appell* on Monday, however, two Dutchmen were missing. Some time later (not the next Sunday, for technical reasons), two more disappeared.

The Germans were worried enough over the first two. They were 'hopping mad' when the number rose to four. When it had risen to six, they forgot even to hop. There was a series of searches of the camp premises, and the park was given a very careful scrutiny. I noticed the Jerries placed bars across the small wooden cover to a manhole in the football ground which had, in any case, one large nut and bolt securing it.

Eventually I managed to worm out of Vandy how he, a comparative newcomer to the camp, had managed with such ease to arrange the escape of his six Dutchmen from the fortress of Colditz.

His trick was so simple that it shook me to think that the rest of us – Poles, French, and British, numbering now some two hundred and fifty – could not have thought of it. The escape was indeed from the manhole in the football ground.

'All very well,' I said to Vandy. 'We've all looked at that manhole cover till we were blue in the face without arriving at a satisfactory scheme.'

'Ah!' he replied, 'Patt, vat is that game the Poles taught you? Gapin? Vell I tought of Gapin and looked at the manhole cover vrom another angle!'

On the first two occasions in question, a few Dutchmen, led by a venerable-looking bearded one named Van Doorninck, had held Bible-reading meetings, curiously enough, around the manhole. Previously they had measured the size of the nut and bolt. During the Bible-reading, the bolt was undone with a pair of large home-made spanners filed out of iron bed-parts. The bolt had about a $\frac{3}{4}$-inch diameter thread. When the sentries' notice was attracted to a football game in progress, two Dutchmen disappeared into the manhole. Now this was the crux. Immediately after the reaction, and before the prisoners returned to the Castle, the football ground was carefully examined, invariably including the manhole, by two or three Jerries appointed for the purpose. They also let loose dogs to trace possible hideouts or graves among the trees.

'How,' I asked, 'did you conceal the opened manhole? That is what beats me.'

'Ve made another bolt; a fery special kind of bolt,' Vandy replied. 'It vas made of glass tubing with a vooden head, and painted just like the real vone.'

That in effect was the secret of this simple yet brilliantly conceived escape. The two escapers in the manhole had the real bolt with them. At nightfall they pushed up the lid, breaking the glass bolt. They cleaned away the bits as best they could before leaving, and replaced the original bolt exactly as it was before, applying mud and dirt to cover any marks left on the iron. Their exit thereafter, only impeded by a high wall and some barbed wire, presented no difficulty in the dark with the nearest guard over four hundred yards away. By this time the Germans had enforced no fewer than four roll-calls on the daily recreation parade: two in the park and two at the courtyard gate. How Vandy managed to cover these he kept a secret for a little while longer!

The first four who escaped were Captains A. L. C. Dufour and J. G. Imit (Royal Netherlands Indies Army) and Lieutenants E. H. Larive and F. Steinmetz (Royal Netherlands Navy), and the latter two reached Switzerland. The other two were caught on the frontier and eventually returned to

Colditz. The third couple disappeared about a month after the others during a Polish-Dutch International Soccer match. They were Major C. Geibel and 2nd Lieutenant O. L. Drijbar, both of the Royal Netherlands Indies Army. They reached Switzerland safely.

The Germans still believed they could make Oflag IV C impregnable (from within), so that escapers, when recaught, were not sent elsewhere according to normal custom but invariably returned to Colditz. For this reason, it was always growing in population; a centre of gravity, towards which escapers moved from all over Germany, when not moving in the opposite direction under their own steam! It was likewise a fortress, which required an ever-increasing garrison. The Germans greatly outnumbered the prisoners. Admittedly our jailers were not class A1 soldiers. The swollen number of the garrison was probably a source of irritation to the German High Command, because they held a series of inspections at one period, including a visit by two German officers who had escaped from Allied hands. One was Hauptmann von Werra, the German airman who gave our POW authorities much trouble and eventually escaped from Canada to the USA. The story has it that he jumped from a train near the St Lawrence River, then stole a motor-boat in which he crossed and eventually reached the German Consulate in New York. He visited our camp during his leave to give the Commandant advice. Shortly afterwards he was reported to have been shot down and killed somewhere on the Russian front.

The return of escaped officers to their original camp provided certain advantages for the inmates, by which we were not slow to profit. It was inevitable, however, that, if the war lasted long enough, in the end the Germans would win the battle of Colditz and the camp would become practically unbreakable, but none of us thought that stage had arrived in the autumn of 1941. In fact, although every escape discovered meant that one more foxhole had been bunged up, the prisoners really never gave up trying until the Allied advance into Germany.

The *Prominente*, as they were called by the Germans, also drifted gradually towards Colditz. Winston Churchill's nephew, Giles Romilly, arrived. He was given the honour and the inconvenience of a small cell to himself, which had a sentry outside it all night. He was free to mix with the other prisoners during the day, but he had to suffer the annoyance of being called for by his guardian angel – a heavy-booted Hun – every night at 9 pm, and escorted to his bedroom and locked in!

Like everybody else, he wanted to escape, but it was naturally more difficult to arrange. I once succeeded in substituting him for one of several French orderlies who were off-loading coal from a lorry in the courtyard. The coal-dust was a helpful disguise – smeared over his face – but he did not pass the first gateway. It was obvious that he was either watched from within the camp by other than his ostensible jailers, or which is equally likely in this case, a French orderly – perhaps the one substituted – reported to the Germans what was happening, to save his own skin. We never found out, but it was Hauptmann Priem himself who entered the courtyard when the lorry was ready to leave and calmly asked Romilly to step down from it. I think he was awarded only a week's solitary confinement and then returned to his normal routine.

It was also in the late summer of 1941, when I was doing one of my customary periods of solitary – three weeks in this case – that the cells became overcrowded and Flight-Lieutenant Norman Forbes joined me for a spell. The cells were tiny, about four yards by three yards. We were given a two-tier bed, however, which helped, but to compensate for this, our cell was built immediately over a semi-basement cellar in which the camp garbage-cans were housed.

Norman and I managed very well and did not get on each other's nerves. One day, shortly before his 'time' was finished, he remarked to me casually that he needed a hair-cut.

'Ah ha!' thought I, 'anything to relieve the monotony!'

'What a curious coincidence,' I said, 'that you should be doing "solitary" with an expert amateur barber. I learnt the art from my school barber, who said I had a natural talent for it.'

'Well, have a shot at mine, then,' was the reply.

Soon I was busy with a pair of nail-scissors and a comb, which I periodically banged together in a professional manner. I tried for a few minutes to cut his hair properly, then realized that a barber's skill is by no means easy to acquire. I carried on, extracting large chunks of hair here and there, until the back of his head looked more like a gaping skull than anything else. At the front of his head I cut a neat fringe. The rest of his head was a jumble. As the front was all that Norman could see in the tiny mirror we had, he was unaware of his predicament until a day or two later, when he rejoined the camp and became a standing joke for several days.

After Norman left, boredom settled on me once again. I was studying economics, but found it heavy reading when continued for weeks on end. One day I thought of my cornet. As a concession I had been allowed to take into 'solitary', along with books and other paraphernalia, my guitar and my brass cornet.

Norman had only just managed to withstand my guitar crooning, and categorically refused to let me practise my cornet. Now I was alone, I thought, and I could practise in peace. But so many objections were raised from nearby cells and also from the courtyard – which my cell faced – in the form of showers of pebbles, shouts, and insults, that I was driven to practising my cornet at the only time (apart from the dead of night) when nobody could stop me, which was during the half-hour of evening *Appell*.

This seemed to satisfy everybody; for the German officers and NCOs taking the parade could hardly hear themselves speak, and the numbers invariably tallied up wrong, necessitating several recounts. By the third evening the hilarity grew to such an extent that the parade almost became a shambles. Apparently many of the German troops thought the cornet practice funny too – which made it all the worse for the German officer-in-charge, who was beside himself. By the fourth day I was feeling so sorry for the Jerries having to put up with the ear-splitting noises which coincided with their commands, that I decided to show a gentlemanly spirit and refrain from practising that evening.

Evidently I was not the only one who had been reflecting, for when the evening *Appell* was assembled, and the German officer-in-charge entered the yard (Hauptmann Püpcke was his name), he made straight for my cell with two soldiers and swung open my door with violence.

'*Geben Sie mir sofort ihre Trompete,*' he shouted.

I was so taken aback by his abruptness after my good intentions and sympathy for the German position that I thought it was my turn to feel insulted.

'*Nein,*' I said. '*Ich will nicht; es ist meine Trompete, Sie haben kein Recht darauf,*' and with that I hid the cornet behind my back. He seized it and we began a violent tug-of-war. He ordered his two men to intervene, which they did by clubbing my wrists and arms with their rifle butts, and I gave up the unlucky instrument.

'You will have a court martial for this,' the officer screamed as he slammed the door behind him.

The court martial never came off, which was a pity, for it meant a journey, probably to Leipzig, and a chance of escape. Instead, I was awarded another month's 'solitary' which I began shortly afterwards in a different cell.

It was late September and the leaves were falling in the park, but all I could see from my tiny window by climbing on to my washstand was the wall of a section of our prison known as the theatre block. It was during one of my long periods of blank staring at this wall-face that light suddenly dawned upon me. If I had not been an engineer, familiar with plans and elevations and in the habit of mentally reconstructing the skeletons of buildings, the idea would probably never have occurred to me. I suddenly realized that the wooden stage of the theatre was situated so that it protruded over a part of the Castle, sealed off from the prisoners, which led by a corridor to the top of the German guardhouse immediately outside our courtyard.

This discovery was a little goldmine. I tucked it away and resolved to explore further as soon as I was free.

CHAPTER 12

THE RIOT SQUAD

As I have said, 'Never a dull moment' might well have been the motto on the armorial bearings of Oflag IV C. I had hardly finished ruminating on my discovery from the cell window when a fusillade of shots sounded from the direction of the park. I was tantalized to know what was happening. Soon the 'riot squad' dashed into the courtyard and headed for the British doorway. Any posse of Goons heading anywhere at the double in an excited manner with fixed bayonets was familiarly known as the 'riot squad'.

They did not leave for hours and there was an incredible amount of shouting and barracking, mostly in French. Eventually I heard the story from Harry Elliott, who passed in a note to me describing what had happened.

He was in the Dutch quarters when the shooting, and much shouting, began from the direction of the park. Everyone rushed to the windows to see what was happening, and they saw two Belgian prisoners (Lieutenant Marcel Leroy and Lieutenant Le Jeune) running up the steep hill towards the wall which surrounded the park. They had climbed the wire (or crawled under it) and were being fired at by the sentries. As the sentries stood in a circle, some of them on the uphill side of the park came close to being hit by the ones below them. The sentries surrounding the Castle walls joined in and a regular fusillade started. The shooting was, as usual, bad, and the Germans were rapidly losing their heads. It was a wonderful opportunity for the prisoners, who wasted no time in trying to distract the sentries by shouting all sorts of abuse at them. The Dutch, who were very correct on all occasions, did not join in with as much enthusiasm as the English. So Harry ran downstairs to the British quarters to assist in the fun from there. By the time he arrived, much of the shooting was directed against the windows of the Castle and bullets were thudding against it. The Belgians had reached the high wall, but found it impossible to climb at that point and eventually stood with their hands up, still being fired at by the

Germans. Luckily they were not hit.[1]

Next, the sentries around the Castle walls came under fire from the sentries in the park, who began firing at the jeering mob at the Castle windows. The bullets were going over their heads, but must have seemed close and they were becoming jittery. The British found this the greatest fun, and continued laughing and teasing the sentries beneath them. Eventually Peter Storie Pugh (Lieutenant, Royal West Kents) produced a Union Jack which had been used in Christmas festivities long ago, and hung it out of the window. This produced an immediate response. The hoarse shouting of the Goons increased to a thunder and the shooting redoubled its intensity until the hills echoed. It was all directed at the Union Jack.

As the walls were of stone, from time to time bullets coming in at the window ricocheted round the room. The prisoners decided it was time to lie down. At this moment the riot squad, composed of the second in command (a major) and about a dozen Goons, with bayonets fixed, clattered into the courtyard. They dashed up the staircase, and burst into the British quarters, the major leading with his revolver in his hand, white to the lips and shaking all over. The riot squad were also terrified.

'Take that flag down,' said the major in German.

None of the prisoners moved – they were lying on the floor, chatting to each other – no one even looked up. There were a few loud remarks, such as:

'They seem pretty windy today', and 'What the hell do they want?'

'The Herr Major says you are to take the flag down,' came from the German interpreter as another round of shots thudded against the walls.

Not a move. The trembling major then went up to an Australian Squadron Leader named MacColm and, pointing a pistol at him, said:

'Take the flag down.'

'Why don't you take it down yourself?' replied MacColm.

The major continued to threaten until MacColm finally crawled over to the window and pulled the flag inside.

All the prisoners in the room were then made to go downstairs and parade in the courtyard. They were encircled by the Goons who kept their rifles in the rabbiting position. Heads started to pop out of windows and the Senior British Officer demanded to know what was happening to his boys.

---

[1] One Belgian, Captain Louis Remy, escaped successfully from the castle in April 1942 with Squadron Leader Paddon (British) and Lt. Just (Polish). The latter two were recaught. Remy reached Belgium, crossed France and Spain and swam to a British ship anchored off Algeciras. He was imprisoned for a month in England on arrival, being released only through the intervention of Paddon, who had again escaped – this time successfully – via Sweden! Remy joined the RAF, serving with Bomber Command (103 Squadron) until the end of the War.

The Goons said: 'They fired first', which caused great amusement.

The POWs waited patiently, making pointed remarks while nothing happened. The French, however, from their windows took up their favourite refrain:

'*Où sont les allemands?*'

'*Les allemands sont dans la merde,*' came the reply from about forty windows. And then the first chorus again:

'*Qu'on les y enforce,*' the reply to that being:

'*Jusqu'aux oreilles.*'

This always provoked the Germans, who understood what it meant, and after the litany had been chanted from the French and English quarters two or three times, the usual happened. The major started shouting at them; loud laughter from the prisoners and a few rude remarks in German; then the usual cry:

'Anyone looking out of the windows will be shot.'

The sentries were in a dilemma; they did not know whether to point their rifles at the British in the courtyard, or at the windows above. Eventually they all pointed at the windows and a few shots were fired. This was the signal for the British to sit down on the cobbles – a pack of cards was produced and four prisoners started playing bridge; the others chatted. When the Goons turned their attention away from the windows again and saw this they were 'hopping mad' and forced everybody to stand up once more at the point of the bayonet, but it was not long before small groups were again sprawling on the cobbles. The German major, having all this time received no orders from his higher command, departed. He was soon followed by the riot squad, who trailed despondently out of the gate, and the anticlimax was complete.

Beer had long since disappeared from the camp, and with the thought of a dreary winter ahead, a few of us put our heads together. With the help of Niki, who had already managed to procure some yeast from a German, we started a brewing society. Someone unearthed a curious medal struck to commemorate a brewing exhibition. I was elected Chief Brewer and dispensed the yeast, and wore the medal attached to the end of a large red ribbon. When asked by curious Goons what the medal represented, I proudly told them it was a war decoration for distinguished service in the boosting of morale.

Brewing soon became a popular pastime and, with a little instruction by the Chief Brewer and his stewards, was highly successful. Soon, at nearly every bedside could be seen large jars or bottles, filled with water and containing at the bottom a mash of sultanas, currants, or dried figs – produced from our Red Cross parcels – together with the magic thimbleful of yeast. Curiously enough, it was eventually found that the yeast was unnecessary, for there was enough natural yeast already on the skins of the fruit to start the fermentation process without assistance. The one difficulty was the provision of gentle heat, because fermentation requires a fairly consistent temperature of about 27 degrees Centigrade. This problem was overcome by the simple use of body heat, or 'hatching' as it was called. It was a normal sight to see rows of officers propped up in their beds for hours on end in the hatching position, with their jars and bottles nestling snugly under the blankets beside them. Fermentation was complete after a fortnight! Some of our amateur brewers were luckier than the ordinary run of broody officers in that their bunks were situated near an electric light. Large incubating boxes were manufactured out of cardboard and lined with German blankets. Jars were arranged in tiers in the boxes and the heat was turned on by placing the electric-light bulbs in the boxes attached to lengths of 'won' electric cable. A flourishing commerce in brewery shares arose and combines were started.

Soon we were having gay evening parties and started entertaining our fellow-prisoners of other nationalities.

One day our Brewing Association invited a 'brilliant lecturer' to expound the secrets of distillation! Human nature being what it was, we were soon distilling briskly. I tore down a long section of lead piping from one of our non-working lavatories and made a coil, which was sealed into a large German jam-tin about twenty inches high. This 'still' became the property of the Brewing and (now) Distilling Society. Almost every night distilling began after 'lights out', and continued into the early hours. We worked shifts and charged a small percentage (of the resultant liquor) for the distilling of officers' brews. I should explain that distillation is merely a method of concentrating any brew or wine. Brandy is distilled grape-wine. We named our liquor simply 'firewater', for that undoubtedly it was.

Over a period of time we used up nearly all the bedboards in the British quarters as fuel for out witches' cauldron. Our rows of broody officers looked more odd than ever reposing on mattresses supported only by a minimum of bed-boards with pendulous bulges in between, the upper bunks in imminent danger of collapsing on to the lower ones. In vain did the Germans make periodical surveys of the bed-boards, even to the extent of numbering them with chalk and indelible pencil. Alas! the numbers were consumed in the flames and did not survive the boards.

The distilling process was an eerie ceremony carried out in semi-darkness around the kitchen stove with the distillers listening over the cauldron for the telltale hiss of gentle distillation – their flickering giant-like shadows dancing on the walls – as the flames were carefully fed with fuel. Distilling required most concentrated attention because the work of a fortnight could be ruined in a minute if a brew, passing through the lead coils, became overheated and the alcohol boiled away. Distillation takes place between roughly 80 degrees and 90 degrees Centigrade.

Having no thermometers, we learned to judge the temperature by sound alone – hence our experts and our right to charge a premium for the process!

The liquor, as it appeared, drop by drop, from the bottom of the still, was pure white in colour. It was bottled and in a very short time the liquor became crystal clear, leaving a white sediment at the bottom. The clear liquid was run off and re-bottled. This was 'firewater'. The white sediment was probably lead oxide – pure poison – but I was not able to check this, and nobody ever died to prove it.

With experience and Polish assistance we produced various flavoured varieties, which the Poles insisted on calling 'vodka'. We did not argue over the name, but I feel sure that our liquor would never have been a suitable accompaniment to caviar. It took the roof off one's mouth, anyway.

It was not long before the British had a good cellar and 'vintages' accumulating. Christmas 1941 looked rosily ahead of us.

CHAPTER 13

A STAGED FOURSOME

I made a reconnaissance of the stage in the theatre, which was on the third floor of the 'theatre block'. By removing some wooden steps leading up to the stage from one of the dressing-rooms, I was able to crawl underneath and examine that part of the floor over the sealed room leading to the German guardhouse. It was as I had hoped. There were no floorboards, only straw and rubble about four inches deep reposing on the lath-and-plaster ceiling of the room in question.

I next looked around for prospective candidates for the escape I was planning. I selected about half a dozen possibilities. To these I mentioned casually that I would get them out of Colditz if they, on the other hand, would produce first-class imitations of German officers' uniforms. It was a challenge and by no means an easy one.

We had made a start, however, on certain parts of German army accoutrements and this was reason for encouragement. What had been left over from the lead piping I removed to make the still had already been melted down and recast into perfect imitations of German uniform buttons and one or two of their insignia. The lead, unfortunately, did not go very far when melted down.

My offer was a test of ingenuity and enterprise, and it produced Lieutenant Airey Neave, R.A., an Etonian and a comparative newcomer to the Castle, and Hyde-Thompson of the 'recumbent palliasse' episode. They had teamed up and Airey promised to make the uniforms. He said he could not make them, however, without Dutch assistance, so eventually, with Van den Heuvel's agreement, two Dutch officers were selected to make the team up to four. The Dutch spoke German fluently, which was a great asset.

Neave and Scarlet O'Hara came to me in distress one day soon afterwards, while I was preparing our next evening's distilling operations. Airey said:

'We're running short of lead.'

Scarlet, who – it is scarcely necessary to mention – had gravitated to Colditz, was our foundry foreman. He added:

'The lead piping you gave me is finished. It didn't go very far. It's too darn thin – cheap German stuff – no weight in it.' He looked towards the still.

'What are you looking at?' I asked. 'I hope you're not hinting.'

'Wouldn't dream of it,' said Scarlet. 'I just don't know where I'm going to get any lead from. We've only got three lavatories working as it is. That's not many for forty officers. If I break one up, there will be a revolution.'

'H'm! This is serious.' I went into a huddle with Dick Howe, who was a keen distiller, and was at that moment repairing a water-leak at the bottom of our still.

'Dick, things look bad for the still. They've run out of lead. How much liquor have we? Would you say our cellar was reasonably stocked?'

'Our cellar is not at all well stocked,' Dick joined in, 'for the simple reason that it's a bottomless pit. But if there's a greater need, I don't see that we can avoid the issue. We'll probably be able to recuperate our loss in due course – from, say, a Dutch or a French lavatory.'

'Very good,' I said to Airey, 'your need is greater than ours. You'd better take the coil,' and then to Dick:

'It's probably just as well to lay up for the time being, as there's a search due one of these days and we've got some stock to carry on with. The still would cause a packet of trouble if found and it's useless trying to hide it.'

Dick stopped tinkering and the lead coil was handed over. It was melted down and poured into little white clay moulds which were prepared from beautifully carved patterns sculptured by a Dutchman. Replicas, conforming perfect as to colour (silver-grey) and size, were made of the various metal parts of German uniforms: Swastikas and German eagles, tunic buttons by the score and troops' belt-clasps with the '*Gott mit uns*' monogram. The Brewing and Distilling Society resumed the title of its earlier days and became 'The Brewing Society Only', a sad reminder of a glory that had passed.

The most important item of the German uniform was the long greatcoat of field-grey, and it was here that the Dutch came in; their greatcoats, with minor alterations, could pass in electric light as German greatcoats. The officers' service caps were cleverly manufactured by our specialists. Leather parts, such as belts and revolver holsters, were made from linoleum, and leggings from cardboard.

At a passing-out test we had to compliment Neave and the various Dutch and Britishers who had done the work. The uniforms would pass – though not in broad daylight at close range, yet under almost any other conditions.

In the meantime I had not been idle, having my share of the bargain to accomplish. From thin plywood I cut out an irregular oblong shape, large enough to fill a hole through which a man could pass. The edge was chamfered to assist in making a snug fit, and I gave one side a preliminary coat of white paint. To the reverse side I fixed a frame with swivelling wooden clamps, and I prepared wooden wedges. The result was christened 'Shovewood IV'!

I asked Hank Wardle to help me in the preparation of the escape. This tall, robust Canadian, with his imperturbable manner and laconic remarks, could be relied upon to do the right thing in an awkward moment. His brain was not slow, though his casual and somewhat lazy manner belied it.

Under the stage in the theatre we quietly sawed through the laths of the ceiling and then through the plaster. Small pieces of it fell to the floor with ominous crashes, but we were able to prevent most of it from capsizing. Then I had to descend with a sheet-rope to the room below, which was empty. The door connecting it to a corridor which passed over the main courtyard gate and thence to the attic of the guardroom was locked. I tested it with my 'universal key'. It opened easily, so I relocked and began work. I had prepared two collapsible stools which fitted one on top of the other. Standing on these, I could reach the ceiling. Hank held 'Shovewood IV' in position while I carved out the plaster of the ceiling to fit it. Eventually, when pressed home and wedged from above, it fitted well enough to give the impression of an irregular oblong crack in the real ceiling. With a pencil I drew lines which looked like more cracks in various directions, to camouflage the shape of the oblong, and remove any impression that an observer might have of a concealed hole.

The colour of the ceiling was exasperatingly difficult to match and it took a long time to achieve a similarity of tint between it and 'Shovewood IV.' This latter work necessitated many visits, as each coat had to dry and then be examined in place.

Airey Neave was ready to go and was becoming impatient. 'Look here, Pat,' he protested, 'I've got pieces of German clothing and gear lying about all over our quarters. It's damn' tricky stuff to hide, and if the search comes I'm finished. When is your hole going to be ready?'

'Keep your hair on, Airey!' I retorted. 'You'll go in due course, but not before it's a finished job. Remember, I want others to use this exit too.'

'I wish you'd get a move on, all the same. The weather is fairly mild now, but remember, we've had snow already and we're going to have a lot more soon. I don't want to freeze to death on a German hillside.'

'Don't worry, Airey! I see your point of view,' I said sympathetically. 'I need two more days. You can reckon on leaving on Monday evening. The "take-off" will be immediately after evening *Appell*.'

Even when I finally launched Neave, I was not completely satisfied with my 'Shovewood'. It was so nearly perfect that I wanted to make it absolutely foolproof. Its position in the sealed-off room was unique, and I felt we could unleash officers at intervals 'until the cows came home'.

I made a reconnaissance along the German corridor and, unlocking a further door, found myself in the attic over the German guardhouse. Probably nobody had been near the attic since Niki climbed in through the skylight and left by the window at the end. The window had not been touched, but that route was no longer possible since a sentry had been positioned to cover the whole of that wall-face beneath the window. A staircase in the attic led down to the guards' quarters below. Layers of dust on everything, including the floor, were my greatest bugbear, and as I returned I had to waft dust painstakingly over fingerprints and footprints by waving a handkerchief carefully in the air over the marks.

The plan was simple enough I would send the escapers out in two pairs on successive evenings immediately after a change of guard stationed at the front entrance to the guardhouse. Thus the new sentry would not know what German officers, if any, might have entered the guardhouse in the previous two hours. The two officers escaping would descend the guardhouse staircase and walk out through the hall. This was the most risky part of the attempt. The stairs and hall would be well lit, and a stray guardhouse Goon might wonder where two strange German officers had suddenly descended from. The moment of descent from the attic had therefore to be chosen when a period of comparative calm in guardhouse activity was anticipated. I insisted that the two officers, on reaching the guardhouse entrance, were to stop in full view of the sentry, put on their gloves and exchange casual remarks in well-prepared German, before marching boldly down the ramp to the first gateway. This 'act' was calculated to absorb any shock of surprise that the sentry might have if, for instance, two strange officers were to issue suddenly from the entrance and quickly march away.

The evening for the attempt arrived. After the last *Appell* all concerned with the escape disappeared into the theatre block instead of to our own quarters. Various senior officers and generals lived in the theatre block and movement in this direction did not arouse suspicion.

The two escapers, Airey Neave and Lieutenant Tony Luteyn (Royal Netherlands Indies Army), were wearing no fewer than three sets of apparel – apart from some delicate pieces of accoutrement, which were carried in a bag. Over everything, they wore British army greatcoats and trousers; underneath came their German uniforms and underneath again they carried their civilian attire.

Although we thought highly of the German uniforms, they were not good enough for a permanent disguise – the cardboard leggings, for instance, would not have looked very well after heavy rain! – and we decided they should be discarded and hidden in the woods outside the Castle.

Our stooges were posted and we climbed – the two escapers with some difficulty owing to their bulk – under the stage. I opened up 'Shovewood IV', and one after the other we dropped quietly into the room below. I led the way, opening the doors, along the corridor and into the German attic. British army attire had already been discarded. The German uniforms were brushed down and everything was checked. I said to Airey:

'It takes me eleven minutes to return, clean up and close "Shovewood". Don't move before eleven minutes are over.'

'Right!' replied Airey, 'but I'm not going to hang around long after that. I shall take the first opportunity of a quiet period on the staircase and landings underneath us.'

'Don't forget to take it easy at the guardhouse doorway,' I reminded him; 'remember, you own the place.

'Good-bye and good luck!' I added, 'and don't come back here. Much as we like you, we don't want to see you again!'

We shook hands and I left them. I relocked doors, redusted traces, mounted the rope of sheets and, with Hank's assistance, wedged 'Shovewood IV' firmly in place. Before Hank and I had issued from under the stage, our watchers reported a perfect exit from the guardhouse. The 'act' went off, the German sentry saluted smartly, and our two passed on. We did not expect much difficulty from the first gate. The guard on duty would see the officers coming and the gate itself was under a covered archway very dimly lit. After this, the two were to pass through the German courtyard under another archway, of which the gates at this hour were open. They would then reach the bridge over the moat, before having to pass the last sentry at the outermost gate. There was a possibility, however, of by-passing this last gate, which might require a password.

I knew of the existence of a small garden gate in the parapet at the beginning of the moat bridge. I had remarked on it on my first entry into the Castle just a year before. This gate gave on to a small path which led downwards into the moat. From what I knew of the geography of the camp, I always suspected this path might lead around to the roadway, down which we passed when going for exercise in the park. If our two officers could regain this roadway, they had merely to pass some occupied German barracks and proceed a hundred yards to a locked gate in the outer wall around the Castle grounds. This gate was not guarded as far as we knew, the area would be in pitch darkness, and the wall with its barbed wire could therefore be climbed.

Our first two disappeared towards the moat bridge, and we heard no more of them.

The next day we covered the two *Appells*. Van den Heuvel arranged this with perfect equanimity. It was another professional secret of his which he promised to reveal if I told him how I launched the escapers!

In the evening I repeated the performance of the night before and Hyde-Thompson and his Dutch colleague departed from the camp.

We could not conceal four absences, so that, at the next morning *Appell*, four officers were found missing. The Jerries became excited and everyone was promptly confined to barracks.

As the day wore on and the German searches proved fruitless, their impatience grew. So did that of the prisoners. Every German who entered the courtyard was barracked until, finally, the riot squad appeared.

With rifles pointed at the windows, orders were issued that nobody was to look out. Needless to say, this made matters worse. The French started shouting their usual colloquy, '*Où sont les allemands?*' and so on. The British began singing, '*Deutschland, Deutschland UNTER alles!*' – our revised version of the German National Anthem – to the accompaniment of musical instruments, imitating a German brass band. Mock heads began bobbing up and down at the windows and the inevitable shooting started, followed by the sounds of splintering glass.

From a protected vantage-point, I suddenly saw Van den Heuvel sally forth into the courtyard, having presumably opened the courtyard door with his own 'universal key'. His face was black with anger. He headed straight for the German officer in charge of operations, and with indignation showing in his every movement, he told the Jerry in his own language what he thought of him and his race and their manner of treating defenceless prisoners. His anger was justified, for hardly had he finished speaking when the French announced in no uncertain terms from their windows that an officer had been hit.

This calmed the Jerries at once. The German officer removed his riot squad and went to investigate. Lieutenant Maurice Fahy had received a ricochet bullet under one of his shoulder-blades. He was removed to hospital and peace settled on the camp once more. Fahy lost the use of one arm through this episode. In spite of this he was never repatriated to France because he was listed as 'Deutschfeindlich', i.e. 'an enemy of Germany'. The personal particulars of every allied officer POW were annotated with either a little green or red flag. The latter meant 'Deutschfeindlich'.

By the winter of 1941–42, when Neave's escape took place, the forging of escapers' credentials had improved considerably. A number of expert forgers were at work, with the result that every British officer was eventually equipped with a set of papers, as well as maps, a small amount of German money and a compass.

Identity papers were reproduced by various means. The imitation by hand of a typewritten document is very difficult. There were only two officers in Colditz capable of doing it, and they worked overtime. The German Gothic script, commonly used on identity cards, while appearing to be even more difficult is, in fact, easier to copy, and our staff employed on this form of printing was correspondingly larger. The day arrived when a Polish officer, Lieutenant Niedenthal (nicknamed 'Sheriff'), made a typewriter. This proved a great boon and speeded up the work of our printing department considerably. The typewriter was of the one-finger variety and its speed of reproduction could not be compared with any normal machine, but it had the great advantage of being dismountable into half a dozen innocent-looking pieces of wood which did not require to be concealed from the Germans. Only the letters attached to their delicate arms had to be hidden.

Each officer was responsible for the concealment of his own papers and aids, the idea being that, under such conditions, it was easier to make use of escape opportunities if they arose without warning. One or two such occasions did arise and were made good use of, thanks to this system. As for concealment of the contraband, many carried their papers about with them, relying on native wit to hide them in the event of a 'blitz' search by the Jerries.

Searches occurred from time to time at unpredictable intervals. Sometimes we had warning; at other times none.

On one of the latter occasions I was busily doing some work with a large hammer when the Goons entered our quarters.

I seized a towel lying on a nearby table and put the hammer in its folds. The method of search was systematic. All officers were herded into a room at one end of our quarters and locked in. The Germans then turned all the other rooms inside out. They tore up floorboards, knocked away chunks of plaster from the walls, jabbed the ceilings, examined electric lights and every piece of furniture, turned bedclothes and mattresses inside out, removed all the contents of every cupboard, turned over the cupboards, emptied the solid contents of all tins on the floor, poured our precious home-made brews down the sinks, broke up games, cut open pieces of soap, emptied water-closets, opened chimney flues, and spread the kitchen fire and any other stove ashes all over the floor.

Then, coming to the last room, each prisoner was stripped in turn, and even the seams of his clothing searched before he was released into the main section of the quarters, there to be faced with the indescribable chaos of the Germans' handiwork. The latter usually found some contraband, though rarely anything of importance.

On this particular occasion when I had the hammer wrapped up in the towel, as soon as my turn came to be searched I put the towel casually on the table beside which the Jerry officer stood, and began stripping. When my clothing had been scrutinized, I dressed, picked up my 'loaded' towel and walked out of the room!

Then there was the time when the Gestapo decided to search the camp and show the German *Wehrmacht* how this should be conducted. They employed electric torches to search remote crevices and borrowed the keys of the camp to make the rounds. Before they had finished, both the keys and their torches had disappeared, and they left with their tails between their legs. The German garrison were as pleased as Punch. We returned the keys, after making suitable impressions, to their rightful guardians.

To return to the thread of my story. The four escapers were well equipped for their journey to the Swiss frontier towards which they headed. They travelled most of the way by train. Neave and Luteyn crossed the frontier safely. Neave was the first Britisher to make a home run from Colditz.[1]

Hyde-Thompson and his companion were caught by station controls at Ulm. They brought back the news that Neave and Luteyn had also been caught at the same station. There had been some RAF bombing, which was followed by heavy controls for the purpose of rounding up plane crews that had parachuted. Neave and Luteyn had, however, managed to escape again from the police-station during a moment's laxness on the part of their

---

[1] Airey Neave has described his adventures in his book *They Have Their Exits* (Hodder & Stoughton). He was elected Conservative Member of Parliament for Abingdon in 1953.

guards. By the time Hyde-Thompson reached Ulm, the Jerries were on their toes. Maybe they had received warning; in any case, once he was suspected, he had no real hope of success.

Hyde-Thompson's bad luck taught us another lesson. We paid for our experience dearly! From now on, no more than two escapers at a time would travel the same route.

CHAPTER 14

THE INFORMER

As I have mentioned, I was not completely satisfied with 'Shovewood IV'. When, after a week, the Germans had calmed down, Hank and I paid a surreptitious visit to the theatre and I applied a new coat of paint to the 'Shovewood', for I knew that when more officers escaped the German efforts to discover the exit would be redoubled.

When the paint was dry we paid another visit to check the colour, and during this visit I had a suspicion we had been followed – a vague impression and no more. I was more careful than ever about our movements and disappearance under the stage. It was curious, though, that the *fouine*, our German 'ferret', paid a visit to the theatre and I even heard him speaking (presumably to a prisoner) close to the stage.

The next two officers were preparing for their exit, due for the following Sunday, when, on Saturday, we learnt that the Jerries had been under the stage and discovered my 'Shovewood'. This was more suspicious than ever, as no traces were left to indicate the position of the 'Shovewood', buried as it was under a four-inch layer of dirt and rubble, which extended uniformly beneath the whole of the stage, an area of one hundred square yards.

My suspicions increased further when the German Regimental Sergeant-Major, Gephard, who on rare occasions became human, remarked in a conversation with Peter Allan:

'The camouflage was *prachtvoll*! I examined the ceiling myself, and would not have suspected a hole.'

'Well, how did you discover it then?' asked Peter.

'*Ach!* That cannot be revealed, but we would never have found it without help.'

'Whose help? A spy?'

'I cannot say,' replied Gephard with a meaning look, then, changing the subject:

'The photographer has been called to take photographs of the camouflage for the escape museum.'

'So you make records of our escapes?'

'*Jawohl!* We have a room kept as a museum. It is very interesting! After
the war, perhaps you shall see it.'

The remark concerning 'help' was reported to the various senior officers
and escape officers. It meant we had to act in future under the assumption
that there was a 'stooge' or 'planted man' in the camp and, sure enough, it
transpired that there was.

Gephard was a strange character. He gave the impression of being sour
and ruthless with his harsh, deep voice and unsmiling face. But he was
probably the most intelligent of the Jerries at Colditz. I am sure he was one
of the first to realize who would win the war! Apart from this, under his
gruffness, there was honesty, and it is possible he disliked the idea of sending
blackmailed spies into a camp, enough to warrant his dropping hints about
it.

The stooge was not unearthed for some time. There was no evidence
from the theatre escape to commit anyone. However, certain Poles had
been keeping their eye on one of their own officers over an extended period
and had slowly accumulated evidence.

Not very long after the theatre escape, we heard a rumour that the Poles
were about to hang one of their own officers. The same day a Pole was
hurriedly removed from the camp.

What I gleaned from Niki and others – the Poles were reticent about the
whole incident – was that they had held a court martial and found the man
guilty of aiding the enemy, though under duress. The officer had been
blackmailed by the Germans, having been tempted in a weak moment
while he was ill in a hospital somewhere in Germany. He was allowed to
return home and see his family, and thereafter was threatened with their
disappearance if he did not act as an informer.

I would go so far as to say that the German army officers in the camp did
not use him willingly. They were probably presented with an informer by
the Gestapo and given orders to employ him. This would also account for
Gephard's reaction in giving us the hint.

In any case, the upshot was that the Polish Senior Officer, rather than
have a dead body on his hands, called on the German Commandant, told
him the facts – which the Commandant did not deny – and gave the latter
twenty-four hours to remove the man.

Towards the end of 1941 the Goons also tried to persuade the French
and Belgian officer prisoners to 'collaborate' and work with them. Their
efforts in Colditz had little success; only two or three Frenchmen

disappeared. The Germans were keen to employ engineers and chemical experts. On a couple of days, a Goon officer addressed the French and Belgian officers at the midday *Appell* – by this time we were having three *Appells* daily – asking if there were any more volunteers for work, saying that officers should give in their names and state their professions in order to see if they could be fitted into the 'Economy of the Reich'. There was no response on the first day, except much laughter and derisive cheers. On the second day a French aspirant, Paul Durand, stepped smartly forward and said:

'I would like to work for the Germans.'

There was a gasp of surprise from the assembled parade and a beam from the Goon officer.

'You really want to work for the Reich?'

'Yes, I would prefer to work for twenty Germans than for one Frenchman.'

More gasps and looks of astonishment from the prisoners!

'All right! What is your name?'

'My name is Durand, and I wish to make it clearly understood that I would prefer to work for twenty Germans than for one Frenchman.'

'Good! What is your profession?'

'Undertaker!'

Jacques Prot, a *Sous-Lieutenant d'Artillerie*, was another Frenchman whose puckishness was irrepressible and whose quick-wittedness won him freedom and later glory. I have mentioned his name along with that of 'Scorgie' Price in connection with the requisitioning of the German dentist's hat and overcoat. Prot contrived to escape during a visit to the German dentist in the village of Colditz. The visit was an unheard-of relaxation, but he worked it. He set off under heavy guard with another Frenchman also suffering from some galloping disease of the teeth. 'Scorgie' Price's teeth did not warrant the visit and he was left behind. The other Frenchman was *Sous-Lieutenant d'Artillerie* Guy de Frondeville. They escaped from the guards when leaving the dentist's house, and that was that.

The two friends separated for safety at Leipzig. Prot, tall, dark, and well-built, aged about twenty-six, went through Cologne to Aix-la-Chapelle. As he neared the frontier he saw to his horror that his false papers were not at all like those in current use. The frontier station was heavily patrolled and guarded. He closely followed the crowd, mostly Belgian passengers, towards the barrier. He was at his wits' end. Then the light dawned! He grabbed a suitcase out of the hand of an astonished fellow-passenger and took to his heels, through the barrier and away. The psychology behind this move was inspired, for the passenger created a tremendous uproar, attracting everybody's attention for a few minutes – then, as soon as the Germans were fully aware of what had happened, they couldn't care less. An escaping French officer might have been something, but a thief running away with a Belgian's suitcase did not raise the slightest interest.

Nine days out from Colditz, Prot arrived in Paris, to the surprise and joy of his family, on Christmas Eve 1941.

He reached Tunis via the French Free Zone in 1942, and joined the 67th Artillery Regiment (Algerian). From Paris he returned the suitcase to the owner, whose address he found inside, and from Tunis he sent to the German dentist a large consignment of real coffee with apologies for the removal of his hat and coat. He fought through the Tunisian campaign to Cassino, where during the First Offensive (Mount Belvedere) on January 29th, 1944, he gave his life for France. May his honoured memory remain long with his countrymen as it is cherished by every Escaper of Colditz!

Christmas 1941 and New Year's Eve were gay affairs. There was deep snow everywhere and there was a spirit of hope, for the Germans were halted in Russia and having a bad time.

Our cellar of wines and firewater added to the fun! Teddy Barton produced another good variety show which played to overflowing houses for three nights. On New Year's Eve, towards midnight, the British started a 'snake chain'; men in single file each with an arm on the shoulder of the man in front. Laughing and singing, the snake passed through the various quarters of the Castle, growing in length all the time, until there must have been nearly two hundred officers of all nationalities on it. As midnight struck, the snake uncoiled itself into a great circle in the courtyard and struck up *Auld Lang Syne*. The whole camp joined in, as the courtyard refrain was taken up from the windows in the Castle. The snow was still falling. It had a peaceful and calming influence on everyone. If we prisoners could ever have felt happy and unrepressed, we were happy that evening.

CHAPTER 15

WINTER MEDLEY

There were many heavy snowfalls during the winter of 1941–42. I used to pass hours in a sleepy trance looking out of my window, hypnotized by the slowly gyrating flakes. I think it was a Chinese philosopher who once said that everything in Nature can be turned to man's advantage, if only man can find the way! I pondered long over the possibilities of using snow in an escape. I thought of snowmen and then of snow tunnels, but the stuff melted so quickly. A short snow tunnel maybe – and as I stared out of my window, once more I saw an opportunity before my eyes.

There below, at the other end of the courtyard, was the canteen, and at a high level above the canteen were the dormer windows of that room into which only Niki had once been, over a year ago, and which was sealed off from the end room (the curved room) of our quarters. There was a small flat roof over the canteen doorway which abutted both a window of the curved room and also a vertical slate-covered gable of the sealed room. The window-sill was at the level of the roof. The snow on the flat roof was nearly three feet thick.

Here was an opportunity not to be missed. I had no idea where we could go from the sealed room, but Niki had reported a further door opening on to the German quarters.

'Scruffy' Orr Ewing and another British officer, Lieutenant Colin MacKenzie, M.C., Seaforth Highlanders, had always wanted to tackle this room, and as they were high on the escape roster I gave them the plan and offered to help. Our curved-room window was, as usual, barred, and the filing of bars would be visible to anyone in the courtyard under normal circumstances. Certainly any persons climbing out of the window would have been seen. Now the snow hid everything.

The bars were cut in no time and Scarlet O'Hara manufactured thin metal sleeves so that the cut bars could be replaced and the sleeves slid over the ends. The metal was worked to a superlative fit and when in place each broken bar could be shaken without its falling out. Quick-drying black paint completed the camouflage after every work-shift.

A short snow tunnel of four yards' length was burrowed. It was shaped like an arch, one foot nine inches high, resting on the flat roof. The snow roof caved in a little at one point but some cardboard helped to prop it. The tunnel did not melt with my body heat but, on the contrary, formed a compact, interior-ice-wall. On reaching the vertical gable I removed some slates and found only laths and plaster beyond. This presented no difficulty. After a day's work the hole was big enough and the three of us crawled through to inspect the sealed room – it was the middle of the afternoon. We were examining the door into the German quarters when we received an alarm signal. Hauptmann Priem and a couple of his stooges on one of their lightning 'catch you out' visits had entered the courtyard. He headed straight for the British door and immediately started a close scrutiny of the British quarters – starting, unfortunately, in the curved room. We were trapped and the bars which had been cut were not in place. It was also standard routine for the Jerries to tap all window bars. For one moment the officers in the room thought the Jerries might overlook our window as it opened into the courtyard and was not therefore as suspect as windows facing the outside of the Castle. But alas! They opened the window, saw the gaping hole in the bars, and then the fun began.

Priem sent an N.C.O. along the snow tunnel. We could see him coming. In a matter of seconds I gathered up the tools we had brought – a hammer, screwdriver, a small saw, a file and some keys, and forcing open one of the dormer windows I have already mentioned, I shouted to a couple of Britishers walking around the courtyard.

'Tools coming out; save them, for heaven's sake!'

Lockwood was one of the two Britishers; he immediately saw the position. The particular window I was at had never been opened since Colditz had become a prison! The tools descended and, before an astonished sentry's gaze, Kenneth collected them and headed for the Polish doorway. He had disappeared before the sentry, who was standing close to the canteen, had recovered from his surprise.

This was not the end; in another five seconds I followed, leaving the window just as the Jerry N.C.O began waving his revolver, with his head and arm protruding through the hole in the gable. I was fed up with repeated 'solitary' confinements; this would mean another month and I was just not going to do it. Although the snow in the cobbled courtyard had been cleared, there was a thin film about half an inch thick on the ground. This might soften the drop, which was about twenty feet after a three-yard slide down to the gutter from the dormer window. I leaped out of the window, slithered, fell, and landed squarely, then doubled up forward, hitting my forehead hard on the ground. I wore a balaclava helmet with only eyes and nose showing, many layers of outer clothing, and thick leather gloves. To the sentry, just recovering from the rain of tools, the descending body must have looked like a man from Mars. As I picked myself up and ran for it, he stood transfixed and I was able to make a clean getaway. Orr Ewing and McKenzie did not follow. By that time the Jerry in the hole had advanced sufficiently to be able to make respectable use of his revolver.

After this setback we had another in which the Dutch came off badly. They lived on the floor just above us, and had discovered the existence of a hollow vertical shaft in the outer wall of the Castle. It was a medieval lavatory. The Castle had many curious buttresses and towers, and once before, during explorations, the Dutch had come across a secret staircase, bricked up in the thickness of one of the walls. Unfortunately, it led only to another floor-level and was of little use for escape purposes. It may have seen curious uses in bygone days!

The vertical shaft, on the contrary, held definite promise. Vandy constructed a superbly camouflaged entrance to it in the urinal wall of the Dutch lavatory. As the urinal was kept wholesome by applications of a creosote-and-tar mixture, Vandy had little difficulty in obtaining a supply of it from the Jerries, which served to hide the shaft entrance from even the most experienced snoop or 'ferret'. The entrance was about three feet from the ground and was closed with a thick concrete slab. Beyond the urinal was a small turret room. Through the outer wall of this turret, Vandy pierced a second hole which he camouflaged equally well by means of a door, made of the original stones of the wall cemented together. The door swung open on pivots and gave directly on to the vertical shaft, which was about one yard by four yards in size. The drop to the bottom was seventy feet. Vandy had a neat rope-ladder made for the descent.

At this stage he came to me with a proposal for a joint escape effort if I would provide him with some experienced tunnellers. This was not difficult. I proposed Jim Rogers, engineer of the long Laufen tunnel in which twelve hundred bedboards were used, and Rupert Barry, the best tunneller of our team, who had constructed the shorter Laufen woodshed tunnel. When Jim Rogers' huge bulk was not tunnelling, it was sitting on a stool playing the guitar. Jim took up the instrument on his arrival at Colditz, saying he would give his wife a surprise when he returned home after the war. He never mentioned it in his letters. By the time he left the prison camp years later, he was a highly proficient player. Without considering the difficult classical music he played, it was sufficiently amazing to watch his massive fists manipulating the delicate strings. His index finger alone could easily 'stop' about three strings at once.

He and Rupert, with Dutch assistants, set to work at the bottom of the shaft, but the going was hard and rocky in parts. Tunnelling continued for a week and then the Jerries suddenly pounced. It was becoming painfully obvious by now that they had sound detectors around the Castle walls. Our tunnellers were experienced, knew exactly what they were up against and could be trusted not to do anything stupid. Yet again they were taken by surprise. This time Priem and his team of ferrets entered the Castle and made straight for the place where the shaft was located at ground-level.

This implied that the Germans knew the invisible geography of the camp, presumably from plans of the Castle in their possession. Without a moment's hesitation, Priem set his men to attack a certain false wall with pickaxes, and in less than ten minutes they had pierced it and a man put his head and arm through and shone a torch up and down the shaft.

The two tunnellers on shift had succeeded in climbing the seventy feet, one at a time – for the rope-ladder was not reckoned strong enough to carry two – and Vandy was busy pulling up the ladder when the torch flashed around the shaft. A few seconds later and the ladder would have been out of sight. The Jerries would have had no clues as to the entrance and the betting was that they would not search for an underground tunnel entrance on the third floor of the Castle. It was such a close shave that Vandy was not even sure they had seen the dangling ladder, but, unluckily for Vandy and his team, they had.

Nevertheless, the tunnellers had time to clear out and Vandy was able to complete the sealing of the two entrances, with the result that when the Jerries arrived in the upper stories they were at a complete loss. Eventually they pierced new openings on the same lines as the 'blitz' hole made down below. They first reached the small turret room, where, unluckily for all, they found important booty. Vandy had hidden much contraband in this room; no fewer than four complete German uniforms – our joint work – were found and also Vandy's secret *Appell* 'stooges'. After this *débâcle* he told me the following story of his 'stooges'.

During one of the periodic visits of the Castle masons, doing repairs, he had managed to bribe one of them into giving him a large quantity of ceiling plaster. The Dutch amateur sculptor had carved a couple of life-size, officer type busts which were cleverly painted (I saw one later) and as realistic as any of Madame Tussaud's waxworks. They were christened Max and Moritz by Vandy. Each bust had two iron hoops fixed underneath the pedestal, which was shaped to rest on a man's arm, either upright, or upside-down hanging from the hoops. A shirt collar and tie were fitted to the bust and, finally, a long Dutch overcoat was draped over the bust's shoulders.

When not in action the dummy hung suspended under the forearm of the bearer, concealed by the folds of the overcoat. In fact, to outward appearances the bearer was carrying an overcoat over his arm. When the *Appell* was called, officers would muster and fall into three lines. With a screen of two assistants and standing in the middle line of the three, the bearer unfurled the overcoat, an army cap was placed on the dummy's head by one assistant and a pair of top boots placed neatly under the coat in the position of 'attention' by the other assistant. The dummy was held shoulder high and the helpers formed up close to one another to camouflage the proximity of the 'carrier' officer to his Siamese twin!

The ruse had worked perfectly for the *Appells* in connection with the Dutch park escape and the theatre escape. Although Max and Moritz were discovered by the Jerries in Vandy's hide, they were found as unclothed plaster busts and Vandy hoped that he might be able to play the trick again.

CHAPTER 16

THE RHINE MAIDEN

Since Niki's last escape attempt over the guardhouse roof, and two successive attempts from hospitals by a Lieutenant Joseph Just, which took him to the Swiss border but alas! not over it, the Poles seemed to retire from the escape front. Of course they were pestered for a long time by the 'informer', whom they must have suspected and who must have hampered their efforts greatly. They were also liable to be blackmailed for the slightest offence, as their families were at the mercy of the Germans. In January 1942, without any warning, they were told to pack. With many regrets we said good-bye, and as we shook hands we expressed the mutual wish:

'*Auf Wiedersehen – nach dem Krieg!*'

We saw very few of them again. They went to semi-underground fortress camps in the Posnan area. A very few managed to trek westward towards the end of the war. Niki died of tuberculosis.

For a long time the Polish rooms were vacant. Then, one spring morning, the 'ghetto' arrived. French Jewish officers sifted out from many camps were gathered together and sent to Colditz. Why were they being incarcerated here? The question made one reflect a little as to what was to be the ultimate fate of all the Colditz inmates. We were 'bad boys', and a public danger and nuisance. I, personally, did not think that we had much hope of surviving the war. If the Allies won, which we considered almost a certainty, Hitler and his maniacs would see that all possible revenge was wreaked before they descended the abyss and their Führer fulfilled the prophecy of his favourite opera, *Götterdämmerung*. The gathering of the French Jews was a bad omen. If the Germans won the war, they, at least, would not survive. Would we?

The French contingent had also been quiet for some time. They seemed to be resting on the laurels of Lebrun's escape for too long.

It was with pleasure therefore, although with considerable misgivings

for its ultimate success, that I received the news of the commencement of a
French tunnel. Its entrance was at the top of the clock-tower, a hundred
feet from ground-level; that, at any rate, I thought, was a good beginning.

So many tunnels, and exits generally, begin at ground-level, that at
Colditz, at least, it was almost a waste of time to start work in the
conventional manner. If someone thought of a tunnel, we examined the
attics; if someone thought of escaping by glider (do not laugh! for one was
made in Colditz and is to this day, as far as I know, concealed there), we
started, if possible, underground! The short Laufen tunnel and the Colditz
canteen tunnel began at ground-level, although the entrances to both were
under German lock and key. Clandestine entrances rose to the second-floor
level in the theatre escape; hovered on the first floor with the snow tunnel;
then rose to the third floor in the Dutch vertical-shaft tunnel, and now, the
French capped all by starting their tunnel at the top of the clock-tower!

The most serious danger, of course, for all tunnel attempts nowadays in
Colditz was that of sound detectors placed around the Castle. The
lightning descents of Priem on our snow tunnel and on the Dutch tunnel
were too speedy compared with what we could expect of normal Jerry
vigilance. At the same time, as far as tunnel entrances were concerned,
German scrutiny of floors and walls decreased in inverse ratio as one
increased one's height from the ground!

The French tunnel was a gigantic undertaking. I shall leave it for the
present at its entrance.

Further French originality displayed itself shortly after their tunnel had
begun. One spring afternoon a mixed batch of French, Dutch and British
were marching through the third gateway leading down to the exercise
ground, or park as it was called. The majority had just 'wheeled right',
down the ramp roadway, when a gorgeous-looking German girl passed by.
She haughtily disdained to look at the prisoners, and walked primly past,
going up the ramp towards the German courtyard of the Castle. There
were low whistles of admiration from the more bawdy-minded prisoners –
for she was a veritable Rhine maiden with golden blonde hair. She wore a
broad-brimmed hat, smart blouse and skirt, and high-heeled shoes – she
was large as well as handsome – a fitting consort for a German Demi-God!

As she swept past us, her fashionable-looking wrist-watch fell from her
arm at the feet of Squadron-Leader Paddon, who was marching in front of
me. Paddon was familiarly known as 'Never-a-dull-moment' Paddon,
because he was always getting into trouble! The Rhine maiden had not
noticed her loss, but Paddon, being a gentleman, picked up the watch and
shouted:

'Hey, Miss! You've dropped your watch.'

The Rhine maiden, like a barque under full sail, had already tacked to port, and was out of sight. Paddon thereupon made frantic signs to the nearest guard, explaining:

'*Das Fraülein hat ihre Uhr verloren. Ja! – Uhr – verloren,*' and he held up the dainty article.

'*Ach so! Danke,*' replied the guard, grasping what had happened. He seized the watch from Paddon's hand and shouted to a sentry in the courtyard to stop the girl.

The girl was, by now, primly stepping towards the other (main) gateway which led out of the camp. The sentry stopped her, and immediately became affable, looking, no doubt, deeply into her eyes from which, unfortunately, no tender light responded! 'Hm!' the sentry reflected, as she did not reply to his cajoling. 'She is dumb or very haughty or just plain rude.'

He looked at her again and noticed something – maybe the blonde hair had gone awry. The second scrutiny, at a yard's distance, was enough for him. By the time our guard arrived panting with the watch, the Rhine maiden stood divested of her *Tarnhelm*, a sorrowful sight, minus her wig and spring bonnet, revealing the head of Lieutenant Bouley (Chasseur Alpin), who unhappily did not speak or understand a word of German.

This escape had been the result of many months of patient effort and was prepared with the assistance of the officer's wife in France. The French were allowed to receive parcels direct from their next-of-kin, which made this possible. He had a complete lady's outfit including silk stockings. The golden hair was a triumph of the wigmaker's art, of real hair, collected, bleached, curled, and sewn together. The wig was put together in Colditz. The large straw bonnet was the product of French patterns and Colditz straw weaving.

The transformation had been practised for weeks and was a conjuring trick which, I regret, I never saw enacted. The 'conjurer' had three accomplices and the usual 'stooges' to distract momentarily the attention of the guards as he turned the corner out of the gateway leading to the park. At this point, the 'conjurer' could count on a few seconds of 'blind-spot', which might be drawn out to, say, ten or twelve seconds by a good 'stooge' attending to the guard immediately behind him. The guards were ranged along the ranks on both sides at intervals of ten yards.

Part of the transformation was done on the march, prior to the arrival at the corner – for instance, strapping on the watch, pulling up the silk stockings, the rouging of lips and the powdering of the face. Once in the gateway, the high-heeled shoes were put on. The blouse and bosoms were in place, under a loose cloak around his shoulders. The skirt was tucked up around his waist. His accomplices held the wig, the hat, and the lady's bag.

There is a moral to this story which is worth recording. I had not been informed of the forthcoming attempt and certainly I sympathized with the French in their desire for complete surprise. It was much better, for instance, that the parade going to the park should be unconscious of what was taking place. The participants behaved naturally in consequence, whereas the least whispering or craning of necks or rising on tiptoe – any conscious movement – might have upset the effort. Yet the fact of having informed me would not have made much difference to all this. Neither would I have been able to warn all the British on the parade; it would have been dangerous. Nevertheless, the moral emerges: the fateful coincidence that I happened to be behind Paddon on the walk; that, if I had been warned, I might have nipped the watch incident in the bud, and the escape would probably have succeeded.

This escape, as usual, closed the park to the prisoners for a period. Hardly had walks recommenced, however, when Vandy announced another attempt to be made by his contingent. I asked from what direction, and he answered, 'Vrom the park, ov course!'

The 'privilege' of going to the park for a two-hour walk around a barbed-wire enclosure at the bottom of the valley was continually being withdrawn by the Goons, because of insubordination of the prisoners, in consequence of escapes, or just to annoy us. During these periods in the late spring of 1942, when the privilege was not withheld, the Dutch used to sit together on the grass in the middle of the wire enclosure while one of them would read to the others. Personally, I did not go very often to the park – it used to depress me. The Goon sentries stood close up to the wire, so that when officers walked round the path of the perimeter, they came within a few yards of them. I am sure the Germans put English-speaking sentries on this job who listened to one's every word. They could not have been edified, because many prisoners made a point of saying exactly what they thought of the Goons, the German race, and the Third Reich in general, for their benefit.

On the day appointed by Vandy, I went there for a change, and noticed the Dutch in their usual group, with a huge, black-bearded man in his army cloak sitting in the centre, reading to them. I happened to notice also that he was fidgeting all the time, as if he had an itch. He held a book and continued reading for an hour and a half. The walk lasted officially two hours, but a quarter of an hour was allowed at the beginning and at the end to line us up and count the numbers present.

The whistle blew and the prisoners slowly collected near the gate where they lined up to be counted before marching back to the Castle. All went off as usual and we started to march back. It was the custom that, as soon as the prisoners left the park, the Goons unleashed their dogs. Suddenly hoarse shouts were heard behind us. We were halted and again counted.

This time the Goons found one prisoner missing.

What had happened was that the huge Dutchman with the black beard had been sitting on a small Dutchman who had been entirely hidden by his black cloak (an alternative to the Dutch colonial army overcoat) and who had dug a 'grave' for himself. The others had all helped to hide the earth and stones and cover the small Dutchman with grass. When the whistle blew they moved towards the gate, leaving the little man in his grave, ready to escape when the coast was clear. They managed to cover up the first count so that the Goons did not notice that a man was missing. By bad luck, one of the Alsatian police dogs took it into his head to chase another. The leading animal ran straight over the 'grave' and the other followed. When he reached the grave the second dog was attracted, possibly by the newly dug earth, and started digging; in a few seconds he unearthed the Dutchman.

Vandy had once more employed a dummy Dutchman – the third he had made. When the alarm was raised, however, he had not used it again. He knew the parade would be carefully scrutinized and he hoped to save the dummy. He was out of luck. The Germans searched all the officers carefully before they re-entered the Castle and the dummy was found in its full regalia.

It was always questionable whether a dog was much use immediately after a parade, unless he found himself almost on top of a body, because the ground must have reeked with the scent of many human beings who had just vacated the area. It cannot be denied, however, that in this case the dogs found the man; whether it was by coincidence or by astuteness, I do not know. The Germans were again having the better of the battle of Colditz. We would have to improve our technique. . . .

PART 3: ESCAPER

CHAPTER 17

THE 1942 FEELING

In April 1942, I asked to be released from the post of escape officer. It was high time someone else took on the job. I had visions of a month or two of rest, followed by an attempt in which I could take part myself. As escape officer it had become morally impossible for me to take part in any escape.

Colonel Stayner replaced Colonel German in the New Year as Senior British Officer, after the latter's departure to another camp. I think Colonel German was the only British officer who was removed from Colditz, once having been incarcerated there. Needless to say he returned about a year later on account of further 'offences' against the German Reich.

I suggested Dick Howe as successor to the post of escape officer. I deputized once again for him in July, while he did a month's 'solitary'. After that he carried on for a long time.

Throughout 1941 the British contingent had slowly risen from a mere handful of seventeen officers to about forty-five. During 1942 the number rose further, until by the summer there were about sixty. Late arrivals included Major Ronnie Littledale and Lieutenant Michael Sinclair, both of Winchester and of the 60th Rifles, and ten Naval officers and two Petty Officers from Marlag Nord. Group-Captain Douglas Bader also arrived.

Ronnie Littledale and Michael Sinclair had escaped together from a camp in the north of Poland and had travelled south. They were given assistance by Poles and lived in a large town somewhere in Poland for a while. When properly organized they headed for Switzerland, but were trapped in Prague during a mass check-up of all its inhabitants on account of the assassination of Heydrich. They were caught and put through the mill, including torture, before they were despatched to Colditz.

Ronnie was a very rare specimen on this earth. There was not a flaw to be found in his character. Quiet and even shy in his ways yet firm in his opinions, he suffered 'the slings and arrows' of this world to strike harmlessly against him. He was very thin, too thin. He had 'been through it'. He looked a little older than his age, with hair thinning unmistakably in front. A sharp nose pointing towards a hatchet chin served to complete the impression of an ascetic, which, in fact, he was. He would never have admitted it, and, indeed, his human kindly side and his alert sense of humour belied his rigid self-discipline and dogged determination.

Fate was to draw us close together.

Before long Michael Sinclair, his colleague, had a court-martial charge read against him for an offence he had committed in his earlier camp. We waved him good-bye as he left for his trial under guard. He was completely equipped for a getaway with transformable clothing, chiefly of RAF origin. His court martial was at Leipzig, but he managed to elude his guards in a lavatory at a Leipzig barracks before it took place, and a few days later turned up in Cologne. There had been heavy Allied bombing and the colour of most of his clothing was unfortunate because a witch-hunt for RAF parachute survivors was in progress. He was caught in the meshes and duly returned to Colditz under a three-man guard.

Returning escapers were bad for morale. Each successful getaway was like a tonic for the rest of the prisoners even though it usually meant one less bolt-hole for those who remained. Michael Sinclair felt this very much, though he had no reason to. His record clearly showed that he was the type of man who would not miss a 'hundred to one against'chance of an escape.

It was, nevertheless, becoming obvious to everybody that, once out of the Castle, it was an escaper's duty to take very heavy risks rather than return to the fold within the oppressive walls of Colditz. It was in the summer of 1942 I resolved I would not come back if I ever escaped again, and I know it was the decision which many others made as the months of 1942 dragged on. We already had one temporarily insane officer on our hands (he recovered after the war). He remained with us for months before the Germans were convinced he was not shamming, and we had to maintain a permanent guard from among our own number to see that he did not attempt suicide. The guard, which was worked on a roster, soon had to do double duty to cope with a second officer who tried to slash his wrist with a razor, but, luckily, made a poor job of it and was discovered in a washroom before he had completed his work. This type of guard duty had a decidedly bad effect on the guards.

Then there was a third British officer who was not so mad as he looked. He confided to me one day, early in 1941, when he was perfectly normal:

'Pat, I think the only way I shall ever escape from Colditz is by going insane.'

'It's not a bad idea,' I replied, 'in so far as the Swiss have at last got things moving over the repatriation of wounded, sick, and insane POWs.'

'I know.'

'Do you realize what it means?' I said. 'Have you thought out all the ramifications?'

'Well, it'll be a long job, I know.'

'Much more than a long job! I read a book before the war called *The Road to En-Dor*[1]. It is the best escape book I have ever read. In it a British officer feigned madness for months – and what he went through was nobody's business. He nearly hanged himself. Yet it was child's play compared with what you would have to do in this war by way of convincing experts.'

'I realize that,' said the officer, 'and I'm prepared for it. I'm ready to behave as insane before the whole camp and convince my friends also that I'm cuckoo.'

'More than that,' I said, 'you'll have to write insane letters to your people at home! Have you considered that?'

'No,' he admitted, 'it might be better not to write at all.'

'You're going to cause a lot of suffering, but if you're determined, go ahead. First, you'll have to have medical advice as to symptoms so that you can develop slowly and correctly. Your insanity will have to become your second nature. Do you realize there if a possibility of its becoming your real nature?'

'I've heard it,' he agreed, 'but I'm prepared to risk it.'

'I shall have to obtain all the medical symptoms for you from the French camp doctor,' I continued. 'You must not approach him yourself because he is one of the first you will have to convince of your authenticity. The job will take six months at least before you get on to a repatriation train.'

'Good, I'm ready to start as soon as you've got all the dope.'

'All right,' I concluded. 'I'll let you know when I have it. I shall not tell anyone. If you mean to succeed, everyone around you must be convinced. It is the only way. If a rumour once starts that you're feigning, it will spread and eventually get to the Germans. Then you're finished for good.'

Two months after this conversation I handed over my job to Dick Howe and told him of the case of our pseudo-lunatic. Dick would not believe me at first. He thought that our pet lunatic (for he was of the harmless type) had pulled the wool over my eyes. It was a tribute to the officer's acting!

The arrival of the Navy in force gave rise to an incident which echoed through the halls of Colditz for many a day. The 'new boys' arrived one evening at about 9 pm. Howard Gee, who had helped in the affair of the canteen tunnel, was a civilian. He had volunteered for the expedition to help the Finns against Russia, had been captured by the Germans in Norway, and inevitably gravitated to Colditz. He was a clever man, aged about thirty, dark and handsome; he loved adventure and sought it out; journalism was one of his hobbies and practical joking was another. He spoke German fluently – so, upon the arrival of the Navy, he dressed up as the German camp doctor in one of our German uniforms (between the Dutch and ourselves there were still several wardrobes available). Our 'medium-sized' RAF officer, as he called himself – he was five-feet – acted

[1]   Now a PAN Book

as his British medical orderly, wearing a white jacket and apron. Entering the room where the Navy had just bedded down and bellowing with rage, Gee ordered them all out of bed to parade in front of him in their pyjamas. He shouted for a *Dolmetscher* – that is, an interpreter – from among them. A fair-haired officer advanced and stood smartly at attention in front of him. In Colditz it was an unwritten law that nobody stood at attention before a German officer (except on *Appell*) unless ordered under threat to do so. The officer's action in this case, being unprecedented, inflamed our 'camp doctor' so much that he promptly ordered the *Dolmetscher* two months' *strenger Arrest*, otherwise 'solitary'. He then delivered a harangue, which the interpreter did his best to translate, saying the Navy were all lousy, that they should never have been allowed into the camp without first passing through the 'delouser' and consequently they would all be court-martialled. Then, with vociferous references to *les papillons d'amour* – he used the French term – he commanded his British orderly to produce the bucket of 'blue'. This is a strong, bright blue-coloured disinfectant which is applied to the body to kill lice, fleas, and so on. It is also a paint which takes weeks to remove. He made the parade strip naked and told the British orderly to apply a lavish coating of 'blue' to the bodies assembled. This done, he inspected the result, calling for more 'blue' where he thought it necessary, and then retired, still muttering threats and Prussian curses. The parade was left standing at attention, a row of bright blue nudists, while the laughter of the twenty or so 'old lags' who occupied the same room could be heard throughout the Castle.

The Navy saw the joke and Gee was known as the 'Herr Doktor' ever after.

Douglas Bader's arrival also heralded an increase in practical joking of the particular form which was known as 'Goon-baiting'. Bader, a character already famous for his exploits, was irrepressible, undaunted by catastrophe, a magnetic leader and a dangerous enemy. He had hardly been in Colditz a few weeks, when he – a man with no legs from the knees downwards – volunteered for partnership in an escape attempt over the roofs of the Castle!

Goon-baiting was a pastime indulged in when one had nothing better to do – a frequent occurrence in a POW camp. It varied from the most innocuous forms, such as dropping small pebbles from a hundred feet or so on the head of a sentry, through less innocent types as the release of propaganda written on lavatory paper and dropped out of windows when the wind was favourable, up to the more staged variety like the case of the 'corpse'.

A life-size 'lay figure' was made out of palliasses and straw by Peter Storie Pugh and clothed in a worn-out battledress. We were having frequent air-raid alarms by the summer of 1942, during which the normally floodlit Castle was blacked out. On one of these raids the 'lay figure' was eased through the bars of a window and left suspended with a long length of twine attached, some of which was held in reserve.

As soon as the floodlights went on again, the figure was jerked into movement and in less than no time the firing started.

After a good 'value for money' volley, the figure was allowed to drop to the ground. Goon sentries immediately rushed to recover the corpse, which thereupon came to life, and rose high into the air again. A Goon approached nearer and the lay figure was promptly dropped on his head!

It was difficult for the Jerries to find the culprits. It was even difficult for them to locate the window from which the figure had sallied, as thin twine was used. The result was the withdrawal of the 'park' privilege for the whole camp during a month.

At first sight it might appear to be unfair that other nationalities should suffer for our sins, but we were not the only sinners and we suffered reciprocally! It was the expression of our unity against the common enemy.

Harry Elliott also indulged in a cold war against the Goons, but of a type which they never actually discovered. In the intervals between escape attempts he was always inventing new ways of waging war inside the prison walls. Thus while languishing in 'solitary' after an 'attempt' from the air-raid shelter on the road to the park along with a Pole, Captain Janek Lados, in which he was caught by the German sleuthhounds, he conceived the 'Razor-blades in the Pig Swill' campaign. With the aid of volunteers and large numbers of broken razor-blades, the camp garbage was heavily and regularly impregnated. All razor-blade pieces were carefully inserted and hidden completely inside rotten potatoes and vegetable remains. The results of the campaign were never known except by inference. The Germans made it a court-martial offence, punishable by most severe sentences including the possibility of the death penalty, to endanger the lives of German animals by tampering with the camp swill. Incidentally, while Harry was hatching this scheme in one prison cell, Janek Lados succeeded in escaping from another – it was conveniently situated in the outer walls of the Castle. Janek cracked his shin-bone in the fall from the cell window. He reached the Swiss frontier, nevertheless, but was recaptured within sight of freedom.

Another campaign which Harry initiated was 'the Battle of the Dry Rot'. In conversation with a fellow-prisoner, Lieutenant Geoffrey Ransone, who was an architect by profession in peacetime, he learnt that dry rot could be propagated by making 'cultures' of it. He argued, quite logically, that whereas an RAF bomb could remove the roof of a building in a second or so, dry rot could do the same thing though in a somewhat longer space of time – say twenty years or so. The war, according to him, might easily last that long, so that in the end his work might equate to the work of a fair-sized bomb, and there was nothing that could please Harry more than the thought that he was dropping a bomb on Colditz – however long the time-fuse.

In less than no time rows of innocent-looking, almost empty jam-jars made their appearance in dark corners under the beds of Harry and his disciples. In each jar was a sliver of wood, but wedged to it somehow was 'the culture'. The jars had to be kept damp and in the dark. On their periodic searches the Jerries were always puzzled by these jars, but they looked so harmless that they never removed them, ignorant of the dangerous 'explosive' they contained. In due course, when ripe, the slivers of wood were distributed throughout the roof timbers of the camp, where no doubt they still repose.

Harry had another habit. At night, after 'Lights Out', he would often hold the stage as we all reclined on our beds in the darkness. A flow of funny stories would issue from the corner where he lay, and then he would start recounting some rather involved incident of his career – I think he did it on purpose. About halfway through it he would stop, and after a pause, during which heavy breathing would become audible, he would say:

'Don't you think so, Peter (or Dick, or Rupert)?'

A long pause was followed by:

'Hm! No answer. Time I turned in.'

And, to the sounds of grunts and rustling straw, Harry would turn in. The silence of 'a prisoner's vigil' would descend upon the rows of wooden bunks, faintly reflecting the glow of the searchlights outside.

CHAPTER 18

ESCAPE STRATEGY

Mike Sinclair's fear that he had closed another bunk-hole for his fellow-prisoners proved groundless. Soon after his attempt, Squadron-Leader 'Never-a-dull-moment' Paddon was called to face a court-martial charge at a former prison camp in the north-east of Germany. He was duly equipped for an escape and left for his destination under heavy guard. It was a long journey and he would be away several days. As the days turned into weeks, Colonel Stayner naturally became concerned, and demanded an explanation from the Camp Commandant. The latter replied with a resigned shrug of the shoulders:

'Es war unmöglich, trotzdem is er geflohen' – 'It was impossible, none the less he escaped!' Paddon eventually reached Sweden and then England safely. He was the second Englishman to do the home run from Colditz.

I was lying on my bunk one hot day in August 1942. 'Lulu' Lawton (Captain W. T. Lawton, Duke of Wellington's Regiment) was lying in another nearby. Lulu had had one short break from Colditz and had been recaught after a few hours' journey outward bound. He was a York-shireman and he naturally preferred the smell of the fresh air outside the precincts of the camp. He lay ruminating for a long time and then in a sad voice, turning towards me, he said:

'As far as I can see, Pat, it's no good trying any more escapes from Colditz - the place is bunged up – a half-starved rat wouldn't find a hole big enough for him to squeeze through.' Then he added soulfully: 'I wouldn't mind havin' another go, all the same, if I could only think of a way.'

'You've got to consider the problem coldly,' I replied. 'The first principle for success in any battle is to attack the enemy in his weakest quarter, but what is always confused in the question of escape is our understanding concerning the enemy's weakest quarter. It isn't, for instance, the apparent weak point in the wire or the wall, for these are his rear-line defences. We have to go a long way before we reach them. It's his front-line defences that count, and they are inside the camp. Jerry's strongest weapon is his ability to nip escapes in the bud before they are ready. This he does right inside the camp and he succeeds ninety-eight per cent of the time. His weakest quarter inside the camp has therefore to be found; after that, the rest is a cakewalk.'

I added: 'For instance, if you were to ask me where the German weak spot in this camp is, I should say it's Gephard's own office. Nobody will ever look for an escape attempt being hatched in the German RSM's office.'

'That's all very well,' said Lulu, 'but Gephard's office has a cruciform lock and an ugly-looking padlock as well.'

'All the better,' I answered. 'You won't be disturbed then.'

'But how do I get in?'

'That's your problem,' I concluded.

I never dreamt he would take the matter seriously, but a Yorkshireman's thoroughness is not to be denied.

There was a Dutchman in the camp, the red-bearded Captain Van Doorninck. He used to repair watches in his spare time, and he even repaired them for the German personnel occasionally, in return for equipment with which to carry on his hobby. Thus, he possessed a repair outfit consisting of miniature tools and various oddments in the way of materials, which were rigorously denied to other prisoners. He never gave his parole as to the employment of the tools.

Van Doorninck was 'brainy'. He had a wide knowledge of higher mathematics, and at one period he gave me, along with one or two others, a university course in Geodesy – a subject I had never thoroughly grasped as a student.

Besides tinkering with watches Van Doorninck was not averse to tinkering with locks, as Lulu Lawton found out, with the result that the former devised a method of lock-picking that any Raffles might have been proud of.

I have described the outward appearance of the cruciform lock before as resembling a four-armed Yale lock. Its essential internal elements consisted of between six and nine tiny pistons of not quite one-eighth of an inch diameter each. In order to open the lock these pistons had to be moved in their cylinders by the insertion of the key.

Each piston moved a different distance, the accuracy of which was gauged to a thousandth of an inch.

The principle involved was the same as that employed in the Yale lock. The keyhole, however, was like a cross, each limb being about one-sixteenth of an inch wide, whereas the Yale has a zigzag-shaped keyway. The latter keyway might have presented more difficulty to Van Doorninck, though I am sure he would have overcome it. However, he solved the cruciform problem by manufacturing a special micrometer gauge, which marked off the amount of movement that each piston required. He then made a key to conform, using his gauge to check the lifting faces of the key as he filed them. The key looked rather like a four-armed Yale key.

Van Doorninck succeeded brilliantly where I had failed miserably. I blushed with shame every time I recollected the tortures I had inflicted on so many wincing sufferers in the dentist's chair! The new key was a triumph. Moreover, Van Doorninck was in a position to 'break' all the cruciform locks, though each one was different. Thereafter, like ghosts we passed through doors which the Germans thought were sealed.

Returning to the door of Gephard's office: once the cruciform lock was 'broken' the other lock, the padlock, presented no difficulty.

The plan evolved. Lulu Lawton had teamed up with Flight-Lieutenant 'Bill' Fowler, RAF, and then made a foursome with Van Doorninck and another Dutchman. Dick Howe, as escape officer, was in charge of operations. He came to me one day.

'Pat, I've got a job for you,' he said. 'Lulu and three others want to break out of Gephard's office window. Will you have a look at it? I'd also like you to do the job for them.'

'Thanks for the compliment,' I replied. 'When do we start?'

'Any time you like.'

'I'm not so sure of the window idea, Dick,' I said, 'but I'll check up carefully. It's pretty close to a sentry and it may even be in his line of sight.'

'Kenneth Lockwood will go sick whenever you're ready,' Dick continued, 'and he'll live in the sick-ward opposite Gephard's office and manipulate all the necessary keys.'

'Good! There's no German medical orderly at night, so I can hide under Kenneth's bed after the evening *Appell* until lights out. Then I can start work. I'll take someone with me.'

'Yes, do,' said Dick, 'but don't take Hank this time. He's an old hand. We've got to train more men in our escape technique. Choose someone else.'

I had a look at the office. It was small and oblong in shape, with a barred window in an alcove at the far end from the door. Gephard's desk and chair were in the alcove. The remainder of the office was lined with shelves on which reposed an assortment of articles. Many of them, such as hurricane lamps, electric torches, dry batteries, and nails and screws, would have been useful to us, but we touched nothing. The window exit was thoroughly dangerous. I saw by careful inspection and a few measurements that with only a little more patience we could rip up Gephard's floor, pierce a wall eighteen inches thick, and have entry into a storeroom outside and below us. From there, by simply unlocking a door, the escapers could walk out on to the sentry path surrounding the Castle. There was one snag. Did the storeroom have a cruciform or an ordinary lock?

This was checked by keeping a watch from a window for many days upon the area of the storeroom. The storeroom door was not visible, but a Jerry approaching it would be visible and, in dure course, a Jerry was seen going to the door holding in his hand an ordinary lever key! Van Doorninck would take a selection of keys and there should be no difficulty. The alternative, which would have taken much longer, would have been for me to construct a camouflage wall and examine the storeroom at leisure. This escape was to be a blitz job. The hole would be ready in a matter of three days. Experience was proving that long-term jobs involved much risk due to the time element alone. I often mused on the chances of the French tunnel which was advancing slowly day by day. . . .

The work would have to be done at night; Gephard's office was in use all day. The office was situated near the end of a ground-floor corridor, on the opposite side of which was the camp sick-ward. This ward was across the courtyard from our quarters, so that the undertaking involved entering the sick-quarters before the main doors were locked up for the night and hiding there, under the beds, until all was quiet – there was a sentry in the courtyard all day and night nowadays. The hospital beds were not high off the ground and were rather crammed together, giving ample concealment for superficial purposes.

I chose Lieutenant Derek Gill (Royal Norfolks) to come along and help me; he was the right type – imperturbable. We started operations as soon as Kenneth was snugly ensconced in his sick-bed, with serious stomach trouble. When the doors were locked and the patrols departed Kenneth manipulated the keys, opened the sick-ward door and then Gephard's door, locked us in for the night and returned to bed.

I removed the necessary floorboards underneath the window and also, incidentally, under the desk at which Gephard sat every day! I started work on the wall. The joints between the stones were old, as I suspected, and by the morning the two of us had reached the far side. I noticed there was plaster on the other side. This was what I'd expected; it was the wall-face of the storeroom. That was enough for the first night. Most of the large stones were removed in a sack, and in the under-floor rubble a passage was cleared at a forty-five-degree angle so that a person could ease himself down into the hole. Blankets were laid down so as to deaden the hollow sound, and the floor under Gephard's desk was then very carefully replaced. Nails were reinserted and covered with our patent dust-paste. All cracks were refilled with dirt. In the early hours, Kenneth, by arrangement, let us out and locked up. We retired to the sick-ward, the door of which also had to be locked, and rested comfortably until the German medical orderly arrived on his morning rounds, when we retired under the beds.

The next night Derek and I went to work again. This time the job was more difficult; the hole in the wall had to be enlarged enough to allow a large-sized man's body (Van Doorninck) to pass through. At the same time, the plaster on the further face was to be left intact. I knew the hole was high up in the storeroom wall, probably eight to ten feet from the floor-level. We finished the task successfully and in the morning retired as before.

The escape exit was now ready. Dick, Lulu, Bill, and myself worked out the plan together. It was based on the fact that German NCOs occasionally came to the storeroom with Polish POWs who were working in the town of Colditz. They brought and removed stores, baskets of old uniforms, underclothing in large wooden boxes, wooden clogs and a miscellaneous assortment of harmless soldier's equipment, as far as we could see. They came at irregular hours, mostly in the mornings, sometimes as early as 7 am and seldom more often than twice a week. These habits had been observed and noted over a period of a month. It was agreed that the escape party should be increased to a total of six. Two more officers were therefore selected. They were 'Stooge' Wardle, our submarine type, and Lieutenant Donkers, a Dutchman. It was arranged that Lulu should travel with the second Dutchman, and Bill Fowler with Van Doorninck.

Sentries were changed at 7 am, so the plan was made accordingly. Van Doorninck, who spoke German fluently, would become a senior German NCO and Donkers would be a German private. The other four would be Polish orderlies. They would issue from the storeroom shortly after 7 am. Van Doorninck would lock up after him. The four orderlies would carry two large wooden boxes between them, the German private would take up the rear. They would walk along the sentry path past two sentries, to a gate in the barbed wire, where Van Doorninck would order a third sentry to unlock and let them pass. The sentries – with luck – would assume that the 'fatigue' party had gone to the storeroom shortly before 7 am. Once through the barbed wire the party would proceed downhill along the roadway which went towards the park. They would, however, turn off after fifty yards and continue past a German barracks, and farther on they would reach the large gate in the wall surrounding the Castle grounds; the same over which Neave and Thompson had climbed in their escape. At this gate, Van Doorninck would have to use more keys. If he could not make them work, he had to use his wits. Indeed, if he managed to lead his company that far, he could probably ring up the Commandant and ask him to come and open the gate!

The plan necessitated the making of two large boxes in sections so that they could be passed through the hole into the storeroom, and yet of such construction that they could be very quickly assembled.

The day for the escape was fixed shortly after a normal visit to the storeroom, in order to lessen the chances of clashing with a real 'fatigue' party. We prayed that a clash might not occur, but the visits were not accurately predictable and we had to take this chance.

The evening before the 'off', after the last *Appell*, nine officers ambled at irregular intervals into the sick-ward corridor. There was other traffic also, and no suspicion was aroused. The sections of the wooden boxes had been transferred to the sick-ward at intervals during the day under coats. Eight officers hid under the beds, while Kenneth retired to his official one and saw to it that the hospital inmates remained quiet and behaved themselves. They were mostly French and were rather excited at the curious visitation. Kenneth had a way of his own of dealing with his brother officers of whatever nationality. He stood on his bed and addressed the whole sick-ward:

'I'll knock the block off any man here who makes a nuisance of himself or tries to create trouble. *Comprenez? Je casse la tête à n'importe qui fait du bruit ou qui commence à faire des bêtises.*'

Of course, Kenneth knew everybody there intimately and could take liberties with their susceptibilities. He continued:

'What is going on here is none of your business, so I don't want to see any curiosity; poking of heads under beds for instance; no whispering. When the patrol comes round everybody is to behave quite normally. I'll be sitting up looking around. If I see the slightest unnecessary movement, I'll report the matter to Gerneral Le Bleu as attempted sabotage.'

Kenneth's mock seriousness had an edge to it. Among those in the sick-ward were a few more or less permanent inhabitants – the neurotic ones. They were capable of almost any absurdity and a firm line was the only one to take in their case.

The sick-ward was duly locked and night descended upon the Castle. Quietly the nine arose, and as Kenneth unlocked one door after another with ease, we 'ghosted' through. Eight of us squeezed into the small office and Kenneth departed as he had come.

'Derek,' I whispered, 'we've got a long time in front of us before we start work. There's no point in beginning too early in case of misfires and alarms.'

'How long do you think it will take to break out the hole?' he questioned.

'About an hour, I should say, but we'll allow double that amount.'

'That means,' said Derek, 'we can start at, say, 4 am.'

'Better make it 3 am. We must allow much longer than we anticipate for pushing this crowd through, along with all the junk. There's also the hole to be made good. Have you brought the water and the plaster?'

'Yes. I've got six pint bottles and enough plaster to do a square yard.'

'Good. What time do you make it now?'

'Nine-forty-five,' Derek replied. We sat around on the floor to pass the vigil.

At midnight there was an alarm. We heard Germans unlocking doors and the voice of Priem in the corridor. He went into the sick-ward for five minutes, then came out and approached Gephard's office door. We heard every word he said as he talked with the night-duty NCO. The latter asked:

'Shall I open this door, Herr Hauptmann?'

'Yes, indeed, I wish to control all,' answered Priem.

'It is the office of *Oberstabsfeldwebel* Gephard, Herr Hauptmann.'

'Never mind. Open!' came the reply.

There was a loud noise of keys and then Priem's voice:

'Ah! of course Herr Gephard has many locks on his door. I had forgotten. Do not open, it is safe.'

The steps retreated and then died away as the outer door was relocked. We took several minutes to recover from this intrusion. Eventually Lulu Lawton, who was beside me, whispered into my ear, 'My God! You were right, and how!'

It was uncanny the way Priem scented us out and nearly caught us in spite of all our precautions.

In the dog-watch, I started work quietly by making a small hole through the plaster and then cutting and pulling inwards towards myself. Minute pieces fell outside and made noises which sounded like thunder to me, but which were not, in reality, loud. In due course the hole was enlarged for a hand to pass through, then the rest was removed with ease. I had a sheet with me to help the escapers down into the storeroom beyond. Van Doorninck went first. He landed on some shelves and, using them as a ladder, descended safely to the floor. A few minutes later he reported that the outside door of the storeroom had a simple lock and that he had tried it successfully. This was good news. The other five officers followed: then the sections of the two boxes; the various bundles of escape clothing; the Polish troops' uniforms; the German soldiers' uniforms, and lastly, the plaster and the water. We could have made good use of a conveyor belt!

Derek and I wished them all good luck and, wasting no time, we started to refill the hole in the wall as neatly as possible, while Van Doorninck on the other side applied a good thick coat of plaster. The wooden boxes would come in very handy for carrying away the empty water-bottles and surplus plaster as well as all the civilian outfits! Finally, as the last stone was ready to go into place, Van Doorninck and I checked watches and I whispered Goodbye and 'Good luck' and sealed the hole.

Derek and I then replaced blankets and floorboards carefully. By 6 am the operation was finished, just as we heard Kenneth whispering through the door: 'Is all well, are you ready?'

'Yes, open up.'

Kenneth manipulated the locks and we retired to the sick-ward.

From there we would not see the rest of the act. The escapers would leave at 7.10 am, while the sick-ward would not open up until 7.30 am. Morning *Appell* was at 8.30. This was where the fun would start!

At about 7.30 am we sallied forth unobtrusively. Dick was waiting for us and reported a perfect take-off!

Van Doorninck's uniform was that of a sergeant. The sentries had each in turn saluted smartly as the sergeant's 'fatigue' party wended its way along the path towards the barbed-wire gate. Arrived here, the sentry in charge quickly unlocked it, and the party passed through and was soon out of sight of our hidden watchers in the upper stories of the Castle.

As minutes passed and there were no alarms, we began to breathe more freely. By 8 am we could almost safely assume they were away.

The *Appell* was going to cause trouble. We had for the time being exhausted all our tricks for the covering of absentees from *Appell*. We had tried blank files, with our medium-sized R.A.F. officer running along, bent double, between the ranks and appearing in another place to be counted twice. We had tried having a whole row of officers counted twice by appropriate distraction of the NCOs checking off the numbers. We had tried bamboozling the Germans by increasing the returns of officers sick. The Dutch dummies were no more.

If the escape had been in the park, we had a greater variety of methods from which to choose. Park parades, in the first place, did not cover the whole prisoner contingent. We could add bodies to begin with; as we had done, for instance, by suspending our medium-sized officer, on occasion, around the waist of a burly Dutch officer, whose enormous cloak covered them both with ease! On another attempt, we had staged a fake escape to cover the real one, by having two officers cut the park wire and run for it – without a hope of escape, of course. The deception, in this case, was that the two officers acted as if a third was ahead of them among the trees. They shouted encouragement and warning to this imaginary one, whom the Jerries chased round in circles for the remainder of the day!

By now we had temporarily run out of inspiration. We might manage to conceal one absence, but six was an impossibility. So we did the obvious thing. We decided to lay in a reserve of spare officers for future escapes. We concealed four officers in various parts of the Castle. There would be ten missing from the *Appell*! With luck the four hidden in the Castle would become 'ghosts'. They would appear no more at *Appells* and would fill in blanks on future escapes. The idea was, by now, not unknown to the Germans, but we would try it.

The morning *Appell* mustered and, in due course, ten bodies were reported missing. There were hurried consultations, and messengers ran to and fro between the *Kommandantur*. We were counted again and again. The Germans thought we were playing a joke on them. Guardhouse reports showed there had been a quiet night, after Priem's visit, with no alarms.

The Germans kept us on parade, and sent a search-party through all the quarters. After an hour, they discovered two of our ghosts. This convinced them we were joking. They became threatening, and finally held an identification parade while the Castle search-party continued its work. Eventually the latter found two more ghosts. By 11 am, not having found any further bodies, they concluded that perhaps six had escaped after all. The identification parade continued, until they had established which officers were missing, in the midst of tremendous excitement as posses of Goons were despatched in all directions around the countryside.

We were satisfied at having increased the start of our six escapers by a further three hours. Later in the day we heard that the Jerries, after questioning all sentries, had suspected our fatigue party, and working backwards to the store room, had discovered my hole. There was much laughter, even among the Jerries, at the expense of Gephard, under whose desk the escape had been made! I leave it to the reader to imagine the disappointment and fury of Priem at our having eluded his grasp so narrowly during the night!

Before the evening was over, we had our disappointment too; Lulu Lawton and his companion were recaught. I was sorry for Lulu. He had put so much effort into the escape. It was largely his own idea and he had displayed cleverness and great pertinacity. These qualities, I thought, deserved better recognition than a month of 'solitary' in the cells.

Lulu told us how Van Doorninck led the fatigue party past the German barracks and onwards to the last gateway. As he approached it, a Goon from the barracks ran after the party and asked Van Doorninck if he wanted the gate opened. 'Naturally,' replied the latter!

The Goon hurried off and returned shortly with the key. He opened the gate and locked it again after them!

A day later, Stooge Wardle and Donkers were recaptured.

Bill Fowler and Van Doorninck carried on happily. They slipped through the net and reached Switzerland safely in six days. That was in September 1942. Two more over the border! We had no reason to be ashamed of our efforts!

CHAPTER 19

FORLORN HOPE

It was high time Bruce, our medium-sized officer, was given a chance of escape. He had done such good work unobtrusively! The opportunity arrived when the Germans decided we had too much personal property in our rooms. It was September, and they issued orders that all private kit not immediately required, as, for instance, summer clothing, was to be packed. The Jerries provided large boxes for the purpose. We were informed on the word of honour of the Camp Commandant that the cases would be stored in the German *Kommandantur* (the outer part of the Castle) and would be made available again in the spring.

The cases were duly packed, closed, and removed on a lorry. Several of them were Tate and Lyle sugar-boxes, about three feet square by three feet high, which had contained bulk consignments of Red Cross food, and in one of these travelled our medium-sized officer!

He had his civilian clothes and escape equipment with him, as well as a knife to cut the cords holding down the lid of his case, and about a forty-foot length of rope in the form of sheets. We knew the cases were to be stored in an attic at the top of a building which we could see from our windows.

Bruce reached Danzig, bicycling much of the way. Unfortunately, he was recaught on the docks, trying to stow away on a neutral ship, and returned in due course to Colditz where he was placed in solitary confinement.

I would like to have heard the full story but I never saw him again. I was doing two successive bouts of 'solitary' in the 'cooler' when he returned, and I did not even meet him during the daily exercise hour.

My 'solitary' was due to two abortive escape attempts. The first was a short tunnel, mostly vertical, built to connect up with the drains in the courtyard, which I have mentioned before. Rupert Barry and Colin McKenzie were my confederates. I had long noticed, on a photograph of the prisoners' courtyard taken before the war, a manhole cover near the entrance gateway. This manhole cover no longer existed and I was sure it had been covered over for a good reason. We were trying to find out why, by means of the tunnel, when the unannounced arrival of a batch of Russian prisoners proved our undoing. Our vertical shaft began in what was known as the 'delousing shed', a temporary structure in the courtyard built to house the portable ovens, which looked like boilers and into which clothing was put and baked in order to kill lice and other pests.

The sudden arrival of the Russians necessitated the use of these portable ovens, and Rupert and I were caught red-handed. McKenzie was lucky. He was doing earth-disposal duty and was not in the shed! The boilers were hardly used once in six months, and it was unfortunate the Russians arrived just during our working hours!

The incident, however, enabled us to meet the Russian soldiers, who were to be housed in the town where normally we should never see them. They were a sight of which the Germans might well have been ashamed. Living skeletons, they dragged their fleshless feet along the ground in a decrepit slouch. These scarecrows were the survivors of a batch ten times their number which had started from the front. They were treated like animals, given no food and put out into the fields to find fodder amidst the grass and roots. Their trek into Germany took weeks.

'Luckily,' said one of them, 'it was summer-time. In the winter,' he added, 'nobody bothered even to move us to the hinterland from the front. We died where we were captured.'

How many times, in my life as a prisoner, did I murmur a prayer of thanksgiving for that blessed document, 'the Geneva Convention', and for its authors! But for its humane principles, I saw myself standing in the place of these wretched creatures. Needless to say, as between Germany and Russia, there were no recognized principles for the treatment of prisoners-of-war. Neither of them had signed the Convention.

My second bout of 'solitary' was due to the fact that I tried to escape from my prison cell. It happened to be in the town jail because, as usual, all the camp cells were full, and the overflow nowadays went to the jail.

By placing my cell table on the bed, I could reach the ceiling of the cell. I had a small saw, which was normally hidden in my guitar. Breaking through the plaster one evening, I started work on the wood. I had to work noiselessly, for the guards lived next door. In spite of every effort, I was not finished by morning and, of course, the jailer saw my handiwork when he came with my bread and ersatz coffee.

I was evidently doomed to spend another winter in Colditz.

September was nearly over. Dick Howe came up to me one day.

'I have another job for you, Pat,' he said. 'Ronnie Littledale and Billie Stephens have teamed up and are clamouring to leave. Their idea isn't in the least original, but that doesn't stop their clamouring,' he added.

He then described to me roughly what they intended to do.

'That old chestnut,' I commented, 'has grown a long beard by now. It has about as much chance of success as the famous camel that tried to go through the eye of a needle! What's the idea, Dick?' I asked. 'I thought we were going to keep that type of lunacy till the very end, and that we wouldn't even consider it until every hole in the camp was completely bunged and we were desperate?'

'We're not desperate, Pat. I hope we never shall be. Still, I don't mind letting them have a shot. I want you to go with them,' he added as an aside, 'just to see they don't get into any trouble!'

'Well! I seem to be doomed. I'll do it for the fun of the thing, but it's a mad idea and it will mean another month in the 'cooler' for me without a shadow of a doubt,' I concluded.

I knew the scheme well. A child could have thought of it. It involved making a sortie from one of the windows of the kitchen over the low roofs of various store buildings in the adjoining German *Kommandantur* courtyard. Then, descending to the ground, one had to cross over the path of a sentry's beat, when his back was turned, and then crawl across the dimly lit area in front of the courtyard, which was visible from our windows. That was as far as the plan went! We were still in the midst of the enemy and how we were supposed to extricate ourselves was a mystery to me.

Dick, Ronnie, Billie Stephens, and myself discussed the plan.

I suggested an addition to the team:

'We may as well be hung for a sheep as a lamb, so why not add a fourth to our group of three! Then, when we get out, *if* we get out, we can travel in independent groups of two each.'

'All right,' said Dick, 'who do you suggest?'

'Well, if Ronnie and Billie are going to travel together, it's rather up to me, I suppose, to choose someone. I think Hank Wardle is the man. It's time he had a turn.'

'Good. I don't think there will be any objections, but I'll just confirm this,' rejoined Dick. 'He's the right man as far as I'm concerned. He has all the qualifications; he's high on the roster and has helped other escapes; and he's RAF.'

Ronnie put in: 'This attempt will be an "All Services" venture then, Billie being a naval type. A good idea, I think!'

'You'll have to travel by different routes, of course,' said Dick. 'What do you suggest?'

'Well, if it's all the same to Ronnie and Billie,' I answered, 'I've studied the route from Penig via Zwickau to Plauen, Regensburg and Munich, and thence to Ulm and Tuttlingen. I'd like to stick to it. How about it, Ronnie? You could go from Leisnig to Dobeln, then via Chemnitz to Nürnberg and Stuttgart.'

'That suits us,' said Ronnie. 'We prefer Leisnig, as it's only a few kilometres away and we reckon to catch a train before the morning *Appell*.'

'All right,' said Dick, 'you're agreed then. We'll go into questions of detail, dress, food, and so on, nearer to the date for the "off". Let me know if you are stuck for anything.'

Lieutenant-Commander William Stephens, RNVR (Billie), had been captured during the St Nazaire raid, when the dock gates were blown up in an effort to imprison a large number of German U-boats. He had tried to escape twice, and was a new arrival at Colditz. In fact, when he arrived he was promptly put into 'solitary' for several weeks to complete his sentences before he was let loose into the camp. His school was Shrewsbury and he came from Northern Ireland. He was handsome, fair-haired, with piercing blue eyes and Nelsonian nose. He walked as if he were permanently on the deck of a ship. He was a daredevil, and his main idea appeared to be to force his way into the German area of the camp and then hack his way out with a metaphorical cutlass.

The one hope I could see was of forcing an entry into the tall block of buildings, at the top of which our medium-sized officer had been deposited in his Tate and Lyle sugar-box. As he had been able to make an exit from there, maybe we could also. It was important to have Bruce's comments, and I managed to pass a message to him in some food and, eventually, had an answer. Once inside his building, it was possible to descend from unbarred windows on the far side into the moat of the Castle. The top floors were unoccupied, but care was necessary to avoid noise as Germans occupied floors below. There was a large heavy door into the building which was visible from our quarters and which gave on to an unused staircase leading to the top.

There were two principal snags: the door mentioned above was visible from almost everywhere and in full view of the sentry in the German courtyard; secondly, the door was locked. We could assume the lock was not cruciform in type, but beyond this we knew nothing. At night, when the floodlights were blazing, this door was in shadow. I might be able to work at the lock, but the risk was tremendous because the door was beside the main path, leading from the outer Castle gateway to the entrance of the *Kommandantur* – all pedestrians passed within a yard of it. Besides, would the shadow be sufficient to hide a man from the eyes of the sentry? Lastly, the door was twenty yards from the pit of which I have spoken – and the nearest place of concealment – so that a person going to and from the door had to flit twenty yards each way in a penumbra where movement would be visible.

When Hank's nomination had been agreed, I broached the subject to him:

'Ronnie and Billie want you and me to join them on about the most absurd escape attempt I know,' I opened by way of invitation.

'One thing seems to be as good or as bad as another in this camp nowadays,' was Hank's reply.

'That means you're not fussy, I take it?'

Hank's answer was a typical shrug of the shoulders and 'I couldn't care less, I've got nothing to do till the end of the war, so it's all the same to me!'

I described the plan to him in fair detail, and when I had finished he said:

'I'll try it with you. I agree there's no hope of success, but we've got to carry on trying just the same.'

The whole scheme assumed that we could reach the pit safely and hide inside it. For all we knew it might have been deep. Our hope that it was shallow was based on the fact that the pit was not balustraded and a man might easily have fallen into it. To reach the pit would be a prolonged nightmare.

The camp kitchen was in use all day. Towards evening it was locked up. It was in full view of the sentry in the prisoners' courtyard. A pane of glass in one of the metal-framed windows was half-broken. I had preparatory work to do in the kitchen and this window was my only means of entry. I employed a stooge to help me. After the evening *Appell* on the first day of operations, he sat on a doorstep near the kitchen, watching the sentry, while I remained out of sight behind the protruding wall of the delousing shed, about five yards from the window. The sentry's beat varied between eight and twelve seconds. I had to be inside before he turned round.

My stooge gave me the OK signal. I ran and hopped on to the sill. Reaching through the broken pane of glass on tiptoe, I could just grasp the lever which opened the window. I pulled it upwards gently, withdrew my arm carefully so as not to break what was left of the glass pane, opened the window and crept through. If the sentry stopped short or turned in the middle of his beat, I was caught. I jumped down on to the kitchen floor and silently closed the window. I was safely inside, with a second to spare.

Leaving the kitchen was a little easier, as one faced the sentry and could see him through cracks in the white paint of the lower glass panes of the window.

I repeated this performance five evenings running along with one assistant. We usually entered after the evening *Appell*, at about 6 pm, and returned again before locking-up time, at 9 pm.

During these periods of three hours, we worked hard. The windows on the opposite side of the kitchen opened on to the flat roofs of a jumble of outhouses in the German courtyard: all the roofs were about twelve feet above the ground. The kitchen windows on this side, as well as the whole wall of the building, were in bright floodlight from dusk onwards.

I opened one of the windows by removing a number of wire clips which were supposed to seal it, and examined the bars beyond. I saw that, by removing one rivet, I could bend a bar inwards, providing enough room for a body to pass. The hole through the bars opened on to the flat roof.

The rivet was the next problem. I could saw off the head, but it was old and rusty and would obviously require great force to withdraw it. Yet the method would involve much less sawing. 'Silence was golden.' A sentry plied his beat just beyond the outbuildings, about fifteen yards away. Luckily the window was not in his line of vision, unless he extended his beat to nearly double its normal length. This he did from time to time. Of course, the window and the flat roof were in full view of all the windows of the *Kommandantur* above the ground floor!

The less sawing I did, the better. Sawing the head off the rivet was the solution, if only I could withdraw it afterwards.

My assistant was ERA 'Wally' Hammond, RN. He was one of the naval types who had been painted blue! He and his friend ERA 'Tubby' Lister arrived by mistake at Colditz, this being an officers' camp, while they were Chief Petty Officers. They made good use of their sojourn.

Soon afterwards, when they were removed to their rightful prison, they escaped, and with the advantage of their Colditz 'education' behind them, they reached Switzerland with comparative ease!

These two submarine men deserve to be placed on pedestals in a conspicuous place somewhere in England. They were the quintessence of everything for which our island stands. If a hundred Englishmen of every rank and county were put together in a pot and boiled down, the remaining crust would be Wally Hammond and Tubby Lister. Their sense of humour was unbeatable. It rose to meet dangers, knocking them on the head with a facetiousness capable of dispersing the most formidable army of adversities.

During their escape, for instance, for lack of a better language they spoke pidgin-English with the Germans throughout, posing as Flemish collaborators. They stayed at middle-class German hotels, and before leaving in the mornings, usually filled any army top-boots which happened to be outside the doors of neighbouring rooms with water, as a mark of their respect for the *Oberkommando der Wehrmacht* – the German High Command! ... Their full story belongs to another book[1]; their journey through Germany was a pantomime.

To return to the story of the rivet which required attention; the head was sawn through during the fourth evening shift. Next, we needed a high-powered silent-working punch which would force the rivet out of its socket.

Wally Hammond made one in the space of a few hours out of a bar used for closing the grate door of a German heating stove. The bar was about a foot long. At each end he made clamps which could be fixed to the iron bar outside the kitchen window. In the centre there was, already, a half-inch-

[1] *The Latter Days at Colditz*, by P. R. Reid (see also page 182).

diameter screw. The end of this was filed to fit the quarter-inch-diameter rivet-hole. The head of the screw was a knurled wheel of two inches diameter. To the latter, Hammond arranged to clamp a lever one foot long.

On the fifth evening of work I applied Hammond's punch, turned the lever, and the rivet, which had been corroded in its position for probably twenty years, slid smoothly and silently out of its hole and the job was done!

I camouflaged the joint with a clay rivet, sealed the window as usual, and, redusting everything carefully, we left the kitchen as we had come.

The escape was on and we wasted no time. Our two groups would travel by different routes to the frontier crossing-point on the Swiss border – a Colditz secret! Although I had never been there, I knew the area in my mind's eye like the back of my hand. Every Colditz escaper's first and last duty was to learn this crossing by heart; for I had forbidden frontier-crossing maps to be carried many months ago. We had the master map in the camp and it was studied by all.

We each had our identity papers, our general maps, money, and compass. We kept them usually in small tubes. I had once received a present from friends in England which actually arrived – two boxes of twenty-five Upmann Havana cigars. The cigars were in light metal containers about five inches long. These cases were much in demand. All the above documents, money, and a compass fitted into the metal tube, which was easily carried and could be easily concealed, even by sleight of hand if necessary.

I had printed my own identity papers. German Gothic script is not easy to copy, but it was possible with practice. We had a primitive, yet highly successful, system of duplicating, and reproduced typewritten orders and letters as desired. A multitude of lino-cut stamps provided all the officialdom necessary, and photographs were managed in various ways. The brown-coloured *Ausweis* was of thick white paper dyed the correct tint with a patent mixture of our own manufacture.

Our clothes had long since been prepared. I would wear one of my mass-production cloth caps, converted RAF trousers, a fawn-coloured windjacket I had concealed for a year, and finally an overcoat (necessary at this time of year, early October) which I succeeded in buying from a French officer who had obtained it from a French orderly who, in turn, had access to the village.

It was a dark-blue civilian overcoat with black velvet lapels and it buttoned, double-breasted, high up on the chest! I imagine it was a German fashion of about 1912. I wore black shoes.

It was essential to remove every single trace of the origin of anything we wore or carried, such as lettering inside shoes, name tags and 'Made in

England' marks. We were to live our false identities, and were prepared to challenge the Germans to prove the contrary, if we were held for questioning. Thus Hank and I became Flemish workmen collaborating with the Germans. As *flamands* we could pass off our bad German and our bad French – a useful nationality! Not being a common one, the Germans would take a long time to find someone who spoke Flemish and could prove we were not *flamands*.

We were concrete or engineering contractors' workmen. My German wallet contained my whole story. I was permitted to travel to Rottweil (some thirty miles from the Swiss border), in reply to newspaper advertisements – I had the cuttings – requiring contractors' men for construction work. I also had a special and very necessary permit to travel close to the frontier. Part of my story was that my fiancée worked at Besançon as a telephone operator for the Germans. She was a Walloon – or French-speaking Belgian girl. I kept a fictitious letter from her (prepared for me by a Frenchman) in my wallet asking me to spend my few days' leave with her in Besançon before going to work in Rottweil. By a curious coincidence the railway line going to Besançon from my direction passed within fifteen miles of the Swiss frontier!

My trump card was a real photo, which I had, of a girl I met in France. One day, while looking through a German weekly newspaper, I had come across a German propaganda photograph showing German and foreign girls working together for the Germans in a post office and telephone exchange. One of the girls in the picture was the double of the girl whose photo I carried. I immediately cut out the press photo and kept it as a treasured possession. It would prove to any German where my imaginary fiancée's loyalties lay. My private snapshot was conclusive evidence and I was prepared to battle with any German who dared to doubt my identity.

The other three of our team had different case-histories, more or less as conclusive as mine.

Towards the end of our final preparations I held a last consultation and, among many items, we discussed food.

'You all realize that we can't take anything with us by way of food except normal German rations,' I pointed out.

'Yes, I agree,' said Billie, 'but all the same I'm taking enough corned beef and tinned cheese to make sure of one good meal before we board the train.'

'Our sugar is all right too,' added Ronnie. 'We can carry that with us indefinitely. It looks the same as the German and would pass.'

'Now I've got a sticky proposition to make,' I began, changing the subject. 'There are a few of those small ersatz leather suitcases lying about – you know, the ones that came with the last batch of parcels. They had army clothing in them. I propose we each carry one.'

'H'm! That's a tall order!' retorted Billie. 'It's going to be hard enough to get out of the camp, climbing over roofs and walls and down ropes, without being pestered with suitcases into the bargain.'

'I agree, but remember, Billie, when we *do* get out of the camp we are a long way from Switzerland and freedom,' I argued; 'it's no use planning only for the beginning and leaving the rest to look after itself. The rest in this case is just as important, and a little extra risk to begin with – in conditions over which we have some control – may be amply repaid later on, in circumstances over which we have no control at all.'

'What does all that imply?' queried Billie.

'It means,' I said, 'that I don't think it's such a tall order. Once outside the camp, a suitcase becomes the hall-mark of respectability and honesty. How many people travel long journeys on main-line expresses in wartime with nothing at all in their hands? Only fugitives and railway officials. And the Germans know this well. They know that to look out for an escaped prisoner means to look out for a man travelling light, with no luggage – without a suitcase.'

'I see your point, Pat,' agreed Billie.

'At railway-station controls or in a round-up, a suitcase will be invaluable,' I continued. 'You can wave it about and make it prominent and the betting is it'll help a lot. Moreover, it will be useful for carrying articles of respectability: pyjamas – without tags and hall-marks – razors, bootbrushes, and German boot polish, German soap, and, of course, your German food. Otherwise your pockets are going to be bulgy, untidy, and suspicious-looking. I know it's going to be hell lugging them with us out of the camp, but I think it will be worth the effort in the end.'

They all agreed and so it was fixed. We procured four of the small fibreboard suitcases and packed away our escape-travelling kit.

I could hardly believe we were going to do the whole four-hundred-mile journey by train. I thought of our naïve escape from Laufen and realized how much experience counted in escaping.

CHAPTER 20

THE WALLS ARE BREACHED

It was October 14th, 1942. As evening approached, the four of us made final preparations. I said '*Au revoir* till tomorrow' to Van den Heuvel, and to Rupert, Harry, Peter Allan, and Kenneth and Dick. Rupert was to be our kitchen-window stooge. We donned our civilian clothing, and covered this with army trousers and greatcoats. Civilian overcoats were made into neat bundles.

In parenthesis, I should explain why we had to wear the military clothes over everything. At any time a wandering Goon might appear as we waited our moment to enter the kitchen, and there might even be delays. Further, we had to think of 'informers' – among the foreign orderlies, for example, who were always wandering about. If orderlies saw one of us leap through the kitchen window, it was just too bad – we might be after food – but it would be far worse if they saw a number of civilian-clothed officers in a staircase lobby – the orderlies' staircase as it happened – waiting, apparently, for their taxi to arrive!

Our suitcases were surrounded with blankets to muffle sound, and we carried enough sheets and blankets to make a fifty-foot descent, if necessary. Later we would wear balaclava helmets and gloves; no white skin was to be visible. Darkness and the shadows were to be our friends, we could not afford to offend them. Only our eyes and noses would be exposed. All light-coloured garments were excluded. We carried thick socks to put over our shoes. This is the most silent method of movement I know, barring removal of one's shoes – which we were to do for the crossing of the sentry's path.

Squadron-Leader MacColm was to accompany us into the kitchen in order to bend the window bar back into place and seal up the window after we had gone. He would have to conceal the military clothing we left behind in the kitchen and make his exit the next morning after the kitchen was unlocked. He could hide in one of the enormous cauldrons so long as he did not oversleep and have himself served up with the soup next day.

Immediately after the evening *Appell* we were ready and started on the first leg of our long journey. It was 6.30 pm.

I was used to the drill of the entry window by now. At the nodded signal from Rupert, I acted automatically; a run, a leap to the sill, one arm through the cracked pane of glass, up with the window lever, withdraw arm carefully, open window – without noise – jump through, and close again softly. I was through. Only two had done it before at any one session. The question was, would five succeed? One after another they came. At least, they had not the window-lever latch to bother about.

The sentry was behaving himself. At regular intervals, as he turned his back, the signal was given. I could not see Rupert – but he was timing perfectly. I could see the sentry from behind the window throughout his beat.

Each time, as the sentry turned away, I heard a gentle scurry. I automatically opened the window, in jumped a body, and I closed the window again, breathing a heavy sigh. The drill was becoming automatic. It was taking as little as five seconds. Then, suddenly, just as the last of the five was due, I sensed – I do not know how – an uncertainty, a hesitation in the manner of the sentry as he turned away. I knew that he would behave oddly during this beat. My heart was in my mouth, for I expected to hear the scurry and anticipated a clash. But there was no scurry, and in the next instant the sentry stopped dead and turned around! It was nothing less than intuition on Rupert's part that saved us.

On the next turn of the sentry's beat, I heard the scurry, opened and closed again. At last all five of us were safe.

We removed our military clothing and handed it to MacColm.

I set about the window overlooking the German courtyard, and as darkness fell and the floodlights went on, I heaved on the bar until it was bent horizontal, and immediately attached to the unbent portion a long strip of black-painted cardboard resembling the bar. This hung downwards in the correct position and camouflaged the opening.

'All set!' I whispered to the others. 'I'm going out now. Hank! Wait until I'm hidden by the shadows of the large ventilator out there. Then join me as quickly as you can. Billie and Ronnie, remember not to follow until we have crossed the sentry's path safely.'

I squirmed through the hole in the bars on to the flat roof beyond. The roof joined the kitchen wall just below our window-sill. I crept quietly forward in a blaze of light. The eyes of a hundred windows glared down upon me.

The impression was appalling. 'Does nobody ever look out of a window at night?' I kept asking myself.

Happily there was shelter from the glare about halfway across the roof. The high square ventilator provided a deep shadow behind which I crawled. Hank soon followed. The sentry plied his beat not fifteen yards away.

For several days we had arranged music practices in the evenings in the senior officers' quarters (the theatre block). The music was to be used for signalling, and we had to accustom the sentry in front of us to a certain amount of noise. While Major Anderson (Andy) played the oboe, Colonel George Young played the concertina, and Douglas Bader, keeping watch from a window, acted as conductor. Their room was on the third floor, overlooking the German courtyard. Bader could see our sentry for the whole length of his beat. He was to start the practice at 7.30 pm, when the traffic in the courtyard had died down. From 8 pm onwards he was to keep rigid control on the players so that they only stopped their music when the sentry was in a suitable position for us to cross his path. It was not imperative that they stopped playing every time the sentry turned his back, but when they stopped playing that meant we could move. We arranged this signalling system because, once on the ground, we would have little concealment, and what little there was, provided by an angle in the wall of the outbuildings, prevented us from seeing the sentry.

At 8 pm Hank and I crawled once more into the limelight and over the remainder of the roof, dropping to the ground over a loose, noisy gutter which gave me the jitters. In the dark angle of the wall, with our shoes around our necks and our suitcases under our arms, we waited for the music to stop. The players had been playing light jaunty airs – and then ran the gauntlet of our popular-song books. At 8 pm they changed to classical music; it gave them more excuse for stopping. Bader had seen us drop from the roof and would see us cross the sentry's path. The players were in the middle of Haydn's oboe concerto when they stopped.

'I shall make this a trial run,' I thought.

I advanced quickly five yards to the end of the wall concealing us, and regarded the sentry. He was fidgety and looked up at Bader's window twice during the five seconds' view I had of his back. Before me was the roadway, a cobbled surface seven yards wide. Beyond was the end of a shed and some friendly concealing shrubbery. As the sentry turned, the music started again. Our players had chosen a piece the Germans love. I only hoped the sentry would not be exasperated by their repeated interruptions. The next time they stopped we would go.

The music ceased abruptly and I ran – but it started again just as I reached the corner. I stopped dead and retired hurriedly. This happened twice. Then I heard German voices throughout the music. It was the duty officer on his rounds. He was questioning the sentry. He was suspicious. I heard gruff orders given.

Five minutes later I was caught napping – the music stopped while I was ruminating on the cause of the duty officer's interrogation and I was not on my toes. A late dash was worse than none. I stood still and waited. I waited a long time and the music did not begin again. A quarter of an hour passed and there was still no music. Obviously something had gone wrong upstairs. I decided therefore to wait an hour in order to let suspicions die down. We had the whole night before us, and I was not going to spoil the ship for a ha'p'orth o' tar.

All this time Hank was beside me – not a word passed his lips – not a murmur or comment to distract us from the job on hand.

In the angle of the wall where we hid, there was a door. We tried the handle and found it was open, so we entered in pitch-darkness and, passing through a second door, we took temporary refuge in a room which had a small window and contained, as far as we could see, only rubbish – wastepaper, empty bottles, and empty food-tins. Outside, in the angle of the wall, any Goon with extra-sharp eyesight, passing along the roadway, would spot us. The sentry himself was also liable to extend his beat without warning and take a look around the corner of the wall where we had been hiding. In the rubbish room we were much safer.

We had been in there five minutes when, suddenly, there was a rustling of paper, a crash of falling tins, and a jangling of overturned bottles – a noise fit to waken the dead. We froze with horror. A cat leaped out from among the refuse and tore out of the room as if the devil was after it.

'That's finished everything,' I exclaimed. 'The Jerries will be here in a moment to investigate.'

'The darn thing was after a mouse, I think,' said Hank. 'Let's make the best of things, anyway. They may only flash a torch round casually and we may get away with it if we try to look like a couple of sacks in the corner.'

'Quick, then,' I rejoined. 'Grab those piles of newspapers and let's spread them out a little over our heads. It's our only hope.'

We did so and waited, with our hearts thumping. Five minutes passed, and then ten, and still nobody came. We began to breathe again.

Soon our hour's vigil was over. It was 9.45 pm and I resolved to carry on. All was silent in the courtyard. I could now hear the sentry's footsteps clearly – approaching – and then receding. Choosing our moment, we advanced to the end of the wall as he turned on his beat. I peeped around the corner. He was ten yards off and marching away from us. The courtyard was empty. I tiptoed quickly across the roadway with Hank at my heels. Reaching the wall of the shed on the other side, we had just time to crouch behind the shrubbery before he turned. He had heard nothing. On his next receding beat we crept behind the shed, and hid in a small shrubbery, which bordered the main steps and veranda in front of the entrance to the *Kommandantur*.

The first leg of our escape was behind us. I dropped my suitcase and reconnoitred the next stage of our journey, which was to the 'pit'. Watching the sentry, I crept quickly along the narrow grass verge at the edge of the path leading away from the main steps. On one side was the path and on the other side was a long flower-bed; beyond that the balustrade of the *Kommandantur* veranda. I was in light shadow and had to crouch as I moved. Reaching the pit, about twenty-five yards away, before the sentry turned, I looked over the edge. There was a wooden trestle with steps. The pit was not deep. I dropped into it. A brick tunnel from the pit ran underneath the veranda and gave perfect concealment. That was enough. As I emerged again, I distinctly heard noises from the direction of the roofs over which we had climbed. Ronnie and Billie, who had witnessed our crossing of the roadway, were following. The sentry apparently heard nothing.

I began to creep back to the shrubbery where Hank was waiting. I was nearly halfway when, without warning, heavy footsteps sounded; a Goon was approaching quickly from the direction of the main Castle gateway and around the corner of the Castle building into sight. In a flash I was flat on my face on the grass verge, and lay rigid, just as he turned the corner and headed up the path straight towards me. He could not fail to see me. I waited for the end. He approached nearer and nearer with noisy footsteps crunching on the gravel. He was level with me. It was all over. I waited for his ejaculation at my discovery – for his warning shout to the sentry – for the familiar '*Hände hoch!*' – and the feel of his pistol in my back between the shoulder-blades.

The crunching footsteps continued past me and retreated. He mounted the steps and entered the *Kommandantur*.

After a moment's pause to recover, I crept the remainder of the distance to the shrubbery and, as I did so, Ronnie and Billie appeared from the other direction.

Before long we were all safe in the pit without further alarms, the second lap completed! We had time to relax for a moment.

I asked Billie: 'How did you get on crossing the sentry's beat?'

'We saw you two cross over and it looked as easy as pie. That gave us confidence. We made one trial, and then crossed the second time. Something went wrong with the music, didn't it?'

'Yes, that's why we held up proceedings so long,' I answered. 'We had a lucky break when they stopped for the last time. I thought it was the signal to move, but I was too late off the mark, thank God! I'd probably have run into the sentry's arms!'

'What do you think happened?' asked Ronnie.

'I heard the duty officer asking questions,' I explained. 'I think they suspected the music practice was phoney. They probably went upstairs and stopped it.'

Changing the subject, I said: 'I heard you coming over the roof. I was sure the sentry could have heard.'

'We made a noise at one point, I remember,' said Ronnie, 'but it wasn't anything to speak of. It's amazing what you can hear if your ears are expecting certain sounds. The sentry was probably thinking of his girl friend at that moment.'

'If it wasn't for girl friends,' I chimed in, 'we probably wouldn't be on this mad jaunt anyway, so it cuts both ways,' and I nudged Hank.

'It's time I got to work,' I added grimly.

My next job was to try to open the door of the building which I have described as the one from which our medium-sized officer escaped. The door was fifteen yards away; it was in deep shadow, though the area between the door and the pit was only in semi-darkness. Again watching the sentry, I crept carefully to the door, and then started work with a set of *passe-partout* keys I had brought with me. I had one unnerving interruption, when I heard Priem's voice in the distance returning from the town. I had just sufficient time to creep back to the pit and hide, before he came around the corner.

We laughed inwardly as he passed by us along the path talking loudly to another officer. I could not help thinking of the occasion when he stood outside Gephard's office and did not have the door unlocked!

Poor old Priem! He was not a bad type on the whole. He had a sense of humour which made him almost human.

It was 11 pm when Priem passed by. I worked for an hour on the door without success and finally gave up. We were checked, and would have to find another exit.

We felt our way along the tunnel leading from the pit under the veranda, and after eight yards came to a large cellar with a low arched ceiling supported on pillars. It had something to do with sewage, for Hank, at one point, stepped off solid ground and nearly fell into what might have been deep water! He must have disturbed a scum on top of the liquid because a dreadful stench arose. When I was well away from the entrance, I struck a match. There was a solitary wheelbarrow for furniture, and at the far end of the cavern-like cellar, a chimney flue. I had previously noticed a faint glimmer of light from this direction. Examining the flue, I found it was an air-vent which led vertically upwards from the ceiling of the cavern for about four feet, and then curved outwards towards the fresh air. Hank pushed me up the flue. In plan it was about nine inches by three feet. I managed to wriggle myself high enough to see around the curve. The flue ended at the vertical face of a wall two feet away from me as a barred opening shaped like a letter-box slot. The opening was at the level of the ground outside, and was situated on the far side of the building – the moat side for which we were heading, but it was a practical impossibility to negotiate this flue. There were bars, and in any case only a pigmy could have wriggled round the curve.

We held a conference.

'We seem to have struck a dead end,' I started; 'this place is a cul-de-sac and I can't manage the door either. I'm terribly sorry, but there we are!'

'Can anyone think of another way out?' asked Ronnie.

'The main gateway, I think, is out of the question,' I went on. 'Since Neave's escape nearly a year ago, they lock the inner gate this side of the bridge over the moat. That means we can't reach the side gate leading down into the moat.'

'Our only hope is through the *Kommandantur*,' suggested Billie. 'We can try it either now, and hope to get through unseen – or else try it early in the morning when there's a little traffic about and some doors may be unlocked.'

'Do you really think we'll ever pass scrutiny at that hour?' questioned Ronnie. 'If we must take that route, I think it's better to try it at about 3 am when the whole camp is dead asleep.'

I was thinking how impossibly foolhardy was the idea of going through the *Kommandantur*. I remembered that other attempt – years ago now it seemed – when we had pumped men through the hole in the lavatory into the *Kommandantur*. I had considered then that the idea was mad. I thought aloud:

'There are only three known entrances to the *Kommandantur*: the main front door, the French windows behind, which open on to the grass patch right in front of a sentry, and the little door under the archway leading to the park. The archway gate is locked and the door is the wrong side of it.'

In desperation, I said: 'I'm going to have another look at the flue.'

This time I removed some of my clothing and found I could slide more easily up the shaft. I examined the bars closely and found one was loose in its mortar socket. As I did so, I heard footsteps outside the opening and a Goon patrol approached. The Goon had an Alsatian with him. A heavy pair of boots trampled past me. I could have touched them with my hand. The dog pattered behind and did not see me. I imagine the smell issuing from the flue obliterated my scent.

I succeeded in loosening one end of the bar and bent it nearly double. Slipping down into the cellar again, I whispered to the others: 'There's a vague chance we may be able to squeeze through the flue. Anyway, it's worth trying. We shall have to strip completely naked.'

'Hank and Billie will never make it,' said Ronnie. 'It's impossible; they're too big. You and I might manage it with help at both ends – with someone pushing below and someone else pulling from above.'

'I think I can make it,' I rejoined, 'if someone stands on the wheelbarrow and helps to push me through. Once I'm out, I can do the pulling. Hank had better come next. If he can make it, we all can.'

Hank was over six feet tall and Billie nearly six feet. Ronnie and I were smaller, and Ronnie was very thin.

'Neither Hank nor I,' intervened Billie, 'will ever squeeze around the curve on our tummies. Our knees are not double-jointed and our legs will stick. We'll have to come out on our backs.'

'Agreed,' I said. 'Then I go first, Hank next, then Billie and Ronnie last. Ronnie, you'll have no one to push you, but if two of us grab your arms and pull, we should manage it. Be careful undressing. Don't leave anything behind – we want to leave no traces. Hand your clothes to me in neat bundles, and your suitcases. I'll dispose of them temporarily outside.'

After a tremendous struggle, I succeeded in squeezing through the chimney and sallied forth naked on to the path outside. Bending down into the flue again, I could just reach Hank's hand as he passed me up my clothes and my suitcase, and then his own. I hid the kit in some bushes near the path and put on enough dark clothing to make me inconspicuous. Hank was stripped and struggling in the hole with his back towards me. I managed to grab one arm and heaved, while he was pushed from below. Inch by inch he advanced and at the end of twenty minutes, with a last wrench, I pulled him clear. He was bruised all over and streaming with perspiration. During all that time we were at the mercy of any passer-by. What a spectacle it must have been – a naked man being squeezed through a hole in the wall like toothpaste out of a tube! To the imaginative-minded in the eerie darkness, it must have looked as if the massive walls of the Castle were slowly descending upon the man's body while his comrade was engaged in a desperate tug-of-war to save his life!

Hank retired to the bushes to recover and dress himself.

Next came Billie's clothes and suitcase, and then Billie himself. I extracted him in about fifteen minutes. Then Ronnie's kit arrived. I gave him a sheet on which to pull in order to begin his climb. After that, two of us set about him, and he was out in about ten minutes. We all collapsed in the bushes for a breather. It was about 3.30 am and we had completed the third leg of our marathon.

'What do you think of our chances now?' I asked Billie.

'I'm beyond thinking of chances,' was the reply, 'but I know I shall never forget this night as long as I live.'

'I hope you've got all your kit,' I said, smiling at him in the darkness. 'I should hate to have to push you back down the shaft to fetch it!'

'I'd give anything for a smoke,' sighed Billie.

'I see no reason why you shouldn't smoke as we walk past the barracks if you feel like it. What cigarettes have you got?'

'Gold Flake, I think.'

'Exactly! You'd better start chain-smoking, because you'll have to throw the rest away before you reach Leisnig. Had you thought of that?'

'But I've got fifty!'

'Too bad,' I replied. 'With luck you've got about three hours; that's seventeen cigarettes an hour. Can you do it?'

'I'll try,' said Billie ruefully.

A German was snoring loudly in a room with the window open, a few yards away. The flue through which we had just climbed gave on to a narrow path running along the top of the moat immediately under the main Castle walls. The bushes we hid in were on the very edge of the moat. The moat wall was luckily stepped into three successive descents. The drops were about eighteen feet and the steps were about two yards wide, with odd shrubs and grass growing on them. A couple of sheets were made ready. After half an hour's rest, and fully clothed once more, we dropped down one by one. I went last and fell into the arms of those below me.

On the way down, Billie suddenly developed a tickle in his throat and started a cough which disturbed the dogs. They began barking in their kennels, which we saw for the first time, uncomfortably near the route we were to take. Billie in desperation ate a quantity of grass and earth, which seemed to stop the irritation in his throat. By the time we reached the bottom of the moat it was 4.30 am. The fourth leg was completed.

We tidied our clothes and adjusted the socks over our shoes. In a few moments we would have to pass underneath a lamp at the corner of the road leading to the German barracks. This was the road leading to the double gates in the outer wall around the Castle grounds. It was the road taken by Neave and by Van Doorninck.

The lamp was situated in full view of a sentry – luckily, some forty-five yards away – who would be able to contemplate our black silhouettes as we turned the corner and faded into the darkness beyond.

The dogs had ceased barking. Hank and I moved off first – over a small railing, on to a path, past the kennels, down some steps, round the corner under the light, and away into the darkness. We walked leisurely, side by side, as if we were inmates of the barracks returning after a night's carousal in the town.

Before passing the barracks I had one last duty to perform – to give those in the camp an idea as to what we had done, to indicate whether other escapers would be able to follow our route or not. I had half a dozen pieces of white cardboard cut into various shapes – a square, an oblong, a triangle, a circle, and so on. Dick Howe and I arranged a code whereby each shape gave him some information. I threw certain of the cards down on to a small grass patch below the road, past which our exercise parade marched on their way to the park. With luck, if the parade was not cancelled for a week, Dick would see the cards. My message ran:

'Exit from pit. Moat easy; no traces left.'

Although I had pulled the bar of the flue exit back into place, we had, in truth, probably left minor traces. But as the alternative message was: 'Exit obvious to Goons' – which would have been the case, for instance, if we left fifty feet of sheet-rope dangling from a window – I preferred to encourage other escapers to have a shot at following us.

We continued another hundred yards past the barracks, where the garrison was peacefully sleeping, and arrived at our last obstacle – the outer wall. It was only ten feet high here, with coils of barbed wire stretched along the top. I was on the wall heaving Hank up, when, with a sudden pounding of my heart, I noticed the glow of a cigarette in the distance. It was approaching. Then I realized it was Billie. They had caught us up. We had arranged a discreet gap between us so that we did not look like a regiment passing under the corner lamp.

The barbed wire did not present a serious obstacle when tackled without hurry and with minute care. We were all eventually over the wall, but none too soon, because we had a long way to go in order to be safe before dawn. It was 5.15 in the morning, and the fifth leg of the marathon was over. The sixth and last stage – the long journey to Switzerland – lay ahead of us!

We shook hands all round and with '*Au revoir* – see you in Switzerland in a few days', Hank and I set off along the road. Two hundred yards behind us, the other two followed. Soon they branched off on their route and we took to the fields.

As we trudged along, Hank fumbled for a long time in his pockets, and then uttered practically the first words he had spoken during the whole night. He said:

'I reckon, Pat, I must have left my pipe at the top of the moat.'

CHAPTER 21

LIBERTY EXPRESS

Hank and I walked fast. We intended to lie up for a day. Therefore, in order to be at all safe we had to put the longest distance possible between ourselves and the camp. We judged the German search would be concentrated in the direction of a village about five miles away, for which Ronnie and Billie headed and in which there was a railway station. The first train was shortly before morning *Appell*. Provided there was no alarm in the camp before then, and if the two of them could reach the station in time for the train (which now seemed probable), they would be in Leipzig before the real search started. This was the course Lulu Lawton had taken, but he had missed the train and had to hide up in a closely hunted area.

Hank and I chose a difficult route, calculated to put the hunters off the scent. We headed first south and then westwards in a big sweep in the direction of the River Mulde which ran due northwards towards the Elbe. In order to reach a railway station we had to trek about twenty miles and cross the river into the bargain. It was not a 'cushy' escape-route and we relied on the Germans thinking likewise.

We walked for about an hour and a half, and when it was almost daylight entered a wood and hid up in a thicket for the day. We must have been five miles away from the camp. Although we tried to sleep, our nerves were as taut as piano wires. I was on the alert the whole day.

'A wild animal must have magnificent nerves,' I said to Hank at one point.

'Wild animals have nerves just like you and I. That's why they are not captured easily,' was his comment.

Hank was not going to be easy to catch. His fiancée had been waiting for him since the night when he took off in his bomber in April 1940. It would plainly require more than a few tough Germans to recapture him. It gave me confidence to know he was beside me.

I mused for a long time over the queer twists that Fate gives to our lives. I had always assumed that Rupert and I would escape finally together. Yet it happened to be Hank's turn, and here we were. I had left old and tried friends behind me. Two years of constant companionship had cemented some of us together very closely. Rupert, Harry, Dick, Kenneth and Peter. Would I ever see them again? Inside the camp the probability of early failure in the escape was so great that we brushed aside all serious thought of a long parting.

Here in the woods it was different. If I did my job properly from now on, it was probable that I would never see them again. We were not going back to Colditz; Hank was sure of that too. I was rather shaken by the thought, realizing fully for the first time what these men meant to me. We had been through much together. I prayed that we might all survive the war and meet again.

As dusk fell we set off across the fields. Sometimes when roads led in our direction we used them, but we had to be very careful. On one occasion we only just left the road in time as we saw a light ahead (unusual in the blackout) and heard voices. A car approaching was stopped. As we by-passed the light by way of the fields, we saw an army motor-cyclist talking to a sentry. It was a control and they were after us. We passed within fifty yards of them!

It seemed a long way to the river. As the night wore on, I could hardly keep my eyes open. I stumbled and dozed as I walked, and finally gave up.

'Hank, I'll have to lie down for an hour and sleep. I've been sleep-walking as it is. I don't know where we're going.'

'OK. I'll stay on guard while you pass out on that bank over there under the tree,' said Hank, indicating a mound of grass looming ahead of us.

He woke me in an hour and we continued, eventually reaching the river. It was in a deep cutting, down which we climbed, and there was a road which ran along its bank. Towards our left, crossing the river and the cutting, was a high-level railway bridge. I decided to cross it. We had to reclimb the cutting. Sleep was overcoming me once more. The climb was steep and over huge rocks cut into steps like those of the pyramids. It was a nightmare climb in the pitch-darkness, as I repeatedly stumbled, fell down, and slept where I lay. Hank would tug at me, pull me over the next huge stone and set me on my feet without a word, only to have to repeat the performance again in a few moments. Halfway up the embankment we stopped to rest. I slept, but Hank was on the *qui vive* and, peering through the darkness, noticed a movement on the railway bridge. It needed a cat's eye to notice anything at all. He shook me and said:

'Pat, we're not going over that bridge; it's guarded.'

'How the hell do you know for certain?' I asked, 'and how are we going to cross the river, then?'

'I don't mind if we have to swim it, but I'm not crossing that bridge.'

I gave way, though it meant making a big half-circle, crossing the railway line and descending to the river again somewhere near a road bridge which we knew existed farther upstream.

Reaching the top of the railway-bridge embankment we crossed the lines, and as we did so we saw in the distance from the direction of the bridge the flash of a lighted match.

'Did you see that?' I whispered.

'Yes.'

'There's a sentry on the bridge, sure enough. You were right, Hank. Thank God you insisted.'

Gradually we edged down the hill again where the river cutting was less steep, and found that our bearings had not been too bad; for we saw the road bridge in the foreground. We inspected it carefully before crossing, listening for a long time for any sound of movement. It was unguarded. We crossed rapidly and took to the bushes on the far side, not a moment too soon; a motor-cycle came roaring round a bend, its headlights blazing, and crossed the bridge in the direction from which we had come.

We tramped wearily across country on a compass bearing until dawn. Near the village of Penig, where our railway station was situated, we spruced ourselves up, attempted a shave and polished our shoes. We entered the village – it was almost a small industrial town – and wended our way in the direction of the station. I was loth to ask our way at this time of the morning when few people were about. Instead, we wandered onwards past some coalyards where a tram-line started. The tracks ran alongside a large factory and then switched over to the other side of the road, passing under trees and beside a small river. We followed the lines, which eventually crossed a bridge and entered the town proper. I was sure the tram-lines would lead us to the station. The town was dingy, not at all like Colditz, which was of pleasing appearance. Upkeep had evidently gone to the dogs. Broken window-panes were filled with newspaper, ironwork was rusty, and the front doors of the houses, which opened directly on to the street, badly needed a coat of paint.

We arrived at the railway station. It was on the far edge of the town and looked older and out of keeping with the buildings around it. It had a staid respectable atmosphere and belonged to a period before industry had come to Penig. We entered and looked up the trains. Our route was Munich via Zwickau. I saw we had a three-hour wait and then another long wait at Zwickau before the night express for Munich. Leaving the station, we walked out into the country again and settled down for a meal and a rest behind a barn near the road. It is dangerous to wait in railway stations or public parks and advisable to keep moving under any circumstances when in a town.

We returned to the station towards midday. I bought two third-class tickets to Munich and we caught the train comfortably. Our suitcases were a definite asset. My German accent was anything but perfect, but the brandishing of my suitcase on all occasions to emphasize whatever I happened to be saying worked like a soporific on the Germans.

In Zwickau, having another long wait, we boarded a tram. I tripped on the mounting-step and nearly knocked the conductress over. I apologized loudly.

'*Entschuldigen Sie mich! Bitte, entschuldigen, entschuldilgen! Ich bib ein Ausländer.*'

We sat down, and when the conductress came round I beamed at her and asked in broken German:

'*Gnädige Fraülein!* If you please, where is the nearest cinema? We have a long time to wait for our train and would like to see a film and the news pictures. We are foreigners and do not know this town.'

'The best cinema in Zwickau is five minutes from here. I shall tell you where to alight.'

'How much is the fare, please, *Fraülein*?'

'Twenty pfennigs each, if you please.'

'*Danke schön,*' I said, proffering the money.

After five minutes the tram stopped at a main thoroughfare junction and the conductress beckoned to us. As we alighted, one of the passengers pointed out to us with a voluble and, to me, incoherent stream of German exactly where the cinema was. I could gather that he was proud to meet foreigners who were working for the victory of 'Unser Reich'! He took off his moth-eaten hat as we parted and waved a courteous farewell.

Zwickau was just a greatly enlarged Penig as far as I could see. Dilapidation was visible everywhere. The inhabitants gave me an impression of impoverishment, and only the uniforms of officials, including the tram conductress, and those of the armed forces bore a semblance of smartness.

Hank and I spent a comfortable two hours in the cinema, which was no different from any other I have seen. German officers and troops were dotted about in seats all around us and made up ninety per cent of the audience. I dozed for a long time and I noticed Hank's head drooping too. After two hours I whispered to him:

'It's time to go. What did you think of the film?'

'What I saw of it was a washout,' Hank replied. 'I must have slept though, because I missed parts of it. It was incoherent.'

'This cinema seems to be nothing more than impromptu sleeping-quarters. Look around you,' and I nudged Hank. The German Army and Air Force were dozing in all sorts of postures around us!

'Let's go,' I said, and, yawning repeatedly, we rose and left the auditorium.

Returning to the station in good time, we boarded the express to Munich. It was crowded, for which I was glad, and Hank and I spent the whole night standing in the corridor. Nobody paid any attention to us. We might as well have been in an express bound from London to the

North. The lighting, however, was so bad that few passengers attempted to read. It was intensely stuffy owing to the overcrowding, the cold outside, and the blackout curtains on all windows. The hypnotic drumming and the swaying of the train pervaded all.

Our fellow-travellers were a mixed bag; a few army and air force other ranks, some workmen, and a majority of down-at-heel-looking business men or Government officials. There was not a personality among them; all were sheep ready to be slaughtered at the altar of Hitler. There was a police control in the early hours. I produced my much soiled German leather wallet, which exposed my identity card or *Ausweis* behind a grimy scratched piece of celluloid. The police officer was curt:

'*Sie sind Auslander?*'

'*Jawohl.*'

'*Wo fahren Sie hin?*'

'*Nach München und Rottweil.*'

'*Warum?*'

'*Betonarbeit*' (that is, concrete work).

Hank was slow in producing his papers. I said:

'*Wir sind zusammen. Er ist mein Kamerad.*'

Hank proffered his papers as I added, taking the officer into my confidence:

'*Er ist etwas dumm, aber ein guter Kerl.*'

The control passed on and we relaxed into a fitful doze as we roared through the night towards Munich – and Switzerland.

We arrived in Munich in the cold grey of the morning – several hours late. There had been bombing and train diversions.

I queued up at the booking-office, telling Hank to stand by. When my turn came I asked for, '*Zweimal dritte Klasse, nach Rottweil.*' The woman behind the grill said:

'*Fünfundsechzig Mark, bitte.*'

I produced fify-six marks, which almost drained me right out. The woman repeated:

'*Fünfundsechzig Mark, bitte – noch neun Mark.*'

I was confusing the German for fify-six with sixty-five.

'*Karl,*' I shouted in Hank's direction, '*geben Sie mir noch zehn Mark.*'

Hank took the cue, and produced a ten-mark note which I handed to the woman.

'*Ausweis, bitte,*' she said.

I produced it.

'*Gut,*' and she handed my wallet back to me.

I was so relieved that as I left the queue, forgetting my part completely, I said in a loud voice:

'All right, Hank, I've got the tickets!'

I nearly froze in my tracks. As we hurried away I felt the baleful glare of a hundred eyes burning through my back. We were soon lost in the crowd, and what a crowd! Everybody seemed to be travelling. The station appeared to be untouched by bombing and traffic was obviously running at high pressure. We had another long wait for the train which would take us to Rottweil via Ulm and Tuttlingen. I noted with relief that the wait in Ulm was only ten minutes. Hyde-Thompson and his Dutch colleague, the second two officers of my theatre escape, had been trapped in Ulm station. The name carried foreboding and I prayed we would negotiate this junction safely. I also noticed with appreciation that there was a substantial wait at Tuttlingen for the train to Rottweil. It would give us an excuse for leaving the station.

In Munich I felt safe. The waiting-rooms were full to overflowing and along with other passengers we were even shepherded by station police to an underground bomb-proof waiting-room – signposted for the use of all persons having longer than half an hour to wait for a train.

Before descending to this waiting-room, however, I asked for the *Bahnhofswirtschaft* and roving along the counter I saw a notice "*Markenfreies Essen*", which meant 'coupon-free meals'! I promptly asked for two and also *Zwei Liter Pilsner*. They were duly served and Hank and I sat down at a table by ourselves to the best meal provided us by the Germans in two and a half years. The *Markenfreies Essen* consisted of a very generous helping of thick stew – mostly vegetable and potatoes, but some good-tasting sausage-meat was floating around as well. The beer seemed excellent to our parched gullets. We had not drunk anything since our repast on the outskirts of Penig when we had finished the water we carried with us.

We went to the underground waiting-room. We were controlled once in a cursory manner. I was blasé by now and smiled benignly at the burly representative of the *Sicherheitspolizei* – security police – as he passed by, hardly glancing at the wallets we pushed under his nose.

In good time we boarded the train for Ulm. Arriving there at midday, we changed platforms without incident and quickly boarded our next train. This did not go direct to Rottweil, but necessitated changing at Tuttlingen. Rottweil was thirty miles, but Tuttlingen only fifteen miles from the frontier! My intention was to walk out of the station at Tuttlingen with the excuse of waiting for the Rottweil train and never return.

This Hank and I duly did. As I walked off the station platform at Tuttlingen, through the barrier, we handed in our tickets. We had walked ten yards when I heard shouts behind us:

'*Kommen Sie hier! Hier, kommen Sie zurück!*'

I turned round, fearing the worst, and saw the ticket-collector waving at us.

I returned to him and he said:

'*Sie haben Ihre Fahrkarten abgegeben, aber Sie fahren nach Rottweil. Die müssen Sie noch behalten.*'

With almost visible relief I accepted the tickets once more. In my anxiety I had forgotten that we were ostensibly due to return to catch the Rottweil train and, of course, still needed our tickets.

From the station we promptly took the wrong road; there were no signposts. It was late afternoon and a Saturday (October 17th). The weather was fine. We walked for a long time along a road which refused to turn in the direction in which we thought it ought to turn! It was maddening. We passed a superbly camouflaged factory and sidings. There must have been an area of ten acres completely covered with a false flat roof of what appeared to be rush matting. Even at the low elevation at which we found ourselves looking down upon it, the whole site looked like farmland. If the camouflage was actually rush matting, I do not know how they provided against fire risks.

We were gradually being driven into a valley heading due south, whereas we wished to travel westwards. Leaving the road as soon as possible without creating suspicion, we tried to make a short-cut across country to another highway which we knew headed west. As a short-cut it misfired, taking us over hilly country which prolonged our journey considerably. Evening was drawing in by the time we reached the correct road. We walked along this for several miles, and when it was dark, took to the woods to lie up for the night.

We passed a freezing, uncomfortable night on beds of leaves in the forest and were glad to warm ourselves with a sharp walk early the next morning, which was Sunday. I was thankful it was a Sunday because it gave us a good excuse to be out walking in the country.

We now headed along roads leading south-west, until at 8 am we retired again to the friendly shelter of the woods to eat our breakfast, consuming most of what was left of our German bread, sugar, and margarine.

We had almost finished our repast when we were disturbed by a farmer who approached and eyed us curiously for a long time. He wore close-fitting breeches and gaiters like a typical English gamekeeper. I did not like his attitude at all. He came close to us and demanded what we were doing. I said:

'*Wir essen. Können Sie das nicht sehen?*'

'*Warum sind Sie hier?*' he asked, to which I answered:

'*Wir gehen spazieren; es ist Sonntag, nicht wahr?*'

At this he retired. I watched him carefully. As soon as he was out of the wood and about fifty yards away, I saw him turn along a hedge and change his gait into a trot.

This was enough for me. In less than a minute we were packed and trotting fast in the opposite direction, which happened to be southward! We did not touch the road again for some time, but kept to the woods and lanes. Gradually, however, the countryside became open and cultivated and we were forced once more to the road. We passed a German soldier, who was smartly turned out in his Sunday best, with a friendly '*Heil Hitler!*' Church bells were ringing out from steeples which rose head and shoulders above the roofs of several villages dotted here and there in the rolling country around us.

We walked through one of the villages as the people were coming out of church. I was terrified of the children, who ran out of the church shouting and laughing. They gambolled around us and eyed us curiously, although their elders took no notice of us at all. I was relieved, none the less, when we left the village behind us. Soon afterwards, the country again became wooded and hilly, and we disappeared amongst the trees, heading now due south.

As the afternoon wore on I picked up our bearings more accurately, and we aimed at the exact location of the frontier crossing. A little too soon – I thought – we reached the frontier road, running east and west. I could not be sure, so we continued eastwards along it to where it entered some woods. We passed a fork where a forest track, which I recognized, joined it. I knew then that we were indeed on the frontier road and that we had gone too far eastwards. At that moment there were people following us, and we could not break off into the woods without looking suspicious. We walked onward casually and at the end of the wooded portion of the road we heard suddenly:

'*Halt! Wer da!*' and then, more deliberately, '*Wo gehen Sie hin?*'

A sentry-box stood back from the road in a clump of trees and from it stepped forth a frontier guard.

'*Wir gehen nach Singen,*' I said '*Wir sind Ausländer.*'

'*Ihren Ausweis, bitte.*'

We produced our papers, including the special permit allowing us to travel near the frontier. We were close to him. His rifle was slung over his shoulder. The people who had been following us had turned down a lane towards a cottage. We were alone with the sentry.

I chatted on, gesticulating with my suitcase brazenly conspicuous.

'We are Flemish workmen. This evening we take the train to Rottweil, where there is much construction work. We must be there in the morning. Today we can rest and we like your woods and countryside.'

He eyed us for a moment; handed us back our papers and let us go. As we walked on I dreaded to hear another 'Halt!' I imagined that if the sentry were not satisfied with us he would, for his own safety, move us off a few yards so that he could unsling his rifle. But no command was given and we continued our 'Sunday afternoon stroll'. As we moved out of earshot Hank said to me:

'If he'd reached for his gun when he was close to us just then, I would have knocked him to Kingdom come.'

I would not have relished being knocked to Kingdom come by Hank and I often wonder if the sentry did not notice a look in Hank's eye and think that discretion was perhaps the better part of valour! A lonely sentry is not all-powerful against two enemies, even with his gun levelled. Our story may have had a vague ring of truth, but none the less, we were foreigners within half a mile of the Swiss frontier!

Soon we were able to leave the road and we started to double back across country to our frontier crossing-point. Just as we came to a railway line and climbed a small embankment, we nearly jumped out of our skins with fright as a figure darted from a bush in front of us and ran for his life into a thicket and disappeared. I could have assured him, if only he had stopped, that he gave us just as big a fright as we gave him!

By dusk we had found our exact location and waited in deep pine woods for darkness to descend. The frontier was scarcely a mile away. We ate a last meal nervously and without appetite. Our suitcases would not be required any more, so they were buried. When it was pitch-dark, we pulled on socks over our shoes, and set off. We had to negotiate the frontier-crossing in inky blackness, entirely from memory of the maps studied in Colditz. We crossed over more railway lines and then continued, skirting the edge of a wood. We encountered a minor road, which foxed me for a while because it should not have been there according to my memory, but we carried on. Hearing a motor-cycle pass along a road in front of us, a road running close to and parallel with the frontier, warned us of the proximity of our 'take-off' point. We entered the woods to our left and proceeded parallel with the road eastwards for about a hundred yards and then approached it cautiously. Almost as we stumbled into it, I suddenly recognized the outline of a sentry-box hidden among the trees straight in front of us!

We were within five yards of it when I recognized its angular roof. My hair stood on end. It was impossible to move without breaking twigs under our feet. They made noises like pistol shots and we would be heard easily. We retreated with as much care as we could, but even the crackle of a dried leaf caused me to perspire freely.

To compensate for this unnerving encounter, however, I now knew exactly where we were, for the sentry-box was marked on our Colditz map and provided me with a check bearing. We moved off seventy yards and approached the road again. Peering across it, we could discern fields and low hedges. In the distance was our goal: a wooded hill looming blacker than the darkness around it, with the woods ending abruptly halfway down its eastern slopes, towards our left. This end of the woods was our 'pointer'. There was no 'blackout' in Switzerland, and beyond the hill was the faintest haze of light, indicating the existence of a Swiss village.

At 7.30 pm we moved off. Crouching low, and at the double, we crossed the road and headed for our 'pointer'. Without stopping for breath we ran – through hedges – across ditches – wading through mud – and then on again. Dreading barbed wire which we could never have seen, we ran, panting with excitement as much as with breathlessness, across fields newly ploughed, meadows and marshland, till at last we rounded the corner of the woods. Here, for a moment, we halted for breath.

I felt that if I could not have a drink of water soon I would die. My throat was parched and swollen and my tongue was choking me. My heart was pounding like a sledge-hammer. I was gasping for breath. I had lived for two and a half years, both awake and in sleep, with the vision of this race before me and every nerve in my body was taut to breaking-pitch.

We were not yet 'home'. We had done about half a mile and could see the lights of the Swiss village ahead. Great care was now necessary, for we could easily recross the frontier into Germany without knowing it, and stumble on a guard-post. From the corner of the wood we had to continue in a sweeping curve, first towards our right, and then left again towards the village. Where we stood we were actually in Switzerland, but in a direct line between us and the Swiss village lay Germany.

Why had we run instead of creeping forward warily? The answer is that instinct dictated it and, I think in this case, instinct was right. Escapers' experience has borne out that the psychological reaction of a fleeing man to a shouted command, such as 'Halt', varies. If a man is walking or creeping the reaction is to stop. If he is running the reaction is to run faster. It is in the split seconds of such instinctive decisions that success or failure may be determined.

We continued on our way at a rapid walk, over grass and boggy land, crouching low at every sound. It was important to avoid even Swiss frontier-posts. We had heard curious rumours of escapers being returned to the Germans by unfriendly Swiss guards. However untrue, we were taking no risks.

We saw occasional shadowy forms and circled widely around them and at last, at 8.30 pm, approached the village along a sandy path.

We were about a thousand yards inside the Swiss frontier. We had completed the four-hundred-mile journey from Colditz in less than four days.

Under the first lamp-post of the village street, Hank and I shook hands in silence. . . .

We beat Ronnie and Billie by twenty-six hours. At 10.30 pm the following evening they crossed the frontier safely!

EPILOGUE

A month after I reached Switzerland, the invasion of North Africa occurred and the Germans took over the south of France. Switzerland became a neutral island in a belligerent's home waters. The British Legation in Berne had only the Swiss Postal wireless telegraphic facilities of communication with London.

I had made a short report on Escape from Colditz in general, which never reached home. In that report, I made a statement which I would like to repeat here. It was:

> Although in one case or another the name of practically every officer could be included in a list of those who worked for the common good at the expense of their own, I mention especially the following – not in order of priority:
>
> Lieutenant-Colonel Guy German, Leicester Regiment; Lieutenant-Colonel G. Young, RE; Major W. F. Anderson, RE; Squadron-Leader H. M. MacColm, RAF; Captain R. Barry, 52nd Light Infantry; Captain R. Howe, RTR; Captain K. Lockwood, QRR; Flight Lieutenant N. Forbes, RAF; Flight Lieutenant H. Wardle, RAF; Lieutenant W. L. B. O'Hara, RTR; Lieutenant D. Gill, Royal Norfolks; Lieutenant 'Rex' Harrison, Green Howards; Lieutenant J. K. V. Lee, RCS; E.R.A. W. Hammond, RN.

In general these officers all placed at the disposal of the camp some flair or technical qualification without regard to personal consequences.

This story brings the war history of Colditz up to November 1942. The camp was relieved by the Americans on April 15th, 1945. The prisoners had therefore nearly another two and a half years in front of them when I left. I pay tribute to their endurance, for I could not picture myself lasting that length of time at Colditz without becoming a neurasthenic.

Two other British officers made successful escapes from the camp: Harry Elliott and 'Skipper' Barnet (Lieutenant R. Barnet, RN). Elliott foxed German Medical Boards for years on end, suffering from terrible stomach ulcers produced on substitute X-ray plates. He lost weight regularly and to an astonishing degree by having himself weighed, to begin with, loaded with bags of sand concealed under his pyjamas. Thereafter, weight-losing was a simple procedure, and like an observation balloon he jettisoned ballast at will. Skipper Barnet practised 'Yoga' for a long time until, by muscular control, he could raise his blood pressure to incredible heights. The Germans finally repatriated him, convinced he would never survive the excitement of a homecoming. Skipper, incidentally, was the boxer at Laufen who nearly knocked Harry Elliott out with a stout door between them.

One or two French officers, also removed to hospital at death's door, managed to rise from their beds and escape successfully to France.

A time came when it was no longer worth while trying to escape. This period probably started around 'D' Day, June 1944. Then it became a question of waiting patiently for the sound of the guns and the arrival of the Allies at the gates of the Castle.

Many events of interest took place, however, before that time. There were several brilliant, though unsuccessful, escape attempts, made under the guidance of Dick Howe. Rupert Barry made another game bid for freedom but was recaught while innocently trundling a wheelbarrow out of the last gateway of Colditz. Michael Sinclair, whose name is rapidly becoming legendary among escape fans, made three attempts. On the first occasion he did not go far; he was shot through the chest at the Castle gateway. He recovered. On his next attempt he reached Rheine, twenty-five miles from the Dutch frontier, along with his companion Flight Lieutenant J. W. Best, RAF, before recapture. On his third attempt he was shot dead some yards from the wire of the Colditz park recreation ground. His memory is especially honoured by every man who knew him.

Best was chiefly known for his 'mole' escape from an Air Force camp (Sagan, I think), which brought him to Colditz. In this attempt he and another officer, Bill Goldfinch, made a sufficiently long tunnel to house themselves with some space to spare for what is known as 'bulking'. They laid in a stock of provisions and had an air-tube. They then carried on digging at their leisure, and eventually surfaced at a reasonable distance from the camp and walked off!

The French tunnel was still under construction when I left. It is worth a chapter to itself. The Dutch departed from Colditz and, unhitching their railway coach in motion on the way to their next camp, the whole contingent escaped in various directions when it came to a standstill! The escape of ERAs Hammond and Lister, which I have mentioned in this book, is among the cream of escape stories. Dick Howe, from somewhere high up in the Castle, eventually made contact with the concealed manhole (which I had tried to reach from the delousing shed) in the prison courtyard. From there he carried on through a maze of drains until he reached the main Castle outfall sewer. The Germans, unfortunately, discovered this attempt before it reached fruition. Dick also took over magnificently concealed wireless sets left by the French and gave the prisoners daily News Bulletins. More *Prominente* arrived of various nationalities – General Bor Komorowsky, Captain the Earl of Hopetoun,

Lieutenant Alexander, Lieutenant Lascelles, First Lieutenant John Winant (USAF), and others. American POWs joined the serried ranks of the hardbitten Colditz convicts! Finally the 'Relief of Colditz' was dramatically exciting, and carried with it a touch of pathos which it would be difficult to describe. All this and much more has been incorporated in my book *The Latter Days at Colditz*, which concludes the Saga of the Fortress Prison.

The Bridge on the River Kwai

Pierre Boulle

No, it was not funny; it was rather pathetic; he was so representative of all the past victims of the great Joke. But it is by folly alone that the world moves, and so it is a respectable thing upon the whole. And besides, he was what one would call a good man.

JOSEPH CONRAD

PART 1

CHAPTER 1

The insuperable gap between East and West that exists in some eyes is perhaps nothing more than an optical illusion. Perhaps it is only the conventional way of expressing a popular opinion based on insufficient evidence and masquerading as a universally recognized statement of fact, for which there is no justification at all, not even the plea that it contains an element of truth. During the last war 'saving face' was perhaps as vitally important to the British as it was to the Japanese. Perhaps it dictated the behaviour of the former, without their being aware of it, as forcibly and as fatally as it did that of the latter, and no doubt that of every other race in the world. Perhaps the conduct of each of the two enemies, superficially so dissimilar, was in fact simply a different though equally meaningless manifestation of the same spiritual reality. Perhaps the mentality of the Japanese colonel, Saito, was essentially the same as that of his prisoner, Colonel Nicholson.

These were the questions which occupied Major Clipton's thoughts. He too was a prisoner, like the five hundred other wretches herded by the Japanese into the camp on the River Kwai, like the sixty thousand English, Australians, Dutch and Americans assembled in several groups in one of the most uncivilized corners of the earth, the jungle of Burma and Siam, in order to build a railway linking the Bay of Bengal to Bangkok and Singapore. Clipton occasionally answered these questions in the affirmative, realizing, however, that this point of view was in the nature of a paradox; to acquire it one had to disregard all superficial appearances. Above all, one had to assume that the beatings-up, the butt-end blows and even worse forms of brutality through which the Japanese mentality made itself felt were all as meaningless as the show of ponderous dignity which was Colonel Nicholson's favourite weapon, wielded as a mark of British superiority. But Clipton willingly gave way to this assumption each time his C.O.'s behaviour enraged him to such an extent that the only consolation he could find was in a whole-hearted objective examination of primary causes.

He invariably came to the conclusion that the combination of individual characteristics which contributed to Colonel Nicholson's personality (sense of duty, observance of ritual, obsession with discipline and love of the job well done were all jumbled together in this worthy human repository) could not be better described than by the single word:

snobbery. During these periods of feverish investigation he regarded him as a snob, a perfect example of the military snob, which has gradually emerged after a lengthy process of development dating from the Stone Age, the preservation of the species being guaranteed by tradition.

Clipton, however, was by nature objective and had the rare gift of being able to examine a problem from every angle. The conclusion he had reached having somewhat calmed the brainstorm which certain aspects of the Colonel's behaviour caused him, he would suddenly feel well disposed and recognize, almost with affection, the excellence of the C.O.'s qualities. If these were typically snobbish, he reasoned, then the argument need be carried only one stage further for the noblest sentiments to be likewise classified as such, until even a mother's love would eventually come to be regarded as the most blatant sign of snobbery imaginable.

In the past, Colonel Nicholson's high regard for discipline had been a byword in various parts of Asia and Africa. In 1942 it was once again in evidence, at Singapore, during the disaster which followed the invasion of Malaya.

When orders came through from Headquarters to cease fire, a group of young officers in his battalion had planned to make their way down to the coast, get hold of a boat and set sail for the Dutch East Indies. Although admiring their zeal and courage, Colonel Nicholson had hindered their scheme with every means at his disposal.

To begin with, he had tried to win them over by pointing out that this venture was a direct contravention of the instructions he had received. Since the Commander-in-Chief had signed the surrender for the whole of Malaya, not one of His Majesty's subjects could escape without committing an act of disobedience. As far as he could see, there was only one line of conduct possible: to stay put until a senior Japanese officer turned up to accept the surrender of himself and his unit and of the hundreds of stragglers who had managed to escape the massacre of the last few weeks.

'A fine example it would be for the men,' he had exclaimed, 'if their officers failed in their duty!'

His argument had been rendered additionally forceful by the piercing look of resolution which he always assumed in moments of crisis. His eyes were the colour of the Indian Ocean on a calm day; and his features, which were always in repose, were the clear reflection of a guiltless conscience. His fair, reddish moustache was the moustache of an unruffled hero; and his ruddy complexion was evidence of a sound heart regulating a smooth, easy circulation perfect in its efficiency. Clipton, who had served under him throughout the campaign, never ceased to wonder at this living example of 'the Indian Army officer', a type which he had always considered legendary, but whose reality was now proclaimed so loudly every day that it invariably caused him these alternating bouts of anger and affection.

Clipton had pleaded the young officers' case. He approved of it and said so. Colonel Nicholson had taken him to task and declared himself painfully surprised to see a middle-aged man in a highly responsible position sharing the wild aspirations of a lot of hot-headed youngsters and encouraging the sort of thoughtless escapade that can cause nothing but harm.

Having explained the reason for his attitude, he had issued strict and definite orders. All officers, N.C.O.s and men were to stay put until the Japanese arrived. Their surrender was not of their own choice; none of them, therefore, should feel in any way humiliated. He, and he alone, would shoulder the responsibility on behalf of the whole battalion.

Most of the officers had given in to him; for his power of persuasion was considerable, and his authority immense, while his unquestionable personal courage made it impossible to attribute his conduct to any motive except sense of duty. Some of them had disobeyed orders and disappeared into the jungle. Colonel Nicholson had been genuinely grieved by their behaviour. He had posted them as deserters, and with growing impatience had waited for the Japanese to appear.

In preparation for their arrival, he had worked out in his head a ceremony which would bear the stamp of quiet dignity. After considerable thought he had decided, as a symbolic act of submission, to hand over the revolver which he wore on his hip to the enemy colonel in charge of the surrender. He had rehearsed the gesture several times and had made certain of being able to take the holster off in one easy movement. He had put on his best uniform and seen that his men tidied themselves up. Then he had ordered them to fall in and pile arms and had inspected them in person.

The first to make contact were some private soldiers who could not speak a word of any civilized language. Colonel Nicholson had not budged. Then an N.C.O. had driven up in a truck and motioned the British to load their arms on to the vehicle. The Colonel had forbidden his men to move. He had demanded to see a senior officer. There was no officer, either senior or junior, and the Japanese did not understand his request. They had turned nasty. The soldiers had assumed a threatening attitude, while the N.C.O. broke out into shrill screams and pointed at the rifles. The Colonel had ordered his men to stay put and not move. Sub machine-guns had been pointed at them, while the Colonel was unceremoniously pushed around. He had kept his temper and repeated his demand. The British began to look rather worried and Clipton was wondering if the C.O. intended to get them all massacred out of loyalty to his principles and for the sake of form, when a car full of Japanese officers at last appeared. One of them wore the badges of rank of a major. *Faute de mieux*, Colonel Nicholson decided to surrender to him. He called his unit to attention. He himself saluted in exemplary fashion and, taking his holster off his belt, presented it with a flourish.

Faced with this gift, the astonished major first stepped back in alarm; then he appeared extremely embarrassed; finally he became convulsed by a long burst of savage laughter in which he was soon joined by his fellow-officers. Colonel Nicholson simply shrugged his shoulders and assumed a haughty expression: none the less he gave his men the order to load their rifles on to the truck.

During the time that he had spent in the prison camp near Singapore, Colonel Nicholson had made a point of observing a strict Anglo-Saxon code of behaviour in face of the enemy's disorderly conduct. Clipton, who had been with him all the time, was not sure even at that early date whether to bless him or curse him.

As a result of the orders he had issued, orders which confirmed and amplified the Japanese instructions, the men in his unit behaved well and fared badly. Bully-beef and other miscellaneous supplies, which the prisoners from other units sometimes managed to 'win' in the blitzed outskirts of Singapore in spite of, and often in connivance with, the sentries, were a welcome supplement to the meagre rations. But this sort of looting was not permitted on any account by Colonel Nicholson. He made his officers give lectures condemning such behaviour as undignified and pointing out that the only way for the British soldier to command the respect of his temporary masters was to set them an example of irreproachable conduct. He saw to it that this order was obeyed by carrying out regular inspections, which were even more thorough than the sentries'!

These lectures on the standard of behaviour which every soldier was supposed to keep up when serving overseas were not the only fatigues which he imposed on his battalion. During that period the unit was by no means overwhelmed with work, since the Japanese had organized no labour to speak of on the outskirts of Singapore. Convinced that idleness was prejudicial to the spirit of the regiment, and frightened at the prospect of a drop in morale, the Colonel had drawn up a full programme for every off-duty hour. He made his officers read out and explain to the men whole sections of *King's Regulations*, after which he examined them and issued rewards in the shape of certificates bearing his signature. Discipline, of course, was not the least important subject in this curriculum. At regular intervals it was brought to the notice of all ranks that correct saluting was compulsory, even in a prison compound. Consequently the privates, who were also obliged to salute every Japanese irrespective of his rank, ran a double risk every time they neglected instructions: on the one hand, they risked the kicks and blows of the sentries; on the other, a dressing down from the Colonel and some punishment imposed by him, such as having to stand to attention for several hours during recreation periods.

The fact that such Spartan discipline had been generally accepted by the men, and that they had voluntarily submitted to an authority which was no longer backed up by the powers-that-be, but was only wielded by an individual at the mercy of the same abuses and ill-treatment as themselves, was a frequent source of amazement to Clipton. He often wondered whether such obedience should be attributed to the personal respect which the Colonel commanded or to the privileges which they enjoyed thanks to him; for no one could deny that his intransigent attitude was successful, even with the Japanese. His chief weapons, when dealing with them, were his insistence on a proper code of conduct, his tenacity, his ability to keep harping on one particular point until he obtained satisfaction, and the *Manual of Military Law* containing the Hague Convention which he calmly waved in the Japs' faces each time a breach of international law was committed. His personal courage and complete disregard for the blows he received were also no doubt largely responsible for the high regard in which he was held. On several occasions, when the Japanese had exceeded the recognized rights due to a victorious army, he had done more than protest. He had personally intervened. He had once been badly beaten up by a particularly brutal guard who had issued an order contrary to international law. He had eventually scored his point, and his assailant had been punished. He had then proceeded to issue his own version of the order, which was far harsher than anything the Japanese could devise.

'The main thing,' he explained, when Clipton suggested that in the circumstances he might exercise a little leniency, 'the main thing is to make the lads feel they're still being commanded by us and not by these baboons. As long as they cling to this idea, they'll be soldiers, not slaves.'

Clipton, who could see both sides of the question, had to admit there was something to be said for this and realized that the Colonel's action was prompted, as usual, by his sterling qualities.

CHAPTER 2

The prisoners now recalled those months they had spent in the Singapore camp as a period of palmy days, and sighed with regret when they compared it with their present plight in this uncivilized corner of Siam. They had reached their destination after an endless train journey right across Malaya, followed by an exhausting march in the course of which they had grown so weak from exposure and malnutrition that bit by bit they had jettisoned the heaviest and most valuable items of their wretched equipment, without any hope of ever getting them back. The rumours about the railway which they were going to build did not cheer them up at all.

Colonel Nicholson and his unit had been moved a little later than the others, and the work was already under way by the time they reached Siam. After the hardships of their cross-country march, their first encounter with the new Japanese authorities had been far from encouraging. At Singapore they had been up against soldiers who, after the initial frenzy of victory, and apart from a few isolated outbreaks of primitive brutality, had proved to be not much more oppressive than any Western army of occupation would have been. The officers in charge of the Allied prisoners on the railway were evidently quite a different proposition. From the very start they had acted like savage chain-gang warders and were liable to turn at a moment's notice into sadistic executioners.

Colonel Nicholson and the remainder of his battalion, which he still prided himself on commanding, had at first been transferred to a vast reception centre serving as a transit camp for all the convoys along this route, part of which, however, was already in use as permanent quarters. They had stayed there only a short time, but long enough to realize what they were in for and how they would live until the job was finished. The poor devils were put to work like beasts of burden. Each of them had to complete a task which was not perhaps beyond the strength of a man in good condition and on an adequate diet; for the pitiful, emaciated creatures that they had become in less than one month, it was a job that kept them busy from dawn till dusk and sometimes half the night. They were worn out and demoralized by the curses and blows which the guards rained down on them at the slightest sign of faltering, and haunted by the fear of even worse punishment to come. Clipton had been appalled by their physical condition. Malaria, dysentery, beri-beri and jungle sores were rife, and the camp M.O. had told him there might be far more serious epidemics, against which he could take no precautions at all. Not even the most rudimentary medical stores were available.

Colonel Nicholson had frowned without saying a word. He was not 'in charge' of this camp, and considered himself almost as a guest there. To the British lieutenant-colonel who ran it under Japanese orders, he had only once expressed what he felt; that was when he noticed that all the officers below the rank of major were doing their share of manual labour on exactly the same footing as the men, in other words they were digging and carting like navvies. The lieutenant-colonel had hung his head. He explained that he had done his best to avoid this humiliation and had given in to brutal compulsion only in order to avoid the reprisals from which everyone would have otherwise suffered. Colonel Nicholson had nodded in a manner that showed he was far from convinced, and had then taken refuge in haughty silence.

They had stayed two days in this reception centre, long enough for the Japanese to issue them each with some meagre haversack rations and a triangle of coarse cloth which fastened round the waist with strings, which they referred to as 'working kit'; long enough also to see General Yamashita perched on a makeshift platform, with his sword at his hip and pale-grey gloves on his hands, and to listen to him first explaining in faulty English that they had been placed under his command in accordance with the wishes of His Imperial Majesty, and then telling them what was expected of them.

The tirade, which lasted over two hours, had been painful to hear and hurt their national pride just as much as the curses and the blows. He had told them that the Japanese had no quarrel with people like them, who had been led astray by the lies of their government; that they would be decently treated so long as they behaved like 'zentlemen', that is to say if they contributed with all their heart and with all their strength to the South-East Asia Co-Prosperity Sphere. They should all recognize their obligation to His Imperial Majesty, who was giving them this chance to mend the error of their ways by contributing to the common cause and helping to build the railway. Yamashita had then explained that in the general interest he would have to impose the strictest discipline and would tolerate no disobedience. Laziness and neglect would be treated as crimes. Any attempt to escape would be punished by death. The British officers would be responsible to the Japanese for their men's behaviour and efficiency.

'Sickness will not be considered an excuse,' General Yamashita had added. 'Reasonable work is the best thing in the world for keeping a man physically fit, and dysentery would think twice before attacking anyone who makes a daily effort to do his duty towards the Emperor.'

He had concluded on an optimistic note, which had driven his audience wild with anger.

'Be happy in your work,' he had said, 'that's my motto. Make it your motto as well from now on. Those who live up to it will have nothing to fear from me, nor from the officers of the Japanese Grand Army which is now protecting you.'

Then the units had been dispersed, each one moving off to the sector it had been allotted. Colonel Nicholson and his battalion had made their way to the camp on the River Kwai, which was quite far off, only a few miles from the Burmese border. The commandant was Colonel Saito.

CHAPTER 3

Some nasty incidents punctuated the first few days in the Kwai camp, where an uneasy undercurrent of tension was at once noticeable in the atmosphere.

The cause of the initial disturbances was Colonel Saito's proclamation stipulating that all officers were to work side by side with the other ranks and on the same footing. This provoked a polite but firm protest from Colonel Nicholson, who outlined his ideas on the subject candidly and methodically, adding in conclusion that the task of British officers was to command their men and not to wield a pick and shovel.

Saito listened to the whole speech without a sign of impatience – which the Colonel interpreted as a favourable omen – then dismissed him, saying that he would think the matter over. Colonel Nicholson returned full of confidence to the squalid bamboo hut which he shared with Clipton and two other officers. There he repeated for his own personal satisfaction some of the arguments he had used to convince the Japanese. To him each of them seemed quite conclusive, but the soundest of all in his eyes was this: the total output of a few men unused to manual labour was negligible, while the extra effort that would be made under the supervision of efficient officers was immense. In the interests of the Japanese, therefore, and to ensure that the work was properly done, it was preferable not to deprive the officers of their position of authority, which they would lose if they were detailed to do the same fatigues as the men. He warmed to his subject as he outlined it once again for the benefit of his own officers.

'Well, am I right or wrong?' he asked, turning to Major Hughes. 'You're an industrialist. Do you think we'd get any results on a job like this without a hierarchy of responsible executives?'

As a result of the losses during the tragic campaign, his headquarters staff now consisted of only two officers apart from the M.O. Clipton. He had managed to keep them together ever since Singapore, for he liked to have their opinion and always thought it advisable to put his views before them as a subject for collective discussion before taking any decision. Neither of them was a regular officer. Major Hughes in civilian life was the director of a mining company in Malaya. He had been attached to Colonel Nicholson's battalion and the latter had at once recognized his administrative ability. Captain Reeves in peace time had been a Public Works engineer in India. After joining as a Sapper, he had been separated from his unit during the initial fighting and had been picked up by the Colonel, who had appointed him to his advisory staff. He liked collecting specialists round him. He was no military dunderhead. He was the first to realize that some civilian concerns are occasionally run on methods which the army might do well to adopt, and he never missed an opportunity of adding to his own knowledge. He had an equally high regard for technicians and executives.

'I think you're quite right, sir,' Hughes replied.

'So do I,' said Reeves. 'If you want to build a railway line and a bridge (I believe there's some scheme afoot for a bridge across the river) you can't afford any shoddy, amateur work.'

'I'd forgotten you're a specialist in that sort of thing,' the Colonel mused out loud. 'So you'll understand,' he added, 'why I hope I've driven a little sense into that fellow's thick skull.'

'And besides,' Clipton chipped in, looking closely at his C.O., 'if the common-sense argument doesn't work, there's always the *Manual of Military Law* and the Hague Convention.'

'There's always the Hague Convention,' Colonel Nicholson agreed. 'I'm keeping that up my sleeve for a second interview, if necessary.'

Clipton spoke in this sarcastic, pessimistic tone because he was very doubtful indeed of the value of an appeal to common sense. He had heard various reports on Saito's character at the transit camp where they had halted during their march through the jungle. The Japanese officer, it was said, was sometimes open to reason, when he had not been drinking; but he turned into an utterly vicious brute as soon as he hit the bottle.

Colonel Nicholson had launched his protest on the morning of the first day, which had been set aside for moving the prisoners into the semi-derelict quarters. Saito thought it over, as he had promised. He felt there was something fishy about the whole business, and started to drink in order to clear his brain. He gradually convinced himself that the Colonel had shown intolerable lack of respect in questioning his orders, and his attitude changed imperceptibly from suspicion to cold fury.

Having worked himself up into a paroxysm of rage by sundown, he decided to assert his authority and called everyone out on parade. He too had made up his mind to deliver a speech. From his opening words everyone realized that there were dark clouds gathering over the River Kwai.

'I hate the British . . .'

He had started off with this phrase, which he had then inserted between every other sentence as a sort of punctuation mark. He was fairly fluent in English, having at one time served as military attaché in a British possession, a post which he had been forced to give up because of his chronic drunkenness. His career had petered out into the ignominious position which he now held, a chain-gang warder without a hope of promotion. The hatred he felt for the prisoners was intensified by all the humiliation he had suffered from not having seen any action.

'I hate the British,' Colonel Saito declared. 'You're here, under my personal command, to carry out a job which is necessary for the victory of the Japanese Grand Army. I want to tell you, once and for all, that I won't have my orders questioned in any way. I hate the British. Noncompliance will be punished really severely. Discipline has got to be maintained. If any of you are thinking of putting up a show of resistance, let me remind you that I've got power of life and death over the lot of you. I shan't think twice about exercising that power in order to bring the work with which His Imperial Majesty has entrusted me to a successful conclusion. I hate the British. The death of a few prisoners leaves me cold. The death of the whole lot of you is a mere trifle to a senior officer of the Japanese Grand Army.'

He had climbed on to a table, as General Yamashita had done. Like him, he had seen fit to don a pair of pale-grey gloves and polished riding-boots instead of the canvas shoes which he had worn during the day. His sword, needless to say, hung from his hip, and he kept slapping the hilt, either to lend more weight to his words or to work himself up into the state of rage which he considered suitable to the occasion. He was a grotesque figure. His head wobbled on his shoulders like a puppet's. He was roaring drunk, drunk on European alcohol, on the whisky and brandy left behind at Rangoon and Singapore.

As he listened to these nerve-wracking words, Clipton remembered the advice he had once been given by a friend of his who had lived for some time with the Japanese. 'Never forget, when you deal with them, that these people believe in their divine destiny as part of an unquestionable creed.' All the same, he thought, there was no race on earth that did not entertain more or less the same religious belief in itself. So he tried to find another reason for this display of self-satisfaction. To be quite honest, he had to admit that in Saito's speech there were certain basic principles to which the whole world subscribed, East and West alike. In the course of it he was able to recognize and identify the various influences behind the words which spluttered on the lips of this Jap: racial pride, a mystic belief in authority, the dread of not being taken seriously, a strange sort of inferiority complex which gave him a jaundiced, suspicious outlook on life, as though he was in perpetual fear of being laughed at. Saito had lived abroad. He must have seen how the British sometimes made fun of certain aspects of the Japanese character, and how comic the affectations of a humourless nation were in the eyes of one to whom humour was second nature. But his uncouth manner of speech and uncontrolled gestures could only be attributed to a legacy of brutish violence. Clipton had felt vaguely uneasy when he heard him talking about discipline, but at the sight of him jumping about like a jack-in-the-box he came to the happy conclusion that there was something to be said for the inhabitants of the Western hemisphere: at least they could take their drink like gentlemen.

With their own men looking on, and with the guards crowding round in threatening attitudes so as to emphasize the commandant's fury, the officers listened in silence. They clenched their fists and deliberately assumed expressions of impassive calm, following the example set by Colonel Nicholson, who had given instructions to meet any hostile demonstrations with a show of quiet dignity.

After this preamble designed to stir their imaginations, Saito got down to brass tacks. He became quite calm, almost subdued, and for a moment they thought they were going to hear a little sense.

'Now listen, all of you. You know what sort of job it is that His Imperial Majesty has been good enough to allocate to you British prisoners. We've got to connect the capitals of Siam and Burma so as to enable the Japanese convoys to get across the four hundred miles of jungle in between, and to provide a way through to Bengal for the army which has liberated those two countries from European oppression. Japan needs this railway to continue her victorious advance, to enable her to overrun India and so bring this war to a rapid conclusion. So this work has got to be finished as quickly as possible: in six months. Those are His Imperial Majesty's orders. It's in your interests as well. When the war's over, you'll probably be able to go home under the protection of our army.'

Saito continued in an even calmer tone of voice, as though the alcohol in his blood had all evaporated.

'Now, do you want to know what your specific task is, you men who are in this camp under my command? I'll tell you; that's why I've called you out on parade. You'll only have two short stretches of line to build, to link up with the other sections. But your particular responsibility will be the erection of a bridge across the River Kwai that you can see over there. That's your main task and you ought to feel proud of it, for it's the most important job on the whole line. It's quite pleasant work, requiring skilled men and not just navvies. What's more, you'll have the honour of being ranked among the pioneers of the South-East Asia Co-Prosperity Sphere.'

'Just the sort of pep-talk a Westerner might have given,' was Clipton's immediate reaction.

'The work, of course, will be under the technical direction of a qualified engineer, a Japanese engineer. For purposes of discipline, you will be under me and my subordinates. So there'll be no shortage of administrative staff. For all these reasons, which I've been good enough to explain, I've given orders for the British officers to work side by side with their men. Things being what they are, I can't have a lot of idle mouths to feed. I hope I shall not have to repeat this order. Otherwise . . .'

Saito relapsed without warning into his initial state of frenzy and started raving like a madman.

'Otherwise I'll have to use force. I hate the British. I'll have you all shot, if necessary, rather than give food to slackers. Sickness will not be considered a reason for exemption. A sick man can always make an effort. I'll build that bridge over the prisoners' dead bodies, if I have to. I hate the British. Work will begin at dawn tomorrow. You will parade here on the first blast of the whistle. The officers will fall in as well. They'll form a separate squad on their own, and they'll be expected to get through the same amount of work as the rest of you. Tools will be issued and the Japanese engineer will give you his instructions. That's all I have to say this evening. But I'd like to remind you of General Yamashita's motto: "Be happy in your work." Just bear that in mind.'

Saito left the platform and walked back to his headquarters with long, angry strides. The prisoners dismissed and returned to their lines, with the incoherent speech still ringing unpleasantly in their ears.

'He doesn't seem to have understood, sir. It looks as if we'll have to fall back on the Hague Convention after all,' said Clipton to Colonel Nicholson, who had remained silently wrapped in thought.

'I believe you're right, Clipton,' the Colonel solemnly replied, 'and I'm afraid we're in for a rather stormy passage.'

CHAPTER 4

At one moment Clipton thought that the stormy passage which Colonel Nicholson had forecast was going to be a short one and would end, almost before it had begun, in terrible tragedy. As an M.O., he was the only officer who was not directly involved in the fuss. Already up to his eyes in work looking after the countless casualties due to exposure in the jungle, he was not included in the labour corps; but this only served to intensify his fear when he witnessed the first clash from the building pompously labelled 'Hospital', where he had reported for duty before dawn.

Woken up while it was still dark by the whistles and the shouts of the guards, the men had gone on parade in an ugly mood, still fuddled and not yet fully recovered from the effects of the mosquitoes and the wretched quarters. The officers had fallen in where they were told. Colonel Nicholson had given them definite instructions.

'We must co-operate,' he had said, 'as far as is compatible with our sense of honour. I, too, shall go on parade.'

It was understood that obedience to Saito's orders would go no further than that.

They were kept there for some time, standing to attention in the cold and damp; then, as the sun rose, they saw Colonel Saito appear, surrounded by junior officers and walking in front of the engineer who was to direct the working parties. He seemed to be in a bad mood, but beamed as soon as he saw the British officers lined up behind their commanding officer.

A truck full of tools brought up the rear. While the engineer was supervising the issue of these, Colonel Nicholson stepped one pace forward and asked to speak to Saito. The latter's face clouded over. He said nothing, but the Colonel pretended to regard this silence as a sign of assent and went forward to meet him.

Clipton could not follow his movements, for he had his back to him. But after a bit he came into view, sideways on, and the M.O. saw him wave a little book in the Jap's face, drawing his attention to one particular paragraph – in the *Manual of Military Law*, no doubt. Saito was taken aback. For a moment Clipton thought that a good night's sleep might have put him in a better frame of mind, but he soon saw what a vain hope that was. After the speech he had made the previous evening, even if he was no longer in a bad temper, the vital importance of 'saving face' now dictated his conduct. He went purple with anger. He had expected to have heard the last of this business, and here was the Colonel bringing it up all over again. Such obstinacy drove him all of a sudden into a fit of raving hysteria. Colonel Nicholson was calmly reading, running his finger along each line, unaware of the transformation that had taken place. Clipton, who could see the change in the Jap's expression, almost shouted out loud to warn his C.O. It was too late. With two swift strokes Saito had sent the book flying and slapped the Colonel in the face. He was now standing straight in front of him, bending forward, his eyes popping out of his head, flinging his arms about and yelling abuse in a grotesque mixture of English and Japanese.

In spite of his surprise – for he had not expected this reaction – Colonel Nicholson kept his head. He picked up his book, which had fallen into the mud, stood up again in front of the Jap, over whom he towered head and shoulders, then calmly announced:

'In that case, Colonel Saito, since the Japanese authorities refuse to abide by the laws in force in the rest of the civilized world, we consider ourselves absolved from our duty to obey you. It only remains for me to let you know what orders I've given. My officers will not do manual labour.'

Having said this, he suffered without a murmur a second, still more savage, attack. Saito, who seemed to have gone berserk, leapt at him and, standing on tip-toe, hammered away at the Colonel's face with his fists.

The situation was beginning to get out of hand. Some of the British officers stepped out of the ranks and advanced in a threatening manner. An angry growl rose from the rest of the unit. The Japanese N.C.O.s shouted a word of command, and the soldiers cocked their rifles. Colonel Nicholson asked his officers to fall in again and ordered his men to stay where they were. Blood was pouring from his mouth, but he still preserved his air of authority, which nothing could alter.

Saito, panting hard, stepped back and made as if to seize his revolver; then he seemed to think better of it. He stepped further back and issued an order in an ominously controlled tone of voice. The Japanese guards surrounded the prisoners and motioned them forward. They marched them off in the direction of the river, to the building-yards. There were one or two protests and a slight show of resistance. A few anxious glances of enquiry were fixed on the Colonel, who made it clear he wanted them to obey the order. They eventually disappeared, and the British officers were left alone on the parade ground, facing Colonel Saito.

The Jap started talking again, in measured tones which Clipton found unnerving. His fears were not groundless. Some soldiers went off and came back with the two machine-guns which were kept at the main gate of the camp. They set them up, one on either side of Saito. Clipton's uneasiness turned to cold terror. He had a view of the whole scene through the bamboo partition of his 'hospital'. Behind him, lying in heaps, were a score of wretches covered in open sores. Some had dragged themselves forward and were looking on as well. One of them gave a hoarse cry:

'Doc, they're not going to . . . surely they can't? That yellow baboon wouldn't dare! But the old man's sticking to his guns!'

Clipton thought it was quite likely that the yellow baboon would dare. Most of the officers standing behind the Colonel were of the same opinion. Mass executions had taken place at the fall of Singapore. Saito had obviously ordered the men off the parade ground so that there should be no tiresome witnesses. He was now speaking in English, ordering the officers to pick up the tools and report for duty.

Colonel Nicholson's voice made itself heard again. He repeated his refusal. No one moved. Saito gave another order. Ammunition belts were slipped in and the guns were trained on the squad.

'Doc,' sobbed the soldier standing next to Clipton, 'Doc, the old man won't give in. I'm telling you, he don't understand. We've got to do something.'

These words spurred Clipton into action; until then he had felt half-paralysed. It was quite clear that the 'old man' did not appreciate the situation. He did not for a moment doubt that Saito would stop at nothing. Something had to be done, as the soldier said; the 'old man' had to be told that he could not sacrifice the lives of twenty others out of sheer stubbornness and for the sake of his principles; that neither his honour nor personal dignity would suffer as a result of giving in to brute force, as everyone else in the other camps had done. The words were on the tip of his tongue. He rushed outside, shouting to Saito.

'Wait a moment, Colonel, wait; I'll tell him!'

Colonel Nicholson rebuked him with a frown.

'That'll do, Clipton. There's nothing more to be said. I'm quite aware of what I'm doing.'

In any case Clipton had not succeeded in getting as far as the squad. Two guards had seized him and pinned him down. But his violent outburst seemed to have made Saito think twice before taking action. Clipton yelled at him, in a rapid torrent of words, so that the other Japanese should not understand.

'I warn you, Colonel, I witnessed the whole scene; and so did the forty men in hospital. You won't succeed in inciting us into a general riot or a mass attempt to escape.'

This was the last desperate card in his hand. Even in the eyes of the Japanese authorities Saito would not be able to justify such an unwarranted execution. He could not afford to leave any British witness alive. Following this argument to its logical conclusion, he would either have to massacre everyone on the sick list, including the M.O., or else abandon all thought of revenge.

Clipton felt he had scored a temporary victory. Saito appeared to give the matter a great deal of thought. He was choking with rage and the shame of defeat, but he did not order his men to fire.

In fact he gave no order at all. The men remained where they were, with their machine-guns trained on the squad. They remained like that for a long time, a very long time indeed; for Saito refused to 'lose face' by ordering them to dismiss. They remained there for most of the morning, without daring to move, until the parade ground was completely deserted.

It was hardly a decisive victory, and Clipton could not bear to think of what lay in store for the recalcitrants. But there was some consolation in the thought that he saved them from their immediate fate. The officers were marched off to the prison camp under escort. Colonel Nicholson was dragged away by a couple of gigantic Koreans, who were part of Saito's personal bodyguard. He was taken into the Japanese colonel's office, a small room which opened out on to his sleeping quarters, thus enabling him to pay frequent visits to his store of drink next door. Saito slowly followed his prisoner inside and carefully closed the door behind him. Shortly afterwards Clipton, who was a sensitive man at heart, shuddered as he heard the sound of blows.

CHAPTER 5

After half an hour's beating-up the Colonel was thrown into a hut where there was neither bed nor chair, so that he was forced to lie down in the damp mud on the floor when he felt too tired to stand up. For food he was given a bowl of rice heavily laced with salt, and Saito warned him that he would keep him there until he decided to obey orders.

For a week the only person he saw was a Korean sentry, a brute who looked like a gorilla, who on his own initiative added still more salt to the daily rice-ration. But he forced himself to swallow a few mouthfuls of it and, after gulping down the whole of his meagre ration of water, he would then lie down on the floor and try to disregard his hardships. He was forbidden to leave the cell, which consequently became as offensive as a cess-pit.

At the end of a week Clipton was at last given permission to visit him. Shortly before, the M.O. had been summoned by Saito, whom he found wearing the sullen expression of an anxious tyrant. He could see that he was wavering between anger and fear, which he did his best to mask behind a cool tone of voice.

'I'm not responsible for all this,' he said. 'The bridge across the river has got to be built, and a Japanese officer can't afford to put up with heroics. Try and make him understand that I don't intend to give in. Tell him that, thanks to him, all his officers are having the same treatment. If that's not enough, his men will have to bear the consequences of his pig-headedness as well. So far I haven't interfered with you, or with those on the sick-list. I've been kind enough to let them off all duties. I shall regard this kindness as a sign of weakness, unless he changes his mind.'

He dismissed him with this threat, and Clipton was taken in to see the prisoner. He was at first horrified by the condition to which the C.O. had been reduced and by the physical deterioration which his body had undergone in such a short time. The sound of his voice, which was barely audible, seemed to be a distant, muffled echo of the tone of authority which the M.O. remembered. But this metamorphosis was only superficial. Colonel Nicholson's spirit had not changed at all; and the words he uttered were still the same, although delivered in a different tone. Clipton, who had fully intended to persuade him to give in, now saw there was no chance of that. He soon exhausted all his carefully prepared arguments, then fell silent. The Colonel did not even answer him, but simply said:

'Please let the others know that I'm still quite adamant. On no account will I have an officer from my battalion working like a navvy.'

Clipton left the cell, torn once again between admiration and anger, a prey to painful indecision, unable to make up his mind whether he should worship the C.O. as a hero or regard him as a complete fool. He wondered whether it would not be best to ask God to crown this dangerous lunatic with a martyr's halo and admit him into His kingdom as quickly as possible, so as to prevent him from turning the River Kwai camp into a scene of frightful tragedy. What Saito had said was no more than the truth. The treatment being meted out to the other officers was only one degree less inhuman, while the men were made regular targets for the brutality of the guards. As he walked away, Clipton thought of the danger that threatened his patients.

Saito must have been waiting for him, for he rushed up, his eyes betraying genuine anxiety as he enquired:

'Well?'

He was quite sober, and looked rather depressed. Clipton tried to judge how far the Colonel's attitude was likely to make the Jap 'lose face', then pulled himself together and decided to take a firm line.

'Well, it's like this. Colonel Nicholson won't give in to force; nor will his officers. And in view of the way he's being treated, I could not advise him to do so.'

He protested against the conditions of the prisoners in detention, quoting the Hague Convention as the Colonel had done, arguing from his professional point of view as a doctor and finally from the simple humanitarian point of view, even going so far as to declare that such monstrous treatment was tantamount to murder. He expected a violent reaction, but none came. Saito merely muttered that the Colonel was to blame for the whole business, and then abruptly walked off. At that moment Clipton felt inclined to believe that he was really not such a bad man at heart, and that his actions were all due to fear of one kind or another: fear of his superiors, who were probably badgering him about the bridge, and fear of his subordinates, in whose eyes he was 'losing face' through his obvious inability to exact obedience.

His natural inclination to generalize led Clipton to identify this combination of two fears, the fear of superiors and of subordinates respectively, as the main source of all human calamities. As he put this idea into words, he felt that somewhere or other he had once come across this very psychological maxim. This gave him a certain sense of satisfaction, which helped to allay his anxiety. He developed this train of thought a little further, but was brought to a stop on the threshold of the hospital by the realization that every calamity, even the worst in the world, could be attributed to men who had neither superiors nor subordinates.

Saito must have thought the matter over. His treatment of the prisoner was more lenient during the following week, at the end of which he went to see him and asked if he had finally decided to behave like a gentleman. He had arrived in a reasonable frame of mind, intending to appeal to the Colonel's common sense, but faced with the latter's refusal to discuss a question which was already cut-and-dried he again lost his temper and worked himself up into a state of hysterical frenzy in which he could hardly be taken for a civilized human being. The Colonel was again beaten up, and the gorilla-like Korean received strict orders for the harsh régime of the first few days to be resumed. Saito even struck the guard as well. He was no longer responsible for his actions when seized by these fits, and he accused the man of being too soft hearted. He rushed about the cell like a raving lunatic, brandishing a pistol and threatening to use it on the guard as well as the prisoner in order to enforce a little discipline.

Clipton, who once more tried to intervene, also came in for a few blows, and his hospital was cleared of all patients who were still capable of standing upright. They were forced to drag themselves to the building-yards and shift heavy loads; otherwise they would have been beaten to death. For several days terror reigned over the River Kwai camp. Colonel Nicholson's answer to his ill-treatment was a stubborn, haughty silence.

Saito's personality seemed to switch from that of a Mister Hyde, capable of every kind of atrocity, to a comparatively humane Doctor Jekyll. Once the period of violence was over, a régime of extraordinary leniency succeeded it. Colonel Nicholson was allowed to draw not only full rations but also a supplementary scale normally earmarked for the sick list.

Clipton was given permission to see him and attend to him, and Saito even warned him that he held him personally responsible for the Colonel's health.

One evening Saito had the prisoner brought into his room and then ordered the escort to dismiss. Alone with him, he asked him to sit down and drew from his stores a tin of American corned beef, some cigarettes and a bottle of liqueur whisky. He told him that, as a soldier, he felt a deep admiration for his attitude, but war was war even though neither of them was responsible for it. Surely he could understand that he, Saito, was obliged to obey the orders of his superior officers? Now these orders stated that the bridge across the River Kwai was to be built as quickly as possible. He was therefore compelled to make use of all the personnel available. The Colonel refused the corned beef, the cigarettes and the whisky but listened with interest to what he had to say. He calmly replied that Saito had not the foggiest idea of how to tackle a work of such importance.

He had reverted to his original arguments. It looked as though the squabble was likely to go on for ever. No one on earth could have told whether Saito was going to discuss the matter sensibly or give vent to another hysterical outburst. He was silent for some time, while the question no doubt was being debated on some supernatural plane unknown to mere mortals. The Colonel took advantage of this and said:

'May I ask you, Colonel Saito, if you're satisfied with the work so far?'

The insidious question might well have tipped the scales on the side of hysteria, for the work was progressing badly – which was one of Colonel Saito's major worries, since his career was at stake as much as his reputation. But this was not the cue for Mister Hyde. He looked foolish, hung his head and muttered some inaudible reply. Then he put a full glass of whisky into the prisoner's hand, poured a large one out for himself and said:

'Look, Colonel Nicholson, I don't think you've really understood. There's no need for us to be at loggerheads. When I said all the officers were to work, naturally I never meant you, the Commanding Officer. My orders only applied to the others . . .'

'Not one of my officers will work,' said the Colonel, putting his glass back on the table.

Saito suppressed a gesture of annoyance and concentrated on keeping calm.

'I've been thinking the matter over during the last few days,' he went on. 'I think I could put majors and above on administrative duties. Only the junior officers would then have to lend a hand . . .'

'None of the officers will do any manual labour,' said Colonel Nicholson. 'An officer must be in command of his men.'

At this Saito could control himself no longer. But when the Colonel returned to his cell, having successfully stuck to his guns in spite of bribes, threats, blows and even entreaties, he felt that the situation was well in hand and that it would not be long before the enemy capitulated.

CHAPTER 6

The work was at a standstill. The Colonel had touched Saito on a raw spot when he asked how the task was progressing, and he was proved right in his forecast that the Japanese would eventually have to yield through sheer necessity.

Three weeks had gone by, and not only was the bridge not yet under way, but the preliminary preparations had been handled so ingeniously by the prisoners that it would take considerable time to repair all the damage that had been done.

Infuriated by the treatment meted out to the C.O., whose courage and endurance they had admired, fretting under the torrent of curses and blows which the sentries rained down on them, indignant at being employed like slaves on work which was useful to the enemy, feeling all at sea now that they were separated from their officers and no longer heard the familiar words of command, the British soldiers competed with each other to see who could be the slackest or, better still, who could commit the most elementary blunders under an ostentatious show of keenness.

There was no punishment sufficently severe to curb their insidious activities, and the little Japanese engineer was sometimes reduced to tears of desperation. The guards were too thin on the ground to superintend all of them, and too stupid to spot the culprits. The lay-out of the two stretches of line had had to be started all over again at least twenty times. Both the straight sections and the curves, which had been accurately computed and pegged out by the engineer, would relapse as soon as his back was turned into a maze of disconnected lines diverging at sharp angles, at which he would afterwards cry out in despair. The two bits on either side of the river, which the bridge was eventually meant to connect, were palpably at a different level and never ended up directly opposite each other. One of the squads would then start digging furiously and succeed in producing a sort of crater which dipped far lower than the level required, while the fool of a guard would gaze with delight at the sight of such feverish activity. When the engineer turned up he would lose his temper, and beat guards and prisoners indiscriminately. The former, realizing they had been fooled once again, would take their revenge; but the harm had been done, and it took several hours or several days to repair it.

One squad had been ordered to cut down some trees as timber for the bridge. They would make a careful selection and bring back the most twisted and brittle ones they could find; or else devote considerable effort to felling a giant tree, which would subsequently tumble into the river and be lost. Or again, they would choose trunks which were eaten away inside by insects and collapsed under the slightest weight.

Saito, who carried out a daily inspection, gave vent to his fury in increasingly stormy outbursts of temper. He dispensed curses, threats and blows, swearing even at the engineer, who would answer back with the retort that the fatigue parties were absolutely useless. At which he would scream and swear louder than ever and try to think of a new form of punishment to put an end to this sullen resistance. He made the prisoners suffer more than if he had been an embittered jailer left to his own devices and scared stiff of being sacked for inefficiency. Those who were caught red-handed in an act of wilful damage or sabotage were tied to trees, beaten with thorn-branches and left out in the open for hours, bleeding and naked, exposed to the ants and the tropical sun. Clipton saw the victims as they came back in the evening; they were carried in by their pals, shaking with fever, their backs stripped raw. He was not even allowed to keep them on the sick list for long. Saito did not forget who they were. As soon as they were capable of standing, he sent them back to work and ordered the guards to keep a special eye on them.

The moral fibre shown by these 'bad-hats' was so moving that Clipton sometimes found himself in tears. He was amazed to see them take such punishment. There was always at least one of them who, when he was alone with him, would find the strength to sit up with a cheerful wink and whisper a few words in a language that was gradually gaining currency among all the prisoners in Burma and Siam:

'The f——ing bridge still isn't built, Doc. The f——ing Emperor's f——ing railway still hasn't got across the f——ing river in this f——ing country. The f——ing C.O.'s right; he knows what he's talking about. If you see him, tell him we're all for him. The f——ing baboon hasn't heard the last of the f——ing British army.'

The most brutal forms of punishment had achieved no result whatever. The men had got used to them. The example set by Colonel Nicholson was a stimulant even stronger than the beer and whisky which they no longer had to drink. If one of them was ever punished beyond the limits of human endurance and could only go on working at the risk of his life, there was always another ready to relieve him. This was a recognized routine.

In Clipton's opinion, they were even more to be praised for refusing to be taken in by the mealy-mouthed promises which Saito made during those fits of depression when he realized he had exhausted every known form of torture and was incapable of inventing others.

One day he made them parade outside his office, having ordered them to stop work earlier than usual – so as not to overtire them, he explained. He issued them all with rice-cakes and fruit bought from the Siamese peasants in the nearest village – a gift from the Japanese army to spur them on to greater efforts. He abandoned all sense of shame and positively grovelled in front of them. He prided himself, he told them, on being one of them, just an ordinary sort of chap, whose only wish was to do his duty with as little fuss as possible. Their officers, he pointed out, were making them all work twice as hard by refusing to work themselves. So he fully understood how resentful they must feel, and did not hold it against them. On the contrary, in order to show his sympathy for them, he had on his own authority reduced the individual quota of work on the embankment. The engineer had fixed this as one and a half cubic yards of earth per man; well, he, Saito, had decided to make it one cubic yard. He was doing this because he felt sorry for them in their present condition, for which he himself was not to blame. He hoped that, in view of this kindly gesture, they would co-operate with him and speed up this easy work, which would help to bring the damn war to an end.

He was almost pleading with them by the time he had finished, but his prayers and entreaties had no more effect than his curses and blows. Next day the quota was fulfilled. Each man consciously dug up and carted off his cubic yard of earth; some even more. But the distance they carried it was an insult to the meanest intelligence.

Saito was the first to yield. He was at the end of his tether; the prisoners' sustained resistance had reduced him to a pitiful condition. He spent the days preceding his final downfall prowling about the camp with the same desperate look in his eye as a beast at bay. He even went so far as to ask the young subalterns to choose for themselves what work they wanted to do, promising them special privileges and extra rations. But they all stood firm and, since a high-level Japanese inspection was imminent, he resigned himself to ignominious surrender.

He prepared to make one last desperate bid to 'save face' and cover up his defeat, but this pathetic attempt did not even deceive his own men. The 7th of December 1942 being the anniversary of Japan's entry into the war, he announced that in honour of the occasion he had undertaken to grant a general amnesty. He had an interview with the Colonel and told him he had adopted a measure of extreme benevolence: all officers would henceforth be exempt from manual labour. In return for this he trusted they would devote themselves to supervising their men's activity so as to ensure the maximum efficiency.

Colonel Nicholson replied that he would see what could be done. Now that the situation was established on a proper constitutional basis there was no longer any reason for trying to oppose the enemy programme. As in every civilized army, the officers — it went without saying — would be responsible for the conduct of their men.

This was total surrender on the part of the Japanese. That evening the victory was celebrated in the British camp by a sing-song, cheers and an extra rice-ration, which had been issued with the greatest reluctance on Saito's orders, as a further gesture of goodwill. That same evening the Japanese colonel retired earlier than usual, wept for his loss of face and drowned his sorrows in a bout of solitary drinking which lasted well into the night, until he slumped dead-drunk on to his bed – a state which he hardly ever managed to reach except in unusual circumstances, for he had an amazingly strong head and could normally stand the most barbaric mixtures.

CHAPTER 7

Colonel Nicholson, accompanied by his usual advisers, Major Hughes and Captain Reeves, went down to the river along the railway embankment on which the prisoners were at work.

He walked slowly. He was in no hurry. Immediately after his release he had scored a second victory by obtaining four days' off duty for his officers and himself by way of compensation for their unjust punishment. Saito had clenched his fists at the thought of this further delay, but had given in. He had even issued orders for the prisoners to be decently treated, and had bashed in the face of one of his own soldiers whom he had caught smiling sarcastically.

If Colonel Nicholson had applied for four days' exemption from duty, it was not only to recover his strength; it was also to give him time to think, to sum up the situation, to hold discussions with his staff and draw up a plan of action, steps which every conscientious commander should take instead of rushing bald-headed at the easiest solution – a thing he hated doing more than anything else in the world.

It did not take long to spot the outrageous mistakes intentionally committed by his men. Hughes and Reeves could not suppress a cry of admiration when they saw the astonishing results of this activity.

'That's a fine embankment for a railway line!' said Hughes. 'I suggest you put the culprits up for a decoration, sir. Just think of an ammunition train trundling over that lot!'

The Colonel did not even smile.

'A splendid job, sir,' echoed Captain Reeves, the ex-Public Works engineer. 'No one in his senses could possibly imagine they intend to run a railway over this switchback. I'd sooner face the Japanese army all over again than take a trip along this line.'

The Colonel looked as solemn as ever and asked:

'In your opinion, Reeves, your opinion as a technician, could this be put to any use at all?'

'I don't think so, sir,' Reeves answered after a moment's reflection. 'They'd do better to abandon this mess completely and build another line a little further up.'

Colonel Nicholson looked more and more preoccupied. He nodded his head and moved on in silence. He wanted to see the whole of the building-yards before forming an opinion.

He reached the river. A squad of about fifty men, stark naked except for the triangle of cloth which the Japanese called 'working-kit', were milling about on the stretch under construction. A guard, with rifle slung, marched up and down in front of them. Some of the squad were engaged on digging a little further away, while the remainder were busy collecting the earth on bamboo carriers and spreading it out on either side of a line marked out with white pegs. This had originally run at right-angles to the bank, but the insidious genius of the prisoners had succeeded in shifting it so that it was now almost parallel to the river. The Japanese engineer was not on the spot. He could be seen on the opposite bank gesticulating in the middle of another squad, who were taken across the river every morning on rafts. He could also be heard.

'Who set out that line of pegs?' the Colonel asked, coming to a standstill.

'He did, sir,' said the British corporal, springing to attention and pointing to the engineer. 'He set it out, but I helped him a little myself. I made a slight improvement as soon as he left. He and I don't always see eye to eye, sir.'

And, since the sentry was not looking, he gave a conspiratorial wink. Colonel Nicholson did not acknowledge this secret message, but remained deep in thought.

'I see,' he said in a voice as cold as ice.

He moved on without further comment and stopped in front of another corporal. This one, with the help of a few men, was devoting considerable effort to clearing the ground of a number of large roots by heaving them up to the top of a slope instead of pitching them down the side of the bank, while another Japanese guard blankly looked on.

'How many are at work in this squad today?' the Colonel asked in ringing tones.

The guard gaped at him, wondering if it was in order for the Colonel to speak like this to the prisoners; but his voice held such a note of authority that he did not dare move. The corporal at once sprang to attention and began to stammer a reply.

'Twenty or twenty-five, sir, I'm not quite sure. One man went sick as soon as we arrived. He suddenly felt dizzy – I can't think why, sir, for he was perfectly all right at reveille. Three or four of the lads were needed, of course, to carry him to hospital, sir, as he couldn't walk by himself. They haven't come back yet. He was the biggest and the toughest chap in the squad, sir. As it is, we shan't be able to get through our quota today. There seems to be a curse on this railway.'

'A corporal,' said the Colonel, 'ought to know exactly how many men he has under him. What is the quota, anyway?'

'A cubic yard of earth per man per day, sir, to be dug and then carted away. But with these damn roots and all, sir, it looks as if it's going to be too much for us.'

'I see,' said the Colonel as coldly as ever.

He moved off, muttering under his breath through clenched teeth. Hughes and Reeves followed behind him.

They went to the top of a rise, from which they could see the river and the whole of the surrounding country. At that point the Kwai was over a hundred yards wide, with both banks high above the level of the water. The Colonel studied the ground from every angle, then turned to his two subordinates. What he had to say was obvious, but he said it in a voice which had recovered all its former tone of authority.

'These people, the Japanese, have only just emerged from a state of barbarism, and prematurely at that. They've tried to copy our methods, but they don't understand them. Take away their model, and they're lost. They can't even do the job they've taken on here in this valley, yet it doesn't need much intelligence. They don't realize they'd save time by planning in advance instead of rushing bald-headed at the thing. What do you think, Reeves? Railways and bridges are in your line, aren't they?'

'You're quite right, sir,' said the Captain, instinctively warming to his subject. 'I've tackled at least a dozen jobs like this in India. With the material available in the jungle and the personnel that we've got here, a qualified engineer could build this bridge in under six months. There are times, I'm afraid, when their incompetence simply makes my blood boil.'

'I agree,' said Hughes. 'I can't help it, but I sometimes feel like screaming at the sight of such inefficiency. You'd think it was quite simple to——'

'What about me?' the Colonel broke in. 'Do you think I'm pleased with this scandalous state of affairs? I'm absolutely appalled by what I've seen this morning.'

'Well anyway, sir,' laughed Captain Reeves, 'I don't think we need worry about the invasion of India if this is the line they say they're going to use. The bridge across the Kwai is not quite ready to take the weight of their trains!'

Colonel Nicholson was deep in thought, but he kept his blue eyes firmly fixed on his two companions.

'Gentlemen,' he said, 'I can see we'll have to take a very firm line if we want to regain control of the men. Through these savages they've fallen into idle, slipshod habits unbecoming to members of His Majesty's forces. We'll have to be patient with them and handle them carefully, for they can't be held directly responsible for the present state of affairs. What they need is discipline, and they haven't had it. It's no good using violence instead. You've only got to look at the result – a lot of disconnected activity, but not a single positive achievement. These orientals have shown how incompetent they are, when it comes to man-management.'

There was a moment's silence while the two officers wondered what he really meant by these remarks. But they were quite clear; there was nothing to read between the lines. The Colonel had spoken in his usual forthright manner. He let his words sink in and then went on:

'I must ask you, therefore – and I'll ask all the other officers as well – to show as much consideration as possible at first. But on no account must our patience be stretched to the point of weakness, or else we'll fall to the level of these brutes. I shall also speak to the men myself. As from today we've got to put a stop to this disgraceful inefficiency. We can't have the men going absent on the slightest provocation. The N.C.O.s must answer any question put to them promptly and clearly. I don't think I need remind you of the need for firm action at the first sign of sabotage or malingering. A railway line is meant to run horizontally and not twist about like a switchback, as you so rightly observed, Reeves . . .'

PART 2

CHAPTER 1

In Calcutta Colonel Green, commanding Force 316, was studying a report which had just come in by the usual roundabout route, a report embellished with the marginal comments of half a dozen military and paramilitary clandestine services. Force 316 (better known as 'The Plastic and Destructions Co., Ltd.') had not yet reached the important position that it later held in the Far East, but it was already taking an active, passionate and exclusive interest in Japanese war establishment in the occupied countries of Malaya, Burma, Siam and China. What it lacked in material resources, it tried to make up for by the boldness and dash of its agents.

'Well, it's the first time I've ever known them all to agree,' Colonel Green muttered. 'We ought to do something about it.'

The first part of his remark referred to the various clandestine services associated with Force 316, each working in a separate watertight compartment and pursuing an individual policy of its own, with the result that they often came to widely different conclusions. This used to infuriate Colonel Green, who was responsible for planning operations from all the intelligence available. 'Ops' was the preserve of Force 316; Colonel Green was not interested in theoretical discussion except in so far as it affected his own line of action. His staff were quite familiar with his views on the matter since he expressed them at least once a day. A large part of his time was spent in trying to sift the truth from these reports, taking into account not only the information itself but also the psychological make-up of the various sources (optimism or pessimism, tendency to exaggerate the facts or, on the other hand, complete inability to interpret them).

Colonel Green had a special grievance against the genuine, the great, the famous, the one and only Intelligence Service, which regarded itself as an exclusively intellectual body and systematically refused to co-operate with the operational staff. Instead, it locked itself up in its own ivory tower, never let its precious documents be seen by anyone who could have made use of them, on the pretext that they were too secret, and carefully filed them away in a safe. There they remained for years, until they were no longer of use to anyone – or, to be more precise, until long after the end of the war, when one of the big-wigs felt an urge to write his memoirs before dying, to leave something to posterity and disclose to an astonished nation how clever the Service had been on one particular date and on one particular occasion, when it ascertained every detail of the enemy plan of campaign: the place and time of the impending attack had been accurately determined in advance. The forecast was a hundred per cent correct, since the enemy had indeed struck in the manner foretold, and with the success that had likewise been foreseen.

That at least was how it appeared, in a rather exaggerated light perhaps, to Colonel Green, who disagreed with the theory of art for art's sake being applied to intelligence matters. He muttered some inaudible remark as he thought of some of the previous ventures; then, in view of the miraculous unanimous agreement on the present scheme, it was almost with disappointment that he felt he had to admit that for once the service had done something useful. He consoled himself with the thought – not entirely a fair one – that the information contained in the report had been known to everyone in India for years. Finally he went through it again and made a mental summary of it, with the idea of taking action on it.

'The Burma-Siam railway is now under construction. Sixty thousand Allied prisoners, drafted by the Japanese into a labour corps, are being employed on it and are working under ghastly conditions. In spite of appalling losses, it is calculated that the task, which is of considerable importance to the enemy, will be completed in a few months. Herewith a rough sketch-map. It shows several river-crossings by means of wooden bridges ...'

At this point in his summary Colonel Green felt in good form again and almost grinned with pleasure. He went on:

'The Siamese people are extremely discontented with the "liberators", who have requisitioned all the rice and whose troops behave as though they were in occupied territory. The peasants in the railway area in particular are showing signs of unrest. Several senior officers of the Siamese army, and even some members of the royal family, have recently established contact with the Allies and are prepared to launch an anti-Japanese underground movement, for which countless peasants have volunteered. They request both weapons and instructors.

'No doubt about it,' Colonel Green decided, 'I'll have to send a team into the railway area.'

Having made his decision, he pondered for some time on the various qualities that would be required by the leader of such an expedition. After ruling out a number of possible candidates, he called for Major Shears, an ex-cavalry officer who had been transferred to Force 316 at the time that special unit had been formed and was, in fact, one of its founder-members. This private army had only seen the light of day thanks to the persistent efforts of a few individualists and the reluctant support of a handful of military experts. Shears had only just arrived from Europe, where he had successfully completed several tricky missions, when he had his lengthy interview with Colonel Green. The Colonel gave him all the information available and outlined the general purpose of his mission.

'You'll take only a few stores in with you,' he said, 'the rest will be dropped to you as and when you need them. About the actual operation, you'll be able to see for yourself on the spot, but don't be in too much of a hurry. I think it'll be best to wait till the railway's finished and deliver a single powerful blow rather than risk giving the whole show away by a series of minor attacks.'

There was no need to specify what form the 'operation' would take or what type of stores would be used. The *raison d'être* of 'The Plastic and Destructions Co., Ltd.' made a fuller explanation superfluous.

Meanwhile, Shears was to get in touch with the Siamese, make sure of their good intentions and loyalty, then start training the partisans.

'As I see it, you'll need to be a team of three,' said Colonel Green, 'for the moment at any rate. How does that strike you?'

'That seems quite reasonable, sir,' Shears agreed. 'We need at least a nucleus of three Europeans. Any more, and we might present too big a target.'

'That's settled, then. Who do you plan to take in with you?'

'I suggest Warden, sir.'

'Captain Warden? Professor Warden? You certainly don't believe in half-measures, Shears. With you, that'll make two of our best agents.'

'I understood it was an important mission, sir,' was Shear's non-committal reply.

'It is. It's a very important mission, from the political as well as the operational point of view.'

'Warden's just the man for that, sir. An ex-professor of Oriental languages. He speaks Siamese and will be able to get on with the natives. He's a level-headed sort of chap and doesn't get the wind up – at least not more than most of us.'

'You can have Warden. Now what about the third?'

'I'll think it over, sir. Probably one of the youngsters who've been through the course. I've seen several who look quite promising. I'll let you know tomorrow.'

Force 316 had established a school in Calcutta where the young volunteers were trained.

'Right. Here's the map. I've marked the possible D.Z.s and hide-outs where the Siamese say you'll be able to lie up without any risk of being discovered. We've already done the air reconnaissance.'

Shears bent over the map and the aerial photographs. He carefully studied the area which Force 316 had chosen as his theatre of unorthodox activity in the wilds of Siam. He felt the thrill which seized him each time he embarked on a new expedition into unknown territory. There was something exciting about any Force 316 mission, but this time the attraction was intensified by the wild nature of the jungle-clad mountains inhabited by lawless tribes of hunters.

'There seem to be several suitable spots,' Colonel Green went on. 'For instance, this isolated little hamlet not far from the Burmese border, about two or three days' march from the railway, apparently. According to the sketch-map, the railway there crosses a river – the River Kwai, if the map's right. The bridge there will probably be one of the longest on the line.'

Shears smiled, as his C.O. had done, at the thought of the number of bridges across the river.

'I'll have to study the question more closely, of course; but for the moment, sir, I should think that place would make a perfect H.Q.'

'Right. Now all we've got to do is arrange for the drop. That'll be in three or four weeks, I should think, if the Siamese agree. Ever done a jump?'

'Never, sir. Parachuting wasn't included in the course until after I'd left Europe. I don't think Warden has, either.'

'Hang on a moment. I'll see if the experts can put you through a few training jumps.'

Colonel Green seized the telephone, asked for a certain R.A.F. office and told them what he wanted. He listened for some time and did not seem at all pleased with what he heard. Shears, who kept his eyes on him throughout the conversation, could see how his mood changed.

'That's really your considered opinion, then?' Colonel Green asked.

He frowned as he listened to the reply, then hung up the receiver. After a moment's hesitation, he finally made up his mind and said:

'Do you want to know the experts' opinion? It's this. They just said: "If you absolutely insist on your chaps doing some training jumps, we'll make the necessary arrangements. But we honestly wouldn't advise it – not unless they can spare six months for a proper course. Our experience of missions dropping into this sort of country can be summed up as follows: if they do only one jump, you know, there's a fifty per cent chance of an injury. Two jumps, it's eighty per cent. The third time, it's dead certain they won't get off scot free. You see? It's not a question of training, but the law of averages. The wisest thing would be for them to do just the one jump – and hope for the best." Well, that's what they said. Now it's up to you.'

'One of the great advantages of the modern army, sir,' Shears calmly replied, 'is that there are experts to solve all the problems for us. It's no good thinking that we know better than them. What they've said obviously shows common sense as well. I'm sure it will appeal to Warden's logical mind; he's bound to agree with it. We'll take the advice and do the one jump – and hope for the best.'

CHAPTER 2

'You don't look altogether happy, Reeves,' said Colonel Nicholson to the R.E. captain, whose face showed every sign of suppressed anger. 'What's wrong?'

'What's wrong! We simply can't go on like this, sir! I tell you, it's hopeless! I'd already decided to approach you on the subject today. And here's Major Hughes who'll back me up.'

'What's wrong?' the Colonel repeated with a frown.

'I agree with Reeves completely, sir,' said Hughes, who had left the building-yards to join the C.O. 'I also wanted to tell you this simply can't go on.'

'But what?'

'It's utter chaos, sir. Never in the whole of my career have I seen such carelessness and lack of system. We're getting nowhere like this, just marking time. Everyone gives contradictory orders. These fellows, the Japs, haven't the vaguest idea of man-management. If they insist on interfering with the work, there's not a hope of ever getting it done.'

The situation had certainly improved since the British officers had been put in charge of the squads, but although there were noticeable signs of progress in the quality as well as the quantity of the work, it was quite clear that things were far from perfect.

'Explain yourselves. You first, Reeves.'

'Sir,' said the captain, taking a sheet of paper out of his pocket, 'I've only made a note of the more glaring blunders; otherwise the list would go on for ever.'

'Go ahead. I'm here to listen to any reasonable complaint, and to consider any suggestion. I can see there's something wrong. It's up to you to tell me what.'

'Well, in the first place, sir, it's utter folly to build the bridge on this bit of ground.'

'Why?'

'It's a quagmire, sir. Who ever heard of a railway bridge being built on shifting soil? Only savages like these would ever think of it. I'm willing to bet, sir, that the bridge will collapse the first time a train goes over it.'

'That's rather serious, Reeves,' said the Colonel, keeping his light blue eyes fixed on the junior officer.

'Very serious, sir. And I've tried to point that out to the Japanese engineer. Engineer indeed! God, what a hopeless bungler! You can't get any sense from a chap who's never even heard of soil resistance, who gapes when you mention pressure tables and who can't even talk the King's English. Yet I've been pretty patient, sir. I've tried everything to make him understand. I even arranged a little demonstration for him, in the hope that he couldn't fail to believe what he saw with his own eyes. Just a waste of time. He still insists on building his bridge in this swamp.'

'A demonstration, Reeves?' asked Colonel Nicholson, whose interest was always aroused at the sound of this word.

'Quite a simple one, sir. A child could have understood it. You see that pile in the water, near the bank? I put that in myself with a sledgehammer. Well, it's gone quite far down already, but it hasn't yet found solid bottom. It's still sinking, sir, just as all the other piles will sink under the weight of a train, I'm sure of it. What we ought to do is lay down a concrete foundation, but we haven't got the materials.'

The Colonel gazed with interest at the pile and asked Reeves if he could repeat the demonstration for his benefit. Reeves gave the necessary orders. Some of the prisoners gathered round and began to heave on a rope. A heavy weight, slung from a scaffolding, dropped once or twice on to the top of the pile, which at once sank visibly deeper.

'You see, sir,' Reeves shouted triumphantly. 'We could go on hammering away till doomsday, it would just go on sinking. And soon it'll be under water.'

'I see,' said the Colonel. 'How far down is it at the moment?'

Reeves gave him the exact figure, which he had noted and added that the tallest trees in the jungle wouldn't be long enough to reach solid bottom.

'Right,' said the Colonel with every sign of satisfaction. 'That's quite clear. As you say, even a child could understand. That's the sort of demonstration I like. The engineer wasn't impressed? Well, I am – and that's the main thing, I assure you. Now what solution do you suggest?'

'Shift the whole bridge, sir. I think there's a good spot about a mile away. Of course, I'd have to check on it ——'

'You must do so then,' the Colonel calmly replied, 'and give me the facts and figures for me to put before them.'

He made a note of this first point and asked:

'Anything else, Reeves?'

'The material they're using on the bridge, sir. Cutting down these trees! That was a fine thing our men started, wasn't it? But at least they knew what they were doing. Well, this hopeless engineer isn't doing much better, sir. He just lets any old thing be cut down, without bothering if the wood's hard or soft, rigid or flexible, or whether it will stand up to any stress laid on it. It's an absolute disgrace, sir.'

Colonel Nicholson made a second entry on the bit of paper which served as a note-book.

'What else, Reeves?'

'I've kept this for the last, sir, because I think it's the most important. You can see for yourself: the river's well over a hundred yards across. It's got high banks. The platform will be over a hundred feet above the water – that's quite a proposition, isn't it? Not child's play. Well, I've asked the engineer several times to show me his working-plans. He shook his head in the usual way, as they all do when they don't know what to say. Well, believe it or not, sir, there isn't a plan! He hasn't made one! And he doesn't intend to! Didn't seem to know what it was all about! So what it boils down to is this: he thinks building a bridge is as easy as throwing a plank across a ditch – some bits of wood here and there, and a few piles underneath! It'll never stand up, sir. I'm absolutely ashamed to be taking part in such sabotage.'

His indignation was so genuine that Colonel Nicholson felt obliged to offer a few words of consolation.

'Don't worry, Reeves. It's a good thing you've got it off your chest. I can quite understand how you feel about it. Everyone has his pride, after all.'

'Exactly, sir. Frankly, I'd rather have another dose of punishment than help to give birth to this monstrosity.'

'I agree with you entirely,' said the Colonel, making a note of this last point. 'It's obviously rather serious, all this, and we can't let things go on as they are. I'll take the necessary steps, I promise you. Your turn now, Hughes.'

Major Hughes was as worked up as his colleague. This was a strange state for him to be in, for by nature he was cool and collected.

'Sir, we'll never get any discipline in the building-yards, or any serious work out of the men, so long as the Japanese guards interfere with our orders – just look at them, sir, absolute oafs. Only this morning I'd split up the squads working on the embankment into three sections each: one for digging, another for carting off the earth, and the third for spreading it and levelling the mound. I'd taken the trouble to arrange the relative strength of each section myself and to organize the various tasks so as to synchronize them properly.'

'I see,' said the Colonel, his interest once more roused. 'A sort of specialization system?'

'Exactly, sir. After all, I do know something about earth-works. I was a works manager before being a director. I've dug wells over three hundred feet deep. Well, anyway, this morning my teams began working according to this system. Everything was going fine. They were well ahead of the schedule laid down by the Japs. Splendid! Then up comes one of these apes and starts chucking his weight about, shrieking and yelling for the three sections to re-form as one. Easier to keep an eye on them, I suppose – the idiot! What's the result? A complete mess-up, utter chaos. They're all on top of each other and can't get a move on. It's enough to make you sick, sir. Just look at them.'

'You're right, I can see that,' Colonel Nicholson agreed after carefully watching the men at work. 'I'd already noticed the lack of organization.'

'But that's not all, sir. These idiots have fixed a quota of a cubic yard of earth per man, without realizing that our chaps under proper supervision could do much more. Between you and me, sir, it's a soft job. When they think each man has dug, shifted and spread his cubic yard, they call it a day. That's why I say they're idiots. If there are still a few clods of earth left to be carted away so as to connect two isolated stretches, do you think they ask for an extra effort? Not a bit of it! They simply order the squad to down tools. In that case, how can I order them to carry on? What would the men think of me if I did?'

'So you think it's a really poor show?' said Colonel Nicholson.

'It's an absolutely rotten show, sir,' Reeves broke in. 'In India, where the climate's just as bad as this, and the ground's much harder, the coolies get through one and a half cubic yards quite easily.'

'That's what I thought,' the Colonel murmured. 'I was once in charge of a job like this myself, building a road in Africa. My men used to work much faster than this. One thing's quite clear,' he concluded decisively, 'we can't go on like this. You were quite right to let me know about it.'

He went through his notes again and, after a moment's reflection, turned once more to his two officers:

'Now listen, both of you. Do you know what I think of all this? Practically the whole trouble can be traced back to one simple cause: complete lack of organization. I'm the first to blame, I know; I should have seen to it in the first place. That's the worst of rushing things, you always waste time in the end. Organization, plain and simple – that's what we need more than anything else.'

'You've said it, sir,' Hughes agreed. 'A job like this is doomed to failure if it's not properly worked out in advance.'

'I think we'd better call a conference,' said Colonel Nicholson. 'I should have thought of that before. Between the Japanese and us. A discussion between both sides is what we need to determine each man's duties and responsibilities. That's it, a conference. I'll go and have a word with Saito right away.'

CHAPTER 3

The conference was held a few days later. Saito did not understand what it was all about, but he had agreed to be present, not daring to ask for an explanation for fear of losing face by appearing ignorant of the customs of a civilization which he hated but which impressed him in spite of himself.

Colonel Nicholson had drafted an agenda, and waited with his officers in the long hut which served as a dining-room. Saito arrived accompanied by his engineer, some of his bodyguard and three captains, whom he had brought along to swell the numbers in his escort although they could not speak a word of English. The British officers stood up and snapped to attention. The Colonel gave a regimental salute. Saito looked quite startled. He had arrived with the intention of asserting his authority, and here he was, already visibly conscious of his inferiority when faced with this ritual performed with a traditional and majestic sense of propriety.

There was quite a long silence, during which Colonel Nicholson shot a glance of enquiry at the Jap commandant, whom he naturally expected to take the chair. The conference could not be held without a chairman. Out of common courtesy the Colonel felt obliged to wait for the other to declare the meeting open. But Saito felt more and more ill at ease and could hardly bear the idea of being the focal point of this gathering. The manners and customs of the civilized world made him feel small. But he could not allow his subordinates to see that he was unfamiliar with them, and he was paralysed with the fearful thought that he might be committing himself by taking the chair. The little Japanese engineer looked even less self-assured.

With a great effort he pulled himself together. In a churlish tone of voice he asked Colonel Nicholson what he had to say. This was the least compromising move he could think of making. Realizing that he would get nothing more out of him, the Colonel decided to take action and embarked on a speech which the English side, with increasing anxiety, had begun to lose hope of ever hearing. He started off with the word 'Gentlemen', declared the meeting open and in a few words outlined his proposals: to establish a proper organization for the construction of the River Kwai bridge and to draw up in general terms a plan of action specifying each individual responsibility. Clipton, who was also present – the Colonel had asked him to attend, since the M.O. was naturally concerned with certain points of general administration – noticed that the C.O. had completely recovered his self-assurance and that his confidence asserted itself in direct proportion to Saito's increasing embarrassment.

After a short formal preamble, the Colonel embarked on the main subject and came to the first important point.

'Before tackling any other question, Colonel Saito, we ought to discuss the position of the bridge. It was fixed, I believe, a little hastily and we now think it ought to be changed. We have in mind a point about a mile further downstream. This, of course, would entail an extra stretch of railway line. It would also mean shifting the camp and building new quarters nearer the site. But I don't think we should let this stop us.'

Saito gave a hoarse grunt, and Clipton thought he was going to lose his temper. It was easy to imagine his frame of mind. Time was running short. More than a month had gone by with no material result being achieved, and now came this proposal for a considerable increase in the work as originally envisaged. He stood up suddenly, his hand clutching the hilt of his sword; but Colonel Nicholson gave him no opportunity of continuing his demonstration.

'Just a minute, Colonel Saito,' he said in ringing tones. 'I've had the matter looked into by my colleague, Captain Reeves, an engineer officer who is one of our bridge-building experts. The conclusions he has reached . . .'

Two days before, after carefully watching the Japanese engineer at work, he had been finally convinced of his inefficiency. He had at once taken a definite decision. He had seized his technical adviser by the arm and exclaimed:

'Listen, Reeves. We'll never get anywhere with this bungler, who knows even less about bridges than I do. You're an engineer, aren't you? Well, you're going to take charge of the whole works and start off again right from the beginning, without bothering about what he says or does. First of all, find a proper position for it. Then we'll see . . .'

Reeves, delighted to be engaged once more on his pre-war occupation, had carefully studied the ground and sounded the depth of the river at various points. He had discovered an almost perfect bottom of hard sand which was quite capable of bearing the weight of a bridge.

Before Saito could find the right words to express his indignation, the Colonel had called on Reeves, who proceeded to state a few technical principles, then quoted certain pressure-and-soil-resistance figures in tons per square inch which proved that the bridge would collapse under the weight of the trains if they insisted on building it over a swamp. When he had finished, the Colonel thanked him on behalf of all present and concluded:

'It seems quite clear, Colonel Saito, that we ought to shift the position of the bridge if we want to avoid disaster. May I ask your colleague for his advice on the matter?'

Saito swallowed his rage, sat down again and embarked on a heated discussion with the engineer. The Japanese had not been able to send their best technicians to Siam since they were needed for the war effort in the capital. This one, then, was not up to the mark. He was obviously lacking in experience, self-confidence and ability to command. He blushed when Colonel Nicholson drew his attention to Reeves's calculations, made a pretence of carefully studying them and finally, too nervous to be able to check them, and in a state of complete confusion, pathetically admitted that his colleague was right and that he himself had come to the same conclusions several days ago. It was such a shameful loss of face on the part of the Japanese that Saito went quite pale and drops of sweat broke out all over his contorted brow. He made a vague gesture of assent. The Colonel went on:

'So we're all agreed on this point, then, Colonel Saito? That means, all the work up to now has been useless. But it would have to be done all over again in any case, as there are serious faults in it.'

'Bad workmen,' snapped Saito, who was out for revenge. 'Japanese soldiers would have built those two sections of line in less than a fortnight.'

'Japanese soldiers would certainly have done better, because they're used to their officers commanding them. But I hope to show you the true worth of the British soldier quite soon, Colonel Saito. Incidentally, I ought to tell you that I've altered our men's quota.'

'Altered it!' Saito screamed.

'I've increased it,' the Colonel calmly replied, 'from one cubic yard to one and a half. It's in the general interest, and I felt this step would meet with your approval.'

The Japanese officer was completely dumbfounded, and the Colonel took advantage of this to put forward another question.

'You must realize, Colonel Saito, that we've got our own methods and I hope to prove their value, provided we're left free to apply them. We're fully aware that the success of this sort of venture depends more or less entirely on basic organization. And while we're on the subject, here are my suggestions, which I should like to submit for your approval.'

At this point the Colonel outlined the administrative plan on which he had worked for the last two days with the help of his staff. It was a fairly simple one, designed to cope with this particular situation, in which each separate department had a proper function. Colonel Nicholson was to be in sole charge, and personally responsible for everyone to the Japanese. Captain Reeves was entrusted with the plans for all the preliminary, theoretical work, at the same time acting as technical adviser on the practical side. Major Hughes, who was good at handling men, was to be a sort of chief foreman, responsible for directing the labour. Immediately under him were the platoon officers, who were to supervise the individual working parties. An administrative department had also been formed, at the head of which the Colonel had appointed his best corporal clerk. His main duties were to be liaison, transmission of orders, control of the quota, distribution and maintenance of tools, etc.

'This department is absolutely essential,' the Colonel explained. 'I suggest, Colonel Saito, that you hold an inspection of the tools which were issued only a month ago. They're in a really scandalous state . . .'

'I strongly recommend that this scheme be accepted,' said Colonel Nicholson, as he looked up again after describing in detail the machinery for the new organization and explaining the reasons which had led to its formation. 'I am, of course, at your disposal to enlighten you further on any point whenever you wish, and I assure you that any suggestion will be carefully studied. Do you agree in principle with these proposals?'

Saito was certainly in need of further explanation, but the Colonel had such a commanding presence as he pronounced these words that he could not refrain from making yet another gesture of assent. With a mere nod he agreed to the whole of this scheme, which deprived the Japanese of all initiative and rendered his own position more or less insignificant. He was prepared to put up with almost any humiliation. He was resigned to any sacrifice in order to see the piles ready to take the weight of this bridge, on which his very life depended. Reluctantly, in spite of himself, he felt confidence in the strange Western preparations for getting the work under way.

Encouraged by his initial success, Colonel Nicholson went on:

'There's another important point, Colonel Saito – the time factor. You realize, of course, how much extra work will be needed for the longer stretch of line. Then the new camp that will have to be built——'

'Why a new camp?' Saito protested. 'Surely the prisoners can march a couple of miles to their work!'

'My colleagues have studied the question from both angles,' Colonel Nicholson patiently replied. 'They have come to the conclusion . . .'

The calculations worked out by Reeves and Hughes showed quite clearly that the total number of hours spent on a daily march was far greater than the time needed to build a new camp. Once again Saito found himself out of his depth when confronted with conjectures based on wise Western forethought. The Colonel continued:

'Besides, we've already wasted over a month, as a result of an unfortunate disagreement for which we're not to blame. To get the bridge finished in the time laid down – and I promise you it will be if you accept my new suggestions – we'll have to start felling the trees and preparing the supports at once, while other teams simultaneously work on the railway line, and others still on the new camp. According to Major Hughes's calculations – and he's had a great deal of labour experience – we shan't have enough men to get all this work done in time.'

Colonel Nicholson paused for a moment in the tense, expectant silence, then continued in a resolute tone:

'This is what I suggest, Colonel Saito. For the moment we'll put most of the British soldiers to work on the bridge. Only a small number will be available for the railway line, so I shall ask you to lend us your Japanese soldiers to reinforce this group, so as to get the first stretch finished as quickly as possible. I think it should also be up to your men to build the new camp; they're more used to handling bamboo than mine are.'

It was at this particular moment that Clipton was swept away by one of his regular floods of affection. Until then he had felt several times like strangling the C.O. Now he could not stop looking at those blue eyes of his which, after glancing at the Japanese colonel, candidly interrogated every other member of the conference in turn, as though to demand an assurance that his last request was a fair one. He felt a momentary suspicion that there might be some cunning Machiavellian process at work behind that apparently artless exterior. Anxiously, earnestly, desperately, he examined each feature of that serene countenance in the wild hope of discovering some sign of treacherous, underhand scheming. After a moment he gave up and looked away.

'It's out of the question,' he decided. 'Every word he said is meant sincerely. He really has tried to work out the best means of accelerating the work.'

He looked up again to watch Saito's face and derived much comfort from the sight. The Jap's features were the features of a victim on the rack, who had reached the limit of human endurance. He was tortured by shame and anger, yet caught in the trap of this relentlessly logical argument. He had little or no chance of getting out of it. Once again he was forced to yield, after hesitating between protest and submission. His only hope now was to regain a little of his authority while the work was actually in progress. He was not yet aware of the abject state to which he was to be reduced by the wisdom of the West. Clipton knew that the Jap could never again retrieve the position he had now abandoned.

Saito capitulated in his usual manner. He suddenly barked out a few orders to his henchmen, speaking in Japanese. Since the Colonel's speech had been so rapid that only he had understood it, he was able to transmit the proposals as his own idea and transform them into words of command. When he had finished, Colonel Nicholson brought up one last point, a detail, but a tricky one, to which he had had to give his full attention.

'We've still got to fix the quota for your men working on the line, Colonel Saito. At first I thought of putting it at one cubic yard so as not to overtire them, but don't you think it would be best if we made it the same as the British soldiers? That would also create a healthy competitive spirit . . .'

'The Japanese soldiers' quota will be *two* cubic yards,' Saito burst out. 'I've already given the orders!'

Colonel Nicholson bowed in assent.

'In that case I expect we'll make good progress. I don't think there's anything more to be said, Colonel Saito. It remains for me to thank you for your kind attention. If there are no other questions, Gentlemen, I think we can declare this meeting closed. We'll start work tomorrow on the conditions to which we have agreed.'

He got up, saluted and withdrew, confident in the knowledge that he had conducted the meeting along the lines he wanted, that common sense had won the day and that a decisive step had been taken towards completing the bridge. He had proved himself a skilful tactician and he knew that he had deployed his forces in the best possible manner.

Clipton left with him, and together they walked back to their hut.

'What fools they are, sir!' said the M.O., looking closely at the Colonel. 'To think that, without us, they would have built their bridge in a swamp and it would have capsized under the weight of their trains loaded with troops and supplies!'

There was a strange glint in his eye as he spoke, but the Colonel's face remained inscrutable. This Sphinx-like character could not reveal his secret since he had no secret to reveal.

'Yes, aren't they?' he solemnly replied. 'They're what I've always said they were: primitive people, as undeveloped as children, who've acquired a veneer of civilization too soon. Underneath it all they're absolutely ignorant. They can't do a thing by themselves. Without us, they'd still be living in the age of sailing-ships and wouldn't own a single aircraft. Just children . . . yet so pretentious as well! Think of it, a work of this importance! As far as I can make out, they're only just capable of making a footbridge out of jungle-creepers.'

CHAPTER 4

There is nothing in common between a bridge, as conceived by civilized society in the West, and the utilitarian scaffoldings which the Japanese forces were in the habit of erecting in the continent of Asia. There is likewise no similarity between the two respective methods of construction. Qualified technicians did exist in the Japanese Empire, but they had been kept behind in the capital. In the occupied territories construction work was the army's responsibility. The handful of engineers who had been despatched to Siam had little skill and even less authority, and for the most part were overruled by the professional soldiers.

The latter's method – which was speedy and, up to a point, fairly efficient – had been dictated by necessity; for during their advance through the countries they had overrun, they had found every installation destroyed by the enemy in retreat. It consisted of driving two rows of piles into the river bed, then crowning these supports with a tangle of mixed timber hastily put together with no thought of plan or design and with a total disregard for the principle of static pressure, and finally adding extra bits of wood at any point which showed obvious signs of weakness.

On this uncouth superstructure, which sometimes reached an enormous height, thick beams were laid in two parallel rows; and on top of these, the only timber to be more or less properly shaped, went the rails themselves. The bridge was then considered to be finished. It fulfilled the need of the hour. There was no parapet, no footpath. The only way to walk across was to step from one beam to another, balancing above the chasm – a feat at which the Japanese were adept.

The first convoy would go jolting across at low speed. The engine sometimes came off the rails at the point where the bank met the bridge, but a gang of soldiers armed with crowbars usually managed to heave it upright again. The train would then move on. If the bridge was damaged at all more bits of timber would be added to the structure. And the next convoy would cross in the same way. The scaffolding would last a few days, a few weeks, sometimes even a few months, after which a flood would sweep it away, or else a series of more than usually violent jolts would make it capsize. Then the Japanese would patiently start rebuilding it. The materials they used were provided by the inexhaustible jungle.

The methods of Western civilization, of course, are not so elementary. Captain Reeves represented an essential element of that civilization – the mechanical – and would never have dreamed of being guided by such primitive empiricism.

But when it comes to bridge-building, Western mechanical procedure entails a lot of gruelling preliminaries, which swell and multiply the number of operations leading up to the actual construction. They entail, for instance, a detailed plan; and for this plan to be made it is essential to determine in advance the section and shape of every beam, the depth to which the piles are to be driven and a mass of other details. Now each section, each shape, and the depth entail further calculations, based on figures representing the resistance of the various materials to be used and the consistency of the ground. These figures, in their turn, depend on coefficients worked out according to 'standard patterns', which in the civilized world are given in the form of mathematical tables. Mechanics, in fact, entail a complete *a priori* knowledge; and this mental creation, which precedes the material creation, is not the least important of the many achievements of Western genius.

There were no tables available on the banks of the Kwai, but Captain Reeves was an expert engineer and his theoretical knowledge enabled him to do without them, but only by increasing the number of preliminary duties and by experimenting with various weights and simple shapes before getting down to his calculations. He was thus enabled to determine his co-efficients by an easy method, using instruments hastily produced for the purpose, since there was not much time to spare.

With the approval of Colonel Nicholson, under the anxious eye of Saito and Clipton's sardonic gaze, he set to work on these tests. At the same time he traced the best possible course for the railway to take, and passed the result to Major Hughes for action. With this off his chest, and with all the necessary data for his calculations ready to hand, he embarked on the most interesting part of the work: the design and planning of the bridge.

He devoted himself to this task with the same professional conscientiousness that he had once shown when engaged on similar work for the Indian Government, and also with a passionate enthusiasm which he had hitherto tried to acquire, in vain, through reading suitable books (such as *The Bridge Builders*), but by which he was now suddenly carried away as a result of a casual remark passed by the C.O.

'You know, Reeves, I'm relying on you entirely. You're the only qualified man we have and I'm leaving everything in your hands. We've got to show we're superior to these savages. I realize how difficult it is in this God-forsaken place where you can't find what you need, but that makes the task all the more worth while.'

'You can count on me, sir,' Reeves had replied, feeling suddenly galvanized. 'I shan't let you down, and we'll show them what we're capable of doing.'

This was the chance he had been waiting for all his life. He had always dreamt of tackling a really big job without being badgered every other minute by administrative departments or maddened by interfering officials who ask ridiculous questions and try to put a spoke in the wheels, on the pretext of economy, thereby frustrating every creative effort. Here he was responsible to the Colonel and to no one else. The C.O. was favourably impressed; although he was a stickler for routine and 'proper channels', he could at least see the other man's point of view and refused to be blinded by convention and protocol as far as the bridge was concerned. Besides, he had openly admitted he knew nothing about engineering, and made it quite clear he intended giving the junior officer his head. Certainly, the job was a difficult one, and there was a shortage of proper material, but Reeves promised to make up for every deficiency by his devotion to duty. He could already feel the breeze of creative inspiration fanning those hungry flames which overcome every obstacle in their path.

From that moment he did not allow himself a minute's leisure. He started by dashing off a sketch of the bridge, as he saw it in his mind's eye whenever he looked at the river, with its four majestic rows of piles meticulously in line, its bold but graceful superstructure towering a hundred feet above the water, its beams assembled according to a process he had himself invented and which he had tried in vain to make the conservative Government of India adopt years ago, its broad platform protected by a strong balustrade, allowing room not only for the railway itself but also for a vehicle track and footpath.

After that he set to work on the calculations and diagrams, and then on the actual design. He had managed to acquire a roll of fairly decent drawing-paper from his Japanese colleague, who kept sidling up behind him to gaze at the work in progress with ill-concealed, bewildered admiration.

He fell into the habit of working like this from dawn till dusk, without a moment's rest, until he noticed that the hours of daylight were over all too soon, until he realized with dismay that the days were all too short and that his task would never be finished in the time he had allowed. And so, using Colonel Nicholson as his intermediary, he got permission from Saito to keep a lamp burning after Lights Out. From that day on, he spent every evening and sometimes half the night working on the design of the bridge. Sitting on a rickety footstool, using his wretched bamboo bed as a desk, with his drawing-paper spread out on a board which he had himself planed smooth with loving care, in the light of the tiny oil-lamp which filled the hut with fetid fumes, he would handle with expert ease the T- and set-square which he had taken such pains to make.

The only time these instruments were out of his fingers was when he seized a fresh sheet of paper and feverishly filled it with further calculations, sacrificing his sleep at the end of each tiring day in order to see his craftsmanship take shape in a masterpiece which was to prove the superiority of the West – this bridge which was to be used by the Japanese trains on their triumphant advance to the Bay of Bengal.

Clipton had at first believed that the preliminary stages in the Western *modus operandi* (the elaborate administrative plans, followed by painstaking research and mechanical tests) would retard the actual building of the bridge even more than the haphazard empiricism of the Japanese. It was not long before he realized how vain these hopes of his were and how wrong he had been to jeer at all the preparatory work undertaken during the long sleepless nights caused by Reeves's lamp. He began to understand that he had been a little too hasty in his criticism of the methods of Western civilization on the day that Reeves submitted his finished plan to Major Hughes and the construction got under way with a speed surpassing even Saito's most optimistic dreams.

Reeves was not one of those people who become mesmerized by symbolic preparations or who postpone taking action indefinitely because they devote all their energies to intellectual activity and think nothing of the practical side. He kept one foot firmly on the ground. Besides, whenever he showed signs of pursuing theoretical perfection too closely and shrouding the bridge in a fog of abstract figures, Colonel Nicholson was there to guide his erring footsteps. The Colonel had the practical sense of a born leader, who never loses sight of his objective or the means at his disposal and who keeps his subordinates perfectly balanced between idealism and reality.

He had consented to the preliminary tests on condition that they were quickly completed. He had also approved the blue-print and been given a detailed explanation of the innovations due to Reeves's inventive genius. All he had asked was that the latter should not overwork himself.

'We'll be getting along nicely, and then suddenly you'll go sick, Reeves. The whole job depends on you, remember.'

So he began to watch Reeves carefully, and appealed to common sense when he came to him one day with a worried look in his eye to inform him of certain particulars.

'There's one point that's bothering me, sir. I don't think we should treat it too seriously, but I wanted to know what you felt about it.'

'What is it, Reeves?' the Colonel asked.

'The wood's still damp, sir. We shouldn't be using freshly-felled trees on a job like this. They should first be left out in the open to dry.'

'How long would it take for these trees of yours to dry, Reeves?'

'It all depends on what sort of wood it is, sir. With some kinds it's advisable to wait eighteen months or even a couple of years.'

'That's absolutely out of the question, Reeves,' the Colonel protested, 'we've only got five months as it is.'

The Captain hung his head apologetically.

'Alas, sir, I realize that, and that's exactly what's worrying me.'

'And what's wrong with using fresh timber?'

'Some species contract, sir, and that might cause cracks and displacements once the work is under way. Not with every kind of wood, of course. Elm, for instance, hardly shifts at all. So naturally I've selected timber which is as much like elm as possible. The elm piles of London Bridge have lasted six hundred years, sir.'

'Six hundred years!' exclaimed the Colonel. There was a glint in his eye as he involuntarily turned towards the river. 'Six hundred years, Reeves, that would be a pretty good show!'

'Oh, but that's an exceptional case, sir. You could hardly count on more than fifty or sixty years in this place. Less, perhaps, if the timber dries out badly.'

'We'll just have to take that chance, Reeves,' the Colonel firmly decided. 'You must use fresh timber. We can't achieve the impossible. If they blame us for any faults in the construction, at least we'll be able to tell them that it couldn't be avoided.'

'Right, sir. Just another question. Creosote, for protecting the beams against insect damage . . . I think we'll have to do without it sir. The Japs haven't got any. Of course, we could make a substitute . . . I'd thought of setting up a wood-alcohol still. That might do, but it would take some time . . . No, on second thoughts, I don't think we'd better . . .'

'Why not, Reeves?' asked the Colonel, who was fascinated by all these technical details.

'Well, there's a difference of opinion on this, sir; but the best authorities advise against creosoting when the timber's not sufficiently dry. It keeps the sap and the damp in, sir; and then there's a risk of rot setting in at once.'

'In that case we'll have to do without creosote, Reeves. You must bear in mind that we can't afford to embark on any scheme beyond our means. Don't forget the bridge has an immediate role to fulfil.'

'Apart from those two snags, sir, I'm quite certain we can build a bridge here which will be perfectly all right from the technical point of view and reasonably strong.'

'That's it, Reeves. You're on the right track. A reasonably strong bridge which is all right from the technical point of view. A bridge, in fact, and not a Heath Robinson contraption. That's what we want. As I've said before, I'm relying on you entirely.'

Colonel Nicholson left his technical adviser, feeling pleased with the simple phrase he had coined to define his objective.

CHAPTER 5

Shears – or 'Number One' as he was called by the Siamese partisans in the remote hamlet where the envoys of Force 316 were now in hiding – was likewise the sort of man who devotes a great deal of thought and care to systematic preparation. In fact the high regard in which he was held at Headquarters was as much due to the caution and patience he showed before taking any action as to his cheerfulness and determination when the time for action arrived. Warden, Professor Warden, his second-in-command, also had a well-earned reputation for leaving nothing to chance unless circumstances dictated otherwise. As for Joyce, the third and youngest member of the team, who was still fresh from the course he had been on at the Plastic and Destructions Company's special school in Calcutta, he seemed to have his head screwed on the right way, in spite of his youth, and Shears valued his opinion. And so, during the daily conferences held in the two-room native hut which had been put at their disposal, any promising idea was carefully considered and every suggestion thoroughly examined.

One evening the three of them were studying a map which Joyce had just pinned up on the bamboo wall.

'Here's the approximate course of the railway, sir,' he said. 'The reports seem to tally pretty well.'

Joyce, who was an industrial designer in civilian life, had been detailed to keep a large-scale map marked with all the intelligence available on the Burma-Siam railway.

There was plenty of information. During the month since they had safely landed on their selected dropping-zone they had succeeded in winning the friendship of the local population over quite a wide area. They had been received by the Siamese agents, and been housed in this little hamlet inhabited by hunters and smugglers and hidden away in a corner of the jungle well away from the nearest line of communication. The natives hated the Japanese. Shears, who was trained to take nothing for granted, had gradually been convinced of the loyalty of his hosts.

The first part of their mission was successfully under way. They had secretly established contact with several village headsmen. Volunteers were ready to rally round them. The three officers had started instructing them and were now training them in the use of the weapons employed by Force 316. The most important of these was 'plastic', a soft brown paste as malleable as clay, in which several generations of chemists in the Western world had patiently contrived to amalgamate the best features of every known explosive and several others besides.

'There are any amount of bridges, sir,' Joyce went on, 'but if you ask me, most of them aren't up to much. Here's the list, from Bangkok right up to Rangoon, complete as far as our information goes.'

The 'sir' was for the benefit of Major Shears, his 'Number One'. Although discipline was strict in Force 316, such formality was nevertheless not usual among members of a special mission; and Shears had asked Joyce several times to stop calling him 'sir'. He had not been able to break him of the habit – a pre-war habit, Shears imagined, which made the young man cling to this mode of address.

Yet so far Shears could find nothing but praise for Joyce, whom he had selected from the Calcutta school on the instructors' reports as well as on the candidate's physical appearance, but most of all on his own instinctive judgement.

The reports were good and the comments flattering. Young Joyce, it seemed, who was a volunteer like all the other members of Force 316, had always given complete satisfaction and had shown exceptional keenness on every part of the course – which was something to be said for him, in Shears' opinion. According to his personal file, he had been a draughtsman on the staff of a big industrial and commercial concern – probably only a minor employee. But Shears had not enquired any further. He felt there was no profession that could not eventually lead to the Plastic and Destructions Company, Ltd., and that a man's pre-war career was his own business.

On the other hand, all Joyce's visible qualities would not have been sufficient to warrant Shears taking him in as the third member of the team, if they had not been backed up by others which were less easy to define and for which he relied on little else but his own personal impression. He had known volunteers who were excellent during training, but whose nerve failed them when it came to certain duties demanded by Force 316. He did not hold this against them. Shears had his own ideas on this subject.

He had therefore sent for this future companion of his in order to try and find out what sort of a man he was. He had asked his friend Warden to be present at the interview, for the Professor's advice in a selection of this sort was always worth considering. He had been favourably impressed by Joyce's appearance. His physical strength was probably not much above the average, but he was fit and seemed a well-balanced type. His clear, frank answers to the questions he was asked showed he had a practical mind, that he never lost sight of his objective and was well aware of what he was letting himself in for. Apart from this, his keenness showed unmistakably in his eyes. He was obviously dying to accompany the two veterans ever since he had heard the rumour of a dangerous mission being planned.

Shears had then brought up a point which he considered important, as indeed it was.

'Do you think you'd be capable of using a weapon like this?' he had asked.

He had shown him a razor-sharp dagger. This knife was part of the kit which members of Force 316 took with them on every special mission. Joyce had not batted an eyelid. He had replied that he had been taught how to handle the weapon and that the course included practising with it on dummies. Shears had repeated the question.

'That's not exactly what I meant. What I want to know is: are you quite sure that you'd be really "capable" of using it in cold blood? Lots of men know how to use it, but aren't able to when it comes to the point.'

Joyce had understood. He had silently thought the matter over, then solemnly replied:

'That's a question I've often asked myself, sir.'

'A question you've often asked yourself?' Shears had repeated, looking at him closely.

'Yes, sir, really. And I must admit, it's worried me quite a lot. I've tried to imagine myself ——'

'And what was the answer?'

Joyce had hesitated, but only for a second.

'Speaking quite frankly, sir, I don't think I'd disappoint you if it ever came to the point. I don't honestly. But I couldn't say for certain. I'd do my very best, sir.'

'You've never had a chance of using one of these in anger, is that it?'

'That's it, sir. My job never called for that sort of thing,' Joyce had replied, as though offering an apology.

He seemed to be so genuinely sorry about it that Shears could not help smiling. Warden had immediately joined the conversation:

'I say, Shears, this chap seems to think that my old job, for instance, is a special qualification for this sort of work. A professor of Oriental languages! And what about you – a cavalry officer!'

'I didn't mean that exactly, sir,' Joyce had stammered in his embarrassment.

'Ours is the only firm I know,' Shears had philosophically concluded, 'in which you'd find, as you say, an Oxford graduate and an ex-cavalryman doing this particular sort of work – so why not an industrial designer as well?'

'Take him,' was all that Warden said when asked for his advice as soon as the interview was over. Shears had done so. Thinking it over, he had been fairly pleased with the candidate's answers. He was just as suspicious of men who overestimated themselves as of those who underestimated. The sort he liked were those who were capable of distinguishing the tricky part of a mission in advance, who had sufficient foresight to prepare for it and enough imagination to see it quite clearly in their mind's eye – so long as they did not let it become an obsession. So from the start he had been satisfied with his team. As for Warden, he had known him for a long time and knew exactly how far he was 'capable'.

They pored over the map for some time, while Joyce pointed out the bridges and described the particular features of each. Shears and Warden listened carefully, with curiously tense expressions, although they already knew the subaltern's report by heart. Bridges always provoked a passionate interest in every member of the Plastic and Destructions Co., an interest of an almost mystical nature.

'These are just footbridges you're describing, Joyce,' said Shears. 'Don't forget, we want a really worth-while target.'

'I only mentioned them, sir, in order to refresh my memory. As far as I can see, there are only three worth bothering about.'

Every bridge was not equally attractive to Force 316. Number One agreed with Colonel Green that they should not put the Japs on their guard before the railway was completed by attacking relatively unimportant targets. He had therefore decided that the team should lie low in the hide-out for the time being and do no more than collate and co-ordinate the information of the native agents.

'It would be silly to spoil the whole show by blowing up a few trucks just for the fun of the thing,' he would sometimes say in order to curb his companions' impatience. 'We want to start off in a really big way. That will enhance our reputation in the country and make the Siamese look up to us. Let's wait till the trains start running.'

Since his firm intention was to start off 'in a big way', it was clear that the less important bridges had to be excluded. The result of the initial blow was to compensate for the long period of inactivity and preparation and to endow the mission, in his own eyes at least, with an aura of success, even if circumstances dictated that nothing else should come of it. Shears knew that one could never be certain of a first attack being followed up by a second. He kept this to himself, but his two companions had realized the reasons for his plan, and the discovery of this ulterior motive had not worried the ex-professor Warden whose rational mind approved of such methods of seeing and foreseeing.

It had not seemed to worry Joyce either, nor had it dampened the enthusiasm he had felt at the prospect of a worth-while attack. On the contrary, it seemed to have spurred him on to greater efforts and made him concentrate all his youthful powers on this probably unique opportunity, on this unhoped for target suddenly flashing in front of him like a lighthouse, casting its brilliant beams of success on to the past for all eternity, lighting up with its magic flames the grey gloom which had so far dimmed his path.

'Joyce is right,' said Warden, as sparing as ever in his speech. 'There are only three worth-while bridges. One of them is Camp Three's.'

'We'll have to give that one up, I'm afraid,' said Shears. 'The open ground doesn't lend itself to attack. Apart from that, it's in flat country. The banks are low. It would be too easy to repair.'

'The other one's near Camp Ten.'

'It's worth considering. But it happens to be in Burma, where we haven't the support of the native partisans. Besides . . .'

'The third one, sir,' Joyce suddenly said, without realizing he was butting in to his C.O.'s conversation, 'the third one's the bridge on the River Kwai. It hasn't any of those drawbacks. The river's four hundred feet across, with steep, high banks on both sides. It's only two or three days' march from here. The area's practically uninhabited and covered in jungle. We could approach it without being observed and command it from a hill from which the whole valley's visible. It's a long way from the nearest large town. The Japs are taking special care over its construction. It's bigger than all the other bridges and has four rows of piles. It's the most important job on the whole line, and the best placed one.'

'You seem to have studied the agents' reports pretty thoroughly,' observed Shears.

'They're quite clear, sir. It seems to me that this bridge . . .'

'I can see that the Kwai bridge is worth considering,' said Shears, as he leaned over the map. 'Your judgement's not so dusty for a beginner. Colonel Green and I had already noted that particular crossing. But our information's not yet sufficiently complete; and there may be other bridges which could be more easily attacked. And how far has the work progressed on this wonderful bridge, Joyce, which you talk of as though you had actually seen it?'

CHAPTER 6

The work was well under way. The British soldier is by nature hard working and puts up with strict discipline without a murmur provided he has confidence in his officers and starts the day off with the prospect of unlimited physical exercise to counteract any nervous tension.

The soldiers in the River Kwai camp had a high opinion of Colonel Nicholson – and who would not have after his heroic resistance? Besides, the sort of work they were doing did not involve much thought. So after a short period of indecision, during which they tried to get to the bottom of the C.O.'s real intentions, they had set to work with a will, eager to show their skill as builders now that they had proved their cunning as saboteurs. In any case Colonel Nicholson had taken steps to avoid any chance of misunderstanding, first by delivering an address in which he explained quite clearly what was expected of them, and secondly by inflicting severe punishments on a few recalcitrants who had not fully understood. This action had seemed so well intended that the victims did not hold it against him.

'Believe me, I know these fellows better than you do,' was the Colonel's retort to Clipton, who had dared to protest against the set task, which he considered too heavy for men who were undernourished and in a poor state of health. 'It's taken me thirty years to get to know them. Nothing's worse for morale than inactivity, and their physical welfare depends largely on their morale. Troops who are bored, Clipton, are troops doomed in advance to defeat. Let them get slack and you'll see an unhealthy spirit developing in the unit. But fill every minute of their day with hard work, and cheerfulness and health are guaranteed.'

'Be happy in your work!' murmured Clipton disloyally. 'That was General Yamashita's motto.'

'And it's not such a bad one, Clipton. We shouldn't hesitate to adopt a principle of the enemy's if it happens to be a good one. If there wasn't any work for them to do, I'd invent some for them. As it is, we've got the bridge.'

Clipton could find no words to express what he felt and could only sullenly repeat:

'Yes, we've got the bridge all right.'

In any case the British soldiers had already revolted on their own against an attitude and code of behaviour which clashed with their instinctive urge to do a job properly. Even before the Colonel intervened, subversive activity had become for most of them a distasteful duty, and some of them had not waited for his orders before using their muscles and tools to proper purpose. It was their natural reaction, as Westerners, to make a loyal and considerable effort in return for their daily bread, and their Anglo-Saxon blood encouraged them to concentrate this effort on something solid and constructive. The Colonel had not been wrong about them. His new régime led to a rise in morale.

Since the Japanese soldier is equally well disciplined and hard working, and since Saito had threatened to string his men up if they failed to prove themselves better workers than the British, the two stretches of line had been quickly completed, while the huts for the new camp had been erected and made habitable. At about the same time Reeves had put the finishing touches to his plans and passed them to Major Hughes, who was thus drawn into the scheme and given a chance to show what he was worth. Thanks to his organizing ability, his knowledge of the troops and his experience of how man-power can be most effectively employed, the labour under his direction achieved tangible results from the very start.

The first thing Hughes did was to divide the personnel into different groups and allot a specific task to each, so that while one was occupied on cutting down trees, another would be trimming the trunks, a third making the beams, while the largest of all was engaged on pile-driving, and many more besides were employed on the superstructure and platform. Some of the teams – not the least important ones, in Hughes' opinion – were made up of various experts in such tasks as the erection of the scaffolding, the transport of the materials and the maintenance of the tools: tasks of secondary importance to the actual construction work, but to which Western foresight devotes – and not without reason – as much care as to the immediately productive work.

This division of labour was a wise move and proved most effective, as it always does when not carried to extremes. As soon as a stack of planks was ready, and the first scaffoldings were in position, Hughes set his team of pile-drivers to work. Theirs was an arduous task, the hardest and most thankless of the whole undertaking. In the absence of all mechanical labour, these new bridge-builders were reduced to using the same methods as the Japanese, that is to say they were obliged to drop a heavy weight on to the head of each pile and repeat this operation until it was firmly embedded in the river. The 'ram', which dropped from a height of eight or ten feet, had to be re-hoisted each time by a system of ropes and pulleys, then allowed to fall once more over and over again. At each blow the pile would sink an infinitesimal fraction of an inch, for the ground was as hard as rock. It was unrewarding, soul-destroying work. There was no visible sign of progress from one minute to the next, and the sight of a group of more or less naked men tugging at a rope reminded one gloomily of a slave-gang. Hughes had put one of the best subalterns in command of this team –

Harper, a man with plenty of drive, who urged the prisoners on better than anyone else by shouting out the time in a booming voice. Thanks to his encouragement, this punishing task was accomplished with zeal and cheerfulness. Under the astonished eyes of the Japanese the four parallel rows gradually crept forward across the water towards the left bank.

At one moment Clipton had almost expected the embedding of the first pile to be celebrated by some solemn ritual, but there had only been a few simple formalities. Colonel Nicholson had confined himself to seizing the rope of the ram and tugging manfully, to set an example, for as long as it took to come down a dozen times.

Once the pile-drivers were well under way, Hughes launched the teams engaged on the superstructure. They in their turn were followed by others employed on laying down the platform with its broad tracks and parapets. The various activities had been so well co-ordinated that from then on work went forward with mathematical regularity.

An observer, blind to elementary detail but keen on general principles, might have regarded the development of the bridge as an uninterrupted process of natural growth. That was certainly the impression that Colonel Nicholson had of it. With a satisfied eye he witnessed this gradual materialization, without connecting it in any way with humble human activity. Consequently he saw it only as something abstract and complete in itself: a living symbol of the fierce struggles and countless experiments by which a nation gradually raises itself in the course of centuries to a state of civilization.

It was in much the same light that the bridge sometimes appeared also to Reeves. He gazed at it in wonder as it simultaneously rose above the water and stretched across the river, reaching its maximum width almost at once, majestically registering in all three dimensions the palpable shape of creation at the foot of these wild Siamese mountains, representing in miraculously concrete form the wealth of fruitful imagination and labour.

Saito too was overwhelmed by the magic of this daily prodigy. In spite of all his efforts, he could not altogether conceal his astonishment and admiration. His surprise was only to be expected. Since he had not fully understood, and had certainly never analysed, the subtler aspects of Western civilization – as Colonel Nicholson so rightly observed – he could not realize to what extent method, organization, calculation, theoretical planning and expert co-ordination of human activities facilitate and eventually accelerate any practical undertaking. The purpose and usefulness of this sort of intellectual groundwork will always be beyond the comprehension of savages.

As for Clipton, he was definitely convinced of his initial stupidity and humbly recognized the folly of the sarcastic attitude he had shown towards the application of modern industrial methods to the construction of the River Kwai bridge.

He inwardly apologized for this, showing a characteristic sense of fair-mindedness mingled with remorse for having been so short-sighted. He was forced to admit that the methods of the Western world had in this case led to positive results. Starting from this premise, he pursued the argument a stage further and came to the conclusion that such 'methods' are invariably effective and invariably produce 'results'. Those who set themselves up as critics of these methods never give them a fair trial. He himself, like so many others, had given way to the temptation of a cheap sneer.

The bridge, growing daily larger and more beautiful, soon reached the middle of the river, then went past it. At this stage it became quite obvious to everyone that it would be finished before the date laid down by the Japanese High Command and would cause no delay to the triumphant advance of the victorious army.

PART 3

CHAPTER 1

Joyce swallowed the drink he had been given in one gulp. His arduous expedition had not told on him. He was still quite fresh and there was a sparkle in his eye. Before he had even taken off the outlandish Siamese disguise, in which Shears and Warden could scarcely recognize him, he insisted on reporting the main events of his mission.

'It's worth having a go at it, sir, I'm certain. It won't be easy – let's face it – but it's possible and definitely worth while. There's thick jungle. The river's a broad one. The bridge runs across a gully. The banks are steep. The train couldn't be cleared, except with a great deal of equipment.'

'Begin at the beginning,' said Shears. 'Or do you want to have a shower first?'

'I'm not tired, sir.'

'Give him a chance,' growled Warden. 'Can't you see he wants to talk, not rest?'

Shears smiled. It was obvious that Joyce was just as eager to make his report as he himself was to hear it. They settled down as comfortably as possible in front of the map. With characteristic foresight Warden handed Joyce a second glass. In the room next door the two Siamese partisans who had acted as the young man's guide were squatting on the floor, surrounded by some of the local villagers. They had already begun to describe their expedition and made flattering references to the behaviour of the white man whom they had accompanied.

'It's been quite a stiff march, sir,' Joyce began. 'Three nights through the jungle, and hard going all the way. But the partisans were splendid. They kept their promise and took me to the top of the hill on the left bank, which commands the whole valley, the camp and the bridge. A perfect O.P.'

'I hope no one saw you?'

'Not a chance, sir. We only moved at night, and it was so dark I had to keep one hand on the shoulder of the chap in front. We lay up during the day in the undergrowth, which was thick enough to discourage any prying eyes. But in any case it's such wild country, even that wasn't necessary. We didn't see a soul till we arrived.'

'Good,' said Shears. 'Go on.'

As he listened, Number One surreptitiously scrutinized Joyce to see if the opinion he was beginning to form of him was justified. To him the values of this reconnaissance were twofold; it gave him a chance of assessing the

young man's abilities when left to his own devices. The first impression he
made on his return was favourable. The cheerful appearance of the two
natives was another good sign. Shears knew that imponderables like these
should not be disregarded. Joyce was certainly a little over-excited not only
by what he had seen but also by the change in atmosphere, by the
comparative peace of these quarters after the countless hazards to which he
had been exposed since his departure.

'The Siamese weren't far wrong, sir. It's a really beautiful job.'

Zero hour drew nearer and nearer as the rails stretched further and
further along the embankment at the cost of countless hardships suffered by
the Allied prisoners of war in Burma and Siam. Shears and his two
companions had followed the daily progress of the line. Joyce spent hours
emending his map and keeping it up to date according to the latest
information received. Every week he added to the line in red pencil which
represented each newly-completed section. The line was now almost
unbroken from Bangkok to Rangoon. The more important river crossings
were indicated by a cross. The particulars of each construction were noted
down on slips of paper, carefully kept up to date by Warden, who liked to
have everything neat and tidy.

With their information on the line growing more complete and more
accurate, their attention was irresistibly drawn to the River Kwai bridge,
which had attracted them right from the start by its many advantages.
With their specialized knowledge of bridges, they had been amazed by the
exceptional number of circumstances favourable to the plan which they
had instinctively started to work out, a plan which combined the practical
sense and the imagination typical of the Plastic and Destructions Co., Ltd.
Prompted by instinct as much as by logic, they had gradually come to pin
all their faith and hopes on the River Kwai bridge and on nothing else.
They had considered a number of other bridges just as carefully and had
discussed their respective advantages, but had ended up by choosing this
one, which seemed naturally and purposely designed for them as an
operational target. The 'big show', which was at first no more than a
vague, abstract idea existing only in the imagination, was now represented
by a concrete body in time and space – a vulnerable target, in other words,
liable to every contingency, to every degradation of which the mind of man
is capable, and especially liable to annihilation.

'This isn't a job for the R.A.F.,' Shears had observed. 'It's not easy to
destroy a wooden bridge from the air. If the bombs find their mark only
two or three arches are damaged. The rest are just knocked a bit. The Japs
can patch it up in no time, they're past-masters at that sort of thing.
Whereas we can not only blow the whole thing sky-high and shatter the

piles at water-level, but also time the explosion for when a train is actually crossing the bridge. Then the whole convoy'll come crashing down into the river, increasing the damage and putting every beam out of action. I've seen it happen before. Traffic was held up for weeks. And that was in a civilized part of the world where the enemy was able to bring up cranes. Here they'll have to make a detour in the line and build the bridge all over again – not to mention the loss of a train and its load of war material. What a show! I can just see it . . .'

All three could imagine what a show it would be. The attack had assumed concrete shape over which the imagination could wander at will. A succession of mental snapshots, some of them underexposed, others in bright technicolour, disturbed Joyce's sleep. The former appertained to the period of clandestine preparation, the latter culminated in such a brilliant picture that the smallest detail stood out amazingly sharp and clear: the train poised above the gully, with the River Kwai sparkling underneath between two blocks of jungle. His own hand was clutching the plunger. His eyes were fixed on a certain point in the centre of the bridge. The distance between the point and the engine was rapidly decreasing. He had to push the plunger down at the right moment. The distance between them was now only a few feet, only one foot. At that very moment he automatically pushed down the plunger. On the bridge which he saw in his dreams, he had already reconnoitred and found a suitable spot, exactly half-way across!

One day he had anxiously exclaimed: 'I only hope the Air Force chaps won't have a go at it, sir, before we do.'

'I've already sent a message to tell them to keep out of it,' Shears had answered. 'I don't think we'll be worried by them.'

During this period of inactivity countless reports had come in, all referring to the bridge which the partisans were keeping under observation from the top of a nearby hill. They themselves had not yet approached it in case the locals got wind of the presence of white men in the area. They had had it described to them hundreds of times, and the more intelligent agents had even made a drawing of it in the sand. From their hide-out they had followed every stage in its construction, and were amazed by the unusual method and system which seemed to govern each successive phase and which were confirmed by every report. They were used to sifting the truth from any rumour, and had quickly detected a feeling akin to admiration in the partisans' description of the bridge. The Siamese were not qualified to appreciate the technical genius of Captain Reeves, nor the organization for which Colonel Nicholson was responsible, but they were fully aware that this was no shapeless scaffolding in the usual Japanese style. Primitive people have an instinctive appreciation of applied art and design.

'God Almighty!' Shears would sometimes cry out in desperation. 'If what our chaps say is true, it's a second George Washington Bridge they're building. They're trying to compete with the Yanks!'

Such unusually lavish work, amounting almost to extravagance – for according to the Siamese, there was a road running alongside the line, which was wide enough for two trucks abreast – was an intriguing but disturbing prospect. An installation of this size would almost certainly be more closely guarded than ever. On the other hand, it might be of even greater strategic importance then he had thought, so that attacking it would be all the more worth while.

The natives had quite a lot to say about the prisoners. They had seen them working almost naked in the scorching sun, working without a break and under strict surveillance. When they heard this, all three of them forgot about their scheme and gave a moment's thought to their wretched fellow-countrymen. Knowing the Japs as they did, they could well imagine how far their brutality would go in order to get a job like this one finished.

'If only they knew we were in the offing, sir,' Joyce had said one day. 'If only they knew this bridge of theirs was never going to be used, it might raise their morale a bit.'

'Perhaps,' Shears had answered, 'but we can't afford to contact them. That's out of the question, Joyce. In our job security's the first essential, even among friends. They'd let their imagination run riot. They'd start trying to help us and might give the whole show away by having a go at the bridge themselves. The Japs would get wind of it, and the only result would be terrible reprisals. No, they've got to be kept out of it. We mustn't allow the Japs even to think of the possibility of the prisoners' co-operating with us.'

One day Shears had suddenly decided to test the reliability of the fabulous reports which were coming in every day from the River Kwai.

'One of us will have to go and have a look. The work will be finished any day now, and we can't go on relying on these chaps' reports, which seem utterly fantastic. You'd better go, Joyce. I want to know what this bridge is really like, understand? How big is it? How many piles are there? I want the exact figures. How can it be approached? How is it guarded? What are the chances of attacking it? Do what you can, but keep your head down. You mustn't let yourself be seen at any price, bear that in mind. But for God's sake get me some proper information on this bloody bridge!'

CHAPTER 2

'I saw it through my glasses, sir, as clearly as I can see you now.'

'Begin from the beginning,' Shears insisted in spite of his impatience. 'How did it go?'

Joyce had set off one night accompanied by two natives who were accustomed to these secret nocturnal expeditions since it was their practice to smuggle wads of opium and cases of cigarettes over the border between Burma and Siam. They claimed that the paths they used were quite safe; but it was so important for no one to know that a European was in the neighbourhood that Joyce had insisted on disguising himself as a Siamese peasant and on dyeing his skin with a brown pigment made up in Calcutta for just such an occasion.

He soon saw that his guides had been telling the truth. The real enemies in this jungle were the mosquitoes and particularly the leeches, which fastened on to his bare legs and climbed up his body; he could feel them sticking to him each time he stroked his skin. He had done his best to overcome his disgust and to disregard them. He had almost succeeded. In any case he could not get rid of them during the night. He refrained from lighting a cigarette in order to burn them off, and he needed all his wits about him to keep up with the Siamese.

'Tough going?'

'Fairly tough, sir. As I said, I had to keep one hand on the shoulder of the chap in front. And these fellows' so-called paths have to be seen to be believed!'

For three nights they had made him clamber up hill and down dale. They followed rocky river-beds blocked here and there with sticking clumps of rotting vegetation, and each time they brushed against these they collected a rich crop of fresh leeches. His guides showed a preference for these paths, in which they were sure they could not get lost. They kept going till dawn. When the first rays of the sun appeared they dived into the undergrowth and quickly ate the boiled rice and cooked meat they had brought for the journey. The two Siamese then squatted under a tree until nightfall, puffing away at a bubbling water-pipe which they always carried with them. That was their method of relaxing after the rigours of the night. From time to time they dropped off between two puffs, without even shifting their position.

Joyce, however, insisted on sleeping properly in order to harvest his strength, for he was anxious to make the best of every circumstance on which the success of his mission depended. He began by getting rid of the leeches which covered his body. Some of them, completely glutted, had fallen off by themselves during the night, leaving a little clot of congealed blood. The others, which had not yet had their fill, stuck to this prey of theirs which the fortunes of war had brought into the jungles of Siam. Under the glow of a burning cigarette their swollen bodies contracted, twisted, then finally let go and fell on the ground, where he squashed them between two stones. Then he lay down on a ground-sheet and went to sleep at once; but the ants did not leave him in peace for long.

Attracted by the drops of congealed blood which bespattered his skin, they took this opportunity to advance in long black and red cohorts. He learnt to distinguish between the two as soon as he felt them, without even opening his eyes. Against the red ones there was nothing he could do. Their sting was like white-hot pincers on his sores. A single one was unbearable; and they advanced in battalions. He was forced to yield ground and find some other spot where he could lie down until they located him again and launched a fresh attack. The black ones, especially the large black ones, were not so bad. They did not sting and their tickling did not wake him up until his sores were alive with them.

Yet he always managed to get enough sleep, quite enough to have enabled him, when night fell again, to scale mountains ten times as high and a hundred times as steep as the hills of Siam. He felt drunk with delight at being on his own during this reconnaissance, which was the first stage in the development of the big attack. It was on his own energy, his own judgement, on his own decisions during this expedition that the success of the operation depended – of this he was certain – and the certainty enabled him to preserve intact his inexhaustible reserves of strength. He kept his eyes firmly fixed on the imaginary bridge, that shadowy form which was a permanent part of his dream-world. The mere thought of it endowed his every gesture with an unlimited magic power which increased his glorious chances of success.

The actual bridge, the bridge on the River Kwai, had suddenly sprung into view when, after a final climb, the stiffest they had so far encountered, they reached the top of a hill commanding the valley. They had kept moving later than on the previous nights, and the sun had already risen by the time they reached the observation post which the Siamese had mentioned in their reports. He looked down at the bridge as though from an aeroplane. Several hundred feet below him a light-coloured band stretched across the water between two strips of jungle; a small gap over on the right enabled him to make out the geometric network of piles and platform. For some time he noticed no other feature of the panorama unrolled at his feet, neither the camp directly opposite him on the far bank, nor even the groups of prisoners at work on the construction itself. It was an ideal O.P. and he felt perfectly safe. The Japanese patrols were hardly likely to risk their necks in the undergrowth between him and the river.

'I saw it as plainly as I can see you now, sir. The Siamese had not exaggerated. It's a big job. It's properly built. It's nothing like any other Japanese bridge. Here are a few sketches, for what they're worth.'

He had recognized it at once. The shock of confronting this materialized ghost of his was not due to surprise but, on the contrary, to its familiar aspect. The bridge was exactly as he had imagined it. He studied it, anxiously at first, then with overpowering relief. The general background also conformed to the patiently worked-out pattern of his imagination and hopes. It differed only in detail. The water did not sparkle as he had seen it in his mind's eye. It was muddy. For a moment he felt almost cheated, but cheered up at the thought that this defect would better serve their purpose.

For two days he lay concealed, crouching in the undergrowth, eagerly observing the bridge through his binoculars and studying the ground over which the attack was to be launched. He had painted a mental picture of the general lay-out and individual features, taking notes and making a rough sketch of the paths, the camp, the Japanese huts, the bends in the river and even of the large rocks protruding here and there out of the water.

'The current's not very strong, sir. The river's an easy proposition for a small boat or a good swimmer. The water's muddy. There's a motor-road over the bridge, and four rows of piles. I saw the prisoners driving them in with a ram – the British prisoners. They've almost reached the left bank, sir, the bank with the O.P. on it. Other teams are following up behind. The bridge'll be ready in a month, I should think. The superstructure . . .'

He now had such a mass of information to report that he could not keep it in its proper order. Shears let him run on without interrupting him. There would be time enough, when he had finished speaking, to question him on specific points.

'The superstructure's a geometric network of cross-beams which looks as if it's been carefully designed. The supports are all squared up and properly put together. I could see the joints in detail through my glasses. A really well-designed job, sir, and a solid one too, let's face it. It'll mean more than just smashing up a few bits of wood. While I was there, sir, I thought of the safest way of dealing with it, and I think it's the simplest as well. I think we'll have to go for the piles in the water, or rather under the water. It's thick with sediment. The charges won't be noticed. That way the whole works will capsize all together.'

'Four rows of piles,' Shears muttered. 'That's a big job, you know. Why the hell couldn't they build this bridge of theirs like all the other ones?'

'How far apart are the piles in each row?' asked Warden, who liked to have exact figures.

'Ten feet.'

Shears and Warden silently made a mental calculation.

'We'll have to allow for a length of sixty feet, to be on the safe side,' Warden finally observed. 'That makes six piles per row, in other words twenty-four to "prepare". It'll take some time.'

'We could do it in a night, sir, I'm certain. Once we're under the bridge there's nothing to worry about. It's wide enough to give ample cover. The water washing up against the piles muffles any other sound. I know——'

'How do you know what it's like under the bridge?' Shears asked, gazing at him with renewed interest.

'Just a moment, sir. I haven't told you the whole story. I went and had a look myself.'

'You went underneath it?'

'I had to, sir. You told me not to get too close, but that was the only way I could get the information I wanted. I climbed down from the O.P., on the blind side of the hill from the river. I felt I couldn't let this opportunity slip through my fingers, sir. The Siamese took me along some wild-boar tracks. . . . We had to move on all fours.'

'How long did it take you?'

'About three hours, sir. We set off in the evening. I wanted to be in position by nightfall. It was a risk, of course, but I wanted to see for myself . . .'

'It's sometimes not such a bad idea to put your own interpretation on the orders you're given,' said Number One, as he glanced across at Warden. 'You got there, anyway – that's the main thing.'

'No one saw me, sir. We fetched up on the river about a quarter of a mile upstream from the bridge. Unfortunately there's a small native village tucked away there; but everyone was asleep. I sent the guides back. I wanted to reconnoitre on my own. I slipped into the water and floated down with the current.'

'Was it a clear night?' asked Warden.

'Fairly. No moon; but no clouds either. The bridge is pretty high, they can't see a thing . . .'

'Let's get things in their proper order,' said Shears. 'How did you approach the bridge?'

'I floated down on my back, sir, completely submerged except for my mouth. Above me . . .'

'Damn it all, Shears,' growled Warden, 'you might think of me when a mission like this crops up again.'

'I'll probably think of myself first if there ever is another one,' Shears replied.

Joyce described the scene so vividly that his two companions succumbed to his own enthusiasm and felt really disappointed that they had missed this part of the fun.

It was on the very day that he reached the O.P. after three nights' exhausting march that he had suddenly decided to do the reconnaissance. He had not been able to wait a moment longer. After seeing the bridge almost within arm's reach, he felt he simply had to go and touch it with his hand.

Flat on his back in the water, unable to make out a single detail in the solid mass of the banks, barely conscious of being carried downstream and unaware of the current, his only landmark was the long horizontal outline of the bridge. It stood out black against the sky. It grew larger as he approached it, soaring up into the heavens, while the stars above him dipped down to meet it.

Under the bridge it was almost pitch dark. He stayed there for some time, hanging motionless on to a pile. Up to his neck in the cold water which still did not cool him down, he gradually managed to pierce the darkness and distinguish the strange forest of smooth trunks emerging from the surrounding eddies. It was no surprise; he was equally familiar with the view of the bridge from this angle.

'It's worth having a shot at it, sir, I'm sure. The best thing would be to float the charges down on a raft. It wouldn't be seen. We'd be in the water. Under the bridge there's nothing to worry about. The current's not strong enough to stop us swimming about between the piles. We could tie ourselves on, if necessary, to avoid being carried away. I went right across and measured the beams, sir. They're not very thick. Quite a small charge would do the trick – under the water. It's thick, muddy water, sir.'

'We'd have to place them fairly deep,' said Warden. 'The water might be clear on the day of the attack.'

He had done all the necessary groundwork. For over two hours he had sounded the piles, measuring them with a piece of string, calculating the gaps between them, making a note of the ones which would cause the most damage if destroyed, engraving in his mind every detail which might be of use in the plan of attack. On two occasions he had heard heavy steps above his head. A Japanese sentry was patrolling the platform. He had crouched against a pile and waited. The Jap had vaguely swept the river with an electric torch.

'Our only worry while we're approaching the target, sir, is if they light a lamp. But once we're under the bridge you can hear them coming a long way off. The sound of their footsteps is magnified by the water. That gives us plenty of time to make for one of the central piles.'

'Is the river deep?' asked Shears.

'Over six foot, sir. I dived to the bottom.'

'How would you set about it?'

'Here's my idea, sir. I don't think we can rely on an automatically detonated fog-signal. We couldn't camouflage the charges. The whole works will have to be under water. A goodish length of electric wire running along the river-bed and coming out on the bank – the right bank, sir, where it would be hidden by the undergrowth. I've found the ideal spot for that – a strip of virgin jungle where a man could easily lie up and wait. And there's a good view of the platform through a gap in the trees.'

'Why the right bank?' Shears broke in with a frown. 'That's the side where the camp is, unless I've got it all wrong. Why not the opposite bank, by the hill? It's covered in thick undergrowth, according to your report, and it would obviously be our line of withdrawal.'

'That's quite true, sir. But just have another look at the map. After this wide bend here the railway winds right round the hill after passing the bridge, and then comes downstream along the river. The jungle's been cleared between the line and the bank, and the ground's quite open. There's not enough cover in daylight. You'd have to lie up much further back, on the other side of the embankment at the foot of the hill. That would need too much wire, sir, and it couldn't be camouflaged where it crosses the line, at least not without a great deal of trouble.'

'I'm not too keen on the idea,' said Number One. 'Why not the left bank, but upstream from the bridge?'

'The bank's too high, sir, there's a steep cliff. And further up still there's that small native village. I went and had a look. I crossed the river again, and then the line. I made a slight detour to keep under cover and came back upstream from the bridge. It can't be done, sir. The only decent spot is on the right bank.'

'Good heavens!' exclaimed Warden. 'You must have spent the whole night wandering round the bridge.'

'Just about. But I was back in the jungle by first light and reached the O.P. early in the morning.'

'And what's your plan for the chap who has to lie up on the right bank?' asked Shears. 'How does he manage to get away?'

'It wouldn't take a good swimmer more than three minutes to get across. That's how long it took me, sir; and the explosion would distract the Jap's attention. I think a rear party posted at the foot of the hill could cover his withdrawal. Once he's across the bit of open ground and on this side of the line, he's safe. A search party would never catch up with him in that jungle. I'm sure that's the best plan.'

Shears thought deeply for a long time as he studied Joyce's map.

'It's a plan worth considering,' he finally announced. 'Now that you've seen the spot for yourself, of course, you're in a position to tell us what you think of it. And the result will be worth taking a risk. What else did you see from your eyrie?'

CHAPTER 3

The sun was well up by the time he had reached the top of the hill. His two guides, who had come back during the night, were anxiously waiting for him. He was worn out. He had lain down to rest for an hour, and had not woken up till the evening. He apologized when he mentioned this lapse on his part.

'Right. I suppose you slept again during the night? That was the best thing to do. And then you went back to the spot you had chosen next morning?'

'Yes, sir. I stayed on a day longer. There was still quite a lot I wanted to see.'

After devoting the first part of his reconnaissance to lifeless objects, he had felt an urge to look at living men. Until then he had been spellbound by the bridge and by the features in the landscape with which his future activity was now closely linked, but suddenly he had felt overwhelmed by the sight of his wretched comrades, whom he could see in the lens of his binoculars, reduced to an abject state of serfdom. He knew what Japanese methods were like in P.O.W. camps. There were stacks of secret reports describing the daily atrocities committed by the exultant enemy.

'Did you see anything unpleasant?' Shears asked him.

'No, sir; not that particular day. But I felt completely shattered at the thought that they had been working like this for months, in this climate, with not enough to eat, rotten huts to live in, no comfort at all, and the constant threat of – well, you can imagine what sort of punishment.'

He had observed each of the teams one after the other. He had scrutinized each individual through his glasses and had been horrified by the state they were in. Number One frowned as he said:

'In our job you can't afford to be too soft-hearted, Joyce.'

'I realize that, sir. But really, they're nothing but skin and bone. Most of them are covered in ulcers and jungle-sores. Some of them can hardly walk. No civilized person would even think of making men work in such a crippled state. You ought to see them, sir. It's enough to make you weep. The team pulling the rope to drive in the last few piles – absolute skeletons, sir. I've never seen such a ghastly sight. It's utterly criminal.'

'Don't worry,' said Shears, 'we'll soon get our own back.'

'Yet I couldn't help admiring them, sir. In spite of their obvious physical hardships, not one of them seemed really beaten. I had a good look at them. They make it a point of honour to behave as though their guards weren't there – that's exactly the impression I had. They behave as though the Japs just didn't exist. They're at work from dawn till dusk, and they've been at it like this for months, probably without a single day's rest. But they didn't look as though they'd lost hope. In spite of their ludicrous dress, in spite of their terrible physical condition, they couldn't be taken for slaves, sir. I could see the expressions on their faces.'

All three fell silent for a moment, each lost in his own private thoughts.

'The British soldier's got any amount of guts when he's really up against it,' Warden finally observed.

'What else did you see?' said Shears.

'The officers, sir, the British officers. They're not being made to work. They're all in charge of their men, who seem to take more notice of them than of the Japanese guards. And they're all in full uniform.'

'In uniform!'

'Badges of rank and all, sir. I could count the pips on their shoulders.'

'Well, I'll be damned!' Shears exclaimed. 'The Siamese had told us about this bridge and I refused to believe them. In every other camp they're making all the prisoners work, irrespective of rank. Were there any senior officers?'

'A colonel, sir. That must be the Colonel Nicholson we've heard so much about, who was tortured when he first arrived. He was out there all day. I suppose he feels he should be on the spot in case there's any more trouble between his men and the Japs – because I bet you there has been trouble. I wish you could have seen those guards, sir. Monkeys dressed up as men! The way they drag their feet and slouch around, you'd never take them for anything human. Colonel Nicholson's a model of dignified behaviour. A born leader, that's how he struck me, sir.'

'He certainly must have an amazing influence, and exceptional qualities as well, to be able to keep the men's morale so high in such appalling conditions,' said Shears. 'I take my hat off to him.'

Surprise had followed surprise in the course of that day. Joyce went on with his story, obviously eager to let the others share in his astonishment and admiration.

'At one moment a prisoner from one of the groups furthest away came across the bridge to speak to the Colonel. When he was six paces off he snapped to attention, sir – in those funny clothes they all wear. Yet there was nothing funny about it. A Jap came rushing up, screaming and waving his rifle about in the air. I suppose that man must have left his team without permission. The Colonel just gave the guard one of those looks of his, sir. I saw the whole thing. The Jap thought better of it and shambled off. Incredible, isn't it? But that's not all. Just before dusk a Japanese colonel came on to the bridge – Saito, probably, the one who's said to be such a brute. Well, believe it or not, sir, when he went up to Colonel Nicholson, he almost kowtowed – there's no other word for it. There are certain ways you can tell. . . . Colonel Nicholson saluted first, of course, but Saito smartly returned the salute – almost nervously, I could see! Then they walked up and down together. The Jap looked exactly like a junior officer being given his orders. It really cheered me up to see that, sir.'

'I can't say I'm sorry to hear about it myself,' Shears muttered.

'Here's to Colonel Nicholson,' Warden suddenly proposed, raising his glass.

'You're right, Warden, here's to him – and to the five or six hundred other poor beggars who are going through such hell because of this bloody bridge.'

'All the same, it's a pity they won't be able to help us.'

'It may be a pity, Warden, but you know what we're up against. We have to go through with it on our own. But let's get back to the bridge . . .'

They spent the whole evening discussing the bridge and studying Joyce's sketch-map in a fever of excitement, occasionally questioning him on some specific detail or other, which he promptly explained. He could have drawn every bit of the bridge and described every eddy in the river from memory. They then got down to the plan he had suggested, making a list of all the operations it would entail, working each of those out in detail, keeping a sharp look-out for any unforeseen snag that might conceivably crop up at the last moment. Then Warden went off to receive the incoming messages on the W/T in the room next door. Joyce was silent for a moment.

'Look, sir,' he finally blurted out, 'I'm the best swimmer of the three, and now that I've been over the ground . . .'

'We'll discuss that later,' said Number One.

Shears realized that Joyce was at the end of his tether when he saw him stagger on his way to bed. After spending three days lying in the undergrowth, studying the lie of the land, he had set off on the return journey during the night and got back to camp by marching without stopping, except for a short halt for food. Even the Siamese had hardly been able to keep up with the pace he had set. They were now busy describing with admiration how the young white man had managed to walk them off their feet.

'You'd better get some rest,' said Number One. 'There's no point in working yourself to death before we start. We want to have you in proper shape when the time comes. Why did you return so quickly?'

'The bridge will probably be finished in less than a month from now.'

All of a sudden Joyce fell asleep, without even taking off the make-up which made him unrecognizable. Shears shrugged his shoulders and did not attempt to wake him. He sat there alone, working out the part that each of them would play in the scene shortly to be enacted in the Kwai valley. He had not yet come to any decision when Warden returned with a handful of messages which he had just deciphered.

'It looks as if the balloon will go up any day now, Shears. Information from H.Q.: the railway's almost finished along the whole of the line. The opening ceremony will probably be held in five or six weeks' time – a "first" train, crammed full of troops and V.I.P.s. A nice little celebration. A fair amount of war material as well. Things are looking up. H.Q. have passed all your plans and are giving you a completely free hand. The R.A.F. won't interfere. We'll be getting a daily sit. rep. The youngster's asleep, is he?'

'Yes, don't wake him up. He deserves a little rest. He did pretty well, you know. Tell me, Warden, do you think we can rely on him in *any* emergency?'

Warden thought the question over before answering.

'He looks all right to me. Of course, one can't be sure *beforehand*, you know that as well as I do. But I know what you're driving at. You want to know if he's capable of taking an important decision in a matter of seconds, or even less, and acting on it. But what made you bring that up?'

'Because he just said: "I'm the best swimmer of the three." And he's not shooting a line. It's true.'

'When I joined Force 316,' Warden growled, 'I didn't realize I would have to be a swimming champion in order to see some action. I'll put in a little practice on my next leave.'

'There's a psychological reason as well. If I don't give him his head, he'll lose confidence in himself, and then he'll be utterly useless. As you say, we can't be sure *beforehand* – even he can't be – and meanwhile he's dying to know. The main thing, of course, is whether he's got as much chance as we have of bringing it off. I think he has . . . and also a chance of getting away with it. We'll know for certain in a few days. I want to see what he looks like tomorrow. Let's not mention the bridge to him for the time being. I don't like the way he gets so worked up by the thought of those wretched prisoners. Oh, I know what you're going to say – what one feels has got nothing to do with how one behaves. All the same, he's rather inclined to get overwrought, to let his imagination run riot, if you know what I mean. He broods a bit too much, that's his trouble.'

'You can't lay down a general rule for our sort of job,' Warden wisely observed. 'Sometimes you get good results by using a little imagination, and even by brooding. Not always, of course.'

CHAPTER 4

Colonel Nicholson also was worrying about the prisoners' state of health, and had come to the hospital to discuss the matter with the M.O.

'We can't go on like this, Clipton,' he said in a solemn, almost threatening tone of voice. 'A man who's dangerously ill can't work, that's obvious; but all the same, there's a limit. You've now got half the personnel on the sick-list! How do you expect us to get the bridge finished in a month? It's well under way, I know, but there's still a lot of work to be done, and with the teams reduced to half-strength, we're just marking time. Even the ones who are still on the job don't seem up to the mark.'

'Look at them, sir,' said Clipton, who was so enraged by these words that he had to struggle to maintain his usual equanimity and show the necessary deference which the Colonel demanded of all his subordinates, no matter what their rank or position. 'If I had listened to the voice of my professional conscience, or simply to the voice of human decency, it wouldn't be half the personnel but the whole lot that I'd certify as unfit for work, especially this sort of work!'

For the first few months the bridge had gone forward at a spanking pace, with only an occasional setback caused by Saito's moodiness. From time to time the Jap felt he ought to regain his position of authority and would try to give himself Dutch courage to overcome his complexes by a show of cruelty. But these outbursts had occurred less and less frequently since it was quite obvious that any attempt at violence did nothing but impede progress on the bridge. For a long time the work had been well ahead of the schedule laid down by Major Hughes and Captain Reeves, thanks to a collaboration which was efficient though not entirely free from friction. But the climate, the nature of the tasks imposed, the diet and the living conditions had all been a drain on the men's health.

Their physical condition was becoming a real anxiety. With no meat, apart from some decrepit old cow which the natives from the nearest village occasionally sold them, with no butter and no bread, the prisoners, whose meals sometimes consisted of rice and nothing else, had been gradually reduced to the skin-and-bone condition which Joyce had found so pitiful. The hard labour of heaving all day long on a rope to lift the heavy weight which dropped back again and again with an ear-splitting crash had become real torture to the men in that particular team. Some of the others were no better off, especially the ones who had to spend hours on end on a scaffolding, up to their waist in water, to hold the piles in position while the ram thudded down over and over again, deafening them each time.

Their morale was still fairly high, thanks to the fine example set by officers like Lieutenant Harper, who showed magnificent drive and energy, shouting cheerful words of encouragement all day long, and willingly lending a hand himself, although he was an officer, tugging at the rope with all his might so as to ease the burden of the weaker men. Their sense of humour was still in evidence on certain occasions, for instance whenever Captain Reeves appeared with his blue-print, foot-rule, spirit-level and other home-made instruments and crept along a rickety scaffolding just above water-level in order to take certain measurements, followed by the little Japanese engineer, who dogged his footsteps, copied every gesture he made, and solemnly recorded some figures in a note-book.

Since all the officers modelled themselves directly on the Colonel, the fate of the bridge was entirely in his capable hands. He knew this, and felt the justified pride of the leader who welcomes and seeks responsibility, but also takes on his own shoulders the burden of worries which that post of honour entails.

The growing sick-list was his chief anxiety. He saw his companies literally whittled down before his very eyes. Bit by bit, day by day, hour by hour, some of the living substances of each prisoner came apart from its individual organism to be swallowed up in the anonymous material universe. This universe of earth, monstrous vegetation, water and mosquito-infested swamp was not perceptibly affected by this human contribution. In arithmetical terms, it was a complete transfer of molecules, which was felt as a severe loss by each individual and could be measured in pounds' weight per man multiplied by five hundred, yet resulted in no appreciable total gain.

Clipton was frightened there might be a fatal epidemic such as cholera, which had broken out in some of the other camps. This scourge had so far been avoided, thanks to strict discipline, but there were still countless cases of malaria, dysentery and beri-beri. Every day he was forced to declare a large number of men unfit for duty and to put them on the sick-list. In the hospital he managed to provide those who were able to eat with a fairly reasonable diet, thanks to a few Red Cross parcels which had escaped the prying hands of the Japanese and had been set aside for the patients. In any case a few days' off-duty was balm to some of the prisoners, who had worn themselves out on the ram and were consequently suffering from nervous prostration, seeing things and living in a continual nightmare.

Colonel Nicholson was fond of his men. At first he had backed Clipton up to the best of his ability so as to justify the size of the sick-list in the eyes of the Japanese. He had anticipated Saito's inevitable protests by demanding a greater effort from the men who were still fit.

But for some time now he had felt that Clipton was going too far. He openly suspected him of abusing his medical privileges and of showing excessive leniency by certifying prisoners who could still be of some use as unfit for duty. The work was due to be completed in a month; this was no time for slacking off. He had come to the hospital that morning to inspect it personally, to thrash the matter out with Clipton and to put the M.O. on the right track – firmly, of course, but also with the courtesy which one had to show, after all, when approaching a staff officer on such a delicate issue.

'What about this chap, for instance?' he said, stopping to speak to one of the patients. 'What's wrong with you, my lad?'

He was walking between two rows of prisoners who lay on bamboo beds, either shivering with fever or in a state of coma, their cadaverous faces protruding from the threadbare blankets.

'Temperature of 104 last night, sir. Malaria.'

'Right. I see,' said the Colonel, moving on. 'And this man?'

'Jungle sores. I had to dig into his leg yesterday – with an ordinary knife; I haven't any other instruments. He's got a hole in him as large as a golf ball sir.'

'So that was it,' muttered Colonel Nicholson. 'I thought I heard someone shrieking in the night.'

'That was it. Four of his pals had to hold him down. I hope I'll be able to save his leg, but it's touch and go,' he added, lowering his voice. 'Do you really want me to send him out to work, sir?'

'Don't talk rot, Clipton. Of course I don't. What you say, goes. But let's get this clear. I'm not trying to force sick and wounded men to work. But we must face this fact: we've got less than a month to finish the job we're doing. It'll require a superhuman effort, I know, but I can't help that. Consequently, each time you take one of the men off work, you make it harder for everyone else. You ought to bear that in mind every moment of the day, do you understand? Even if a man's not at the top of his form he can still make himself useful and help on light duties – the trimmings and finishing touches, for instance; the general wash and brush-up that Hughes will soon be organizing, you know.'

'I suppose you're going to have the thing painted, sir?'

'Don't even think of such a thing, Clipton,' said the Colonel testily. 'The most we could do would be to give it a coating of lime – and a fine target that would make for the R.A.F., wouldn't it! You seem to forget there's a war on!'

'You're quite right, sir, there's a war on.'

'No, there'll be nothing fancy about it. I'm all against that. All we want is a decent, properly finished job. That's what I came here to tell you, Clipton. You must make the men understand they've all got to pull their weight. This fellow, now . . .'

'A nasty arm wound, sir, which he got from hoisting beams for that

bloody bridge of yours,' Clipton burst out. 'I've got twenty others like him
on my hands. Naturally in their present state the wounds won't heal and
they get infected. I've got nothing to treat them with . . .'

'I wonder,' persisted Colonel Nicholson, pursuing a single train of
thought and overlooking Clipton's improper language, 'I wonder if in a
case like this fresh air and light duties wouldn't do them more good than
lying cooped up in this hut of yours. What do you think, Clipton? After all
it's not our usual policy to send a man to hospital just because he's
scratched his arms. If you stop to think for a moment, Clipton, I'm sure
you'll feel the same as I do.'

'Not our policy, sir! No, not our policy!'

He raised his arms in a gesture of impotent despair. The Colonel took
him aside, away from the patients, into the ante-room which served as a
surgery, and went on pleading his case, using every argument available to a
commander who wants to persuade rather than give orders. Finally, since
Clipton seemed far from convinced, he put forward his most cogent reason:
if Clipton insisted on pursuing this course, the Japanese would take it on
themselves to evacuate the hospital completely and would show no
discrimination in the process.

'Saito has threatened to take drastic steps,' he explained.

That was a white lie. Having at last realized that violence had no result,
Saito had now stopped using it and, in his heart of hearts, was delighted to
see the best installation on the whole line being built under his direction.
Colonel Nicholson had indulged in this distortion of the truth, even though
it pricked his conscience. He could not afford to disregard a single factor
which might accelerate the completion of the bridge – this bridge
representing the dauntless sort of spirit which never acknowledges defeat
but always has some inner resource to draw on as proof of its invincibility,
this bridge which needed only a few more yards before it would straddle the
Kwai valley in a single unbroken line.

Faced with this threat, Clipton cursed the Colonel but was forced to
yield. He discharged about a quarter of the patients, in spite of the terrible
moral problem that confronted him each time he had to make a choice. In
this way he sent back to work a crowd of limping cripples, walking
wounded and malaria cases still shaking with fever but capable of dragging
themselves along.

They did not complain. The Colonel had the sort of faith which moves
mountains, builds pyramids, cathedrals or even bridges, and makes dying
men go to work with a smile on their lips. They succumbed to his appeal
that they should pull their weight. They went down to the river without a
murmur. Some of the poor devils, with one arm out of action thanks to a
dirty or slipshod dressing, seized the rope of the ram with their only good

hand and tugged at it all together with what remained of their will and strength, putting all their reduced weight behind it, contributing the additional sacrifice of this painful effort to the sum total of suffering which was slowly bringing the River Kwai bridge to a successful conclusion.

With this fresh impetus the bridge was soon finished. All that remained now was what the Colonel called the 'trimmings', which would give the construction that 'finished' look in which the practised eye can at once recognize, in no matter what part of the world, the craftsmanship of the European and the Anglo-Saxon sense of perfection.

PART 4

CHAPTER 1

A few weeks after Joyce's expedition Warden followed the same route as the lieutenant and, like him, reached the O.P. after an exhausting climb. It was his turn now to lie flat on his face in the ferns and observe the Kwai bridge down below.

Warden was anything but romantic. At first he gave no more than a rapid glance, just sufficient to enable him to recognize with satisfaction the construction that Joyce had depicted and to confirm that it was now complete. There were four partisans with him. He told them he did not need them for the moment. They sat down in their favourite position, lit their water-pipes and watched him quietly get down to work.

He first set up his W/T aerial and tuned in to several stations. One of these, an absolute boon in occupied territory, gave him a daily intelligence report on the forthcoming departure of the big convoy which was to inaugurate the Burma-Siam railway. The messages he received were encouraging: the orders still stood.

After that he arranged his sleeping-bag and mosquito-net as comfortably as possible, carefully laid out the contents of his sponge-bag, then did the same for Shears who was to join him on this hill-top. Warden was a man of foresight, older than Joyce and more level-headed. He was also more experienced. He knew the jungle from the various expeditions he had been on during his pre-war vacations. He knew how highly a white man values his tooth-brush at certain times and how much longer he can carry on if properly installed and if fortified by a cup of tea in the morning. If they were hard pressed after the attack, they would have to jettison these goods and chattels of the civilized world; they would no longer be needed. But they would have helped to keep them fighting fit up to the moment they went into action. Satisfied with his arrangements, he ate some food, slept for three hours, then went back to the O.P. and tried to think of the best method of carrying out his mission.

In accordance with Joyce's plan, which, after countless modifications, had been finally adopted by all three of them and on which Number One had now decided to take action, the Force 316 team had split up. Shears, Joyce and two Siamese volunteers, accompanied by a few porters, had set off in single file for a point on the river upstream from the bridge, so as to avoid launching the explosives in the vicinity of the camp. They had gone rather far out of their way, making a wide detour to by-pass some native settlements. The four men were to move down to the bridge at night in order to prepare the material. (It would be a gross mistake to think that blowing up a bridge is a simple operation.) Joyce was to remain in hiding on the enemy bank and there wait for the train. Shears was to rejoin Warden and, with him, share the responsibility of covering the withdrawal.

Warden was to remain at the O.P., maintain radio contact, observe what went on round the bridge and reconnoitre possible positions from which to give Joyce covering fire. The scope of the mission was not strictly limited. Number One had allowed him a certain amount of initiative. He would have to act for the best according to the circumstances.

'If you see any chance of following up with a subsidiary attack,' Shears had told him, 'then I won't try to stop you – provided, of course, that there's no risk of your being discovered. The principles of Force 316 still hold good. But the bridge is our number one target and on no account must you jeopardize our chances of success in that direction. I'm relying on you to be sensible and at the same time forceful.'

He knew he could rely on Warden to be both sensible and forceful. Whenever there was time, Warden methodically weighed up the consequences of every gesture he made.

After an initial reconnaissance of the sky-line Warden decided to place his pocket artillery – two light mortars – right on top of the hill and to man this post during the attack with the two Siamese partisans, so that the wreckage of the train, the troops trying to escape after the explosion, and the soldiers rushing up to help them, would all be under constant fire.

This was perfectly in keeping with the implicit instructions contained in Number One's reference to the principles of Force 316. These principles could be summed up as follows: 'Never assume an operation is complete in itself; never be satisfied while there's still a chance, however slight, of causing the enemy further alarm and despondency.' (The typically Anglo-Saxon 'finishing touches' were as much in evidence in this sphere of activity as elsewhere.) Now, in this case it was obvious that a hail of mortar shells falling on the survivors, like bolts from the blue, would be calculated to demoralize the enemy completely. The O.P., which commanded the whole valley, was almost miraculously placed from this point of view. At the same time Warden saw yet another advantage in prolonging the attack: it would divert the enemy's attention and so indirectly help to cover Joyce's withdrawal.

Warden spent a long time creeping through the ferns and wild rhododendrons before finding gun-emplacements entirely to his satisfaction. When he did find them, he called up the Siamese, chose two of them, and told them exactly what they would have to do when the time came.

They were quick on the uptake and seemed to like the idea.

It was about four in the afternoon by the time Warden completed his preparations. He then started to think about the subsequent arrangements to be made, when he heard the sound of music in the valley. He returned to his observation, his field-glasses trained on foe and friend alike. The bridge was deserted, but there was something strange going on in the camp, over on the far side of the river. Warden at once realized that, in order to celebrate the successful conclusion of their labours, the prisoners had been allowed, or perhaps even obliged, to throw a party. A signal received a few days ago had notified him of these festivities decreed by the loving kindness of His Imperial Majesty.

The music emanated from some instrument which must have been knocked together by a local craftsman, but the hand plucking the strings belong to a European. Warden knew the barbaric tunes of the Japanese well enough not to be mistaken. Besides, the sound of singing soon reached his ears. In feeble, faltering tones, but with an unmistakable accent, a voice was singing an old Scottish ballad. The words echoed round the valley and were taken up in chorus. This pathetic concert heard in the solitude of his O.P. moved Warden to the point of tears. He made a conscious effort to repel these gloomy thoughts and managed to drive them out of his mind by concentrating instead on the requirements of his mission. He lost all interest in what was happening inside the camp, except in so far as it affected the impending attack.

Shortly before sundown it looked as if a banquet was being prepared. Prisoners began to crowd round the cook-house. There was a noticeable stir in the direction of the Japanese quarters as well, where several soldiers were rushing about, shouting and laughing. The Japanese, it appeared, were also preparing to celebrate the conclusion of their labours.

Warden's mind worked fast. His cool, calculating temperament did not prevent him from pouncing on the first opportunity that occurred. He made the necessary arrangements for going into action that very night, having suddenly decided to follow a plan which he had thought of long before he reached the O.P. His profound understanding of human nature told him that in a God-forsaken patch of jungle like this, with a chronic alcoholic like Saito in command, and with soldiers subject to a régime almost as ruthless as that of the prisoners themselves, every Jap in the place was bound to be blind drunk by midnight. Here was an exceptionally favourable opportunity for him to take individual action, with a minimum of risk in accordance with Number One's instructions, and to lay a few of those subsidiary traps, which give to the main attack that additional zest to which every member of Force 316 is partial. Warden weighed up the pros and cons, came to the conclusion that it would be criminal not to exploit this miraculous coincidence, decided to move down to the river, and started making up a small charge . . . for, even against his better judgement, why should not he too, just for once, have a close view of that bridge?

He reached the foot of the hill shortly before midnight. The party had ended exactly as he expected it would. He had been able to follow each stage of it from the increasing din punctuating his own silent progress: savage yells, like a parody of the English singing, had stopped some time ago. The silence was now complete. He called a final halt and listened carefully, crouching with two partisans who had accompanied him behind the last curtain of trees not far from the railway line, which at this point ran along the river after crossing the bridge, just as Joyce had described it. Warden signalled to the Siamese. Carrying the sabotage material, the three men cautiously moved off in the direction of the railway.

Warden was convinced he could perform the operation in complete security. There was no sign of the enemy on this bank. The Japanese had enjoyed such complete peace in this out-of-the-way corner that they had lost all sense of danger. By now all the soldiers, and all the officers too, must have passed out, all of them blind drunk. But just to make sure, Warden posted one of the Siamese as a sentry, then methodically got down to work, assisted by the other.

What he had in mind was a straightforward, text-book operation. It was the first lesson taught in the Plastic and Destructions Company's special school in Calcutta. It is quite a simple job to loosen the gravel which is used as ballast on a railway line from either side of the rails and from underneath them, so as to make a small cavity capable of holding a plastic charge fastened to the inside of the metals. The properties of this chemical compound are such that a two-pound charge, if cleverly placed, is all that is needed. The energy stored in that small amount is rapidly released, by the action of a detonator, in the form of a gas which reaches a speed of several thousand feet per second. The strongest steel is incapable of standing up to the splintering effect of this sudden expansion.

The detonator, then, is inserted in the plastic. (Pressing it in is as easy as sliding a knife through a pat of butter.) A length of so-called 'instantaneous' fuse connects it to a wonderfully simple little mechanism which is likewise hidden in a hole made underneath the rail. This device consists of two blades kept apart by a strong spring, with a primer inserted between them. One of the blades is placed against the metal, while the other is firmly wedged with a stone. The detonating cord itself is buried below the surface. A team of two experts can lay this charge in less than half an hour. If the work is done carefully, the trap is invisible.

When one of the wheels of the engine presses down on the mechanism, the two blades are crushed together. The primer then sets the detonator off through the action of the instantaneous cord. The plastic explodes. A length of steel is reduced to powder. The train is derailed. With a little luck and with a slightly larger charge, the engine can be overturned. One of the advantages of this method is that the mechanism is released by the train itself, thus enabling the agent who has laid it to be a mile or more away at the time. Another is that it cannot go off prematurely if an animal treads on it. A really heavy weight, like a locomotive or a railway-coach, is needed.

Warden, in his logical, systematic way, pursued the following argument: the first train will come from Bangkok along the right bank and so, in theory, will be blown up at the same time as the bridge and crash into the river. So much for target number one. The line is consequently cut, and traffic comes to a standstill. The Japanese then work like fiends to repair the damage. They are anxious to repair it as quickly as possible in order to open up the line again and avenge this outrage, which is also a serious blow to their prestige. They rush forward any amount of labour-gangs and work without stopping. They toil away for days, for weeks, perhaps even for months. When the line is at last cleared, and the bridge rebuilt, another convoy comes along. This time the bridge holds together. But a little later – the next train to cross blows up. That is bound to cause an adverse psychological effect, apart from material damage. Warden lays a slightly larger charge than is strictly necessary, and places it so that the train will come off the rails close to the river bank. If all goes well, the engine and some of the coaches will land in the water.

Warden quickly completed these initial stages of his work. He was a past-master at this sort of job, having trained himself to shift the gravel without making a sound before moulding the plastic and setting the booby-trap. He operated almost mechanically and was pleased to find that the Siamese partisan, though new to the game, was nevertheless an able assistant. His instruction had been good – much to the delight of Professor Warden. There was still some time to go before first light. He had brought with him a second contraption of the same type but slightly different, which he placed a few hundred yards further up the line in the opposite direction to the bridge. It would be criminal not to take full advantage of a night like this.

Warden had shown his usual foresight. After two attacks in the same sector the enemy usually got suspicious and proceeded to inspect the line systematically. But one never knew. Sometimes, on the contrary, he could not imagine the possibility of a third outrage, precisely because there had already been two. In any case, if the trap was well camouflaged, it might escape the most searching scrutiny – unless the search-party reluctantly decide to rake through every bit of gravel in the ballast. Warden set his second 'toy', which differed from the first in that it was fitted with a device to vary the effects of the explosion and cause another sort of alarm. The mechanism worked on a kind of delayed-action principle. The first train did not set it off, but simply started the mechanism working. The detonator and plastic themselves were only affected by the weight of the following train. It was quite clear what the Force 316 technicians had in mind when they perfected this ingenious device which so delighted Warden's rational mentality. Quite often, when a line had been repaired after a whole series of accidents, the enemy sent the next important convoy through behind a screen of a couple of coaches loaded with stones and pulled by a useless old engine. Nothing untoward happened to the leading train. And so the enemy was convinced that his run of bad luck was over. Full of confidence, and without any further security measure, he launched the train that really mattered and hey-presto, the train that really mattered blew up!

'Never assume an operation is complete unless the enemy has been caused as much alarm and despondency as possible' was the *leitmotiv* of the Plastic and Destructions Company, Ltd. 'Always strive to multiply the number of unpleasant surprises and to invent fresh traps so as to sow confusion among the enemy just when he thinks he has at last been left in peace' was the firm's ceaseless exhortation. Warden had taken these doctrines to heart. After setting his second trap and leaving no trace of it, he again wracked his brains and tried to think of yet another trick to play.

He had brought with him a few other 'toys', just in case. He had several specimens of one of these, consisting of a round of ammunition fitted into a loose board which pivoted on its axis and snapped back on to a second, fixed, board pierced with a nail. These were anti-personnel devices. They were hidden under a thin layer of earth. They were the most simple sort of mechanism imaginable. The weight of one man was all that was needed to snap the round down on to the firing-pin. The bullet went off and pierced the man's foot or, with any luck, hit him in the forehead if he happened to be walking leaning forward. The instructors in the special school in Calcutta recommended scattering large numbers of these 'toys' in the neighbourhood of a 'prepared' railway line. After the explosion, when the survivors (there were bound to be a few) were rushing about in panic, the traps would go off and add to their confusion.

Warden would have liked to get rid of the whole lot as cunningly as possible, but his caution and reason prompted him to abandon this final delight. There was a risk of their being discovered, and the priority target was too important to warrant such a risk. A sentry coming across one of these traps would be enough to put the Japs on their guard against a possible sabotage attack.

Dawn was approaching. Warden wisely but reluctantly decided to go no further and started back for the O.P. He was fairly pleased to be leaving behind a well-prepared area seasoned with spices designed to give an added zest to the main attack.

CHAPTER 2

One of the partisans made a sudden movement. He had heard an unusual crackling in the forest of giant ferns which covered the hill-top. For a few seconds the four Siamese kept absolutely still. Warden had seized his tommy-gun and stood ready for any eventuality. Three low whistles were heard a little below them. One of the Siamese whistled back, then waved his arm and turned to Warden.

'Number One,' he said.

Presently Shears and a couple of natives joined the group at the O.P.

'What's the latest?' he anxiously asked as soon as he caught sight of Warden.

'Everything under control. Nothing new. I've been here three days. It's all set for tomorrow. The train leaves Bangkok some time during the night and should get here about ten in the morning. What about you?'

'Everything's ready,' said Shears, lowering himself to the ground with a sigh of relief.

He had been horribly afraid that the Japanese plans might have been changed at the last moment. Warden too had been on tenterhooks since the evening before. He knew that the bridge was being prepared that night and had spent hours listening blindly for the slightest sound from the River Kwai, thinking of his two friends at work in the water just below him, constantly weighing up their chances of success, visualizing each successive stage of the operation, and trying to think of any snag that might possibly crop up. He had heard nothing unusual. According to the programme, Shears was to rejoin him at first light. It was now past ten o'clock.

'I'm glad you've turned up at last. I was getting a little worried.'

'We were hard at it all night.'

Warden looked at him more closely and saw that he was utterly exhausted. His clothes, which were still damp, steamed in the sun. His drawn features, the dark circles under his eyes, the growth of beard on his chin, made him look like nothing on earth. He handed him a flask of brandy and noticed how he fumbled as he seized it. His hands were covered with scratches and cuts, the dead-white skin wrinkled and hanging in strips. He could hardly move his fingers. Warden gave him a dry shirt and a pair of shoes which he had put out for him, then waited.

'You're quite sure nothing's planned for today?' Shears repeated.

'Absolutely. Another signal came in this morning.'

Shears took a gulp, then gingerly started massaging his limbs.

'Rather a tough job,' he remarked with a shudder. 'I think I'll remember that cold water for the rest of my life. But everything went off all right.'

'What about the youngster?'

'The youngster was terrific. Didn't let up for a second. He was at it harder than I was, yet showed no sign of fatigue. He's now in position on the right bank. He insisted on settling in at once and staying put until the train arrives.'

'Supposing they get wind of him?'

'He's well concealed. It's a risk, I know, but it's worth it. We've got to avoid a lot of movement round the bridge at this stage. And then the train might turn up earlier than we think. I'm sure they won't catch him napping today. He's young, and he's tough. He's lying up in a thicket which can only be reached from the river, and the bank there is steep. We can probably see the place from here. All he can see, through a gap in the branches, is the bridge. But he'll be able to hear the train approaching.'

'Did you go there yourself?'

'I went with him. He was right. It's a perfect position.'

Shears took out his field-glasses and tried to spot the place in a landscape which was strange to him.

'It's hard to pin-point it,' he said. 'It all looks so different from here. But I think it's over there, about ten yards behind that large red tree with its branches trailing in the water.'

'So now everything depends on him.'

'Yes, everything depends on him, and I feel completely confident.'

'Has he got his knife?'

'He's got his knife. And I'm sure he'll be capable of using it.'

'One can never really tell till the time comes.'

'I know one can't. All the same, I'm pretty sure.'

'And afterwards?'

'It took me five minutes to get across the river, but he swims nearly twice as fast as I do. We'll be able to cover his withdrawal.'

Warden told Shears what arrangements he had made. The evening before, he had climbed down from the O.P., this time before it was quite dark, but had not gone as far as the stretch of flat, open ground. On his way he had selected a suitable spot for the team's light machine-gun and had reconnoitred positions for the partisans who were to provide rifle fire in the event of a counter-attack. Each position had been carefully noted down. This barrage, in conjunction with the mortar shells, would provide ample protection for quite a long time.

Number One approved of the plan in general. Then, since he felt too tired to sleep, he described to his friend how the previous night's operation had been carried out. As he listened carefully to this account, Warden felt almost relieved that he himself had not taken part in the preparations. Meanwhile, there was nothing else for them to do until the next day. As they had said, everything now depended on Joyce – on Joyce and the fortunes of war. They tried hard to curb their impatience and to stop worrying about the principal actor, who now lay hidden in the bushes over on the enemy bank.

As soon as he had decided to put his plan into action, Number One had drawn up a detailed programme. He had assigned the various roles so as to enable each individual member of the team to think out in advance what he would have to do and to rehearse each move that he would have to make. In this way, when the time came, they would all be able to keep their minds free to deal with any unforeseen eventuality.

It would be childish to think that a bridge can be blown up without a great many preparations. Working from Joyce's sketch and notes, Warden, like Captain Reeves, had made a plan – a destruction plan: a large-scale drawing of the bridge in which every pile was numbered and every charge marked in at the exact spot where it would be needed, the intricate network of electric wire and detonating cord which would set the whole thing off being indicated in red pencil. Each of them soon had this plan engraved on his memory.

But these paper-work preparations had not been sufficient for Number One. He had made them go through several rehearsals at night on an old derelict bridge lying across a stream not far from their camp, the charges, of course, being represented by sacks of earth. The men who were to fix the explosives in position – himself, Joyce and two local volunteers – had practised swimming silently, pushing in front of them a light bamboo raft specially built for the purpose, on which all the kit was fastened. Warden was the umpire. He had been quite ruthless and had made them repeat the drill until the operation was a hundred per cent perfect. The four men had got used to working in the water without making a splash, fastening the dummy charges firmly on to the piles and connecting them together by means of the intricate network of fuses worked out in the destruction plan. At last they had managed to do it to Number One's satisfaction. All that now remained was to prepare the genuine material and see to a mass of important details, such as waterproof sheeting for whatever needed protecting from the damp.

The party had then started off. Along paths known only to themselves, the guides had taken them to a point on the river a long way upstream from the bridge, where the launching could take place in complete security.

Several native volunteers were acting as porters.

The plastic was made up into twelve-pound charges, each of which had to be fastened to a separate pile. The destruction plan catered for the preparation of six consecutive piles in each row, making a total of twenty-four charges. All the supporting beams would thus be shattered for a stretch of nearly thirty yards, which would be quite sufficient to bring the bridge down under the weight of a train. Shears had wisely brought a dozen extra charges in case of accident. They might eventually be fixed in some suitable position to cause the enemy further alarm. He was not one to forget the maxims of Force 316.

These various quantities had not been chosen at random. They had been determined after much calculation and long discussion, and were based on the measurements that Joyce had taken during his reconnaissance. A formula, which all three knew by heart, gave the weight of charge required for shattering a beam of any given material, according to its shape and size. In this case six pounds of plastic would have been enough, in theory. With eight, the margin of security would have been ample for any ordinary operation. Number One eventually decided to increase the amount still further.

He had good reasons for adopting such measures. Another of the Plastic and Destructions Company's principles was to add a little on to every figure provided by the technicians. At the end of the theoretical training Colonel Green, who ran the Calcutta school at a very high level, used to deliver a short address on this subject, based on common sense and his own personal experience of engineering.

'When you work out the weight needed by means of the formula,' he would say, 'make a generous allowance – then add even a little more on. On a tricky operation you must make absolutely certain. If you're in the least doubtful it's better to use a hundred pounds too much than a pound too little. You'd look pretty silly if, after slaving away, for several nights perhaps, in order to prepare the target, after risking your life and your men's lives, after getting so far after God knows how many difficulties – you'd look pretty silly if, for the sake of saving a few pounds of explosive, the destruction was only a partial success – beams knocked about a bit but still in position, and so quite easy to repair. I'm speaking from personal experience. That's what happened to me once, and I can't think of anything in the world that's more demoralizing.'

Shears had sworn he would never allow such a disaster to happen to him, and he generously applied the principle. On the other hand one had to guard against going to the opposite extreme and cluttering oneself up with a lot of useless material when there was only a small team available.

In theory, the launching of the material presented no difficulty. One of the many qualities of plastic is that it has about the same density as water. A swimmer can easily tow quite a large amount of it behind him.

They had reached the River Kwai at dawn. The porters had been sent back. The four men had waited till nightfall, hidden in the undergrowth.

'The hours must have dragged by,' said Warden. 'Did you manage to get to sleep?'

'Hardly at all. We tried to, but you know what it's like just before zero hour. Joyce and I spent the whole afternoon chatting. I wanted to keep his mind off the bridge. We had the whole night to think about that.'

'What did you talk about?' said Warden, who wanted to know every detail.

'He told me a little about his civilian life. A rather sad type at heart, that lad. A pretty dull career on the whole – draughtsman in a big engineering firm; nothing brilliant about it, and he doesn't pretend there was. A sort of glorified office-boy. I'd always imagined it was something like that. Two dozen chaps of the same age sitting all day long over their drawing-boards in a communal work-room – can't you see what it was like? When he wasn't drawing, he was working out sums – with formulae and a slide-rule. Nothing particularly exciting. I don't think he was too keen on the job – he seems to have welcomed the war as the chance of his lifetime. Strange that a chap chained to a desk should have landed up in Force 316.'

'Well, after all, there are professors in it as well,' said Warden. 'I've known quite a few like him. They're not necessarily the worst of the bunch.'

'And not necessarily the best either. You can't make a general rule about it. But he's not at all bitter when he talks about his past. Just rather sad, that's all.'

'He's all right, I'm sure. What sort of drawing did he have to do?'

'By a strange coincidence the firm had something to do with bridges. Not wooden bridges, of course. And they didn't handle construction work either. Articulated bridges in metal – a standard model. They used to make them in separate pieces and deliver them all together to the contractors – just like a meccano set! He was never out of the office. For two years before the war he drew the same piece over and over again. Specialization and all the rest of it – you can imagine what it was like. He didn't find it terribly exciting. It wasn't even a very big piece – a girder, that's what he said. His job was to work out the shape that would give the greatest resistance for the smallest weight of metal, at least that's what I understood him to say. I don't know anything about the subject. It was a question of economy – the firm didn't like wasting material. He spent two years doing that – a boy of his age! You should have heard him talk about that girder! His voice was trembling. You know, Warden, I think the girder was partly responsible for his enthusiasm for the present job.'

'I must admit,' said Warden, 'I've never seen anyone quite so keen on the idea of destroying a bridge. I'm beginning to think, Shears, that Force 316 is a heaven-sent opportunity for men like that. If it didn't exist, we'd have had to invent it. Take yourself, now; if you hadn't been fed up with regimental soldiering . . .'

'And if you, for instance, had been completely satisfied with lecturing at a university . . . Well, whatever the reason, at the outbreak of the war he was still completely absorbed in that girder. He told me quite seriously that in two years he had succeeded in saving a pound and a half of metal, on paper. That wasn't too bad, it seems, but the firm thought he could do still better. He would have had to go on like that for months on end. He joined up during the first few days. When he heard about Force 316, he could hardly wait. And people still say there's no truth in vocation! It's a funny thing, though. If it hadn't been for that girder, he probably wouldn't at this very moment be lying flat on his face in the undergrowth a hundred yards from the enemy, with a knife in his belt and an instrument of wholesale destruction by his side.'

CHAPTER 3

Shears and Joyce had chatted like this all day, while the two Siamese conversed in an undertone about the expedition. Shears had an occasional twinge of conscience, wondering whether he had chosen the right man for the most important role, the one who of the three of them had the best chance of succeeding; or whether he had simply succumbed to the earnestness of his entreaties

'Are you quite sure you'll be able to act as decisively as Warden or myself no matter what the circumstance?' he had solemnly asked for the last time.

'I'm absolutely certain now, sir. You must give me this chance.'

Shears had not pressed the point and had not reconsidered his decision.

They had started the launching just before dusk. The bank was deserted. The bamboo raft – which they had themselves built, since they trusted no one else to do the job properly – consisted of two separate, parallel sections, to make it more easy to carry through the jungle. They slid it into the river and fastened the two halves together by lashing a couple of shafts across them. When in position, they made a rigid platform. Then they fixed the charges on as firmly as possible. There were other parcels containing the rolls of cord, the battery, electric wire and the generator. The fragile material, was wrapped in waterproof sheeting. As for the detonators, Shears had brought an extra set. He had given one to Joyce and carried the other himself. They were wearing them in their belts. These were the only really tricky things to carry, plastic being in principle immune to rough handling.

'All the same, you must have felt uncomfortably weighed down with those parcels round your waist,' Warden observed.

'You know, one never thinks of that sort of thing – anyway that was the least dangerous part of the voyage. Yet we were shaken about, I can tell you. Damn those Siamese who promised us an easy stretch of water!'

According to the information of the natives, they had calculated that the trip would last less than half an hour. So they had not set out until it was pitch dark. Actually, they had taken over an hour, and it was heavy going all the way. The current in the River Kwai, except for a calm stretch round the bridge, was like a torrent. As soon as they started, the rapids swept them away into the darkness, past rocks which they could not avoid, while they clung desperately on to their precious, dangerous cargo.

'If I had known what the river was like, I would have chosen a different line of approach and taken the risk of launching the stuff nearer the bridge. It's always the simple information like this that turns out false, Warden, whether it comes from native sources or European. I've often noticed that. I was led up the garden path once again. You can't imagine how hard it was to manœuvre the submarine in that torrent.'

The 'submarine' was the name they had given the raft, which, weighted down at each end with bits of iron, floated half under water most of the time. Its trim had been carefully worked out so as to make it only just buoyant when launched. In this way the mere pressure of a finger was enough to submerge it completely.

'In the first rapids, which sounded as loud as Niagara, we were tossed around, buffeted about and whirled over and under the submarine from one bank to the other, sometimes scraping the river bed, at other times the branches. When I got things more or less under control (which took me some time – I was half-drowned) I ordered each man to hang on to the submarine and not let go at any price, to concentrate on that and nothing else. That was all we could do, and it's a miracle no one had his head bashed in. A really splendid tonic, just what we needed to put us in the right mood for the serious job ahead. The waves were like a storm in mid-ocean. I was nearly sea-sick; and there was no way we could avoid the obstacles. Sometimes – would you believe it, Warden – sometimes we could not even tell if we were going backwards or forwards. Do you think that's strange? When the river begins to narrow and the jungle closes over you, I defy you to know for certain what direction you're moving in. We were being swept down with the current, you'll say. Yes, but compared to us, the water, apart from the waves, was as calm as a lake. It was only the obstacles that gave us some idea of our direction and speed – when we bumped into them. A question of relativity! I wonder if you can imagine . . .'

It must have been an extraordinary sensation. He did his best to describe it as accurately as possible. Warden was intrigued as he listened to him.

'I can well imagine it, Shears. And the raft held together?'

'Another miracle! I could hear it cracking whenever my head happened to be above water-level, but it did hold together – except for a second. It was the youngster who saved the situation. He's first class, Warden. It was like this. At the end of the first rapids, when we were just beginning to get used to the dark, we crashed into a huge rock bang in the middle of the river. We were literally thrown up in the air, Warden, on a cushion of water, before being snatched down again by the current and dragged over to one side. I should never have thought it possible. I saw the obstruction looming up when we were only a few feet off. There was no time. All I could think of doing was shooting out my legs and straddling a bit of bamboo. The two Siamese were chucked off. Fortunately we picked them up again a little further down. Pure luck! But do you know what he did? He only had a split second to think. He flung himself flat on his stomach right across the raft. Do you know why, Warden? To keep the two halves together. Yes, one of the ropes had snapped. The shafts were slipping and the two bits were beginning to come apart. The bump must have shaken them loose. A disaster – he took it all in at a glance. He thought fast. He had the sense to act and the guts to hold on. He was in front of me. I saw the submarine rise out of the water and leap into the air, like a salmon making upstream – just like that – with him underneath, clinging on to the bamboo sticks. He did not let go. Later on we fixed the bits together as best we could. In that position, you realize, his detonators were in direct contact with the plastic, and he must have taken a hell of a toss. I saw him right above my head, I tell you. Like a flash of lightning! That was the only moment I was conscious of the explosives we were carrying. It didn't matter, of course. There wasn't the slightest danger, I'm sure. But he had realized that in a split second. He's an exceptional chap, Warden, I know it. He's bound to succeed.'

'A wonderful combination of sound judgement and quick reflex-action,' Warden agreed.

Shears went on in a low voice:

'He's bound to succeed, Warden. This job is part of him, and no one can stop him going through with it. It's his own personal show. He knows that. You and I are only onlookers now. We've had our day. All we've got to think about now is making his task as easy as possible. The fate of the bridge is in good hands.'

At the end of the first rapids there had been a lull, during which they had put the raft together again. Then they had another rough passage through a narrow gap in the river. They had wasted some time in front of a pile of rocks which obstructed the proper flow of water, causing a vast slow-moving whirlpool upstream, in which they had been caught for several minutes without being able to move any further.

At last they had escaped from this trap. The river had widened, going suddenly sluggish, which had given them the impression of being washed out on to a huge, calm lake. Soon afterwards they had caught sight of the bridge.

Shears broke off and gazed in silence at the valley.

'Strange to be looking at it like this, from above, and seeing the whole thing. It's got quite a different appearance when you're down there at night. All I saw of it were separate bits flashing past, one after the other. It's those bits that matter to us right now – and also afterwards, for that matter. But when we arrived it was outlined against the sky surprisingly clearly. I was scared stiff someone would see us. I felt we were as visible as though it was broad daylight. Just an illusion, of course. We were up to our necks in the water. The submarine was submerged. It even showed signs of sinking completely. Some of the bamboos had caved in. But everything went off all right. There was no light. We glided silently into the shadow of the bridge. Not even a bump. We tied the raft up to one of the central piles and got down to work. We were already quite numb with cold.'

'Any particular trouble?' asked Warden.

'No *particular* trouble, I suppose, Warden – unless you think this sort of job is all in the day's work.'

He fell silent again, as though hypnotized by the bridge, which he could see still shining in the sun, the light-coloured wood showing clear above the yellowish water.

'All this seems to be happening in a dream, Warden. I've had that feeling before. When the time comes, you wonder if it's true, if it's real, if the charges are really there, if it's really true that one touch to the plunger of the generator is all that's needed. It all seems so utterly impossible. There's Joyce, less than a hundred yards away from the enemy lines. There he is, behind that tree, watching the bridge. I bet he hasn't moved an inch since I left. Just think what could happen before tomorrow, Warden. If a Jap soldier should happen to amuse himself by chasing a snake into the jungle . . . I shouldn't have left him there. He shouldn't have got into position until this evening.'

'He's got his knife,' said Warden. 'It's up to him. Tell me about the rest of that night.'

After a long immersion in water a man's skin becomes so soft that mere contact with a rough object is enough to bruise it. Hands are particularly sensitive. The slightest scrape tears strips off the fingers. The first difficulty had been untying the ropes which had been used to fasten the kit on to the raft. They were rough native cords bristling with thorny prickles.

'It sounds like child's play, Warden, but in the state we were in . . . And when you've got to work under water, and without making a noise. Look at my hands. Joyce's are the same.'

Once again he peered out over the valley. He could not stop thinking about the other man waiting over there on the enemy bank. He lifted his hands, examined the deep cuts which had congealed in the sun, then, with a shrug of his shoulders, went on with his account.

They had both carried sharp knives, but their frozen fingers could hardly handle them. And then, even though plastic is a 'tame' explosive, digging into it with a metal instrument is not exactly recommended. Shears had soon realized that the two Siamese were not going to be of any further use.

'I was frightened of that all along, and had said so to the youngster before we set off. I told him we would have to rely on ourselves and no one else to get the job done. They were completely done for. They stood there shivering and clinging to one of the piles. I sent them back. They waited for me at the bottom of the hill. We were left on our own. For work like that, Warden, plain physical stamina isn't enough. The lad stood it magnificently; I only just did. I think I was at the end of my tether. I must be getting old.'

They had unpacked the charges, one by one, and fixed them in position according to the destruction plan. They had to struggle every minute to avoid being swept away by the current. Clinging to each pile with their toes, they had to lower the plastic a sufficient depth into the water for it to be invisible, then mould it against the wood so that the explosive would act with maximum efficiency. Fumbling about underwater, they tied it on with those awful, prickly, searing ropes, which scored bloody furrows across their palms. The mere gesture of tightening the cords and tying the knots had become sheer torture. In the end they were forced to bob down and do it with their teeth.

This part of the operation had taken most of the night. The next task was less arduous, but more tricky. The detonators had been inserted at the same time as the charges were fixed. They now had to be linked together with a network of 'instantaneous' fuse, so that all the explosions would occur simultaneously. This is a job that demands a cool head, since a slip could cause a nasty mess. An explosives 'circuit' is much the same as an electric circuit, and each separate element has to be in its proper place. This was a fairly complicated one, for, in order to be on the safe side, Number One had doubled the number of fuse-lengths and detonators. These cords were fairly long, and the bits of iron which had been used to trim the raft had been fastened to them so as to make them sink.

'At last everything was ready. I don't think we did too badly. I thought I had better make a final inspection of the piles. It wasn't necessary. With Joyce, I needn't have worried. Nothing will shift out of place, I'm sure.'

They were worn out, bruised and battered, shivering with cold, but they grew more and more exultant as they saw the end of their work in sight. They had dismantled the submarine and had let the bits of bamboo float off, one after the other. All that remained was to float downstream themselves, swimming towards the right bank, one carrying the battery in its waterproof case, the other paying out the wire which was weighted at intervals and kept afloat by the last hollow stick of bamboo. They had reached dry land at the spot they had reconnoitred. The bank there rose in a steep slope and the vegetation came down to the water's edge. They had camouflaged the wire in the undergrowth, and then hacked their way a dozen yards or so into the jungle. Joyce had set up the battery and generator.

'Over there, behind that red-coloured tree with its branches trailing in the water. I'm sure that's it,' Shears repeated.

'Everything seems to be under control,' said Warden. 'Today's nearly over and he hasn't been discovered. We should have seen from here. No one's been anywhere near him. There's not much going on in the camp itself, either. The prisoners left yesterday.'

'The prisoners left yesterday?'

'I saw quite a large column leaving camp. That party must have been to celebrate the end of their tasks, and the Japs obviously don't want to keep a lot of men hanging about here doing nothing.'

'That makes things still better.'

'There were a few who stayed behind. Casualties, I suppose, who weren't able to walk. So you left him over there, did you, Shears?'

'I left him over there. There was nothing more I could do and it was nearly dawn. I hope to God no one gets wind of him.'

'He's got his knife,' said Warden. 'Everything's working out perfectly. It's getting dark now. The Kwai valley is already in shadow. There's no chance of anything happening now.'

'There's always a chance of something happening when you least expect it, Warden. You know that as well as I do. I don't know exactly why it is, but I've never yet come across a single instance of things going according to plan.'

'That's true. I've noticed that myself.'

'I wonder what we should expect to happen this time. When I left him, I still had a little bag of rice and a flask of whisky on me – the last of our provisions, which I had been carrying as carefully as the detonators. We drank a mouthful each and I left him the rest. He assured me for the last time that he felt perfectly confident. I left him there on his own.'

CHAPTER 4

Shears listened to the constant murmur of the River Kwai echoing through the jungle of Siam, and felt strangely perturbed.

He was now quite familiar with this ceaseless accompaniment to his every thought and gesture, yet this morning he was unable to recognize either its rhythm or volume. He stood motionless and uneasy for some time, all his faculties on the alert. Gradually he became aware, without being able to define it, of something unaccountably strange in the actual physical surroundings.

It seemed to him that in these surroundings (which were part and parcel of his very being) some transformation had taken place during his one night in the water and his one day spent on top of the mountain. The first sign of it had been his feeling, shortly before dawn, of inexplicable surprise. This had been followed by an odd impression of uneasiness which had gradually seeped up through his subconscious and developed into an actual thought – vague at first, but desperately struggling to express itself in more precise terms. Now, at sunrise, he was still unable to put it more clearly than in these words: 'Some change has occurred in the atmosphere round the bridge and above the river.'

'Something has changed. . . .' He whispered the words over and over again. His special sense of 'atmosphere' hardly ever deceived him. His uneasiness developed into real anxiety, which he tried to dispel by logical argument.

'Of course, there's been a change. It's perfectly natural. Sound varies, depending on the place from where you listen. Here, I'm in the forest, at the foot of the mountain. The echo is not the same as on a hill-top or on the water. If this job lasts much longer, I'll end up by hearing things . . .'

He looked through the branches, but noticed nothing unusual. The river was barely visible in the dawn light. The opposite bank was still nothing but a solid grey mass. He forced himself to concentrate exclusively on the plan of battle and the disposition of the various groups waiting to go into action. Zero hour was not far off. He and four partisans had climbed down from the O.P. during the night. They had settled into the positions chosen by Warden, close to the railway line and just above it. Warden himself and two other Siamese had stayed with the mortar. From up there he would be able to command the whole theatre of operations and be ready also to lend a hand after the attack. That was Number One's decision. He had told his friend that they had to have a European in command at each important post, to act on his own initiative if necessary. It was impossible to foresee everything or to give detailed orders in advance. Warden had understood. As for the third, the most important member of the team, the whole operation depended on him. Joyce had now been over there, exactly opposite Shears, for over twenty-four hours. He was waiting for the train. The convoy had left Bangkok during the night. A signal had reported its departure.

'Something's changed in the atmosphere . . .' Now the Siamese with the light machine-gun was also showing signs of alarm. He was squatting on his haunches, looking at the river.

Shears could not get rid of his feeling of uneasiness. The vague thought was still struggling to express itself more clearly, yet still defied analysis. Shears' brain was intent on solving this exasperating mystery.

The sound, he could swear, was now no longer the same. A man with Shears' training was quick to note the symphony of the natural elements; he recorded it instinctively. This ability had served him well on two or three previous occasions. The shimmering eddy, the particular gurgling sound of water rushing over sand, the crack of branches bending with the current, all these this morning formed part of a different, less noisy concert – certainly less noisy than last night's. Shears seriously wondered if he was not going deaf. Or perhaps his nerves were not quite so steady?

But the Siamese could not have gone deaf at the same time. There was something else. All of a sudden another aspect of his impression flashed through his mind. There was a different smell as well. The smell of the River Kwai this morning was not the same as it had been. An oozy, dank miasma predominated, like the exhalation from a mud flat.

'River Kwai down!' the Siamese suddenly exclaimed.

And as the light began to reveal the details of the opposite bank, Shears suddenly realized. The tree, the big red tree where Joyce was hiding up, no longer had its branches trailing in the water. The River Kwai had sunk. The level had fallen during the night. How far? A foot perhaps? In front of the tree at the bottom of the bank was now a pebbly beach still sparkling with water and shining in the rising sun.

The moment he realized this, Shears felt relieved to have found the explanation for his uneasiness and regained confidence in his nerves. His instinct had not let him down. He was not yet going mad. The eddies were no longer the same, neither those in the water nor those in the air above. It was really the whole atmosphere that had become affected. Newly-exposed earth, still wet, explained that dank smell.

Disaster never makes itself felt at once. The mind's natural inertia enforces a delay. Shears realized the fatal implications of this commonplace occurrence, one by one.

The River Kwai had sunk. In front of the red tree could be seen a broad flat area, which yesterday had been under water. The wire – the electric wire! Shears uttered an obscene oath. He took out his field-glasses and anxiously scanned the area of solid ground which had emerged during the night.

There was the wire. A long piece of it was now high and dry. Shears scanned it all the way from the water's edge up to the bank: a dark line dotted here and there with tufts of grass swept up by the current.

All the same, it was not too noticeable. Shears had managed to see it because he was looking for it. It could pass unnoticed if a Jap happened to come along that way. But the bank which previously had been inaccessible! There was now an unbroken beach at the foot of the slope, which stretched perhaps as far as the bridge (from here the bridge was out of sight) and which, to Shears' agonized glance, seemed designed to attract the attention of any passer-by. Still, while waiting for the train, the Japs were bound to be engaged on duties which would prevent them from sauntering along the river. Shears wiped his brow.

An operation never takes place according to plan. At the last moment there is always some small, trivial, sometimes grotesque, occurrence which upsets the most carefully-worked-out programme. Number One blamed himself, as though he was personally responsible, for his negligence in failing to foresee the fall of the river. Of all nights, it had to happen now – not one night later, nor two nights earlier!

That open beach without a blade of grass on it, lying naked, as naked as truth itself, absorbed his whole attention. The river must have sunk considerably. By a foot? By two feet? Perhaps more? Oh God!

Shears suddenly felt faint. He clung to a tree to prevent the Siamese from seeing how his limbs were trembling. This was the second time in his life that he had felt so upset. The first was when he had felt an enemy's blood trickling through his fingers. His heart literally, actually, stopped beating and his whole body broke out in a cold sweat.

By two feet? Perhaps more? God Almighty! The charges! The charges of plastic on the piles of the bridge!

CHAPTER 5

After Shears had shaken his hand and left him alone in the hide-out, Joyce had felt completely fuddled for some time. The realization that he now had no one to rely on but himself went to his head like fumes of alcohol. He was physically insensible to the fatigue of the previous night and the clammy discomfort of his sodden clothes. He was not yet conscious of that feeling of power and conquest which absolute isolation affords, whether on a mountain-top or in the bowels of the earth.

When his head cleared, he had to reason with himself before he could finally decide to take certain necessary steps before dawn so as to avoid giving in to his lassitude. If this decision had not entered his head he would have stayed there without moving, leaning against a tree, his hand on the plunger, gazing at the bridge whose dark shape could be seen, outlined against a corner of starlit sky above the thick mass of low bushes, through the less thick foliage of taller trees. He had instinctively adopted this position as soon as Shears left.

He got up, took off his clothes, wrung them out and massaged his frozen limbs. He put his shorts and shirt on again; although still wet, they were some defence against the chilly early-morning air. He ate as much as he could of the rice that Shears had left him, then took a long swig of whisky. He felt it was too late now to leave his hide-out to go and fetch some water. He used some of the spirit to wash the wounds which speckled his limbs. He sat down again at the foot of the tree and waited. Nothing happened that day. He had not expected anything to happen. The train was not due until the morning; but he felt more able to dictate the course of events by being here on the spot.

Several times he saw some Japanese on the bridge. They obviously suspected nothing and no one looked in his direction. As in his dream, he had picked out an easily distinguishable landmark on the platform, a cross-beam of the parapet which was in line with himself and a dead branch. This was exactly half-way across, that is to say at one end of the 'prepared' section of piles. When the engine reached it, or rather when it was still a few feet off, he would apply his full weight to the plunger. With the picture of an imaginary engine in his mind, he had disconnected the wire and practised this simple gesture twenty times over, so as to make it an automatic reaction. The machine was in perfect working order. He had carefully dried it and wiped it clean, conscientiously removing the slightest blemish. His own reflexes were also working well.

The day went by quite quickly. When it was dark he scrambled down the slope, swallowed several mouthfuls of muddy water, filled his bottle, then returned to his hide-out. He allowed himself to doze leaning against a tree, without shifting his position. If, for some extraordinary reason, the train's schedule were to be changed, he would still be able to hear it in the distance, he felt certain. When one has lived for some time in the jungle, one quickly develops the instinctive wariness of a wild beast.

He slept by fits and starts, punctuated by long bouts of insomnia. In between, visions of his present adventure alternated strangely with memories of that past life of his which he had described to Shears before launching out on the river.

He was once again in the dusty workroom in which some of the best years of his life had been spent sitting day after day and for long gloomy hours in front of a sheet of drawing-paper under a projector-lamp. The girder, that bit of metal which he had never actually seen, was responsible for the mathematical symbols in two dimensions which had occupied the whole of his youth. The plan, the outline, the elevation and countless cross-sections came to life before his very eyes, with all the details of the structure on which a staff of experts had managed to achieve a saving of a pound and a half of steel after two years of tests and experiments.

Superimposed on this picture, against the background of this structure, were the small brown squares, like those Warden had drawn, fixed to the twenty-four piles on the large-scale plan of the bridge. The heading, over which he had sweated so painfully and so many times, the final heading came into focus, then grew blurred as he watched it. He tried in vain to decipher the letters. They were dotted all over his drawing-paper, until at last they fused together again, as sometimes happens at the end of a film on a cinema screen, to form a single word. It was the word DESTRUCTION, in heavy black letters written in shiny ink, which reflected the light of the projector-lamp and bewilderingly filled the whole screen, leaving no room for any other character.

He was not really obsessed by this sight. He could avoid it whenever he wanted. All he had to do was open his eyes. The dark corner in which the River Kwai bridge stood outlined in black banished these dusty ghosts of the past and summoned him back to reality; his present reality. His life would no longer be the same after this. He was already tasting the fruits of success while witnessing his own metamorphosis.

At first light, about the same time as Shears, he too felt uneasy on account of the perceptible change in the emanations from the river. The alteration had been so gradual that in his fuddled state he had not even been aware of it. From his hide-out he could see only the platform of the bridge. The river was out of sight, but he was certain his feelings were justified. This certainty soon became so overwhelming that he felt he could no longer remain inactive. He pushed his way through the undergrowth towards the river, reached the last curtain of branches and looked out. He saw the reason for his uneasiness at the same time that he noticed the electric wire lying exposed on the pebble beach.

Following the same course as Shears, his mind slowly grasped the significance of this irreparable disaster. In the same way he felt his whole body quiver at the thought of the plastic charges. From his new position he would be able to see the piles. He had only to raise his eyes. He forced himself to do so.

It took him a fairly long time to appreciate how much the risk had been increased by the River Kwai's whimsical behaviour. Even after close observation he could not assess the extent with any degree of accuracy, but oscillated between hope and despair at each of the thousand ripples which the current created round the bridge. At first glance a wave of voluptuous optimism eased his nerves, which were tense with the horror of his original fears. The river had not sunk so very much. The charges were still under water.

At least they seemed to be, from this position rather far down. But from above? From the bridge? And even from here? Concentrating still more closely, he now noticed a fairly large wave, like one created by a flow of water round a grounded wreck, washing round the piles, those piles which he knew so well and which he had left encrusted with strips of his own flesh. The waves round those particular piles were larger than the rest. And on one of them he thought he could see a patch of brown against the lighter colour of the wood. This emerged from time to time like a fish's dorsal fin, yet a moment later there was nothing to be seen but the eddy. The charge was probably just below the surface of the water. A keen sentry would certainly be able to spot those on the outside rows simply by leaning over the parapet.

And what if the level should fall still further? In a moment, perhaps, the charges would be visible for all to see, still dripping with water, sparkling in the harsh light of the Siamese sun! He was numbed by the grotesque absurdity of the picture. What time was it? How long would it take? The sun was just beginning to light up the valley. The train was not due before ten o'clock. Their patience, their toil, their anxiety, their suffering, all had suddenly been rendered pitiful and almost ludicrous by the inhuman whim of this trickle from the mountains. The success of the big attack, for which he had for good and all sacrificed his hitherto neglected reserves of stamina and strength after thriftily saving them up for years, was now again in the balance, being weighed once more on scales which took no heed of his soul's ambition. His destiny was to be fulfilled during the minutes that remained before the train's arrival, fulfilled regardless of himself, fulfilled on a higher plane; consciously fulfilled, perhaps, but in an external consciousness, a pitiless consciousness scornful of the impulse which had carried him thus far, a consciousness which directed human affairs at such a high level that no human wish could sway it, neither entreaty nor despair.

This feeling that the discovery or non-discovery of the explosives was now independent of anything he could do made him, paradoxically enough, a little calmer. He stopped thinking about it, and even stopped hoping. He could not afford to waste an ounce of energy on things that were taking place on a supernatural plane. He had to forget about them, so as to concentrate all his resources on the factors which were still within the scope of his own initiative. It was on these, and these alone, that he now had to bring his mind to bear. The operation was still feasible; he only had to envisage what form it was likely to take. He was still wondering what his reactions would be. Shears had noticed him doing that before.

If the charges were discovered, the train would be stopped before it reached the bridge. He would then thrust the plunger down before being discovered himself. The damage would be easily repaired. It would be only a partial success, but he could not help that.

It was a different situation when it came to the electric wire. This could be seen by anyone walking along the beach a few feet away from him. In that case there was still a chance of taking independent action. Perhaps there would be no one on the bridge at that moment, and no one on the opposite bank who could see him. And the slope hid the pebble beach from the Japanese in the camp. The man would probably hesitate before sounding the alarm. In that case he, Joyce, would have to act, and act fast. And to do that, he would have to keep both bridge and beach in view.

He thought again, returned to his previous hide-out and brought his gear back to the new position behind a flimsy screen of undergrowth from which he could see at the same time the bridge and the patch of open ground now bisected by the wire. An idea crossed his mind. He took off his shirt and shorts. He kept on his pants. This was more or less like the prisoners' working kit. From a long way off he might be mistaken for one of them. He carefully set up the generator and knelt down beside it. He took his knife out of its sheath. This important item of equipment, which was included on every Plastic and Destructions Company expedition, he placed on the grass by his side. Then he waited.

The time passed desperately slowly, at a snail's pace, as sluggishly as the diminished flow of the River Kwai; it was measured for him in endless seconds by the muffled murmur of the water nibbling imperceptibly into a future fraught with danger, storing up in the past a few flashes of security, each invaluable but infinitesimal and tragically out of proportion with his anxiety. The tropical light flooded the dripping valley and shimmered on the wet black sand of the recently exposed river bed. After outlining the cross-beams in the superstructure of the bridge, the sun, hidden for a moment by the platform, rose above this obstruction, casting before it the gigantic shadow of this example of human artifice. It crossed the pebble beach in a straight line parallel to the wire, was distorted in the water where it writhed in countless curves, then melted away on the other side into the shape of the hills beyond. The heat hardened the cuts on his tattered hands and made the wounds on his body smart horribly in the grip of multi-coloured legions of ants. But physical pain did not distract his thoughts; it was only an agonizing accompaniment to the obsession which had been wracking his brain for the last few minutes.

A fresh fear had assailed him just as he was trying to imagine what form the action would have to take if, during the next few hours, his fate-line were to be crossed by one particular event – a Japanese soldier wandering idly along the river and stopping to investigate the pebble beach. He would be surprised to see the wire. He would stop. He would bend down to take hold of it and stand still for a moment. It was then that he, Joyce, would have to intervene. It was essential for him to visualize his own actions in advance. As Shears had said, he brooded too much!

Picturing the action was enough to tie his nerves in knots and paralyse every muscle. He could not help it. He had a deep instinctive feeling that this action was imperative, that it had been ordained a long time ago, that it was the natural conclusion of events leading inevitably to this final test of his capabilities. It was the most dreaded, hateful test of all, which he could throw on to one or the other side of the scales, a test sufficiently fraught with horror and sacrifice by itself to tip the scales on the side of success by snatching him from the hungry grasp of destiny.

He exercised all his brain cells with this final end in view, feverishly going over in his mind the school instructions, trying to devote himself body and soul to the dynamics of the job on hand, yet still unable to banish the nightmare of the immediate consequences.

He remembered the worrying question which his C.O. had once asked him: 'When the time comes, would you be "capable", in cold blood, of using this weapon?' He had been uneasy about his instinctive reactions and will-power. He had not been able to give a definite answer. At the moment of launching out on the river he had been absolutely certain; now he was not sure of anything. He looked at the weapon lying on the grass beside him.

It was a sharp long-bladed knife with a short metal hilt just big enough to ensure a reasonable grip, blade and hilt being all in one piece. The backroom boys of Force 316 had modified its blade and handle several times. The instructions in its use had been specific. It was not simply a question of clenching one's fist round it and striking blindly; that was too easy; anyone could do that. Every form of destruction requires its own individual technique. The instructors had taught him two methods of using it. For purposes of defence, against a man rushing forward, it was advisable to hold it in front of one, with the point tilted slightly upwards and the cutting edge uppermost, and to strike with an upward thrust as though disembowelling an animal. The gesture itself was not beyond his powers. He could have done it almost automatically. But in this case he would not have to. There would be no enemy rushing forward. He would not have to defend himself. For the action which he was anticipating, he would have to use the second method. It needed hardly any strength, but a lot of skill and utter ruthlessness. It was the method by which the trainees were taught to wipe out a sentry in the dark without giving him the time or opportunity to raise the alarm. It necessitated striking from behind; but not in the man's back (that, too, would have been too easy). It necessitated cutting his throat.

The knife had to be held palm downwards, with the nails underneath, the thumb running along the root of the blade to ensure proper control, with the blade itself held horizontal and perpendicular to the victim's body. The thrust had to be made from right to left, firmly but not violently enough to turn it off its course, and directed at a certain point an inch or two below the ear. This point and no other had to be aimed at and hit, to prevent the man from crying out. Such was the general plan of the operation. It also involved several further subsidiary gestures, secondary but no less important, which had to be carried out immediately after the blade's penetration. But the advice on this subject, which the Calcutta instructors gave so light-heartedly, Joyce did not even dare whisper to himself.

He could not dispel his mental picture of the immediate consequences. So he forced himself instead to examine it closely, to build it up in his mind in every detail of its shape and horrid colour. He made himself analyse its most frightening aspects, in the mad hope that he would thereby get used to it and so reach that state of detachment which is born of habit. He relived the scene a dozen times, twenty times over, and gradually managed to create not a ghost, nor even a vague imaginary shadow, but a human being, a real flesh and blood Japanese soldier standing on the beach in uniform, wearing his funny cap, his ear projecting underneath it, and a little lower down the small patch of brown skin which he aimed at as he silently lifted his outstretched arm. He forced himself to feel, to judge the resistance to the blow, to see the blood spurting and the body jerking as the knife in the palm of his clenched fist went through the subsidiary gestures and his left arm flashed down and bared the victim's throat. He steeped himself for hour after hour in the worst horror he could imagine. He made such an effort to train his body to be nothing more than an insensible obedient machine that he felt overwhelming fatigue in every muscle.

He was still not sure of himself. He was appalled to see that this method of preparing himself was not effective. The threat of failure taunted him as relentlessly as the realization of his duty. He had to choose between two courses: the first ignominiously scattering, in an eternity of shame and remorse, the same horror that the second concentrated in a few seconds of ghastly action – an ignominious but passive course, demanding only inactive cowardice and so all the more attractive for providing the insidious temptation of the easy way out. He came to realize that in cold blood and in full possession of his faculties he would never be capable of the action which he insisted on picturing to himself. He felt, on the contrary, that he would have to banish it from his mind and find either a stimulating or sobering alternative which would turn his thoughts elsewhere. He needed more help than he could derive from the paralysing contemplation of this terrifying task.

Outside help? He looked round him in despair. He was alone and naked in a strange land, skulking in the undergrowth like a wild beast, surrounded by enemies of every kind. His only weapon was this dreadful dagger burning a hole in the palm of his hand. He searched in vain for some support from any feature in the landscape which had fired his imagination. Everything now looked hostile in the Kwai valley. The shadow of the bridge faded as the minutes went by. The bridge was now nothing but a lifeless, useless structure. There was no hope of help. He had nothing more to drink, nothing to eat. It might have been comforting to gulp down some sort of food, any sort.

He could expect no outside help. He was left entirely to his own devices. This was what he had wanted, what he had welcomed. He had felt proud and inspired. His personal powers had seemed invincible. Surely they could not all of a sudden fade away, leaving him stranded like some machine with a sabotaged engine! He closed his eyes on the surrounding world and looked inwards on himself. If there was any hope of rescue it lay there, and not on this earth beneath these skies. In his present misery the only gleam of hope he could see was the hypnotizing flame of those mental pictures which are born of hallucination. His imagination was his only refuge. Shears had been worried by that. Warden had wisely not declared whether it was a virtue or a fault.

He had to combat the evil effects of obsession by the counter-poison of self-imposed obsession; to unwind the film on which the representative symbols of his spiritual capital were inscribed; to examine with an inquisitor's fury every spectre in his mental universe; to hunt passionately through these immaterial witnesses of his existence until he found a sufficiently absorbing figure to occupy the whole realm of his consciousness without leaving a single gap. Feverishly he reviewed them all. Hatred of the Japanese, sense of duty – these were ludicrous irritants which could not be expressed in a sufficently clear form. He thought of his superior officers, of his friends who were relying on him entirely and who were now waiting on the opposite bank. Even that thought was not sufficiently real. It was barely sufficient to induce him to sacrifice his own life. Even the intoxication of success was now of no avail. Or else he would have to envisage victory under a more palpable guise than that half-extinguished halo of glory whose fading beams could no longer find material element on which to shine.

A thought suddenly flashed through his mind. It flashed with startling clarity for a split second. Even before realizing it, he had the feeling that it was sufficiently significant to give him hope. He struggled to retrieve it. It flashed again. It was last night's vision: the sheet of drawing-paper under the projector-lamp; the countless designs for the girder on which the brown squares were superimposed and which were dwarfed by a heading endlessly repeated in huge shining letters: the words DESTRUCTION.

It went on flashing. From the moment that it was instinctively recalled and triumphantly occupied his thoughts, he felt that this alone was sufficiently consistent, sufficiently complete, sufficiently powerful to make him rise above the disgust and horror of his wretched carcase. It was as exhilarating as drink and as soothing as opium. He gave in to it completely and took care not to let it escape him again.

Having reached this state of self-induced hypnosis, he was not surprised to see some Japanese soldiers walking along the bridge over the River Kwai.

CHAPTER 6

Shears also saw the Japanese soldiers, and lived through another nightmare.

For him, too, time was passing at a relentlessly slow pace. After the dismay caused by the thought of the charges, he had pulled himself together. He had left the partisans in position, and climbed a little further up the slope. He had stopped at a point from which he could see the bridge as well as the river. He had noticed the little waves round the piles and examined them through his field-glasses. He imagined he could see a patch of brown rising and falling with the movement of the eddies. Instinctively, involuntarily, and from a sense of duty, he had wracked his brains to discover what personal action he could take to avert this stroke of misfortune. 'There is always something further to be done, some extra action to take', so the Force 316 authorities asserted. For the first time since he had been engaged on this sort of work Shears could think of nothing to do, and he cursed himself for his impotence.

For him the die was cast. He had no more chance of retaliating than had Warden, who from up there had no doubt also discovered the treachery of the River Kwai. Joyce perhaps? But had he even noticed the change? And who could tell if he would have the necessary initiative and instinct to deal with such a catastrophe? Shears, who was used to judging the size of the obstacles to be overcome in situations of this sort, bitterly regretted not having taken his place.

Two endless hours had dragged by. From the spot he had reached he could see the hutments of the camp. He had noticed some Japanese soldiers moving about in full-dress uniform. A hundred yards away from the river there was a whole company of them waiting for the train, lined up in honour of the authorities who were to open the railway line. Perhaps the preparations for this ceremony would occupy all their attention? Shears hoped so. But a Japanese patrol had emerged from the guardroom and was now on its way to the bridge.

Now the men, led by a sergeant, were moving along the platform in two ranks, one on either side of the track. They walked slowly along in a rather dreamy manner, their rifles carried carelessly at the slope. Their mission was to make a final inspection before the train arrived. From time to time one of them stopped to lean over the parapet. Clearly it was only to salve their conscience, to carry out their orders, that they were performing this task. Shears tried to persuade himself that their hearts were not in the job – which was probably true. No accident could happen to the bridge over the

River Kwai whose growth in this God-forsaken valley they had personally witnessed day by day! 'They're looking without seeing,' he told himself as he watched them advance. Each step they took echoed through his head. He forced himself to keep his eyes on them and follow every movement they made, while he silently delivered a vague prayer to whatever god or devil or other mysterious power there might be. He automatically judged their speed and the distance they moved along the bridge in every second. They were now more than half-way across. The sergeant leaned over the parapet and spoke to the leading man, pointing at the river. Shears bit his hand to keep himself from shouting out loud. The sergeant laughed. He was probably making some remark about the fall in the level of the water. They moved off again. Shears was right: they were looking without seeing. He felt that by following them like this with his eyes, he would be able to exercise an influence on their sense of perception – a miracle of telepathic suggestion. The last man had gone past. They had noticed nothing.

Now they were coming back. They were moving along the bridge in the opposite direction at the same ambling pace. One of them leaned head and shoulders right over the dangerous section, then stepped back into the ranks.

They had gone past again. Shears mopped his brow. They were moving away. 'They have seen nothing'; automatically he whispered these words to himself, to convince himself all the more of the miracle. Anxiously he kept them under observation and did not take his eyes off them until they had rejoined the company. Before allowing his hopes to soar he was seized by a strange feeling of pride.

'If I'd been one of them,' he muttered, 'I shouldn't have been so careless. Any British soldier would have spotted the sabotage. Ah well, the train won't be long now.'

As though in answer to this last thought, he heard a harsh voice shouting out orders on the enemy bank. There was a stir among the men. Shears looked into the distance. On the horizon of the plain a small cloud of black smoke proclaimed the approach of the first Japanese convoy to cross into Siam, the first train, loaded with troops, munitions and high-ranking Japanese generals, which was about to cross the bridge over the River Kwai.

Shears' heart softened. Tears of gratitude to the mysterious power ran down his cheeks.

'Nothing can stop us now,' he whispered. 'Fate has no more tricks to play. The train will be here in twenty minutes.'

He quelled his anxiety and returned to the foot of the mountain in order to take command of the support group. As he scrambled down, bent double and taking care to keep under cover, he was unable to see the fine upstanding officer in the uniform of a British colonel approaching the bridge from the opposite bank.

At the very moment that Number One got back in position, still in a flurry of emotion, with every faculty concentrated on the anticipated sight of a blinding explosion followed by the fire and wreckage that spell success, Colonel Nicholson in his turn started to cross the bridge over the River Kwai.

With a clear conscience, at peace with the universe and with God, gazing through eyes that are bluer than the tropical sky after a storm, feeling through every pore of his ruddy skin the satisfaction of the well-earned rest that is due to any craftsman after a difficult task, proud of having overcome every obstacle through his personal courage and perseverance, glorying in the work accomplished by himself and by his men in this corner of Siam which he now feels almost belongs to him, light at heart at the thought of having shown himself worthy of his forefathers and of having contributed a far from common chapter to the eastern legends of empire-builders, firmly convinced that no one could have done the job better, confirmed in his certainty of the superiority of his own race in every field of activity, glad of having furnished ample proof of this during the last six months, bursting with the joy that makes every commander's effort worth while once the triumphant result is there for all to see, drinking the cup of victory in tiny sips, delighted with the quality of the construction, anxious to see for himself, and for the last time, the sum total of its perfection compounded of hard work and intelligence, and also in order to carry out a final inspection, Colonel Nicholson strode with dignity across the bridge over the River Kwai.

Most of the prisoners, and all the officers, had left two days before, on foot, for an assembly point from which they were due to be sent to Malaya, to the islands or to Japan, in order to undertake other duties. The railway was finished. The ceremony which His Imperial Majesty in Tokyo had graciously ordained, and imposed, on all the groups in Burma and Siam, had been held in honour of its completion.

It had been celebrated with particular pomp in the River Kwai camp. Colonel Nicholson had seen to that. All along the line it had been preceded by the usual speeches from Japanese officers, generals and colonels, perched on a rostrum, wearing black boots and grey gloves, gesticulating with their arms and heads, making an extraordinary parody of the language of the Western world in front of a legion of white men, men who were crippled, sick and covered in sores and still in a daze after living through several months of hell.

Saito had spoken a few words, of course, in praise of the South-East Asia Sphere, and had condescended to add his thanks for the loyalty which the prisoners had shown. Clipton, whose temper had been sorely tried for weeks, during which he had seen dying men dragging themselves to the workyards in order to finish the bridge, felt almost like weeping with rage. He had then had to put up with a short speech from Colonel Nicholson, in which the C.O. congratulated his men, extolling their self-sacrifice and fortitude. The Colonel had ended up by declaring that their hardships had not been suffered in vain and that he was proud of being in command of such fine fellows. Their conduct and demeanour in the face of adversity would be an example to the whole country.

After that came the festivities. The Colonel had lent a hand and taken an active part in them. He knew that nothing was worse for the men than inactivity, and had ordered a mass of entertainments, the organization of which had kept them breathless for several days. There were not only several concerts, but also a comic turn performed by soldiers in fancy dress, and even a ballet of men made up as dancers which provoked a hearty laugh.

'You see, Clipton,' he had said, 'you criticized me once, but I stuck to my guns. I've kept the morale of the unit high, and that's the main thing. The men have stuck it out.'

This was true. A fine spirit had been maintained in the River Kwai camp. Clipton had to admit this when he looked at the men round him. It was obvious that they were taking an innocent, childish pleasure in these celebrations, and the sincerity of their cheers left no room for doubt about the level of their morale.

The next day the prisoners had moved off. Only the seriously ill and the cripples had stayed behind. They were to be evacuated to Bangkok in the next train from Burma. The officers had left with the men. Reeves and Hughes, to their great regret, had been obliged to join the convoy and had not been allowed to see the first train cross the construction which had cost them so much toil and effort. Colonel Nicholson, however, had been given permission to travel with the sick men. Because of the services he had rendered, Saito had not been able to refuse him this favour, which he had requested in his usual dignified manner.

He now walked along, taking lengthy brisk strides which resounded triumphantly on the platform. He had won the day. The bridge was ready. There was nothing fancy about it, but it was a sufficiently 'finished' job to advertise the qualities of the Western world in large letters across this Siamese sky. This was where he deserved to be, in the position of a commander reviewing his troops before a victorious march-past. It was unthinkable that he should be elsewhere. His presence was some consolation for the departure of his faithful assistants and his men, all of whom deserved to share in this honour. Luckily he at least was here. The bridge was soundly built, he knew. There was no weak spot. It would stand up to what was expected of it. But nothing can take the place of a final examination by the man responsible for it, of that he was also certain. One can never foresee every eventuality. Years of experience had taught him that something always tends to crop up at the last moment, that there is always some fly in the ointment. If it does, even the best junior officer is incapable of taking the necessary steps to deal with it. Needless to say, he placed no faith in the report made by the Japanese patrol which Saito had sent out that morning. He had to see to things himself. As he strode along, his glance confirmed the firmness of each support and the soundness of each joint.

When he was a little over half-way across he leant over the parapet, as he had done every five or six yards on the way. He caught sight of a pile and stood rooted to the spot with surprise.

His trained eye had at once noticed the extra ripples on the surface of the water caused by one of the charges. Examining them more closely, Colonel Nicholson thought he saw a brown patch against the wood. He hesitated for a moment, then moved on and stopped a few yards further off, above another pile. Once again he leant over the parapet.

'That's funny,' he muttered.

Again he hesitated, then crossed the line and looked over the other side. Another patch of brown was visible a bare inch below the surface. This made him feel vaguely annoyed, like the sight of a blot disfiguring his work. He decided to walk on, went as far as the end of the platform, turned round and retraced his steps, as the patrol had done before him, then stopped once more, wrapped in thought and shaking his head. Finally he shrugged his shoulders and turned towards the right bank. He kept talking the whole time.

'That wasn't there two days ago,' he mumbled. 'The water level was higher, it's true. Probably some muck that's been washed up against the piles and stuck there. Yet . . .'

The ghost of a suspicion flashed through his mind, but the truth was too extraordinary for him to grasp it immediately. Yet he was no longer in a cheerful mood. His morning was spoilt. He turned round again to have another look at the anomaly, found no explanation, and finally stepped off the bridge still feeling rather puzzled.

'It can't be true,' he muttered, as he contemplated the vague suspicion skimming through his brain. 'Unless it's one of those Chinese Communist bands . . .'

Sabotage was firmly associated in his mind with gangster activity.

'It can't be true,' he repeated, still unable to recapture his light-hearted mood.

The train was now in sight, though still some way off, struggling up the line. The Colonel calculated that it would take at least ten minutes to arrive. Saito, who was strolling up and down between the bridge and the company, watched him approach and felt embarrassed as he always did in the Englishman's presence. Colonel Nicholson suddenly made up his mind as he drew level with the Japanese.

'Colonel Saito,' he declared in a lordly manner, 'there's something rather odd going on. We'd better look into it more closely before the train goes across.'

Without waiting for an answer, he scrambled quickly down the slope. His intention was to take the small native canoe moored under the bridge and make a tour of inspection round the piles. As he reached the beach he instinctively swept it with his trained glance and noticed the length of electric wire on the shining pebbles. Colonel Nicholson frowned and walked over towards it.

CHAPTER 7

It was while he was scrambling down the slope, with an ease born of the daily habit of light exercise and the peaceful contemplation of everyday truths, that he came into Shears' field of view. The Japanese colonel followed close behind him. It was only then that Shears realized that adversity still had a card up its sleeve. Joyce had been aware of this for some time. In the state of trance to which he had managed to force himself he had seen the Colonel's behaviour on the bridge without any further feeling of alarm. But he seized his dagger as soon as he saw the figure of Saito following behind him on the beach.

Shears noticed that as Colonel Nicholson approached he seemed to be dragging the Japanese officer along in his wake. In face of this incoherent situation he felt himself give way to a sort of hysteria; he began babbling to himself:

'But the other fellow's leading him to it! It's our own colonel who's taking him there! If only I could explain, have a word with him, just a word!'

The sound of the puffing engine could be heard in the distance. All the Japanese were probably now on parade, ready to present arms. The two men on the beach were invisible from the camp. Number One made an angry gesture as he instantly grasped the whole situation and instinctively realized what action would have to be taken, the action which a situation of this sort required and demanded of every man who had enlisted in the ranks of the Plastic and Destructions Company. He too seized his knife. He tore it out of his belt and held it in front of him according to the school training, palm downwards, the nails underneath, the thumb running along the root of the blade – not in order to use it, but in the wild hope that he would be able to influence Joyce by suggestion, and moved by the same instinct which had induced him a little earlier to follow the movements of the patrol.

Colonel Nicholson had stopped in front of the wire. Saito was coming up behind him, waddling along on his stumpy legs. All the emotions that Shears had felt in the morning were nothing to what he felt at that moment. He began talking out loud, brandishing the dagger in front of him above his head.

'He won't be able to do it! There's a limit to what you can expect of a lad of that age who's been brought up in the ordinary way and spent his whole life in an office. I was mad to let him have his way. It was up to me to take his place. He won't be able to do it!'

Saito had caught up with Colonel Nicholson, who had bent down and picked up the wire. Shears felt his heart thumping against his ribs.

'He won't be able to do it! Three minutes more, just three minutes, and the train will be here. He won't be able to do it!'

One of the Siamese partisans crouching by his rifle gazed at him in terror. Luckily the jungle muffled the sound of his voice. He was hunched up, clenching his fist round the knife which he held motionless in front of him.

'He won't be able to do it! God Almighty, make him lose his head; make him fighting mad – just for ten seconds!'

As he uttered this wild prayer, he noticed a movement in the undergrowth, and the bushes parted. He stiffened and held his breath. Joyce was silently creeping down the slope, bent double, with his knife in his hand. Shears fastened his eyes on him, and kept them there.

Saito, whose mind worked slowly, was crouching at the water's edge with his back to the forest, in the Oriental's favourite position which he instinctively adopted whenever any unforeseen event made him forget to guard himself against it. He too had picked up the wire. Shears heard a few words spoken in English:

'This is really rather alarming, Colonel Saito.'

After that there was a short silence. The Jap was pulling the strands apart in his fingers. Joyce had arrived unobserved behind the two men.

'My God,' the Colonel suddenly yelled, 'the bridge has been mined, Colonel Saito! Those damn things I saw against the piles were explosives! And this wire . . .'

He had turned round towards the jungle, while Saito let the weight of these words sink in. Shears watched still more intently. As his fist flashed across from right to left, he saw an answering flash on the opposite bank. He at once recognized the familiar change that had come over the man crouching there.

'So he had been able to do it! He had done it. Not a muscle in his tensed body had faltered while the steel went in with hardly any resistance. He had gone through the subsidiary gestures without a tremor. And at that very moment, partly in order to obey the instructions he had received and partly because he felt the overwhelming need to cling to something human, he had brought his left fist down on to the neck of the enemy whose throat he had just slit. In his death-spasm Saito had begun to straighten his legs and was in a semi-upright position. Joyce had clasped him with all his strength against his own body, partly to stifle him and partly to still the trembling which had started in his own limbs.

The Jap had collapsed. He had not uttered a sound, apart from the death rattle, which Shears only heard because he was expecting it. For a few seconds Joyce lay paralysed underneath his adversary, who had fallen on top of him and was drenching him with his blood. He had had the strength to win the first round. Now he was not sure that he had enough will-power to struggle free. At last he gave a heave. In a single movement he threw off the lifeless body, which rolled half into the water, then looked round.

Both banks were deserted. He had won, but his pride could not dispel either his horror or disgust. With an effort he got up on to his hands and knees. There were still a few simple things he had to do. First of all, explain himself. Two words would be enough. Colonel Nicholson had remained rooted to the spot, petrified by the suddenness of the scene he had witnessed.

'Officer! British officer, sir!' Joyce muttered. 'The bridge is going up. Stand clear!'

He could not recognize his own voice. The effort of moving his lips caused him untold labour. Yet this fellow here did not even seem to hear him!

'British officer, sir!' he repeated in despair. 'Force 316 from Calcutta. Commandos. Orders to blow up the bridge.'

Colonel Nicholson at last showed some sign of life. A strange light sparkled in his eyes. He spoke in a hollow voice:

'Blow up the bridge?'

'Stand clear, sir. Here comes the train. They'll think you're in on it too.'

The Colonel still did not move.

This was no time for argument. He would have to act. The puffing of the engine could be heard quite distinctly. Joyce realized that his legs would not carry the weight of his body. On all fours he clambered up the slope, back to his position in the undergrowth.

'Blow up the bridge!' the Colonel repeated.

He had not moved an inch. He had blankly watched Joyce's painful progress, as though trying to grasp the meaning of the words. Suddenly he moved and followed in his footsteps. He tore through the curtain of branches which had just closed behind him and stumbled on the hide-out with the generator, on which he at once laid his hand.

'Blow up the bridge!' the Colonel once more exclaimed.

'British officer, sir!' Joyce stammered almost plaintively. 'British officer from Calcutta. Orders . . .'

He did not finish the sentence. Colonel Nicholson had launched himself at him with a yell:

'Help!'

CHAPTER 8

'Two men lost. Some damage done but bridge intact thanks to British Colonel's heroism.'

Such was the concise report which Warden, the only survivor of the trio, sent to Calcutta on his return to base.

When he read this signal Colonel Green felt that there were a lot of points which needed clearing up in this strange business, and asked for an explanation. Warden replied that he had nothing further to say. His C.O. then decided that he had been long enough in the jungle of Siam and that a man could not be left on his own in that dangerous spot when the Japanese were probably going to search the area. At this stage of the war Force 316 was in a strong position. A second team was dropped on to a D.Z. some distance away to maintain contact with the Siamese, and Warden was recalled to H.Q. A submarine came to take him off from a secret beach in the Bay of Bengal, which he managed to reach after an eventful two weeks' march. Three days later he was in Calcutta and reported to Colonel Green.

He gave him a brief summary of the preparations for the attack, then came to the operation itself. From the top of the hill he had witnessed the whole scene; not a detail had escaped him. He began speaking in the cool, calculated tone which he normally used; but as he went on with his story his voice changed. During the last month that he had spent as the only white man surrounded by Siamese partisans a flood of unexpressed sensations had been surging through him. Each episode in the drama constantly recurred, bubbling through his brain, yet with his usual love of logic he instinctively struggled to find a rational explanation and to reduce them all to a handful of universal principles.

The outcome of these conflicting mental exercises came to light one day in the offices of Force 316. He had not been able to confine himself to a dry military report. He had felt an urgent need to unleash the storm of his fears and anxiety, his doubts and rage, and also to reveal quite candidly the reasons for the grotesque sequel in so far as he could fathom them. He was impelled by his sense of duty to give in addition a factual account of what had happened. He tried to stick to this and occasionally succeeded, only to give way again and again to the torrent of his uncontrollable temper. The result was a strange combination of almost incoherent invective mingled with the elements of an impassioned address, sprinkled here and there with extravagant contradictions and only an occasional 'fact'.

Colonel Green listened patiently and attentively to this piece of fantastic rhetoric, in which he could see no sign of the cool reasoning for which Professor Warden was famous. He was interested in facts more than anything else. But he interrupted the junior officer as little as possible. He had had some experience in dealing with men returning from similar missions, to which they had devoted themselves heart and soul only to see their efforts result in an ignominious failure for which they themselves were not responsible. In such cases he made a fairly liberal allowance for the 'human element', closing his eyes to their aberrations and pretending to overlook the occasional lack of respect in their tone of voice.

'I suppose you'd say the lad behaved like a fool, sir. Well, yes, he did; but no one in his place could have done better. I watched him. I didn't take my eyes off him for a second. I could guess what he was saying to that colonel. He did what I should have done in his place. I watched him as he dragged himself off. The train was almost there. I didn't know what was happening myself until the other fellow rushed at him. I only realized later, when I'd had time to think. And Shears claimed that he thought too much! My God, he didn't think too much; he didn't think enough! He should have been more perceptive, more discerning. Then he would have understood that in our job it's no good cutting any old throat. You've got to cut the right one. Isn't that so, sir?

'More insight, that's what he needed; then he would have known who his enemy really was, realized it was that old bull-shitter who couldn't stand the idea of his fine work being destroyed. A really perceptive mind would have deduced that from the way he strode along the platform. I had my glasses trained on him, sir; if only it had been a rifle! He had the sanctimonious smile of a conqueror on his lips, I remember. A splendid example of the man of action, sir, as we say in Force 316. He never let misfortune get him down; always made a last effort. It was he who shouted to the Japs for help!

'That old brute with his blue eyes had probably spent his whole life dreaming of constructing something which would last. In the absence of a town or a cathedral, he plumped for this bridge. You couldn't really expect him to let it be destroyed – not a regular of the old school, sir, not likely! I'm sure he had read the whole of Kipling as a boy and I bet he recited chunks of it as the construction gradually took shape above the water. "Yours is the earth and everything that's in it, and what is more, you'll be a man, my son" – I can just hear him!

'He had a highly developed sense of duty and admired a job well done. He was also fond of action – just as you are, sir, just as we all are. This idiotic worship of action, to which our little typists subscribe as much as our great generals! I'm not sure where it all leads to, when I stop to think about it. I've been thinking about it for the last month, sir. Perhaps that silly old fool was really quite a decent fellow at heart? Perhaps he really had a genuine ideal? An ideal as sacred as our own? Perhaps the same ideal as ours? Perhaps all that hocus-pocus he believed in can be traced back to the same source that provides the impetus which lies behind our own activities? That mysterious atmosphere in which our natural impulses stir us to the point of action. Looking at it like that, perhaps, the 'result' may have no meaning at all – it's only the intrinsic quality of the effort that counts. Or else this dream-world, as far as I can see, is simply a hell afflicted with devilish standards which warp our judgement, lead the way to every form of dishonesty and culminate in a result which is bound to be deplorable. I tell you, sir, I've been thinking about all this for the last month. Here we are, for instance, blundering into this part of the world in order to teach Orientals how to handle plastic so as to destroy trains and blow up bridges. Well . . .'

'Tell me what happened in the end,' Colonel Green quietly broke in. 'Nothing matters, remember, apart from action.'

'Nothing matters apart from action, sir . . . Joyce's expression when he came out of his hide-out! And he didn't falter. He struck home according to the text-book, I'll vouch for that. All he needed was just a little more judgement. The other chap rushed at him with such fury that they both rolled down the slope towards the river. They didn't stop till they were almost in the water. To the naked eye they looked as if they were both lying there quite still. But I saw the details through my glasses. One was on top of the other. The body in uniform was crushing the naked blood-stained body, crushing it with all its weight, while two furious hands were squeezing the other's throat. I could see it all quite clearly. He was stretched out with his arms flung wide, next to the corpse in which the dagger was still embedded. At that moment, sir, he realized his mistake, I'm sure. He realized, I'm sure he realized, that he had misjudged the Colonel.

'I saw him. His hand was close to the hilt of his knife. He seized it. He stiffened. I could almost see his muscles flexing. For a moment I thought he had made up his mind. But it was too late. He had no strength left. He had given all he had. He was unable to do anything more – or else he was unwilling to. He dropped his knife and gave in. Total surrender, sir. You know what it's like, when you have to give up completely? He resigned himself to his fate. He moved his lips and uttered just one word. No one will ever know if it was an oath or a prayer, or even a polite conventional expression of utter despair. He wasn't bloody-minded, sir, or if he was he didn't show it. He always treated his superior officers with respect. Good God, Shears and I only just managed to stop him springing to attention each time he spoke to either of us! I bet you he said "sir" before passing out, sir. Everything depended on him. It was all over.

'Then several things happened all at once, several "facts", as you would no doubt call them, sir. They were all muddled in my mind, but I've sorted them out since. The train was arriving. The roar of the engine was growing louder every second; but it wasn't loud enough to drown the yells of that lunatic, who was shouting for help at the top of his voice in parade-ground tones!

'There I was, unable to do anything, sir. I couldn't have done better than he did. I certainly couldn't; no one could – except, perhaps, Shears. Shears! It was then that I heard someone else shouting. Shears' voice, that was it. It echoed right round the valley. The voice of a raving madman, sir! I could only make out the one word: "Strike!" He too had realized, and sooner than I had. But it was too late now.

'Some time afterwards I saw a man in the water. He was swimming towards the enemy bank. It was him. It was Shears. He too worshipped action, action at any price. A crazy thing to do. He had gone mad, just as I had, as a result of that morning. He didn't have a chance. I felt like dashing out to join him, but it would have taken over two hours to climb down from the O.P.

'He didn't have a dog's chance. He was swimming frantically, but it took him several minutes to get across. And in that time, sir, the train was already on the bridge, the splendid River Kwai bridge which our comrades-in-arms had built! Just then – just then, I remember, I saw a group of Japanese soldiers; they had heard the yells and were stumbling down the slope.

'They were the ones who dealt with Shears as he climbed out of the water. He got rid of two of them. Two thrusts of his knife, sir, I didn't miss a thing. He wasn't going to let himself be captured alive, but a rifle butt came down on the back of his head. He collapsed. Joyce was also on the ground, lying quite still. The Colonel was getting to his feet. The soldiers had cut the wire. There was nothing more we could do, sir.'

'There's always some further action to take,' Colonel Green observed.

'Always some further action to take, sir . . . After that there was an explosion. The train, which no one had thought of stopping, had blown up on the fog-signal I had laid this side of the bridge, just below the O.P. A bit of luck, that! I'd forgotten all about it. The engine came off the track and plunged into the river, bringing two or three coaches down with it. A few men were drowned. A fair amount of stores lost; but the damage could be repaired in a few days – that was the net result. But it caused quite a lot of excitement on the opposite bank.'

'A pretty fine sight, I should think, all the same,' Colonel Green consoled him.

'A very fine sight, sir, for those that like that sort or thing. So I tried to think how I could make it look even finer. I didn't forget the principles of the Force, sir. I really wracked my brains at that moment to see if there was anything more I could do in the way of action.'

'There's always something more to be done in the way of action,' Colonel Green dreamily remarked.

'Always something to be done . . . That must be true, since everyone says so. That was Shears motto. I remembered it.'

Warden stopped talking for a moment, overcome by this last thought; then went on in a softer tone of voice.

'I thought hard, sir. I thought as hard as I possibly could, while the group of soldiers swarmed round Joyce and Shears. Shears was certainly still alive, and so perhaps was Joyce, in spite of what that dirty dog had done to him.

'I could see only one possible way of taking action, sir. My two partisans were still in position with the mortar. They could fire just as easily on the group of Japs as on the bridge, and the group was just as easy to hit. I gave them that as their target. I waited a little longer. I saw the soldiers pick up the prisoners and start carrying them off. They were both still alive. It was the worst that could have happened. Colonel Nicholson brought up the rear, hanging his head as though he was deep in thought. I wonder what he was thinking, sir. I suddenly made up my mind, while there was still time.

'I gave the order to fire. The Siamese understood at once. We had trained them pretty thoroughly, sir. It was a splendid fireworks display. Another fine sight for those in the O.P. Close cross-fire. I handled the mortar myself, and I'm not such a bad shot.'

'Good results?' Colonel Green broke in.

'Good results, sir. The first shells burst right among the group. A stroke of luck! Both our chaps were blown to pieces. I confirmed that by looking through my glasses. Believe me, sir, please believe me, I didn't want to leave the job half-done either. All three of them, I should have said. The Colonel as well. There was nothing left of him. Three birds with one stone. Not bad!

'After that? After that, sir, I fired all the shells I had. There were quite a lot. Our hand-grenades as well. The position had been well selected. We sprayed the ground pretty thoroughly. I was a bit overwrought, I admit. The stuff was falling a bit indiscriminately, on the rest of the company rushing out of the camp, on the derailed train, in which everyone was shrieking, and also on the bridge. The two Siamese were as worked up as I was. The Japs fired back. Soon the smoke spread and crept up as far as us, more or less blotting out the valley and the River Kwai. We were cut off in a stinking grey fog. There was no ammo, nothing else to fire. So we retired.

'Since then I've often thought about that decision of mine, sir. I'm now convinced I couldn't have done anything else. I took the only line of conduct possible. It was really the only proper action I could have taken.'

'The only proper action,' Colonel Green agreed.

The Battle of
the River Plate

Dudley
Pope

FOREWORD

by ADMIRAL SIR EDWARD PARRY, KCB

The battle of the River Plate received a great deal of publicity at the time, largely because it was fought during the first winter of the war when little else was happening. Moreover, the picture of a comparatively large enemy vessel being pursued by two smaller British ships appealed to the imagination. To this day I do not know why the *Admiral Graf Spee* did not dispose of us in the *Ajax* and the *Achilles* as soon as she had finished with the *Exeter*.

This book gives a far more complete story of the battle, and of the events leading up to it, than any that have previously been written. The author has made full use of the German naval records captured by us at the end of the war. He is therefore able to trace the rebirth of the German Navy after its defeat in the First World War, and the intentions of that great strategist who planned its growth, Grand Admiral Raeder.

Dudley Pope reminds us that a battle is the culmination of years of planning, of production, and of practice. On our side we certainly owed our success to our pre-war training. It is perhaps fortunate that, on the German side, Hitler did not always follow the far-seeing advice of his naval staff.

This book poses some very interesting questions. Why did the captain of the *Admiral Graf Spee* think that his ship was so seriously damaged that he must make for a neutral port instead of finishing off his two small opponents?

Why was he so easily persuaded that large British warships were waiting for him outside Montevideo, when in fact there was only one new arrival, far inferior in gunpower to his own ship?

Why, even when he received definite intelligence that the *Ark Royal* and *Renown* had arrived at Rio de Janeiro, a thousand miles away, and were therefore not in the River Plate estuary, did he persist in his plan to scuttle his ship? And why were his ship's company considerably demoralized by the comparatively light hammering they had received, whereas the officers and men of the far worse damaged *Exeter* behaved so magnificently?

My last question may appear to give an answer to the others. Yet we must not think that the German Navy was inefficient or that its officers and men were lacking in courage. On the contrary, one can but admire the maintenance of their morale throughout the war, and particularly that of their submarine crews, in spite of the appalling losses which they suffered.

If therefore the answer to my questions is that Captain Langsdorff felt that he had been defeated, and if consequently he was determined not to fight it out, his decision is a real tribute to the dominating influence of Commodore Harwood's leadership in the battle.

How I wish that he could have written the foreword to this book!

PREFACE

by ADMIRAL SIR CHARLES WOODHOUSE, KCB

I served in the South America Division under Commodore Harwood for more than a year before the war. He was then in command of HMS *Exeter*, I was in HMS *Ajax*.

No one could have been kinder and more helpful to a captain in his first command than Harwood. He was the sort of man to whom one wanted to take one's doubts and difficulties in the certainty that one would get a sympathetic hearing and wise advice.

Harwood was constantly considering the special problems with which the South America Division would be faced in war, and thinking out the best means of dealing with every foreseeable contingency.

Apart from seeing to the fighting efficiency of his ships, he took endless trouble to explain to all those whose understanding cooperation would be required in an emergency the measures which he anticipated would be necessary.

He had a gift for winning the confidence and esteem of those he met, whether leading government officials or British residents in South America.

Dudley Pope's book gives a picture of the problem of protecting our trade against surface raiders in the early days of the war, and describes the success which rewarded Harwood's years of work on his station. It fell to him to strike the blow with perhaps the least powerful of the several forces which, under the direction of the Admiralty and commanders-in-chief, were all seeking the *Graf Spee* with the same determination to find her if they could, and to fight her wherever she was found.

AUTHOR'S
INTRODUCTION

This is the story of a British naval victory, written from the British and German official records with the help of the men who fought in it. That it was won at a time when it had great propaganda value is incidental to my narrative, which aims to show what goes into such a victorious battle – the last of the great naval actions fought before aircraft and radar[1] completely changed sea warfare and put an end to tactics that Nelson might have used.

Had Nelson or one of his 'band of brothers' been in Commodore Harwood's place at the Battle of the River Plate, where we were fighting an enemy which had a heavier armament, they would undoubtedly have adopted similar unorthodox tactics. A few months afterwards, radar, aircraft and U-boats revolutionized naval warfare, thus severing the link between the tactics which stemmed from Nelson and those employed after 1940.

But apart from the actual battle – in itself only the calculated end of a strategic concept – I have tried to tell of the men behind it: Britons, Germans, neutrals, diplomats, admirals, able-seamen and spies. And one should not forget how the men and women working in the government offices, in factories, dockyards and the harvest fields all contributed to the final victory.

I have done this because it is not enough to give details of how three battleships, three aircraft carriers and fourteen cruisers hunted the *Graf Spee*, and how three cruisers found her; that is not a tenth of the full story. Mistakes were made by both sides, and since I have tried to present an objective account they are described as impartially as possible.

One fact must be borne in mind by the reader who wants to comprehend the *significance* of the story: the success of the commerce raider cannot be measured in terms of her scoreboard of sinkings. The *Graf Spee* sank nine ships, totalling 50,089 tons, in just over three months at sea; but she would have been no less useful to the Germans and dangerous to the Allies had she sunk half or ten times that number.

A commerce raider has another, even more important task: to disorganize her enemy's seaborne commerce. She can do this by simply letting the enemy know she is at sea. Twenty powerful ships in nine hunting groups were eventually hunting the *Graf Spee* – and all but a few of them had to be withdrawn from other theatres of operations where they were badly needed.

---

[1] The *Graf Spee* had a simple type of rangefinding radar which was of little or no use for search purposes.

Thus the fact that the *Graf Spee* was at sea ultimately affected the ships sailing the oceans of the world and soldiers and airmen fighting on many battlefields; and although she was destroyed in the last days of 1939, the Allies were still reaping the benefit of Commodore Harwood's victory in 1943 and 1944.

But victories at sea are, in the final analysis, the scoring of hits on enemy ships by shells or torpedoes; shells and torpedoes made by thousands of civilians involved in such widespread jobs as coal-mining, iron-smelting, lathe-operating, ammunition-filling – and even typing – and fired by men both skilled and resolute. That, then, is why this story does not open dramatically with the thunder of broadsides from the *Ajax*, *Achilles* and *Exeter*, and end at sunset off Montevideo with the pocket battleship *Admiral Graf Spee* blowing up like an erupting volcano.

Many people have given me valuable assistance in writing this narrative, and I am especially grateful to Admiral Sir Edward Parry, KCB, and Admiral Sir Charles Woodhouse, KCB, both of whom gave me a great deal of help and advice. They also read the completed manuscript and suggested certain alterations. I am most grateful to Lady Harwood for her help and encouragement.

The Board of Admiralty were kind enough to grant me access to all the British and German documents I needed to write this account, and I am particularly indebted to members of the Historical Section, Records Section, Information Room, Foreign Documents Section, and Department of the Chief of Naval Information.

Officers who served in the three cruisers have provided me with a great deal of detail, and I am especially grateful to Rear Admiral R. E. Washbourn, DSO, OBE, RN, formerly Gunnery Officer of the *Achilles*; Captain E. D. G. Lewin, CB, CBE, DSO, DSC, RN, formerly of the *Ajax*; Cdr R. B. Jennings, DSO, DSC, RN (Retd), formerly Gunnery Officer of the *Exeter*; Lt-Cdr A. P. Monk, DSC, RN (Retd), formerly of the *Ajax*; Surgeon-Cdr J. Cussen, MB, BCh, RN (Retd), formerly of the *Exeter*; and Mr C. A. Pittar, MB, BS, FRACS, surgeon of the *Achilles*.

It remains to thank two people unconnected with the Navy – Count Henry Bentinck, a friend with whom I spent many hours discussing the construction of my narrative, and my wife, who was perhaps my sternest critic, and who typed the manuscript.

Times given in the narrative are frequently zone times; and much of the naval terminology and procedure in use in 1939 has now been changed.

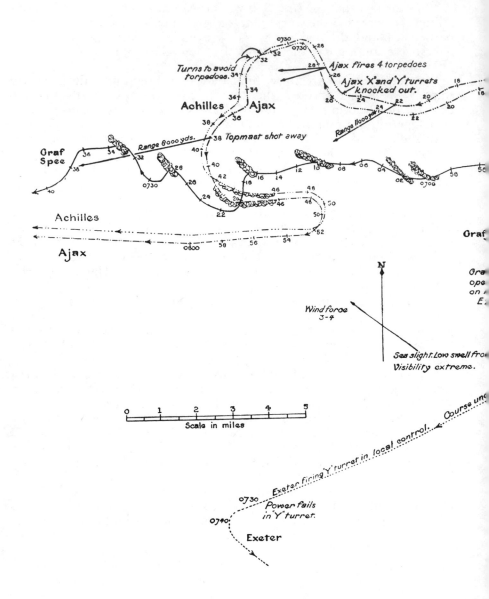

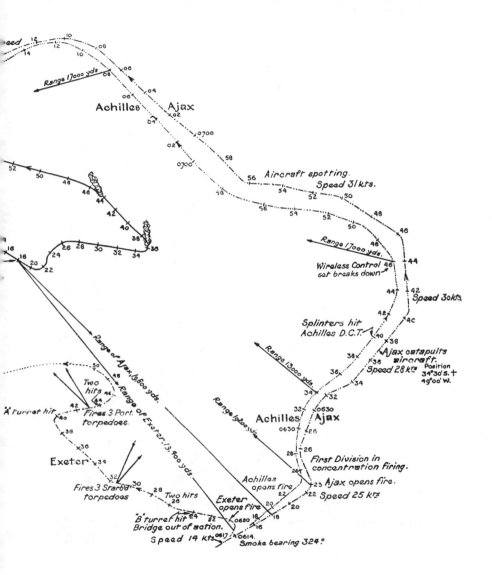

Admiral Graf Spee

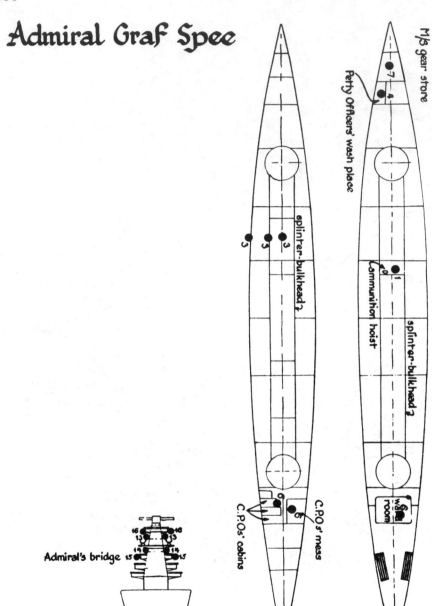

315

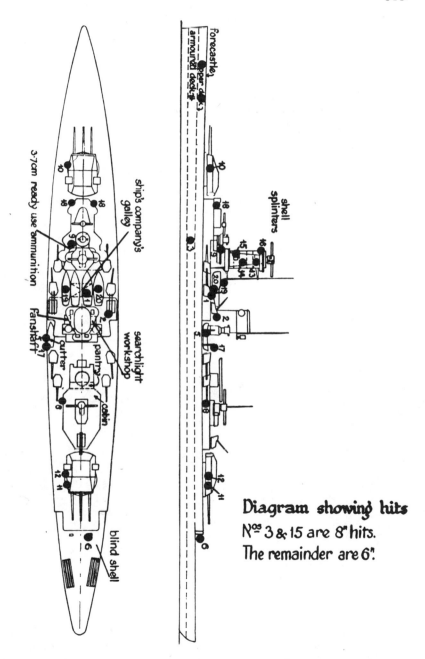

Diagram showing hits
Nᵒˢ 3 & 15 are 8" hits.
The remainder are 6".

forecastle
upper deck
armoured deck

shell splinters

3·7cm ready use ammunition

ship's company's galley

fanshaft

cutter

searchlight workshop

pantry

cabin

blind shell

*To those who fought
in The Battle of the River Plate
13 December 1939*

CHAPTER 1

LOADING THE DICE

On 6 January 1936 rain was falling over most of Europe, and the suave voices of radio commentators speaking in many languages had warned of gales sweeping the coasts. In France the rain was torrential; in Paris fire pumps stood by as the Seine rose three feet and work stopped when many commercial quays flooded. Swollen rivers teeming through other parts of Northern France damaged road and rail bridges, and at Poitiers flood waters submerged the station amid much shrugging of Gallic shoulders.

Apart from the weather, London was a cheerful city; people wanting to see a good film at a West End cinema that evening had the usual moments of indecision while choosing between Charles Laughton in *Mutiny on the Bounty* at the Empire, Leicester Square; George Arliss in *The Governor* at the Rialto, or Conrad Veidt and Helen Vinson in *King of the Damned* at the Tivoli.

Those who preferred a play were trying to get seats for Bobby Howes in *Please Teacher* at the Hippodrome or the Old Vic's inevitable *School for Scandal* in the Waterloo Road. For the millions staying at home beside the fire there was always the wireless, and Claude Hulbert was due on the Regional Programme at 7.45 in *The Scarlet Caramel*, a gentle skit on Baroness Orczy's elusive hero.

There was not much of interest in the evening newspapers: Lloyd George was planning to sell 3,000 head of poultry at his farm in Churt; gossip-writers were describing the interior of the new liner *Queen Mary*, due to sail shortly on her maiden voyage; Sir Alan Cobham had a new scheme for refuelling aircraft in mid-air; and Mr Anthony Eden had been elected president of the London Naval Conference which had just started meetings. Radiograms were advertised at ten guineas each.

Although it was not reported in the evening papers, it had been quite a stirring day for the German Navy at Kiel, where Hitler's third and latest pocket battleship, the £3,750,000 *Admiral Graf Spee*, had been ceremonially commissioned amid rain, Nazi pomp and noisy circumstance.

She was a ship of which Germany could be justifiably proud: as the world's latest capital ship she incorporated many new ideas. The plates and frames of her 609-foot hull were electrically welded and, in a vessel of her size, that was something new and showed daring on the part of her designers. In addition she had diesel engines instead of steam turbines, and these gave her a relatively high economical speed and increased her radius of action.

Her 11-inch guns were the new Krupp model which fired a 670-lb shell and had a range of fifteen miles; her rangefinders and other such gear were the finest that German technicians could devise. A radar set for obtaining accurate ranges was being secretly developed. Altogether, the builders at the Wilhelmshaven yard where she was laid down in October 1932 and launched on 30 June 1934 were proud of the *Panzerschiffe* which they had created.

But perhaps the proudest man in Germany on that wet day in January 1936 was Captain Patzig, the *Admiral Graf Spee*'s commanding officer. He paraded his crew of just under a thousand men on the quarterdeck and read a message from Admiral Erich Raeder, the Navy's Commander-in-Chief.

The uninhibited message pointed out that the ship bore the name of the Admiral who commanded the German Cruiser Squadron 'on the glorious day [of] Coronel and in the heroic battle at the Falkland Islands'. It added that 'the motto of the battleship's complement, like that of Admiral Graf von Spee and his men, would be now and for all time "Faithful unto Death"'.

So the *Admiral Graf Spee*[1] joined her two sister ships, the *Deutschland* and the *Admiral Scheer*, and Admiral Raeder was satisfied. He had explained to Hitler that building up a balanced fleet from nothing was a slow process, but unfortunately the Fuehrer did not understand naval strategy. Still, like the build-up of the entire German armed forces, it was at least a steady one.

Germany had been – at least ostensibly – limited by the Treaty of Versailles, and the naval clauses held her to a navy comprising a maximum of 15,000 men, with six heavy ships, six light cruisers, twelve destroyers and twelve torpedo boats, with a limit on displacement in each class. The construction of U-boats was entirely forbidden. But Germany had been secretly breaking the Treaty for some years.

In 1928, for example, within ten years of the end of the First World War and five years before Hitler came to power, the construction of a pocket battleship had begun. She would be much larger than allowed under the Treaty, but by then the former Allies were complacent in enforcing its terms, and by using the description 'pocket battleship' and giving false displacement figures, with the explanation that new methods of welded construction and diesel propulsion saved weight, the Germans had made sure no awkward questions were asked.

When Hitler was appointed Chancellor he had given Raeder a free hand to go ahead with his construction plans and set about ridding himself of the terms of the Versailles Treaty, which was repudiated in 1935. This was little more than a formality – although the Treaty limit for capital ships

[1] The *von* was dropped from the ship's name.

had been 10,000 tons, the pocket battleships exceeded that and Raeder already had under construction the battle cruisers *Scharnhorst* and *Gneisenau*, each of 32,000 tons, while submarines were built secretly in Holland and Finland.

In 1936 the Anglo-German Naval Treaty was signed. Although he had seen that Britain and France had shown an almost lackadaisical unconcern about enforcing the naval clauses of the Versailles Treaty, Hitler was careful to make sure the British negotiators left the conference table content. It was agreed that Germany could build to thirty-five per cent of the British naval strength, and could have submarines. In terms of ships it meant five capital ships, two aircraft carriers, twenty-one cruisers and sixty-four destroyers. Hitler was quite content because it was the maximum number that German shipyards could build for the next few years, and by then he knew he would be in a position to repudiate that Treaty too.

But Germany was not a party to either the Washington Naval Agreement or the London Conference, under which Britain, France and the United States could not – and did not – build battleships of more than 35,000 tons. Meanwhile Hitler allowed Raeder to build the *Bismarck* and *Tirpitz*, each of 45,000 tons ...

Thus by early 1937, while Britain, France and the USA had voluntarily tied their own hands by treaties, the great expansion of the German Navy went ahead. In making his long-term plans, Raeder had two courses open to him:

(a) Build up to the Treaty limit of thirty-five per cent of the Royal Navy, planning to reach that total by 1940, on the assumption war would break out then.
(b) Assume war would start later – possibly in 1944–5 – and plan a more balanced fleet. This would mean having a weaker fleet in the meantime.

Although Raeder chose the second course, by 1938 he felt that Britain's reaction to the European crisis caused by Hitler's activities was stiffening (a view not shared by Hitler) and drew up the so-called Z Plan, which provided for a more immediately powerful offensive force and to a certain extent abandoned the idea of a fully balanced fleet.

Since the actual strategy that a navy can follow is governed by the types of ships it has, Raeder visualized that under the Z Plan Germany's naval operations against Britain would be directed more against the merchant shipping in her sea lanes than Britain's fighting fleet. In the circumstances this was sensible strategy, particularly since the U-boat arm was being built up.

By the time it was completed in 1945, the Z Plan was intended to provide

Germany with a formidable navy comprising thirteen battleships, thirty-three cruisers, four aircraft carriers, 250 U-boats and a large number of destroyers. And every ship would be of a modern design, compared with the majority of the larger ships of the Royal Navy which dated from the First World War. The Anglo-German Naval Treaty would, of course, have long since been repudiated by Hitler.

Yet the Z plan was soon aborted by Hitler's changes of policy. Although a voracious reader, much of the material which Hitler read passed through his brain without leaving much impression. But he was an instinctive and effective politician, his major mistake being that he considered himself a statesman. He dreamed of himself as a master strategist, following great soldiers like Napoleon. And in some ways he did resemble Napoleon – initial successes on land in Europe led to the same suicidal attack on Russia, and at no time did he understand naval strategy. Nor was any member of the German Navy, least of all Raeder, among Hitler's 'inner circle'.

But for these factors, he might well have kept his hands off Poland until the Z Plan was more advanced, if not completed. In addition he believed that Britain could be persuaded to stay out of a continental war. It is certain he never visualized a long war – yet, in the event, there were only two places where he could effectively attack Britain, the only enemy left in the field against him.

One was at sea, but his timetable wrecked the Z Plan and prevented Raeder from building a navy capable of decisive action. The other was in the Mediterranean, the only area where he could bring Britain to battle on land. Of the two, Britain could only be defeated at sea.

Early in 1939 Admiral Raeder was still working to his Z Plan when Hitler began planning the actual invasion of Poland and in April issued a directive to the Armed Forces to prepare the details. The directive said, 'Policy aims at limiting the war to Poland, and this is considered possible in view of the internal crisis in France and consequent British restraint ...'

Raeder disagreed over Britain's probable role, quite apart from his dismay at being faced with a war for which he had a completely unbalanced navy. A month later another directive, indicating that Hitler too was now having doubts, gave instructions for the 'economic war and the protection of our own economy', and said that the Navy and *Luftwaffe* were to prepare for the immediate opening of economic warfare against Britain and, as a second priority, against France. The Navy, Hitler added, was to plan for a war against British and French merchant shipping.

In fact, because of Raeder's doubts, the Naval War Staff was already drawing up its Atlantic Trade Warfare Plan, and in order to understand the significance of the subsequent operations by the *Graf Spee*, described in this volume, it is necessary to discuss briefly the strategy of commerce raiding as planned by Raeder.

There are two main objects of commerce warfare: the obvious one of the destruction of enemy ships, and the less obvious one of so disorganizing the sailing of merchant ships that restrictions on the enemy's seagoing trade become unbearable and finally impossible.

The surface raider can assist in three ways:

1. Sinking or capturing ships.
2. Dislocating normal traffic through the fear of her presence (or by minelaying), thus slowing up the regular arrival of food, supplies and raw materials. This eventually cuts down imports so much that the blockaded country collapses economically.
3. By making the enemy so scatter his surface warships hunting for the raiders that other arms – the submarines and aircraft, for example – have a better chance of successfully attacking convoys whose escorts (both close escorts and the more remote patrols by larger ships) have been weakened.

So when one tries to estimate the value of a surface raider one has to take these three points into consideration: the actual total sinkings or captures is only a part – and a small part – of the story, as will be seen in the case of the *Graf Spee*.[1]

In the First World War, as very few merchant ships had radio transmitters or receivers, the surface raider had it more or less her own way, especially as she used coal and could easily refuel from captured colliers. The task of discovering her whereabouts and destroying her was incredibly difficult. In August 1914 the Germans had in fact stationed their warships abroad in favourable positions. But although the losses inflicted by these raiders were not great, the potentialities of this type of warfare were enormous: and it was this which made a great impression on Admiral Raeder's mind when planning the course of a possible second war against Britain. The ships used in the First World War by the Germans had not been really suitable for the task of commerce raiding, and Admiral Raeder, reviewing the results, concluded that independence and deception were more useful qualities in a raider than speed and gunfire, and the cruiser designed for Fleet work was unsuitable. Some other designs of warship was therefore needed.

While still outwardly limited by the Versailles Treaty, the German Naval Staff had decided to concentrate on the construction of a type of warship which, while ostensibly keeping inside the tonnage restrictions of the Treaty, would have long endurance and a reasonably high speed.

The three twenty-eight-knot pocket battleships, with six 11-inch, eight

---

[1] Commerce raiders in both wars claimed only a small proportion of total Allied ship losses – 4.1 per cent in the First World War and 6.2 in the Second. (See Appendix C.)

5.9-inch, six 4.1-inch (high-angle) guns, torpedo tubes and two aircraft, were the result. Their power was underestimated by the British, who assumed they were inside the then Treaty limit of 10,000 tons. If this had been the case, either operational range, speed or armour would have had to be sacrificed. As it was they were of more than 12,000 tons and had a great range, sufficient armour and a speed appropriate to their role.

With an OKW[1] directive of 3 April setting down the date for the attack on Poland for any time after 1 September, events moved fast in Germany. While the Operations Division of the Naval War Staff drew up detailed plans for commerce raiding by the *Admiral Graf Spee* and the *Deutschland*, Raeder was now not unnaturally far from satisfied with the Navy he had created.

The 45,000-ton *Bismarck* and *Tirpitz*, of advanced design and the most powerful warships under construction by any European power, were not yet completed; the 32,000-ton battlecruisers *Scharnhorst* and *Gneisenau* were neither operationally satisfactory nor fully worked up. The new 8-inch heavy cruisers *Admiral Hipper* and *Prinz Eugen* were not yet available, and by August one of the three pocket battleships, the *Admiral Scheer*, would be in need of a long overhaul.

However, he had the consolation that the pocket battleships were brilliantly conceived ships. He considered that the combined British and French Navies had only five or six ships individually capable of both catching and sinking any one of them.

The odds against the pocket battleships in ocean raiding against British and French merchant shipping were not as heavy as Germany's numerical weakness and lack of foreign bases might suggest. The sheer vastness of the oceans is not often fully appreciated: the Atlantic comprises more than 34,000,000 square miles and the Indian Ocean 28,000,000, compared with the area of Europe (3,947,000), South America (6,970,000), Africa (11,688,000) and Asia (17,276,000). Any British warship searching for a pocket battleship in perfect visibility could at best hope to sight her at a range of about twelve miles, so the problem in the Atlantic was finding a ship while looking round a circle with a diameter of twenty-four miles in an area twice the size of Asia and its offshore islands.

In addition, the raider inevitably enjoys the initiative. To fulfil her objective of disrupting trade – far more important than actually sinking ships – she need do little more than make her presence known in one area and move swiftly to another.

After sinking a ship in one position, the *Graf Spee* could be 500 miles away within twenty-four hours without using up fuel at an excessive rate. Cruising at twenty knots, she could easily travel in a week the distance between London and New York.

---

[1] *Ober Kommando Wehrmacht* – the High Command of the Armed Forces.

The German plan, as yet untried, for operating the pocket battleships at sea for long periods anticipated using auxiliary vessels specially designed for fuelling, supplying and prison-ship duties. These supply ships, usually disguised as neutral tankers, were to cruise in the general area of the raiders' operations, making rendezvous as ordered and when possible waiting in unfrequented areas of the ocean.

So the spring of 1939 gave way to a lazy summer. 'Munich', with all that it implied, had passed and British public opinion was rapidly realizing that Neville Chamberlain's 'Peace in our time' was to be measured in months rather than years. In Berlin the Naval War Staff had completed its Atlantic Trade Warfare Plan and, because of the increasing international tension, put it into operation.

On 27 July secret orders were sent to Captain Heinrich Dau, master of the tanker *Altmark*, telling him to store his ship with three months' supplies by 2 August so that the ship could sail to the United States, embark fuel oil and be under way again before war broke out. The *Altmark* was to be a supply ship for a commerce raiding pocket battleship.

Dispatching Dau's orders was the first actual move made by Germany against Britain, and it was swiftly followed by several more. The pocket battleship *Graf Spee*, at sea on torpedo-firing exercises, was recalled to Wilhelmshaven on 17 August to be docked, overhauled and secretly stored at top speed.

Meanwhile the *Altmark* had crossed the Atlantic and was in Port Arthur, New Mexico, taking on 9,400 tons of diesel fuel as the *Graf Spee* entered Wilhelmshaven. Two days later, on 19 August, Dau sailed after receiving orders in cipher from the Naval War Staff telling him to make for an area near the Canary Islands, where he was to wait for the *Graf Spee*.

The detailed operational orders for the *Graf Spee* and *Deutschland* had been ready since 4 August. They told the two captains that as far as the political situation was concerned, in the event of war with Poland, it was now considered that Britain and France would intervene, and Italy would probably be on Germany's side. Russia's attitude would be uncertain but neutral at first.

The ships' task in wartime, the orders added, would be 'the disruption and destruction of enemy shipping by all possible means'. Enemy naval forces, even if inferior in strength, were to be engaged only if it furthered the principal task of commerce raiding. Frequent changes of position in the specified operational area 'would create uncertainty and will restrict enemy shipping'.

While these orders were being digested, the *Graf Spee*'s men, helped by ratings from the barracks, got on with the work in Wilhelmshaven. The second in command, Kapitän zur See Kay, made sure of the stowage of food and supplies for the fifty-four officers, 217 petty officers, 833 ratings, twenty-four civilians and six Chinese, forming the *Graf Spee*'s crew – and enough paint and gear to keep the ship smart and, if necessary, alter her appearance with dummy funnels from time to time. It was Kay's job to have the ship running smoothly – he was responsible to Kapitän zur See Langsdorff, the *Graf Spee*'s present captain. One last-minute job he had when it was made known that the ship was going to the tropics was to find out if every man had his own sleeping quarters. He discovered forty-seven men had not. After arguing with the staff on shore it was agreed to cut down the number of the crew, and Kay used this opportunity to get rid of some unreliable men. He also had to find accommodation for Reserve officers forming boarding parties. Several of these were carefully chosen former Merchant Marine officers who had served in South American and African waters.

The Chief Gunnery Officer, in charge of the main armament, was Fregattenkapitän Ascher: he had the job of making sure he had enough shells, charges and spares stowed away for the 11-inch and 5.9-inch guns. The Second Gunnery Officer, Korvettenkapitän Meusermann, was responsible for the 4.1-inch high-angle guns; his shells, too, had to be stowed in magazines and ready-use lockers.

Kapitänleutnant Brutzer was the Torpedo Officer: his task, in addition to handling the torpedo tubes on the *Graf Spee*'s quarterdeck, included the checking and stowing of the bombs which would be used to sink captured merchant ships.

The man who would be responsible for navigating the *Graf Spee* was Korvettenkapitän Wattenberg: in the pocket battleship's chart room he had stowed folios of charts enough to navigate the warship round the world – along with the latest Lloyd's Register of Merchant Ships, *Jane's Fighting Ships*, and German and British pilot books for all coasts.

Perhaps the busiest man in these hurried days was Korvettenkapitän (Ing) Klepp: he was the Chief Engineer. In addition to taking hundreds of tons of oil fuel on board through snaking hose, he had to order and stow thousands of spare parts – from electric light bulbs to pieces of metal weighing several hundredweights – for the great diesel engines.

Late on 20 August the Captain, Hans Langsdorff, reported to the Naval War Staff[1] that the *Admiral Graf Spee* was ready for sea. For this slim, elegant young commander the test was just beginning: all his adult life had been spent in preparation for the day when he would be captain of his own ship at sea – and at war.

That night, 20 August, was the last the *Graf Spee* was destined to spend in

[1] Control of the *Graf Spee* and the *Deutschland* and eleven U-boats was retained by the High Command instead of being left to the C-in-C, West, at Wilhelmshaven.

a home port; and although the sailing date and destination was a closely guarded secret since the world was still at peace, few men on board the grey-painted pocket battleship could fail to realize that they were on the eve of departure.

In Britain the three Services were rapidly preparing. While the Admiralty put the finishing touches to their own plans, Coastal Command were having a full-scale exercise to test out their search scheme designed to prevent surface raiders breaking out of the North Sea.

At the completion of the exercises the squadrons of planes were to fly to their war stations and, although war had not started, they were to begin with war-time reconnaissance flights over the North Sea immediately. The days chosen for the exercise were 15 August to 21 August, the last flights ending at dusk . . .

Monday, 21 August, started off as a hot summer's day and rapidly the temperature in London and the south-east of England rose to about 27°C. From Brussels came reports that King Leopold was inviting representatives of several small nations to Brussels for a conference to discuss the sending of a peace appeal to the great nations.

In London, the Prime Minister, Mr Neville Chamberlain, was talking with his Foreign Secretary, Lord Halifax, about the latest reports of the situation in Danzig. Reports of big purchases of copper, lead and rubber on the London market came in at noon, and all were for early delivery. 'In some cases,' reported the *Evening News*, 'Dutch firms have made the first inquiries, but on coming down to details have readily disclosed that the deliveries are ultimately to reach a German destination . . .'

At the Oval the West Indies had passed England's total with five wickets in hand, and by lunchtime the atmosphere was oppressive with a damp and heavy, foreboding heat. In the afternoon the thunder clouds which had been gathering swirled into a heavy storm; lightning flickered and struck houses (at Ilford several people were killed). Many London roads were flooded and railways were affected.

As usual there was a good choice of films, plays and cabaret for those who wanted entertainment in the West End. So if you wanted fun that evening you could have had it. But on that evening, when the Coastal Command's exercise over the North Sea had finished, eight sets of diesel engines in the *Graf Spee* started their rhythmical thumping and her two great bronze propellers spun almost lazily as Captain Langsdorff took her at 8 pm out of Wilhelmshaven down the Jade River, through the Schillig Roads, and into the North Sea.

Quietly, without fuss, the propellers increased their spinning until dials recorded 250 revolutions, taking the pocket battleship at full speed north-

north-eastward past the rock that is Heligoland, past the island of Sylt and
Horns Rev off Denmark ... By noon next day Langsdorff wanted to be in a
position west of Bergen.

The ship was sailing on a route already taken by several U-boats since 19
August as they headed for their war stations in the Atlantic, and by 29
August seventeen of them were to have sailed. Thus that night an operation
began which, as the Germans themselves observed, not only made the
heaviest claims on the strength, endurance and constant operational
readiness of the ships' officers and men, but in demands on technical
resources and material efficiency.

Carefully Langsdorff moved his ship northward through the night,
keeping thirty miles off the Norwegian coast and altering course as soon as
a ship's lights were sighted. Only one ship and several fishing vessels had
been seen by noon on the 24th, when the *Graf Spee* was south-east of
Iceland.

Now he was at sea, Langsdorff was able to digest his instructions more
easily. The operational areas allocated to him were (a) the South
American-Cape Verde Islands-Biscay trade route; and (b) the South and
Central Atlantic sea area, the Cape Town-Cape Verde Islands route, or
the South Indian Ocean. However, these orders were not binding on
Langsdorff: he was free to choose his operational area according to the
opposition he encountered and the density of the traffic. Until the war
began, his instructions said, the *Graf Spee* was to wait in an area to the
north-westward of the Cape Verde Islands. In the meantime the pocket
battleship was to maintain wireless silence. The next move would come
from the Naval High Command.

The supply ship *Westerwald* sailed on 22 August for a position south of
Greenland, where she would work with the pocket battleship *Deutschland*;
and on the same day Hitler added to the confusion in the minds of the
Naval High Command by a speech at Obersalzberg (near Berchtesgaden,
in Bavaria, where Hitler had his mountain retreat, the Berghof) to the
Commanders-in-Chief of the Armed Forces.

He was in a jubilant mood, and first he told them that a pact was about
to be signed with Russia – which meant Poland was isolated. But, he said,
he did not know whether Britain and France would go to Poland's help
when she was attacked. He felt the pact with Russia would deter them.

The next day, 23 August, saw one of the first British operational moves
which affect this story: the cruiser *Exeter* was at Devonport with her crew on
foreign-service leave when she was recalled to South American waters.
Captain F. S. Bell assumed command of the ship two days later, and
she continued to fly Commodore Henry Harwood's broad pendant as
Commodore, South American Division. That evening she sailed.

The *Deutschland* sailed on Thurdsay, 24 August, from Wilhelmshaven under the command of Captain Paul Wenneker. Her operational area was the North Atlantic, and she was due to rendezvous with the *Westerwald* south of Greenland. The Air Ministry in London, warned by the Admiralty that something of this nature was happening, gave orders to Coastal Command to start dawn reconnaissance with the object of shadowing, 'in an unobtrusive manner', any German forces sighted.

On the same day Hitler announced to a surprised world that a non-aggression pact had been signed in Moscow between Germany and Russia. In Poland the Government knew that Hitler's net was closing in on them. Help was many hundreds of miles away, and now the Kremlin was backing Hitler.

It was the same Thursday that the Admiralty signalled orders to the Home Fleet and all ships at home ports to proceed to their war stations, and this was followed on Tuesday, 29 August, by the order to mobilize the Fleet 'in accordance with instructions for war with a European power ...'

Slowly and perhaps almost unwillingly the British moved towards readiness for war. Two days later, on 31 August, a signal reached the Admiralty saying there was some indication that a large German ship had left Wilhelmshaven pm on 30 August or am on the 31st. This was followed by a signal from the First Sea Lord, Admiral Sir Dudley Pound, ordering all forces to proceed to sea and patrol in the area between the Shetlands and Norway; but they found nothing ... the *Graf Spee* had passed through ten days and the *Deutschland* seven days earlier ...

On the same day Hitler issued his 'Directive No. 1 for the Conduct of the War'. He said that now all political possibilities of disposing of the situation on the Eastern Front were exhausted, 'I have determined on a solution by force.' *Fall Weiss*, the attack on Poland, was to start next day. The time, 4.45 am, was inserted in red pencil. The German land frontiers in the west, he added were not to be crossed, and 'the same applies to warlike actions at sea, or any which may be so interpreted.'

At dawn next day German forces swarmed across the Polish frontier at the time written down by Hitler's red pencil. *Fall Weiss*, and with it the Second World War, had started. It was to be a war the like of which had never been seen; a war waged by the Germans in complete disregard of international law and humanitarian considerations; and which saw them, among other things, establish *Einsatzkommandos* (Extermination Squads) expressly to murder Jews.

CHAPTER 2

TOTAL GERMANY

On the morning of Sunday, 3 September, the voice of the Prime Minister was heard through radio loudspeakers in almost every home in Britain saying that a state of war now existed with Germany. Almost immediately the air-raid sirens sounded and the great silver barrage balloons rose into the sky over a strangely hushed and sunlit London.

From the Admiralty the following signal was broadcast in plain language to all home commands and ships: *11 AM COMMENCE HOSTILITIES AT ONCE AGAINST GERMANY*. A similar signal was also sent to all British merchantmen by the powerful Rugby transmitter. (One of the ships that picked it up was the *Graf Spee*, giving Captain Langsdorff the first news that the war had begun.) To its own ships at sea the Admiralty radioed the prearranged signal *TOTAL GERMANY*.

Almost at once, German U-boats struck their first blow, torpedoing the liner *Athenia* in the Atlantic. Four ships heard her SSS signal[1] and managed to rescue 1,300 civilians, including many children, before the ship sank, drowning about 100 people. However, the *Athenia* was not the war's first casualty although she was the first merchant ship sunk without warning.

The credit for being the first warship to capture and sink an enemy merchant ship in the Second World War fell to the British cruiser *Ajax*, which was later to play a major part in the destruction of the *Graf Spee*. Commanded by Captain Charles Woodhouse, she was in Rio de Janeiro the week before the war began, and as events in Europe reached a climax Captain Woodhouse found himself responsible for 4,000 miles of coastline while being nearly 2,000 miles from the nearest British base. There are few men who would not have felt lonely under these circumstances, and he admitted he was not one of them.

There were a large number of German merchantmen at sea and in port along his 'beat', some reported by Intelligence to have guns on board and to be manned by Nazis. Feeling that war was imminent, Woodhouse decided he ought to be at sea, so that the Germans would not know where the *Ajax* was, and the prospect of being intercepted by a British cruiser might deter some ships from sailing. He was heading for the River Plate area when he received the Admiralty signal *TOTAL GERMANY*, and three hours later a merchant ship was sighted.

She proved to be the *Olinda*, bound for Germany from Montevideo with a cargo of wool, hides, cotton, scrap iron and wood. Her crew was taken off

---

[1] The traditional SOS was superseded by SSS for attack by submarine, RRR for attack by a surface raider, and AAA for aircraft.

and since it was not practical to make a prize of her, she was sunk by gunfire. Next day, yet another German merchantman, the *Carl Fritzen*, was sighted and her crew taken off. One of the *Ajax*'s first shells happened to hit a tank just above the *Carl Fritzen*'s waterline, so that instead of sea water rushing in the hole the British were rather embarrassed to see fresh water pouring out!

Three days later in Berlin Admiral Raeder had his first war conference with Hitler, and the main problem he raised was the future role of the two pocket battleships already at sea. In view of the French restraint 'and the still hesitant conduct of British warfare', he said, the pocket battleships should be withdrawn from their operational areas. British trade was being stopped and British forces were being sent out in planned attacks against raiders, so 'the risk was out of all proportion with the chances of success'. After listening to the Admiral, Hitler agreed that the *Graf Spee* and *Deutschland* 'are to hold back and withdraw for the present'.

So far we have dealt only with German naval policy, but the broad lines of Admiralty policy had been approved by the Board eight months before the outbreak of war. The United Kingdom's geographical position has for centuries been one of the most important factors in British power: it has formed a barrier and a fortress between Northern Europe and the Atlantic, and all ships bound for the oceans of the world have to pass either through the Channel or round the north of Scotland. The arrival of high-speed surface vessels, submarines and aircraft had increased the importance of that factor since the gap between Scotland and Norway, the so-called northern passage, is a scant three hundred miles. In the Second World War German ships could get in or out only by passing through the northern passage. If the Royal Navy could prevent this, then Germany would be blockaded and her Navy trapped.

However, there was another side to this, even if the Royal Navy controlled all the ocean highways to Britain completely but lost control round our coasts – to German aircraft, submarines, surface craft or even minefields – then Britain would still be cut off. Her supply ships would be sunk almost literally at the harbour entrance after sailing perhaps half-way round the world.

Some idea of the magnitude of the Navy's commerce-protection task is given by the fact that in 1939 more than 3,000 foreign-going merchant ships were registered in Britain, and more than 1,000 coasters. An average of 2,500 ships flying the Red Ensign were at sea on any one day in positions ranging from the east coast of England to the far ends of the Pacific. So the first priority in the Admiralty's plan was the defence of home waters. Second was the Mediterranean, across which came tankers with oil from the Middle East, and ships with cargoes from India and the Far East. Third came the Far East itself where Japan, with a vast and powerful fleet, stood smiling and inscrutable.

After the bitter experience of the First World War, the Admiralty had always maintained that the minimum number of cruisers needed to meet our commitments was seventy. When the Second World War began, we had only fifty-eight, some of which were unsuitable because of age or lack of endurance. The shortage was due to many things, all political, and the most important of which were the limitations caused by naval treaties. The Washington Conference produced the large 8-inch cruisers, which the Navy never wanted. Later the 8-inch tonnage allowed to each nation was limited and resulted in our last two, the *Exeter* and *York*, having only six instead of eight 8-inch guns.

Although its estimate of the potential of the German pocket battleships (based on their supposed displacement) was wrong, the Admiralty was accurate in its forecast of the way Raeder would make use of commerce raiding, and its War Memorandum specified 'traditional and well-proved methods' of protecting the trade routes. These, it said, consisted in the dispersal of shipping (i.e. the special and often devious routing of ships to keep them away from known or suspected danger spots); the stationing of naval patrols in focal areas (one might almost call them the ocean crossroads where one trade route crossed another or several met off a large port) and where cruisers could concentrate in pairs; and the formation of adequately escorted convoys. Detachments from the main fleet could be used if required.

The plans outlined in the Memorandum came into force the day war broke out, but British ships were obviously extremely vulnerable for several weeks after that, since many of them on their way to and from Britain were already scattered along regular trade routes.

Changes had just been made concerning the naval command in the South Atlantic, where the events to be described in this volume took place. The designation of Vice-Admiral George D'Oyly Lyon was changed from Commander-in-Chief, Africa Station, to Commander-in-Chief, South Atlantic, and he transferred his headquarters from the Cape to Freetown, in Sierra Leone – a move which brought him 3,000 miles north and put him in a better position to control British warships ranging over the whole of the South Atlantic.

At the same time the South America Division of the America and West Indies Squadron (based at Bermuda) was transferred to his command. The Division at the time comprised the cruisers *Exeter* and *Ajax* and was under the immediate command of Commodore Henry Harwood, who had been in South American waters for the past three years.

Commanded by Captain F. S. Bell, the *Exeter* was an 8,390-ton cruiser carrying 1,900 tons of fuel, giving her a range of only 10,000 miles at eleven to fourteen knots – not nearly enough for the task the Admiralty had given her, as will be seen later. She was a far from satisfactory warship, apart from her short range, the treaty limitations forcing her to carry only six 8-inch guns, instead of eight, leading those taking a charitable view to assume she was built to sell to a potential enemy.

Commodore Harwood was anxious to meet his new Commander-in-Chief, so when the *Exeter* sailed from Devonport she made for Freetown, where she could also refuel. She arrived there the day Hitler marched into Poland.

The situation Commodore Harwood described to Admiral Lyon was a difficult one. The South America Division was operating off an entirely neutral coastline. The nearest British base was in the bleak Falkland Islands, 1,000 miles south of Buenos Aires and Montevideo, and nearly 2,000 miles from Rio de Janeiro. This meant that if a cruiser like the *Exeter*, with her range of 10,000 miles, had to go from Rio to fuel at the Falklands and return, she would have to use nearly half her fuel to get there and back – and that was assuming she did not exceed fourteen knots.

The entry of belligerent warships into neutral ports was governed by international law and varied from country to country (although they were all very similar and based on the 13th Hague Convention of 1907). Whereas a belligerent soldier or aircraft landing in a neutral country was automatically interned, a warship could stay for twenty-four hours, and this period could be extended for certain reasons, which include repairs to make the vessel seaworthy.

Although the Hague Convention did not specify the number of times a warship may visit a neutral port, it did say she could take on enough fuel to reach the nearest port in her own country. Some neutral countries interpreted this as allowing a warship to fill up all spaces built to carry fuel, but once having done this she could not fuel again in the same country for three months. This meant, in fact, that Harwood could only refuel his ships in any port belonging to each of the three neutral republics once every three months. The main ports were Buenos Aires (Argentine), Montevideo (Uruguay) and Rio de Janeiro (Brazil). However, the interpretation of the rules finally rested with the neutral governments concerned, and it was vitally necessary for Britain to be on friendly terms with them.

After discussions with the Admiral, Commodore Harwood sailed for Rio de Janeiro where he had to sort out various problems. Arriving on the 7th, he talked with Sir Hugh Gurney, the British Ambassador, knowing that fuelling was now going to be even more of a problem since the 8-inch cruiser *Cumberland* was on her way from Plymouth to reinforce him and two destroyers, the *Hotspur* and *Havock*, were coming from Freetown.

It is on these occasions that the value of the peacetime 'showing the flag' cruises is revealed. The Commodore's three years on the South America Station had been well spent. He was a good mixer and had taken the trouble to learn Spanish. He was noted more for his brave attempts than his fluency; but nevertheless the South American governments had a high regard for him. They considered him a typical Englishman whom they could trust, and the fact that he could talk to them in somewhat unconventional Spanish helped considerably – his grammatical errors were guaranteed to liven up any diplomatic party.

Whereas Drake was famous for his game of bowls, it might well be said that Commodore Harwood's golf and pleasing, 'typically British' personality were two factors which did much to ensure that at the outbreak of war the South American republics (despite the high percentage of Germans living there and forming a virulent and noisy Fifth Column) were all pro-British and willing to stretch a point or two in Harwood's favour.

Over the next few days Harwood received permission from Brazil to fuel at frequent intervals 'provided that such visits were made discreetly and at different ports'. The Commander-in-Chief of the Argentine Navy raised no objections to Harwood's force refuelling from a British tanker in the Plate estuary, going so far as to suggest a particularly sheltered anchorage. The Uruguayan Government was equally helpful, but in each case Harwood had to bear in mind that concessions applied to both belligerents: he could not ask for anything that would also benefit the Germans.

In addition to the twin handicaps of a small force of ships and the difficulty of fuelling them, Harwood suffered to some extent from being afloat. While at sea, his ship had to keep wireless silence. She was of course free to receive signals from the Admiralty or Admiral Lyon in Freetown, but transmitting any message meant she gave her position away to the enemy.

These were the three basic handicaps facing Harwood and the South America Division. And on 8 September, when the *Exeter* sailed from Rio after a stay of less than twenty-four hours, Harwood received a signal from the Admiralty which underlined them. Three German merchant ships, the Admiralty warned, were assembling off the Patagonian coast (at the extreme tip of South America). The position was more than 2,000 miles to the south of the *Exeter*.

The three ships could do a number of things, from mounting guns and acting as surface raiders to launching an attack on the undefended Falkland Islands. So while the cruiser *Ajax* went south to guard the Falklands, the Commodore started short-distance convoys from the Plate and Rio de Janeiro, the merchantmen being escorted clear of the coast and dispersed at night on different routes.

However, unsuspected by either the Admiralty or Harwood, a German pocket battleship was already ranging the South Atlantic.

CHAPTER 3

MAKE THE CHALLENGE

The *Graf Spee*'s voyage down towards the Tropics had been uneventful. On 24 August, the day the *Deutschland* sailed from Wilhelmshaven, she was midway between Iceland and the Faeroes; by the 27th the noon position noted in her log put her on the same latitude as London and midway between Britain and Newfoundland. On the 28th Berlin passed a radiogram from the SKL giving the position for a rendezvous with the tanker *Altmark* on 1 September.

The world was still at peace and the merchant ships steaming along well-defined shipping lanes of the Atlantic carried the normal navigation and accommodation lights. Since it was essential that the *Graf Spee* reach the waiting area near the Cape Verde Islands, off the West African coast, without being sighted, Langsdorff decided to cross the shipping lanes at night with his ship darkened. And whether it was daylight or darkness, he knew that his lookouts in their positions high over the bridge, scores of feet above sea level, and other men watching through the immensely powerful rangefinder which revolved twenty-four hours a day, would see lights or smoke long before any other ship would sight the *Graf Spee*.

And — even though it was always breaking down — the *Dt-Geraet* was useful for dodging ships. *Dt-Geraet* was the rudimentary radar set mounted in a revolving pillar on the foretop. Although intended for rangefinding, it could be used, with its eighteen-and-a-half-mile range, for searching. The trouble was that the vibration all over the ship from the diesel engines caused breaks in the cables feeding the set. However, when it was working it was quite accurate and one great advantage was that the British did not know the Germans had a form of radar installed.

Thus, using his speed, the *Dt-Geraet* and the rangefinders, Langsdorff could evade surface ships. The only thing he had to worry about was aircraft, and he was sufficiently far out into the Atlantic not to have any great fears. The mainstay of the British Coastal Command, the Anson, then had a range of only 510 miles at 144 knots; not even enough for it to reach the Norwegian coast from England and return.

So the hours slipped by as her diesel engines thrust the pocket battleship through the Atlantic swell. Korvettenkapitän (Ing) Klepp, the Chief Engineer, made his daily report to the Captain: all was well, the engines were behaving perfectly, and every man in the engine room, down to the greasers responsible for lubricating the two great propeller shafts, was settling down to the sea routine. And it was a good time for exercising all the guns' crews. Even Kapitänleutnant Brutzer had a chance of exercising his men at the torpedo tubes.

The man with the least work on his hands was Dr Kartzendorff, the ship's surgeon. Apart from the usual cases of sea-sickness and constipation he had no sick or injured men to attend to. However, he had a chance to sort out instruments and check up on the spare supplies – which he might well be wanting within a very short time.

The two busiest men, apart from Langsdorff, were undoubtedly Kay, the second in command, and Wattenberg, the Navigating Officer. Kay was responsible to Langsdorff for the state of the ship and the crew. It was his task to see that all the departments ran smoothly, that the crew were efficient, and the ship was in good trim. And if anything happened to Langsdorff he would take over the command.

In worsening weather the *Graf Spee* ploughed her way to the south-west. The *Dt-Geraet* searched with its invisible eye; the powerful motor slowly revolved the big rangefinder; and ratings, their faces pressed to the rubber-rimmed eye-pieces, watched for the first telltale sign of smoke on the horizon which would mean a quick warning to the bridge and an alteration of course to keep the ship clear.

Watches were changing with what was becoming monotonous regularity. The Navigating Officer, Wattenberg, and his assistant regularly took sun sights, plotted their position on the large North Atlantic track charts, and made neat entries in the log which Wattenberg signed. The amount of cloud, strength of wind, height and length of sea, amount of fuel consumed, courses steered, visibility, revolutions at which the propellers were turning – all were noted at hourly intervals and initialled by the officer of the watch. With a comparatively inexperienced crew the note for 26 August, 'great deterioration in weather', also told a story of widespread sea-sickness.

On 31 August, as Commodore Harwood approached Freetown in the *Exeter*, the *Graf Spee* was more than 1,500 miles away to the north-west, steering south for her first meeting with the tanker *Altmark*; and that evening an officer went as fast as dignity allowed from the wireless office to the Captain's cabin, knocked on the door and entered. He had just deciphered a long signal and he handed a signal pad to Langsdorff. 'Radiogram from Berlin, sir,' he said.

It was from the Naval War Staff and signed by Grand Admiral Raeder. The radiogram contained the gist of Hitler's 'Directive No. 1 for the Conduct of the War' – *Fall Weiss*, the invasion of Poland, was timed to begin at 4.45 am next day; and Langsdorff was expressly ordered that, owing to the uncertain attitude of the Western Powers, the *Graf Spee* was to open fire only if attacked ...

During the night Wattenberg was busy with his sextant taking star sights to get a final fix before meeting the *Altmark*. After the usual session in the chart room solving neat problems in spherical trigonometry, Wattenberg announced that the *Graf Spee* should sight the *Altmark* – providing Captain Dau was in position – at about 0800.

Shortly after dawn next day, Friday, 1 September, Langsdorff was on the bridge, joining a group of officers who had also gone up there – although they were not on watch – to wait for one thing: the meeting with the *Altmark*.

Suddenly, at 0805, there was a shout from a lookout: 'Two masts in sight fine on the starboard bow'. The operator at the rangefinder could, at first, see a double image of the two masts, then he quickly spun a dial until they merged into a single image. Another rating read off the range of the strange vessel and this was passed to the bridge.

Was it the *Altmark* or was it, by some awful coincidence, a British cruiser? Langsdorff waited for more reports from the rangefinder. 'It's a tanker ... about 10,000 tons ...'

'Make the challenge,' Langsdorff ordered; and the shutter of the big searchlight directly above the bridge rattled as a signalman tapped out the Morse letters.

On the bridge of the *Altmark* all available binoculars were trained on the warship, still almost hull-down on the horizon. Was it, wondered Captain Dau, the *Graf Spee* or a British cruiser? If it was the Royal Navy he stood a good chance of bluffing his way out – there were plenty of merchant ships about (he had dodged several in the previous few days), and the *Altmark* bore little resemblance to a German supply ship. The Norwegian flag was flying aft and the name painted on either bow was *Sogne*[1], and it was repeated on the stern, with the port of registry underneath – 'Oslo'.

The chances were, reasoned Dau, that a British cruiser would come close alongside, identify her as Norwegian and therefore neutral, and after asking her destination, steam on and leave him in peace.

Dau and his Chief Officer, Paulsen, spelled out the Morse letters: it was the *Graf Spee*. He ordered the answer to be made, and in a few seconds a rating with a signal lamp was flashing the reply. Rapidly the word spread round the *Altmark*'s crew and they lined the rails to watch the pocket battleship approach.

---

[1] The Norwegian *Sogne*, of Oslo, was not listed in Lloyd's Register.

Since the two ships were approaching at a mean speed of thirty-five knots, it was a matter of minutes before the details of the *Graf Spee* could be picked out with the naked eye, and Dau rang down to the engine room to stop engines. Slowly *Altmark* lost way and started to wallow gently while the *Graf Spee* manoeuvred to within a cable length and stopped.

Soon Dau was in Langsdorff's cabin where he was introduced to Kay and the other senior officers, including Wattenberg, the Navigator, who had brought along a roll of charts.

After hearing his report, Langsdorff told him that he considered the *Graf Spee* had, so far, not been sighted. Dau, although overawed by Langsdorff, could not help making a joke about the fact that the *Altmark*'s lookouts had sighted the *Graf Spee*'s smoke before her masts had come in sight over the horizon.

This astonished Langsdorff, especially since the *Graf Spee* had diesel engines. Making a lot of smoke in wartime, for a battleship or a humble merchantman trying to keep station in convoy, is a great offence, apart from being a standing invitation to an inquiring enemy.

So the entry appeared in *Graf Spee*'s log on 1 September: 'Sighted *Altmark* 0805 in 24° 25′ north, 36° 15′ west. *Altmark* reported they were able to sight our smoke before seeing masts'. And Korvettenkapitän (Ing) Klepp, the *Graf Spee*'s Chief Engineer, was warned that it must not happen again.

Then Langsdorff, Dau, Kay and Wattenberg discussed future operations. Wattenberg had the *Graf Spee*'s first operational area – between 5° and 10° north, and 25° and 35° west (some 400–500 miles due west of Freetown) marked on his chart; but until the diplomatic situation cleared itself up, Langsdorff told Dau, the *Altmark* would steam in company with the *Graf Spee*.

While the officers talked, a large hose was being passed across to the *Graf Spee*, and as soon as it was connected pumps started the precious oil fuel flowing into the pocket battleship's bunkers. They did not stop until 785 cubic metres of it had poured across.

The *Graf Spee* had brought Dr Harting to join the *Altmark*, but as she already had a doctor on board, Dau and Langsdorff decided he should stay in the *Graf Spee*. After transferring some signalmen and certain stores to the *Altmark*, the two ships got under way and moved southward in company. And all the time the wireless operators in both ships were listening to broadcasts from European stations giving the latest news of the Fuehrer's march on Poland.

All seemed to be going well the next day, Saturday, 2 September; and everyone on board was jubilant. Only the more thoughtful of them stopped to wonder if Britain and France would honour their pledges to Poland.

Still the two ships moved southward at slow speed. All the time they were moving into warmer water and Dr Kartzendorff had to treat some of the *Graf Spee*'s crew, who had unwisely bared their Nordic skin for too long under the tropical sun.

During the morning the *Altmark* altered course from time to time so that her position varied in relation to the *Graf Spee*. This gave the *Graf Spee*'s gunnery officers a chance to exercise their men. Both the *Dt-Geraet* and optical rangefinders were used and the results were compared.

Later Langsdorff was brought an intercepted radio signal from the British Admiralty to all British merchant shipping homeward bound, warning them to follow certain routes. At dusk both ships altered course to the northward; by midnight the officer of the watch noted the weather as being fine, with a Force 3–4 easterly wind.

At 0800 on Sunday, 3 September, the *Graf Spee* was just over three days from her first operational area, according to Wattenberg, and course was altered south again. As usual, a receiver in the radio room was tuned in to the Rugby transmitter to see what the British were talking about, and a startled operator took down a plain-language (i.e. not in cipher) broadcast in English of an Admiralty special telegram which said: *11 AM COM-MENCE HOSTILITIES AT ONCE AGAINST GERMANY.*

This was rushed to Langsdorff, who called his officers together and read it to them. Over the ship's loudspeakers, the crew were told that Britain had declared war against Germany. Then, thirty-nine minutes after the Rugby broadcast, operators in Berlin started to transmit a radiogram in code addressed to the *Graf Spee* from the *Seekriegsleitung*. It read: *COM-MENCE HOSTILITIES WITH ENGLAND IMMEDIATELY.*

Later that evening a further message from SKL told Langsdorff that from 1700 hours France considered herself at war with Germany; but it added that French shipping was not to be attacked, so that Hitler's efforts to dissuade the Western Powers from assisting Poland would not be prejudiced.

As Langsdorff observed in his War Diary, these orders tied his hands even more in relation to French shipping than they were tied over neutral vessels. French ships could report the position of the *Graf Spee* by wireless, and he could take no action to stop them; whereas with neutral ships the ban on the use of wireless for unneutral purposes could be enforced.

At this time Langsdorff had a reasonably clear idea of what opposition he was up against, thanks to *B-Dienst*. This consisted of a group of cipher experts on board the *Graf Spee* whose only task was to take enemy cipher signals as they were received and try to break down the code.

In many cases they were able to do this successfully; and the signals often revealed present or future movements of British warships. This infor-mation, coupled with similar reports from Berlin, where other signals were intercepted, was often invaluable to Langsdorff. The *Graf Spee* was equipped with special wireless receivers which automatically combed all the frequencies, and stopped at any one on which a message was being transmitted. If it was in code which the *B-Dienst* group could not break, it was – if wireless silence was not vital – rebroadcast to the SKL in Berlin. There a special computer was set to work on it. The SKL boasted at this time that the computer could break down a code in twenty minutes.

On 7 September another long radiogram addressed to Langsdorff was received from SKL in Berlin, and it gave the gist of Raeder's conference with Hitler, ending up with the order to the *Graf Spee* to move away from the operational area.

By now thoroughly exasperated, Langsdorff decided, in view of these orders, to move rapidly to the open wastes of the South Atlantic, where both the *Graf Spee* and the *Altmark* could wait without fear of being spotted.

The area he chose was a triangle 2,500 miles to the south-east, and just to the westward of Ascension and St Helena. Langsdorff considered that it would be free of merchant ships, unpatrolled by warships, and the weather would be calm enough for both the *Altmark* and *Graf Spee* to carry out such necessary tasks as overhauling engines, storing and fuelling.

On the following Sunday, 10 September, the *Graf Spee* and *Altmark* arrived at the northern limit of the waiting area chosen by Langsdorff as being free of British ships, and at noon slowed down so that they just had steerage way. Langsdorff, however, was wrong. The next day was a Monday, 11 September, and he ordered that refuelling was to start early; but just as a precaution the pocket battleship's reconnaissance aircraft, an Arado 196 float-plane, would take off and make a wide sweep round their position to ensure they were not disturbed.

Just after dawn the plane's tanks were filled, and the pilot, Flugzeug Unteroffizier Heinrich Bongardts, and the observer Oberleutnant zur See Spiering, donned their flying clothes. At 0610 Bongardts opened up the throttle of the Arado's single engine and took off.

Spiering told Bongardts to steer a south-westerly course, and as the Arado climbed, the two men carefully watched for any sign of smoke or ships. After a few minutes, when they had flown thirty miles and reached latitude 9° south, Spiering gave the pilot another course – this time due north.

Still they sighted nothing until they had covered twenty-nine miles; then, almost on the horizon to the north-east, they saw a ship. While Spiering watched it closely through binoculars, Bongardts swung the Arado away to starboard through 180 degrees, until they were flying back along their own track. The time was 0638.

Had they been sighted? Spiering was not sure – but as they were almost at extreme visibility range he thought they probably had not. Unless, of course, the ship carried *Dt-Geraet*.

However, Spiering was certain of two things – the ship was steering a course of 170 degrees when sighted, but she had then turned to 200 degrees and increased speed. And he was fairly certain she was a British cruiser.

It was far too risky to send a wireless signal to warn the *Graf Spee* that an enemy cruiser was only twenty miles away and might any second alter course directly towards the *Graf Spee* to the south-eastward. Bongardts opened the throttle and steered south for about ten miles until Spiering gave him an easterly course which would bring them to the *Graf Spee* and the *Altmark*, lying stopped and unaware of the danger they were in.

By the time the two ships were in sight Spiering had the signal lamp ready and Bongardts put the aircraft into a shallow dive towards the pocket battleship. Rapidly Spiering called her up, received the answering signal, then passed the warning. Immediately Langsdorff ordered all boats to return to their respective ships and passed a signal to the *Altmark* that he intended moving away east-south-east.

In the meantime the *Dt-Geraet* operators were given an approximate bearing to search, and the *B-Dienst*, the code experts, were told to stand by as the *Graf Spee*'s wireless operators listened on the enemy wavelengths to see if any increase in signalling would give an answer to the vital question as to whether or not Spiering's aircraft had been sighted.

But the enemy cruiser – if indeed it was a cruiser – was too far away for the radar, and there was no sign of smoke on the horizon. Soon the operators reported that there was no increase in wireless traffic on the enemy wavelengths. In fact there were no indications, Langsdorff decided, that the pocket battleship's presence in the Atlantic had been discovered. But it had been an extremely narrow escape. It was not that he considered the cruiser was any particular menace to him, but apart from any damage she might do, which would perhaps prove impossible to repair without a base, there was the danger that one brief signal to the British Admiralty would bring swarms of powerful warships hunting for him – from Freetown, Gibraltar, Bermuda, the South American coast and from South Africa.

However, the danger passed. For the moment the problem was to refuel from the *Altmark* and get the stores on board. Shortly before 0715 Langsdorff told Kay that the two ships could stop and resume their interrupted task. As the Arado aircraft was running short of fuel it came in, landed nearby and was hoisted on board.

Within a few minutes launches were plying between them; cases were lowered overside from the *Altmark*, taken over to the *Graf Spee* and taken on board. The long hose and its floats were being prepared when suddenly a lookout in the *Altmark* shouted excitedly to Captain Dau and pointed to the south-east.

Through binoculars the tops of two masts could be seen on the horizon. From the angle they made, Dau roughly estimated the ship was steering a course of 220 degrees and was making about fifteen knots. Within seconds a signal lamp was flickering a warning to the *Graf Spee*. But the unknown ship was steaming fast and soon two thin yellow funnels could be seen.

As 'Action Stations' alarms rattled through the *Graf Spee*, Langsdorff decided that the ship was probably an armed cruiser; and once again the launches were hurriedly retrieved and the pocket battleship, followed by the *Altmark*, turned and steered north-eastward at full speed, away from the unknown ship. Again operators listened carefully for any wireless signals which might indicate that the *Graf Spee* had been sighted; but they picked up nothing. It seemed that Langsdorff's luck was holding.[1]

The first ship sighted by the Arado, and which Spiering thought was a cruiser, was in fact the *Cumberland*. As mentioned earlier, she had left Plymouth after being detached from the 2nd Cruiser Squadron of the Home Fleet with orders to reinforce Commodore Harwood in the Rio de Janeiro area.

She had arrived in Freetown, Sierra Leone, on the 7th, refuelled, and then sailed again next day for Rio, more than 2,000 miles to the south-west. Three days earlier Langsdorff had chosen his waiting area – and the *Cumberland*'s course for Rio ran through the northern end of it. So, after steaming more than 4,000 miles from Plymouth to join in the hunt for possible commerce raiders in the South Atlantic, the *Cumberland*, by one of those strange and dangerous coincidences that happen in war, was at 0637 steering 170 degrees – a course which would have taken her within ten miles of the *Graf Spee*. But at 0638 she altered course thirty degrees to starboard, on one leg of a zig-zag, to 200 degrees.

Had she steered a course which took her ten miles farther to the south-east she would probably not have been sighted by Spiering in the Arado and would have come upon the *Graf Spee* and *Altmark*. How the course of the ensuing action would have gone is not hard to guess. The *Cumberland*'s eight 8-inch guns would have been outranged by the *Graf Spee*'s six 11-inch, and Langsdorff would have had to choose between risking engaging the *Cumberland* and possibly being severely damaged by hits or withdrawing and trying to nullify the enemy's advantage of speed by using his superior fire power.

But far more important is the fact that the *Cumberland* would firstly transmit the all-important enemy report. This would have been picked up at Freetown and passed to the Commander-in-Chief, South Atlantic, and to the Admiralty in London. Then the *Cumberland* would have tried to fulfil

---

[1] The identity of this second ship has never been discovered.

the cruiser's traditional role of shadower. However, we cannot speculate too much: the *Cumberland* did in fact alter course 30 degrees at 0638 and was spotted by Spiering at extreme visibility range, and by that chance the *Graf Spee* escaped detection.

For the next fortnight the *Graf Spee* and *Altmark* cruised in the waiting area. Langsdorff kept his ship's company exercising and the Arado float-plane was sent up frequently to act as 'target' for Mausermann's anti-aircraft guns. From time to time the two ships stopped to carry out machinery overhauls, and by the 13th the *Graf Spee*'s navigator noted that the pocket battleship had so far covered 7,079 miles. Langsdorff was wisely keeping her fuel tanks topped up, so that although the *Graf Spee* could operate for six weeks without refuelling, oil was taken in on 12, 20 and 22 September.

So the days slipped by, one very much like another, until the 25th. Although it was to prove a turning point in the *Graf Spee*'s career, it started off badly. She and the *Altmark* had stopped early in the morning in a calm sea to transfer more crates and barrels of stores. Among the barrels was one containing three months' supply of special oil for the pocket battleship's refrigeration equipment (which was required for the magazines as well as food). As it was being hoisted on board from one of the *Altmark*'s launches, a sling slipped and the barrel fell into the sea, sinking immediately.

However, that was soon forgotten when the *Graf Spee*'s wireless operators picked up a long coded radiogram from Berlin which Langsdorff was overjoyed to read: the SKL announced an imminent change of objective for the *Graf Spee* from a passive waiting (*Abwarten*) to an active participation in the trade war.

The radiogram also gave a list of British warship dispositions. From agents' reports and radio intercepts, SKL placed the cruisers *Cumberland*, *Exeter*, *Ajax* and *Despatch*, the destroyers *Hotspur* and *Havock*, and the submarine *Severn* on the east coast of South America, and three cruisers and a submarine on the West Africa coast.

With this information, plus all radio traffic intercepted by his own operators and decoded by *B-Dienst*, Langsdorff was able to build up a fairly clear picture in his mind of the naval situation in the South Atlantic and make plans to begin commerce raiding the moment the SKL sent the order.

Although Langsdorff did not know it, the signal warning of a change of objective was the result of a long argument with Hitler two days earlier. Eventually the Fuehrer had agreed to lift restrictions on French ships and, on being told that 'it will be necessary to commit the pocket battleships by about the beginning of October so that their supplies will not be exhausted or their morale undermined', finally gave permission. On 26 September, more than three weeks after the beginning of the war, the SKL ordered Langsdorff to 'commence active participation in the trade war'.

On the day the war began, Admiral Raeder had written: 'Today the war against France and Britain broke out, the war which, according to the Fuehrer, we had no need to expect before about 1944 . . .' After the events and political reassurances of the previous years, he added: 'The surface forces, moreover, are so inferior in number and strength to the British Fleet that, even at full strength, they can do little more than show that they know how to die gallantly . . . The pocket battleships – with the outbreak of war only the *Deutschland* and *Graf Spee* are ready for operations in the Atlantic – if skilfully used should be able to carry out cruiser warfare on the high seas for some time . . .'

After the end of the war the man who had succeeded Admiral Raeder in command of the German Navy, Admiral Karl Doenitz, wrote: 'Once Germany was committed to war against the United Kingdom, her whole naval effort was directed against British shipping and sea communications. If this campaign failed to achieve decisive results, then Germany's defeat, whatever form it might happen to take, became inevitable.'

Both men were correct, and the SKL's signals to the *Graf Spee* and the *Deutschland* were the beginning . . .

The day after receiving the SKL's signal, Langsdorff noted down in his War Diary his thoughts on the future, and his salient points were:

(a) The choice of operational areas is limited to south of 5° south because of defects in the *Graf Spee*'s refrigerating plant affecting magazine temperatures. [Certain explosives are very sensitive to heat changes and for safety's sake must be kept below a certain temperature. The refrigeration plant had been giving trouble for some time and had constantly affected Langsdorff's decisions. It was eventually repaired.]

(b) The South American trade route is more vital to the British and French than the Cape route since the Mediterranean is open to the Allies and in any case provides a shorter route to Europe from the Far East.

Langsdorff decided to take the *Graf Spee* to an area off Pernambuco (in Brazil, forming the easternmost part of South America) and then sweep south to find the British shipping route off the Brazilian coast. After finding a convoy and attacking it energetically, he intended withdrawing at high speed eastward across the Atlantic to attack again on the South African shipping routes off the Cape of Good Hope.

Shortly after noon on 27 September, when Langsdorff had told Captain

Dau of his plans and arranged to rendezvous on 14 October, the *Graf Spee* left the *Altmark* in the waiting area and moved off to the north-west at cruising speed.

For all the fifty-four officers and more than one thousand other men it was a moment of elation: all the days and weeks of wearisome preparations on board the pocket battleship were now going to pay dividends. For Langsdorff it was the culmination of years of study and training which started as midshipman in the Kaiser's Navy. Now, at long last, he was commanding one of Germany's greatest warships and he was steering her into action.

But first he must tell the crew what lay ahead of them. He told Kay to muster as many men as could be spared at 1700 because he wanted to address them. They fell in and Langsdorff, smart in his uniform, the Iron Cross pinned on his left breast, came out to deliver his speech. Briefly he outlined the situation. The waiting period was over; the Fuehrer had ordered that from now on the *Graf Spee* was to act as a commerce raider. Even as he spoke, he said, they were heading for their first operational area off the Brazilian coast, where they would find some prey on the old peace-time shipping routes. Their task, he concluded, was not going to be an easy one: the *Seekriegsleitung* had signalled the whereabouts of several enemy cruisers, but the *Graf Spee* would have to run from them if she was to fulfil her role as a commerce raider successfully. 'Heil Hitler,' he said.

'Heil Hitler,' they replied, and their cheers showed Langsdorff that he had struck just the right note and he went back to his cabin well satisfied. He was quite pleased that they were not too keen on the idea he had for fooling the enemy – it showed they were proud of their ship. He had realized, however, that once raiding started it would be impossible to stop the enemy knowing a big German warship was at large, but it would confuse them if her victims gave her conflicting names. From now on, then, the *Admiral Graf Spee* was to become the *Admiral Scheer*.

The second in command, Kay, supervised the painting out of the name *Admiral Graf Spee* on the stern, replacing it with *Admiral Scheer*, written in the same Gothic lettering. All the names on lifebelts, boats and other equipment were altered; and the crew were given new cap bands which bore the *Admiral Scheer*'s name in gold letters.

Thanks to the *Altmark*, the pocket battleship's fuel tanks were full; if necessary she could carry on for another six weeks without meeting the tanker again. There was plenty of food on board, the ammunition outfit was complete, and apart from the refrigerating plant there were no defects to report. Steadily the pocket battleship moved towards Pernambuco; the noon sights recorded in the log showed her oblique progress towards the Equator – on the 28th she was 15° south of it, and on the 29th, 11° 05′ south.

That evening another signal was received from the SKL, and it read:

> *At the present time England is in need of successes; any gain in prestige by England is therefore undesirable. On the other hand attacks on shipping by the pocket battleship are to be carried out to the fullest extent. Restriction of operations to specified areas is hereby cancelled. In the North Atlantic battle cruisers and aircraft may be encountered, but not yet in the South Atlantic.*

At noon on Saturday, 30 September, Wattenberg took a sun sight and within a few minutes noted in the log the *Graf Spee*'s noon position – 9° 21' south, 33° 40' west. The *Graf Spee*, under the guise of the *Admiral Scheer*, was about to make her first kill.

CHAPTER 4

SINKING THE *CLEMENT*

1300. Steamer sighted. (From the log of the *Graf Spee*.)

The wind was easterly, blowing about Force 4, the sea was moderate, and the British steamer *Clement*, 5,050 tons, was within 200 miles of the end of her voyage from New York to Bahia (Salvador). Stowed in her holds were 20,000 cases of kerosene.

Third Officer H. J. Gill was on watch and the master, Captain F. C. P. Harris, was in his cabin, one deck below the bridge. By ship's time it was just after 1115[1], and in his report[2] later Gill said: 'I sighted a battleship four points on the port bow on the horizon. From the time I sighted it, it was making a beeline for us all the way ...'

Captain Harris reported that the Third Officer called down the speaking tube from the bridge to his cabin. '"There is a man-o'-war about four points on the port bow, coming in fast." I said, "I expect that is the *Ajax*," which I knew was on the Brazilian coast, "or a Brazilian cruiser," which had left Pernambuco the day before.'

'I could see no flags,' the Captain's report continued, 'only that it was a man-o'-war. It was about four or five miles off with a huge bow wave as if

---

[1] The *Graf Spee* kept German time but the *Clement* kept local time in common with other British merchantmen and warships.

[2] Survivors were interrogated for Admiralty Intelligence and records purposes.

he was coming in at thirty knots.'

> *1330. Aircraft flown off to stop it. The aircraft signalled to the steamer:*
> *'Stop – no wireless transmitting'. (Graf Spee's log.)*

Gill continues: 'Three or four minutes later a plane appeared – more on the port quarter. She circled round the *Clement* and flashed a message to the battleship giving the information he wanted – whether we were armed or not, I suppose.

'The seaplane circled round again, then opened fire. She was painted very dark grey and the black iron cross was just in front of the tail on the port-side fuselage. We stopped engines and the plane kept up his fire until the ship's way was lost, firing at the bridge – the wheelhouse went up in the air ...'

Captain Harris, who was standing with Gill on the bridge, heard a buzzing sound and saw the aircraft flying past. He continued in his report: 'I was not worried as I knew the *Ajax* had one. We exposed the name board.

'The plane circled and came over the ship again, and started firing. I stopped the engines. Just then the Chief Officer looked up and said "Look, Chief – a German. I can see the markings." I could see that there was some black on the plane but could see no definite markings.

'I could see no flag on the cruiser, which was end on. I said "Swing the boats out, lower them and get the crew in." About five minutes later the ship was stopped.'

He then ordered the confidential books to be thrown over the side in their special weighted canvas bag; and he continues, 'I got the Second Officer to telephone and send out the RRR signal, giving the ship's position. The operator reported that he had got this message through and that it had been picked up by a Brazilian steamer.'

> *Ship is ss* Clement. *Crew took to boats and were left. Captain and Chief Engineer taken off and kept in* Graf Spee. *(Graf Spee's log.)*

As Captain Harris ordered his crew to abandon ship, a picket boat was hoisted out from the *Graf Spee*. On its bows was painted the false name *Admiral Scheer*. All the ratings in the picket boat wore false cap bands bearing that name, and the ruse was successful, as is shown by the following reports.

The picket boat first went to the lifeboat commanded by Third Officer Gill, and a German officer said: 'Proceed to the ship. Where is your Captain?'

As Gill and his men rowed towards the pocket battleship the picket boat went over to the number one lifeboat and took off Captain Harris and the

Chief Engineer, Mr W. Bryant. It then went alongside the *Clement* and the two men were taken back on board again.

Mr Bryant reported: 'When I was on board the *Clement* with the boarding party one man with a revolver in his hand took charge and said "Come down to the engine room," and when there he told me to open the sea valves. I immediately opened the tank injection; he did not seem to know much about it. These valves would merely fill the ballast tanks and would not flood the ship. We then came up. While I was with this officer the other men were going round the ship putting bags of bombs around the vessel.'

After the German boarding party had searched all the officers' cabins, wireless room and chart room for any documents, the two British officers were taken in the picket boat to the *Graf Spee*, and Captain Harris's account for the next few hours says: 'The Boarding Officer went and reported to the Captain. We followed an officer up the ladder on to the bridge.

'When there, we met the Captain [Langsdorff] and ten officers. He saluted me and said "I am sorry, Captain, I will have to sink your ship. It is war." Shortly afterwards he said "I believe you have destroyed your confidential papers?" I said "Yes." He answered "I expected it. That is the usual thing."'

Chairs were then brought to the bridge for both Captain Harris and Mr Bryant, and the *Graf Spee* moved closer to the *Clement*. Captain Harris continues: 'Then they said "We are going to fire a torpedo." They fired a torpedo from the starboard quarter aft from the deck tube at about half a mile range, and it passed about fifty feet ahead of the *Clement*. The Captain did not seem at all pleased with this . . .

'Then they fired a second one. It passed about twenty-five feet astern . . . Then they said "We are going to use the guns." They steamed round then under the quarter of the *Clement*. The two ships were then stern to stern and the German ship was 2,500 yards off the *Clement*.

'They started with the 6-inch guns and fired about twenty-five rounds. They were not happy about that either – some were going short and some were hitting. Some of the officers could speak English well, and one said "If we were farther away we would hit, but we are too close." They gave us cotton wool during the firing to put in our ears.'

1530. Clement sunk by gunfire. (Graf Spee's log.)

Finally, after using heavier guns, they managed to sink the steamer. Captain Harris was kept on the bridge another hour. Then 'The Commander [Kay] said to me that the Captain wished to speak to us. The Captain, speaking in good English, said "If you will give me your word not to attempt any sabotage or espionage, and do exactly as we tell you, you will be left free. Otherwise I will have to put a guard on you." I said "You can take my word. Neither the Chief nor I will attempt anything." He said "All right, shake hands."'

Kay took them down to his cabin and offered them cigars and iced beer. He then wrote out in English an order about sabotage, and the two Britons signed it. After that they were given a meal consisting of a large dish of cold meat, tongue and sausage, bread and butter, tea, and some rum to put in it. Later some officers came into the cabin and one of them said, 'You may be here a week or a fortnight. Would you like a razor or will you go to the barber's shop? There is a barber's here.'

After the *Clement* had sunk, the *Graf Spee* then continued southward and two and a half hours later sighted another steamer. As they closed, it was seen that she was a neutral, the Greek *Papalemos*. She was ordered to stop and a picket boat took Captain Harris and Mr Bryant across to her. The *Papalemos*, with the two Britons on board, was then allowed to continue her voyage on condition she did not use her wireless within an area of 600 miles of her present position.

Later Langsdorff ordered a signal to be sent to Olinda, the radio station at Pernambuco. Using the call sign DTAR – which belonged to the *Admiral Scheer* – the signal said: *Please save the lifeboats of the* Clement. *0945 south, 3404 west.* Olinda replied: *Thanks. OK Hasta Luego.*

A second signal sent by Langsdorff was addressed to the *Seekriegsleitung* in Berlin. It gave the *Graf Spee*'s position and reported the sinking of the *Clement*, saying that 'because they used their radio the aircraft used machine guns'.

The *Graf Spee* then altered course eastward to pass between Ascension Island and St Helena, as Langsdorff had previously planned.

After narrowly missing the *Graf Spee* and *Altmark* on the 11 September, the *Cumberland* arrived in Rio de Janeiro to find orders from Harwood telling her to start 'out' convoys with the destroyer *Havock*. The destroyer *Hotspur* was due to meet the Commodore in the *Exeter* to start similar convoys from the River Plate. The *Ajax* was in the Falklands investigating the report of the three German merchantmen off the Patagonian coast.

Meanwhile a vast number of reports concerning the coasts of South America were reaching the Operational Intelligence Centre at the Admiralty in London. These reports came from a variety of sources since the Admiralty had set up a worldwide network which not only helped control merchantmen but provided intelligence information as well.

In most ports there were Naval Control Service Officers (NCSO) and in the major ports naval attachés as well. In neutral countries the NCSOs were appointed as additional consular officers, so that they had the right status for carrying out what was really war work on neutral soil. The official task of an NCSO was to interview the captains of Allied merchant ships arriving in port, giving them routing instructions, and report their movements to the nearest Staff Officer, Intelligence, who in turn relayed the information to the Admiralty. But the NCSO was well placed to pass on information about German ship movements and any other useful intelligence he might discover.

At the Admiralty the movements of merchant ships had been taken over by the Trade Division, while control of warships was handled by the Operations Division. The Plans Division, as its name shows, was responsible for all naval planning, and all three worked closely with the Naval Intelligence Division.

The result was that a complete record of the whereabouts and condition of the larger warships was kept – with almost hourly alterations – on operational plots in the underground rooms at the Admiralty which formed the nerve centre of the Royal Navy at war. Thus, working closely with the Naval Intelligence and Trade Divisions, the Operations Division could switch them about – like a vast and fast-moving game of chess where you do not see your opponent's moves but can only guess them – to meet any eventuality.

Nearby were the trade plots, showing the positions of British merchant ships on the world's sea lanes, and kept up to date by the Trade Division from information arriving hourly from NCSOs, consular officials, intelligence agents, air reconnaissance, naval attachés, shipping companies and their agents.

It was through this complex grapevine that Commodore Harwood received much of his information, and we can resume the narrative with an example. On 10 September, the day before the *Graf Spee*'s Arado sighted the *Cumberland*, intelligence reached the Admiralty that the German merchant ship *Montevideo* was sailing from Rio Grande do Sul for Florianopolis (Brazil). This information was immediately radioed to Commodore Harwood in the *Exeter*, patrolling off the River Plate.

The Admiralty had provided the information; it was up to the Commodore to decide what to do. If he used the *Exeter* to try to intercept her, it meant diverting the cruiser 500 miles from the focal area off the Plate. He had to balance the possible interception of a German merchantman against the possible sinking of several Allied merchantmen if a German raider arrived in the Plate area while the *Exeter* was away. He decided the *Montevideo* would have to be left alone.

These 'What have I to gain compared with what I might lose?' decisions had to be made almost daily by Harwood, although the *Montevideo* is a minor example compared with the one he faced on 24 September, two days before Langsdorff received the order to start operations. The naval attaché at Buenos Aires signalled Harwood that 'according to reliable source' a number of German ships – including two previously reported among those assembling off the Patagonian coast – and a U-boat were to rendezvous south-west of Ascension Island in four days' time.

The position was 1,900 miles from the *Cumberland* at Rio and nearly 3,000 miles from the *Exeter* off the Plate. Harwood promptly signalled the *Cumberland* to steam to the rendezvous at full speed while Captain Woodhouse in the *Ajax* at the Falklands was ordered nearly 2,000 miles north to take the *Cumberland*'s place at Rio de Janeiro. At the same time Admiral Lyon sent two destroyers from Freetown. The ships searched, but found nothing, and the *Cumberland* went on to Freetown to refuel.

The first month of the war ended in the South Atlantic with Harwood's two destroyers being recalled to England because of a serious shortage in the Home Fleet. His plan for Plate and Rio convoys was working well, and although some German merchantmen were managing to slip through on their way home to the Fatherland, no British ships had been lost. But, as we have already seen, the *Graf Spee* was on the eve of striking her first blow. Overnight the whole course of the war at sea in the north and south Atlantic was about to change, and we can now view the *Graf Spee*'s activities from the British side.

CHAPTER 5

RRR – *CLEMENT* GUNNED

The wireless operator in the British cableship *Norseman* was listening in as usual on Saturday, 30 September, with his set tuned to 600 metres. His small cabin was almost lined with grey-finished equipment, and to anyone unused to a wireless office he faced an apparently bewildering number of dials and tuning knobs.

The time was 1452 GMT and suddenly he heard hurried Morse coming through his earphones. The first three letters galvanized him – dot-dash-dot, dot-dash-dot, dot-dash-dot . . . It was the beginning of a raider report, and quickly he wrote on his signal pad:

RRR RRR RRR . . . 3404 W Clement *gunned.*

He had not been able to read the middle of the message, but it was clear enough; the steamer *Clement* was being attacked by a raider. He called the

Captain and anxiously continued listening in.

Three minutes later, through the crackle of atmospherics, came more Morse, and he automatically wrote it down:

RRR RRR RRR 0908 S 3404 W Clement *gunned*.

A minute later the same desperate message was again transmitted, and he was able to check the figures in the complete message. By now the Captain was standing beside him in the wireless office, and after four minutes, at 1500, he heard more Morse and noted it down:

PPA DE KIXZ QRT (Amaralina, Bahia, Radio Station from ss Mormacrio – *stop transmitting*).

This was followed a minute after by another signal from the steamer *Mormacrio*, telling Amaralina Radio Station:

If you would listen on 600 metres you would hear ss Clement *in distress*.

The *Norseman*'s operator continued listening; and as he waited for some ship or shore station to acknowledge the call for help, the wireless operator on board the *Clement* reported to Captain Harris that he had got the raider report through.

And while Captain Harris gave the order to abandon ship, and the *Graf Spee* lowered boats to carry a boarding party over to the steamer, the Master of the *Norseman* continued waiting anxiously. When it was obvious to him that no one had answered, he decided he would have to break wireless silence so that the Admiralty could be warned. This was an extremely dangerous thing for him to have to do, since a raider could fix the *Norseman*'s position by direction-finder as she transmitted it; but he realized that far more than the safety of his own ship was involved.

So the *Norseman*'s operator started calling Portishead Radio Station, more than 3,000 miles away in the Bristol Channel. The time was 1512, only seventeen minutes after the last signal from the *Clement*, but the *Norseman* was unlucky; Portishead did not hear her calling-up signal.

There was only one thing for the *Norseman* to do now, and the Captain told his operator to re-broadcast the *Clement*'s raider report on 600 metres, and at 1520 the dramatic signal started crackling out again and again.

But no reply was noted in the *Norseman*'s log; and her Captain decided to try to get a message passed to the British authorities in South America, which was of course much nearer but still out of range of the *Norseman*'s radio. So at 1525 she called up the steamer *Mormacrio*, which was near the coast and whose signals would be powerful enough to reach a shore station.

The operator tapped out:

Will you take a message for re-transmission to Olinda Radio? How are my signals?

The *Mormacrio*'s operator answered:

Go ahead with your transmission.

In the verbal 'shorthand' used by wireless operators the *Norseman* then sent:

CTD CDE Clement *1 10 30 1452 GMT via Western D RM British Consul Pernambuco – RRR 0908 S 3404 W* Clement (secret call sign)[1] *AR K.*

The *Mormacrio* replied: R QRA? (Message received, what is the name of your station?) and continued: *Are U* Clement? *Don't get who from.*

The *Norseman* was not anxious to give her name, since any German raider could – and probably would – be listening and fixing her position; but, providing the *Norseman* did not reveal who she was, there was no reason for any raider to suppose she was not a neutral ship. So she replied:

SRI NO QRA (Sorry, will not give the name of my station).

A minute later came another signal from the *Mormacrio*, which, since she was an American vessel, was perhaps understandably rather puzzled:

If you are Clement *why not send direct PPO* (Olinda Radio). *Only 50 miles.*

The *Norseman* answered:

Not Clement. *Too far away to raise.*

By now the *Mormacrio* was extremely suspicious of the whole thing, and at 1536 asked:

Are U DTAR? (Are you *Admiral Scheer*)

No, British. Unable to give QRA (name of station), the *Norseman* replied; and the *Mormacrio* then sent:

Will not take as message, will take as note for PPO (Olinda).

The *Norseman*'s operator then heard the *Mormacrio* calling up Olinda, and as soon as the shore station replied she passed the message to the British Consul at Pernambuco which was to start the opening moves of the greatest hunt ever known up to then.

---

[1] The secret call sign would identify the *Norseman* to the British Consul.

Three hours later the *Norseman*'s wireless operator heard the following breezy conversation between two ships (probably American) which were working without call signs:

> *SA OM WOT QRA OF DT DTAR* (Say, old man, what was the name of that German warship?)
>
> *Think it's* Admiral Scheer, *one of their battlewagons.*

Just before lunch-time on Sunday, 1 October, while people in Britain walked home from church, dug their allotments, had a quiet morning doing nothing, or talked of the disaster in Poland (where Warsaw had fallen to the Germans four days earlier), a wireless signal in code arrived at the Admiralty in Whitehall.

It was one of dozens already received that morning, only it was from the Naval Control Staff Officer at Pernambuco, and it said:

> *British ship MBBL* (Clement) *sunk by surface raider 75 miles south-east of Pernambuco 1400 local time yesterday.*

It took only a second to realize its significance: the Admiralty's suspicion that a pocket battleship was at large might now be confirmed, although the raider that had sunk the *Clement* could be merely an armed merchant ship. Nevertheless a German raider had revealed herself in the Atlantic for the first time; and this was the minute the First Sea Lord, Admiral Pound, had been waiting for. But the most important fact to establish was the identity — and thus the strength — of the raider.

An hour and a half after the first signal from the NCSO at Pernambuco a second arrived at the Admiralty, from the NCSO at Bahia:

> *W/T message from British ship* (Clement) *received by cable ship GBVS* (Norseman) *and British ship GLTK* (Almanzora) *about 1400 Brazilian time 30 September consisted of 'Rs' and possibly 'As' and word 'gunned'. Position 009 degrees 08 minutes south, 034 degrees 08 minutes west. British ship GLTK arrived and suspended sailing pending instructions.*

While plans were drawn up in case the raider was a pocket battleship and not just one of the many German merchant ships which had sneaked out of the sanctuary of a South American port and armed herself, the Admiralty signalled to Admiral Lyon and Commodore Harwood that the order recalling the destroyers was cancelled and they were 'to be retained in the South Atlantic for the present'.

A further signal said that Admiral Lyon's command would be strengthened by the cruisers *Effingham, Emerald, Enterprise, Norfolk* and *Capetown*.

The battleships *Resolution* and *Revenge*, and the aircraft carrier *Hermes* would proceed to Freetown or Jamaica.

Meanwhile, just before 0800 that same Sunday morning, the Brazilian steamer *Itatinga* was steaming along the South American coast some miles off Pernambuco when the officer on watch spotted a ship's boat. The steamer stopped and picked up the men in it. They were Third Officer Gill and twelve other survivors from the *Clement*. The master of the *Itatinga* then sent a wireless message to the port he was bound for, Bahia, reporting his find. He also added that he was due at Bahia early on 3 October.

At the same time three other lifeboats from the *Clement*, one of them commanded by the *Clement*'s Chief Officer, were heading for the South American coast; and the Greek ship *Papalemos*, which had been stopped by the *Graf Spee*, was heading for the Cape Verde Islands with Captain Harris and the Chief Engineer on board.

So the first day of October ended with the Admiralty knowing only that there was a raider in the South Atlantic. Whether it was a German cruiser, pocket battleship or simply an armed merchant ship was a mystery. Mr Churchill and Admiral Pound, as well as the Operations and Planning Divisions, could only wait for more news.

They did not have to wait long. Next day, 2 October, the first signal came shortly after 0900 from the wide-awake Naval Control Service Officer at Bahia:

> Brazilian ship PUKW (Itatinga) *expected to arrive Bahia early 3 October with thirteen survivors of British ship MBBL. Immediate report will be sent on arrival.*

This was followed three hours later by a signal from the NCSO at Pernambuco, who reported:

> British ship MBBL *was machine-gunned by seaplanes and Chief Officer slightly wounded. Later sunk by secondary armament. The Captain and Chief Engineer taken prisoner.*

A few minutes after that came a signal from Maceio which gave the first definite news of the identity of the raider (apart from those which referred to the fact that the call sign DTAR used by the enemy was that of the *Admiral Scheer*. That was naturally regarded at the Admiralty as a possible ruse which could be used by any vessel).

The message from Maceio, quickly decoded and taken to Admiral Pound, said:

> Ship's lifeboat from British ship MBBL (Clement) *arrived here today Monday with eleven crew including Chief Officer who was slightly*

wounded. Chief Officer confirms name of German armoured ship Admiral Scheer *and reports that two other lifeboats following on with remainder of crew except Captain and Chief Officer who were taken on board German ship.*

The First Sea Lord presided over a meeting of the heads of divisions in the Upper War Room at the Admiralty later that day to discuss ways of trapping and sinking the raider. If she was in fact a pocket battleship, with six 11-inch guns, then each 'killing unit' would have to comprise one battle-cruiser, or two 8-inch cruisers with, if possible, an aircraft carrier. It was decided to form 'Force K', the *Renown* and the carrier *Ark Royal*, and orders were given for them to leave the Home Fleet and make for the South Atlantic. The French Ministry of Marine was also asked to provide ships, and they agreed.

While the Admiralty worked out plans for forming hunting groups – as they were later called – Admiral Lyon at Freetown and Commodore Harwood in the *Exeter* were doing the best they could with what forces they had. When the first signals arrived on 1 October, Harwood was far from sure at that stage that the vessel had been a pocket battleship, and was reluctant to abandon the River Plate area because of the large amount of shipping using it – far more than used Rio de Janeiro, the nearest 'focal area' to the raider's last known position near Pernambuco.

Harwood thought it more likely that the German plan behind the appearance of a raider off Pernambuco was that they expected him to move his force northwards, leaving the wide River Plate estuary open to attack by a second raider waiting in readiness. Given the considerable number of German merchantmen round the South American coast, and which could have been carrying guns ready to be fitted when war began, this was a distinct possibility.

He finally signalled to Admiral Lyon that he had decided to concentrate the *Exeter* and *Ajax* off Rio, send the destroyer *Hotspur* to cover the Rio-Santos area, and keep the *Havock* patrolling the Plate area. The NCSOs at Rio and Santos were told to suspend sailings for four days to give the *Hotspur* time to arrive and take over the area which was being vacated by the *Ajax*. Harwood's signal crossed with orders from Admiral Lyon telling him to concentrate the *Exeter*, *Ajax* and two destroyers in the Rio area. Harwood had in fact already anticipated part of the order.

The *Exeter* fuelled and confirmation arrived that the raider was in fact a pocket battleship. A few hours earlier the Admiralty had sent a welcome signal – Harwood's force was to be reinforced with the cruiser *Achilles*, a sister ship of the *Ajax* and belonging to the New Zealand division of the Royal Navy. She had been operating on her own along the Pacific coast of South America.[1]

---

[1] The *Achilles* joined three weeks later. There was no New Zealand Navy at this time.

Later in the day Admiral Lyon signalled that when the *Cumberland* rejoined – she was at that time refuelling in Freetown after the abortive search off Ascension Island – the *Ajax*, *Achilles* and the two destroyers should be used for trade protection in the focal area while the two 8-inch cruisers, *Cumberland* and *Exeter*, formed a hunting unit.

Meanwhile plans were being changed at the Admiralty: a meeting presided over by the First Sea Lord cancelled the plan made four days earlier and abandoned the patrolling of focal areas visualized in the War Memorandum. Instead, as a telegram told Admiral Lyon, since a full convoy system in the South Atlantic and Indian Ocean would 'result in unacceptable delay even if escorts could be provided', eight hunting groups were to be formed. These comprised mostly pairs of 8-inch cruisers, some with an aircraft carrier. 'The strength of each hunting group is sufficient to destroy any armoured ship of the *Deutschland* class or armoured cruiser of the *Hipper* class', the signal said.[1]

Bearing in mind that at this point the *Graf Spee* had sunk only one merchant ship, the way that a powerful commerce raider can disrupt and disperse the enemy's strength is shown by the composition of the hunting groups:

Force	Composition	Area
F	*Berwick*, *York*	North America and West Indies
G	*Cumberland*, *Exeter*	East coast of South America
H	*Sussex*, *Shropshire*	Cape of Good Hope
I	*Cornwall*, *Dorsetshire* and *Eagle*	Ceylon
K	*Renown*, *Ark Royal* and one 6-inch cruiser to be detailed by C-in-C South Atlantic.	Pernambuco-Freetown
L	*Dunkerque*, three 6-inch cruisers and *Bearn*	Brest [north west France]
M	Two 8-inch cruisers	Dakar [West Africa]
N	*Strasbourg*, *Hermes*	West Indies

[1]. The Admiralty still believed the pocket battleships were within the 10,000-ton treaty limit. They were, of course, bigger, and this led the Admiralty to assume (quite correctly) that it was impossible to pack six 11-inch guns *and* plenty of ammunition *and* powerful engines *and* strong armour into a ship of 10,000 tons – only 1,500 tons larger than the *Exeter*, which had only six 8-inch guns.

But the Admiralty were well aware of a raider's vulnerability, and the signal to Admiral Lyon said: 'It is also to be remembered that raiders are vitally dependent on their mobility, being so far from repair facilities. Hence a weaker force, if not able to effect immediate destruction may, by resolute attack, be able to cripple an opponent sufficiently to ensure a certain subsequent location and destruction by other forces.'

The effect of forming the eight groups was immense and world-wide – Force F consisted of ships diverted from Halifax, Nova Scotia; Force H from the Mediterranean; Force I from China and Force K from the Home Fleet. But that was not all – in addition to the hunting groups, the battleships *Resolution* and *Revenge* and cruisers *Enterprise* and *Emerald* were to sail to Halifax to escort homeward-bound Atlantic convoys, and were followed later by *Repulse*, *Furious* and *Warspite*, while a battleship and aircraft carrier were sent through the Suez Canal to form a ninth hunting group in the Indian Ocean.

CHAPTER 6

PRISONERS IN THE *ALTMARK*

After destroying the *Clement*, Captain Langsdorff kept to his plan of withdrawing quickly to the eastward, passing south of Ascension Island and north of St Helena, and by 1 October, the day after the sinking, the *Graf Spee* had already covered a quarter of the distance.

Rapidly the pocket battleship's longitude noted in the log decreased – it was 28° 56′ west on the 1st, 22° 51′ on the 2nd, 16° 42′ on the 3rd and 10° 44′ on the 4th. The crew were cheerful and fit, and as the days passed without the *Graf Spee* being spotted, Langsdorff began to have high hopes for the future.

After passing between the two islands on the 4th, Langsdorff altered course to the north-east, and a sudden call to the bridge at 0630 next morning told Langsdorff that it had probably been a lucky change: smoke had been sighted on the horizon. Alarm bells rang, sending the crew hurrying to their action stations.

Langsdorff decided to steer straight for the smoke, and twelve minutes later two masts and a funnel of a merchant ship could be seen. Rapidly officers and men prepared for action. A group of men assembled under Leutnant zur See Schunemann, and this time it was a prize crew and not a boarding party: Langsdorff had decided that the next ship captured undamaged should be kept as an accommodation vessel for the crews of further victims. So Schunemann had engineers, wireless operators, junior officers capable of standing a bridge watch, and ratings standing by.

Every minute reports came through from the rangefinder, and when the calibrated dials recorded 1,800 metres Langsdorff ordered the 'Heave to' and 'Do not transmit' flag signals to be run up. Still the *Graf Spee* was bows-on to the merchant ship, and at the last moment she swung round, dropped the Tricolour, hoisted the German ensign and hove to. Through glasses Langsdorff and the other officers on the bridge watched the British steamer slowing down and stopping. The *Graf Spee*'s 5.9-inch guns swung round to point menacingly at the merchantman. Would she transmit a distress signal?

As soon as the way was off the *Graf Spee* a launch was lowered to take Schunemann and his prize crew to the victim. As they approached a telephone buzzed on the *Graf Spee*'s bridge. It was a message from the wireless room: the British ship was transmitting a distress signal, but it was very weak.

In a few minutes Schunemann signalled from the steamer's bridge that everything was under control: she was the 4,651-ton *Newton Beech*, and most of her cargo appeared to be maize. He was now sending the British crew over to the *Graf Spee* . . . Within two hours, with the *Newton Beech* in company, the pocket battleship was under way again. This time her speed was governed by the merchantman, and Langsdorff had second thoughts about the distress message her operator had managed to transmit. Finally he shrugged his shoulders. The transmission was weak; it was a hundred-to-one chance against anyone else picking it up, especially as it had been sent outside the normal hourly period for ships with only one operator.

Shortly after dawn next day the Arado 196 took off and flew a triangular course of more than 300 miles without sighting more ships, and Langsdorff decided to search farther to the south-east, closing in towards the direct Freetown-Capetown, and Freetown-Lobito trade routes. But daylight on Saturday, 7 October, revealed a clear horizon. The *Graf Spee* was almost in the Gulf of Guinea, and Langsdorff went to his cabin for breakfast, having decided to send up the Arado again later.

He was called at 0824; smoke had been sighted on the horizon to the south-west. Once again on the bridge, with his high spirits restored, Langsdorff went through the now familiar routine: action stations, boarding party stand by, 'Heave to' and 'Do not transmit' signals bent on, the Tricolour hoisted, the 5.9-inch guns loaded, and the German prize crew in the *Newton Beech* warned.

The steamer was the 4,222-ton *Ashlea*, owned by the Cliffside Shipping Company. She was carrying a cargo of 7,200 tons of sugar and was on her way from Durban to Freetown, where she was to pick up a homeward-bound convoy. Like most merchants ships at this time, she was unarmed.

The *Ashlea* had a crew of thirty-five, and this is how her Master, Captain C. Pottinger, later described the next few minutes: 'At about 8 am GMT[1] the Second Officer sent down a report that he had sighted a man-of-war on the horizon bearing east-north-east. Our course was about west-north-west and our speed eight and a half knots.

'I went on to the bridge and saw a man-of-war coming towards us on our starboard bow. She seemed to be coming from the direction of the Cameroons. Her fighting top gave me the impression she was either the *Dunkerque* or *Strasbourg* [French battleships] so I carried on.

'She approached very rapidly and kept bows-on all the time she was approaching. She carried on like this until about a quarter of a mile off. It was not possible to see any ensign, and we still thought she was a French warship.

'Suddenly she ran up a signal "Heave to, I am sending a boat across". Then her next signal was "Don't use your radio or we will fire". By that time a launch was already in the water half-way across to us.

'She then altered course to come broadside on to us and then I saw the German ensign. I did not risk putting the Confidential Books over the side in case they could hook them up with a boathook, so I put them in the furnaces.'

The *Graf Spee*'s boarding party were quick and thorough. They scrambled on board and split up, some men going to the wireless office to make sure no distress signals were transmitted, while Schunemann went to the bridge and others to the Captain's cabin. Schunemann demanded the Confidential Books from Captain Pottinger, but was told they had been destroyed. Pottinger was then told he and his men had ten minutes to leave the ship.

The officer of the watch wrote in the *Graf Spee*'s log:

> Steamer was ss Ashlea. *Crew taken off and put on* Newton Beech. *Part of cargo of* Ashlea, *two tons of sugar, taken on board* Graf Spee. Ashlea *sunk by cartridge charges.*

Langsdorff was pleased with himself: in the first place he had been correct in assuming he was somewhere on the wartime trade route from South Africa to Freetown, and his method of approach – keeping bows-on to the victim until the last moment so that his identity would not be discovered – and the boarding had been a complete success, so much so that the *Ashlea* had not managed to transmit a distress signal.

He decided to move northward again, and the *Graf Spee* moved off, followed by the *Newton Beech*. The steamer was proving rather a nuisance,

---

[1] The *Graf Spee*'s times were now one hour ahead of GMT.

he decided. Schunemann had already tried her out at her maximum speed and it was not nearly fast enough. She was going to limit the pocket battleship's mobility – her most valuable weapon.

Next day he made up his mind: the *Newton Beech* must be sunk and he would have to risk having the *Graf Spee* overcrowded with prisoners. A signal was passed to Schunemann, and both ships stopped. The pocket battleship's launch took a party across carrying the scuttling charges and then brought over the thirty-five men from the *Ashlea*.

The cartridge charges were set to explode at 1816, and the launch took off the last of the prize crew. Langsdorff and his officers watched the minutes tick by, and exactly on time the charges exploded. But the *Newton Beech* did not sink. All that happened was that she settled in the water a little.

Langsdorff was extremely angry: the farce of sinking the *Clement* was still fresh in his mind, and the *Graf Spee*'s log records the story with understandable reticence:

> *1816.* Newton Beech *sunk by cartridge charges. (Did not sink until 2347 owing to maize cargo.)*

After sinking the *Newton Beech* Langsdorff headed the *Graf Spee* back west-north-westward, turning west on the 9th and south-east on the 10th. Later that day, at 1739, the familiar cry sounded from the lookouts: 'Smoke in sight'.

By the time Langsdorff reached the bridge the ship's masts could be seen, and as the *Graf Spee* approached from her usual bows-on position, he could see through binoculars that the steamer was bigger than any they had caught up to now.

Once again Schunemann stood by with a boarding party, and when the rangefinders showed the steamer was just under a mile away the *Graf Spee* turned broadside on, stopped and lowered a launch. Within seven minutes Schunemann was climbing on board.

He had a surprise waiting for him: Chief Officer A. M. Thompson recognized him as the former Master of the German coaster *Rudfidgi*, lying in Beira. Schunemann later told Thompson that he had been called back for service in the German Navy and had been appointed to the *Graf Spee* some days before war broke out. He had been on leave in Hamburg from Beira.

Soon Schunemann was signalling across to the pocket battleship that the steamer was the ss *Huntsman* of 8,196 tons, and with a crew of eighty-four on board. Langsdorff read the signal with mixed feelings. It was one thing to destroy an enemy ship of 8,196 tons, but it was quite another to dispose of eighty-four prisoners. It was certain he could not have them on board the

Graf Spee – it would impair his fighting efficiency since he had left forty-seven men behind in Wilhelmshaven because he had no room for them. Already he had the crews of the *Newton Beech* and *Ashlea* on board ...

His own wireless operators had warned him that the *Huntsman* had managed to transmit a distress message, but it was in the off-watch period and no one had been heard to reply. So he decided to keep the *Huntsman*, leaving the prisoners on board in the charge of a prize crew. Later they could be transferred to the *Altmark*.

One other point worried Langsdorff. He realized that the presence of his ship in the South Atlantic must now be known – the *Clement*'s lifeboats would have been found, and the *Papalemos* must have landed Captain Harris and his Chief Engineer by now – and that within a very short time the *Newton Beech*, *Ashlea* and *Huntsman* would be reported overdue.[1]

One way of throwing his pursuers off the scent, he reasoned, would be to make them think the ships had been sunk by U-boats. He therefore ordered a false distress signal, giving a different position and apparently coming from the *Newton Beech*, and using the prefix 'SSS' denoting an attack by a submarine, to be sent out on the *Huntsman*'s wireless.

That afternoon, Tuesday, 10 October, a German operator sat at the *Huntsman*'s wireless and transmitted[2] on 600 metres:

> *SSS SSS SSS Position 7 20 S 7 57 W* Newton Beech *torpedoed.*

After laying the false trail, the *Graf Spee*, with the *Huntsman* in company, moved away to the south-westward. Next day the wireless officer reported that they were having rather more success in intercepting British signals and the *B-Dienst* were busy decoding the latest of them. Finally a signal was brought to Langsdorff telling him that the *Ajax* had refuelled at Rio de Janeiro the previous day, 10 October. As Rio was more than 1,800 miles away, he had nothing to fear.

However, the time had come to alter course to meet the *Altmark* at the next rendezvous on the 14th. Langsdorff decided to send the *Huntsman* on alone to a special rendezvous; this would allow the *Graf Spee* to go ahead and meet the *Altmark*, refuel and then return northward with the tanker to find the much slower *Huntsman*. The rendezvous was signalled to Schunemann and at 1600 on the 12th the *Graf Spee* forged ahead, leaving the prize crew feeling rather lonely aboard the merchant ship.

About this time the radar gear broke down once again and the electricians reported it as the old trouble – vibration affecting the power cables. Langsdorff was not unduly worried – the *Graf Spee*'s optical rangefinders were among the finest afloat and in good visibility were

---

[1] The *Ashlea*'s owners wrote to the Admiralty on 13 November expressing concern over her non-arrival at Freetown on 13 October. The *Ashlea*, *Newton Beech* and *Huntsman* were officially listed as overdue on 22 November.
[2] Ironically enough, this was never picked up.

almost as effective as the *Dt-Geraet*, and certainly a good deal more reliable.

In the evening a long radiogram arrived from the *Seekriegsleitung* giving Langsdorff the latest Intelligence report of the whereabouts of British warships. The most startling news was that capital ships were moving from the Mediterranean into the Atlantic.

The night was an uneasy one for him, and reports from the monitors in the wireless room next day, the 13th, really worried Langsdorff. They told of a great increase in W/T traffic between the British stations along the African coast.

He now feared that the presence of the *Graf Spee* on the Cape route had been discovered – this could easily be the result of the sinking of the *Newton Beech* and *Ashlea* and the capture of the *Huntsman* – and the British would probably increase protective measures considerably and start sailing their merchant ships in convoy.

Any strengthening of the Cape Town-Freetown trade route, he reasoned in his War Diary, would probably mean the British would use St Helena and Ascension as auxiliary bases as much as Freetown and Cape Town. That would make the *Graf Spee*'s present operational zone an extremely dangerous spot to be in. The time had come, in fact, to change his plans.

Within a short while he had made up his mind, and, as usual, described his thoughts, reasoning and decisions at great length in his War Diary: he would store and refuel from the *Altmark* at the earliest possible moment (they were due to meet next morning), transfer all the prisoners from the pocket battleship to the *Altmark*, and then return with the tanker to the *Huntsman*. The *Altmark* would take off the eighty-four prisoners from the British ship, the *Graf Spee* would retrieve her prize crew, and the *Huntsman* would then be sunk.

The waiting area would be shifted to the westward, clear of the Cape Town-St Helena-Ascension-Freetown route, and once again the pocket battleship would be free to move about at will instead of worrying about a slow merchant ship loaded with prisoners following along astern.

At dawn next day the *Graf Spee* was within a few miles of the rendezvous and at 0824 lookouts reported masts in sight. After the usual brief minutes of anxious doubt over whether it was a merchant ship or a British cruiser, the vessel was identified as *Altmark*.

Soon the two ships were lying stopped within a few hundred yards of each other, and then the *Altmark* manoeuvred so that the hose could be passed across for fuelling to start. At 1000 a launch brought Captain Dau over from the *Altmark* – which was still sailing under the name of *Sogne*.

Dau was not very pleased to hear that Langsdorff proposed to use the *Altmark* as a prison ship, and he pointed out that he had no accommodation to spare. However Langsdorff was quite adamant and impressed on Dau that the prisoners must be well treated. He had taken four British ships without a life being lost. He told him he was sending across an officer and some men from the *Graf Spee* who would help guard the prisoners (it was unlikely that Dau missed the point of that latter move: he was notorious for his hatred of the British, but the *Graf Spee* officer would ensure that Langsdorff's wishes were carried out).

Oil had been flowing across the pipeline between the two ships since 1105, and it continued for the rest of the day and well into the night. For what Langsdorff had in mind he wanted full tanks, since that would ensure him six weeks' cruising before having to meet the *Altmark* again.

CHAPTER 7

NINE SHIPS SUNK

Rid of the *Huntsman* and free of the *Altmark*, Langsdorff settled down with his War Diary and recorded his future programme, starting with '*Graf Spee* will continue her trade war as long as possible. Its object is not only disruption of the enemy mercantile marine, but also to force the enemy to deploy greater forces to protect the merchantmen.'

In view of the state of the ship's engines, the food supply and the refrigeration plant, a refit at a home port was to be aimed at, he added; and a provisional date for a break-through to Germany would be the new-moon period in January. Meanwhile, the pocket battleship's operational zone was to be the Cape route south-east of St Helena ...

Next day another long radiogram arrived from the SKL and this time it was welcome news – two German ships were on their way to meet the *Graf Spee* with more supplies. They were the motor ship *Dresden*, which had left Coquimbo the previous day, and the tanker *Emmy Friederich*, which had sailed from Tampico (Mexico).

The pocket battleship arrived in her new operational zone on 22 October, shortly after midnight, and Langsdorff and Wattenberg had carefully worked out a search plan. They already knew some of the courses being used by British steamers from secret route orders found in one of the captured merchantmen.

Shortly before daylight the crew went, as usual, to Dawn Action Stations and Langsdorff received his usual call which gave him time to dress and go to the bridge before the visibility started increasing. But this morning he was disappointed; there was nothing in sight – only the endless sea horizon which had circumscribed their little world now for several weeks. Had the British changed the merchant ship routes? Were they now sailing their vessels in convoys? Langsdorff ordered the Arado to be catapulted off to make the prearranged search, in the hope that an unsuspecting freighter might be steaming along just out of sight of the *Graf Spee*'s lookouts.

Spiering had not been in the air long before he saw smoke on the horizon, and he told the pilot, Bongardts, to approach in a wide sweep. Within a few moments he had identified the vessel as a merchant ship, and noted her course, approximate speed, and her position.

Bongardts then turned the Arado and headed back for the *Graf Spee* at full speed. As soon as she was in sight he put the aircraft into a shallow dive and then circled her while Spiering signalled the news.

More than three hours passed before the steamer was sighted, and then she was rapidly overhauled. The *Graf Spee* approached bows-on as usual, and, when only a few hundred yards away, she turned and ran up the flag signal 'Heave to, I am sending a boat' and then, 'Do not transmit or I will open fire.'

The steamer was the 5,299-ton *Trevanion*, homeward-bound from Port Pirie with a crew of thirty-three and a cargo of 8,000 tons of concentrates. Her Master, Captain Edwards, reacted quickly; he ordered Radio Officer N. C. Martinson to transmit an RRR report. This was picked up immediately by the *Graf Spee*'s monitors and reported to the bridge, and Langsdorff ordered the *Trevanion*'s bridge and upper deck to be sprayed with machine-gun fire.

Captain Edwards wrote later: 'They were about a hundred yards away at the time, and they swept her right the way along. I was on the top bridge, and I blew the signal for the men to come on deck. Then the Wireless Operator stopped sending the message and the battleship stopped firing.

'I ran down to the wireless room and asked him if he had got the whole message out, and he said, "No, I have only got half out." I then said that I would stand behind him while he sent the whole message, and I told him not to be nervous about sending it. He then got on with the message and sent the whole of it out from start to finish.

'Immediately the battleship started to machine-gun the ship again and they certainly made a mess of the bridge. They were firing tracer bullets, and one or two of them came on to the table, which knocked the Wireless Operator backwards, and I also fell backwards too. The Wireless Operator told me that he was positive that he had got the whole of the message out correctly.'[1]

---

[1] Despite the gallantry of these two officers, and of others whose ships fell victim to the *Graf Spee*, no awards were ever made. This in spite of the fact that the sending of an RRR report is an extremely unselfish act which cannot benefit·the sender.

Captain Edwards then went to the bridge and found that, although it was wrecked, none of his men had been wounded. He just had time to throw the secret papers overboard before the boarding party arrived. Three men, brandishing revolvers, came up to the bridge and announced to Captain Edwards: 'This ship has been captured by the Reich. You have ten minutes to get clothes, etc, before going into the boat.' The Germans then placed cartridge charges, timed to go off in fifteen minutes, round the ship and the crew were taken off. The charges exploded and the ship sank an hour later.

Once on board the *Graf Spee* (Captain Edwards wrote), 'Captain Langsdorff came up to me and said, "I am very sorry to have had to sink your ship. Are you hurt?" I just smiled at him and said nothing. He then said, "Are any of your crew hurt? War is war, Captain." I just stood there and did not bother to speak to him when he reached across me and caught hold of my hand to shake hands with me.'

Next day the aircraft spotted another ship, and the *Graf Spee* altered course to intercept. However, at the time the ship should have been in sight the horizon was clear. Although Langsdorff carried on for another half an hour there was still nothing to see. Positions, courses and speeds were checked with the Arado's observer and the *Graf Spee*'s navigator, but there had been no mistakes. There seemed only one possible explanation – the ship had sighted the Arado and immediately altered course. And the ship might have guessed the aircraft belonged to a German raider and radioed a warning to the British which the *Graf Spee*'s operators had failed to detect ... even now British hunting groups might be converging on the area ...

Langsdorff decided to move off to the westward at high speed to get well clear, and within a short time the *Graf Spee*'s engines were turning at full speed for the first time in several weeks while Langsdorff waited anxiously to see if the monitors, their wireless sets automatically combing all wavelengths, noticed any increase in enemy W/T traffic, and he was relieved when they reported it was about the same as usual.

That night Langsdorff sent a signal to the SKL reporting his move and asking them to tell the *Altmark* to move the next rendezvous 600 miles to the west. The two ships met on the 28th, and while fuel was transferred the *Trevanion*'s crew were taken over to the *Altmark*.

Langsdorff still had not decided on his new move. For two months he had operated his ship away from a base, and he had sunk five ships, crossing the Atlantic twice in the process. The last four had been intercepted on the Freetown-Cape route, and it was reasonable to suppose the British would be concentrating their search there. The hours Langsdorff spent making his decision were lonely ones. As captain of the pocket battleship he had his duty to perform as a commerce raider, and he was personally responsible for the life and death of more than a thousand men ...

Six days earlier he had received a signal from the SKL telling him to consider moving unexpectedly into the Indian Ocean if enemy pressure in the Atlantic became stronger. This gave him a lead, showing the SKL were well informed on the problems he faced.

Finally, during the afternoon, he made up his mind: he would take the *Graf Spee* right round the Cape of Good Hope into the Indian Ocean. There, he noted in his diary, his course of action would be 'to carry on the trade war south of Madagascar', and 'create alarm there and draw off the British forces'. He would leave the *Altmark* behind in the Atlantic, arranging four provisional rendezvous, the last being for 26 November.

By 8 November the *Graf Spee* was in her new operational area in the Indian Ocean, east of Durban and south of Madagascar, and zig-zagging across the shipping routes. The Arado was launched daily and several hundreds of square miles were searched, but nothing was sighted as the *Graf Spee* worked her way northwards towards Madagascar.

After five days Langsdorff was forced to change his plan: up to now he had been avoiding neutral ships, but it was vital that he made his presence known to the British, otherwise his presence in the Indian Ocean would not cause them to divert their forces as he had planned.

Langsdorff's decision was noted in the *Graf Spee*'s log:

> *Purpose of operation: to create alarm in Indian Ocean. Only possible if present plans enlarge. Decision: (1) To proceed up the Mozambique Strait and search north-east of Lourenço Marques; (2) Failing that, to attack South African coastal traffic; (3) Possible attack on Durban by* Graf Spee's *aircraft.*

The *Graf Spee* then altered course west-north-west to carry out the first part of Langsdorff's decision, reaching a position close to the coast off Lourenço Marques on 14 November. That night, in heavy seas, they sighted a small ship and identified her by searchlight as a Dutch coaster. Since she was neutral and knowing she would think the *Graf Spee* was a British warship, Langsdorff left her, hoping for better luck after daylight.

And it came soon after noon when a steamer was sighted. The *Graf Spee*'s crew ran to action stations with the prospect of the first bit of excitement for more than three weeks. Again the French Tricolour was hoisted, and the 5.9-inch guns were loaded – after the *Trevanion* incident Langsdorff had decided machine guns were useless in dissuading British wireless operators from transmitting RRR reports.

From the *Graf Spee*'s bridge the approaching steamer looked quite small and was not far off when she suddenly bore away and then headed back the way she had come. Langsdorff ordered more speed and the signal flags were hoisted. Still the merchantman continued steaming away. Langsdorff ordered a warning shot to be fired, and one of the 5.9-inch guns on the port side barked out, to send a shell spinning over towards the little coaster.

The steamer was in fact the *Africa Shell*, 706 tons, bound from Juelimare to Lourenço Marques. She had a crew of twenty-nine and her master was Captain P. G. G. Dove, who later reported[1] that when a warship was sighted he at first thought it was French. Later, however, he became suspicious and 'I turned my stern on him and ran for it. We kept going and we were about four miles from where we first sighted him when suddenly I saw a flash and a big brown splash about a quarter of a mile astern of me. I realized that the warship meant business and that we had better do something, so I slowed down to half speed. By this time the battleship was about two miles away.'

He and the rest of the crew then saw that the warship was German and he immediately took bearings on Cape Quessico and Cape Zavora and reported to Captain Dove that they were two miles off the beach.[2]

The *Graf Spee* slowed down and lowered a launch, which immediately made for the *Africa Shell*, and at 1145 a boarding party of nine ratings and two officers clambered on board the merchantman, revolvers in their hands, and told Captain Dove they were going to sink his ship.

'They said they would give us ten minutes to get ready and we could take all we could collect,' Captain Dove continued. 'They also said we could either go on to the cruiser or go ashore if we liked. I decided to go ashore.

'I called all hands up, we cleared away the boats and lowered them. The Chief Officer got into one off the port side and the Second Officer into the other, with the rest of the crew. The port boat pulled away, the Second Officer's boat waited for me.

'The [German boarding] officer then said he wanted to see our papers, the ship's Register, and the Articles. The Secret Service officer in plain clothes searched the ship. He searched everything. He came across the book for working out salaries, etc, and he took that away as there were a lot of figures in it.

'While this search was going on I made my protest that my ship was in territorial waters, and they could not sink it. The officer said, "Oh no, you are not." Apparently the cruiser had meanwhile come round and was between us and the beach, making a complete circle round us.

'He told me that I could make a protest if I liked, so I started to write out that the ship was in territorial waters. I had to dash out to the lifeboat to tell

[1] In a report to the British authorities on the sinking.
[2] i.e. one mile inside Portuguese territorial waters.

them to wait for me as I was coming in a few minutes. There was an awful commotion going on, and then a man came in and said that the Captain of the warship had signalled that I was not to go ashore, but was to go on board the warship, so they rushed me into the waiting launch.

'They took three or four bags of food, typewriting paper, typewriters, torch batteries, all the sextants and the chronometer.

'I protested that I had no clothes, as I had only had on a pair of shorts and a shirt. The officer asked me where they were. I said they were in the lifeboat, so we went over to it in the launch and they handed me one small suitcase and half a bottle of whisky to see me through.

'My boats pulled to the shore and I was taken on board the warship. When we left the *Africa Shell* the [German] sailors put a time bomb on the port side of the engine room ...

'I had left my Ensign up and I saluted it for the benefit of the Germans watching. The last I saw of the ship, she had a heavy list and I understood she turned over and drifted ashore.

'I climbed up a ladder on board the warship and they took me below to the Navigator's cabin. They asked me to have a cigarette, saying they thought they had just one left from the *Clement*. Then the cruiser went full speed for another ship which had been sighted ...'

This vessel turned out to be Japanese, the *Tihuku Maru*, and as she was neutral she was allowed to pass unmolested.

By this time the lifeboats from the *Africa Shell* had reached the shore and Langsdorff decided it was high time the *Graf Spee* made her escape. As it was obvious that they would be under observation from Zavora lighthouse, he ordered the pocket battleship to be steered towards the north-east – as though going through the Mozambique Channel – until they were out of sight of the coast; then he altered to 120 degrees, a course which took them south-eastward and clear of the coast.

Next day, just before noon, another ship was sighted and the *Graf Spee* prepared a boarding party. But they were disappointed – the vessel was the *Mapia*, flying the Dutch flag, and she was left to continue her voyage.

This ended the *Graf Spee*'s operations in the Indian Ocean, and Langsdorff had achieved his objective of diverting the British hunting groups. He headed away south-east on the 16th, altering south-west next day. The log noted '*2130 – journey round Cape begun*'.

Langsdorff knew that the *Africa Shell*'s survivors would by now have been interrogated and, from their descriptions, their attacker would have been identified as a pocket battleship.

Having trailed his red herring, he had now to try to guess what the British would do with their net; and what they did depended on what they guessed his own future actions would be. Would the British expect him to return to the Atlantic after sinking the *Africa Shell*? Or would they think he would go farther into the Indian Ocean, perhaps seeking the rich cargoes from the Far East which converged on the Red Sea, making their way through the Suez Canal to Britain?

He decided on the latter; and that meant he would probably fool them if he doubled back into the Atlantic, and the main danger would lie in accidentally meeting any of the forces which would be diverted from the Atlantic round the Cape into the Indian Ocean. These hunting forces, Langsdorff guessed, would be in a hurry and take the shortest route, keeping close inshore. If he rounded the Cape westwards keeping 500 to 600 miles off, he should be fairly safe.

And this is what he did, altering course westward on the 19th and entering the Atlantic the next day. He set a course for the last of the four rendezvous with the *Altmark* – he was too late for the previous three.

The two ships met shortly after dawn on 26 November and once again the pipeline was towed across to the pocket battleship. She had used up a lot of fuel, and pumping started at 0815, by which time several launches were ferrying over tons of stores. Langsdorff wanted the *Graf Spee* to be fuelled and provisioned so that she could operate until February 1940 without meeting a supply ship.

That night the pocket battleship's officers, with some from the *Altmark*, had a big party on board. Perhaps they realized that the operations of their great ship were reaching a climax, or maybe they were pleased at the way they had hoodwinked the British – as they assuredly had, it seemed. They invited Captain Dove, the jovial master of the *Africa Shell*, but he refused. However, Langsdorff and his officers had an admiration for the redoubtable Briton, and during the evening arrived at his cabin with several bottles and noisily drank his health. They told him in all seriousness that he 'would be a prisoner shortly'.

Earlier in the day Langsdorff had written a nine-page review in his War Diary of the situation and the intentions of the *Graf Spee*. The main points were that there were no deficiencies in the ship's main armament, and she had 2,841 tons of fuel on board – enough for her to remain at sea until the end of February – with another 3,600 tons available in the *Altmark*. The marine growth on the ship's bottom had 'increased considerably but in general considering the circumstances, the state of preservation is good'. The ship's machinery required a dockyard overhaul 'in the near future' – in October this had been envisaged for January.

Turning to operations, Langsdorff noted that while the *Graf Spee* would continue attacking enemy shipping for as long as possible, he had to bear in mind instructions from Germany that the enemy must obtain no prestige from the destruction of a pocket battleship. The need for machinery overhaul within two or three months meant that the period of commerce raiding was nearing an end and, Langsdorff wrote, 'in consequence the necessity for avoiding action damage can no longer be so pressing. If the *Graf Spee* were to close the range it could be anticipated that her powerful armament would at least so damage an opponent, with the exception of the *Renown*, as to eliminate her as a pursuer.'[1]

'On the other hand,' he continued, 'it would be difficult to achieve decisive results or shake off fast shadowers in the bright moonlight nights of the South Atlantic.'

This and several previous references in his War Diary during the preceding weeks show that Langsdorff underestimated the problems of night shadowing, even in the clear visibility of the South Atlantic. In the event, as will be described later, the out-gunned British cruisers had difficulty in shadowing the *Graf Spee* at a safe distance even when she was silhouetted against the lights of the city of Montevideo.

Despite the powerful enemy forces disposed against the *Graf Spee*, Langsdorff wrote, no effort had apparently been made to search the area she used for fuelling. In addition, the absence of sinkings in the South Atlantic for the past month had probably led to the enemy relaxing counter-measures. 'This favourable situation must be utilized for further disruption of traffic in the Atlantic before returning to Germany,' Langsdorff noted.

He concluded that, after completing a minor machinery overhaul, he would operate again on the Cape-Freetown route in the area where he found the *Trevanion* until about 6 December. Then, depending on the state of the machinery, the *Graf Spee* would either return home or operate against the River Plate traffic.

For the next two days Langsdorff kept his men busy altering the appearance of the *Graf Spee* as much as possible. She had a very distinctive shape, quite unlike any British capital ship. Her fighting top was built up solid, instead of the more usual British system of having a platform on top of a tripod; and of course she had only one turret forward and one aft, whereas a British cruiser, battlecruiser or battleship (with the exception of the distinctive *Nelson* and *Rodney*) usually had two turrets forward and two aft.

First of all the crew got busy chipping, scraping and patching up the rusty spots in the hull and upperworks with red lead. After that they started painting the ship with various shades of grey. Langsdorff told Captain Dove that he wanted to make the *Graf Spee* look like a British battleship.

---

[1] This reference is the only possible clue to the often-asked question of why Langsdorff, when he found he was engaging three cruisers, did not make an all-out attempt to break off the action right at the beginning of the subsequent Battle of the River Plate.

Describing what he saw, Captain Dove reported later to the British authorities: 'He rigged up a dummy funnel just aft of his forward turret, even painting a black strip along the top. He also rigged a dummy turret forward, and the Captain and officers went off in a launch four miles away to see the effect.

'He came back and said he was very pleased with the work. He said, "We shall now look like the *Repulse* as shown in *Jane's Fighting Ships*." He told me it was for the benefit of neutrals because when he went back to Germany, if he was sighted by a neutral ship and they were asked by a British ship if they had seen the *Graf Spee*, the neutrals would say they had seen a ship with two funnels and a double turret forward, and then the British ship would think it was the *Repulse* . . .

'He put *Deutschland* on the stern of the ship, painting in letters of gold on a tin plate in German script. He said this was also for the benefit of neutrals. On the other side of the plate was *Von Scheer* . . .'

On 29 November, after being together for three days, the *Graf Spee* left the *Altmark* after giving Captain Dau new positions for meeting in December. Langsdorff steered east-north-east for the position where the *Trevanion* had been sighted, and he had high hopes of sighting a victim almost immediately.

But an empty horizon greeted the men on the pocket battleship's bridge at dawn on the 30th; nor did they have any better luck on 1 December. When nothing was sighted during the rest of the day, Langsdorff ordered the Arado to be ready to fly off early next morning.

Once again the crew were at Dawn Action Stations on 2 December; once again the only people to see anything on the horizon were those whose livers were not in good order. At 0700 the Arado took off to search on either side and ahead of the *Graf Spee*, and it had to return two and a half hours later, because of fuel shortage, to report nothing in sight.

At noon the navigators took their usual sights and they had just finished working them out and were entering the pocket battleship's latest position in the log when a cry came from the tiny lookout position above the rangefinder on the fighting top: 'Smoke in sight'.

The alarm bells sounded, sending the crew to Action Stations; the rangefinders swung round to the bearing given by the lookout; the 3.7-cm guns were manned. As Langsdorff hurried to the bridge, wireless operators switched on the Marconi radio set, which had been taken out of the *Newton Beech* before she was sunk, and tuned it in. The Germans were taking even more precautions, should the unknown ship try to send out an RRR report: the Marconi set would be used to jam any transmission, and the 3.7-cm guns would open fire.

Within a few minutes various reports from all over the ship told

Langsdorff that the crew were prepared – gunners, wireless operators, engineers, boarding party and everyone remotely connected with the task in hand. The rangefinder and *Dt-Geraet* operators gave the range as 220 hectometres and as the range stayed the same during the next few minutes it was obvious the vessel was steaming away at high speed.

That could mean only one thing: she was not a warship – that much could be seen even at this range – so she must be a large and fast merchant ship. At last the *Graf Spee* was going to make a worthwhile capture ...

Langsdorff ordered an increase in speed, and gradually the distances reported by the rangefinders and radar decreased. At 1337, an hour and twelve minutes after the smoke was sighted, Langsdorff ordered a warning shot to be fired and the word 'Stop' to be signalled in plain language by searchlight. The steamer slowed down, but three minutes later the monitors in the *Graf Spee* warned the bridge that she was tuning in her wireless. The British were obviously getting suspicious, and Langsdorff ordered 'No wireless' to be flashed by searchlight.

But he was too late. Captain W. Stubbs, the master, had ordered Radio Officer William Comber to transmit a raider report as fast as he could. Immediately the *Graf Spee*'s operators started jamming with the Marconi set from the *Newton Beech* and one of the 3.7-cm guns thundered out another warning shot, which fell very close to the steamer. Langsdorff was told that transmission had now stopped.

Four minutes later, however, Comber started transmitting again. The *Graf Spee*'s operators continued their jamming and reported that they thought they were being successful.

Langsdorff did not want to continue shelling the merchantman because she was bigger than anything else he had caught, and she would make a good prize. Through binoculars he could see the steamer's crew swinging out the lifeboats and preparing to abandon ship, and fifteen minutes later the *Graf Spee* turned, less than 500 yards from the steamer, and lowered a boat.

The prize crew were soon on board and signalled across to the pocket battleship that the steamer was the *Doric Star*, 10,086 tons, bound from Auckland to the United Kingdom with a cargo of meat and dairy produce. A further signal, however, upset Langsdorff's plans – the *Doric Star*'s Chief Engineer had damaged the engines, so she could not be got under way ...

The prize crew were then told to bring off the British, along with some provisions from the steamer's cargo. Scuttling charges were placed and shells and a torpedo were also used to sink her. The *Doric Star* finally submerged at 1710.

Not at all sure that the jamming of the *Doric Star*'s RRR reports had been completely successful, Langsdorff lost no time in moving away to the south-west at high speed, and in the meantime the *Graf Spee*'s monitors listened in as their wireless sets combed the wavelengths. The *B-Dienst* group were ready to break down any enemy cipher signals. They had to wait a minute short of two hours after the sinking of the *Doric Star*: at 1909 a powerful signal was picked up from a ship using the British procedure, and within a short while *B-Dienst* reported to Langsdorff that a British warship had just sent a very urgent message to Simonstown naval radio station.

At 1923 the *Graf Spee*'s operators intercepted a signal which dashed Langsdorff's hopes that the Marconi set from *Newton Beech* had successfully jammed the *Doric Star*'s raider report. It was from Simonstown, addressed to all British warships in the South Atlantic, and it said:

> *1417 RRR 19.15 S, 5.5 E.* Doric Star *gunned. Battleship.*

Langsdorff noted that the position given in the raider report, which Simonstown Radio was now repeating, was five miles farther south than the *Graf Spee*'s navigators had calculated – not that it made any difference in the circumstances. However, the signal told him that his original decision made two hours earlier, that the *Graf Spee* had to get clear quickly, was a correct one.

What he did not know was that the chance of meeting with the *Doric Star* at 1225 that day – which resulted in him sinking his biggest capture up to date – also meant the beginning of the end for the *Graf Spee*. It meant the death of thirty-seven of his men, the wounding of fifty-four more, and it meant his own suicide a short while after. Yet Langsdorff did not know that death was near when he took his pocket battleship away to the south-west at full speed; and in any case the *Graf Spee* still had more victims to claim.

Next morning, shortly before daybreak, the crew went as usual to Dawn Action Stations; and, just as they had done every morning since the voyage had begun back in August, the officers on watch waited anxiously for dawn to light up the horizon and reveal if there was a victim – or a hunter – nearby.

This time, on 3 December, they were not disappointed: at 0518 they sighted a steamer on the port quarter, and the *Graf Spee* swung round towards her. As the crew were already at Action Stations it was only a question of having a prize crew standing by.

By 0551 the *Graf Spee* was close enough to the steamer to run up flags ordering her 'Heave to, I am sending a boat', and 'Do not transmit or I will shoot'.

Within a few minutes – as soon as the flags had been read by the men on the bridge of the steamer – she began to slow down. Suddenly a warning reached the *Graf Spee*'s bridge from the wireless monitors that the steamer was transmitting, and Langsdorff ordered the 3.7-cm guns to open fire at the bridge. For two minutes the guns kept up a rapid fire, shells bursting on the chart house. Then the monitors reported that transmission had ceased, and the guns stopped firing. Two minutes later, while the smoke of the shell bursts was still clearing, the steamer started transmitting again, and again the 3.7s opened fire, shells exploding on the bridge. The wheel and binnacle were smashed and transmission finally ceased altogether.

As the shelling started Captain Starr, the steamer's master, ordered all hands to the boats. As the men ran to their positions shells were still bursting, wounding three of them. By this time the *Graf Spee* had stopped and her prize crew – for Langsdorff intended using the steamer as a tender – were in the launch. Six minutes after the shooting had stopped they had boarded her and were soon reporting details to the *Graf Spee* by signal lamp: the steamer was the *Tairoa*, of 7,983 tons, bound from Melbourne to Freetown to join a convoy for the rest of the voyage home. She was carrying a cargo of meat, wool and lead. She had heard the *Doric Star*'s raider report when four days out from Cape Town; and Captain Starr had promptly altered course to keep clear of the position.

The boarding officer ordered Captain Starr to get under way; but he told the German the wheel had been smashed. Semaphore messages were sent across to the *Graf Spee* and Langsdorff decided he would have to sink her instead, and take the crew of eighty-one on board the pocket battleship. That meant his ship was getting very crowded again, since he already had the *Doric Star*'s crew on board.

At 0920 the *Tairoa* was sunk by torpedo, and a tribute to her gallant wireless operator was written in the *Graf Spee*'s log: 'The first 3.7-cm shells hit the chart house and radio cabin. At the end the radio operator was lying on the deck attempting to transmit his report until finally shrapnel [sic] put the transmitter out of order.'[1]

The *Graf Spee* moved off at twenty-two knots, heading across the Atlantic towards South America, 2,000 miles to the westward. Langsdorff planned to refuel from the *Altmark* on 6 December and then continue to an area between Rio de Janeiro and the River Plate. After sinking any ships he found, he would go south to the River Plate and stop a neutral ship so that the British would think he was going south round Cape Horn and into the Pacific. Instead he would double back and start the long voyage back to Germany.

On 4 December he received a far from cheering signal from SKL giving the latest estimated enemy positions. The *Ajax*, *Achilles*, *Exeter* and *Cumberland* were in the Rio-Plate area, a powerful British and French force, including an aircraft carrier, was on the West African coast, and two cruisers were at the Cape.

[1] As in the case of the *Trevanion* and *Doric Star*, no award was made by the British Government.

The *Graf Spee* met the *Altmark* as planned on the 6th and refuelled. All the prisoners, with the exception of a few British officers, were transferred to the *Altmark*, and Captain Dau was given new positions for a rendezvous after the River Plate foray and for the journey home. At 0800 next day, 7 December, the two ships parted. Although no one on board either ship realized it, they would never see each other again. Their hunting days as a team were over, and the notorious Dau had the crews of six British ships on board. He talked a good deal of how he was eventually going to take them back to Germany, but instead they were to be rescued by the British destroyer *Cossack* as the *Altmark* hid in a snow-rimmed Norwegian fjord.

After leaving the *Altmark*, the *Graf Spee* continued to the westward and later that day, at 1746, smoke was sighted. A few minutes afterwards the lookouts identified a small merchant ship and once again the pocket battleship closed for the kill.

The steamer was the *Streonshalh*, of 3,895 tons, bound from Montevideo to Freetown, where she was to join a convoy for England. She was owned by the Marwood Steamship Company, of Whitby, and was carrying a cargo of 5,654 tons of wheat. The crew numbered thirty-two and her master, Captain J. R. Robinson, later told the British authorities:

'I was sitting on the lower bridge reading. The Chief Officer came down and said he thought he had seen a sailing ship on the horizon. I went up to the top bridge and put my telescope on her and made her out to be the fighting[1] top of a cruiser.

'I had heard the *Doric Star*'s distress signal recently and knew that there was a raider in the vicinity. However, in this case I thought it was a British cruiser but took no chances regarding this.

'I got all hands on deck, and had the boats swung out and had provisions put in them. I kept the ship going on her course.

'The cruiser approached us, bows-on all the time. She was not camouflaged but had some signals flying. I could not make out what they were as she was stem on to us, until she was about two ships' lengths away on my starboard side.

'She steamed right round on to my course and then at last I observed she was German. The signals read: "If you transmit on your wireless I will open fire immediately."'

A boarding party came over and with it was the usual man in civilian clothes who ransacked the bridge and cabins in the usual fruitless search for secret papers or anything else he thought might be of use.

Captain Robinson and his crew were then taken over to the pocket battleship, and he continued in his report: 'We were taken to the Navigator's cabin, where two officers, one of whom was Lt Hertzberg, gave us a glass of beer, and tried to find out about the routes from the Plate to Freetown.

[1] 'Flying' in the verbatim report.

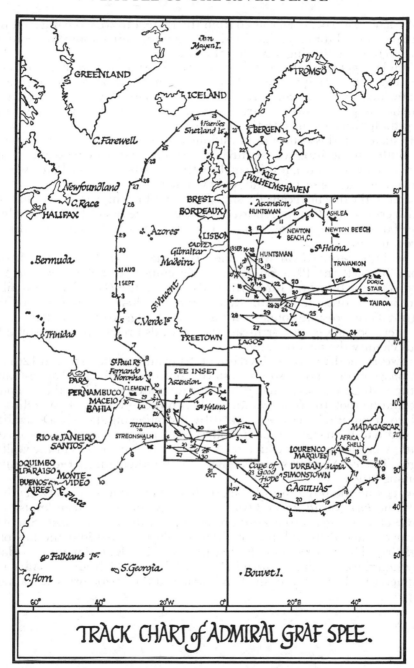

TRACK CHART of ADMIRAL GRAF SPEE.

'We had, it is true, been routed from the Plate, but we were miles off the ordinary route. I told him that I did not know anything about routes at all as we were not following any special route.'

Unable to get any help from Captain Robinson, Langsdorff had to guess at where the wartime steamship lane ran from Buenos Aires and Montevideo to Freetown. The course the *Streonshalh* was steering when sighted was plotted on a chart to see if that gave any indication, and Langsdorff altered course to the south-west.

He stayed on this course until midnight and then came round more to the south, but nothing was sighted on the 8th. Next day he came round further to the westward, headed in directly towards the River Plate, so that by noon he was some 1,200 miles off Montevideo.

Later in the day he received a signal from Berlin which told him that the British cruiser *Achilles* was reported to be at Montevideo. It also gave him some far more important news – the movements of some big British merchant ships.

The 14,000-ton Royal Mail liner *Highland Monarch*, said the Berlin signal, had left the Plate on about 5 December, and the *Andalusia Star* (owned by the Blue Star Line, which also owned the *Doric Star*) had sailed from Buenos Aires on the 8th. After estimating their speeds and carefully plotting their possible courses on his chart, Langsdorff estimated that if they were bound for the north-east (i.e. towards Freetown) they would be in his vicinity the next day.

However, nothing was sighted on the 10th; and on the 11th and 12th the *Graf Spee* continued on a south-westerly course towards the Plate estuary. By the 12th Langsdorff reached what he estimated would be the shipping lane and he took the *Graf Spee* along it with the intention of patrolling to and fro across it during the night. If by the following day, 13 December, nothing had been sighted, he intended to turn right round and cross the South Atlantic again to an area off the West African coast near the Gulf of Lagos. There he would search along and on either side of the peacetime shipping lanes.

So it came about that shortly before dawn on Wednesday, 13 December, 1939, the *Panzerschiff Admiral Graf Spee* was cruising at fifteen knots on a course of 155 degrees in a position 34° 27′ south, 49° 55′ west. She had destroyed nine British ships, totalling 50,089 tons, without the loss of a single life. The man who made that proud claim, Kapitän zur See Hans Langsdorff, was at that moment in his sea cabin on the bridge, his task as a commerce raider nearly finished and his life, at the age of forty-two, almost over.

CHAPTER 8

ACHILLES JOINS THE PARTY

We left Commodore Harwood's force of the *Ajax*, *Exeter*, and the destroyers *Havock* and *Hotspur* off Rio, waiting for the *Cumberland* to join them from Freetown. The Admiralty had formed the hunting groups; interrogation of the *Clement*'s survivors had established beyond all doubt that the raider was a pocket battleship – apparently, thanks to Langsdorff's subterfuge, the *Admiral Scheer*; and the real search of the South Atlantic trade routes was about to start.

The Commodore's first orders from Admiral Lyon were that as soon as the *Cumberland* arrived, she and the *Exeter* would form a hunting group and carry out a sweep northwards from Rio towards Pernambuco, off which the *Clement* had been sunk. The *Ajax*, *Achilles* (when she arrived from the west coast of South America) and the two destroyers would patrol the focal areas protecting the merchant shipping.

The Commodore's plan was that if he met a pocket battleship in daylight he would shadow until dusk – he had the advantage of speed and would be able to keep out of range. After darkness had fallen he would then go into action. If, however, he found the enemy at night his destroyers would immediately attack her with torpedoes.

The position therefore on 5 October (the *Clement* had been sunk on 30 September) was that Harwood's force was concentrated off Rio de Janeiro ready to engage the pocket battleship should she come south from Pernambuco, and that the *Achilles* was passing through the Magellan Straits on her way to join him.

On that day the British steamer *Martand* intercepted a raider report from a British merchant ship saying that she was being attacked by a German armed raider. The *Martand* had not managed to get the whole signal and did not know the name of the vessel. [She was in fact the *Newton Beech* which the *Graf Spee* had sighted at dawn 900 miles away on the Cape-Freetown route.]

Later that day the *Martand* met the *Cumberland*, which had left Freetown two days earlier and was due to rendezvous with Commodore Harwood on the 9th; and while Leutnant zur See Schunemann and his prize crew aboard the *Newton Beech* steamed along with the *Graf Spee*, the captain of the *Martand* told the *Cumberland* of the distress message his radio operator had picked up.

The *Cumberland* was then 700 miles from Freetown and her captain assumed that the message would be intercepted by the other merchant ships much nearer on the Cape-Freetown route and passed on to Admiral Lyon at Freetown, even if it was not intercepted by shore stations. He also considered wireless silence particularly important and decided against breaking it.

However, the *Newton Beech*'s distress signal – reported by the *Graf Spee* as having been weak – does not appear to have been picked up by any other British ship, and the Admiralty remained in ignorance of the fact that shortly after dawn that morning the position of the *Graf Spee* was 9° 20′ south, 6° 19′ west. Admiral Lyon, in a subsequent official report[1] said that in his opinion this information, if acted upon, might have led to the early destruction of *Graf Spee* and the *Altmark*. (As it was, he knew nothing of it until 21 January 1940.)

Meanwhile many conflicting reports continued to arrive at the Admiralty, giving the alleged positions of German ships and U-boats; and it was the task of the Director of Naval Intelligence to assess them. The *Admiral Scheer* is in the St Helena area ... two German cruisers and six U-boats along the South American coast ... German merchantmen sailing from various South Atlantic ports on a variety of likely and unlikely operations ... so the reports flowed in.

During the first half of October the Commodore's force protected various convoys leaving Rio and the Plate, and steamed here and there following up Intelligence reports on German shipping. They were busy days with little rest for the officers and men of the British warships; and on the 13th Harwood told Admiral Lyon that as the *Exeter* needed certain repairs he proposed taking her to the Falklands on the 17th, returning on the 27th.

Admiral Lyon, however, said that he would prefer the *Exeter* to stay until the Commodore transferred to the *Ajax* on the 27th, when the *Achilles* was also due to arrive. Then she and the *Cumberland* could operate as Force G until the *Exeter*'s return. It had previously been agreed that the Commodore should transfer from the *Exeter* to the *Ajax* because Force G would have to maintain wireless silence. Thus Harwood could continue patrolling the focal areas and still keep in touch with Admiral Lyon. At the same time the Commodore pointed out the endurance differences of the *Exeter* and *Cumberland*, and suggested that the former should be replaced by a 10,000-ton cruiser as soon as possible.

On 26 October the *Cumberland* entered Montevideo and an hour later the *Achilles* joined the *Exeter* off the Plate. She was the first British warship the New Zealand cruiser had sighted since before the war.

The *Achilles* had returned to Auckland, New Zealand, on 18 August from a

---

[1] Given in an Admiralty account: *The Chase and the Destruction of the* Graf Spee.

typical peacetime cruise of the Pacific Islands, and the following week had been spent carrying out exercises with the cruiser *Leander*. On 25 August both ships were ordered to prepare for war. Two days later they were stored and provisioned and at twelve hours' notice to sail for any part of the world ...

The New Zealand Government had decided they would retain only one of their two cruisers, and the *Achilles* was chosen to go. Captain W. E. Parry, her commanding officer, received his sailing orders at 0900 on 29 August. During the morning fifty extra ratings from HMS *Philomel* and two RNR officers from the *Leander* joined the ship.

Groups of relatives appeared at the dockside to say goodbye – including Captain Parry's wife, who had just arrived in New Zealand: they had only been able to spend two weekends together before being parted again. At 1330 the *Achilles* left her berth, bound for a secret destination. One officer scrambled aboard as the last hawsers were being cast off: he was another doctor, Surgeon-Lieutenant Pittar. He had been warned only one and a half hours earlier and immediately dropped a flourishing ophthalmic practice to join the *Achilles*.

As soon as the cruiser cleared Rangitoto the bugle sounded 'Everybody aft', and Captain Parry briefly told his crew the plans for the *Achilles*: they were bound for the West Indies, via the Panama Canal, and they would come under the orders of the C-in-C, America and West Indies Station.

So the *Achilles* headed for Panama, 6,500 miles away. The northerly winds made her roll, and there was an air of excitement in the ship. The BBC news bulletins became gloomier and gloomier; and warning telegrams from the Admiralty in London and the Navy Office in New Zealand arrived thick and fast.

On 2 September Captain Parry's new C-in-C ordered *Achilles* to Valparaiso, where he was to meet the Naval Attaché and 'in the event of hostilities to take such immediate action as is considered necessary'.

Late the next evening a signal was received on board. It consisted of two words: '*TOTAL GERMANY*'.

Captain Parry wrote later: 'As in 1914, when I was in the *Grasshopper* at Malta, I heard this news from my bed; and it did not cause me a sleepless night, for which I was grateful ... I think we all felt rather pleased to be going on a lone job, away from fleets and squadrons. Certainly it is much more interesting for me.'

For the next six weeks the *Achilles'* task was to protect Allied shipping and stop enemy trade on the west coast of South America. That meant covering the 4,100 miles between Panama and Cape Horn alone ...

At the beginning of October orders arrived from the Admiralty telling Captain Parry to take the *Achilles* through the Magellan Straits to the South

Atlantic, where he would come under the orders of Admiral Lyon. The cruiser left Valparaiso on 13 October, passed through the Magellan Strait on the 19th, and arrived at Port Stanley, in the Falkland Islands, on 22 October. The islands are large and bleak, consisting mainly of sparse moorland intersected by ridges of rocky hills, and the Sailing Directions describe the climate as 'stormy, and a day without wind is unusual. Sudden and severe squalls may occur at any time, or gales which blow heavily'.

The islands' strategic value was proved in the First World War, although in 1939 they had not been developed as a naval base. There were no stores, except fuel, and no repair facilities. As often as not ships had to keep steam on the main engines because of the danger of dragging anchors. In fact it was a base only in name.

After the *Achilles* met the *Exeter* on 26 October, the two ships carried out manoeuvres together and then the *Achilles* went to oil from the *Olwen*. Meanwhile Captain Parry went on board the *Exeter* to meet Commodore Harwood. They were both torpedo specialists but had met only once previously – in HMS *Vernon*, the torpedo establishment at Portsmouth.

The position which the Commodore outlined to Captain Parry during their two-hour talk was not a very cheering one: he was suffering to some extent from divided control since – as mentioned earlier – Admiral Lyon could override his plans,[1] particularly with regard to Force G. If he could not allocate this force to one of the focal areas he could not compete ... The Admiralty were insistent over not accepting any benevolence from neutrals which might also be useful to the Germans if granted to them. For instance he had to stop keeping his oiler at Montevideo when she was not being used, since we did not want the Germans to be allowed a similar privilege.

The *Achilles* sailed the same day to meet the *Cumberland* off Lobos with orders for both ships to cover the Rio-Santos area as Force G. The *Ajax* arrived from the Rio area and took all the fuel remaining in the *Olwen*, which was going north to the West Indies. Next morning Commodore Harwood and his staff transferred to her and his Broad Pendant was hoisted. Captain Bell then sailed the *Exeter* to the Falkland Islands, where his crew could rest and repairs be effected.

Meanwhile the *Cumberland* and *Achilles* went on patrol. As the captain of the *Cumberland* was three years' senior to Captain Parry, *Achilles* had to 'Follow Father' which, as he commented at the time, 'at least gave our watch-keeping officers some badly needed practice in station keeping'.

As Force G now comprised only an 8-inch and a 6-inch cruiser (instead of two 8-inch cruisers), it was not considered strong enough to tackle a pocket battleship in daylight; and Commodore Harwood gave them definite instructions that if they made contact they were to shadow by day

[1] In practice this rarely if ever happened, and their relationship was a cordial one.

but attack by night.

Captain Fallowfield, of the *Cumberland*, planned that the two ships should work out to the eastward of the enemy in daylight so that they could close in at dusk and have her silhouetted against the afterglow of the sunset. That would enable the cruisers to see her at a greater range than she could see them. The *Achilles* would steam ahead of *Cumberland* in an attempt to fire torpedoes (the *Cumberland* had none); but of course the two ships would stay within supporting distance of each other. As Captain Parry rather wryly commented, 'I am not sure that the prospect is altogether a pleasant one, though I take some comfort from the possibility that the enemy is likely to put his main armament on *Cumberland* and only his secondary armament on us ...'

CHAPTER 9

CASTING THE NET

By 21 October the Admiralty knew for certain that the *Deutschland* was at large because of reports from her victims, and the whereabouts of the raider which sank the *Clement* on 30 September became even more of a mystery. In fact, despite the reports of the survivors who landed in South America on 3 October, and of the Master and Chief Engineer who had been transferred to the Greek steamer *Papalemos* by the *Graf Spee* and landed at St Vincent, Cape Verde Island on 9 October[1] (when they were interrogated by two naval officers and the British Vice-Consul), there was doubt in the minds of some people as to the identity of the raider.

The mystery was partially solved the very next day, 22 October, when in the afternoon the British liner *Llanstephan Castle* intercepted a garbled signal from an unknown ship which said:

Gunned in 16° south, 4° 3'[2] east at 1400 GMT.

But unfortunately there was no confirmation of the report. [The victim was the *Trevanion*, which had been ordered to heave-to by the *Graf Spee* at 1420. As described earlier, her bridge had twice been machine-gunned as her wireless operator transmitted an RRR report.]

So apart from the brief and incomplete signal intercepted by the liner, the Admiralty were no wiser: they did not know the identity of either attacker or victim. The message could have been a hoax, transmitted in the first instance by a U-boat or a German armed merchantman.

---

[1] Not 9 November, as mentioned in certain official reports.
[2] The *Graf Spee* logged the position as 19° 40' south, 4° 2' east.

Although the southern half of the Cape-Freetown route had been swept by Force H (*Sussex* and *Shropshire*) between 14–22 October, Admiral Lyon decided, in view of the *Llanstephan Castle*'s signal, on a new and complete sweep along the whole route. The two cruisers were ordered to search up to St Helena while Force K (*Ark Royal* and *Renown*) with the *Neptune* and four destroyers, sailed from Freetown to cover the northern end.

Both searches were unsuccessful – although the German steamer *Uhenfels*, which had escaped from Lourenço Marques, was spotted by one of the *Ark Royal*'s aircraft and taken in prize by the destroyer *Hereward*.

The first half of November was, as far as the British were concerned, comparatively quiet on both sides of the Atlantic; and on the 3rd the Admiralty told Admiral Lyon that all German capital ships were apparently in home waters. It appeared, therefore, that the pocket battleship – still thought to be the *Admiral Scheer*, thanks to Langsdorff's ruse – had returned home, and the raider reported by the *Llanstephan Castle* was only an armed merchantman.[1]

Here, then, was a good opportunity for resting the hunting groups, and at the same time the Admiralty ordered that Force G (*Cumberland* and *Exeter*) should change places with Force H (*Sussex* and *Shropshire*), so that Commodore Harwood should have the balanced and long-endurance hunting group that he so greatly desired.

Admiral Lyon had planned that the *Sussex* and *Shropshire*, which had arrived at the Cape on 7 November, should sweep towards Durban, arriving there on the 11th. This would have taken them within 160 miles – five hours' steaming – of the *Graf Spee* when she sank the *Africa Shell* on 15 November.

But on the 5th, however, he ordered the two cruisers to sail on the 11th for a position off St Helena to change over with the *Cumberland* and *Exeter*. Despite the fact that on the 8th the Admiralty cancelled their signal about German capital ships being in home waters, and said that the *Admiral Scheer* was now believed to be in the Indian Ocean, Admiral Lyon still sailed the two cruisers for St Helena, away from the Indian Ocean.

Bad weather delayed the departure of the *Cumberland* and *Exeter* from the Plate, where the latter had been damaged when her oiler cast off in a heavy sea. Before the exchange could take place it was cancelled.

The reason was not hard to guess: the *Graf Spee* had, under the guise of the *Admiral Scheer*, struck again. The Naval Officer-in-Charge, Simonstown, signalled to the Admiralty on the 16th that the *Africa Shell* had been attacked off Lourenço Marques the previous day and sunk by time bombs. The crew 'believed a battleship was responsible'. After that, messages poured in. The crew, shown photographs, identified their attacker as either

---

[1] Unfortunately the Admiralty could not have been more wrong: the *Graf Spee* was then 400 miles south of Cape Town, and the *Deutschland* was off Greenland.

the *Graf Spee* or the *Admiral Scheer*. From Intelligence sources, incidentally, the Naval Attaché in Buenos Aires reported that the ship was the *Graf Spee*, the only person to identify her correctly until after the battle.

Immediately the presence of an enemy raider in the Indian Ocean was confirmed, the Admiralty's Operations Division in Whitehall started a wholesale movement of warships to hunt and destroy her. Unfortunately all the hunting groups were badly placed for an immediate search, and valuable days were bound to be lost.

The First Sea Lord and his staff, meeting in the Upper War Room at 2200 on the 16th, had to put themselves in the position of the captain of the German raider and of the German Naval War Staff. They would know the British were by now aware the raider had struck more than twenty-four hours earlier. The question was – which way would the raider move? Or, more correctly, which way had she moved, since she had the vital twenty-four-hour lead?

She had plenty of ocean to choose from. She could double back into the Atlantic and then either go northward or stay in the south, down towards the Antarctic ice barrier; stay in the Indian Ocean and go northward between Madagascar and the African mainland, and strike at the shipping always converging on the Red Sea; cross the Indian Ocean diagonally towards Ceylon, and play havoc with the trade routes there; move over towards the Dutch East Indies and Bay of Bengal, focal points for the Far East sea traffic; or steam along the open wastes of the Southern Indian Ocean to attack the vulnerable shipping round Australia and New Zealand.

Every alternative – with the exception of lying in wait off the Antarctic – would provide her with plenty of merchant ships to sink or capture; any move she chose to make would achieve one of her main tasks – drawing off powerful British warships from other theatres where they were badly needed. She could pick any one of four oceans as her hunting ground.

It was late that evening before the meeting finished, having decided that the battleship *Malaya* was to stay with Force J (in the East Indies); the battleship *Ramillies* to be placed at the disposal of the C-in-C, East Indies (in whose waters the raider, by moving towards Madagascar, was now apparently operating); the cruiser *Kent* and the French *Suffren* would form Force M at Dakar, if the French agreed; Force H (*Sussex* and *Shropshire*) would return to the Cape; and Force G (*Exeter* and *Cumberland*) were to remain on their station. They also suggested that the *Renown* and *Ark Royal* should steam direct to Mauritius to fuel, thus avoiding Cape Town where their presence might be reported to the Germans. Shortly after midnight signals started going out from the Director of Operations Division (Foreign), Captain R. H. Bevan, to start the movements of these ships.

Next morning, 17 November, two German merchant ships, the *Adolph Woermann* and *Windhuk*, were reported to have sailed the previous day from Lobito, and Admiral Lyon decided that the *Sussex* and *Shropshire*, now heading for the Cape, were in a good position to intercept them. He therefore signalled them to close Lobito 'at best possible speed'. Both ships swung eastwards, and increased to more than thirty knots. The destroyers from Force K were also ordered to join in the hunt, but they were unsuccessful. However, a British merchant ship found the *Adolph Woermann* and shadowed her until the *Neptune* had time to get to the position. The Germans, however, scuttled their ship.

As the search for the German merchantman had taken Force K nearly 200 miles to the eastward of the original course from Freetown, Vice-Admiral Wells decided to steam towards the Cape by the route inside St Helena to save fuel. This may have resulted, according to Admiral Lyon, in the escape of the *Altmark*, which was waiting in the unfrequented areas west of the Cape-Freetown shipping route. The *Ark Royal* and *Renown* would have swept through these areas had they not been diverted.

The day after the scuttling of the *Adolph Woermann*, 23 November, the hunting groups were in the following positions:

Force

F	*Berwick*: in dock at Portsmouth.
	York: at Bermuda.
G	*Cumberland, Exeter*: patrolling off S America.
H	*Ajax*: off Montevideo.
	Achilles: off Rio de Janeiro.
I	*Cornwall, Eagle*: at Colombo.
	Dorsetshire: in Ceylon area.
J	*Malaya, Glorious*: Aden area.
	Ramillies: off Aden.
K	*Ark Royal, Renown*: on way to Madagascar.
L	*Furious, Repulse*: covering Atlantic convoys.
M	*Kent, Suffren*: patrolling off Sumatra.
X	*Hermes* and 2 French cruisers with
Y	*Strasbourg, Algérie*: patrolling between Pernambuco and Freetown.

From this it will be seen exactly what Langsdorff had achieved in his efforts to draw off Allied warships. [On that day *Graf Spee* was already back in the Atlantic, having returned round the Cape, and was more than 600 miles west of Simonstown. She was due to meet the *Altmark* on the 26th south-west of St Helena.]

New orders went out from the Admiralty to the *Ark Royal* and *Renown*, and the *Sussex* and *Shropshire* on 27 November to patrol south of the Cape. The plan was that they should prevent a raider passing from the Indian Ocean to the Atlantic or vice versa and, according to Admiral Lyon, 'was a good one in theory' but found to be unsuitable in practice because of local weather. This allowed aircraft to fly off from the *Ark Royal* only once in five or six days, so the patrol could not be extended far enough south to intercept a raider 'bent on evasion'.

When the *Exeter* and *Cumberland* returned to the South American coast they were sent to patrol off Rio de Janeiro while the *Achilles* fuelled from the *Olynthus* on the 22nd, ready to relieve them. It was the *Ajax*'s turn to go to the Falkland Islands for a rest and repairs, so the *Exeter* and *Cumberland* were told that at the end of their patrol they were to refuel and then take over the Plate area. Before he sailed, the Commodore told Captain Parry to move a further 800 miles to the north of Rio, and make sure the German ships in Pernambuco, reported to be ready to sail, knew that he was around. He was to return to Rio at once if any raiders were reported in the South Atlantic.

By the beginning of December the *Graf Spee*, as we have already seen, was about to strike again. Nothing had been heard of her since she sank the *Africa Shell* on 15 November; and on 22 November four British ships had been reported overdue at Freetown – the *Newton Beech* and the *Ashlea* which should have arrived on 13 October, the *Huntsman*, due on the 17th, and the *Trevanion* on 1 November.

There had, in the meantime, been plenty of rumours and conflicting reports arriving at the Admiralty, and the Director of Naval Intelligence was kept busy weeding out the crop. Again the majority originated in South America, where there was a fairly complete network of British agents and where, of course, so many German ships were waiting for an opportunity to escape back to the Fatherland.

CHAPTER 10

SUMS ON A SIGNAL PAD

On Saturday, 2 December, the British steamer *Port Chalmers* was steering a north-westerly course at fifteen knots. Many miles ahead lay the island of St Helena, where the exiled Napoleon had dragged out the last, bitter years of his life.

No one aboard the steamer realized that their own radio operator was shortly to play an anonymous but vital part in the destruction of the *Graf Spee*. But at 1245 he intercepted a signal, the first three letters of which revealed its urgency:

> *RRR RRR RRR 19° 15′ south, 05° 05′ east*, Doric Star *gunned battleship.*

The *Port Chalmers'* master, Captain Higgs, was immediately called, and four minutes later the same signal again flashed out from the *Doric Star*.

Then there was silence until 1300 when the *Doric Star* started transmitting a long dash which suddenly ceased. For many anxious minutes Captain Higgs and the wireless operator listened for any messages which would show that shore stations had received the raider report or reveal why the steamer had broken off the signal.

But none came, and at 1313 Captain Higgs ordered the *Doric Star*'s raider report to be repeated and signed with the *Port Chalmers'* signal letters, EADG. This was done, and once again the operator listened in vain for a reply.

Then at 1349 a station with the call sign GOTA was heard repeating the signal – but that was all. Once again, at 1416, the *Port Chalmers* transmitted the message and a minute later a weak station using no call sign signalled *RRR Received.*

Nothing more was picked up until seven minutes after midnight, when they were relieved to hear Walvis Bay Radio Station (in South Africa) transmitting the *Doric Star*'s raider report as repeated by the *Port Chalmers*. Six minutes later they heard Slangkop Radio, also on the South African coast, sending it. Captain Higgs was now satisfied he had done his duty: shortly the signal would be in the Admiralty and appropriate action would be taken.

But within five hours the *Port Chalmers* was again helping in the hunt for the German raider: at 0501 her wireless operator once more heard a signal being transmitted,[1] beginning with the fateful letters 'RRR'. This time the

---

[1] This was from the *Tairoa*.

Morse as received was jumbled up and the words were run together. The message he managed to write down on his pad was incomplete, but said:

RRR 21° 20′ south 310 battleship Von Scheer.

Two minutes later the ship started transmitting 'RRR' and then stopped. Nothing more was heard. No shore station acknowledged the raider report; no ship repeated it. Captain Higgs had been called and he decided at 0529 to repeat the signal. This was done ... but no one replied. It was repeated again.

Several hours later Simonstown was heard to signal a reference to aircraft from a raider attacking a ship, and as this seemed to refer to the message *Port Chalmers* was repeating[1] Captain Higgs ordered it to be re-broadcast with an explanation.

Early that Saturday, before the *Doric Star* was attacked, the First Sea Lord had signalled to Admiral Lyon that on Force I (*Cornwall, Dorsetshire* and the carrier *Eagle*) approaching the Madagascar area from Ceylon, it was possible that any raider operating there would move into the Atlantic; and because of this Force H (*Sussex* and *Shropshire*) and Force K (*Ark Royal* and *Renown*) should fuel immediately and then return to their present area. This was south of the Cape on a patrol line which should prevent a raider slipping through. Admiral Lyon, as soon as he received this order, signalled it to the two hunting groups and they immediately altered course for the Cape.

Then at 1530 that day Admiral Lyon at Freetown and the First Sea Lord in Whitehall received the dramatic signal they had been waiting for since the *Africa Shell* was sunk on 16 November. It was from the Naval Officer-in-Charge at Simonstown and said a raider report from the *Doric Star* (re-broadcast by *Port Chalmers*) had been picked up by Slangkop and Alexander Bay radio stations.

So once again the mystery of the whereabouts of the raider was partially solved, thanks – as already described – to the bravery of the *Doric Star*'s captain and her wireless operator, who stayed at his Morse key despite gunfire from the *Graf Spee*, and the alertness of the operator of the *Port Chalmers*.

Speed was now vital if the raider was to be trapped. Which way would she go? Westward into the vast wastes of the South Atlantic, north to break through into the North Atlantic, or round the Cape into the Indian Ocean? (It must be borne in mind that the Admiralty did not know the identity or possible speed of the raider, nor where she had come from.)

To the *Ark Royal, Renown, Sussex* and *Shropshire*, Admiral Lyon immediately signalled: *Force K, H to proceed with all dispatch to the Cape fuelling*

---

[1] The Morse letter 'R', standing for a raider attack, is dot dash dot, and could be confused with 'A', referring to aircraft attack, which is dot dash.

ports. The ships were already on their way and the signal said nothing of the sinking of the *Doric Star*; yet it told the four ships that something dramatic had happened. The wording of naval signals follows a time-honoured tradition: no ship is ordered to 'go' from one place to another – it is always instructed to 'proceed'. And 'proceed' means steaming at an economical speed – economical from both the oil fuel and Treasury point of view. But the phrase 'proceed with all dispatch' is a discreet and dignified way of conveying the need to go flat out because there is something in the wind.

Four minutes later a further signal from Admiral Lyon gave them rather more scope for speculation. It said briefly that the *Sussex* and *Shropshire*, without waiting for the *Ark Royal* and *Renown*, were to proceed immediately after fuelling to cover the trade route between the Cape and the latitude of St Helena.

It was too late for the *Ark Royal* and *Renown* to reach the area between Freetown and Pernambuco and 'seal the gap' in order to intercept a raider breaking out into the North Atlantic. Instead, Admiral Lyon wanted them to steam from the Cape to a position west of where the *Doric Star* had been sunk.

In a signal to the Admiralty he said: *Believe appearing from previous experience that raiders after tip and run attack on trade routes disappear to unfrequented areas, and if the raider is proceeding south and east, she will probably proceed well clear of trade routes.*

It seems from this that Admiral Lyon thought the raider was perhaps on her way to the Indian Ocean, and that she was not responsible for the previous attacks (i.e. the *Clement* and *Africa Shell*, since they were the only ones known to the Admiralty). Anyway, Admiral Pound, the First Sea Lord, did not agree, and signalled: *It should be assumed that raider will not repetition not proceed round the Cape.*

On 3 December the *Sussex* and *Shropshire* reached Simonstown three-quarters of an hour before the *Ark Royal* and *Renown* arrived at Cape Town. The Vice-Admiral Aircraft Carriers, Vice-Admiral Wells, was then ordered by Admiral Lyon to make for a position southwest of St Helena. At Vice-Admiral Wells' request this was changed to a point 500 miles farther south so that he would be in a more central position to go to Freetown, the Falklands or Rio de Janeiro.

But early next morning, while oil fuel was being pumped into the ships of the two hunting groups and mechanics aboard the *Ark Royal* worked hard to get her aircraft serviceable, the *Graf Spee* struck again and for several hours the *Port Chalmers* struggled to get the raider report from the *Tairoa* (for that was the ship) through to a shore station.

Once again Admiral Lyon received the news from the Naval Officer-in-Charge at Simonstown. At 1030 the signal arrived in Freetown saying that

Slangkop had intercepted the following garbled message from an unknown ship, assumed to be the *Tairoa*:

> *AAA Von Scheer de Madn. 0501. LOtt 21° 20' south, 3° 10' (?) datarshpt?*

This was followed by a further signal saying that a full raider report, re-broadcast by the *Port Chalmers* had been intercepted at 0530.

At 1700 that afternoon the *Sussex* and *Shropshire* left Simonstown at twenty knots and headed north-westward. The hunt for the elusive *Graf Spee* across the broad waters of the Atlantic was once more in full swing. Had long-range Coastal Command aircraft of the type that swept the North Atlantic later in the war been available, the hunting groups might have had a chance; as it was, the search for a proverbial needle in a haystack was, by comparison, an easy task. The two cruisers were followed next day by the *Ark Royal* and *Renown*.

Although Admiral Lyon had been told to assume that the raider would not go round the Cape into the Indian Ocean, and as there were clear indications from the positions radioed by the *Doric Star* and *Tairoa* that she was moving westward, the First Sea Lord was taking no chances, and the Admiralty ordered the *Cornwall* and *Gloucester* and the carrier *Eagle*, in the Indian Ocean, to establish a new patrol off the Cape.

More than ever before it was now necessary for the British to put themselves in the position of a lone raider and try to guess which way she would go next. Admiral Lyon estimated that if the enemy went northward at fifteen knots she would cross the Freetown-Pernambuco line between 9–10 December.

He therefore arranged with Vice-Admiral Duplat, the French Senior Officer of the new Force X (the cruisers *Dupleix* and *Foch*, the British carrier *Hermes* and two French destroyers, *Milan* and *Cassard*) that he should take the *Neptune* and her destroyers under his command and patrol the gap between Freetown and Pernambuco from 10 to 13 December.

Meanwhile the *Sussex* and *Shropshire* searched the area where the *Graf Spee* had been operating, but the pocket battleship was already a thousand miles away to the westward. The *Ark Royal* and *Renown* had no better luck, crossing her track on 9 December, four days too late to intercept her.

The sequence of events during the next few days, leading up to the Battle of the River Plate, are necessarily rather complicated, so it is proposed to separate the actual hunt from the rest of the story.

Once again contradictory reports started arriving at the Admiralty to confuse the issue even more. On 4 December, for instance, the French reported that the *Deutschland* had been off Pernambuco on the 2nd. This was quite feasible if the raider which sank the *Doric Star* and *Tairoa* was the

Admiral Scheer; and the possibility of having two pocket battleships marauding in the South Atlantic was an alarming one. Fortunately the men most likely to be immediately affected – those manning the merchant ships steaming in that area – were in a state of ignorance, even if not bliss.

In the meantime the *Ashlea*, *Newton Beech*, *Trevanion* and *Huntsman*, previously reported overdue, were officially considered lost. It seemed certain they had been sunk by a raider. On 7 December the *Graf Spee* sank her last victim, the *Streonshalh*; fortunately she managed to send out a raider report, part of which was received by the Admiralty, although not enough to reveal her name.

At the beginning of December, Commodore Harwood's ships were scattered along South America's Atlantic seaboard. The *Ajax* and *Exeter* were at Port Stanley in the extreme south for a much-needed rest and self-refit; the *Cumberland* was in the River Plate. The *Achilles* was a good deal farther north patrolling the Rio de Janeiro area.

On Saturday, 2 December, Commodore Harwood took the *Ajax* north from the Falkland Islands, bound for the River Plate. The whole ship's company had benefited from the rest, despite the fact that there was little social life ashore in Port Stanley. However, almost anything was a relief from the almost constant steaming of the past months, even if the Falklands were a particularly windy place and the only entertainment ashore was drinking beer out of tins.

Before leaving the islands Commodore Harwood had made certain plans. December 8 was the 25th anniversary of the Battle of the Falklands, and thinking the enemy might attempt to try to avenge the defeat, he had ordered the *Cumberland* – which was also in need of an urgent refit – to join the *Exeter* there on the 7th and patrol the islands for two days before entering Port Stanley.

Then on the same afternoon that the *Ajax* sailed a coded signal arrived in the *Ajax*'s wireless office addressed to the Commodore Commanding South America Division and marked 'Immediate'. It told Commodore Harwood that the *Doric Star* had been attacked by a pocket battleship in 19° 15′ south, 5° 5′ east. The *Ajax* continued moving northward and before dawn the Commodore was handed another 'Immediate' signal: an unknown ship had been attacked by a pocket battleship 170 miles south-west of the *Doric Star*'s position at 0500.

What was the enemy's next move to be? At present the pocket battleship was more than 3,000 miles from any of the South American focal areas. And 3,000 miles was a great distance. Yet Harwood recognized that the enemy's next objective might well be the valuable shipping off the South American coast, since it was there he could do the most damage.

In the *Ajax*'s chart room Harwood and his staff worked over a small-scale chart of the South Atlantic, and the raider's last known position was plotted. Using a cruising speed of fifteen knots, a remarkably accurate estimate, as captured German documents subsequently proved, Harwood worked out in pencil on a signal pad how long it would take the *Admiral Scheer* (for this was still the supposed name of the raider) to reach the focal areas, and how quickly the *Exeter* could come north.

The *Admiral Scheer*, he estimated, could be at Rio de Janeiro on the morning of 12 December; or the River Plate by the morning of the next day; or the Falkland Islands by the morning of the 14th. Which would she choose? It was 1,000 miles from the Falklands to the Plate, and a further 1,000 to Rio. If Harwood made a mistake in his choice the raider would escape again; if he was correct it could mean its destruction ...

Admiral Lyon had concluded that the *Admiral Scheer* would go north; but Harwood subsequently wrote: 'I decided that the Plate, with its larger number of ships and its very valuable grain and meat trade, was the vital area to defend. I therefore arranged to concentrate there my available forces in advance of the time at which it was anticipated the raider might start operations in that area.

'In order to bring this about, I made the following signal to the South America Division timed 1315 of 3 December 1939:

> *In view of report pocket battleship, amend previous dispositions,* Cumberland *self-refit at Falkland Islands as previously arranged but keep at short notice on two shafts.* Achilles *leave Rio de Janeiro so as to arrive and fuel Montevideo 0600 (Zone plus 2) 8th December,* Exeter *leave Falkland Islands for Plate AM 9th December, covering ss* Lafonia *with returning volunteers.* Ajax, Achilles, *concentrate in position 35° south, 50° west at 1600 (Zone plus 2) 10th December.* Exeter *to pass through position 090° Medanos Light 150 miles at 0700 12th December. If concentration with* Ajax *and* Achilles *not effected by that time further instructions will be issued to* Exeter ...'

His decision was now made. He had ten days to wait before he would know whether it was the right one – ten days in which the raider could round the Cape and circle Madagascar in the Indian Ocean, reach up north-westward to strike round the West Indies, go up to the Canaries, off North Africa, move down to the ice limits of the Antarctic – or make for Rio, the Falklands, or the Plate ...

The *Achilles* had been having a busy but not unenjoyable time in the north, rattling the bars outside Pernambuco and Cabadello, where German ships were caged. 'Our appearance so far north was unexpected,' Captain Parry wrote later, 'and we were reported by the Brazilian Air Force as a pocket battleship, which caused a flutter until C-in-C, South Atlantic, heard the truth.'

During this trip the crew passed the time with competitions – including an obstacle race which started off with twenty yards in diving boots, standing long jump, and an original item, a singing relay, in which each team ran right round the ship and then sang a popular song. For them, war seemed a long way off, but Captain Parry wrote: 'I remember thinking how fit and well and happy they all seemed; and how damnable it would be, if we got into action with the enemy, to face heavy casualties amongst such a fine lot of men.'

Then Commodore Harwood's signal arrived and the *Achilles* turned south for Montevideo, increasing speed to $19\frac{1}{2}$ knots in order to arrive on time. Once at Montevideo they had a great reception, and the Uruguayan authorities berthed the New Zealand cruiser alongside and instituted a very thorough guard to prevent possible sabotage. Meanwhile the *Ajax* was steaming northward. Admiral Lyon signalled the Commodore on the 5th that the cruiser *Dorsetshire* would arrive in Port Stanley on 23 December to relieve the *Exeter*, which would then cross the South Atlantic and refit at Simonstown where there were plenty of dockyard facilities.

On the same day the British Naval Attaché at Buenos Aires signalled that the 7,800-ton German steamer *Ussukuma* had left Bahia Blanca at 1900 the previous evening. The Commodore promptly ordered the *Cumberland*, which was by now on her way south to the Falklands, to search the southern arcs of the *Ussukuma*'s possible course, and at the same time he headed the *Ajax* southward at twenty-two knots in case the German ship, which was known to be short of fuel, should try to reach Montevideo inside territorial waters.

At 1910 that day smoke from a steamer was sighted and within a short time the vessel was identified as the *Ussukuma*. She was ordered to heave to and a boarding party from the *Ajax* was put aboard. But they were too late – the Germans had started scuttling. By the time they reached the engine room sea water was covering the valves. Captain Woodhouse recalled them when the ship took on a dangerous list and the ship sank during the night. Her crew were made prisoners, and they were transferred to the *Cumberland* when she arrived shortly after dawn next day and the *Ajax* went in to refuel from the *Olynthus* in San Borombon Bay.

On 10 December at 1000 the *Achilles* joined the *Ajax* in a position 230 miles east of Montevideo, and at 0700 two days later the *Exeter* joined them. It was the first time three of Commodore Harwood's ships had ever worked together.

He wrote: 'I then proceeded towards position 32° south, 47° west. This position was chosen from my Shipping Plot as being at that time the most congested part of the diverted shipping routes, i.e. the point where I estimated a raider could do most damage to British shipping.'

At noon Commodore Harwood made a signal to Captain Parry in the *Achilles* and Captain Bell in the *Exeter*, which gave, in a few words, his plan for battle. It was brief and it was clear. In Nelson's time the two captains would have joined him and Captain Woodhouse for dinner aboard the *Ajax* and he would have discussed it with them over a bottle of good port.[1]

The three captains would then have talked over every eventuality with him; and they would have gone back to their ships knowing exactly what move to make at a given flag signal. In that way signalling would be kept down to a minimum, and in an emergency each captain could act on his own initiative knowing exactly what Nelson had in mind and what he would have ordered them to do. But in 1939, more than a century later, it was not necessary.

Modern weapons had not, at this stage, complicated the tactical issue; they only increased the number of specialist officers and ratings carried on board. Harwood had had many weeks to consider the tactics he would use: since the attack on the *Clement*, which revealed a raider's presence, any one or two of his cruisers might have happened on a pocket battleship.

Now, on 12 December, if his assessment was correct, he would be employing those tactics within a few hours. And in a few more hours, if he was still alive, he would know whether they had been the correct ones.

In most men's lives there comes a time when the whole future is precariously balanced. For Nelson it had been the few hours before the Battle of the Nile, which for him could have ended in disaster but in fact resulted in fame, further opportunities, and the final victory at Trafalgar.

Now Henry Harwood, a month short of his fifty-second birthday and hardly known outside the Royal Navy and his own circle of friends, had also reached that point. Nelson had won at the Nile by brilliant, daring and totally unexpected tactics. Had they failed his enemies and the politicians would have had him sent home in disgrace. That was the price for losing when gambling with high stakes.

Harwood's small force, which would be outgunned from the start, could only sink or cripple a pocket battleship by superior tactics. There would be no scope for the unexpected move which would take the enemy unawares that Nelson had employed at the Nile; but there was just as much scope for mistakes.

So at noon, as the signal giving his plan was sent, Harwood had reached the crisis for which thirty-six years of naval training had prepared him. Britannia Naval College in 1903 as a cadet; service as a midshipman in the

---

[1] It had been variously reported that before the battle the captains did in fact meet on board the *Ajax*; but this was not the case, and the suggestion detracts from Conmmodore Harwood's feat.

London and *Bulwark*; Torpedo Officer in the cruiser *Sutlej* in the Atlantic and the *Royal Sovereign* in the Grand Fleet during the First World War; the cruiser *Southampton*; Plans Division at Admiralty; the Third Battle Squadron; Commander in the *Cumberland*; the Imperial Defence College; commander of the cruiser *London* as Flag Captain and Chief Staff Officer, First Cruiser Squadron; on the staff of the RN War College between 1934 and 1936; and then, in September 1936, the proud moment when he hoisted his Broad Pendant in the *Exeter* as Commodore Commanding the South America Division.

The future held what? Bitter disappointment or death after failing to destroy the pocket battleship, a task most senior officers in the Navy would give up a pension to attempt? Or victory, promotion, and all that goes with it? Or was his deduction wrong in any case, and the pocket battleship now hundreds of miles away, steaming in a different direction?

Supposing the enemy was steaming for Rio de Janeiro when he had placed his three cruisers off the Plate? Supposing the pocket battleship was approaching the Falkland Islands, to attack and slip into the broad waters of the Pacific? Supposing ...

There were plenty of questions that day; but there were no answers.

The Commodore planned to attack immediately by day or by night, and he would split his force into two divisions – the *Exeter*, with her heavier 8-inch guns forming one, and the *Ajax* and *Achilles*, with their less effective and shorter-ranged 6-inch guns, forming the other. Both divisions would attack from slightly different directions so that each could spot the other's fall of shot (flank marking) and also force the enemy to divide his attention. This splitting of his main force was unorthodox – it would have been more usual to keep the three ships concentrated – but it might keep the enemy guessing.

As mentioned earlier, Harwood's signal to his captains was a masterpiece of brevity; and as Captain Parry wrote later, 'His intentions were so clear that practically no signals were made during the action, because we all knew exactly what to do.'

The signal said:

> *My policy with three cruisers in company versus one pocket battleship. Attack at once by day or night. By day act as two units. 1st Division* (Ajax *and* Achilles) *and* Exeter *diverged to permit flank marking. First Division will concentrate gunfire. By night ships will normally remain in company in open order. Be prepared for the signal ZMM, which is to have the same meaning as MM^1 except that for Division read single ship.*

---

[1] MM – 'Commanders of Divisions are to turn their Divisions to course ... starting with the rear Division.'

He amplified this signal later as follows:

> *My object in the signal ZMM is to avoid torpedoes and take the enemy by surprise and cross his stern. Without further orders ships are to clear the line of fire by hauling astern of the new leading ship. The new leading ship is to lead the line without further orders so as to maintain decisive gun range.*

That evening the three ships practised the manoeuvre and also carried out concentration and flank marking exercises. Concentration of gunfire means that two or more ships act as one – the *Ajax* and *Achilles* in this instance. The *Ajax* would pass all the necessary orders, ranges, deflection and firing signals to the *Achilles*, which would apply corrections for her distance and bearing from the *Ajax*.

Concentration increases the hitting rate and prevents confusion in spotting the fall of shot since theoretically all the shells from both ships should fall simultaneously and in much the same piece of water. The two ships therefore spent some time testing the communication procedure.

The flank-marking exercises were for much the same purpose. If the two Divisions, *Exeter*, and *Ajax* and *Achilles*, could keep the enemy so that their individual lines of fire were roughly at right angles, then each could report how far 'short' or 'over' the other Division's shells were falling.

Otherwise all that the gunnery control officer in each of the three ships could do was to correct the salvoes which fell in line with the enemy. So the three cruisers passed imaginary spotting signals to each other and exercised using this information on the gunnery fire control equipment.

While they were doing that, the rest of the hunting groups were in the following positions:

Force H (*Sussex* and *Shropshire*) sweeping off the West African coast, more than 4,000 miles away;

Force I (*Eagle*, *Cornwall*, and *Gloucester*) were at Durban, more than 4,100 miles away, short of fuel after a wild goose chase into the Indian Ocean;

Force K (*Ark Royal* and *Renown*) the most powerful hunting group in the South Atlantic, were off Pernambuco, 2,000 miles northwards;

Force X (*Hermes* and the French cruisers *Dupleix* and *Foch*) with the *Neptune*, *Hardy*, *Hostile* and *Hero*, were still farther north, off St Paul Rocks.

The *Cumberland* was at the Falkland Islands; and the *Dorsetshire* was on the eve of sailing from Simonstown to relieve the *Exeter*. The submarine *Severn* was half-way between St Helena and Bahia, on her way to the Falklands, and the submarine *Clyde* was approaching Dakar.

That, then, was the scene in the South Atlantic on 12 December 1939, the eve of the Battle of the River Plate.

CHAPTER 11

GRAF SPEE IS TRAPPED

The time was 0552 on 13 December. In four minutes the upper margin of the deep-red orb that was the sun would edge above the horizon; and it would find a clear sky and a south-easterly breeze from the trade winds ruffling the low swell into lazy wavelets.

While Kapitän zur See Hans Langsdorff rested in his bridge cabin the great pocket battleship *Admiral Graf Spee* slipped through the water at fifteen knots, seeming graceful as the bow wave curved up and outwards with geometric precision from her stem; yet the easy light of early dawn could not soften the harsh shape of the six 11-inch guns jutting aggressively from the curved armour plating of their turrets.

The quartermaster at the wheel was having an easy watch — it was no trouble for him to keep the ship on her course of 155 degrees, and he was lost in his own thoughts. In eight minutes' time he would receive a curt order to come round to 335 degrees, north-westward, the next course laid out by the Navigator to ensure a thorough search of the area.

There had been something of an anti-climax at first light: Langsdorff's hopes of finding a British merchantman in sight — for visibility was soon twenty miles, somewhat reduced by mirages — were dashed. He half-expected to find a liner, the *Highland Monarch*; and today, just when he wanted it, the Arado float-plane was out of action. An engine block had cracked the day before and that had meant dismantling the whole engine. The wings too, had been dismantled, so that the aircraft looked like a trussed turkey waiting to be put in an oven.

Four minutes to sunrise on 13 December 1939 ... lookouts leisurely swung their binoculars through their allocated arcs, each watching a segment of a circle of which the *Graf Spee* formed the centre. Each searched his sector with the ease of precision which comes only with long practice.

With the first light it was always a tense job, since the rolling back of darkness could reveal a powerful enemy within gunshot; but now, with the whole sky becoming blue and the sun soon to rise, confidence came back as usual and barely comprehended fears slid back into the limbo of men's spirits.

Then suddenly one man perched high up above the bridge saw, fine on the starboard bow, two thin masts on the horizon, looking like pins stuck on the far edge of a vast grey-green pin cushion. The curvature of the earth hid the ship to which they belonged; but a lone raider has no friends. All masts, all smoke, all aircraft – all belong to the enemy.

A quick check on the bearing, a harsh call to the bridge: two masts in sight. Then binoculars back on the bearing with eyes straining to see if they belong to a merchantman or a warship . . .

The officer of the watch rapidly passed the word for the Captain; and that was hardly done before lookouts were reporting four more thin masts. Langsdorff reached the bridge just as the first estimated ranges arrived – about seventeen miles. Someone passed him a pair of binoculars.

'Maintain course and speed,' he said. 'Action Stations.'

Alarm rattlers clattered throughout the ship to startle hundreds of men from sleep. Pulling on clothing with the near-conditioned reflexes of trained but sleepy seamen, they started running to their action stations – to the guns, to rangefinders, to magazines and damage control centres, to first-aid stations and a dozen other positions. Water-tight doors clanged shut, hatches slammed down and were secured with clips. In a few seconds the ship became a honeycomb of water-tight compartments.

Fregattenkapitän Ascher, the Chief Gunnery Officer, went to the Director Control Tower with his team of spotting observers, layers and trainers, and the great rangefinder high above the bridge moved a few degrees until the nearest masts appeared in the eyepieces. Ranges were called into telephones and Ascher waited . . .

Korvettenkapitän (Ing) Klepp, the Chief Engineer, was soon in the engine room reporting all was well with the great diesels; Kapitänleutnant Brutzer, was standing by his beloved torpedo tubes; all over the ship fifty-four officers and 1,080 petty-officers and ratings waited for orders from Langsdorff: orders which could lead to the destruction of another British merchantman, or – and nine 'kills' without trouble were making them over-confident – the remote possibility of action against a British warship. In any case, hadn't they been told the *Graf Spee* was almost invincible?

As Langsdorff made his way to the flying bridge an officer reported to him that the pocket battleship was cleared for action. The time was 0600, four minutes after sunrise.

By now more than a dozen powerful binoculars, as well as the main rangefinder on the fighting top, and the smaller one on the foretop, were trained on the ships ahead.

What were they? Merchantmen? If so, what size? Any sign of an escort? What was their course? Where were they bound? In a few moments an excited lookout reported he could identify the one farthest to the right: she was the British cruiser *Exeter* . . .

An officer hurriedly grabbed a reference book, leafed through the pages and started reading out details of her guns, armour and speed. The photograph showing her very tall masts was compared with the vague silhouette on the horizon. There was no doubt about it – she was the *Exeter*, with six 8-inch guns . . .

Then more reports from the lookouts: the two ships to the left had low-lying superstructure. Two destroyers, Langsdorff noted. They would be screening the cruiser in case there were any U-boats about.

Briefly he summed up his views to his officers gathered round him on the bridge: the *Exeter* and the destroyers were obviously protecting a convoy which at the moment was out of sight. He would attack immediately – the *Graf Spee* had not much to fear from the *Exeter* – and close to an effective fighting range before the *Exeter* had raised enough steam to make her best speed. Then the *Exeter* and her attendant destroyers disposed of, the *Graf Spee* could finish off the convoy.

The bridge telegraphs were altered and in the engine room corresponding indicators pointed to full speed, and the pocket battleship's diesels increased their thundering power. On deck, ratings clawed at halyards and her Battle Ensigns ran up to flap in the wind, now increased to almost gale force by the ship's forward speed. At the same time a masthead flag was reported to have been run up by the *Exeter*.

Five minutes later an officer turned to Langsdorff: the two smaller ships, he said, were not destroyers. They were cruisers of the *Ajax* class. He added – quite unnecessarily, since Langsdorff knew the details by heart – that they mounted eight 6-inch guns and had a designed speed of thirty-two knots . . .

Thus, in a few seconds, the whole situation had changed alarmingly . . . and while Langsdorff thought, the *Graf Spee* raced at twenty-four knots towards the cruisers crossing her bow. Each couple of minutes' thought brought the ships nearly a mile closer . . . A lucky hit by an 8-inch shell from the *Exeter* and nowhere to repair the *Graf Spee* . . . These British cruisers could make at least thirty knots compared with his twenty-four . . . If he could not sink them could he shake them off in daylight – darkness was more than fifteen hours away? . . . Or would they dog him like terriers round a slower, snarling badger, their yelps bringing up more powerful reinforcements?

Rapidly Langsdorff made up his mind and changed his original plan.

From the Graf Spee's *Action Report: At 0612 course was changed to 115 for a running fight to starboard. The enemy steered an easterly course. The light cruisers pulled ahead to the east at high speed so that their distance from the Exeter quickly increased . . .*

At 0617 at 197 hectometres [21,000 yards] the Graf Spee *opened fire with its main battery on the* Exeter. *Four salvoes of each turret shot at first base-fused shells for better observation purposes, afterwards impact fuses (Kz) were ordered in order to obtain the greatest possible damage to the lightly-armoured turrets and superstructure and through hits on its hull to reduce the ship's speed . . .*

CHAPTER 12

OPEN FIRE. G 25

If your name was Henry Harwood, Commodore, Royal Navy, then at 0610, as the *Graf Spee* identified[1] the two smaller cruisers, you were having a well-earned rest in your bunk in the *Ajax*, which was steaming at fourteen knots and zig-zagging about a mean course of 060 degrees, followed by the *Achilles* and *Exeter*.

From 0450 to 0540 the crews of all three cruisers had been at Dawn Action Stations as usual. Night had almost imperceptibly merged into the grey of dawn; and then it had been daylight, with visibility quickly lifting from a few hundred yards to twenty miles.

And there was no sign of the German raider – or indeed, any ships at all. The whole 360 degrees of the horizon was empty. For Harwood there was a moment of disappointment and the thought that his conclusion that the enemy raider would be lured to the Plate area might be wrong: that while he was waiting here more merchant ships 1,000 miles away might already have been sunk without being able to send out RRR reports . . .

But he had made his decision and acted: there was no going back on it now. He could only wait – wait until his lookouts spotted something, or his wireless operators picked up a signal addressed *To CCSAD:* IMMEDIATE . . . which would give him news.

With the last of the dawn, he had exercised his three ships, using the signal *ZMM*, in the manoeuvres they would use in action against a pocket battleship. A practice shoot together, since the *Ajax* and *Achilles* would concentrate their gunfire, was planned for later in the day.

Finally, at 0540, the crews went from Dawn Action Stations to Day Defence Stations. Only one gun in each turret was left manned and certain of the ships' boilers were shut off to save fuel.

If your name was Edgar Duncan Lewin, Lieutenant, and pilot of the *Ajax*'s Seafox aircraft, you were officer of the watch and standing on the cruiser's bridge talking to Lt-Cdr Richard Pennefather. You had control of a vessel which cost £1,480,097 to build and needed another £133,000 a year to maintain. Yet if she went into battle your Action Station would be in the Seafox, spotting the fall of shot.

If your name was Charles Woodhouse, Captain and Commanding Officer of the *Ajax*, ultimately responsible for everything connected with the cruiser and the thirty-nine officers and 554 men who made up her crew, you were in your sea cabin after spending the previous hours on the bridge,

[1] Her much taller fighting top gave her a far greater visibility range than the cruisers.

manoeuvring under the command of Commodore Harwood.

But if you were one of five officers and forty-eight ratings in the *Exeter*, or four ratings in the *Achilles*, or seven ratings in the *Ajax*, you had less than two hours to live.

Lt Richard Washbourn, a New Zealander, was the Principal Control Officer in the *Achilles*, and at the first sign of dawn he had gone to Action Stations – as every warship had done each morning since 28 August. Captain Parry had climbed up to the bridge and taken over from Washbourn, who had then scrambled up to the Director Control Tower. After the usual testing of electrical circuits and communications he had reported to Captain Parry 'Main armament closed up and cleared away', using the voicepipe to the bridge. Then had come the usual exercises, which stopped as night slowly changed into the grey of dawn. While visibility increased, he and his men in the DCT used their powerful binoculars and telescopes to watch the diffuse and indeterminate line where the sea merged with the sky.

There had been nothing on the horizon and as broad daylight brought maximum visibility Washbourn had reported to the Captain, 'Horizon clear, Sir. May I fall the quarters out?' With the order 'Sound the disperse. Close up the cruising watch', Washbourn had climbed down to the bridge where Captain Parry was standing with the Navigator, Lt Cowburn.

Normally Captain Parry went straight down to his cabin to shave and have a bath; but this morning he stayed on the bridge longer than usual, talking to Washbourn about the gunnery exercises planned for later in the day. He was on the point of going to his cabin when the bridge lookout reported 'Smoke bearing Red one double oh, Sir.'[1]

The smoke had been sighted a minute earlier in the *Ajax*, at 0610. It was a vague blur just above the horizon on the port beam when Leading Signalman Swanston reported it to Lewin. It was probably from a British or neutral merchantman bound for the Plate. But today all smoke had to be regarded with a certain amount of suspicion. It might be caused by best-quality Welsh steaming coal shovelled into a furnace by perspiring Scots stokers, or by the oil-fired engines of a neutral liner. Or by a German pocket battleship.

Still, it was unlikely that an enemy raider would advertise her presence with a lot of funnel smoke; and in any case they were in fact due to meet a particular merchantman. The Commodore had previously given a coded signal to the *Exeter* so that she could pass it to a British steamer, which would, on arriving at Montevideo, pass it on to the British Consul. In this

[1] For lookout purposes the horizon is divided into two 180-degree arcs – from 0 degrees (dead ahead) to 180 (astern) on either side. 'Red' signifies the port side, green the starboard. Thus 'Red one double-oh' is 100 degrees on the left side – 10 degrees abaft the beam.

way the cruisers could avoid breaking wireless silence.

So Lewin went to the voicepipes and told first Captain Woodhouse of the sighting, and then Commodore Harwood. The Commodore told him to order the *Exeter* to investigate and, if it was a British ship, pass the signal. In the meantime the *Exeter* had sighted the smoke and ran up a flag signal *Smoke bearing 320 degrees.*

A few seconds later Leading Signalman Swanston was sending the Commodore's order to Captain Bell:

> *Investigate smoke bearing 324 degrees. If this is a British merchantman bound for the Plate due to get into harbour soon, transfer your signal to her.*

The time was 0614. The *Exeter* acknowledged the order and hauled round to port out of the line, towards the smoke lying to the north-west.

A few moments later Swanston reported to Lt Lewin that he thought there was a pocket battleship under the smoke. Lewin and Pennefather both had a good look with their binoculars and decided that what looked like a warship's fighting top was in fact a plume of black smoke.

Very soon, however, Lewin became converted to Swanston's point of view, and sounded the alarm rattlers. He would face a good deal of leg-pulling if he was wrong, but precious minutes would be saved if he was right.

Captain Woodhouse came to the bridge and Lewin explained the position. Pennefather, who was still rather doubtful about the identity of the strange ship, was sent aloft, where he would have a better field of view.

By now the *Exeter* and the *Graf Spee* were approaching each other at a mean speed of forty miles an hour. Every second found them climbing towards each other over the curvature of the earth. In the *Graf Spee* 1,134 men prepared to meet an enemy; in the *Exeter* everyone was alert, waiting to see if they would find a friend.

The *Graf Spee* had the advantage of height: from the lookout position high on her fighting top she could see farther over the curve of the earth than the smaller cruisers. This, plus the fact that she knew she had no friendly ships at hand, was giving her nearly twenty-four minutes start[1] in the battle for her life which was to be called The River Plate.

Less than two minutes after the *Exeter* turned towards the smoke the fighting top of a warship was seen and at 0616 Captain Bell ordered the following signal to be flashed to Commodore Harwood in the *Ajax*:

> *I think it is a pocket battleship.*

The Torpedo Officer, Lt-Cdr C. J. Smith, then definitely identified her as a pocket battleship of the *Admiral Scheer* class.

Immediately flag 'N', a yellow triangle with a blue tongue, followed by

---

[1] On the assumption that the times given in the German report are correct.

the numerals 322, was run up: *Enemy in sight bearing 322.*

The Graf Spee would be opening fire any minute ... Action Stations was sounded, the main wireless office in the *Exeter* was warned, and all depth charges in the traps were released – there was no point in having high explosive lying around waiting for an enemy shell to detonate it.

Then her Battle Ensigns were run up. They were White Ensigns which streamed at the fore- and main-mastheads, from the yardarm and from the gaff. There were four in case one was shot away; and they would only be hauled down at the end of the battle. If they were hauled down before then it would mean only one thing – the *Exeter* had surrendered.

Now, with her crew at Action Stations, her guns loaded, aimed and ready to fire, her boilers rapidly increasing to full power, and Battle Ensigns flying, the *Exeter* was ready for the unequal fight.

In the *Ajax*, while Pennefather was beginning his laborious climb, Captain Woodhouse called to the Director Control Tower above and behind the bridge to see if they could see anything; but apart from the smoke they had nothing to report.

Then Pennefather, from his vantage point up the mast, shouted down to the bridge. What was he saying? The wind and the noise carried his voice away. Captain Woodhouse, straining his ears, was conscious of a signalman reading a message coming from the *Exeter*. Pennefather shouted again: 'It's a pocket battleship!' At that moment the signalman reported the *Exeter*'s message.

The Commodore had been right.

After the alarm rattlers had sounded earlier throughout the cruiser the Commodore had come up to the compass platform. On the port beam his enemy appeared as a blur of smoke stemming from a small, dark and vague shape on the horizon; the *Achilles* was astern; and on the port quarter the *Exeter* headed towards it, her Battle Ensigns being run up.

His three ships were already in the formation he wanted them – the *Exeter* hauled out of the line and preparing to attack from one direction, and the *Ajax* and *Achilles* forming another division to attack from another direction. There was no need to hoist *ZMM*.

Now he had the *Graf Spee* within range; but she might wipe out his small force by the sheer weight of her 11-inch shells[1], or keep them at arm's length and escape at night. He had first to send an enemy report – which would also bring reinforcements – as soon as possible, and within a few minutes his wireless operators were transmitting his signals. To the *Cumberland* 1,000 miles to the south, waiting at Port Stanley, to the Senior

---

[1] A broadside of the *Graf Spee*'s 11-inch guns weighed roughly 4,140 lbs against the 900 lbs of each of the 6-inch cruisers and the 1,600 lbs of the *Exeter*. The *Graf Spee*'s secondary armament of 5.9-inch was, of course, only a fraction smaller than the smaller cruisers' 6-inch guns.

Officer of Force K (*Renown* and *Ark Royal*) 2,000 miles to the northward, off Pernambuco; and to the Senior Officer of Force X (the French cruisers *Dupleix* and *Foch* and the British carrier *Hermes*) and the *Neptune* and three destroyers still further north of St Paul Rocks, went the signal:

IMMEDIATE. *One pocket battleship 034° south 049° west, course 275 degrees.*

By this time Harwood could see the *Graf Spee*'s shells falling round the *Exeter*; the splashes showed she was shooting fairly accurately. Then, through his binoculars, he saw the *Exeter*'s guns belching smoke. The time was 0618.

Suddenly shells from the *Graf Spee* threw up gouts of water near the *Ajax*; she had turned one 11-inch turret on to the First Division.

'It appeared at this stage as if the enemy was undecided as to her gunnery policy,' Harwood wrote later. 'Her turrets were working under different controls, and she shifted target several times before eventually concentrating both turrets on the *Exeter*.'

Then, as the *Exeter*'s shells fell near the *Graf Spee*, Harwood saw the pocket battleship begin to turn to port, away from the *Exeter* and on to a course parallel with the *Ajax* and *Achilles*. Was she going to keep the cruiser in range of her 11-inch but far enough away to be out of range of the 8-inch and 6-inch guns?

As Rate Officers in the three cruisers rapidly passed the *Graf Spee*'s new course to the transmitting stations and Director Layers trained their sights round further to starboard, the turrets followed obediently. In accordance with his plans Harwood's first order, after seeing that the 'enemy report' had been sent, was to alter course towards the *Graf Spee*.

A brief order and within seconds a signal was being sent to the *Achilles*:

Alter course together to 340 degrees.

The time was 0620.

Then a second order was sent to the *Achilles*:

Open fire. G 25.[1]

Captain Langsdorff noted: 'The first salvo was observed to be short. The following ranging salvo located the target and about four minutes after opening fire the first hit was observed on the *Exeter*'s fo'c'sle. *Exeter* returned the fire about two minutes later. Her first salvoes were short.'

The Battle of the River Plate had begun.

---

[1] G 25 – speed 25 knots.

CHAPTER 13

BROADSIDES ... SHOOT

When the lookout in the *Achilles* had called out 'Smoke bearing Red one double-oh, Sir,' Captain Parry and Lt Washbourn had walked un-hurriedly over to the port wing of the bridge. Both of them had heard scores of similar reports before, and each time a merchant ship had come into sight. There was no tension, only boredom ...

Captain Parry levelled his binoculars at the smoke and Washbourn looked through the Principal Control Officer's sight – powerful binoculars mounted on a moveable arm.

There was, however, no mistaking what they saw. There was a thin feather of orange-brown smoke hanging low on the horizon. Beneath it they could see a gunnery control tower and a mast; but it was a gunnery control tower and a mast of a peculiar and unmistakable design.

They both turned to each other.

'My God,' said Captain Parry, 'it's a pocket battleship. Sound the alarm, Pilot. Warn the engine room that we will be going on to full speed shortly, and are going into action.'

He wrote later: 'I remember a rather sickening feeling in the pit of my tummy as I realized we were in for an action in which the odds were hardly on our side. Luckily there wasn't much time to think about that.'

As Washbourn started to climb back to the DCT the Chief Yeoman of Signals, Lincoln Martinson, reported: '*Exeter* has hoisted Flag N, Sir ... "Enemy in sight".'

On the bridge Cowburn had automatically taken over from Washbourn as officer of the watch and from now on would give all helm and engine orders (Captain Parry would give him all the instructions, addressing him as 'Pilot').

The first order had come very promptly.

'Open out to about three or four cables from the *Ajax*, Pilot, and keep loose formation. Weave when the pocket battleship fires at us, but don't use too much rudder.'

By that time the ship's company were racing to their Action Stations. Having fallen out at 0550, almost every one of them not at Defence Stations had turned in again. Sleep was very precious in wartime, and the forty minutes before 'Call the hands' at 0630 was not to be missed.

As the alarm rattlers had sounded, followed by a bugle's urgent doh soh-soh, doh soh-soh calling them to 'Action' (which was not preceded and followed by the 'G' indicating 'exercise'), they tumbled out of their hammocks and ran to their quarters in all sorts of garb – pyjamas, underclothes, shorts or anything they could grab on the way.

Down in the engine room Lt Jasper Abbott, a small, precise man with a neatly-trimmed black beard, worked under the Commander (E) in the ever-present task of using sluggish fuel oil to turn water into super-heated steam – a transformation undreamt of by ancient alchemists intent on changing base metals into gold, but far more valuable. It was steam which at 700 degrees Fahrenheit was invisible, yet three times hotter than boiling water; steam which could strip the flesh from a man's body within seconds.

Each pair of the *Achilles*'s six boilers supplied steam to an engine room, forming a self-contained unit. If one unit was damaged and flooded, another could keep the ship moving at a reasonable speed.

While the men in the engine room were hard at work providing more steam for the ever-hungry turbines, the guns' crews were getting ready. Lt Washbourn had climbed into his seat in the Director Control Tower and pulled on headphones and the microphone transmitter. In a moment he would be in communication with all the gun turrets and the Transmitting Station. He was preparing to unleash more destructive power in one minute than a medieval emperor dreamt of in a lifetime.

He switched on the microphone.

'Control, TS. Testing communications ... Report when closed up ... Enemy in sight bearing Red nine oh ... All quarters with CPBC[1] and full charges load!'

These orders, repeated with loud shouts in the gun turrets, caused an exchange of meaningful glances: the men, in their hurried dash to their positions, had no time to glean any news. Now they realized something was very definitely in the wind.

By this time the whole Director Control Tower had trained round towards the enemy, like an owl with many eyes. Washbourn was looking through stereoscopic binoculars at the *Graf Spee* on the horizon. Between his knees was the gun-ready lamp box with eight indicators on its face. Each of these would glow red as the gun it represented was loaded and ready to fire.

Sitting on Washbourn's right was the Spotting Officer, Sergeant Samuel Trimble. This big, red-faced Ulsterman was better known as 'Baggy' Trimble, and his job was spotting the fall of the *Achilles*'s shells and reporting them to the Transmitting Station.

On Washbourn's left was the Rate Officer, Mr Eric Watts. Rotund, placid and very competent, he was the Gunner. He had the difficult job of estimating the *Graf Spee*'s course and speed, and any alterations she might

[1] Common Pointed Ballistic Capped: the then latest six-inch armour-piercing shell. The 'ballistic cap' was a light steel nose fitted on the shell to streamline it and so increase the range for a given charge.

make, and reporting constantly to the Transmitting Station.

Behind these three men were Telegraphist Frank Stennett, who would be the link with the *Ajax* when the two ships' gunfire was concentrated, Telegraphist Neville Milburn, who would pass on flank-marking reports from the *Exeter*, and Boy Dorsett, a young New Zealand lad who operated the telephones to the turrets.

Above the telegraphists, was the Position-in-Line (PIL) Rangetaker, Able Seaman Shirley, a New Zealander. Using a special instrument, and with his head stuck out of the DCT, he was taking the range of the *Ajax* to get the correction for the position in line when gunfire was concentrated and the *Achilles* was using the *Ajax*'s fire orders.

In the forward section of the DCT, sitting lower than the others, were four more men. Two of them operated the Director Sight, the master eye by which all the ship's guns were aimed. And they were men hand-picked by Washbourn: men who had keen eyes and keen minds, who would not get flustered or frightened, and who could be relied on, whether the ship was rolling or pitching in a heavy sea, zig-zagging, burning or sinking, to go on turning the hand wheels which would keep the Director Sight, and, in turn, the guns aimed at the chosen enemy.

Working at the left side of the sight, an eye glued to a stabilized telescope, was the Director Layer, Petty Officer Alfred Maycock. He was responsible for laying the guns vertically on the enemy (elevation) and, when ordered, pressing the trigger which would fire them simultaneously. On his right was the Director Trainer, Petty Officer William Headon. Using his special telescope, he trained the guns horizontally.

The other two men with them were the Range to Elevation and Deflection unit Operator, Able Seaman Shaw, and the Cross-Level Operator, Ordinary Seaman Rogers.

Below the DCT was the rangefinder. It worked like a pair of vast human eyes except that Chief Petty Officer William Bonniface and a New Zealander, Able Seaman Gould, focused them; and instead of a brain to register the range, there were dials which were repeated in various parts of the ship.

But although the DCT and the rangefinder were the ship's eyes and the kingdom of the Gunnery Officer, a mechanical 'brain' several decks below, protected by armour, worked out all the complicated mathematics which would ensure that the shells, if Headon and Maycock aimed the Director Sight correctly, arrived on the target.

This 'brain' was officially called the Admiralty Fire Control Table and it was situated in the Transmitting Station. It was a fantastic product of scientific designing, and when it had certain information fed into it, it transmitted a series of answers, or corrections, to the guns.

When the enemy position (from the Director Sight), range (from the rangefinders), speed and course (from the Rate Officer), and fall of shot (from the Spotting Officer), were fed in, it—

Indicated how much the guns had to be trained left or right;

Gave the correct angle of elevation for them;

Worked out precisely where the *Achilles'* shells had to fall, allowing for the problem that she and the *Graf Spee* would each be going in different directions at upwards of twenty-five knots, and the shells would be in the air for almost a minute, and applied the necessary correction;

Allowed for the fact that the right-handed spin given to the shell by the rifling of the gun made it wander to the right;

Allowed for the effect of wind on the shell while it was in flight, and for the temperature and barometric pressure;

Caused the aim of each gun to converge on the target (if the guns were aimed in the same direction they would shoot on parallel lines and the shells would fall the same distance apart as the guns were in the ship. This spread would be far too great);

Allowed for the fact that, when firing over the bow, each gun would be at different distances from the enemy and would require slightly different elevations.

Thus, as Maycock and Headon aimed the Director Sight at the *Graf Spee*, the enemy's elevation and bearing were transmitted to the 'Table' and also to the guns, which trained round in the same direction.

But the Director Sight was aimed directly at the enemy. Since the shells would be in the air for a minute, the guns would have to be aimed at where the *Graf Spee* would be in a minute's time. This 'aim off', called 'deflection', was worked out by the Table and sent electrically to the guns.

But in far less time than it took you to read this, Washbourn was giving his next order:

'Broadsides.'

Every gun in A and B turrets forward and X and Y turrets aft was now loaded with a 112-lb shell and a 30-lb cordite charge. Breeches were closed, and in each breech was placed a small tube like a rifle cartridge with the bullet removed. In the base of the tube – which was filled with explosive – was a thin iridio-platinum wire, and when the Director Layer pressed the trigger an electric current would flow across and fuse it, firing the explosive which would in turn explode the cordite charge.

Quickly the gun-ready lamps in the box between Washbourn's knees flickered on – one, two (X turret, manned by the Royal Marines, was the first to be ready), three, four, five . . .

Washbourn leaned over and spoke into the voicepipe to the bridge.

'Captain, Sir.'

'Yes, Guns?' replied Captain Parry.

'Ready to open fire.'

'Open fire.'

Washbourn glanced at the gun-ready box: all eight lamps were glowing. He spoke into the microphone:

'Shoot!'

The fire going in the DCT sounded its 'ting ting' and Petty Officer Headon, his left hand automatically spinning the elevating hand wheel to keep the Director Sight aimed at the base of the *Graf Spee*'s foremast, squeezed the trigger and completed the circuit.

Electricity flowed across the iridio-platinum bridges – far more than their resistance of 0.9 ohm could take – and fused them. Spurts of flame leapt out to explode the 30-lb charges of cordite, packed like long strings of macaroni in silk bags, and turn it into gas – far more than the chambers could hold without bursting. Something had to give way – and it was the shells.

They were thrust up the barrels, spinning one and a half times as they engaged in the thirty-six grooves of the rifling, and leaving at more than 2,000 miles an hour. They would rise nearly 19,000 feet into the atmosphere before plunging down 60.89 seconds later; and they would burst between twenty-two and twenty-seven millionths of a second after striking with a velocity of 1,500 feet per second.

But once the shells left the barrels the guns' crews were concerned with the next broadside. Each gun, weighing six and three quarter tons was flung back by the enormous power of the cordite and stopped after thirty and a half inches by the recoil cylinder, and then thrust into position again by the run-out springs.

Another shell and another charge came up the hoists to each gun from the magazines, which were hidden behind armour well below the waterline; the breeches were flung open and blasts of compressed air automatically cleared the cordite chambers of any burning residue; soaking-wet rammers – better known as 'woolly 'eaded bastards' – were thrust up the chambers to clean them and cool the mushroom head of the breech block; shells were swung into the chambers and rammed home; charges were slid in after them; the tubes were changed and the breeches closed.

One after another the eight gun-ready lamps in front of Washbourn flicked on again.

Maycock and Headon were still keeping the Director Sight on the *Graf Spee*; Sergeant Trimble was still waiting for the shells to land and Watts was reporting on the pocket battleship's course and bearing. The Deflection had come up from the Table to train the guns round slightly.

'Shoot!' said Lt Washbourn in the *Achilles*.

'Shoot!' said Lt Desmond Dreyer in the *Ajax*.

'Shoot!' said Lt-Cdr Richard Jennings in the *Exeter*.

The *Achilles* had opened fire at 0622, and the *Ajax* at 0623. The range was just over 19,000 yards. The *Ajax*'s first broadside fell short. This was signalled to the Transmitting Station, and the Table did many more calculations so that the next salvo would fall where the *Graf Spee* should be sixty seconds after the shells left the guns.

When Lt Dreyer, the Control Officer, ordered 'Up ladder, shoot', the elevation of the guns was adjusted up the scale and the guns fired again. The shells burst over. The range was corrected and a zig-zag group – the guns being so elevated that the salvoes would fall in a zig-zag pattern – fired.

A rapid group was being fired when suddenly the *Ajax* was straddled by a salvo of 11-inch shells from the *Graf Spee*. Immediately Commodore Harwood ordered a thirty-degree turn to starboard to dodge the next salvo and the *Ajax*, steaming at twenty-five knots, heeled as she swung round, followed by the *Achilles*.

The guns of both the cruisers were thrown out by this sudden alteration of course; but rapidly the DCTs and Transmitting Stations brought the turrets round again. Two minutes later the Commodore altered back to the original course, and Captain Parry, whose orders were to conform loosely with the *Ajax*'s movements, brought the *Achilles* round again.

From the *Graf Spee*'s log: 'The light cruisers pulled rapidly ahead so that at 0625 from their twenty-eight-degree to twenty-five-degree relative bearing there was a danger of torpedo attack. The Captain decided ... to slowly turn away on to a northerly course. At the same time he ordered a change of target on to the left, light cruiser ...

'At 0631 the main batteries had another target change to the *Exeter*. At the same time[1] the light cruisers opened fire against the *Graf Spee* without at first scoring any hits.

'The *Exeter* turned to starboard on to a westerly course [and] *Graf Spee* turned with rudder hard to port to a course of 270 degrees. The light cruisers were now quartering off to port and turning slowly to port.

'About 0634 the *Exeter* turned sharply away after heavy hits – only Turret C was still firing – making heavy smoke and for the time being was out of sight.

'The light cruisers were travelling at full speed off the starboard quarter. They could be brought under fire with B turret and secondary batteries

[1] In fact the *Achilles* opened fire at 0622 and the *Ajax* at 0623.

several times, but only for short periods because of their use of smoke and fog.'[1]

As soon as he saw the *Graf Spee* swinging round to port at 0637, Commodore Harwood ordered Captain Woodhouse to steer first north and then west to close the range again. As she moved north-westward, away from the three British ships, the pocket battleship started making smoke. Billowing black and brown clouds soon hid the ship for long periods.

The rate officers could see she was zig-zagging violently to avoid the salvoes of the three cruisers; and there was the satisfaction that it threw off the *Graf Spee*'s gunners more than it did the British.

Lt Lewin, the pilot of the *Ajax*'s Seafox, was anxious to get into the air. After the *Graf Spee* had opened fire he asked Captain Woodhouse: 'Can I take off?'

The aircraft would be useful for spotting; but X and Y turrets were firing within a few feet of the aircraft as it stood on its catapult. At this stage Captain Woodhouse was more concerned with the rate of fire. 'If you can,' he said, 'but I'm not going to hold fire for you.'

That was enough for Lewin. With Kearney, his observer, he went aft to the Seafox which had been prepared for catapulting by Pennefather and Warrant Engineer Arthur Monk. Blast from the muzzles of the guns in X and Y turrets was shaking the aircraft as the two men climbed into their seats. The catapult was trained round and, with her engine at full throttle the tiny Seafox was flung into the air.

Just before this, Kearney discovered that the Seafox's wireless was tuned into the reconnaissance wave of 230 kcs instead of the spotting wave of 3800 kcs. To save time he decided to use 230 kcs instead of re-tuning the set, and made a visual signal to the flagdeck telling them to warn the W/T office. This message was never passed on, and the omission was to have a serious result in the early part of the action.

While Lewin climbed to 3,000 feet, the *Achilles* was concentrating her gunfire with the *Ajax* and after thirteen broadsides a salvo of 11-inch shells from the *Graf Spee* erupted in the sea along her port side. Hundreds of splinters spun into the air, several of them cutting through the light plating round the bridge. Six sliced through the 1-inch armour of the DCT, making it look like a tin savaged by a large tin opener.

Captain Parry woke up to find himself prostrate on the deck with Martinson, the Chief Yeoman of Signals, lying nearby and moaning.

He stood up, conscious that all the *Achilles*'s guns had stopped firing. Then he saw that they were pointing in the wrong direction ... Previously, when the *Graf Spee*'s gunfire had been getting unpleasantly close, he had told Cowburn: 'Alter *towards* the splashes, Pilot. That will probably upset

[1] The cruisers were not deliberately making smoke at this stage.

his gunnery more than anything else we can do.'

Cowburn had been playing this game very skilfully – Captain Parry was later to attribute the *Achilles'* apparent invulnerability to this – and as soon as the salvo landed along the port side Cowburn had ordered a high-speed turn to port.

The idea behind this was that the *Graf Spee*, spotting her own salvoes, would make an 'up' correction for 'shorts' and a 'down' correction for 'overs'. By steering the *Achilles* towards the splashes, Captain Parry would always be steering away from where the second (and corrected) salvo would fall.

Realizing the Gunnery Control was not functioning Captain Parry went to the voicepipe and called up to the Director Control Tower. There was no reply.

At that moment someone said: 'Look at your legs!' Captain Parry glanced down. Blood was streaming down the back of one of his calves. He sat down on the edge of the monkey island, the platform round the two compasses, and within a few moments the first-aid party arrived.

They found that Martinson's left leg had been hit with splinters and he had a compound fracture of the tibia. Splints were tied on and he was taken away on a stretcher – still asking whether 'my boys' were all right.

The Sick Berth Petty Officer bandaged one of Captain Parry's legs and then said, 'Now the other leg, please, Sir.' Preoccupied with the battle, Captain Parry said, 'Oh, what's wrong with that?' Looking down he saw that it, too, had been badly cut with splinters.

Up in the DCT the situation was far worse. Washbourn – in his official report he wrote 'I was conscious of a hellish noise and a thump on the head' – came round to find the tiny compartment in a shambles. There were several jagged holes in the armour and the wind whistled in.

Behind him both the telegraphists, Milburn and Stennett, had collapsed, killed outright. One of the bodies had fallen through into the tiny rangefinder compartment below (CPO Bonniface was later to report 'A good bit of vibration was set up inside the rangefinder by our own speed and gunfire. Ranging was otherwise comfortable bar the fact of having a corpse at the back of the neck most of the time made it unpleasant. AB Gould kept calm during the action and did not take any notice of the extra ventilation we were getting. He got a bit peeved over a foot sticking in his ear, but soon settled down after it was removed . . .').

The Concentration Link Rangetaker, Edgar Shirley, had dropped off his stool and was bleeding badly from wounds in his thighs and face. Sergeant Trimble had been severely wounded in the back but he said nothing and carried on with his job so that no one would know he had been hit.

Shaw, the R to ED Unit Operator, was dead from multiple wounds in his chest; but he had slumped over his instrument in such a way that no one knew he had been hit. Washbourn saw that both Headon and Maycock were still all right at the Director Sight, and Boy Dorsett was still alive.

Mr Watts, the Rate Officer, spoke quickly into his microphone: 'DCT has been hit. After Control take over.'

Then he stood up and said to Washbourn:

'Come on, Sir. Running repairs.'

Washbourn, still rather dazed, did not understand. 'What's up? I'm all right.'

He put his hand to his head, and it came away sticky. He climbed off his stool as Watts took down a first-aid bag, extracted a bandage, and tied up the scalp wounds.

Climbing back into his seat, Washbourn called down the voicepipe:

'Control: bridge.'

Cowburn answered almost immediately.

'Tell the Captain that the DCT has been hit and the After Control is now controlling. Send up first-aid parties.'

That dealt with, he called out to the surviving DCT crew: 'What's out of action?'

Headon turned from his telescope to say: 'Director seems all right, Sir.'

Meanwhile the *Achilles* started shooting again, but the gunfire was extremely ragged because the After Control position was very ineffective. The two men manning it had been experiencing the continuous blast from the muzzles of X turret guns and were completely deafened and nearly stupid from concussion. Although they were also being sick from time to time they carried on as best they could.

Washbourn, realizing it was essential that the DCT started operating again as soon as possible, said:

'We'll see what happens. Switch to DCT controlling.'

Everything seemed to work all right, and while Watts deftly tied a tourniquet on Shirley's leg to stop some of the bleeding, Washbourn went to work.

'DCT controlling,' he said into the microphone. 'Broadsides . . . Shoot!'

Nearly a dozen broadsides had been loosed off before Petty Officer Maycock turned round from the Director Sight and reported: 'Archie's had it, Sir.'

Washbourn stooped in his seat and looked down into the forward part of the DCT. He saw that Shaw, sitting at his instrument in a natural position, was in fact dead.

He called to the cross-level operator: 'Rogers, take over Shaw's job.'

It was fortunate that Washbourn, in the previous weeks of practice, had made sure that all the men in the DCT could do every job. Rogers, who took over his new task without a word, could not move Shaw's body; and he had to sit on it to operate the instrument until later in the action.

It was about this time that Boy Dorsett, who had escaped unscathed, could be heard talking angrily into the telephone to the turrets. Somehow the rumour had got around that he had been killed.

'I'm *not* dead', he said. 'I tell you I'm not *dead*. It's me who's speaking to you.'

When the DCT was hit all wireless communication with the *Ajax* failed and concentrated gunfire was impossible. It is unlikely that Washbourn was very upset by this – no self-respecting Gunnery Officer likes to have the control of his guns taken away from him.

CHAPTER 14

SEVEN HITS ON *EXETER*

From Captain Bell's report: '... At 0620 A and B turrets opened fire at a range of 18,700 yards, Y turret joining in 2¼ minutes later, having been given permission to disregard the aircraft. At this time the ship was being straddled. At 0623 a shell bursting just short amidships killed a tube's crew, damaged communications, and splinters riddled the searchlight, funnels and starboard aircraft ...'

The *Exeter* had been steaming with four boilers in B boiler room, and as the alarm was sounded all the boilers in A boiler room were flashed up and connected. At 0620 Captain Bell ordered full speed, and by that time the Damage Control Headquarters in the Engineer's Workshop was closed up and the majority of the outlying parties had reported correct.

The Gunnery Officer, Lt-Cdr Jennings, had straddled the *Graf Spee* with his third salvo of 8-inch shells. The prospects looked promising and he ordered a zig-zag group.

At that moment one of six 11-inch shells from a broadside fired by the *Graf Spee* landed in the water close alongside the *Exeter*, just short of amidships. A shower of splinters spattered the ship like a handful of rubble flung at a window.

Some spun aft, cutting down and killing most of the crew of the starboard torpedo tubes; others pierced the thin steel plating of the ship's side and killed two of the decontamination party waiting in the Chief Stoker's bathroom and started a small fire among clothing and towels.

Still more sprayed the searchlights, the two funnels and the starboard aircraft. Electric leads were cut and holes pierced in the upper deck. All the gun-ready lamp circuits and the fall of shot hooter went out of action, making Lt-Cdr Jennings' job as Gunnery Officer doubly difficult. Now he was unable to tell when all his guns were loaded, how many splashes to look for, or when his salvoes were falling.

Immediately reports started coming into the Damage Control Head-quarters and parties were sent up to start repairing the damage. Men began to douse the fires, plug the holes in the ship's side and upper deck, and shore down hatches in the compartments below. The bodies were dragged away from the torpedo tubes and fresh men took over. Wounded were led or carried to the Medical Stations.

A few moments later the *Graf Spee* scored her first direct hit on the cruiser. An 11-inch shell smashed through the embarkation hatch on deck abaft B turret, ploughed into the Sick Bay, and went outwards through the ship's side into the sea without bursting.

A Sick Berth Chief Petty Officer was walking back from the fore part of the Sick Bay with bottles of morphine sulphate solution when the shell came through and sent splinters flying through the bulkhead. He was knocked unconscious and the precious bottles fell from his hands and smashed. Men in agony from wounds were waiting for the relief that morphine would give them . . .

When he came round he realized what had happened and stumbled back through the smoke and fumes to get more solution. Coughing and half suffocated, he could not find any bottles so he brought back morphine ampoules. But his troubles were only just starting – the task of helping the wounded had to alternate with dealing with the water flooding through the splinter-ridden deckhead, and the *Exeter* was still to be struck by another six 11-inch shells.

But within a minute of this hit the *Graf Spee* was to deliver an almost decisive blow.

> From Captain Bell's report: '. . . After the eighth salvo B turret received a direct hit from an 11-inch shell and was put out of action. The splinters also killed or wounded all the bridge personnel with the exception of the Captain, Torpedo Control and Firing Officers, and wrecked the wheelhouse communications . . .'

As mentioned earlier, the *Graf Spee*, after firing four salvoes of base-fused shells, switched over to impact fuses 'in order to obtain the greatest possible damage to the lightly-armoured turrets and superstructure and through hits on its hull to reduce the ship's speed'.[1]

One of these shells landed on B turret just between the two guns, ripping off the front armour plate and killing eight men at the front of the gunhouse.

They had fired seven broadsides and the Number Ones of the two guns were just about to ram home the next rounds when the shell burst. All the lights went out, leaving the gunhouse in darkness, and dense, acrid fumes started to burn the nostrils and throats of the stunned survivors.

Sergeant Arthur Wilde, RM, groped for the Number Ones who should have been either side of him, but they were not in their seats. Then he saw daylight coming in through the left rear door of the gunhouse, which had been blown open, and he made his way out on deck.

'As I was going aft,' Wilde reported later, 'Marine Attwood called for me to assist him with Marine W. A. Russell. I turned and saw Russell had lost a forearm and was badly hurt in the other arm.

'Attwood and I assisted Russell down to the port 4-inch gundeck and as we reached it there was another violent explosion which seemed to be in the vicinity of B turret. I dropped to the deck, pulling Russell with me.

'After the splinters had stopped, I cut off two lengths of signal halyard, which were hanging loose, and put a clove hitch for a tourniquet around both of Russell's arms above the elbows.

'I went to the Sick Bay and told someone that I had left Russell sitting against the funnel casing, port side. I proceeded down to the waist and turned forward, intending to go to B magazine and shell room, but was ordered back as the gangway was blocked by CPO Evans who was attending to a man who was seriously injured around the legs ...

'Sometime later I collected Marines Camp, Attwood and Thomas, and we went back to B turret to see what could be done. I observed several small fires, some of which were put out by sand, the fire hydrants being dry.

'Marine Thomas drew my attention to a small fire near the left elevating standard, and I sent him for water and sand. Then, remembering I had seen water in the starboard waist, I went down for some. When I returned Lt Toase, assisted by Marine Thomas, had extinguished the fire and we proceeded to take the cordite from both rammers and pass it overboard ...'

While this was being done, the badly-wounded Russell, his clothing bloodstained and his arms still bound with signal halyard, walked round making cheering remarks and, in the words of Captain Bell, 'encouraging all by his fortitude'. (He stayed on deck until after the action, when he collapsed.)

While the guns' crews were handling the dangerous cordite charges, Sergeant Puddifoot was dealing with the magazine and shell room below. When the shell burst, 'We heard a violent crash and felt a shock from

[1] Later in the action she reverted to base-fused shells.

above, and simultaneously the turret pump stopped', Puddifoot wrote later.

He called the gunhouse several times but there was no reply. Two men just above them told him they were sure it had gone. He ordered two ratings to continue calling the gunhouse, opened the escape hatch to the magazine, and then told everyone to abandon it.

'When this had been done,' Puddifoot wrote, 'I once more challenged the gunhouse and still having no reply I decided to abandon and ordered everybody on to the Boys' and Torpedo messdecks to await further orders ... When I reached the messdeck the Sergeant-Major informed me that he had reported by phone to Damage Control Headquarters and that we were to await further orders, and acting on instructions from SPO Knight, in command of Fire and Repair Parties in that sector, we lay down clear of the gangways.

'Shortly after this the ship was struck by the shell which damaged the CPOs' flat and I told SPO Knight to use my people as he liked, and I tried to get aft to ascertain the proximity of the fire with reference to the magazine. Owing to the intense heat and glare it was impossible at that time to enter the CPOs' flat and in view of the fact that the magazine was immediately below I decided to flood, and went below to the handling room.

'The lights were out but ERA Bond, equipped with a torch, followed me down, and together we unshipped the hopper guards, battened down the doors, flung what cordite we could find through the escape door, battened that, and then opened up the flood and seacock ...'

But although the shell had hit B turret, the worst damage was done on the bridge just above: a withering shower of splinters, like spray from a big sea, had been flung up at more than the speed of sound and cut through the thin armour and window openings, ricocheted down from the metal roof and killed or wounded nearly every man standing on the bridge.

Within a fraction of a second the *Exeter* was changed from a perfectly-handled fighting ship to an uncontrolled machine. The wheelhouse was wrecked; all communications to the engine room and Lower Steering Position were cut. Captain Bell had been wounded in the face. Among the dead were the Navigating Officer, plotting staff and the men standing either side of Captain Bell.

It took Captain Bell only a few seconds to realize that, with all controls gone, he could not fight the ship from the bridge any longer, and he would have to take over from the After Conning Position. He gave his orders and with the survivors made his way aft as quickly as possible.

The *Exeter*'s guns – with the exception of B turret – were still firing; but with no one on the bridge to con the ship she was slowly turning to starboard.

Just after Captain Bell and the rest of the survivors had left the bridge to hurry aft, Sub-Lieutenant Clyde Morse, who was in the Air Defence Officer's Position, happened to look down at the bridge and saw no one there – except for dead and badly-wounded men lying about in grotesque attitudes among the wreckage.

Realizing the ship was out of control and seeing the wheelhouse was wrecked, yet not knowing quite what had happened, he jumped down and ran to the buckled voicepipe communicating with the Lower Steering Position. Above the thunder of A and Y turrets' guns and the cries of the wounded he managed to shout down 'Steer 275 degrees'.

In the meantime the Torpedo Officer, Lt-Cdr Charles J. Smith, who had been knocked down by the blast of the bursting shell, was on his way aft to join Captain Bell. He had not gone far before he saw that the *Exeter* was turning to starboard, away from the enemy: in a minute or two, he realized, she would be so far round that the 'A arcs'[1] would close and A turret would not be able to fire.

Running back to the bridge he found Morse had managed to get one message through to the Lower Steering Position, and he was able to pass the order 'Port 25' to bring her round again.

Captain Bell, wounded in the face, arrived at the After Conning Position to find the steering-order transmitter and the telephone had been put out of action, so that the whole position was isolated. Midshipman Bonham, whose action station was the After Control Position, ran down to the After Steering Position with helm orders while a chain of ratings was being formed to repeat Captain Bell's orders.

As soon as this was done, Captain Bell sent Bonham forward to the bridge to hoist the Not-under-control balls.[2] He reached the bridge safely despite splinters flying up from near misses, and with the help of Yeoman Harben, who was wounded in the thigh, hoisted them on one of the few remaining halyards. They had been up only a few seconds when the halyard parted.

Stoker John Minhinnet had previously been ordered by Captain Bell to go to the engine room and tell them to change over to the After Steering Position. He made his way down to the control platform and, above the din of the turbines, now spinning at full speed, passed the message.

He was told to go on to the After Steering Position and give the order direct to the Engine Room Artificer in charge; but on the way there a shell bursting close alongside wounded him. A first aid party took him to the after medical station, but Minhinnet refused any treatment until he was sure his message was delivered.

But the *Exeter* was hitting back at the *Graf Spee*. Mr Cook, the Director

[1] The bearings on which the main armament could fire.
[2] Two black balls which, when hoisted vertically, indicate that a vessel is not under control.

Gunner, reported: 'I think it was with our fifth or sixth salvo that we straddled and obtained a hit[1] near the funnel. In different salvoes after this I saw several hits, while the whole of one salvo appeared to burst just along the waterline. The Control ordered an up correction, having taken this as a short. Soon after the fall of this salvo the enemy made smoke and altered course.'

About this time the Chief Quartermaster, Petty Officer William Green, was seriously wounded. Green was at the Upper Steering Position when the bridge was wrecked, and at once went below to make sure that the Lower Steering Position was undamaged and fully manned. Finding everything all right there he started to make his way aft when he was hit.

Meanwhile the two aircraft had been riddled with splinters and twisted by blast. The one on the port side had been fuelled at dawn and petrol was by now spurting from the tanks and blowing aft over the deck and the After Conning Position.

The triatic stay linking the two masts had been cut by blast or splinters, and the heavy wire had fallen across the starboard aircraft. But Leading Seaman Shoesmith realized that both the planes would have to be jettisoned very shortly.

Without waiting for orders, and despite the fact that the blast from Y turret's guns and the enemy shells dropping round the ship might set alight his petrol-soaked clothes or explode the fuel in the tanks, he climbed up on to the wing and dragged the heavy wire clear.

The Gunner, Mr Shorten, had been round to try and help the men wounded at the torpedo tubes when he met Cdr Graham, who had already been wounded. He ordered Shorten to get the charges for firing the catapults to get rid of the two damaged aircraft. The Gunner had already made them up the night before and he collected them and took them along to the catapults. But the catapults had been damaged and were not yet ready.

Less than five minutes had elapsed since the hit on B turret. Captain Bell was successfully conning the ship from aft, using a chain of messengers, and heading north-west at high speed. The *Graf Spee* was by now about 13,000 yards away on the starboard bow heading on a parallel but opposite course.

> From Captain Bell's report: '... The ship had received two more hits forward and some damage from splinters set up by shells bursting short ...'

The first of these two shells burst on the sheet anchor, tearing a hole six feet by eight feet in the *Exeter*'s side above the waterline. Splinters ripped into the paint store – where a fire started – and Bosun's store and riddled No. 10 watertight bulkhead.

[1] See page 435.

Stoker Petty Officer Albert Jones had immediately started taking his No. 1 Fire Party forward to deal with the damage, but more shells from the *Graf Spee* burst in the water nearby. A splinter hit him and he collapsed; but he realized the next salvo would probably be even nearer, and his men were in a dangerously exposed position. He shouted to them to shelter behind A turret. It was his last order before he died, and it saved their lives. A few seconds later a shell burst on the deck ahead of them, ripping open a twelve-feet-square hole abaft the cable-holder. Again splinters did a great deal of damage, and soon fires were burning.

The Fire Party then ran forward, avoiding the blast from the two guns of A turret, to plug up the holes with hammocks, deal with fires, and examine the watertight bulkheads.

Engine Room Artificer Frank McGarry had been up forward since the beginning of the action, and without waiting for orders he had flooded the petrol compartment – where one spark, let alone a flash from a shellburst, would cause an explosion.

Then the shell had hit the anchor, only a few feet from him. Dense fumes from the explosion had streamed in; men had fallen, killed or wounded by splinters. He was trying to see how much damage had been done when the other shell burst on deck abaft the cable-holder and the blast flung him against a bulkhead and temporarily stunned him. Then, half suffocated by the acrid smoke of the shell bursts, he set about getting shipwrights to investigate the damage, organize stretcher parties and deal with fires.

Sub-Lieutenant Morse, who had jumped down to the bridge when he had realized it was deserted, now saw a fire burning on the fo'c'sle after the shell bursts, and ran down to organize a party of men to deal with it. He quickly realized he had too few men to tackle it and ran aft to collect more. He found Midshipman Cameron, who was in charge of the 4-inch guns. Cameron, since his guns were not wanted at the moment, had used his men for rigging hoses to the forward part of the ship, but after B turret was hit it had been reported to him that there was no water coming through them and a fire was burning on the fo'c'sle.

Cameron had immediately sent half his guns' crews forward to help while most of the remainder struggled to get the hoses patched up and the water flowing. At that moment Morse arrived, asking for more men and water. Cameron told him that all the men he could spare had already gone forward, and the others were doing the best they could with the hoses.

Morse hurried back to the fo'c'sle to supervise the men. Then the second shell exploded very close to him. He was never seen again, and it is believed that his body was blown over the side.

By now the forward part of the ship was slowly flooding. Water streamed out of a shattered fire main and from hoses pouring water on to the fo'c'sle fire; and the sea was spurting in through splinter holes caused by the hit on the anchor and the many near misses. The flow was increased by the forward thrust of the ship, which was now steaming at full speed.

> *From Captain Bell's report: '... At 0631 the order to fire torpedoes was correctly anticipated by the Torpedo Officer and he fired the starboard torpedoes in local control ...'*

After passing the order to the Lower Steering Position which brought the *Exeter* round to starboard again, Lt-Cdr Smith, the torpedo officer, realized that the *Graf Spee*, on her present course, would very soon be a good torpedo target. But there was no time for him to wait for orders from Captain Bell.

Many of the torpedo tubes' crew had been wounded by the near miss at the beginning of the action. Among them was the Torpedo Gunner's mate, Petty Officer Charles Hallas. However, he was in charge of the tubes and as soon as they were trained he stood by waiting for the order from Lt-Cdr Smith.

Smith waited as the ship slowly swung round; then he gave the order to fire. Compressed air thrust the torpedoes over the side into the sea, and gyroscopes inside took over to keep them on a straight course as they sped at more than forty knots towards the pocket battleship.

But the *Exeter*'s luck was out: they had been running only two minutes when the *Graf Spee* suddenly swung round 150 degrees to port, away from the three British cruisers – and away from where she was to have had a rendezvous with the torpedoes. At the same time she started laying a thick smoke screen to hide her movements and confuse the British gunners.

Immediately Captain Bell, passing his orders through the chain of messengers, swung the *Exeter* round to starboard towards the *Graf Spee* so that the port torpedoes could be fired; but as she turned, the pocket battleship struck twice more.

> *From Captain Bell's report: '... Two more 11-inch hits were received, one on A turret putting it out of action, and one which penetrated the Chief Petty Officers' flat where it burst, causing very extensive damage ...'*

Just before the Chief Petty Officers' flat was hit another shell, not mentioned in the above report, hit the Navigating Officer's cabin, passed through the Armament Office, killed five telegraphists and went on for sixty feet before bursting on the barrel of 'S-one' (Starboard one) 4-inch gun, killing or wounding several more men.

The foremost ready-use locker, containing 4-inch shells, immediately caught fire and the ammunition started bursting, sending up showers of debris and splinters. At that moment a man ran up to Midshipman

Cameron, in command of the 4-inch guns, and warned him that the fore topmast was just about to fall down.

'I gave the order to clear the fore end of the gun deck,' Cameron reported later. 'As it did not appear to be coming down immediately I started the crews working again.'

The men in A turret had fired between forty and fifty rounds when, at this moment, an 11-inch shell hit the right gun. Once again the explosion tore at the armour plate on the front of the turret. Inside all the lights were put out and fumes streamed in.

Petty Officer Pierce tried to get through to the bridge by telephone, but it was wrecked. Ordering the telegraphists to stay at their posts, he climbed out of the gunhouse to go up to warn the bridge, but finding it had already been wrecked he went back to the gunhouse to tell the men to abandon it.

By this time an 11-inch shell had burst in the Chief Petty Officers' flat and started a bad fire above the 4-inch magazine. After checking that it was being dealt with, Midshipman Cameron returned with Ordinary Seaman Gwilliam to find the 4-inch ready-use ammunition locker still burning from the earlier hit.

'There were still several live shells in the bottom of the locker. Without any hesitation Gwilliam removed his greatcoat and attempted to smother the flames with it,' Cameron reported later. 'At the same time somebody else threw a bucket of sand over it. The flames were extinguished and we proceeded to throw over the side what was left in the locker.

'Gwilliam reported to me that there were still several cans of petrol underneath the port catapult. These we threw overboard.

'As the fire on the messdecks was still raging I got more hands on to the job of carrying buckets to it. At the same time Lt Kemball and I kept the remainder occupied in breaking up blocks of holystone in an effort to make sand out of them . . .

'At this time an effort, which subsequently proved to be successful, was being made to get the planes over the side, they having been badly holed and showering out quantities of petrol.'

The shell which burst in the CPOs' flat did so much damage that the *Exeter* later had to discontinue the action. It penetrated the light plating of the ship's side amidships, as if it were cardboard, cut through three bulkheads and then burst on the lower deck above the 4-inch magazine and the torpedo gunner's store, blasting a hole measuring sixteen feet by fourteen feet.

The explosion was felt all through the ship, as though she had been punched in her solar plexus. Blast and fumes thrust back along the starboard passage; one bulkhead door was blocked with debris and bodies, and another with the wreckage of kit lockers; the Chief Petty Officers' flat was in darkness and filled with dense fumes and steam escaping from a punctured heating pipe.

A fierce fire broke out in the lower servery flat, and the crews of the switchboard and forward dynamo rooms were trapped, the whole space filling with fumes, steam and water spraying out from a burst fire main.

Splinters from the shell cut a large number of electric leads, among them vital ones supplying power to the Transmitting Station, the main armament's 'brain'. Because the Fire Control Table could work no longer, the Transmitting Station was abandoned.

More splinters pierced the lower deck and slashed the fire hoses. Water poured into the Lower Steering Position and the Number One low-power room below. Generators and compass alternators were flooded and this put the compass repeaters out of action.

Other splinters sliced through a bulkhead into A boiler room; but fortunately the boilers were saved by spare firebricks which had been stacked up out of the way – otherwise it is probable that every man in the boiler room would have been killed by superheated steam.

The immediate task for the Damage Control parties was to get at the men trapped in the forward dynamo room and the switchboard.

Number Four Fire Party were the first to try. Smoke and fumes would have suffocated any man along the starboard passage in a few moments, so they pulled on their anti-gas respirators and started dragging their hoses towards the fire. But debris and the bodies of seamen killed by the explosion blocked the way.

It seemed impossible to force an entrance into the Chief Petty Officers' flat to see exactly what had happened and what was on fire, so another party was sent up on deck to try to break in from forward: every minute counted now because the trapped men were being badly affected by the fumes.

In the meantime, however, Stoker Patrick O'Brien was trying to break through alone to the main switchboard. In darkness, tripping over twisted metal, bodies and smashed equipment, and almost suffocating from the high-explosive fumes and steam, he managed to clamber and crawl through the apparently impenetrable Chief Petty Officers' flat and shout a message down the main switchboard hatch, which was blocked by debris.

After that he crawled to the hatch over the dynamo room. This, too, was blocked by twisted metal and all sorts of debris; but O'Brien managed to call to the Engine Room Artificer, Thomas Phillips, who was in charge of the trapped party.

Phillips had been struggling in the thick fumes and smoke to get a dynamo going. It had stopped as the shell burst above, and the exhaust fan had broken down. Having made contact with the trapped men, O'Brien then crawled and scrambled out on to the upper deck, and ran back to his fire party and led them into the reeking flat.

In the meantime Petty Officer Herbert Chalkley, who had also been in the forward dynamo room, had managed to force open the door in the escape trunk and crawl over the wreckage to the switchboard hatch. It was jammed, with a good deal of wreckage piled on top of it.

Amid the swirling smoke and barely able to see what he was doing, Chalkley pulled and pushed at the wreckage, trying to lever pieces off to free the hatch. But he could not move it.

Realizing he would not be needed again in the dynamo room, he guessed his best move would be to get out on to the upper deck so that he could then guide fire parties to his trapped shipmates. He carefully made his way back through the smoke and steam to the escape trunk and climbed up it. Once in the open air again he found the fire parties and went back to help fight the fires in the servery and CPOs' flats.

By now the blaze in the servery flat was raging fiercely and almost out of control. The 4-inch magazine, bomb room, and the magazine of B turret were in danger from the heat and fumes.

The 50-ton pump supplying water for the hoses forward had failed four or five times and it was at this point that, as mentioned earlier, Sergeant George Puddifoot, in B magazine, realized the fire overhead was getting out of hand and, with ERA Frank Bond, decided to flood the magazine.

Bond then went to the main centre of the fire to check up how much damage had been done – and found that the flooding valve spindle had been shot away and the fire main shattered. However, there was sufficient water from the burst mains pouring into the magazine through shell and splinter holes, so he went on to help fight the fires.

This was proving a difficult task: the ship was so badly riddled with splinters by this time that many hoses and fire mains had burst. Midshipman Robert Don, for instance, was having great difficulty in running hoses to the burning Marines Barracks and also in fighting the fire over the Lower Steering Position. He was one of several men searching for the wounded lying amid the smoke and debris, and dragging them to safety.

The *Exeter's* tall topmasts were still in danger. Flying splinters had cut through many of the wire shrouds supporting them, and when finally the triatic stay joining the heads of the two masts was severed they had started to whip so violently that all the main aerials parted and the ship's wireless link with the Commodore was cut. As soon as the sets had gone dead Chief Petty Officer Telegraphist Harold Newman began the dangerous and laborious job of rigging jury aerials.

The topmasts were so tall that they undoubtedly helped the *Graf Spee*'s gunners in finding the range; and had the weather not been exceptionally calm they almost certainly would have toppled down.

As mentioned earlier, the Transmitting Station and the Fire Control Table were out of action. Mr Dallaway, the TS Officer, reported that when communications with B Turret ceased he did not know it was because it had been hit. 'Thinking B turret may have some mechanical trouble,' he wrote, 'I decided to send the Ordnance Artificer from the TS to 'B' to see if he could be of any assistance, realizing that he would not have far to go, and also that while everything was running smoothly in the TS he was wasting his talent.

'With that object in view I ordered the TS hatch to be opened so that he could get out of the TS. Before I had time to tell him what to do there was a slight blast effect felt and the TS started to fill with dust and fumes. The TS crew, with the exception of the TS Officer and Communications Number, put on their gasmasks and carried on with their jobs.

'Lights in the TS then went off with the exception of two which remained burning dimly ... The effect was that the TS was practically in darkness, and combined with the dust it was hardly possible to see anything.

'Everything appeared to happen at once ...' he added. 'A turret reported they were going on to "local" firing, the range receiver unit stopped working, and then the compressed air working the Fire Control Table failed.

'I did manage to see the Ordnance Artificer playing around with the air valves, but still no air was available on the Table. To work hunters by hand in the existing light was impossible, and that combined with the report from A turret that pointers were not working forced me to the conclusion that the TS was useless. I reported this fact to the Gunnery Officer and then the order to go into local control was passed. Communication to A turret was then lost.

'I then asked permission for the TS crew to go on the Marines' messdeck in order to use them for work. This was agreed to by the Gunnery Officer.

'The crew could not get out of the TS as they were told that the upper hatch was closed. I went up to investigate the possibility of opening the hatch and found it open. The crew then came up. Everywhere was in complete darkness, but I tried to get into the servery flat, which I soon discovered to be in a shambles.

'Realizing that a gangway through there was impossible, I shouted back to the remainder to work their way forward, which they did. For some reason or other I could not get out of the flat by the same way that I had entered, and I have recollections of being lost among the debris. Eventually

I managed to make the starboard waist where I found the TS crew and other ratings.'

Despite all the bitter punishment the *Exeter* had taken in forty minutes of battle, she was still in action: Y turret, right aft, was still firing in local control. Lt-Cdr Richard Jennings, the Gunnery Officer, had gone aft to see what was happening, and while standing outside the After Control Position talking to the After Control Officer, Y turret trained round on to an extreme forward bearing and fired. Both men were badly shaken by the blast. Jennings then sent Sub-Lt Wickham, the After Control Officer, to take charge of Y turret while he stationed himself on the roof of the turret, where he could see better, and, ignoring the blast and flying splinters, shouted spotting corrections down through a manhole.

The position at 0700, therefore, was that:

1. A and B turrets were out of action from direct hits;
2. Y turret was still firing in local control;
3. The bridge, DCT and Transmitting Station were out of action;
4. A fierce fire was raging in the CPOs' and servery flats;
5. Minor fires were burning on the Marines' messdeck and in the paint shop;
6. There were no telephone communications – orders could be passed only by messengers;
7. The ship was down by the bows by about three feet because of flooding forward, and had a list of from seven to ten degrees to starboard – due to about 650 tons of water, which had flooded in;
8. Only one 4-inch gun could still be fired;
9. Both aircraft had been jettisoned;
10. Wireless communications had completely broken down.

But mercifully the engine room was undamaged and the ship was steaming at full speed. The heat was so great in the furnaces that the floors were becoming almost fluid, and because of the list the molten brickwork had run over to the starboard side.

Many gallant actions in those forty minutes went almost unnoticed; it needed bravery to carry out even normal duties in the ravaged cruiser. An order to take a message to a position twenty yards away could mean sudden death from an invisible rain of shell splinters; young ratings were making split-second decisions which meant life or death to many of their shipmates. But fortunately months of drill under keen and able officers paid dividends.

Already more than fifty officers and men had been killed and others were so seriously wounded they would die before the day ended; more than twenty others had been badly hurt.

There was, for instance, the cold-blooded gallantry of Captain Bell, one of the few men left alive in the ship who knew all the facts and dangers. Despite the damage caused by the almost undivided attention of a pocket battleship which could match each of his 8-inch shells with an 11-inch shell at the beginning of the action, and now still had six 11-inch guns firing to his two 8-inch (and one of them had stopped firing for a short while), the *Exeter*'s Battle Ensigns were still flying and the ship continued in action against the *Graf Spee*.

From the After Conning Position Captain Bell was having to steer the ship with the help of a compass taken from a whaler – the compass repeaters had been damaged some time earlier. But the compass needle was so badly affected by the magnetism of the steel all round that it did almost everything except spin round like a catherine wheel.

There was the gallantry of Chief Shipwright Anthony Collings, who, although seriously wounded and badly burned, continued to supervise and direct the work of the shipwrights repairing damage in the forward part of the ship. He only stopped when he fell unconscious. A few moments before that he had been asking for a report on the condition of a damaged hatch.

There was Commander Robert Graham, who was wounded in the face and leg early in the action. Yet despite that he cheerfully carried on walking round the ship seeing what was damaged or on fire and giving orders to deal with it.

There was Midshipman Bonham. After hoisting the 'not under control' balls he had been ordered to find some flexible voicepipe so that Captain Bell could communicate with the engine room.

He took two ratings and unrigged the flexible lead from the bridge to the armament office, and while doing this he found a man lying outside Captain Bell's sea cabin. He had both legs blown off but was still alive, so Bonham sent a rating to warn the sick bay.

After searching various places in the ship for more voicepipe he went back to the After Conning Position. He saw that some more had been found and was being rigged, and he was sent forward to the fire still raging amidships.

'I went down through the sick bay flat into the Marines' messdeck where I met Midshipman Don,' he reported later, 'and together we got a hose in, and we were getting it down through the hatch outside the bookstall when he fell through the hatch and vanished. I heard voices below so assumed he was all right, and continued getting more hose and switching on the water.

'I had to go outside several times as the smoke was very bad . . .

From the Exeter's log: '. . . 0729, Y turret ceased firing owing to failure
of electricity supply. 0730, Broke off action. 0750, Enemy disappeared to
westward pursued by Ajax and Achilles . . .'

Strangely enough, it was not the *Graf Spee*'s hits which forced Captain Bell
to break off the action, but her near misses. As long as he had a gun which
worked, Captain Bell was determined to keep the *Graf Spee* under fire, but
at last water flooding in through splinter holes in the *Exeter*'s side abreast of
No 216 bulkhead stopped the power supply.

With his last turret out of action, and only a boat compass to steer by,
Captain Bell was now able to devote all his attention to keeping his ship
afloat.

CHAPTER 15

SHELLS AND SNOWBALLS

From Commodore Harwood's dispatch: '. . . Ajax and Achilles hauled
round to the north-westward at 0656 to open their A arcs. Graf Spee made
frequent alterations of course to throw out our gunfire and from 0700
onwards she made great use of smoke; she appeared to have some form of
chloro-sulphonic apparatus aft and used this as well as smoke floats . . .'

The *Graf Spee* was now heading away to the north-westward at full speed
with the two cruisers pursuing on her starboard quarter. The *Achilles* had
recovered from the damage to the Director Control Tower, her four turrets
were in action again, and Lt Lewin and Lt Kearney were spotting the fall of
shot from the Seafox aircraft.

At first their reports were not picked up in the *Ajax* because, as
mentioned earlier, they were using the reconnaissance wavelength and
Kearney's message to the flag deck before taking off had not been passed
on to the main wireless office. It was not until 0649 that their first report
was received.

Shortly before this, after the *Achilles*'s DCT had been hit and the wireless
link for concentration firing broken, Lt Washbourn had begun firing in
individual control.

However, neither Kearney in the Seafox nor the *Ajax*'s Gunnery Officer,
Lt Dreyer, knew this, and it led to the *Achilles*' salvoes being reported to the

Ajax by the aircraft and Dreyer naturally regarded them as referring to his own and corrected accordingly. The *Ajax*'s salvoes, as a result of this, were falling well over the *Graf Spee* for a short while.

The two men in the Seafox had a fine view of the battle although there was no time to sit around and appreciate the grandeur of the scene. Lewin had climbed to 3,000 feet, where there was slight cloud, because he knew the enemy had two aircraft, each of which had forward-firing machine guns, and if they came up after him it might well be convenient to dodge into a cloud to escape their attention.

He took the Seafox to a position a mile off the *Ajax*'s disengaged bow and Kearncy started passing his spotting reports. It was quite easy for him to see the splashes of the near misses, but hits on the *Graf Spee* were more difficult to discern, mainly because of the smoke from the pocket battleship's 11-inch guns.

On one occasion Lewin took the aircraft too close to the pocket battleship, which immediately opened fire from her anti-aircraft guns. The first few rounds burst short but the German gunners quickly corrected and for two minutes the shells were bursting far too near for either Lewin or Kearney to have an easy mind. A splinter from one shell went right through both the starboard wings, and Lewin turned the aircraft and climbed up into a cloud for a few moments to give the German gunners a rest.

The position at 0707, when the *Exeter* had only one turret left in action, was that the *Graf Spee* was eight and three-quarter miles from the *Ajax* and *Achilles*, constantly zig-zagging to throw the British gunners off their aim, and streaming out funnel smoke and dropping smoke floats.

Thus in the first phase, from 0618 when the *Graf Spee* opened fire until 0638 when she put down a smoke screen and hid behind it, the *Exeter* had suffered considerably and the other two ships had escaped unharmed. In the second phase the enemy had scored several times on the *Exeter* and damaged the *Achilles*. Her smoke screen was hampering the British gunners, and later on, although the *Ajax* and *Achilles* were shooting fast, their fire was inaccurate because of the spotting mix-up.

In other words, the gunfire of the three British ships had deteriorated badly, giving Langsdorff, had he known it, a golden opportunity. But fortunately he did not take it. Instead he swung the *Graf Spee* round in a big alteration of course to port, away from the First Division.

For the last half an hour the battle had been indecisive. Although the range was just right for the *Graf Spee*'s 11-inch guns, it was still high for Commodore Harwood's 6-inch guns. So he decided to close the *Graf Spee* as quickly as possible even though it meant halving the number of guns which he could bring to bear. It was a bold decision and one reached amid the brain-numbing crash of his own ship's broadsides and while the *Graf Spee*'s shells were bursting close. It could mean victory at a terrible cost for the *Ajax* and *Achilles*, or it could mean annihilation.

While the message was passed to the *Ajax*'s engine room his order was also signalled to the *Achilles*: *Proceed at utmost speed.*

The *Ajax* came round to port, followed by the *Achilles*, and now, the spotting sorted out, their shooting was fast and accurate. On an average, the 'gun-ready' lamps flickered on three times a minute in each DCT, and Dreyer and Washbourn ordered 'Shoot'; and all the while each Director Sight was being skilfully trained round to keep the guns aimed at the *Graf Spee*, with the Fire Control Tables supplying the bearing and elevation.

> *From Commodore Harwood's dispatch: '... At 0716* Graf Spee *made a drastic alteration of course to port under cover of smoke, but four minutes later she turned to the north-west and opened her A arcs on the First Division.* Ajax *was immediately straddled three times by 11-inch at a range of 11,000 yards, but the enemy's secondary armament was firing raggedly, and appeared to be going consistently over, between* Ajax *and* Achilles *...'*

As the *Graf Spee* made this sudden turn to port, Commodore Harwood immediately concluded she was moving down to finish off the crippled *Exeter* – now steaming in a pall of smoke only eight miles to the south – and would then concentrate all her guns on the First Division.

He promptly ordered the *Ajax* and *Achilles* to turn to starboard at once so that all their guns would bear on the enemy; his only chance of rescuing the *Exeter* was to provoke the pocket battleship to shift all her gunfire on to the First Division.

And their shooting was magnificent: Kearney, up in the Seafox aircraft, signalled 'Good shot', and a few moments later the red glow of a 6-inch hit was seen amidships in the *Graf Spee*, followed by a fire which burned fiercely.[1]

This determined attack seemed to do the trick, and Harwood saw the *Graf Spee* turn to the north-west so that she could bring both her 11-inch turrets to bear on the *Ajax* and *Achilles*. It soon appeared to the Commodore that she had taken the bait and now intended to neglect the *Exeter* and give the First Division her undivided attention.

Harwood was, however, not a torpedo expert for nothing: guessing that she would hold her present course, at 0724 he ordered the *Ajax* to fire a salvo of torpedoes. She turned to starboard to bring her port tubes to bear, and at 0727 four torpedoes were loosed off at the *Graf Spee* 9,000 yards away to the westwards.

Unfortunately all four broke surface after being launched, and from the

---

[1] This was in fact the Arado aircraft blazing.

splashes it must have been obvious to wide-awake lookouts in the *Graf Spee*
that they were on their way. Anxiously the Commodore, Captain
Woodhouse and the Torpedo Officer waited and waited.

Then they saw the great pocket battleship start swinging round to port,
away from them – 10 . . . 20 . . . 50 . . . 60 . . . 100 . . . and finally 130 degrees.
Although the chance of hitting with torpedoes at 9,000 yards was never
very rosy, there was none at all now; and three minutes later, the danger
passed, the *Graf Spee* came back on to her original course, still laying a
smoke screen.

A few moments later there was a sudden explosion aft in the *Ajax* and the
whole cruiser shuddered: an 11-inch shell had burst somewhere inside the
ship. Almost immediately Lt Dreyer reported from the DCT that both X
and Y turrets were out of action.

But neither the Commodore nor Captain Woodhouse had a moment to
spare, apart from seeing that the ship was still afloat and steaming at full
speed. Almost before the shaking of the explosion had stopped, Kearney, in
the Seafox aircraft, signalled: *Torpedoes approaching; they will pass ahead of you.*

Harwood, however, was taking no chances and ordered an eighty-
degree turn to port and, so as to blank her fire for as little time as possible,
signalled to the *Achilles: Cross my stern.*[1]

Now the *Graf Spee* was on the *Ajax*'s starboard side and rapidly A and B
turrets swung right round, obediently following the Director Sight. Both
cruisers were now hitting the pocket battleship frequently and the range
was closing rapidly; by 0738 it was only four miles – close range for the *Graf
Spee*'s 11-inch guns. Yet despite the number of times the two cruisers were
scoring hits, there was very little apparent damage. The pocket battleship's
vitals were protected by a belt of armour five and a half inches thick, and
even at four miles' range a 6-inch shell had very little chance of penetrating
it.

Nevertheless, the hits were worrying the *Graf Spee* because she turned
south-west and once again brought all her guns to bear – 11-inch, 5.9-inch
and anti-aircraft guns firing time-fused shells.

> *From Commodore Harwood's dispatch: '. . . By 0738 the range was down
> to 8,000 yards. At this time I received a report that* Ajax *had only 20 per
> cent of ammunition left and had only three guns in action, as one of the
> hoists had failed in B turret and X and Y turrets were both out of action.*
>
> *'*Graf Spee's *shooting was still very accurate and she did not appear to
> have suffered much damage.*
>
> *'I therefore decided to break off the day action and try to close in again
> after dark. Accordingly at 0740* Ajax *and* Achilles *turned away to the
> east under cover of smoke . . .'*

[1] Apart from 'Open fire' and speed signals, this was the Commodore's first
order to *Achilles* and is an indication of how well the two ships worked together.

By this time a messenger had reached the *Ajax*'s bridge to report to Captain Woodhouse the extent of the damage. The 11-inch shell had hit the upper deck at an angle of thirty-five degrees, ploughed through three cabins – belonging to Captain Woodhouse, his secretary, and the Commander – and struck X turret ammunition lobby. There the splinters it ripped from the deck and bulkheads killed four men, and wounded five more. It then hit the horizontal angle irons and shot upwards through the working chamber killing two more men, finally bursting in Commodore Harwood's sleeping cabin.

The heavy base plug of the shell was blown straight aft, denting the armoured ring and jamming Y turret. Splinters cut through the upper deck, slicing through the power main[1] and causing flooding.

X turret had naturally received the worst damage. The gunhouse crew were all flung into the back of the turret, and when the Officer of the Quarters, Lt Ian de'Ath, picked himself up he saw smoke and sparks pouring up the hatch from the lobby below, and smoke was coming from the cordite hoists. Each of the buckets of the hoist had a 30-lb charge in it. Realizing the whole lot might explode any second, he ordered the hoists to be drenched with water.

Sergeant Raymond Cook, at the left gun, dragged a hose to the hatch, but no water came out when the valve was turned on – the main had been smashed below.

De'Ath then ordered the cordite charges to be taken out of the top buckets of the hoist and flung over the side. Then he had a look down the hatch. Clouds of smoke were pouring out and flames could be seen below, but all the lighting was out of action and it was impossible to see exactly what was going on.

Another hose was dragged in from the quarter-deck, but this was found to have been pierced by splinters. A third hose was brought along by a fire party, and fortunately this worked. It was thrust down the hatch, where Stoker Bertram Wood, who had broken into the lobby, was tackling the blaze single-handed.

In the flat below the turret the explosion had flung men across the deck, several being killed or hurt by splinters. All the lights were put out and the whole flat filled with fumes and smoke. Visibility was cut down to less than arm's length so torches were useless, and while men struggled to find their way round, small electrical fires were started.

Then the atmosphere began to clear – helped by compressed air escaping from a bottle in X lobby – but water and oil started flooding in from burst fire mains and fuel pipes. It swilled from side to side as the ship

[1] About 150 electrical cables were cut during the action. Twenty per cent were destroyed by the 11-inch shell before it burst, fifteen per cent by the explosion, fifty per cent by splinter from the same shell, and fifteen per cent by other splinters.

rolled and greatly hindered the fire and repair parties.

It was about this time that Commodore Harwood, worried by the possibility of running out of ammunition, asked Captain Woodhouse to see how much was left in the *Ajax*. This was passed on and the answer came back that there were fifty rounds a gun left.

This meant that each turret had fired about 300 rounds – 150 broadsides in an hour's action ... But if there were only enough for another fifty broadsides the Commodore realized he was dangerously short.[1] It was this knowledge, plus the apparent lack of damage to the *Graf Spee*, which made him break off the action. He commented: 'we might just as well be bombarding her with a lot of bloody snowballs ...'

Just as the *Ajax* was about to turn away she was damaged again: 11-inch shells straddled her and one of them hit the main topmast and cut it in two. The shell was not seen to burst, but all the wireless aerials were brought down and the Commodore could not pass any more wireless signals until jury aerials were rigged.

So with the *Ajax* turning away and signalling to the *Achilles: Make smoke*, the third phase of the Battle of the River Plate ended.

CHAPTER 16

GRAF SPEE RUNS AWAY

The *Graf Spee*, however, had not escaped as lightly as Commodore Harwood thought. At 0631,[2] when the *Exeter* had turned to fire her first salvo of torpedoes, the *Graf Spee* was using her two 11-inch turrets against her, and the Torpedo Officer had just passed a message to Langsdorff warning him that there was also danger of torpedo attacks from the other two cruisers.

At this time the *Ajax* and *Achilles* were not scoring any hits, and when Langsdorff saw the *Exeter* moving off to the west he turned hard a port, away from the two light cruisers.

But at 0634 he could see the *Exeter* was being hit hard by his own guns, and suddenly she turned away, making heavy smoke and with only Y turret firing.

---

[1] In fact the report was wrong: it referred only to A turret which had fired far more than the other three turrets, but at the time was thought to refer to all the turrets.

[2] All German times are approximate and must be taken only as a general indication.

The *Ajax* and *Achilles* were now moving up fast on the *Graf Spee*'s starboard quarter. Only B turret, aft, and the 5.9-inch batteries could fire at them; and since both British ships were hidden in smoke the German gunners had to break off from time to time.

At 0700 the *Exeter* came in sight again. From the flying bridge Langsdorff could see that her A turret guns were trained fore and aft, while B turret pointed to starboard. Only Y turret was firing at him.

The *Graf Spee* opened fire with her B turret and soon the Germans saw the *Exeter* being hit again, and once more she turned away under thick black smoke.

In the meantime the *Ajax* and *Achilles* had closed the range, as Commodore Harwood intended, and since the *Graf Spee*'s B turret was firing at the *Exeter*, only the 6-inch guns could engage them.

> From Captain Langsdorff's log: '. . . They fired very fast, their fire being at times very effective, the ship receiving in this part of the action a large number of hits . . .'

A 6-inch shell came in on the starboard quarter, passed through the starboard boat deck, the crew's gallery, the upper deck on the port side, and burst against the splinter bulkheads.

This was to become the most important shell-hit in the action, as will be seen later. Apart from wrecking the gallery, it destroyed an ammunition hoist and the electric supply to the 15-cm shell hoists forward.

An earlier 6-inch shell from either the *Ajax* or *Achilles* had come in on the starboard bow, passed through the armoured shield of the starboard 4-inch anti-aircraft gun, penetrated the bakery and burst in the searchlight workshop. The gun was wrecked, the starboard ammunition hoist for the 4-inch guns put out of action, and the searchlight workshop and a sick bay destroyed.

One of the *Exeter*'s 8-inch shells had hit the armour belt above the armoured deck and splinter bulkheads and exploded. The armoured deck was dented and cracked but the shell did not penetrate it. Water flooded in and the whole area was filled with fumes, but the leaks were quickly sealed by repair parties.

A 6-inch shell from the starboard quarter passed through the fo'c'sle and detonated on the port side, tearing a hole three feet by six feet above the waterline. The fifth hit was also a 6-inch shell which went through the wooden cutter on the port side, wrecked the 4-inch ammunition hoist and rained splinters over the engine-room ventilation hatches.

The sixth hit was something of a surprise to the Germans. Earlier, in the B turret of the *Achilles*, there had been a temporary delay in the shell supply, and the gunhouse crews took the ready-use shells from their racks and fed them into the guns. When they ran out of armour-piercing shells they came to two practice projectiles resting in their racks.

'Go on, stuff them in too,' said Sub-Lieutenant Somerville, who was the Officer of Quarters.

And off they went. One of them missed. The other was described in the *Graf Spee*'s Damage Control report thus:

> *A 15-cm drill shell* [sic] *came from the starboard quarter, passed through the starboard hawser reel behind the officers' mess, the starboard torpedo loading station, the warrant officers' mess, and several warrant officers' lockers on the port side between decks. Damage Control telegraph, Damage Control telephone and service conduits* (Wirtschaftsleitung) *between decks in Section III were destroyed.*

The seventh hit was on the fo'c'sle and the explosion started a fire in the Damage Control storeroom and caused a leak on the port side. The next, also a 6-inch shell, hit the shielded port of Captain Langsdorff's cabin and exploded in the pantry.

The forward AA command post was put out of action by the ninth hit, which struck the foremast, the ready-use ammunition locker of a starboard 3.7-cm gun, and exploded in the command post. Everyone at the gun was killed and the ammunition was set on fire and exploded.

There were several occasions when the 6-inch shells hit the *Graf Spee*'s armour and ricocheted outboard to burst in the sea. Three hit the armoured front of B turret, but the steel was too tough, and each ricocheted overboard without causing any damage.

The thirteenth hit wounded Captain Langsdorff. This was another 6-inch shell which went through the starboard side of the foremast underneath the flying bridge, through the deck directly underneath and the port side of the mast without exploding. But a large number of splinters flew off and one of them struck Langsdorff. He had previously been slightly wounded by a splinter.

This time he ordered his second in command, Captain Kay, to come to the flying bridge; but Langsdorff continued in command.

The next shell also hit the foremast, destroying the radio-photo room, and the fifteenth hit, an 8-inch shell from the *Exeter*, went through the Admiral's bridge and the mast without exploding. Successive 6-inch hits destroyed a 5.9-inch gun and killed its crew, wrecked the Night Control Station, and smashed two boats.

Although the pocket battleship had been hit several times without suffering a great deal of damage, splinters from hits and near misses had by this stage put a good deal of equipment out of action.

In the forward conning tower the training mechanism was destroyed, the big rangefinder on the flying bridge was wrecked, the aircraft was badly damaged, most of the searchlights were put out of action, and there were six leaks below the waterline.

The reserve radio transmitter was wrecked by shock, along with the radar ranging apparatus for the guns.[1]

The men in the most terrible of all plights were the British Merchant Navy officers who were prisoners in the *Graf Spee*. Locked in their quarters, they stood a good chance of being either killed by British shells or drowned should the *Graf Spee* be sunk.

As soon as the alarms had sounded all over the pocket battleship – after the *Exeter*'s mast had been sighted – their doors had been locked.

Captain Pottinger, of the *Ashlea*, wrote later:[2] 'We were told afterwards by Captain Langsdorff that we were in the safest part of the ship, also that we were behind armour.

'We could see nothing. At about 6 am the battle commenced. There were repeated concussions, like the firing of big guns. We could not tell whether these were the guns being fired by us or shells striking us. We zig-zagged continually at high speed and heeled over so much that at times I thought we were going to capsize.

'At about 8 AM the firing eased a bit but we continued to zig-zag and fired occasional salvoes from our after 11-inch guns.

'The only view we could get of what was going on was through a small hole in the door through which we could get a running commentary on what could be seen by our several observers.

'We could see some men working an ammunition hoist. They all looked very anxious. From what we could tell, things were not going too well with them. The dead were being piled up outside and the stench was awful. We could see men with rubber gloves on washing down the corpses with hoses. This may account for the report we used gas.

'We could also hear and see men being sick all over the place, some probably from fear and others from the gruesome sights around them.'

Captain Edwards, of the *Trevanion*, had an even better view. In his report he says that the *Graf Spee* was hit first about two minutes after she first opened fire,[3] and later on he could feel more shells bursting on board.

The shell which wrecked the pantry came through a bulkhead and hit a beam above them, making a hole. Captain Edwards climbed up to look

[1] It is not clear from German reports whether the radar was working at all during the action. It frequently broke down because of vibration from the ship's engines.

[2] In his report of the sinking of his ship.

[3] This may well have been the hit referred to by the *Exeter*'s Director Gunner (see page 418): he reported a hit near the funnel with the fifth or sixth salvo.

out, and he could see one of the aircraft had vanished.

At 0740 when Commodore Harwood decided to break off the action until nightfall, thirty-seven of the *Graf Spee*'s officers and men had been killed and fifty-seven wounded. And Langsdorff had had enough.

After receiving a report of the damage he went round the ship to make his own survey with his second in command, Captain Kay. He chatted with the wounded, praised certain men, and did what he could to cheer up his crew. But they were far from being the cheerful, confident youngsters who had gone into battle.

Returning to the bridge after seeing for himself what damage the three small cruisers had caused, he said to his Navigator, Korvettenkapitän Wattenberg: 'We must run into port, the ship is not now seaworthy for the North Atlantic.'[1]

> The Captain expressed this opinion with certainty, and ordered the Navigating Officer to check whether Montevideo or Buenos Aires was the best harbour for that purpose.
>
> The Navigating Officer advised Montevideo, considering the shallow water of the Indio Channel (possibility of fouling the engine cooling water with mud.)
>
> The Captain agreed with this proposal. The strong dependence of Uruguay on England from a political standpoint was not known to him to the full extent.[2]

It now remained to report to Berlin, and Langsdorff drafted a signal to the Operations Division of the *Seekriegsleitung* in which he briefly described the battle and the *Graf Spee*'s action damage.

The log of the pocket battleship said:

> The Captain signalled his desire to enter Montevideo at the same time as he reported on the battle to the Operations Department. He understood that it would be impossible to sail out again, and thought the ship would be interned. Before he ran into Montevideo he received the answer from Operations. 'Agreed, Commander-in-Chief'.

Wattenburg laid off a course for the River Plate, and Langsdorff ordered a speed of twenty-three knots. On the horizon to the north-east and south-west were the two British cruisers. Ahead, although no one realized it, lay the graves of the *Graf Spee* and her Captain.

---

[1] From the *Graf Spee*'s action report.
[2] Ibid.

CHAPTER 17

GUARDING *ACHILLES'* HEEL

'When the action was broken off,' Captain Parry wrote later, 'my own feelings were that the enemy could do anything he wanted to. He showed no sign of being damaged; his main armament was still firing accurately; the *Exeter* was evidently out of it; and so he only had two small cruisers to prevent him attacking the very valuable River Plate trade . . .

'It was therefore rather astonishing, when we turned back a few minutes later, to find the enemy steaming off at fairly high speed to the westward.'

Commodore Harwood ordered the *Ajax* to shadow from the *Graf Spee*'s port quarter and the *Achilles* from her starboard quarter. The time was 0830, the weather was perfect, apart from the increasing wind, which was kicking up a bit of sea; and the *Graf Spee*, despite her diesel engines, obligingly continued to make fairly continuous funnel smoke, so the task of shadowing at long range – then about fifteen miles – presented no difficulties.

Earlier the Commodore had naturally been very anxious about the *Exeter*, the heavyweight of his team, and before the *Ajax* lost her wireless aerials he signalled to Captain Bell: *Join me. What speed have you available?*

But the *Exeter* did not reply: Chief Petty Officer Telegraphist Harold Newman had not yet succeeded in rigging his jury aerials. *Ajax* called her up for more than twenty minutes, not knowing what had happened. Deciding finally that her wireless had been put out of action, Commodore Harwood ordered the Seafox to find her. To Lt Lewin went the signal: *Tell Exeter to close.*

Lewin returned after half an hour and signalled: Exeter *severely damaged and joining you as best she can.* Even from the aircraft the cruiser had looked a terrible mess. Kearney, the observer, reported: '*Exeter* was closed about eighteen miles south of the action. She was obviously hard hit and in no condition to fight another action. The position, course and speed of the squadron was passed to her, the aircraft flew over her in the direction of the Flag, and returned to *Ajax*.'

Lt Lewin wrote later: 'I have never seen such a shambles, anyway in a ship which survived. Her mainmast was moving perceptibly as she rolled.'

The Commodore had now to let the Admiralty, merchant ships in the area, Admiral Lyon, and the *Cumberland* know what was going on. His first signal, which was to give the Admiralty the news that he had found the *Graf Spee*, was, as mentioned earlier, at 0615:

IMMEDIATE: *One pocket battleship 034° south 049° west course 275 degrees.*

This had been followed with a signal to the *Cumberland* to join him as soon as possible. Then at 0637 the *Ajax* transmitted a curt and dramatic signal:

Am engaging one PB; Exeter, Achilles *in company.*

This was followed by a further 'pot-boiler' at 0717 to keep Admiral Lyon, the Admiralty and the *Cumberland* in the picture:

Am engaging one PB in lat 34° south, long 49° west.

Later, when the *Ajax*'s wireless was out of action, Commodore Harwood signalled to the *Achilles*:

Broadcast in plain language to GBMS:[1] *One PB 34° south, 50° west, steering 275 degrees, report to Admiralty.*

The *Achilles* then found that all her own aerials were down and it took some time to rig new ones. By then the Commodore had sent a further signal, this time to the *Cumberland*. Captain Parry later reported to him that the messages had been sent but 'I have only one leg of aerial left.'

Then, to the Admiralty and Admiral Lyon, Harwood made the following signal:

IMMEDIATE: *HMS* Ajax, *HMS* Achilles, *HMS* Exeter *have been heavily engaged. Have withdrawn from daylight close action owing to shortage of ammunition. HMS* Exeter *hauling away due damage, two turrets out of action in HMS* Ajax. *Pocket battleship has undoubtedly been hit. I am shadowing.*

On board the three cruisers there was now plenty to be done. In the *Exeter* there was the task of making the ship seaworthy, in the *Ajax* and *Achilles* repairing damage and shadowing.

All three also had the heartbreaking job of preparing for the burial service. In the *Exeter* it took place at 1545, and her log records: 'Buried at Sea Capt H. R. D. Woods, RM, Lt-Cdr J. Bowman-Manifold, Sub-Lt D. H. Tyler, Midshipman J. Rickcord and forty-seven ratings killed in action. Missing believed killed in action Sub-Lt C. A. L. Morse and one rating.'

Despite all that the ship's doctors could do, several more ratings died of wounds later in the day. (When the ship arrived at the Falkland Islands three days later fifty-nine ratings were taken ashore to hospital, and one man died six hours after she anchored.)

The *Ajax* hoisted the Seafox inboard after Lt Lewin made a fine landing – the observer later reported: 'Conditions were the worst of any in which

---

[1] GBMS – General Broadcast to Merchant Ships.

the aircraft had previously been recovered.'

In the *Achilles*, as Captain Parry's wounded legs were stiffening up, he gave Lt Washbourn permission to leave the DCT to visit each gun turret, have a yarn with the men and tell them what was going on. He later reported to Captain Parry: 'I found everyone in magnificent heart ...'

Then there was the question of the reward to be settled. Captain Parry had said, soon after the war started, he would give £1 to the first man to spot a German warship, and the time had now come to pay up. The rating who had reported the first sight of smoke to Washbourn was sent for, and Captain Parry handed over a pound note.

The rating, after pocketing it, said 'Well, sir, it wasn't me that first saw it; it was ——.' Thus the *Graf Spee* cost Captain Parry another pound.

While the ship settled down into the shadowing routine, Captain Parry glanced over the side of the bridge and noticed a number of men wandering around, apparently aimlessly, on deck. He asked what they were doing and was told, 'They're collecting souvenirs, sir.'

By then it was time for the much-delayed breakfast – huge slices of bread with fried bacon in between were taken round to all the quarters. The guns' crews, still fresh after firing an average of 156 rounds a gun, left their turrets and sat on deck in the sunshine to attack their meal, sum up their chances, and digest the news given them by Lt Washbourn.

It was then that Washbourn heard the comments made about him at the beginning of the action by a stoker, who had not then appreciated that the *Graf Spee* had arrived on the horizon.

The stoker had emerged from a hatchway grumbling about 'Flicking gunnery shoots so flicking early in the flicking morning and why couldn't the flicking Gunnery Jack (Officer) wait till after breakfast?'

At that point in his colourful monologue three large fountains, the manifestation of three 11-inch shells from the *Graf Spee*, rose close alongside. The stoker, commenting 'Cor, this ain't no flicking place for me!', hastily returned down his hatchway.

Outwardly all that the *Achilles* had to show of the action were splinter holes, damage on the upper deck – mostly caused by the after guns firing on a forward bearing – and the paint very badly blistered along the barrels of the guns.

So the two ships continued to shadow the *Graf Spee*, and an indication of how they felt is given by an extract from a letter written by one of the *Achilles'* officers six weeks later: '... We talk loudly now about that phase of the operations as "The Chase", but it didn't seem like that at any time then. It was incredible to us that she should be running away from one and a half rather battered little cruisers, both very short of ammunition. And why, oh why, didn't she turn aside to polish off *Exeter* and make it something of a material victory if a moral defeat?'

At 1010 she did turn aside to snap at the *Achilles*, which, over-estimating the pocket battleship's speed, came up too close on her tail. She turned suddenly and fired three salvoes of 11-inch shells. The first fell short, and Captain Parry immediately altered course to dodge the second salvo, which burst close alongside as the cruiser turned. The third burst in her wake and would have probably hit had Captain Parry not rapidly side-stepped.

On this occasion a Marine, before making for cover, paused a moment as the shells burst close astern to comment: 'Blimey, they're after our Heel.' It was with this in mind that Captain Parry put down a smoke screen and zig-zagged at a more respectful distance.

During the next hour both ships were able to make a proper check on the armament and ammunition left, and it was found that the original hurried estimates, made while the guns were still firing, were wrong.[1] The *Achilles* had roughly estimated that she had 60 rounds for A turret, 90 for B, 90 for X and 100 for Y; now she reported to the Commodore that she had 173 for A, 239 for B, 140 for X and 100 for Y. The *Ajax*, too, found she had roughly double her original estimate.

This was cheering news, since no one was very certain what the *Graf Spee* was going to do next, and the prospect of being caught without ammunition and with fuel running low was not very encouraging for anyone.

The *Achilles'* ammunition report had just been signalled to the *Ajax* when, at 1103, a merchant ship was sighted close to the *Graf Spee* and seemed to be blowing off steam. A few minutes later the *Graf Spee* called up the *Ajax* by wireless, using the cruiser's pre-war call sign, and said:

Please pick up lifeboats of English steamer.

This was the first indication that the enemy was the *Graf Spee* and not the *Admiral Scheer*, and the *Ajax* did not reply; but within fifteen minutes she was close enough to the steamer to see that her boats were still hoisted and there were men aboard. She was the ss *Shakespeare*, and the *Ajax* signalled:

Are you all right? If so hoist International 'C'.

Flag C of the International Code was hoisted on one of the *Shakespeare*'s signal halyards.

Have you received message from Admiral Graf Spee?

Yes, replied the *Shakespeare*, whose crew were still agreeably surprised to

---

[1] In the whole action the *Achilles* fired 340 rounds from A turret, 349 from B, 290 from X and 263 from Y turret. Altogether she fired between 210 and 220 broadsides.

find themselves alive after the passage of the pocket battleship.

Do you require assistance? If not, hoist 'No'.

Once again the flag hoist was run up in the *Shakespeare*: no, she did not need help.

Keep continuous watch on 500[1] kcs, ordered Commodore Harwood, and the *Ajax* steamed off after the *Graf Spee*.

For the *Shakespeare* it had been a very narrow escape. The *Graf Spee*'s log records: 'While steering towards La Plata a large 5,000-ton English steamer was ordered to stop with a warning shot and to send the crew into the boats. The Captain had the intention of torpedoing the steamer if the crew left the ship. He radioed a message to the *Ajax*.

'Since the crew of the steamer did not leave the ship, the Captain abandoned his intention of sinking the ship in view of the probable reception of his own crew in Montevideo.'

So the chase continued; and for a while it became almost routine. Both the cruisers continually altered course and speed to keep the *Graf Spee* in sight, zig-zagging from time to time in case Langsdorff should be tempted to open fire again.

At noon the *Exeter*, her jury wireless aerials rigged, answered the Commodore's signal asking her maximum speed:

> *Eighteen knots. One gun in Y turret available in local control. All other main armament permanently out of action. One 4-inch gun available only. No air in ship.*

This was followed twenty minutes later with: *All guns out of action.*

Half an hour later Captain Bell asked: *Do you know where Admiral Scheer is?*

He was having great trouble steering a reasonable course since he had only a boat compass, and he could not steam at more than eighteen knots because the damaged bulkheads would not stand it. Although the list to starboard had been taken off by pumping fuel oil over into the tanks on the port side, the *Exeter* was still three feet down by the bows.

The Commodore realized now that the gallant ship had no further fighting value, and he ordered Captain Bell to make for the Falkland Islands.

> *From Captain Parry's report: '1534–1542. The masts of a vessel were sighted to the north-westward and reported to you [Commodore Harwood] by V/S. When first seen the masts had the appearance of a merchant vessel, but six minutes later a streamlined funnel appeared . . .'*

[1] The international Distress frequency.

The lookout reported masts bearing Green 45 and Washbourn had swung the *Achilles'* DCT round on to it. He was unable to recognize what little he could see of the ship; but the over-all impression was ominous. She appeared to have a truncated funnel and the high fighting superstructure of a man-o'-war.

She was like nothing in the recognition manuals – everyone in the DCT was agreed on that point. They had not been given any photographs of the *Admiral Hipper* class of German cruisers, but a recent signal had given them enough details to sketch a rough silhouette.

The idea quickly caught on, and Washbourn called down the voice pipe to Captain Parry: 'The ship bearing Green 45 looks very like a *Hipper* to us.'

Whatever thoughts crossed Captain Parry's mind at being told that one of Germany's latest heavy cruisers, mounting eight 8-inch and a dozen 4-inch guns, was likely to join in the already unequal fight, he merely said: 'I think I'll close a little further before reporting, Guns.'

Washbourn decided to get another opinion and climbed up through the hatch in the top of the DCT with the silhouette card and handed it down to the Captain of Marines, saying: 'See what you make of it.'

He looked at the card and then took up his binoculars. After what seemed an age he put them down and said glumly: 'That's her all right.'

Washbourn climbed back into the DCT and reported to Captain Parry: 'I am afraid there's no doubt now, Sir . . .'

'All right,' Captain Parry replied, 'I'll make the enemy report.'

In a few moments a signalman was flashing to the *Ajax*: *Emergency. Enemy in sight bearing 297 degrees.*

The strange ship was broad-on the *Achilles'* starboard bow, while the *Ajax* was nine miles away on the port beam. The Commodore signalled: *What is it?*

Captain Parry replied: *Suspected 8-inch cruiser. Am confirming.*

For the Commodore this was grim news. The two cruisers were in no state to take on another enemy in a fight which could have only one result. But the sudden appearance of a German heavy cruiser would explain the *Graf Spee*'s anxiety to get away to the westward – she had led them into a trap.

Harwood ordered the *Achilles* not to engage the new enemy and sent off a signal to the *Exeter* warning her to keep away from the coast. Lewin was told to get ready to fly off again in the Seafox.

By then, however, the hull of the strange ship had risen over the horizon and could be seen from the *Achilles*. Everyone was vastly relieved when she was identified as a British merchantman – the ss *Delane*. Her streamlined funnel had given her the appearance of one of the *Hipper* class at long range.

And very thankfully Captain Parry signalled to the *Ajax*: *False alarm.*

While the two cruisers broadcast warnings to Allied merchant ships who might be lying in her path, the *Graf Spee* continued on her westward course, and the Commodore was by now fairly certain she would enter the Plate.

That raised several problems for him. The estuary of the River Plate, dividing Uruguay on the east from Argentina on the west, is in fact a huge bay forming a half circle, with the river entering in the middle. Its size can be gauged by the fact that from Lobos Island on the Uruguayan side of the bay to Cape San Antonia on the Argentinian side is 120 miles of open sea.

Yet three widely separated deep-water channels can be used to enter the River Plate. The northernmost is between the English Bank lightship and Cumberland Shoal, the second between English Bank and Rouen Bank, and the southernmost, which is nearly thirty miles wide, between Rouen Bank and the Argentine coast.

The city of Montevideo lies on the east bank of the river where it empties into the bay, while Buenos Aires lies 115 miles farther up-river on the Argentine side, being reached by the Indio Channel.

The *Graf Spee* was approaching the great bay obliquely; and if she was in fact making for the Plate she would enter on the eastern side. But she could round English Bank and double out again in the darkness, since night would have fallen before she reached the coast.

There were several things Langsdorff could do; and the Commodore, like a maritime Sherlock Holmes, tried to put himself in the German's position and deduce what his intentions were.

To do this successfully Harwood had to ask two questions – how badly damaged was the *Graf Spee*, and why had she broken off the action? Unfortunately, he could only guess at the answers.

Briefly, Harwood had to plan for the pocket battleship entering either Montevideo or Buenos Aires, or doubling back in the darkness and making a dash for the broad Atlantic, trying to escape the pursuing cruisers in the night – not a difficult task, since these were the days before radar; and although Langsdorff did not know it, they would be out of fuel long before reinforcements arrived.

Shortly before 1400 the Commodore signalled to Captain H. W. McCall, the Naval Attaché at Montevideo, that the *Graf Spee* was heading direct for the Plate, and requested him to arrange for Lobos, English Bank, the Whistle Buoy off Montevideo entrance, Recalada light vessel and San Borombon Bay – on the west side – to be watched. He stressed the need for negative reports from areas in which the *Graf Spee* was not sighted.

Within nine hours Captain McCall reported that all arrangements had been made and the areas would be watched by tugs and aircraft.

To Captain Parry the Commodore signalled:

If enemy passes west of Lobos Achilles *is to follow him.* Ajax *will proceed south of English Bank in case he doubles out. Be careful you are not caught at dawn up sun as even if he anchors he may come to sea at any time. He is not to be relied on to respect territorial waters.*

Shadowing continued without incident until 1852, when lookouts in the *Ajax* saw the *Graf Spee* altering course to starboard and noticed her after turret training round in their direction. The three guns started elevating, and at once Captain Woodhouse put the *Ajax* on a zig-zag course in case the Germans started shooting.

The range was thirteen miles, and for a few minutes nothing happened. At 1913 the pocket battleship started making white smoke, then she fired a salvo which burst between 400 and 600 yards short. Immediately Captain Woodhouse altered course to port and a second salvo burst in the cruiser's wake as she turned.

The *Graf Spee*, her gesture of defiance apparently made, turned back on to her original course.

Sunset was due at 2048, and the after-glow would obviously silhouette the *Graf Spee* very nicely, whereas the two cruisers would be hidden against the darker eastern sky. But in order to keep in touch after dark the two cruisers would have to close the range before 2000, and they started creeping nearer.

By this time the coast of Uruguay was in sight, and Captain Parry took the *Achilles* as close inshore as possible. He had edged up to within eleven miles of the *Graf Spee* at 2055, and this no doubt irked the touchy Germans: they put down a smoke screen and fired three salvoes at the *Achilles*. The first two fell short and the third close astern.

This provoked Captain Parry into replying, so he too put down a smoke screen and fired five salvoes as he turned away. The *Ajax*, who was in a good position for flank marking, signalled that she had seen the *Graf Spee* straddled.

The Germans opened fire at the *Achilles* three times during the next hour; but Captain Parry did not take the bait. He was sure the Germans could not see his ship in the twilight and if he replied they would be able to plot his exact position from the flashes of his guns.

'None of these last efforts fell anywhere near us,' Captain Parry wrote later. 'But his cordite smoke being unexpectedly black, these salvoes created a smoke screen which made him very difficult to see; and it was not till two hours after sunset that he could again be distinguished unmistakably. His position then showed he was passing north of English Bank.'

The *Ajax* had earlier signalled *I am leaving her to you this side. Make frequent enemy reports*, and turned to port to guard the south-western exit from the Plate; at 2213, by altering course to the south slightly, Captain Parry had the pocket battleship neatly silhouetted against the lights of Montevideo, a city at peace where young couples danced in night-clubs, brightly-illuminated shop windows displayed their wares and war seemed a lifetime away; but at that moment it was less than seven miles.

> *From Commodore Harwood's dispatch: '. . . Graf Spee proceeded north of the English Bank and anchored in Montevideo roads at 0050.'*

'My chief preoccupation at that time,' he wrote, 'was how long did *Graf Spee* intend to stay there. The primary necessity was to keep to seaward of the *Graf Spee* if she came to sea again, and at the same time to avoid being caught against the dawn light.

'At 2350 I ordered *Ajax* and *Achilles* to withdraw from the Plate. *Achilles* to patrol the area from the Uruguayan coast to a line 120 degrees from English Bank, and *Ajax* the southern area, both ships to move back into the Plate in their respective sectors after dawn.'

Everyone in both ships remained closed up at Action Stations all night while they kept guard on the stable doors. There was every chance that Captain McCall would be able to warn them if the *Graf Spee* got under way again; but once she was out of sight of the harbour she would rapidly disappear into the darkness unless one or other of the two waiting cruisers could get her silhouetted against the lights of the coastline and estimate her course.

For the captains of the two cruisers it was a worrying time; and both of them stayed on their bridges the whole night until after dawn.

CHAPTER 18

NO HELP AT HAND

For the time being, then, the two small cruisers, manned by weary but resolute men, stood alone between the enemy and the sea. If the *Graf Spee* could sink or elude either of them, then she would almost certainly escape into the vast area of the South Atlantic or even the Antarctic. Both the ships had been heavily engaged, and were short of fuel and ammunition (the nearest supply of the latter was at Trinidad). They had no hope of destroying the *Graf Spee* unless they could engage her together; but this was likely to be impossible – at least at the beginning – since they had to watch different channels across the 120-mile stretch of the estuary.

The difficulties and dangers were many and great; and Commodore Harwood could look for little immediate assistance. The only trump cards now had to be played by the diplomats ashore; and the *Graf Spee* always had the last trick – she could weigh anchor and slip out whenever she wanted to, whatever the diplomatic rights and wrongs of the situation.

The Commodore wrote: 'I requested His Britannic Majesty's Minister, Montevideo [Mr E. Millington-Drake], to use every possible means of delaying *Graf Spee*'s sailing, in order to gain time for reinforcements to reach me. I suggested he should sail British ships and invoke the twenty-four-hour rule[1] to prevent her leaving.

'I learned that the *Ark Royal*, *Renown*, *Neptune*, *Dorsetshire*, *Shropshire* and three destroyers were all closing the Plate, but none of them could reach me for at least five days.

'*Cumberland* reported that she would arrive in the Plate at 2200/14th December, having made the passage from the Falkland Islands in thirty-four hours ...'

Meanwhile, in London the Admiralty was making its plans. Commodore Harwood's original enemy report had been received in Whitehall at breakfast time, and the signal was immediately taken to Admiral Pound, the First Sea Lord.

He realized the unequal odds facing Harwood, but there was not much he could do until he had more news. And he had to wait more than two hours before the Commodore's signal arrived saying that the *Exeter* had been badly damaged and that he was breaking off the daylight action.

Here, in order, are the majority of the relevant signals which arrived at Admiralty that day.

---

[1] If a merchant ship of a belligerent nation sails from a neutral port, under International Law a warship of the opposing country is not allowed to sail for twenty-four hours.

Commodore Harwood to Forces K and X (intercepted by Admiralty):

IMMEDIATE: *One pocket battleship 034° south, 049° west course 275 degrees.*

Harwood to the *Cumberland* and Admiralty:

IMMEDIATE: *HMS Ajax, HMS Achilles, HMS Exeter have been heavily engaged. Have withdrawn from daylight close action owing to shortage of ammunition. HMS Exeter hauling away due damage, two turrets out of action in HMS Ajax. Pocket battleship has undoubtedly been hit. I am shadowing.*

Staff Officer (Intelligence), Freetown, to Admiralty:

British ship GCVQ (Doric Star) due 9 December has not arrived.

Harwood to Admiralty and Admiral Lyon (at Freetown):

MOST IMMEDIATE. *Position, course and speed of pocket battleship 034° 44' south, 051° 40' west, 260 degrees, 22 knots, using call sign DTGS. HMS Ajax and HMS Achilles shadowing.*

HMS Exeter very badly damaged. One gun in local control remains in action. Speed reduced maximum eighteen knots. Have directed her to proceed to Falkland Islands. Aircraft reports twenty-five to thirty hits obtained on pocket battleship but he still has high speed.

Staff Officer (Intelligence), Freetown, to Admiralty:

British ship Tairoa due here 11 December has not arrived.

Admiral Lyon to the *Cumberland*:

Proceed to sea with all dispatch and endeavour to make contact with HMS Exeter and/or Commodore CSAD who reports contact with pocket battleship ...[1]

Staff Officer (Intelligence), Montevideo, to Admiralty:

Pocket battleship sighted fifteen miles east from Punta del Este being engaged by two cruisers.

Admiral Lyon to the *Neptune*:

If fuel permits, proceed to Rio de Janeiro, complete with fuel, and join CCSAD off River Plate. If necessary take in fuel from [oiler] Cherryleaf to reach Rio de Janeiro.

---

[1] *Cumberland* had received only garbled signals from the Commodore but her captain, on his own initiative, had already put to sea.

Staff Officer (Intelligence), Montevideo, to Admiralty:

> MOST IMMEDIATE: *German pocket battleship anchored in Montevideo Roads 2350 today Wednesday.*

Staff Officer (Intelligence), Montevideo, to Admiralty:

> *German armoured ship understood locally to be* Admiral Graf Spee *now anchored in Montevideo.*

While these cryptic signals were gradually building up the picture for the First Sea Lord, he made the first moves to send reinforcements to help Commodore Harwood. But apart from the *Cumberland*, already steaming north from the Falkland Islands at thirty knots to get to the Commodore 1,000 miles away, there were no British warships within 3,000 miles of the Plate.

Force I (the cruisers *Cornwall* and *Gloucester* and the carrier *Eagle*) were at Durban, more than 4,000 miles from the Plate, and as they were at the disposal of Admiral Lyon he ordered them to Cape Town 'with all dispatch', intending to give them further orders when they arrived, since by then the situation would be clearer.[1]

The cruisers *Sussex* and *Shropshire*, Force H, were on their way to Cape Town, and Admiral Lyon ordered them to proceed to the Cape 'with all possible speed', refuel and sail for Freetown. However, when he lost Force I he ordered both ships to stay at the Cape.

The *Dorsetshire*, which was at the Cape on the day of the battle, was ordered to sail for the Plate 3,600 miles to the westward. The *Shropshire* followed her two days later, also bound for Montevideo. She was due to arrive on 23 December.

Three thousand miles to the north along the South American coast, 600 miles from Pernambuco, the carrier *Ark Royal* and the *Renown*, Force K, were on their way to meet the *Neptune*, which was coming south with her destroyers when the Commodore first sighted the *Graf Spee*.

The *Renown* was short of fuel, and as she had barely enough to reach the Plate and none for a long chase, Admiral Lyon ordered Vice-Admiral Wells, commanding Force K, to meet the *Neptune* and then go to Freetown to refuel. This would take them in the opposite direction to the Plate, but Freetown was the nearest British port to which Admiral Lyon could send them to fuel; and from his point of view diplomatic difficulties might prevent him from using a neutral port.

The First Sea Lord, directing operations in the Admiralty, quickly realized this and had the power to invoke the Foreign Office's help. He

---

[1] A few hours later, after they had left Durban, the Admiralty put these ships under the command of the C-in-C, East Indies, for work in connection with some important convoys, and they were recalled to Durban.

signalled to Admiral Lyon:

> *Force K is to proceed to River Plate, fuelling at a South American port or from an oiler.*

This would save them more than 2,000 miles, but the diplomats would have to put in some hard work. The First Sea Lord then signalled to Admiral Lyon:

> *Report where Force K will fuel. Pressure is being applied by Ambassador so that they can fuel at Bahia or Rio de Janeiro should you select either of these places.*

These signals were repeated to Vice-Admiral Wells in the *Ark Royal* and the First Sea Lord followed them up with a message telling him to leave the destroyers (*Hardy*, *Hostile* and *Hero*) behind if they were likely to delay him. Admiral Lyon then ordered him to refuel at Rio de Janeiro, which was on the direct route and 1,000 miles north of the Plate. He at once increased speed to twenty-five knots.

Thus the *Ark Royal* and *Renown* could reach Rio by 17 December and would want twelve hours to refuel, and they would still be 1,000 miles – forty hours' steaming – from the Plate; the *Neptune* would reach Rio about twelve hours after Force K; the *Dorsetshire* would not get to Montevideo from South Africa before 21 December, and the *Shropshire*, which had later been ordered to sail, was not due until 23 December.

So at dawn on 14 December, when the Commodore's two cruisers began their daylight vigil in the Plate estuary, they knew that, apart from the *Cumberland* joining them that evening, there would be no further reinforcements until the *Ark Royal* and *Renown* and *Neptune* arrived in five days, and the *Dorsetshire* in seven days.

CHAPTER 19

LANGSDORFF DECIDES TO SCUTTLE

Daybreak on the 14th found every available man in the *Graf Spee* hard at work. The bodies of the thirty-seven men killed in the action were being prepared for burial, and the fifty-seven wounded were to be moved ashore for treatment. Repair parties were busy plugging innumerable splinter and shell holes – the pocket battleship was estimated to have been hit more than fifty times – clearing away wreckage, repairing electric leads and making a list of special equipment necessary to make good some of the more extensive damage.[1]

The load on Captain Langsdorff's shoulders was, to a certain extent, being eased. At sea he had no one with whom he could discuss decisions – command of a ship is a lonely, isolated task. Now he had an abundance of talent to help him and was in direct contact with Berlin.

The German Naval Attaché at Buenos Aires immediately flew over to Montevideo with German civilian constructors and boarded the *Graf Spee*. The German Ambassador at Montevideo, Dr Otto Langmann, was already on board by the time he arrived.

Captain Langsdorff, by now almost completely exhausted by lack of sleep and worry, outlined the position to the two men: the *Graf Spee* was unfit to go to sea because of action damage and he could not feed his men properly because the galley was wrecked. He had sixty-one British Merchant Navy officers on board and he proposed to free them almost immediately. And it was essential that he should discover what British reinforcements were due.

Dr Langmann, a stockily-built and testy little man who wore pince-nez, then told Langsdorff of the mistake he had made in entering a Uruguayan harbour, instead of going up to Buenos Aires where the atmosphere would probably have been more cordial.

The British and French Governments, he said, would very soon be exerting the strongest pressure on the 'politically weak' Uruguay to make sure the *Graf Spee* was either allowed to stay no more than the seventy-two hours[2] allowed by International Law or that she was interned if she overstayed that period.

Then both Langmann and the Naval Attaché went ashore for a conference with the Uruguayan Foreign Minister, Dr Guani.

Meanwhile the *Graf Spee*'s Engineer, Korvettenkapitän Klepp, and the

---

[1] See Appendix D.
[2] In fact Britain was pressing for only twenty-four hours on the ground that as the *Graf Spee* had steamed into harbour at high speed she was obviously seaworthy.

German civilian constructor from Buenos Aires were making a detailed inspection of the whole ship to estimate how long it would take – bearing in mind local facilities – to get her ready for sea. The major items on their list were four small leaks in Sections I–III and several more about six inches in diameter at and under the waterline at Section XIII on the starboard side, and two in Sections V and XIV, and one about five inches in diameter at the waterline at Section X on the port side. The underwater holes had been plugged, but the others, along with several eight-inch holes in the upper deck, would have to be welded. The galley would also need a good deal of work on it. There was some damage to fighting equipment which would have to be made good if the *Graf Spee* was to go into action effectively again. And there was also an unexploded British shell, embedded in the hull, to be removed.

Klepp and the constructor talked it over and decided that a minimum of fourteen days would be needed for the crew and civilian workmen with equipment to get the ship ready for sea. They reported their findings to Langsdorff. He immediately passed them on to Dr Langmann, who found himself in something of a quandary. He wanted to get as long a stay as possible for the *Graf Spee*; but on the other hand he did not want to reveal to the British the extent of the damage. In the end he sent a Note to the Uruguayan Foreign Minister requesting permission for a stay of fourteen days.

At the conference at the Foreign Ministry, Langmann and the Naval Attaché put their case to Dr Guani as strongly as they could; and it was finally agreed with him that a Uruguayan Technical Commission should inspect the ship later that afternoon to determine what repairs were needed.

So at 1900 a Uruguayan Navy commander and an engineer officer arrived on board and were shown round by Klepp. They agreed some repairs were necessary to make the ship seaworthy, but no amount of questioning by the Germans would get them to say how long they considered would be required. They had first to report to their superior officers, they explained.

Thus, in a way hardly satisfactory to the Germans, the *Graf Spee*'s first day in Montevideo ended. In Berlin, Grand Admiral Raeder had received a brief radio report from Captain Langsdorff describing the damage and his immediate intentions; and with Ribbentrop, the German Foreign Minister, was anxiously awaiting a cable from Dr Langmann giving Uruguay's decision on the time to be allowed.

In Whitehall that day the Admiralty had been working closely with the Foreign Office. All available warships were, as described earlier, steaming to Commodore Harwood's assistance; now it was up to the diplomats to do their juggling.

Ideally, the Admiralty would have liked to see the *Graf Spee* interned; but failing that they wanted her to be allowed to stay for four or five days until the British reinforcements arrived off the Plate.

But it was vitally important that the Germans should not guess that. Otherwise, as soon as the *Graf Spee* realized that there was still only the *Ajax* and *Achilles* waiting for her outside, she might well make a dash for it and sink both the cruisers before escaping.

There were, therefore, three things to be done. The first one was to kick up a fuss in Montevideo and request that the *Graf Spee* should not be allowed to stay more than twenty-four hours, thus making it appear that Britain was anxious for the *Graf Spee* to sail as soon as possible. The Germans would naturally assume the British had several warships just over the horizon, waiting to fall on the pocket battleship with vicious enthusiasm.

The second was to 'plant' stories that British heavy warships were in fact already in position; and the third was to make sure the *Graf Spee*, despite Britain's apparently sincere and stern protests, did *not* sail. As Commodore Harwood had already suggested, this could be done for a few days by sailing British merchant ships and claiming twenty-four hours' grace.

Instructions were cabled to Mr E. Millington-Drake, the British Minister in Montevideo, and the following signal was sent to Commodore Harwood, in the *Ajax*, and to Admiral Lyon in Freetown:

> *Foreign Office have instructed HM Minister, Montevideo to use every endeavour to get* Spee *interned. Arguments to be used are (A) if ship is seaworthy, Hague Convention does not permit repairs and she must leave after twenty-four hours or be interned, (B) if she is not seaworthy same is true, as there is wide support for the view that no shore facilities or extension of time may be granted for repairs and damage sustained in action.*
>
> *Foreign Office have added for Minister's own information that if Uruguayan authorities will not accept these arguments we should prefer that ship remains four or five days.*

Meanwhile the *Ajax* and the *Achilles* continued on guard during the day and night of 14 December. The Commodore received various signals telling him when it was anticipated the reinforcements would arrive. The *Cumberland* joined him at 2200 after her dash from the Falkland Islands, and he ordered her to cover the sector between Rouen Bank and English Bank, with the *Achilles* to the north of her and the *Ajax* to the south.

'Should *Graf Spee* come out,' he wrote later, 'she was to be shadowed and all ships were to concentrate sufficiently far to seaward to enable a concerted attack to be carried out.'

That night after dark Captain Parry decided to take the *Achilles* right in close, and he found that it was possible to see anything moving in the entrance channel silhouetted against the lights of the town.

However, the Commodore said they must not commit any warlike act so close in. Although it was outside the three-mile limit, which was the only form of territorial waters which Britain recognized, Argentina and Uruguay between them claimed the whole Plate Estuary.

Next day, Friday, 15 December, Captain Langsdorff had the melancholy task of attending the funeral of the *Graf Spee*'s dead in a cemetery outside Montevideo. Hundreds of people lined the streets watching the cortège – a naval band forming a vanguard of brassy melancholy – move through the city, and a few German sympathizers gave Nazi salutes.

At the cemetery Langsdorff, in white uniform, with seven medals on his left breast and the Nazi eagle emblem sewn on the right, his left hand on the hilt of his sword, spoke a short funeral oration over the coffins, each of which was draped with a Nazi flag.

He then stepped to each of the coffins in turn and sprinkled earth over it. His face was drawn, and there were dark rings under his eyes. His uniform was creased and he looked very weary. Finally he stood back, flanked by the German petty officers who were the pall-bearers, and with the German Ambassador and several civilians standing behind him. Every German man and woman present then stood to attention and raised their right arms stiffly, in the Nazi salute. All except Langsdorff. His left hand still clasping the hilt of his sword, he brought his right hand up to the peak of his cap in the old naval salute. He was oblivious to the sharp eyes of Dr Langmann, who realized that the photographs being taken by Press cameramen would very shortly be printed on the front pages of newspapers all over the world

One of those newspapers, the *Washington Post*, wrote of 'the tribute offered by the English merchant seamen who were formerly prisoners of Captain Langsdorff. They, at the graveside, honoured the German sailors killed by the British guns ... Restored to freedom in Montevideo, they placed on the coffins of the German dead a wreath inscribed "To the memory of brave men of the sea from their comrades of the British Merchant Service".'

Later in the day Langsdorff, back on board the *Graf Spee*, received disturbing reports from the German Embassy in Buenos Aires about the strengthening of British forces off the Plate. It was said that the *Ark Royal* and *Renown* had left Cape Town on 12 December[1] for an unknown

[1] When they were, in fact, off Pernambuco.

destination; and furthermore chartered private planes flying over the Plate Estuary had sighted four British cruisers.

Then, to cap this, one of the *Graf Spee*'s gunnery officers personally reported sighting from the Director Control Tower a large warship which he considered to be the *Renown*; and on the horizon he saw what seemed to be the *Ark Royal* and two or three destroyers.

People ashore working for the Germans reported sighting several warships and the *Cumberland* was 'definitely identified'.

So the rumours and reports came in to Langsdorff. Some were inspired by the British Admiralty and some by people genuinely wishing to help the Germans. But it was the gunnery officer's report which worried Langsdorff most of all.

At the same time the German Ambassador was being told of the Uruguayan Government's decision on the *Graf Spee*'s stay in port. She was to be allowed seventy-two hours, and any extension 'was not acceptable'. Their decision was based on the report of their Technical Commission, which said that seventy-two hours was adequate to make good the damage.

'The Uruguayan Government and populace were not unfriendly to the Germans,' the Germans later recorded, 'and the Foreign Minister had agreed that the time should commence from the time of the return to the shore of the Uruguayan Technical Commission. By this time *Spee* would have been nearly ninety-six hours in harbour from the time of her arrival.

'The German Ambassador, in his telegram to the Foreign Office, attributed the Uruguayan Government's decision to "the extraordinary economic pressure with which they were being treated by England and France".'

Early next day, 16 December, after spending the night considering the news from Dr Langmann, Captain Langsdorff dispatched a signal to the Naval High Command in Berlin, in which he outlined the situation and requested instructions. He said:

(1) Renown *and* Ark Royal *as well as cruisers and destroyers off Montevideo. Close blockade at night. No prospects of breaking out to the open sea and getting through to Germany.*

(2) *Intend to proceed to the limit of neutral waters. If I can fight my way through to Buenos Aires with ammunition still remaining I shall endeavour to do so.*

(3) *As a break-through might result in the destruction of* Spee *without the possibility of causing damage to the enemy, request instructions whether to scuttle the ship (in spite of the inadequate depth of water in the Plate estuary) or to submit to internment.*

To his appreciation of the situation the German Ambassador added his own version in a telegram to the German Foreign Office:

> *No argument concerning the legal rights can alter the necessity for an urgent decision regarding* Spee. *Superior enemy naval forces which have been clearly observed from on board* Spee *make it appear to the Commanding Officer quite out of the question to shake off shadowers and thus achieve a successful break-through to Germany. From this point of view the fourteen days' stay would not alter the situation and could only assist the concentration of enemy naval forces.*
>
> *I am at one with the Naval Attaché regarding the internment of the vessel as the worst possible solution in the circumstances. It would be preferable in view of the shortage of ammunition to blow her up in the shallow waters of the Plate and to have the crew interned.*

In Berlin, however, the Foreign Office still seemed unable to grasp the situation. Ribbentrop, whose temper when thwarted always overcame his limited reasoning powers, was unused to having small countries standing up to him. The rule of law was of little interest and had no bearing on the situation as far as he was concerned. Was not he the man Hitler – after the signing of the treaty with Russia – described as 'a second Bismarck'?

But apparently he failed to realize that Uruguay was not standing alone: eleven American Republics, including the United States, had a vital interest in the outcome, since the Havana Convention of 1928, to which the United States and several South American countries were signatories, was involved.

The British request for no more than twenty-four hours' stay was, of course, based on three Articles of the Hague Convention of 1907 – Article XI which forbids belligerent warships, unless individual nations have local laws to the contrary, to stay more than twenty-four hours in the territorial waters of a neutral power; Article XIII, which obliges a neutral country to notify a belligerent warship to leave its waters within twenty-four hours; and Article XIV, under which a belligerent warship may not prolong its stay beyond twenty-four hours except on account of damage or stress of weather.

Regarding this last Article, the ruling of the Havana Convention was that 'damage' did not cover damage caused by enemy action.

The British Minister had also drawn Uruguay's attention to Article XVII of the Hague Convention which said that repairs to belligerent warships must be only those absolutely necessary to make her seaworthy and must not add to her fighting efficiency.

Thus the Uruguayans had been more than fair in granting seventy-two hours, starting after the twenty-four hours the *Graf Spee* had already spent in port.

Nevertheless, Ribbentrop replied to Dr Langmann by cable saying that the Uruguayan Government's decision was completely incomprehensible 'having regard to the condition of the *Spee* and of the legal position'. Dr Langmann and Captain Langsdorff were ordered to seek to prolong the authorized stay and to 'counter with the greatest possible energy the influence of the British'.

At Dr Langmann's meeting later in the day with the Uruguayan Minister of Defence, this armchair directive proved impossible of fulfilment as the Minister appeared 'completely in the English camp and was the person chiefly responsible for the unfavourable decision[1] of the Uruguayan Cabinet'.

Further evidence of the German Foreign Office's wishful thinking and lack of realism came in another telegram an hour or so later:

> *According to English Press reports the* Ark Royal *is in the Plate area. As you know we believe the* Ark Royal *has been sunk. By order of the Fuehrer you are to attempt to take photographs of the supposed* Ark Royal. *Signal results and forward photographs.*

The Germans were unable to charter an aircraft to make a reconnaissance ...

Whatever Berlin's view of the situation, neither Dr Langmann nor Captain Langsdorff was very optimistic. Various articles considered to be of historic interest were taken ashore from the *Graf Spee* for dispatch to Berlin. They included the Battle Ensign worn during the action, a picture (which was damaged by shell splinters) of the late Admiral Graf von Spee, and the ship's bell.

In Berlin, having received Captain Langsdorff's signal, Admiral Raeder reported to Hitler at 1300 to put forward his suggestions concerning the pocket battleship and to get a decision on her fate. Also present at the meeting were Brigadier-General Jodl, who was Chief of the Operations Staff of the German High Command, and Commander von Puttkamer, a member of Admiral Raeder's staff.

The minutes of the meeting say that Admiral Raeder reported that at least two weeks were needed to make the *Graf Spee* seaworthy and that Uruguay had granted only seventy-two hours. The Foreign Office had been requested to continue their efforts to gain more time but 'this appears hopeless, however, as Britain and France are exerting great pressure, and Uruguay will conform to their wishes. Uruguay is unreliable as a neutral,

---

[1] Nevertheless, the Uruguayan Chamber of Deputies, which ordinarily is far from being a unified body, subsequently voted unanimously unqualified approval of all that the Government had done with regard to the *Graf Spee*.

and is not able to defend her neutrality. Internment in Montevideo is therefore out of the question.

'A break-through to the Argentine, which is stronger,' Raeder added, 'could be considered, since this would permit us to retain greater freedom of action. The captain of the *Graf Spee* has proposed a break-through to Buenos Aires, and he requests a decision as to whether, if the prospect is hopeless, he should choose internment in Montevideo or scuttle the ship in the fairly shallow waters of the Plate.'

Raeder then read out Langsdorff's signal, and gave his views. He could not recommend internment in Uruguay, and the right course, he said, would be an attempt to break through, or, if necessary, to scuttle the ship in the River Plate. He read the signal he proposed sending to Langsdorff.

Hitler, who had been listening carefully to what Raeder had to say, then declared he too was opposed to internment 'especially since there is a possibility that the *Graf Spee* might score a success against the British ships in the break-through'. He approved of the proposed instructions for Langsdorff.

These instructions, sent as Radiogram 1347/16 to the *Graf Spee* at 1700 said:

(1) *Attempt by all means to extend the time in neutral waters in order to guarantee freedom of action as long as possible.*

(2) *With reference to No. 2. Approved. [Langsdorff's proposal to put out to the neutral boundary and, if possible, fighting through to Buenos Aires.]*

(3) *With reference to No. 3 [if destruction was certain, should Langsdorff scuttle the ship or allow her to be interned]. NO internment in Uruguay. Attempt effective destruction if ship is scuttled.*
Signed: Raeder.

Later that evening Dr Langmann cabled from Montevideo that he had attempted to get the time limit extended but had failed, and Admiral Raeder sent a further signal to Captain Langsdorff:

As envoy reported impossibility of extending time limit, instructions according to Radiogram 1347/16 Nos. 2 and 3 remain in force.

During the afternoon and evening of 16 December, while Raeder and Hitler discussed these instructions, Captain Langsdorff had been preparing for a break-through. He had received reports from Rio de Janeiro and other sources which he and the Naval Attaché considered reliable, that the *Renown* and the *Achilles* had requested permission to enter the port, the latter to put wounded ashore. The *Ark Royal* was also reported off Rio de Janeiro, outside territorial waters.

Then the Harbourmaster of Montevideo informed Captain Langsdorff that a British steamer had sailed at 1815 that day and that in consequence the *Graf Spee* could not, under the Hague Convention, put to sea until twenty-four hours had elapsed – i.e. until 1815 next day.

This news appalled Langsdorff. His best chance of making a successful break-through depended mainly on being able to make a dash for it, hoping to take the waiting British warships by surprise. But now, unable to sail before 1815 on the 17th, with his seventy-two hour time limit expiring at 2000, he had only one and three-quarter hours in which to select a sailing time.

The British had obviously sailed the steamer with this fact in mind, commented Langsdorff. He called a meeting which was attended by Kay, his Executive Officer, Wattenberg, his Senior Navigating Officer, two other officers, and the German Naval Attaché to consider the alternatives to breaking through to Germany.

Langsdorff began the meeting by saying that the seventy-two hours granted were not enough to patch the holes in the ship's hull and restore her seaworthiness. In other respects too, he considered the condition of the *Graf Spee*, as already described, precluded any idea of breaking through to Germany, even should she succeed in getting through the British forces off the Plate.

But, he told them, there was a possibility of putting to sea and, with the ammunition remaining, destroying one or more of the enemy; but the shallow water of the Plate was a handicap. If the *Graf Spee* should receive a hit and have her draught increased by flooding, she would ground and then be more or less defenceless, and the British would be able to shoot her to pieces. They might then be unable to prevent secret equipment falling into enemy hands.

On the other hand, said Langsdorff, it was out of the question to stay longer than the authorized time: if the *Graf Spee* stayed in harbour after 2000 next day, it was likely that the British ships would be summoned in and a naval battle would develop in the port.

'The severance of relationships between Uruguay and Germany would be the inescapable result of such an incident,' he added.

The break-through to Buenos Aires was then discussed, and it was agreed that it was impossible. The main reason was that, with the cooling-water intakes for the engines in the ship's bottom, there was the danger, in the shallow and muddy waters of the Plate, that they would get blocked up, causing the engines to run hot, and the ship, perhaps already in action with the enemy, would run into difficulties. In addition, they agreed, it was very questionable whether the Argentine would allow any longer period for repairs than Uruguay. The long approach channel to the Plate would also be disadvantageous for any subsequent attempts to put to sea.

Admiral Raeder's instructions forbade internment. Thus, said Langsdorff, the only alternative was to scuttle the ship outside territorial waters ...

He gave instructions for his officers to prepare for this eventuality, but he warned them that scuttling was not to be ordered until he conferred again with the Ambassador.

The Ambassador, as mentioned in Raeder's second telegram to Langsdorff, had had a two-hour interview with the Uruguayan Foreign Minister that evening, and at times the conversation became very heated.

Dr Langmann, desperately seeking a few more days' grace, had demanded sufficient time to permit friendly negotiations; but the Foreign Minister was adamant. Seventy-two hours was all the time that could be permitted under international law.

Langmann was playing for high stakes and he put up every argument he could muster, but the Foreign Minister would not budge. Finally the angry Ambassador requested an audience with the President, but the Minister insisted that no interview could be granted unless the Ambassador acknowledged the seventy-two-hour time limit. Langmann realized he was beaten. Hot and angry, he left the room to report to Berlin and to Langsdorff.

It was well after midnight that Langsdorff, with a heavy heart, then wrote a long official letter to the Ambassador in which, at the end, he made known his decision. It said:

Admiral Graf Spee   Montevideo
                                                         17:12:39
To: The German Ambassador Otto Langmann.
Your Excellency,

[The letter begins with the usual courtesies and he thanks the people of Uruguay for the reception he and his crew had been afforded.]

It was to my great regret amid these demonstrations of true human sentiments a jarring note was struck.

(1) By reason of what you have told me regarding your interview with the Foreign Minister of the Republic of Uruguay I am forced to regard as final and binding the time limit fixed as 2000 on 17:12:39 – before which time the *Admiral Graf Spee* must put to sea even if the repairs vitally necessary to make the vessel seaworthy cannot be completed by then.

I hereby register a formal protest against the decision of the Government of Uruguay.

(2) In accordance with Article 17, Chapter XIII of the Hague

Convention, permission for warships of belligerent powers to remain in a neutral port may be granted for a period sufficient to carry out such repairs as are essential for the safe navigation of such vessels.

As far back as the year 1914 there was a precedent for this in South America. For several weeks the cruiser *Glasgow* lay in port carrying out repairs.

After an expert survey of the damage, I requested a period of fifteen days to carry out repairs in respect of the damage which compromised the seaworthiness of my ship.

The commission of experts sent by the Uruguayan Government was in a position while on board my ship to ascertain that the fighting capacity of my vessel (by which I mean the engines and armament) had suffered to such a small extent that there was no need for me to utilize the period of time I originally requested in order to increase her fighting capacity.

The said commission was able to ascertain that the hull of my ship gave evidence of damage, the repair of which was essential to the seaworthiness of the vessel.

In addition, it was patently obvious to this commission that the cooking installations and bakery on board were in a damaged condition – and that it was essential (considering the large crew borne) that these installations be in good working order before a long period on the high seas could be contemplated.

Article 17, Chapter XIII of the Hague Convention is concerned with damage such as this which I have described.

On the basis of a communication made to you by His Excellency the Foreign Minister, a committee of experts appointed by the Minister of Defence declared that a period of seventy-two hours would be sufficient to make good the damage. The decision of the Uruguayan Cabinet was based on this.

In spite of strenuous efforts it was not possible, in the time allotted, to repair the damage to my ship with the means at our disposal in Uruguay. This could have been ascertained beyond all doubt at the time, if a further investigation had been carried out on board.

(3) I hereby make formal declaration that the constructor entrusted with repairing the damage to my ship was obstructed by the port authorities on 16 December for a space of some hours after 1800, none of the men engaged for the work was permitted to come aboard. Permission for this was finally granted only after an official from the German Embassy had intervened.

I hereby declare that the decision of the Government of Uruguay compels me to leave the harbour of Montevideo with a ship which could not be sufficiently repaired to ensure the maximum safety of navigation.

To put to sea in such a vessel would bring danger upon my crew (over 1,000 men) by negligence. When I say 'danger' I do not mean such danger as would be involved in an action with the enemy. I am referring exclusively to the danger that would inevitably menace a ship at sea in such a condition.

(4) The decision taken by the Cabinet of the Republic of Uruguay is therefore a flagrant violation of the efforts to humanize warfare which led to the signing of the International Convention of the Hague.

It is abundantly clear that the difference between the attitude of the Uruguayan people and the Uruguayan officials (except with the instance I have dealt with under Clause 3) on the one hand, and the position of the Uruguayan Government on the other hand, is attributed only to the influence of some interested parties.

Although I had the technical facilities to hand, I personally refrained from bringing to bear pressure of any kind.

Early on the morning of 13 December, I engaged the British cruiser *Exeter* on the high seas. The British cruisers *Ajax* and *Achilles* took part in this action. After the *Exeter* had been put out of action I decided to make for Montevideo to repair the damage to my vessel. I was aware that the British Government recognizes only the three-mile zone (even in the waters of the River Plate). As soon as my ship had reached the zone over which the countries contiguous to the Plate claim national condominium (and in spite of the British interpretation of this claim as it was known to me) out of respect of the two peace-loving nations I abstained from further part in the action. I should stress particularly the point that in spite of a favourable tactical position and in spite of good visibility I did not open fire on a British cruiser standing off the Isla de Lobos until the enemy had fired on my ship and shot had fallen close.

(5) I do not recognize the grounds for the decision of the Government of Uruguay – nevertheless I shall respect the time limit imposed. Inasmuch as the Government of Uruguay refuses to grant me time to make my ship seaworthy as laid down in the Hague Convention, I am not minded to place my ship (which has suffered no diminution of its fighting powers during the action) under the control of that Government.

Under these circumstances I have no alternative but to sink my ship. I shall blow her up close inshore and disembark my crew if this may be possible.

Signed: Langsdorff (Captain)

This letter to the Ambassador was almost certainly written for its possible propaganda value at a later date; and it throws little real light on the subject.

In the first place, having arrived in Montevideo and landed his wounded, both Langsdorff and the *SKL* in Berlin might have guessed that few if any effective reinforcements could reach Commodore Harwood for many hours. It was obvious that the *Ajax* and *Achilles*, waiting outside, must be even shorter of ammunition than the *Graf Spee* professed herself to be. And Langsdorff was certainly not desperately short of fuel – the *Tacoma* was in any case in Montevideo, civilian supplies were available, and the *Altmark* was still at sea.

His own public assessment of the action damage affecting the *Graf Spee*'s seaworthiness does not tally with damage reports from the ship which were subsequently captured by the Allies after the war.[1] Her engines and fighting efficiency, he admits, were not affected. He was at present unable to cook hot meals for his crew and there were holes in the hull – but all were temporarily patched and shored up.

It is possible the ship might be said not to have been in first-class condition to face a winter's gale in the North Atlantic; but with the *Altmark* waiting for him to the south, still undetected, there was no reason why he should not wait in a more equable climate until the spring before attempting to get back to Germany.

The knowledge that the *Ajax* and *Achilles* were still waiting outside could not, on the 14th, have been a very great deterrent to a determined ship should Langsdorff have sailed from Montevideo in the darkness. Captain Bell had managed to get the shattered *Exeter* back to the Falklands; and the damage to the *Graf Spee* was negligible by comparison. Once clear of the lights ashore, the chances of evading the cruisers were good. Commodore Harwood, at least, was under no illusions about the difficulties he faced. Referring to 16 December, after the *Cumberland* had joined him and a few hours before the time limit expired next day, he wrote with typical understatement: 'The difficulty of intercepting *Graf Spee* who had so many courses of action open to her will, I feel sure, be realized.' He told his captains afterwards that he put their chances at about thirty per cent, and to his wife, while the *Ajax* steamed up and down on guard, he wrote: 'Things are tricky at the moment as we don't know if he is coming out again. I have a most difficult problem to catch him again. If he escapes me all the good we have done will be upset – not all, but a lot of it. The mouth of the Plate is so wide and there are so many ways out that it is very difficult. Probably another battle – and who knows? I hope for the best. If yes or no, you will know before you get this . . .'

A British officer in one of the cruisers wrote later to a friend describing the action, and added: 'Our wait outside, the "Death Watch" as the Yankee [radio] running commentaries called it, with our little "pop guns" was perhaps a little more trying. As you probably know by this time the

[1] See Appendix D.

fleet which assembled outside were entirely the products of the distorted imagination of the BBC announcer ably aided by TL [Their Lordships – the Admiralty], I presume. After thirty-six hours one lumbering great mastodon, *Cumberland*, blundered up, but we had little faith in her, except as the obvious target for the Teutons' first attentions.'

CHAPTER 20

GRAF SPEE SCUTTLES HERSELF

Early on 17 December, shortly after writing his letter to the Ambassador, Captain Langsdorff received a signal from Berlin approving his decision to try to break through to Buenos Aires, but for the reasons mentioned he had already decided instead to scuttle his ship.

Shortly before 0300 he returned on board to supervise the preparations. From the chart of the Plate Estuary, it was obvious that the *Graf Spee* would not be totally submerged when scuttled because the water was so shallow, and the Germans had to ensure that as much equipment as possible should be destroyed so that prying British eyes would not be able to discover too much afterwards.

Arrangements were also made during the morning for the disembarkation of officers and men from the *Graf Spee*, and also for tugs to take off the personnel who would actually form the scuttling party. Langsdorff decided his crew should be taken to Buenos Aires, since he hoped for better treatment from the Argentine Government. Dr Langmann also agreed to take several of the pocket battleship's officers on the staff of the Embassy at Montevideo, in the hope that some of them would be able to get back to Germany and report personally on the cruise and the last days of the *Graf Spee*.

During the morning it was rumoured that the previously reported intention of the *Renown* to enter Rio de Janeiro had been abandoned, and by now she could be off the River Plate. But there was no further news for Langsdorff about the *Ark Royal* and *Achilles*.

Then at 1300 the German Ambassador in Rio de Janeiro sent an urgent message: the *Ark Royal* and *Renown* had just arrived there. Langsdorff received the news philosophically. Perhaps he wondered if the Embassy staff at Rio were taking photographs of the allegedly sunken carrier in order to convince Berlin that she was still afloat. He considered the arrival of the two warships did not disprove the fact that they had been seen off the

Plate from the *Graf Spee* on the 15th, since they could have covered the 1,000 miles to Rio in two days.

He then estimated that the British force waiting outside Montevideo included cruisers (among them the *Cumberland*), which in the event of the *Graf Spee*'s departure would shadow in order to bring the *Ark Royal* and *Renown* and eventually further powerful forces into contact, and he therefore saw no cause to alter his decision to scuttle.

The BBC, the Press and the agents of both sides had done a good job in creating a powerful British force lurking over the horizon just off Montevideo – indeed, they had been helped by the *Graf Spee*'s officers as well; but in fact on 17 December it was still the mixture as before – the *Ajax*, with Commodore Harwood on board, the *Achilles* and the *Cumberland*.

As the hours went by, the tension in the three ships was increasing. The *Graf Spee* had to sail by 2000, and it was generally felt she would leave with a skeleton crew on board and fight it out. The prospect was not altogether a pleasing one.

The *Ajax* and *Achilles* had been guarding the entrance to the Plate for four days now. On the 15th, after the *Cumberland* had joined him, the Commodore decided to start refuelling his force. The *Olynthus* was ordered to go to the Rouen Bank and the *Ajax* met her there. The Commodore told the *Cumberland* to wait in sight to the northward, so that she could give a warning should the *Graf Spee* slip out without her sailing being reported from Montevideo itself.

The weather, however, was bad and a strong wind kicked up a nasty sea in the shallow waters of the Estuary. Only 200 tons of oil had been pumped over to the *Ajax* before wires – including the spans of two hurricane hawsers – started parting.

During the morning the Commodore had completed his plans for guarding Montevideo and he sent the following policy signal to the other two cruisers:

> *My object destruction. Necessitates concentrating our forces. Increased risk of enemy escape accepted.* Achilles *is now to watch north of English Bank and* Cumberland *to west of English Bank, latter showing herself off Montevideo in daylight. If enemy leaves before 2100, ships in touch shadow at maximum range – all units concentrate on shadower. If enemy has not left by 2100, leave patrol positions and concentrate in position 090 degrees San Antonio 15 miles by 0030;* Ajax *will probably join* Cumberland *on her way south.*
>
> *If enemy leaves Montevideo after sunset,* Cumberland *is at once to fly off one aircraft to locate and shadow enemy, if necessary landing in a lee,*

risking internment, and trying to find a British ship in the morning. If plan miscarries, adopt plan 'B', all units concentrate in position 36° south 52° west at 0600.

The only criticism of the plan was made by a few officers who, referring to the first words of the signal, asked rather wryly: 'Who's going to be destroyed?'

The Commodore then sent the *Cumberland* the same signal that he had dispatched to the *Exeter* and *Achilles* the day before the battle,[1] describing how on the signal *ZMM* they would divide into two divisions. The *Cumberland*'s name was substituted for that of *Exeter* which appeared on the original. Thus in the event of going into action against the *Graf Spee* the *Ajax* and *Achilles* would again form the First Division and the *Cumberland*, with her eight 8-inch guns, would form the Second.

The Commodore was, as mentioned earlier, receiving valuable information every two hours from the Staff Officer (Intelligence) in Montevideo. He reported that the *Graf Spee* had landed a funeral party that morning and, later, had been granted an extension of her stay up to seventy-two hours.

'It appeared that she had been damaged far more extensively than I had thought likely,' the Commodore wrote afterwards, 'and had been hit 60 to 70 times in all.

'The British ship *Ashworth* was sailed at 1900 and *Graf Spee* accepted the edict that she would not be allowed to sail for 24 hours after this. At the same time I could feel no security that she would not break out at any moment . . .'

In London, the Admiralty of course were busy with the task of concentrating more warships in the Plate area and, by discreet propaganda, spreading alarm and despondency among the Germans in both Montevideo and Berlin.

As it seemed quite possible that the SKL might well have ordered U-boats to head for the Plate area to help the *Graf Spee* escape, and since cruisers make good targets yet are ill-fitted for tackling submarine attacks, Force K was warned by Admiral Lyon that the destroyers should join as soon as possible, although the *Ark Royal* and *Renown* were not to wait for them.

This was followed up by a signal from the First Sea Lord telling Vice-Admiral Wells that the *Ark Royal* was to arrive in the Plate area as soon as possible and not wait for the *Renown*.

By this time the First Sea Lord had received reports from Montevideo about the interrogation of the British Merchant Navy Officers freed from the *Graf Spee* – reports which told an extraordinary story of a tanker named

---

[1] See page 394.

the *Altmark* which had been acting as a supply ship to the pocket battleship, and which now held more than 300 British prisoners of war. The only details available were her tonnage, probable speed, rough silhouette, the fact that she carried concealed guns, and that she had last refuelled the *Graf Spee* on 6 December in an unknown position.

As the commanding officer appeared to be a complete Nazi, it seemed probable that the only way to rescue the Britons on board would be by capturing the vessel.[1] The submarine *Severn*, on her way to the Plate, was therefore ordered to reconnoitre Trinidada Island to see if the *Altmark* was hiding in the vicinity. The First Sea Lord's signal ordered 'As 300 British merchant seamen on board [she] should be shadowed but do not torpedo.'

On Saturday, 16 December, the *Ajax*, *Achilles*, and *Cumberland* met as planned at 0030 and together they steamed towards Montevideo. The *Ajax*'s Seafox was catapulted off to make a reconnaissance of the harbour, but Lt Lewin had strict instructions not to fly over territorial waters. However, he and Kearney did not have any luck – thick mist prevented them seeing anything, but they reported being fired on in the vicinity of the Whistle Buoy.

This seemed to indicate that the *Graf Spee* was trying to break out, taking advantage of the mist, and all three ships went to action stations. However, a report by radio from the Staff Officer (Intelligence) in Montevideo shortly afterwards indicated that she was still in harbour. No one was very disappointed: the prospect of blundering into a pocket battleship in the mist, possibly at a range of a few yards, was not a welcome one, even for keen and hardy gunnery officers.

'I informed His Britannic Minister, Montevideo, of the firing on our aircraft,' the Commodore wrote, 'and suggested that an investigation into this might be a way of delaying *Graf Spee* sailing. He replied, however, that it was definitely not *Graf Spee* who fired, and that it had possibly been the Argentine guard gunboat at Recalada, or in some other position.'

Lewin, by this time, was very tired and had developed a habit which was worrying Kearney. He was keeping watch on and watch off in the *Ajax*, as well as making extensive reconnaissance flights over the Estuary, and sometimes he almost dropped off to sleep. Kearney would not notice this

---

[1] The *Altmark* in fact evaded all British warships until 15 February 1940, when she was reported off Trondheim, Norway. The destroyer *Cossack* was one of a force of ships ordered to sweep along the Norwegian coast. The *Altmark* was sighted and she ran into Jossing Fjord, inside territorial waters. The Norwegians were obstructive and the First Sea Lord ordered Captain Vian, commanding the *Cossack*, to offer the Norwegians joint escort of the *Altmark* to Bergen or, failing that, to board her. The Norwegians would not co-operate and the *Cossack* went in, slid herself alongside and boarded the *Altmark* with the now-famous cry 'The Navy's Here!'

until the aircraft started doing strange things, and he used to shout at the top of his voice to warn Lewin before matters got out of hand.

While the cruisers had been closing Montevideo, the First Sea Lord sent the Commodore a signal which indicated Britain's attitude towards the claim for a twelve-mile limit on territorial waters. It said:

> IMMEDIATE: *You are free to engage* Graf Spee *anywhere outside the three-mile limit.*

The Commodore wrote: 'I decided to move my patrol into the area north and east of English Bank, as I considered that a battle in the very restricted water just outside the three-mile limit off Montevideo was impracticable, owing to the lack of sea room and possibility of "overs" landing in Uruguay and causing international complications.'

The latest news from Montevideo was to the effect that the *Graf Spee* was still repairing damage, having obtained assistance from the shore, and had provisioned. 'It was reported as unlikely that she would sail that night; on the other hand, once again I did not feel able to rely on such an optimistic report,' Harwood commented.

During the evening a more welcome signal arrived for the Commodore, and the first thing he noticed when it was handed to him was that instead of being addressed to 'Commodore Commanding South America Division' it was prefixed 'Rear-Admiral Commanding South America Division'. It said:

> *From Naval Secretary.*[1] IMMEDIATE. *In recognition of the gallant and successful action fought by HM ships* Ajax, Achilles *and* Exeter *against the German battleship* Graf von Spee [sic], *the First Lord desires me to inform you that His Majesty has been pleased to appoint Commodore Henry Harwood to be Knight Commander of the Most Honourable Order of the Bath; and that Captains W. E. Parry, HMS* Achilles, *C. H. L. Woodhouse, HMS* Ajax, *and F. S. Bell, HMS* Exeter, *to be Companions of the same Order.*
>
> *Commodore Harwood has also been promoted to be Rear-Admiral in His Majesty's Fleet to date from 13 December, the date of the action.*

This was followed by a signal from the First Sea Lord, which said:

> *Their Lordships desire to express to you, the captain, officers and ship's company of HM ships* Ajax, Achilles *and* Exeter, *their high appreciation of the spirit and determined manner in which the action against the* Admiral Graf Spee *was conducted.*

It was a fitting and stimulating end to the day. Tomorrow the *Graf Spee*'s time limit expired and a battle seemed likely. Harwood ordered that

[1] i.e. Sir R. H. Archibald Carter, Secretary to the Board of Admiralty.

instead of the three ships remaining all night in the first degree of readiness (i.e. everyone at their night action stations), they could assume the third degree (a proportion only to be closed up).

The spirit of the men, who had had very little sleep for four days and nights, was shown by the fact that when the order was passed round a unanimous request was received from all quarters that they would prefer to remain closed up all night.

The Squadron spent the night patrolling on a north and south line five miles to the east of the English Bank Light Buoy, and the *Olynthus* went to sea with orders to be at Rouen Bank by 1000 if the *Graf Spee* had not broken out.

The events of the next day, Sunday, 17 December, are best told in the words of Rear-Admiral Harwood:

'I ordered *Achilles*, who was getting low in fuel, to oil from *Olynthus* off the Rouen Bank during the forenoon. *Ajax* and *Cumberland* acted as lookouts at visibility distance during the operation. The squadron then cruised in company off the south-east of the English Bank, remaining concentrated throughout the afternoon and ready again to take up the same night patrol as on the previous night.

'The SO (I), Montevideo, reported that *Graf Spee* had landed all her borrowed welding apparatus during this forenoon. We all expected that she would break out at any moment. I would like to place on record the fact that at this stage the most cheerful optimism pervaded all ships in spite of the fact that this was the fifth night of waiting for the enemy.

'At 1540 I received a signal that *Graf Spee* was transferring between 300 and 400 men to the German ship *Tacoma* lying close to her in the ante-port. At 1720 a further report stated that over 700 men with their baggage and some provisions had now been transferred, and that there were indications that *Graf Spee* intended to scuttle herself.

'Shortly after this *Graf Spee* was reported as weighing.

'I immediately altered course to close the Whistle Buoy, and increased to 25 knots. *Ajax*'s aircraft was flown off and ordered to proceed towards Montevideo and report the position of *Graf Spee* and also *Tacoma*.

'*Graf Spee* left harbour at 1815 and proceeded slowly to the westward. *Tacoma* also weighed, and followed her out of harbour.

'I ordered my squadron to assume the First Degree of Readiness, in case *Graf Spee* intended re-transferring her crew from *Tacoma* outside the harbour, or intended to break out with or without her surplus crew ...'

In Montevideo itself Captain Langsdorff, weary and disheartened, had almost completed the plans which would destroy the ship that had been his greatest command and would provide the Allies with powerful propaganda. From his own personal point of view he could not get away from the fact that, whatever mitigating factors there were, he would be a naval officer who had scuttled his ship. And having spent his early, formative years in the Kaiser's High Seas Fleet, he was considerably more sensitive about his personal honour than the type of men normally absorbed into the Nazi régime.

But to his own officers and men he remained outwardly as cheerful as ever, and he gave no indication of the struggle which was going on in his own mind. He was a Nazi and believed wholeheartedly in Germany; but like many other naval officers he had been shocked by Hitler's alliance with Russia. He believed that Bolshevism was the greatest enemy, and it may well be that the seeds of his apparent disillusionment with Hitler were sown with the signing of the Treaty.

Langsdorff considered it quite likely that the British cruisers, warned as soon as he weighed anchor, would steam in towards Montevideo and attack the *Graf Spee* as she was being scuttled; and if this happened there might be a heavy loss of life among his men.

To safeguard against this as much as possible he decided that the actual scuttling party should consist of only forty-three men – himself, Ascher, the Senior Gunnery Officer, Wattenberg, the Navigator, Klepp, his engineer, a sub-lieutenant and thirty-eight petty officers and ratings.

The bulk of the *Graf Spee*'s crew would be transferred to the *Tacoma*, anchored nearby in the harbour, before he sailed. But he dared not risk having the *Tacoma* make for Buenos Aires in case she was intercepted by the British cruisers. Instead he arranged for two Argentinian tugs and a barge to meet the *Graf Spee* and the *Tacoma* out at sea and take off all the German officers and crew, and the *Tacoma* could then return to Montevideo. Langsdorff guessed that the British, even if they realized what was going on, would not dare intercept three neutral vessels inside their own territorial waters.

There was much to do before the *Graf Spee* sailed on her last voyage, and the minutes sped by. All the secret papers on board which were not wanted by the Embassy were destroyed, and Langsdorff was furious when he found that one overzealous officer had burned the Action Report which he had written. It was the only copy, and with it were the gunnery, damage control, torpedo and action control centre reports.

Between 1400 and 1600, boatloads of the *Graf Spee*'s crew were transferred to the *Tacoma*, and among the crowds of people watching from the shore were Britons whose task it was to relay the latest information to the waiting British cruisers. They counted the Germans in the boat as best they could, and estimated that in those two hours 900 men had been taken off the pocket battleship.

Langsdorff had already sent word to the Harbourmaster that the *Graf Spee* would sail at or shortly after 1815, and this news soon became common knowledge among the crowd. Langsdorff was told that a launch would lead him out of the harbour.

By now the great warship had become the centre of world attention: dozens of newspaper reporters and radio commentators of many nationalities had been gathering in Montevideo during the past three days, and several radio stations were broadcasting direct commentaries, which were, not unnaturally, being listened to with some interest aboard the British cruisers.

For the people of Montevideo it promised to be a dramatic Sunday afternoon, and crowds gathered along the Prado and other vantage points, eagerly watching the pocket battleship and commenting vociferously on every movement made by the Germans.

Then, a few moments after 1700 local time, a large Nazi ensign was broken out from the *Graf Spee*'s foremast, followed by a second from the mainmast, and slowly one anchor was weighed. A few minutes later the second cable rumbled up from the sea bed, and almost imperceptibly the pocket battleship began to move.

To the crowd the *Graf Spee* seemed a majestic sight as, without the help of tugs, Langsdorff manoeuvred her round until she was heading seaward. Then he increased speed; and with the Nazi ensigns streaming in the wind, the *Graf Spee* passed out through the breakwater on her last voyage. Fifteen minutes later the *Tacoma* sailed out, following the same course.

The crowd, by now numbering three-quarters of a million and standing on quays, breakwaters, piers and along the shore, were silent as the pocket battleship moved out through the seaward channel to the south-eastward. She still looked a powerful fighting machine, and many believed she would go into action, and that the talk of scuttling her was merely a ruse to mislead the British.

They could see an aeroplane – presumably British, flown off by one of the cruisers – approaching the warship, and farther out to sea were two tugs and a barge. What were they doing there? The crowd, the newspaper reporters and the radio commentators speculated freely and, as it happened, inaccurately.

Suddenly they saw the *Graf Spee* start altering course. She came round to starboard until she was heading westwards, towards the setting sun. She was going to Buenos Aires! She wasn't going to fight the British or scuttle herself after all!

The *Graf Spee* was now steering for the Recalada pontoon, marking the entrance to the channel to Buenos Aires, but she had not gone far on her new course when she slowed down and then stopped. The two Argentinian tugs and the barge came alongside, and the rest of the pocket battleship's crew, with the exception of the scuttling party, scrambled over the side to the safety afforded by neutral flags. They had signed their own private peace, and few of them regretted it.

All this, however, was only the overture to the Wagnerian masterpiece, the preliminary bars which built up the tension while the late-comers of the audience shuffled into their seats and made themselves comfortable.

As the barge and the tugs drew away, the screws of the great warship started to turn almost reluctantly, and at Langsdorff's order a touch of the helm turned her towards the westward, where the sun, by now a deep crimson ball, was almost touching the rim of the land round the Estuary.

But, unlike the Ulysses of Tennyson's inspiration, it was too late to seek a newer world; Langsdorff's purpose held, but it was not to sail beyond the sunset, and the baths of all the western stars, until he died; it was, more prosaically, to sail a few cables until the pocket battleship's bows nosed on to a mudbank. That was to be the *Graf Spee*'s Happy Isles; and it was ironic that Tennyson's next line reads 'And see the great Achilles whom we knew ...'

Held on the mudbank, the overture ended with the rattling of the cable as an anchor was let go, and it mattered little whether there was good holding ground. At a signal launches came across from the *Tacoma*, now waiting 3,000 yards away, and went alongside.

Langsdorff waited alone with his hopes and fears while his men set the fuses of the scuttling charges, walking through an empty ship in which, for the first time in many months, there was no sound other than the metallic echo of their footsteps.

The time was 2040, and the scuttling party, their task completed, climbed into the launches and were taken off to the tugs. All the vessels then moved off to a respectful distance.

The time selected for the fuses to go off had been chosen with the Teutonic flair for heavy drama, because at 2054, as the sun dipped below the coastline, a sudden flash of flame leapt from the ship, followed by a vast double explosion. The centre of the *Graf Spee* seemed to dissolve into swirling black smoke which twisted upwards in tortured spirals towards the darkening sky.

The pocket battleship's crew, scattered in the tugs, the barge and the *Tacoma*, stood to attention, giving the Nazi salute; and this indeed was the twilight of a god, a welded-steel god worshipped by nearly fifty score Nazi adolescents, and which was now disintegrating before their awe-struck eyes and upraised arms. Was it for this end that they had fought? They themselves did not ask the question; the Fuehrer had apparently said so, and therefore it was so. Blind faith supplies its own balm to bruised spirits.

But the first rumbling reverberation had not lost itself in receptive space before another curtain of flame leapt up aft, high above the masthead, to be followed by another explosion which seemed to erupt under the *Graf Spee*, lift her, and drop her back crumpled into the waiting sea. Wreckage showered out in neat parabolas, the mainmast collapsed like a stalk of corn before a scythe, and the great after turret, which had successfully withstood the shells of the British cruisers, was flung upwards as the magazine beneath exploded.

Now the violent dying spasms were over and self-induced cremation was to follow. Eager, seeking flames swept along the whole length of the ship; and ashore, while excited radio commentators regained their breath, the German Naval Attaché sent a cable to Berlin. Had his lords and masters wished to use it as a dramatic libretto to this Wagnerian sham they would have been disappointed. It said:

> Pocket battleship Graf Spee *left Montevideo 1820* [German time];
> *blown up by her crew 1954. Crew at present embarked in* Tacoma.

Just as the *Graf Spee* blew up, a British officer, Lt Cassells, was sent from Montevideo to report on the activities of the tugs and the barge.

'On arriving at the dockside,' he wrote, 'we heard the explosion in the *Graf Spee* and immediately boarded our tug. We had barely cast off when we were hailed by one of the port officials and instructed by him to take him on board.

'As we proceeded at full speed towards the wreck, it was evident that the port official knew absolutely nothing of what had taken place, and in fact he thought that some of the German crew were still aboard when the explosion occurred.

'We arrived alongside the *Tacoma* within twenty minutes of the explosion and found that the crew of the *Graf Spee* had already boarded one barge and two tugs ... The port official hailed the ships and asked them under what instructions they were acting. He was informed that they were bound for Argentina in accordance with instructions from their company.

'The senior port official, Senor Riquero, then appeared in another tug and orders were received from him that the tugs were not to move away. However, one of these tugs proceeded away to the westward at full speed and was pursued.

'In addition to the tugs there were four of the *Graf Spee*'s boats under their own power, in one of which was Captain Langsdorff. As difficulty was being experienced in giving instructions to the German crew, Captain Langsdorff came aboard our tug to act as interpreter. The port official informed Captain Langsdorff that as he had no knowledge that the tugs and barge had orders to leave Uruguayan waters, it was imperative for them to return to Montevideo.

'The Captain at first thought that he had been stopped because of being accused of blowing up his ship in Uruguayan waters, and hastened to explain that he had been led to a pre-arranged spot, three miles off the coast, by a Uruguayan official tug and then gone one mile farther on his own initiative in order to avoid future arguments.

'In this connection the Captain remarked: "The English do not recognize a neutral territorial zone of more than three miles: that is why I sank my ship one mile farther out than the limit, so that I was free to act as I chose with the Argentine tugs and barge and the crew in them."

'The port official then pointed out it was not a question of the sinking of the *Graf Spee* but the behaviour of the Argentine tugs and barge with which he was concerned.

'He insisted on an explanation of their apparently unauthorized transport of men and baggage and of their movements generally. Captain Langsdorff reported that he had received full permission from the Uruguayan authorities to proceed to Argentina.

'As the port official had no knowledge of this, he was not prepared to accept the Captain's statement and it was therefore decided to hail a Uruguayan naval gunboat which had just arrived on the scene.

'The commander of the gunboat had also received no instructions and he therefore sent a wireless message for orders. The reply was that the Germans were to be allowed to proceed without hindrance.'

Rear-Admiral Harwood and his three cruisers heard the news when Lewin and Kearney, who had watched the whole act, signalled:

Graf Spee *has blown herself up.*

Captain Parry wrote later: '... One realized that the drama was over. Both *Ajax* and ourselves simultaneously had ordered all hands on deck; and CSA then ordered us to take station ahead of him.

'We were both steaming as fast as we could in the shallow water some thirty miles east of Montevideo, which made the ships almost unmanageable. But as we passed *Ajax* everybody went mad and cheered and yelled themselves hoarse.

'We then eased down while *Ajax* hoisted in her aircraft. Her pilot complained that no one seemed to be taking any interest in him. However, in he came. By this time it was dark. I suddenly heard another roar coming out of the darkness, and there was *Ajax* passing us only about 100 yards away, while both ships' companies again yelled at the tops of their voices.

'Ahead of us there was visible a red glow in the sky, flickering up and down like a bonfire; and as we approached it turned into a sort of witch's cauldron blazing away in the sea a few miles west of the Montevideo channel . . .

'Soon after midnight, having gazed our fill on this unique sight, we turned south; and all those who could do so turned in to enjoy their first real night's rest for some days.'

CHAPTER 21

LANGSDORFF SHOOTS HIMSELF

Captain Langsdorff and his crew were housed in the Naval Arsenal in Buenos Aires, and while the *Graf Spee* still burned like a livid torch, a grim warning to those who cared to accept it, Berlin tried to turn her ignominious end into a propaganda victory. But even by Nazi standards they had little enough to go on.

An hour after the scuttling the German Ambassador in Montevideo protested to the Uruguayan Foreign Minister that the neutrality laws had not been properly observed; and at the same time he published Captain Langsdorff's letter which set out the alleged contraventions.

The first official announcement made in Berlin about the scuttling was to have said briefly, 'The time necessary to make the *Graf Spee* seaworthy was refused by the Government of Uruguay. In the circumstances Captain Langsdorff decided to destroy his ship by blowing it up.' According to Admiral Raeder, however, the second sentence was altered to include the phrase 'on the personal orders of the Fuehrer' (underlined) and later altered again to read '. . . Under the circumstances the Fuehrer ordered Captain Langsdorff to destroy the ship by blowing her up. This order was put into effect outside the territorial waters of Uruguay.'

At the same time an urgent telegram was sent from Berlin to the German Ambassador in Montevideo:

> *Please give no further releases or reports of any sort to the Press concerning the sinking of the* Graf Spee. *This applies also to Langsdorff's letter. Anything further that is to be revealed will be released from here. Signed, Ribbentrop.*

The Nazi Foreign Minister was still smarting from the rap over the knuckles applied by Uruguay with her strict interpretation of international law; and he did not want to risk any indiscretions by his envoys or, for that matter, by Langsdorff.

The *Tacoma*, meanwhile, had been ordered back to Montevideo by a Uruguayan warship, and her captain was put under arrest, charged with violating port regulations. Four members of the *Graf Spee*'s crew were found on board and they too were arrested and charged with blowing up their ship. (They were subsequently released.)

On Monday morning Captain Langsdorff awoke in Buenos Aires to find himself attacked in the local newspapers as a coward and a traitor to the tradition of the sea because he had not gone down with his ship. This came as a deep shock to him, since he had expected a great welcome from the Argentinians.

Now, with thirty-seven of his men buried on Uruguayan soil, twenty-eight in hospital at Montevideo, four more in jail there and the rest detained in Argentina, he considered his duty was almost done.

One task remained: to prevent, if possible, the internment of his crew. During the day representations were made to the Argentine Government, claiming that as the *Graf Spee*'s crew were now shipwrecked seamen they were not subject to internment.

However, the Cabinet decided next day that they should be interned and the cost would be charged to the German Government. This news was taken to Captain Langsdorff by the German Ambassador, Baron von Thermann, and it was unofficially stated that it meant, in effect, that officers would be interned in Buenos Aires city under parole, and the crew would be sent to the interior, under the control of local authorities.

During the late afternoon Langsdorff decided that he would like to speak to all his crew in private, and they were assembled in a large room while guards kept all unauthorized people away from the building. Subsequent reports of what he said to his men vary considerably. Some say that he told them of a telephone conversation with Hitler in which he declared that the *Graf Spee* ought to sail out and fight, but that Hitler ordered him to scuttle her. However, in the light of the documents subsequently captured at the end of the war, excerpts from which have already been given in this narrative, this has been shown to be completely untrue. Langsdorff had never pressed to be allowed to fight, and he certainly never had a telephone conversation with Hitler, whose instructions were given in the first instance to Admiral Raeder.

All the reports agree on one thing, that his closing words to the men assembled before him were:

'A few days ago it was your sad duty to pay the last honours to your dead comrades. Perhaps you will be called on to undertake a similar task in the future.'

Only a few of the officers fully understood the significance of his words;

and they were confirmed later when Langsdorff gave his personal effects, including his camera, as keepsakes to certain officers, saying, 'Take these; I will not need them any more.'

After saying good-night to his crew and saluting them – using the old Navy salute, not the Nazi one – he left with some of his senior officers. When approached by newspaper correspondents, he said, with his usual courtesy, 'There's no story tonight, but there will probably be a big one for you in the morning.'

Then, after talking with him for three hours, his officers left the room. It was now nearly midnight, and Langsdorff sat down at a desk and wrote three letters. One was to his wife, another to his parents, and a third to Baron von Thermann. It said:

Buenos Aires
19:12:39.

To: The Ambassador, Buenos Aires.
Your Excellency,

After a long struggle I reached the grave decision to scuttle the pocket battleship *Graf Spee* in order to prevent her from falling into enemy hands. I am convinced that under the circumstances no other course was open to me, once I had taken my ship into the trap of Montevideo. For, with the ammunition remaining,[1] any attempt to fight my way back to open and deep water was bound to fail. And yet only in deep water could I have scuttled the ship after having used the remaining ammunition, and thus been able to prevent her falling to the enemy.

Rather than expose my ship to the danger of falling partly or completely into enemy hands after her brave fight, I have decided not to fight but to destroy the equipment and scuttle the ship. It was clear to me that the decision might be consciously or unwittingly misconstrued by persons ignorant of my motives as being attributable partly or entirely to personal considerations. Therefore I decided from the beginning to bear the consequences involved in this decision.

For a captain with a sense of honour, it goes without saying that his personal fate cannot be separated from that of his ship.

I postponed my intention as long as I still bore responsibility for decisions concerning the welfare of the crew under my command. After today's decision of the Argentine Government, I can do no more for my ship's company. Neither will I be able to take an active part in the present struggle of my country. I can now only prove by my death that the fighting services of the Third Reich are ready to die for the honour of the flag.

I alone bear the responsibility for scuttling the pocket battleship *Admiral Graf Spee*. I am happy to pay with my life for any possible reflection on the

---

[1] In fact he had nearly half the 11-inch outfit left: see Appendix D.

honour of the flag. I shall face my fate with firm faith in the cause and the future of the nation and of my Fuehrer.

I am writing this letter to Your Excellency in the quiet of the evening, after calm deliberation, in order that you may be able to inform my superior officers, and to counter public rumours if this should become necessary.

(signed) LANGSDORFF,
Captain.
Commanding Officer of the sunk
pocket battleship *Admiral Graf Spee*

This letter completed and sealed, Langsdorff unwrapped an ensign of the old Imperial German Navy, and took out his revolver.

At 0830 next morning one of his officers came to the room and found Langsdorff dead, his body lying on the ensign. The fact that he had not used the Nazi ensign is perhaps the best indication of Langsdorff's final attitude to that régime.

During the afternoon the German Embassy issued a communiqué which said: 'According to a letter he wrote to the German Ambassador he said that he had decided from the first moment to share the fate of his superb vessel.

'Only by exercising powerful self-control, and by considering the responsibility which devolved upon him for the safe disembarkation of the crew, composed of more than a thousand young men, was he able to postpone his decision until he had fulfilled his duty, and made a complete report to his superiors.

'This mission was completed last night, and the destiny of a brave sailor, who has written another glorious page in Germany's naval history, was fulfilled.'

The funeral of Captain Langsdorff took place the next afternoon at the German cemetery in Buenos Aires, and was attended by the *Graf Spee*'s officers and crew, members of the Argentine armed forces, the German Ambassador, and Captain Pottinger, master of the *Ashlea*, who represented the captains of British merchantmen who had been prisoners in the pocket battleship.

EPILOGUE

After an uneventful fortnight following the scuttling, Rear-Admiral Harwood arranged to visit Montevideo in the *Ajax* and sent the *Achilles* to Buenos Aires. Both ships were given great receptions, and on 5 January they met off English Bank for the last time. The *Ajax* was to sail for England, and Rear-Admiral Harwood transferred his flag to the *Achilles*, which for the next twenty-four days remained the flagship of the South America Division.

When the *Achilles* was due to leave for New Zealand to have a refit, the cruiser *Hawkins* arrived to take over as flagship and early on 29 January the Admiral transferred to her. The *Achilles* steamed off to collect mail off the Whistle Buoy at the entrance to Montevideo and rejoined the *Hawkins* in the evening.

Then the *Achilles* received a signal telling Captain Parry to proceed in execution of previous orders. The time had come for the last of the three cruisers which fought the Battle of the River Plate to say goodbye to Rear-Admiral Harwood, leaving him flying his flag in a ship manned almost entirely by reservists and which had no association with the events of the past few weeks.

The *Achilles* steamed close to the *Hawkins*, with the band playing 'For He's a Jolly Good Fellow', and the crew singing at the tops of their voices. They ended with an entirely spontaneous three cheers and the 'Maori Farewell'.

The Admiral signalled 'My best wishes to you all. I have so enjoyed flying my flag in your happy ship. Goodbye and good luck'.

While aboard the *Achilles* the Admiral had taught the wardroom a new South American method of cutting for drinks with dice, called 'Bidai Bidou'. Now several officers asked Captain Parry's permission to signal 'Bidai Bidou'. This was given, but the two words had to be repeated several times before *Hawkins*'s signalman understood it. The Admiral answered '653' – the one throw that defeats 'Bidai' and 'Bidou'.

Just before he transferred to the *Hawkins*, the Rear-Admiral received a letter from the First Sea Lord, and it said:

11th January, 1940

My dear Bobby,
    You can have no doubt in your mind about what we feel here and your determined and courageous handling of the Graf Spee.

I do not mind telling you that when we got the news of the first sighting I thought the Huns had all the luck as the first contact of one of his pocket battleships was being made in that area in which we had the weakest hunting unit, and what is more, not only were the two ships of the unit separate, but they were running up against the weakest ship of the pair.

I think the manner in which all your ships went for her baldheaded must have had a great moral effect and largely influenced the Spee's subsequent unintelligible actions. She must have realized that Exeter had only one gun in action when she dropped out of the fight, and why the Spee did not turn on her and finish her off, I cannot imagine.

Even if all our ships had been sunk you would have done the right thing. As things turned out I am delighted that you did not have Cumberland with you – so even had you sunk the Spee it would not have been so glorious an affair.

Your action had a great effect in two ways. Firstly it has set a standard for this war, a matter of great importance.

Secondly it has reversed the finding of the Troubridge court martial and shows how wrong that was.

Little did we think when we were shipmates so many years ago in the Mediterranean what Fate had in store for us, but Fate has been kinder to you even than to me, because you have been allowed to command a British force in a successful action at sea. That can never be my lot.

You seem to have had a wonderful reception at Montevideo, but not more than you deserve.

Yrs ever
DUDLEY POUND

APPENDIX A

Extracts from an analysis, dated February 1940, of the role of the *Admiral Graf Spee* in the Battle of the River Plate, produced by the German Inspectorate of Naval Ordnance, the Naval Gunnery Experimental Command, and the Naval Gunnery School:

'*Assumptions Regarding the Action:*
Before considering the method of using the guns, it must be mentioned that, according to the available reports, the fight would not have taken place if *Spee* had not desired it.

Her decision was based on the erroneous assumption that she had only one cruiser and two destroyers against her. For *Spee* sighted the mastheads of the enemy as early as 0552, range 31,000 metres, while she, owing to her smoke, was not identified until 0610.

Gunnery Tactics:
The *Spee*, with a broadside of six 11-inch guns and four 5.9-inch guns opposed by *Exeter* with six 8-inch guns and *Ajax* and *Achilles* with a total of sixteen 6-inch guns.

Fire was opened at 0617.

In principle no enemy ships should be left uncovered by our guns; a division of armament to engage three targets (that is one turret on *Exeter*; one on *Ajax* and the secondary armament on *Achilles*) is precluded because of the slow rate of fire of the main armament and the consequent technical difficulties.

The principle must be: "Use the main armament against the main enemy". Therefore under the conditions of the action the following distribution of fire would have been correct:

Main armament against *Exeter*; secondary armament against *Ajax* and *Achilles*.

Despite the contradictory British statements it may be assumed the *Spee* distributed her fire in this way. The short shift of target to the light cruisers when they threatened the *Spee* with their torpedoes was ineffective; therefore the main armament, which had been holding the *Exeter* well, was taken off its target, thus giving *Exeter* temporary relief after several hits which she had suffered after opening of fire.

Unfortunately the reports do not show *which* ship turned *first*. Was it *Spee* to avoid danger from torpedoes, or was it *Exeter* in order to avoid *Spee*'s fire, or was it a manoeuvre made "in accordance with a predetermined plan"?

According to the track chart *Exeter* turned about 0623, while *Spee* followed round at 0625. It is not clear why *Spee* did not immediately turn about, but left off firing at *Exeter* and turned her fire on to the light cruisers for a short period. If the *Spee* considered the light cruisers (which had in the meantime approached to within 16,000 metres) as the more dangerous enemy, then only the fire of the main armament over a longer period would have had any prospect of damaging the light cruisers or of forcing them away.

The northerly course chosen by *Spee* made it temporarily more difficult for the cruisers to fetch over to the other side; this move by *Spee* increased *Exeter*'s range. In spite of this, between 0631 and 0634 *Spee* inflicted such severe hits on *Exeter* that she had to turn away to the south making black smoke.

If at 0634 *Spee* had followed this move by turning to the south-west then, whilst maintaining or reducing the range, she could have engaged the already damaged opponent with her main armament from a favourable position in regard to the wind. If, because of smoke, *Exeter* was out of sight, then on a still more southerly course *Spee* could have engaged the light cruisers for a longer period not only with her secondary armament but also with her main armament. From the course steered by *Spee* this was possible intermittently with the after turrets.

It may be assumed that, if *Spee* had decided at that time to continue to use her main armament on the *Exeter*, the latter would have been put completely out of action much earlier; and *Spee* would not have encountered the difficulties in engaging the light cruisers which occurred between 0710 and 0715 when *Exeter* was actually disabled.

According to our analysis the British light cruisers, independently of the courses of *Spee* and with more progressive closing range, obtained a position far more unfavourable to the pocket battleship.

The actual course of the engagement resulted in the light cruisers in time becoming the main opponent, so that *Spee* should have used her main armament against these. She could do this the more easily since two turrets were already out of action in *Exeter* at the latest by 0710, and since *Exeter* had scored no decisive hits on *Spee*.

This statement is made without prejudice to the earlier possibility of sinking the *Exeter* (after 0634).

However, as soon as she was being effectively hit by the British light cruisers she had to shift target to them. It would therefore have been desirable by 0710 at the latest for *Spee* to have used the whole of her main armament against the British cruisers. Every minute after this increased the danger of torpedoes.'

The German experts go on to enlarge on this theme and then say:

'From 0712 onwards, however, *Spee* engaged in a purely retreating action which was dictated by the worries about torpedo hits – apart from the possible considerations as to the operational use of the ships.

Although torpedo hits were avoided, this was at the cost of numerous shell hits which were sustained by the ship. The effective use of *Spee*'s gunnery was reduced by the constant changes in course, the unfavourable bearings and the hindrance through smoke and blast, and finally the frequent changes of target.

The *longer* the ship's guns can fire on one target with a steady ship's course the *greater* are the chances of success. As can be seen from this action, this principle has not been changed despite new mechanical devices.

Effective Gunnery:
Apparently the main armament of *Spee* inflicted most severe damage on the *Exeter* which reduced her speed and finally made her useless as a fighting unit. According to reports the effect of the secondary armament was unsatisfactory and – at least against the *Exeter* – not of decisive importance.

According to available data the least danger for pocket battleships is at a range of between 16,000–18,000 metres, where an 8-inch shell does not yet penetrate the horizontal armour with a favourable angle of impact . . .[1]

Conclusions:
It must be stressed that these criticisms are the result of "armchair" deliberations and are in no way meant as a criticism of the decisions of the Commanding Officer of *Spee* during the action.'

APPENDIX B

Extract from the War Diary of the Operations Divisions of the German Naval Staff, 16 January 1940:

'The task of commerce raiding was very well carried out by the *Spee*. . .

Conclusion from the action: Timing unfavourable. Battle was deliberately accepted. The question as to whether disengagement was subsequently possible cannot be answered, but if the decision was once made to fight it out then it was necessary for the action to be pressed home with all

[1] By this, the Germans presumably meant that at a range of *less* than 16,000 metres an 8-inch shell might penetrate the vertical armour, while at a range *greater* than 18,000 metres it would be falling so steeply that it might get through the horizontal armour. Between 16,000–18,000 metres, apparently, neither would happen.

resources until the principal opponent had been sunk.

The course of the action demonstrates the great difficulty and abnormal risk for a pocket battleship in engaging two or three cruisers, since even a few relatively minor but unlucky hits can rob her of the utilization of her main asset – the wide Atlantic.

The strategic effect of the *Spee*'s operation was very considerable.'

APPENDIX C

British, Allied and neutral merchant shipping losses 1939–45

Cause	Tons	Ships	Percentage
U-boat	14,687,231	2,828	68.1
Aircraft	2,889,883	820	13.4
Mines	1,406,037	534	6.5
Surface raiders[1]	1,328,091	237	6.2
E-boats	229,676	99	1.1
Unknown	1,029,802	632	4.7
	21,570,720	5,150	

[1] The total consists of:

Warships	498,447	104	2.3
Merchant raiders	829,644	133	3.9

It will be seen that although only 6.2 per cent was sunk by surface raiders, the actual tonnage is considerable.

APPENDIX D

Battle damage to the *Admiral Graf Spee*, 13 December 1939: reports of departments. (These documents were captured at the end of the war.)

GUNNERY

Main battery:
1. Foretop rangefinder destroyed by fragments, otherwise nothing out of action, no derangement of fire-control and turrets.
2. Ammunition supply: 324 rounds (ammunition expenditure during the battle 378 rounds).

Secondary battery:
1. Starboard target indicator in the conning tower.
2. Current supply for the hoist for the forward magazine group.
3. Ammunition hoist, No 1, port, destroyed.
4. Port, No 3, 15-cm gun mount: gun shield badly battered, elevating mechanism jammed.
5. Ammunition supply: 423 rounds.

Anti-aircraft:
1. Forward AA command post out of action from a hit in the foundation.
2. AA No 1 from a hit in left half.
3. Right gun barrel of AA No 11, dented from a large shell fragment, barrel unusable.
4. Starboard forward 3.7-cm elevating gears and left sighting mechanism damaged from shell fragments.
5. Starboard chain hoist for 10.5-cm ammunition hoist destroyed.
6. Chain hoist bushing of the port 10.5-cm ammunition hoist shot away (temporarily out of action).
7. Ammunition supply: 2,470 rounds of 10.5-cm; full supply of 3.7-cm and 2-cm.

Searchlights:
1. Cables for searchlights No 2 and No 6 shot away.
2. Mirror for searchlight No 5 destroyed by fragments (replaced).

Torpedo:
Caused by hits –
1. Port torpedo train angle indicator (*TRW – Torpedo-richtungsweiser*), through direct hit in the foundation, all cables shot away.
2. Starboard foremast director (shock effect of a shell passing through the platform railing and from fragments).
3. Torpedo distance converter (*l/e Wandler*), through detonation of a 20.3-cm shell in the transverse corridor, between decks, Section XI.
4. Head telephone, torpedo reporting station, through fragments.
5. Starboard loading station, through a direct hit.
6. Starboard spread firing apparatus (lamps destroyed by vibration, apparatus in use later without illumination).

Through other causes –
1. Current supply for the spread firing apparatus and training mechanism, groups 1 and 2 of the port set of tubes. (Cause unknown. Current was at a later time available. A disturbance, which appeared often during practice of battle exercises, and at that time was found to be caused by a poor circuit connection at the switch panel.)
2. From gas pressure [blast] from B turret: effect on the tube banks.
3. Wall telephone of the torpedo work room.

Communications:
1. Dispatch tubes sending and receiving room shot away.
2. Transmitter of the reserve radio room fouled.
3. Both DF rangefinders (*Goniometerkreuzrahmen*).
4. A long-wave and three short-wave aerials, four receiving aerials and four on the funnel.
5. Radio photo post from direct hit.
6. Radio directionfinder from shock. Radar gear from shock.

Ship's hull:
Large hole in the ship's side, Section XV port, in the upper-deck (sealed off by damage control).

Personnel losses:
37 dead.
57 wounded.

――――――

After running into Montevideo, the following damage outboard was determined:
1. An approximately 15 cm-long crack in the between decks, section IV, port.

2. Several leaks about 15 cm diameter in the upper deck, section VIII, port.

3. A dent in the upper deck, section VIII starboard, about 15 cm long.

4. A leak about 10 cm in diameter at the waterline of section X port. A trim tank full of water.

5. Several leaks about 15 cm in diameter at and under the waterline, section XIII, starboard. (Trim tanks XII 4.6 and XII 4.8 full of water.)

Battle damage which could not be repaired with the equipment and materials aboard the Admiral Graf Spee:

    Forward AA command post.
    Starboard AA gun mounting.
    Right barrel, port AA gun mounting.
    Starboard chain hoist.
    15-cm hoist 1, port.
    Rangefinder, foretop.
    Starboard foremast apparatus.
    Port torpedo training mechanism.
    Torpedo ranging device.
    Torpedo tube 11.
    Spread (torpedo) apparatus, starboard.
    Starboard torpedo filling room.
    Turning gear for [aircraft] catapult.
    Bow protection gear.
    Radiators for after part of ship.
    Service conduits, after part of ship.
    Fire-fighting piping, section X, upper deck. [Firemains.]
    Deck duty petty officers' bath.
    Hole in the freeboard, Section XV, port.

APPENDIX E

Gun installations put out of action in the Admiral Graf Spee *during the battle and time required for repairs.*

Hit No	Place	Damage	Time required
1	Detonation of a 15-cm shell in upper deck by amm hoist, No 1 port, secondary battery.	Port, No 1 hoist out of action. Current supply of forward group re-established with emergency power supply.	5 hours.
2	Shell through left side No 1 AA mounts.	Destroyed part cut away. English sight from 7.5-cm gun sight built in. AA shooting impossible. Only to side.	On 16 Dec. ready for use.
2	Detonation by the starboard 10.5-cm amm supply installation, upper deck.	Stbd chain hoist of 10.5-cm amm hoist destroyed.	Not repairable.
3	20.3-cm shell between decks, Section IX.	Cable and remote controls to foretop damaged.	Repaired by noon, 14 December.
5	Shell through chain hoist port 10.5-cm amm hoist	Brass bushing shot away. Bushing exchanged.	
9	Splinter in starboard 3.7-cm gun mount forward.	Elevating mechanism overhauled, shafts put in order.	6 hours.

Hit No	Place	Damage	Time required
9	Detonation in the foundation of forward AA command post.	Gyroscope section out of action, cables and telephone connection repaired.	7 hours.
17	15-cm shell hit left side protective shield of port No 3 gun mounting.	Bent portion of shield cut away, cable repaired, helix shaft overhauled, elevating gear still works with difficulty.	Conditionally operative on 15 Dec.
18	Shell through night-control station.	Cables for searchlights 2 and 6 shot away; cable for searchlight 6 repaired.	4 hours.
near miss	Splinter in forward post.	Gearing dismantled, helix and 'segment' overhauled.	6 hours.
near miss	Splinter in flying bridge rangefinder.	Apparatus for range-finding out of action.	Not repairable.
near miss	Large fragment in right barrel of AA 2.	Right barrel dented and unusable.	Not repairable.
near miss	Splinter in searchlight 5.	Mirror destroyed: exchanged with a spare reflector.	3 hours.

APPENDIX F

Additional awards to officers and men of the cruisers *Ajax*, *Achilles* and *Exeter*.

Appointed to the Distinguished Service Order:
    Captain D. H. Everett, MBE (*Ajax*); Cdr D. M. L. Neame (*Achilles*); Cdr R. R. Graham (*Exeter*); Lt I. D. de'Ath, R. M. (*Ajax*), Lt R. R. Washbourn (*Achilles*); Cdr (E) C. E. Simms (*Exeter*).

Conspicuous Gallantry Medal:
    Able Seaman W. G. Gwilliam (*Exeter*); Sgt S. J. Trimble, R. M. (*Achilles*); Marine W. A. Russell (*Exeter*); Stoker P. O'Brien (*Exeter*).

HMS AJAX

DSC
    Lt-Cdr D. P. Dreyer; Lt N. K. Todd; Lt E. D. G. Lewin; Warrant Shipwright F. H. T. Panter; Warrant Engineer A. P. Monk; Gunner R. C. Biggs.

DSM
    Petty Officer A. E. Fuller; Chief Mechanician W. G. Dorling; Stoker B. Wood; Stoker F. E. Monk; Shipwright D. Graham; Electrical Artificer J. W. Jenkins; Sgt R. G. Cook, RM; Marine T. S. R. N. Buckley; Petty Officer C. H. C. Gorton; Petty Officer J. W. Hill; Leading Seaman L. C. Curd; Able Seaman R. D. Macey; Able Seaman R. McClarnan; Stoker R. Perry.

HMS ACHILLES

DSC
    Lt G. G. Cowburn; Surgeon-Lt C. G. Hunter; Gunner E. J Watts; Gunner H. T. Burchell.

DSM
    Able Seaman E. V. Shirley; Ordinary Seaman I.T. L. Rodgers; Boy A. M. Dorsett; Chief Petty Officer W. G. Boniface; Petty Officer W. R. Headon; Petty Officer A. Maycock; Able Seaman H. H. Gould; Acting Chief Mechanician L. Hood; Chief Stoker W. J. Wain; Chief Yeoman L. C. Martinson; Chief Petty Officer Telegraphist W. L. Brewer; Chief Ordnance Artificer G. H. Sampson; Cook A. G. Young; Sgt F. T. Saunders, RM.

HMS EXETER

DSC

Cdr C. J. Smith; Cdr R. B. Jennings; Lt A. E. Toase, RM; Surgeon-Lt R. W. G. Lancashire; Midshipman R. W. D. Don; Warrant Shipwright C. E. Rendle.

DSM

Engine Room Artificer J. McGarry; Engine Room Artificer F. L. Bond; Sgt A. B. Wilde, RM; Acting Petty Officer H. V. Chalkley; Sick Berth Chief Petty Officer C. D. Pope; Petty Officer C. F. Hallas; Stoker J. L. Minhinett; Acting Leading Airman E. A. Shoesmith; Plumber G. E. Smith; Joiner F. Knight; Petty Officer W. E. Green; Chief Mechanician J. A. Rooskey; Able Seaman A. J. Ball; Petty Officer S. J. Smith; Engine Room Artificer T. G. Phillips; Master-at-Arms S. A. Carter; Sick Berth Attendant E. T. Dakin.

The
Dam Busters

Paul
Brickhill

BRIEFING

Once I asked an Air Marshal what he thought 617 Squadron was worth, and after a while he said, 'Well, one can't really say but I suppose they were worth ten other squadrons.' He pondered a little longer and added: 'No, that isn't quite so either. Ten other squadrons couldn't have done what they did, and then of course you've got to consider that inventor chap and the freak weapons he gave them. I suppose 617 was the most effective unit of its size the British ever had.'

This is a story of quality as against quantity, demonstrating that exceptional skills and ingenuity can give one man or one unit the effectiveness of ten. It seems that this is a rather British synthesis of talents, and perhaps this story will reassure those who are dismayed by the fact that the British and their allies are outnumbered in this not too amicable world.

What is probably more important, the talents that made 617 what they were evolved a new form of precision bombing which enabled a specific military target to be hit accurately and destroyed. Already this is pointing a way towards the end of 'carpet' bombing of cities, that dreadfully inescapable feature of recent war.

Forgive me for cloaking occasional characters in tactful anonymity. They are still alive.

There is so much to tell that some of the 617 men, like David Wilson, Arthur Kell, Bunny Clayton, Bob Knights and many others cannot be given full credit for their brave competence. Likewise there are too many to name in thanking those who told me about 617. They were too modest to talk about themselves, so I got them to tell me about the others. And *vice versa*.

The famous dams raid was just the start of it all. Guy Gibson wrote some of the wonderful story of this affair towards the end of his excellent 'Enemy Coast Ahead'. Any full account must draw on this, and I am most grateful for permission to do so, in addition to my own researches. My thanks also to Air Commodore Pat Huskinson for the anecdote from 'Vision Ahead'; to Air Vice-Marshal C. N. H. Bilney; John Nerney, Chief of RAF Historical Records; Tom Cochrane, Deputy Chief Information Officer; Mr A. J. Charge, Keeper of Photographs at the Imperial War Museum; and, by no means last, to Wing Commander Willie Tait for the inspiration of his fine accounts.

PAUL BRICKHILL

*To the men living and
dead who did these things*

CHAPTER 1

A WEAPON IS CONCEIVED

The day before the war started Barnes Wallis drove for five hours back to Vickers' works at Weybridge, leaving his wife and family in the quiet Dorset bay where they had pitched tents for a holiday.

He had that morning reluctantly decided that war was not only inevitable but imminent, and he was going to be needed at his drawing-board. No point bringing the family back yet to a house near an aircraft factory till it became clear what influence the Luftwaffe was going to have on one's expectation of life.

Wallis did not look like a man who was going to have much influence on the war; he looked more like a diffident and gentle cleric. At 53 his face was unlined and composed, the skin smooth and pink and the eyes behind the horn-rimmed glasses mild and grey; crisp white hair like a woolly cap enhanced the effect of benevolence. Many people who stood in his way in the next three years were deceived by this, having failed to note the long upper lip which gave stubbornness to the mouth and was the only visible clue to his persistent refusal to be diverted from his purpose. Even his friends did not quite understand this because Wallis, in a vaguely indefinable way, was a little insulated from the rough and tumble of ordinary life by a mind virtually on another plane, immersed in figures and theories. They knew him as a gentle, if rather detached, aircraft designer, and it was not till later that they began to use the word 'genius'.

He spent the last night of peace alone in his house near Effingham, and in the morning, like most people, listened to the oddly inspiring speech of Chamberlain's. Afterwards he sat in silence and misery, not even swearing because the strongest words in his vocabulary were inadequate.

One thought had been haunting him since the previous morning's decision: what could he, as an aircraft designer and engineer, do to shorten the war? The thought stayed with him for a long time and through remarkable events before it was honourably discharged. None of the strange ideas that emerged from it came in a flash of inspiration. There was no one moment in which Barnes Wallis shouted, 'Eureka, I have it!' Scientific minds seldom work in that spectacular and convenient fashion. Ideas germinated slowly in his head, a fertile breeding ground, feeding on study and thought, amorphous and unrecognizable at first like any embryo till gradually they took shape and were recognized.

He had been designing for Vickers since before the first world war. When that started he was designing an early British airship, but a potentate in the upper strata of government decided that work on it should stop as the war was not going to last longer than three months; so Wallis enlisted in the Artists' Rifles as a private. As the war, after three months, was disconcertingly remote from ending, the potentate ordered work to be resumed on the airship, and Wallis was brought back to his drawing-board.

In the twenties he designed the R.100, the most successful British dirigible. In the thirties he invented the geodetic form of aircraft construction and, using this, designed the Wellesley which captured the world's non-stop distance record, and the Wellington, which was the mainstay of Bomber Command for the first three years of the war (and in 1951 was still being used for advanced training).

Vickers' works, nestled in the banked perimeter of the old Brooklands motor-racing track, was turning out Wellingtons as fast as it could, and Wallis was designing its proposed successor, the Warwick. At this time he was on the design of the Warwick's tailplane, which was being troublesome. Clearly any additional work would have to be done in his own spare time and there was, also quite clearly, not going to be much spare time.

Bombers and bombs were the directions in which he was most qualified to help. Bombs, particularly, seemed a fruitful field. He knew something about RAF bombs, their size, shape, weight and so on; the knowledge had been essential when he was designing the Wellington, so that it could carry the required bombs over the required distance. It was not knowledge which, in Wallis, inspired complacency. The heaviest bomb was only 500 lb, and aiming was so unpredictable that the Air Force was forced to indulge in stick bombing – you dropped them one after another in the pious hope that one would hit the target. One hoped then that it would go off. Too many didn't. Years of placid peace and the diffidence of the Treasury had inhibited development of bombs, a natural consequence of a war to end all wars but regrettable in the face of reality. Lack of development had been assisted by the presence here and there in the Services of a few of those officers who thrive only in peacetime, lacking neither in courage nor devotion to Regulations and afternoon tea but lamentably deficient in the vitality and intellectual resilience that lead to actual work being done.

RAF bombs, too, were old, very old. Nearly all were stocks hoarded from 1919. There had been an attempt in 1921 to design a better bomb, and in 1938 they actually started to produce them, but in 1940 there were still very few of them. Both new bombs and old were filled with a mediocre explosive called amatol (and only 25 per cent of the weight consisted of explosive). There *was* a far better explosive called RDX but production of that had been stopped in 1937. (It was not till 1942 that the RAF was able to use RDX-filled bombs.) Meantime Luftwaffe bombs contained a much more powerful explosive than amatol – and half the weight of the German bomb was explosive.

Wallis knew there had been an attempt in 1926 to make 1,000-lb bombs for the RAF but they never even got to the testing stage. The Treasury was against them; the Air Staff thought they would never need a bomb larger than 500-lb, and anyway Air Force planes were designed to carry 500-pounders. Thousand-pound bombs would need new and costlier planes for the whole Air Force and the country could not afford it. Not till 1939 did the Air Staff begin to think seriously again of the 1,000-pounder, and six months *after* the war started they placed an order for some.

These shortcomings were not so obvious then, particularly as (as Wallis knew) all air forces favoured small bombs designed to attack surface targets. The blast of bigger bombs was curiously local against buildings, and a lot of little bombs seemed better than an equal weight of larger ones. Even larger bombs needed a direct hit to cause much damage and there was more chance of a direct hit with a lot of little bombs.

To Wallis's methodically logical mind there was a serious flaw to all this. Factories and transport could be dispersed; in fact *were* dispersed all over Germany. Bombing (vintage 1939) would not damage enough factories to make much difference.

He started wondering *where* and *how* bombing could hurt Germany most. If one could not hit the dispersed war effort perhaps there were key points. Perhaps the sources of the effort. And here the probing mind was fastening on a new principle.

The sources of Germany's effort, in war or peace, lay in power. Not political power (that was dispersed too, and hidden in deep shelters at the approach of aircraft). Physical power! Great sources of energy too massive to move or hide – coal mines, oil dumps and wells, and 'white coal' – hydro-electric power from dams. Without them there could be no production and no transport. No weapons. No war.

But they were too massive to dent by existing bombs. One might as well kick them with a dancing pump! The next step – in theory anyway – was easy. Bigger bombs. Much bigger!

But that meant bigger aircraft; much bigger than existing ones. All right then – bigger aircraft too.

That was the start of it. It sounds simple but it was against the tenets of the experts of every air force in the world.

Wallis started calculating and found the blast of bigger bombs *was* puny against steadfast targets like coal mines, buried oil and dams. Particularly dams, ramparts of ferro-concrete anchored in the earth.

Then perhaps a new *type* of bomb. But then Wallis did not know enough about bombs and the logic stopped short.

The war was a few weeks old when the dogged scientist dived into engineering and scientific libraries and at lunchtimes, when he pushed the problem of the Warwick's tailplane aside for an hour or so, he sent out for sandwiches, stayed at his desk and started to learn about bombs.

His designing office was evacuated to an old house at Burhill, near Weybridge, which had been built by Wellington, and there he studied the chemistry and behaviour of high explosives, aerodynamic bomb design, the forging, casting and milling, the theories of light and heavy case bombs, the fusing and the aiming. And at night at home he did the same, absorbed and lost to his family for hours. If a bomb had gone off near by he possibly would not have noticed, or if he did his first thought would probably have been to inquire into the chemical nature of its explosive or the type of casing, or the charge/weight ratio. As the hard winter of 1939 arrived he progressed to the study of the sources of power.

Coal mines! Impossible to collapse the galleries and tunnels hundreds of feet underground. Possible, he decided, that a heavy bomb might collapse the winding shaft so that the lift would not work. No lift. No work. No coal. But that could soon be repaired.

Oil! Rumanian oil fields were too far for existing bombers, but a possibility for a future bomber. Germany's synthetic refineries were massive and well defended; perhaps a target for bigger bombs.

Dams! Three German dams stood out – the Moehne, the Eder and the Sorpe. All in the Ruhr, they accounted for nearly all the water supply to that monstrous arsenal. Wallis knew that the German method needed between 100 and 150 tons of water to produce a ton of steel. The possibilities were intriguing.

The Moehne dammed Moehne Lake where the Heve flowed into the Ruhr River, maintaining the level so that barges with coal and steel and tanks could go to and from the foundries. Moehne Lake held 134 million tons of water. The Eder dammed the Eder River in Eder Lake, 212 million tons of water. It controlled the level of Germany's second most important waterway, the Mittelland Canal. Even Kassel, forty miles away, got its water from the Eder. The Sorpe dammed another tributary of the Ruhr River in Sorpe Lake.

The Moehne was 112 feet thick at the base, 130 feet high and 25 feet thick at the top where a roadway ran; the Eder was even bigger. Wallis acknowledged that they were formidable. A 500-lb bomb would hardly scratch the concrete. No less formidable was the Sorpe, an earth dam, with two sloping mounds of earth sealed and buttressed in the centre by a core of concrete.

In an engineering library Wallis unearthed accounts of their construction compiled by the proud engineers who had built them and found it hard to discipline his excitement as he read what the effects of breaching the dams would be.

It would not merely destroy hydro-electric power and deprive foundries of essential water, but affect other war factories which needed water for their processes. Disrupting them might cause a dozen critical bottlenecks in the completion of tanks, locomotives, guns, aircraft – almost anything one cared to name. It would deprive the populace of water, too, which was no cause for joy in a gentle soul like Wallis but would at least induce in them a lessening of zest for the war as well as some testy sentiments directed not only at the RAF but at Hitler too. Humanity is not inclined to limit its censure for discomfort to the direct cause only. Indirect sources get their share; another and intriguing way, thought Wallis whimsically, of attacking the enemy at the source of power.

There was still more to it. Breaches in the dams would send enormous floods ripping down the valleys, tearing away roads, bridges and railway lines, smashing factories and houses, so that some factories, rather than be deprived of water, would receive somewhat too much.

All this was fine, Wallis thought . . . logical ideas; but again one big flaw. The dams were so colossal that bombs twenty times bigger than existing ones were not going to hurt them.

His figures showed that when a 1,000-pounder exploded the charge expanded as a gas bubble, but at the end the bubble was only 20 feet across. A lot of damage was done beyond this 10-foot radius, however, by flying fragments, by blast and by the pressure pulse, or 'shock wave'. Wallis well remembered the pedantic description of shock waves . . . 'there is no motion of the transmitting medium other than the usual oscillation of particles to and fro about their position of rest as the wave passes through them.' Thin air gave scope to flying fragments and blast but the shock wave soon dissipated.

It would vibrate a structure, but not enough. To be destructive, shock waves had to travel through a more solid medium than air. And somewhere in Wallis's brain a little cell awoke and stirred restlessly, an old memory, locked up and almost forgotten. He felt there was something he knew about shock waves that he should remember, tried to think what it was – it was a long time ago – but the harder he tried the farther it receded. Memory can be so tantalising. He thought about it for the rest of the day, trying irritatedly to isolate it, but it had gone. Memory is like a woman; it was only when he put it out of his mind that it sneaked insidiously back to him again.

It was something he had read, something about concrete. And then it hit him. Waterloo Bridge! Concrete piles being driven into the bed of the

Thames! That was years ago. The piles had kept shattering mysteriously and there had been an investigation. He started searching his notebook and in a quarter of an hour had found it, an article in a 1935 journal of the Institution of Civil Engineers. The great drop-hammers had been slamming the piles into the river bed and the tops of the piles had been exploding upwards.

Investigation narrowed the cause to the shock waves. The sudden blows sent shock waves shivering down the piles; at the bottom they met the blunt resistance of the clay and bounced back up the pile at something like 15,000 feet a second, reached the top just after the hammer had bounced off, so there was nothing to rebound from again and they passed out and away, and in their wake you got a tension after the compression. A sort of crush and then a sharp stretch, almost in the same moment; enough to make a structure split – to shatter it.

Concrete, the article concluded sagely, well resisted compression but poorly withstood tension. Wallis docketed the fact in his mind, thinking of dams.

You needed a solid medium to get destructive shock waves!

Of course, if you could bury a bomb *deep* in . . . But you couldn't slice a big bomb deep into ferro-concrete. No, but you might be able to inject it deep into some less solid medium before it exploded. You'd get the shock waves then. The expanding gas effects would be greater too; tamped by the encircling solids they would have to burst their way out.

He was aware that bombs and shells often buried themselves 3 or 4 feet in the ground before exploding, but that was so shallow the explosion forced its way easily to the top, causing a small crater, and the shock waves dissipated into the air. It was less effective than a surface explosion because the blast and shock waves went straight up instead of outwards.

But if you could *lock* the explosion underground so it could not break out you would get a sort of seismic disturbance . . . an earthquake! An earthquake bomb!

The idea shaped in his mind while he was sitting in a deep chair in his home at Effingham, an unspectacular setting for the birth of something so powerful.

But how to sink a bomb deeply into a resisting medium? You could not put one deep into a concrete dam. But a dam is set in water!

Water! It might not transmit a shock wave as well as earth but it would do so better than air. The tamping effect of water would produce a concentrated explosion and carry the 'shock' punch. Wallis was starting to feel he might be getting somewhere.

And how about sinking the bomb in earth? A schoolboy knew the two principles. The heavier the bomb, the more power and speed it developed in falling. Wallis had learned the classic example in school. Drop a mouse down a well and at the bottom it will be able to get up and run. Drop a horse down and the horse will probably burst. Because it was heavier it would hit *harder*. And the *farther* it fell, the *faster* it would fall!

So there it was: a bomb as heavy as possible (and as slim as possible) dropped from as high as possible.

Wallis looked up more books, studied the propagation of waves in soil, the effects of underground explosions at depth, and even found pages on the penetrative powers into soils of shells and light bombs. There was a piece about an enormous land mine exploded under a German-held hill at Messines Ridge in World War I. A colossal charge sent shock waves ripping into the earth, the hill was destroyed and the shock was felt in Kassel – 300 miles away.

Wallis pulled out a pad and pencil and worked for a week, covering sheets with calculations, equations, formulae – accelerations, resistances kinetic energy, stresses, friction, charge/weight ratios – and came up with a preliminary theoretical answer. A 10-ton bomb, with 7 tons of explosive in an aerodynamically-designed case of special steel, dropped from 40,000 feet, would reach a speed of 1,440 feet per second, or 982 mph – well over the speed of sound. At that rate it should penetrate an average soil to a depth of 135 feet.

A charge of that size should theoretically 'camouflet' (not break the surface) at a depth of 130 feet. What it *would* do is cause a violent earthquake movement on the surface resulting in a hump forming.

'Such earth movements,' said a learned paper, 'are capable of doing much damage at great distances.'

It looked as though Wallis had found his answer. Or part of it.

He worked out theoretical effects, more pages of figures, and decided that there was a chance that a 10-ton bomb exploding deep in water by a dam wall would punch out a hole a hundred feet across.

Supposing the bomb did not go as deeply into the earth as the figures predicted? Wallis worked out the effects of a 10-tonner exploding about 40 feet deep. In theory it would throw out the staggering amount of 12,000 tons of earth, leaving a crater 70 feet deep, with lips 250 feet across. He worked out the circumferences of the crater and from that the maximum number of men and machines that could gather round the edges. Working day and night they could not fill it in under fourteen days! Supposing one such bomb was dropped accurately in a marshalling yard! Or on a vital railway or canal or road where ground contours prohibited a detour!

CHAPTER 2

– AND REJECTED

Wallis did not get too excited. No bomber in the world would carry a 10-ton bomb. Or for that matter even a 5-ton bomb far enough to get it to a target.

Back to pencil and paper. He knew the limitations of aircraft design in 1940 and in a couple of weeks he knew it was possible to build a 50-ton bomber to carry a 10-ton bomb 4,000 miles at 320 mph and a height of 45,000 feet. He drew up rough specifications and christened it the 'Victory Bomber'.

The methodical mind did not overlook anything. At 40,000 feet would constant cloud obscure the targets? Back to the library. The weather should be clear enough on one day in three. That was reasonable.

Could a bomb-aimer pick up a small target from 40,000 feet? Wallis came across a scientific report which showed that a test object a few feet wide could be visible from 35,000 feet.

Winds? Stratospheric winds sometimes reached 200 mph. He set that against bomb-aiming techniques and decided that, whatever the faults of present bomb-aiming, the winds could be allowed for.

And the aiming of bombs – notoriously hit and miss, mostly miss. Wallis found that increasing heat did not greatly increase the problems and estimated that new bomb sights being developed and special training could put the bombs near enough to a target to destroy it.

That was the beauty of this 10-ton bomb. It should not have to be a direct hit! The earthquake shock would be so great that a near miss should shake a target to destruction. And another thing – a big bomb exploding 130 feet deep would not crater the surface but cause a huge subterranean cavern. Put such a bomb alongside a bridge or viaduct, and if the shock wave did not shake it to pieces the cavern underneath would knock its support away. An opening trapdoor – a hangman's drop! The bridge would collapse into it.

There was one other possibility in it – perhaps the greatest of all. A few such bombs, accurately aimed, might shatter the roots of a nation's war effort. That could mean the end of the dreadful 'Guernica' carpet bombing, which saturated an area with bombs so limited in effect that the area had to be saturated to make their use militarily worth while. Wiping out cities and civilians at the same time!

But it was only a revolutionary and complicated theory. The Army,

Navy and Air Force were deluged with revolutionary, complicated and crackpot theories. The next problem – maybe the biggest – was to get them to listen to this one, to believe and accept it.

Wallis spent weeks setting it all out on paper and took it to people he knew in the RAF and the Ministry of Aircraft Production. It was Dunkirk time. A potent new weapon had never been better timed.

Wallis's paper on the 'earthquake bomb' roused three main emotions in officials: (1) Lukewarm interest. (2) Incomprehension. (3) Tactful derision.

One man understood and did what he could: Arthur Tedder, a quiet, intensely likeable man smoking a pipe, chained to a desk in Whitehall. But he was only an air vice-marshal then and did not have the influence he acquired later as Eisenhower's deputy in the invasion, and then as Lord Tedder, Marshal of the RAF and Chief of the Air Staff. He brought the bomb and Victory Bomber to the attention of several people in high places but the only result seemed to be a ubiquitous manifestation of courteous but implacable inactivity, often the only defence of hard-working officials plagued by importunate and impractical inventors. Every machine in the country was working overtime on other vital things and the ambitious and excellent four-engined bomber project was just getting under way. It was a fair assumption that it might be disastrous to dislocate that in favour of the Victory Bomber, which would inevitably take much longer to develop. That automatically prejudiced the shock-wave bomb, because there was therefore no aircraft in sight which could drop it from Wallis's prescribed height of 40,000 feet. The new bombers would probably not be able to lift it or, if they could, to carry it far enough to drop it from higher than 20,000 feet, which was not likely to be enough.

And then on July 19, out of the blue, Wallis got an urgent summons to see Lord Beaverbrook, the bright-eyed fire-cracker who was Minister for Aircraft Production. With 'The Beaver' interested anything could happen, and probably at speed. He caught the first train to London, cooled his heels a few minutes in an ante-room and then the big door opened and a young man said: 'Lord Beaverbrook will see you now, sir.'

Wallis jumped up, cuddling his calculations under his arm, and crossed the threshold, nervous with anticipation; and there was the little man with the wide, mobile mouth, sitting slightly hunched in his chair. It was the speed with which things happened that shook Wallis as much as the things themselves. No gracious, measured preliminaries. He was still in the middle of the floor, walking, when the little man barked: 'Will you go to America for me?'

For a moment Wallis was rattled. He collected himself.

'I'd rather stay here for you, sir.'

'What would you do for me here?' Crisply and fast, like repartee.

'Build you a ten-ton bomb and a Victory Bomber to carry it, sir.' Wallis was standing his ground better than most. The little man looked at him a moment.

'What good would that do?'

'End the war,' Wallis said simply. 'An earthquake bomb. I've got it set out here,' he touched the papers under his arm.

'All right, never mind that now. Have a look at this,' and Beaverbrook tossed over a newspaper clipping. 'Look into it and come back and see me tomorrow.'

Wallis lost track of the interview after that, probably because there was no more interview. He found himself outside the door; from start to finish it had lasted a bare forty seconds and as his thoughts reassembled he felt disappointment like a shock. Beaverbrook had never heard of his ideas; it was some other wretched thing he had wanted. Automatically he began to walk away and it was not till he got to the front door that he began to wonder what the other thing was and remembered the clipping.

It was not in his hand. He searched his pockets. Not there. It was a pretty position; he did not even know what Beaverbrook wanted and he had to advise him tomorrow about it. He could not go back and ask what the subject was . . . he shuddered slightly at the thought. Agitated, he ploughed through his pockets again and in the last one, a fob, when hope had gone, he felt the cutting, drew it out and read it.

It was a report from America about work on pressurised aircraft cabins for high flight. 'The Beaver' evidently wanted him to go across and see how it was done.

Very amusing! Wallis had already done experimental work on pressurised cabins and knew how it was done. He went back to Weybridge.

Next day he saw Beaverbrook again, armed this time by experience and was not rattled. He told the Minister he had all the information needed on pressurising aircraft cabins and there was no need to go to America.

'All right,' said Beaverbrook. 'What's this about a ten-ton bomb?'

Wallis told him as concisely as he could; difficult for a scientist, who always feels compelled to go into technicalities, but he kept it short and lucid and Beaverbrook was interested.

'You know how short we are of stuff,' he said. 'This thing's only a theory. We'd have to stop work on other vital things to make it and then it might be a flop.'

'It won't be that,' Wallis said stubbornly.

'We'd still have to stop work on other things.'

'It will be worth it.'

'Take too long, wouldn't it?' said 'The Beaver'. 'A ten-ton bomb and a bomber twice the size of anything else sounds like something in the distant future.'

'We can do it in stages, sir,' Wallis said. 'I've got drawings for two-ton and six-ton bombs on the same principle. My Wellingtons can carry the two-tonner all right. The new four-engined ones can carry the six-tonner. They'll be operating in a year.'

'Well, I'll see my experts about it,' Beaverbrook said. 'If it's going to mean diverting too much effort I don't like your chances.'

Wallis came out with a sigh of hope and relief, spent some days simplifying his designs and on 9 August took a train to Sheffield to get the advice of steel experts on manufacture of the tempered castings. They would have to be immensely strong to withstand the shock of hitting at 1,000 mph without breaking, and as light and roomy as possible so the maximum amount of explosive could be crammed into them. Big bomb design is incredibly complicated, but the blitz had started and it was a good time for discussing big bombs to throw back.

Little seemed to happen for a while but behind the scenes things were moving in a ponderous government way. Little snippets filtered through to Wallis, particularly from that astute ally, Arthur Tedder. Nothing much; just that So-and-so had consented to look into the idea and that So-and-so had expressed mild interest. Out of this came one or two more converts. One was Air Commodore Pat Huskinson, a grey-haired, burly man who was Director of Armament Developments for the RAF, renowned for his blunt aggression in forcing new weapons through bottlenecks. But most of Huskinson's time was filled with dozens of other problems, and then a bomb fell on his flat. Huskinson lived but was blinded.

Wallis thought the prospects were still favourable. Sir Charles Craven, managing director of Vickers, was sympathetic and felt confident enough on 1 November to write to Beaverbrook suggesting he gave permission to go ahead on both 10-ton bomb and Victory Bomber.

Then Tedder was posted to take over the RAF in the Middle East and Wallis had lost his keenest supporter in the sacred and essential precincts of Whitehall. It was soon after that Craven sent for him.

'I'm afraid I haven't very encouraging news for you,' Craven said as kindly as he could. 'Air Council seem too wary of big bombs. They still believe stick bombing is necessary.'

'But can't they *see* what a really big bomb would do?' Wallis said pleadingly.

'Apparently not. They say that from experience they would rather drop four 250-pound bombs than a thousand-pounder. Much less a 22,000-pounder.'

'Could they understand my calculations, sir?'

Craven did not comment on their understanding. He said diplomatically that he doubted whether the members would have the *time* to go individually through all the calculations. Which was probably true. And then gently: 'They say that anyone who thinks of ten-ton bombs is mad.'

Wallis went back to Weybridge in anger, but in the morning the anger had mostly gone and in its place was outraged stubbornness. He started writing a treatise on his 10-ton bomb and called it 'A note on a method of attacking the Axis Powers', the kind of obscure title so favoured by scientists; the word 'note' being particularly misleading, as such things are often as long as a book.

Wallis's was. He started by outlining his theory of crippling an enemy by destroying the sources of energy, and went on to discuss in exhaustive detail the physical qualities of the targets, shock waves, blast, penetration, bomb design, aircraft design, charge/weight ratios, aiming problems, possible effects, repair potentialities, backed up with pages of graphs and formulae and equations. It was a *tour de force*, explaining step by step so lucidly that a layman could follow it if he took the mathematics for granted.

The 'note' took Wallis several months, and then he had it roneoed and bound and posted copies to seventy influential men in science, politics and the services.

Results were not long coming. A secret service man called on him with a copy of the 'note' under his arm.

'Did you send this to Mr—?' he asked.

'Yes,' Wallis said. 'Why?'

'I'm afraid you shouldn't have done so, Mr Wallis.'

'Why?'

'It's very secret stuff. This sort of thing must be handled very carefully and only reach authorised persons. Mr— was very surprised when this arrived in the post. We were concerned too. I quite realise you didn't mean to be . . .'

'I sent out seventy of them,' Wallis said calmly, and the Secret Service was appalled.

'Seventy!' he said. '*Seventy*! Who? To whom? But you shouldn't have. This is vital and very secret!'

'Is it?' said Wallis mildly. 'When I showed it to the authorised persons they said I was mad. I'm supposed to be a crackpot and this is regarded by authorised persons as fiddle-faddle.'

The secret service man said, 'Oh!' He asked for the names of the seventy. Wallis read them out and the secret service man, who seemed a little uncertain of his ground, went back to London to investigate further.

He appeared again a couple of days later.

'Well, it's all right,' he said, 'this time. We've decided that as so many were sent out so openly it's actually rather a good form of security. No one will dream it's all so secret. But please don't do it again.'

Wallis bowed gravely. 'I hope it will not be necessary again,' he said and the incident was closed.

A few days later there was another result. A copy had reach a Group Captain Winterbotham, who had an office in the City and was used to dealing with unorthodox aspects of the war. He had found it convincing, called on Wallis, and Wallis explained more fully. Winterbotham caught some of his enthusiasm. He knew Sir Henry Tizard, who was scientific adviser to the Ministry of Aircraft Production, and drew his special attention to Wallis's paper.

Tizard read it carefully; as a scientist he could follow the intricate calculations. He went down to see Wallis at Weybridge and was impressed.

'I'd better form a committee to study this more fully,' he said. 'It would have to have pretty solid backing from expert opinion. You'll understand, I know. It would divert effort from other important things if we were to go ahead with it and we've got to be reasonably sure it would be worth while.'

'Of course,' Wallis said. He felt like singing.

Not long after, Wallis met the committee. At the head was Dr Pye, Director of Scientific Research at the Ministry of Supply, and the others were scientists too. Wallis explained his ideas and described the probable effect on Germany's war industries if the dams were breached. There was only one really worthwhile time of the year to breach them, and that was in May, when the storage lakes were full after the winter thaw and spring rains, and before the sluice gates were opened to water the country and canals for summer. Then you would get the greatest floods, the most serious loss of water and power. Dr Pye said the committee would be a few days considering.

A week later Wallis faced the committee to hear their findings. His worst fears were soon over; the report was favourable, but, as they read on, a little disappointingly so. They thought that the dams showed possibilities and the upshot was another committee. This one focused the aim more definitely; it was to be called 'The Air Attack on Dams Committee'.

The members were again scientists and engineers and in a mood to be interested in something new because even German bombs, though they were more efficient than RAF bombs and killed thousands of civilians, had demonstrated the limitations of small bombs. The machine shop in an English factory, for instance, had been hit by seven Nazi 250-lb bombs and they had damaged only twenty-four out of the 500 machines in the factory.

All except two were repairable and the machine shop was running as usual almost immediately. Because aiming was so inaccurate it was obvious that 75 per cent of such bombs were wasted.

'With this big bomb,' Wallis earnestly impressed on them, 'you don't have to get a direct hit. I think a ten-ton bomb dropped fifty feet away stands a good chance of knocking a hole in a dam like the Moehne. A near miss like that ought to be simple enough to organise.'

One of the members, Dr Glanville, of the Road Research Laboratories at Harmondsworth, suggested building a model dam and testing the theories with scaled-down charges of explosive. Wallis accepted delightedly.

Over the next few months, whenever he could spare time from his arduous work at Vickers, Wallis helped Glanville design and painstakingly build a model dam one-fiftieth the size of the Moehne with tiny cubes of concrete, scale models of the huge masonry blocks in the real dam. The model was about 30 feet long, 33 inches high and up to 2 feet thick, a low wall arched between earthen banks, secluded from prying outside eyes in a walled garden.

They flooded the ground at one side to simulate the lake, and Wallis exploded a few ounces of gelignite under the surface 4 feet from the model to give the effect of a 10-tonner going off 200 feet away. There was a commotion on the water and a fountain of muddy water gushed up on the model and a couple of patches of concrete flaked and chipped.

'Not so good there,' Wallis said. 'Let's try it closer.'

He exploded more gelignite 3 feet from the dam, and there was a little more damage. He set off another charge 2 feet away and still found only minor chipping.

At a distance of 12 inches (representing a 10-tonner 50 feet from the dam) the gelignite caused a couple of cracks in the outer structure; but they were small cracks, not enough to harm the dam significantly. They tried several more charges but the cumulative effect was not encouraging.

Months had passed since the first hopeful meeting of the committee, and Wallis could see that their early co-operation was congealing. Glanville built another model, and Wallis tried bigger charges to see what *would* smash the models at a distance. One day a few extra ounces of gelignite a foot away sent a mushroom of water spraying over the wall round the garden and as the spume cleared they saw the water of the little lake gushing through the burst dam. Slabs of concrete had cracked and spilled out and there was the breach that Wallis had been wanting. He calculated the scaled-up charge which, dropped 50 feet away, would smash such a hole in the Moehne. The answer was something like 30,000 lb of the new explosive RDX, and the gentle scientist did not need pencil and paper to estimate the significance.

Thirty thousand pounds was nearly 14 tons. That was the explosive alone. Add the weight of the thick case of special steel – another 40,000 odd lb. It meant a bomb weighing 70,000 lb – over 30 tons, and the Victory Bomber, still only on paper and straining the limits of feasible aircraft construction, would carry only a 10-tonner.

The next meeting of the Air Attack on Dams Committee was in a fortnight and it required little thought to foresee it would be the last meeting.

Wallis would not give up.

Supposing, he thought, a bomb could be exploded *against* the dam wall. The shock wave punch would be much greater. So the explosive needed would be much smaller. So would the bomb casing.

But how to get a big bomb in the exact spot – deep enough for the shock punch and pressed against the wall to make the most of it? Or, as it might require more than one bomb, how could you get them all in the exact spot? A torpedo? But the dams had heavy torpedo netting in front of them, and so torpedoes were out. You could drop a bomb from very low level for accuracy, but bombs don't 'simply drop'. Just after release they carry a lot of forward speed, giving them almost a horizontal trajectory for a while. If you drop a bomb – even a whopper – from very low to get the accuracy it would simply skid off the water; so that was no good. If you dropped it high enough to enter the water cleanly, you only had about one chance in a thousand of putting it right in the exact spot.

Wallis probed at this problem for days and every time he probed he came up against the same problem – the only way would be to drop something from very, very low and somehow make it go and stay where it was supposed to be. But that seemed impossible.

Off and on he puzzled about it and then one day out of vague memories he remembered his last holidays with the children just before the war began when they had been skipping stones across the smooth water of a little pond. How on earth, he thought, could I toss a stone low like that and stop it skipping just where I wanted it. Drop any shape of bomb very low at a couple of hundred miles or more an hour and heaven knows where it would skip to.

When dams are full there is practically no space between the level of the water and the top of the dam wall and in his wry imagination he visualized a series of huge and grotesque bombs bounding over the dam wall and flying harmlessly downstream. What a pity, he thought idly, that you couldn't make a torpedo do a bit of bouncing – over an anti-torpedo net for instance.

Hullo! That was an idea! If a bomb could hurdle a dam wall it could also hurdle an anti-torpedo net. Such nets were a good hundred yards away from dam walls to keep any explosion at arm's length. But a bomb didn't have to keep skipping further. Maybe it could be so judged to skip the torpedo net and not skip the dam wall. He felt sudden excitement surging inside him. There would probably be three or four feet of dam wall above the water side of the dam. Supposing the skipping of the bomb were timed (if it could be done) so that it was slithering to a stop on the water as it reached the wall. Why then, the wall would stop it dead and it would simply sink into the water, by the wall, as deep as you like. You could have the fuse fixed with a hydrostatic trigger so that the bomb would go off when the water pressure reached the right amount. Set it for thirty feet down or fifty or a hundred. Please yourself, according to the effect. Hang it, the more he thought about it the more he liked the idea, even if it did sound a bit odd.

But the very shape and operation of a torpedo made that sort of timing virtually impossible. Supposing there were a missile of a different and more tractable shape – something that would skip and then be subject to some form of control or judgement. He began thinking of those pebbles again and the way they reached the point where they skipped no longer but sank under the water.

Wallis went home, dragged a tub into the garden of his house at Effingham and filled it right to the top with water. Then he rigged up a rubber catapult a few feet away, a few inches above the level of the water. A few feet on the other side of the tub he stretched a string between a couple of sticks so that the string was also just above the level of the water. Logic told him that at some time there would be a point where an object might skip the first few times and then slither to a halt and sink.

He borrowed a marble from his young daughter, Elizabeth, and shot it from the catapult at the water. It skipped off and cleared the string by several inches. Elizabeth and the other children looked on wondering what he was up to. Elizabeth brought the marble back and Wallis fired it again, this time with a little less tension on the rubber of the catapult. The marble slipped off the water, and only just cleared the string. 'Ah,' thought Wallis, 'it can be controlled.'

He and the youngsters spent the whole morning playing with the catapult, trying different combinations of power and height while Wallis was finding out how much he could control the skip. To his deep joy he found out that with a regular shape and weight like a marble on smooth water he could control it well enough for it to be distinctly encouraging.

But could he control several skips, which might be necessary? That remained to be seen. They went in to lunch eventually, all thoroughly splashed. Wallis was very cheerful and also, the children thought, very mysterious about it.

Always sensitive to ridicule, Wallis told no one the details, not even his friend Mutt Summers, chief test pilot for Vickers and the man who had tested his old warhorse, the Wellington. Captain Summers was a hefty extrovert and not the type to take a freak idea seriously. Unable to keep completely silent, he did say to Summers cagily:

'Mutt, I think I've got an idea about these dams. Something I saw on my last holiday with the youngsters.' He would say no more. Summers looking at him curiously, noted that he was 'quite excited'.

The day of the meeting of the Air Attack on Dams Committee he went early to London, buttonholed the chairman, Dr Pye, and privately explained his new theory, so earnestly that Pye did not laugh though he looked a little sideways.

'I'd rather you didn't tell the others yet,' Wallis said. 'They might think it a bit far-fetched.'

'Yes,' said Dr Pye. 'I see that. What do you want me to do?'

'Give me time to find out how much RDX will blow a hole in the Moehne Dam if it's pressed up against the wall.'

Pye talked eloquently to the committee without giving Wallis's secret away. The members were reluctant when they heard the results of the last model's test and Wallis was like a cat on hot bricks till they consented to one more experiment.

Glanville built him a new model dam, and Wallis started with small charges, sinking them in the water and exploding them when they were lying against the slabs of concrete. The effect was shattering – literally. He smashed wall after wall seeking the smallest charge needed, and soon he knew that in a contact explosion tamped by water a tiny plug of a few ounces of gelignite blasted a satisfying hole through a concrete wall 6 inches thick. From that he calculated he would need only 6,000 lb of RDX to breach the Moehne Dam. With his new idea he could cut the case weight down to a little over 3,000 lb, making the complete bomb about 9,500 lb. Less than 5 tons. The new four-engined Lancasters would carry that to the Ruhr without trouble.

CHAPTER 3

THE GREEN LIGHT

Armed with sums and theories, Wallis faced the task of convincing officials in their brick and stone lairs along Whitehall and other influential thoroughfares that he could put his bomb in the exact spot, an awkward task because they were all allergic to weird inventions. Literally one in a thousand was any good, and that usually not good enough to justify diverting effort. Most were obviously 'crackpot', and Wallis's must have looked like one of those. He called on Professor Patrick Blackett, director of an 'operational research' branch, and Blackett, a spare, rather intense man, listened to his ideas, carefully examined the calculations, riffled them back into a neat pile and said quietly:

'We've been looking for this for two years.' Wallis was electrified.

'I'd like you to leave these with me for a while,' Blackett said. 'There are one or two people I know who would be interested.'

Blackett moved fast. As soon as Wallis had left he went to see Sir Henry Tizard and told him what he had heard. Tizard also moved with unorthodox haste, driving down to Weybridge next morning, where Wallis eagerly explained it all again.

'It seems,' Tizard said when he had finished, 'that the main thing to establish is whether this freak of yours will really work, and if so how we go about putting it into practice.'

At Teddington, he said, was a huge ship-testing tank which would be ideal for experiments. He also thought there should be more tests to check how much explosive would theoretically punch a hole in a dam.

'I think I know just the thing,' said Wallis, whose 'damology' researches had been fanatical. 'There's a small disused dam in Radnorshire; no earthly use any more as a dam and won't ever be. We could try and knock it down.'

'Who owns it?' Tizard asked.

'Birmingham Corporation.' Wallis knew all the answers.

'We'll try them,' Tizard said, and Birmingham Corporation, with a little prodding, said yes.

It was a nice little dam, about 150 feet long and quite thick, curving gracefully across the mouth of a reach of Rhayader Lake, high in the Welsh hills west of Leominster. The corporation had built a bigger dam across the mouth of the lake to feed a little river that tumbled out of the hills.

Wallis estimated that the old dam should have a fifth of the resistance of the Moehne, an ideal test model. He calculated the smallest charge that should knock it down and set off with a packet of RDX and some explosives engineers. Wrapped against the raw mountain wind, he wasted little time, measured out the charge, tamped it in a sealed casing and lowered it deep into the water against the dam wall. Behind the rocks, his mouth dry with anxiety, he pressed the plunger and the hills echoed with sound. Water spurted a hundred feet high, the lake whipped into fury, and as the water plunged back into the void the concrete crumbled and a hissing flood burst into the main lake. Wallis, pink with glee, saw there was a ragged hole in the dam 15 feet across and about 12 feet deep.

For the next five months he experimented whenever he could in the ship tank at Teddington, an enormous thing hundreds of feet long. He wanted to find out exactly how to control a skipping missile, so that after a given number of bounces over a given distance he could make it reach a certain given point at a particular speed and height. At this ultimate spot the missile would have to be either slithering across the water or only, moving slowly, just a fraction above it. He had to find out the best combinations of weight of missile, and height, speed and power of release. Using an adjustable spring-loaded catapult so that he could measure the force behind it, he started firing marbles at first. Obviously a missile of regular shape, such as a sphere, was needed so that no matter how it might flick or spin after the first impact, it would still hit the water with an identical shape on the next and subsequent bounces. An irregular shape might produce the same amusingly eccentric hops after it hit, but this wasn't child's play any more.

But soon he noticed something inconsistent about the bouncing marbles. More often than not they tended to dig in and sink after the third bounce or thereabouts. Maybe it was the small size of the marbles that made them unstable. Maybe some imperceptible ripple on the water affected them. The only consistent pattern was that they never bounced as far as the far end of the tank – except for one or two strong shots that hit the end and always bounced back too far. There would obviously be ripples on the lake's surface held back by the dams. Something bigger and heavier might not be so affected. He tried using golf balls, but they were as unpredictable as the marbles. Then he tried using 2 lb spheres of steel, but they were no better either.

Why? He asked himself; and his family could hardly get a word out of him for days while he cogitated. It was on a Sunday afternoon that he found what seemed to be the answer, while he was mulching some spring daffodils in his garden. Metaphorically (and typically) he kicked himself for not thinking of it before. It seemed so simple, really.

The first bounce gave the marble or golf ball or steel sphere a pronounced top-spin and that was why they tended to dig themselves into the water. Of course one could try a flattish shape like a disc type stone but heaven knows how one could control the skips. There was one other answer – just one! The spherical projectiles must be fired with a pronounced back-spin. Wallis rigged up a cradle for the spring-loaded catapult that allowed him to spring the missile backwards just before release.

He got a double-bonus! For one thing, virtually every shot hit or slithered against the far end of the tank. And even more important – the residual back-spin still on the small projectile made it crawl under the water at the far end, flat against the far wall of the tank. It was exactly what he wanted to happen when the missiles reached a dam wall.

Now another problem cropped up. Wallis had been calculating the size of the sphere that would carry enough RDX explosive inside a steel case strong enough to stand the impact of hitting both the water and the dam wall. Hitting water at something well over 200 mph would be like hitting concrete.

He started to work out the required diameter of the sphere. He already knew he would have to take both bomb bay doors off the Lancasters and suspend the bombs under the belly with 'legs' that stuck down underneath with some sort of belt or chain drive from some power source to get them spinning backwards before the drop.

Finding the necessary size of the sphere wasn't difficult. He soon worked it out, and damn! the sphere was going to be too big. It had to be slung close to the centre of gravity of the aircraft and low enough to clear the tunnel of the fuselage above. And if he slung it low enough for that, the base of the missile was going to be crushed hard against the ground. In fact you could only load the missile in place by jacking the aircraft up till the under-carriage wheels were clear of the tarmac.

Once you took the jacks away either the 'legs' would buckle and the missile burst through the fuselage floor, or the aircraft would break its back, or both. And you couldn't sufficiently lift the fuselage floor of a Lancaster (or other suitable aircraft) because the space around the centres of gravity and lift (or balance) was already overcrammed with immovable mainspar (wing), crew and equipment.

Any way you looked at it, neither aircraft nor missile would be getting off the ground. Neither it seemed would the entire project. It was pointless making the sphere smaller. That would either weaken the casing too much or cut down the explosive contents too much and apparently it had to be a sphere. So even if you got it loaded it could not be anything more than a study in still-life until you took the jacks away, and then the scrap metal wouldn't be funny.

It looked like the end of a disappointing (and humiliating) road. But to the stubborn Wallis this was only a challenge – not yet a defeat. Science and stubbornness often produce an answer. He thought constantly about it – and for a few days got nothing out of it except insomnia.

Again he could not pinpoint the exact moment he began thinking about gyroscopic principles. He was only rummaging in his mind and bound to strike it sooner or later.

If you make something spin fast enough around an axis it needs a surprising amount of force to tilt it off that axis. The earth is one example of spinning on an axis. It stays on that same axis (thank God) but it doesn't have to be a sphere. A lot of youngsters have little gyroscopes as toys. Yank hard on a string and a caged disc spins like mad, and people are intrigued at the strength it needs to budge it from its axis. Or take a child's top. It stays upright when it is spinning fast enough and falls over when it isn't. (That's a top secret!) A lot of aircraft blind flying instruments depend on gyroscopic action, such as an artificial horizon.

Wallis knew that he had to reduce the diameter of his missile. And he knew it still had to hit the water on every bounce with the same shape surface as before. He already knew his missile had to drop with a lot of back-spin on it to control the bounces, and also to make it crawl underwater flat against the dam wall when it hit. So why not a missile shaped like a portly barrel with enough back-spin to keep it gyroscopically on an identical axis all the way.

That would reduce the diameter without lengthening the 'barrel' shape too much. It seemed all so easy. All one had to do was think it out first.

His assistants carved on lathes a series of fat, barrel-shaped models, each with differing weight-size-shape ratios and all of them with a potential diameter small enough to be carried under a Lancaster.

Wallis tested each repeatedly with varying combinations of backspin, catapult velocity and height. Consistently they skipped across the water in the tank in little flashes of spray but seldom tilting off their horizontal axis, presenting at each skip the same pot-bellied shape to the water. By trial and error he found at what speeds each model would slither against the far end of the tank and crawl under the water hugging the wall (with the residual back-spin). He filled a notebook with details of each shape, and by simple elimination was able to choose the model with the widest range of reliable performance.

The rest was largely doing sums, such as how fast a five-ton 'barrel' could be safely spun backwards before release from an aircraft and achieve enough gyroscopic stability for half a mile or more of bouncing bumps. Wallis made it between 450–500 revolutions per minute backwards.

By the middle of 1942 he was satisfied he could make a five-tonner do what he wanted it to. The only thing he didn't know was whether to call it a barrel, a bomb, a mine or a missile. Not that it mattered.

Tizard was pleased, but Tizard was an adviser, not all-powerful; the task was to get executive officials keen. Wallis thought he had proved his point, and as an innocent scientist he can perhaps be excused for optimism. In government there are 'proper channels' and few short cuts, and the proper channels were preoccupied with other vital work.

Wallis saw several officials, received tea and courtesy, even compliments, but not enough action to please him. Two high executives in particular who could have started things moving seemed irritatingly cautious. They shall be nameless, because they are good men who worked hard and brilliantly in other directions, and no honest man should be censured for failing to understand Wallis any more than he should be condemned for failing to follow Einstein.

But it was so *maddening*! Wallis knew he had proved his theories and still he was up against a barrier that seemed as solid as a dam wall. He got the ear of a great scientist who had access to Churchill, expounded his ideas and showed his calculations. The scientist was not impressed, and said so. Yet there were other officials, like Dr Pye, who were encouraging him.

The phone rang one day and a man named Lane, speaking from London, said he wanted to talk to Wallis about 'a secret matter'. He was, he said, from one of the committees dealing with new and secret weapons. Wallis felt his heart skip. 'What's it about?' he asked.

'It's to do with aircraft and water,' said the man, 'but I mustn't say any more over the phone. Can I come and see you?'

'Tomorrow,' said Wallis, 'as early as you like.'

Lane walked into his office in the morning, an alert young man, and Wallis welcomed him warmly. Lane showed his credentials and said:

'Do you remember an idea of yours back in 1941 about putting a smoke screen round a fleet?'

'Smoke screen?' Wallis said, not understanding for a moment; and then he remembered. Many other things besides earthquake bombs had germinated in his fertile mind since 1939, and one of them had been for a radio-controlled pilotless plane which could be catapulted from a cruiser or battleship to lay a smoke screen; cheaper and faster than laying a screen by destroyers.

'Yes,' he said heavily. 'I remember.'

'We're interested in it,' Lane said. 'Have been for some time, but we couldn't do everything at once. Can you tell me a little more about it?'

Wallis spent the next hour going into detail, and when he had finished and Lane was thanking him and rising to go Wallis said a little wistfully:

'You know, it's very disappointing. I thought you wanted to see me about my pet idea that nobody seems to want.'

'Oh?' said Lane politely, reaching for his hat. 'What's that?'

Wallis started to tell him, and as he described his tests the casual attention on Lane's face changed to a look of startled interest. He sat down again and listened for another hour; afterwards, when he rose to go again, he said, 'I'll tell my chief about this one. I think he might be interested.'

Lane's chief rang Wallis next morning and an hour later he was in Wallis's office in the old house at Burhill, listening. Hours later he went back to London as nearly convinced as a man can be by figures.

He spent just under 48 hours chewing it over and soft-talking one of the two Doubting Thomases. Then he conveniently 'forgot' the other Doubter and picked up the phone to call Wallis.

It happened to be lunch-time, when there was a standing order that no calls should be put through to Wallis. That was his sacred hour for dreaming up new ideas while he munched a cheese sandwich and an apple at his desk. Even the gentle Wallis had his limits, and breaking his train of thought at that hour evoked loud protest. Backed by the mystique of Government Authority, the official forced the switch-girl to put him through. Despite her warnings the frustrated protest in his earphone still startled him. When he edged his name audibly into the noise, Wallis subsided into his normal courtesy.

'I thought you might like to know,' said the official, 'you can go ahead and make six half-size prototypes of your bomb thing. You can convert a Wellington to test-drop them and we'll both keep our fingers crossed. Purely for experiment, you know.'

It took a few seconds for it to sink in before Wallis could express his fervent thanks to the official and all concerned. At the end he said, 'I'll write a note of thanks to Sir Blank Blank right away.'

'Oh my God no!' said the official. 'Don't. Don't make a sound. I'll carry my share of the can if it doesn't work, but you don't have to throw it at me in advance.'

Converting a Wellington was simple enough. Wallis had the bomb-doors taken off a production model. Two sturdy steel struts were bolted in their place so that they hung down like stiff, short little legs. Each had a bearing gear at the base so that a 'bomb' could be slung between them with freedom to revolve. Wallis was alight with enthusiasm, anticipating each little problem before it arose. One bearing had a sprocket attachment for chain drive and twin quick-release shackles were no problem. Well before this was completed Wallis was poking around the stores of odd bits of machinery that accumulate in any large experimental and production factory. He was looking for a compact, light-weight motor to rotate the bomb and soon found what he wanted – an electric motor salvaged from the gizzards of an obsolete Vickers submarine broken up in some marine knacker's yard. He mounted this in the fuselage of the Wellington. Rigging the chain drive and switches was no trouble.

By this time the castings of the six half-size $2\frac{1}{2}$-ton prototype bombs were finished and balanced, then filled with harmless substitute the same weight as RDX. Wallis had been too busy to worry about the outcome, but suddenly, overnight, it was all ready. The moment had come!

At 3 pm on 4 December 1942, the converted Wellington took off from Weybridge with the first bomb slung below and Mutt Summers in the pilot's seat. Wallis, hopeful butterflies fluttering in his stomach, crouched in the nose as bomb-aimer to test-drop off Chesil Beach on the south coast.

The strange shape hanging underneath changed the outline of the plane. Naval gunners at Portland could not make out the strange aircraft, so they rightly gave themselves the benefit of the doubt and opened fire and the gentle scientist was intrigued to see black puffs of flak staining the sky. He thought they were tiny clouds and his scientific mind wondered at the phenomenon until a wing tip flicked up and the Wellington peeled off out of range. Wallis saw Summers muttering explosively, realized what had happened and thought, wryly, the flak was carrying official obstructionism a little too far.

They were not going to worry much this time about precise speed and height. About 200 feet and 200 mph, and for the time being never mind exactly how far the bomb went. It should, however, bounce on cleanly about half a mile. Something near that would do for the first test. The main thing was to see whether a couple of tons of spinning steel *would* bounce according to theory.

Wallis was lying on his stomach in the nose, looking through the bomb-aimer's perspex floor panel for a clear stretch of water. He sighted one and briefly, over the intercom, guided Summers towards it. As Summers wheeled and then started a shallow dive, Wallis switched on the electric motor just in front of him. It started to whine, louder and louder, and as its speed increased Wallis could feel the growing vibration through the aircraft as the bomb spun backwards, faster and faster towards the 8 revs a second mark. He couldn't see much of the actual bomb but it wasn't making any nasty thumping noises. Coming up to the clear water, Summers levelled out fairly low and reported briefly, 'Speed two-two-zero indicated.'

Right! Now! Wallis pressed the button and watched the spinning black thing slip clear of its stowage. It took so long to drop that it seemed like slow-motion, especially as its forward trajectory kept it still under the aircraft, but slowly losing speed and falling behind. Then, quite suddenly, it hit and vanished in a sheet of hissing white spray.

Wallis watched with painful anxiety for it to appear. Just for a moment nothing seemed to happen and then out of the foam lurched the black thing looking vaguely misshapen in its aura of spray. It fell back into the water quite quickly, lurched drunkenly up again, hit once more, skipped another short distance, then slithered a few yards and vanished into the green depths. It didn't seem to have travelled more than about two hundred yards and Wallis looked down, puzzled, not quite knowing what to think. It had worked, but not the way it was supposed to. Something was wrong. Summers turned the aeroplane back towards Weybridge and Wallis, on the way back, trying to imagine what could have gone wrong, remembered the misshapen look about the bomb. He decided that the casing had not been strong enough. It must have crushed a little under the impact, making the bounces unpredictable and sluggish. When they landed he ordered the cases of the remaining bombs strengthened.

On 12 December he and Summers took off with a strengthened bomb, Summers prudently avoiding Portland. Off Chesil Beach, Wallis watched the bomb going down, holding his breath and feeling his mouth dry with anxiety. Again the hissing sheet of spray as it hit, and then, oh the thrill, out of the spray the black barrel came soaring a hundred yards across the water, hit with another flashing feather of spray and soared out again, hit again, and again, the distances shortening every time until at last, after nearly half-a-mile, it slithered to a foaming stop and sank. Summers had banked the aeroplane round and they could both look down on that glorious sight of the long necklace of white foaming scars on the water where the bomb had hit. Wallis had never known such a moment of triumph. He crawled half-way out of the nose to look up and grin at Summers above in the cockpit. The engines were making too much noise to talk but Summers grinned down at him, gave him the thumbs-up sign and an enormous wink.

In the next three days he and Summers dropped three more bombs and they worked every time. They took a movie cameraman with them on these flights and got undeniable evidence that it worked.

After that things happened very quickly. From Somewhere on High Wallis got instructions to try the small prototype bomb in a small Mosquito bomber against a battleship moored in a remote naval station.

This time the aircraft was faster and the bomb bounced further till it hit the side of the battleship virtually amidships and crawled below under the hull (battleships were armoured above the water but not below).

They made several runs and the results were similar in every case – these subsequent runs being filmed by an aircraft flying alongside and following the track of the bouncing bomb.

Next an urgent summons to the Admiralty, together with his films, and there he found the First Sea Lord, Admiral of the Fleet, Sir Dudley Pound, a gaggle of other Admirals and the Chief of the Air Staff, Marshal of the RAF, Lord Portal. In a private cinema the films were run through of the missiles hitting the battleship and a startled murmuring burst forth. Wallis did not catch all the conversation but there was one Admiral who remarked audibly, 'My God, if we can get a bit of extra range into the Mosquito we can blow that damned *Tirpitz* sky high.' (The *Tirpitz* was moored in northern Norway and a constant threat to the convoys carrying war materials to Russia.)

There was another Admiral who said, 'So we might, too, but don't forget if the Germans wake up to how it is done we've got a damn sight more big ships to be sunk than they have.' Portal did not say very much and the meeting broke up into discussion groups, some apparently in favour and some having distinct qualms.

In the next couple of days Wallis was asked to show his films to the German-born Lord Cherwell, the controversial scientist who had direct access to Churchill over all matters scientific, to the great resentment of a number of distinguished scientists who objected both to his opinions and to his manner. Cherwell saw the films and indicated in a most lukewarm manner that he did not think the dams were a very important target – though he didn't outwardly condemn the idea.

It is unlikely that anyone will ever know the precise story of the intrigue that went on behind the scenes in the next couple of days. It is known that the Navy was in favour of an attack against the *Tirpitz* but apprehensive about the secret leaking out to the Germans. Cherwell was generally recognized as opposed to the whole proposition, including the dams which he said frankly did not seem to be a very important target. With him was Air Marshal Linnell. Undecided was Dr Pye of the Attack on Dams Committee. Keen and enthusiastic were Sir Henry Tizard, Prof. Sir Patrick Blackett and Sir Thomas Merton who also had considerable influence with Churchill. In the end it was apparently Churchill who made the decision to get the dams project moving. He issued instructions to one of the cautious ones to instruct Wallis to go ahead with the preliminary design of a full-size bomb and Wallis felt the fierce joy of a front row forward who has heaved manfully in the scrum and gained a couple of inches. The official tempered his joy by telling him not to expect too much. Further work would depend on whether it would dislocate work on a new bomber. It is perhaps fair to say that the official *had* to be cautious. He couldn't do everything he wanted to.

This was early February, 1943, and the best time to smash the dams was in May, when they were full. To leave it later might annoy the Germans

but not seriously incommode them. There was still just time. Wallis worked
late over his plans and on the eighth day had them virtually finished when
the bombshell dropped. One of the cautious ones phoned, ordering him to
stop work on the big bomb. There was to be no further action on it.

Wallis went grimly next day to the big tank at Teddington, sank two
glass airtight tanks in the water, put an arc light in one and induced a slight
young woman to go into the other with a movie camera. She and the
camera could just fit in. He dropped a model bomb into the water and the
girl filmed its under-water progress. It was a beautiful film; clearly it
showed the bomb plunging under the surface and crawling into position
against the side of the tank.

Next he called up Summers and demanded an interview with Air
Marshal Sir Arthur Harris, chief of Bomber Command. Summers had
known Harris for years, well enough to call him by his first name, which few
people dared to do. Harris, it was freely acknowledged, could crush a
seaside landlady with a look.

Summers and Wallis drove into the wood outside High Wycombe where
Harris had his headquarters, and as Wallis put his foot on the threshold of
Harris's office the booming voice hit him like a shock wave:

'What the hell is it you want? I've no time for you damned inventors. My
boys' lives are too precious to be wasted by your crazy notions!'

It was enough to strike fear into the heart of the sturdiest inventor. Wallis
almost baulked, then pressed on and there was the bulky figure of Harris,
grey eyes staring coldly over the half-moon glasses perched on his nose.

'Well?' Harris was a man of few words and forceful ones.

'I have an idea for destroying German dams,' Wallis said. 'The effects on
Germany would be enormous.'

'I've heard about it. It's far-fetched.'

Wallis said he'd like to explain it, and Harris gave a grunt which Wallis
took for yes and went ahead, trying not to be too involved and yet show
how he had proved the theory. At the end the bomber chief had absorbed it
all. Not that there was any encouraging reaction. Harris said bluntly: 'If
you think you're going to walk in and get a squadron of Lancasters out of
me you've made a mistake. You're not!'

Wallis started to bristle and Summers, who knew Wallis's obstinacy and
Harris's explosive temperament, kicked Wallis's shin under the desk.
Wallis controlled himself.

'We don't want a squadron,' he said, '. . . yet. We'd like a chance to
prove it in trials with one Lancaster first.'

Harris eyed him stonily. 'Maybe,' he said. 'You *really* think you can
knock a dam down with that thing?'

'Yes,' Wallis said. 'Or it may take three or four. We can put them all in
the same place.'

Summers said peaceably, 'We'll prove it'll work, Bert.'

'Prove it and I'll arrange a squadron,' Harris said, and then with his old fierceness, staring at Wallis, 'but I'm tired of half-baked inventors trying to run things.'

Summers kicked Wallis once more under the desk and broke the tension by saying, 'We've got some films here that show clearly how it works.'

'All right. Let's see them.' They trooped out to the Command projection room, picking up Harris's chief lieutenant, Air Vice-Marshal Saundby, on the way. Harris curtly told the projectionist to clear out. 'If it's as good as you say,' he told Wallis, 'there's no point letting everyone know. Saundby can run the films through.'

Saundby's training had not concentrated much on film projection work and for a while there was a tangle of celluloid, but eventually he sorted it out, clicked the lights off and they watched in silence the antics of the bombs dropped at Chesil Beach and the tricks of the model under the water at Teddington.

When the lights went up Harris had his poker face on. 'Very interesting,' he grunted. 'I'll think it over.'

Wallis and Summers went back to Weybridge; Summers, who was a tough customer, amused by the interview, and Wallis with mixed feelings. He did not know why Harris distrusted inventors so much.

[It started (so the story goes) back about 1916, when Major Arthur Harris led a squadron of fighters in England whose job it was to down German Zeppelins. An inventor was sent to him to try out a new idea, to dangle an explosive charge like a football on a long line under a fighter, which then flew over a Zeppelin so that the football grenade hit the Zeppelin, to the mortification of the Germans. Harris, already a firebrand, tried it and found that the long clothes-line dangling underneath was more of a menace to the plane.

'. . . So why not,' he said to the inventor, 'dispense with the clothes-line and just drop the grenade?'

'Ah, that's a good idea,' said the inventor. 'Let's try that.'

'Just a minute,' Harris said. 'If you're going to drop it by itself wouldn't it be better to streamline it so it'll fall faster and more accurately?'

'Yes, yes,' the inventor said. 'Excellent. Let's do that.'

'Just a minute,' said Harris, and pointed to his plane standing near by. 'What the hell d'you think those are under the wings?'

'Those' were little anti-Zeppelin bombs.]

Not long after, Wallis got a summons to a senior executive whom he knew quite well and who in the past had encouraged his bomb work.

'Wallis,' he said. 'I've been asked by –' (one of the two cautious ones) 'to tell you to stop your nonsense about destroying dams. He tells me you're making a nuisance of yourself at the Ministry.'

For a moment Wallis was stunned, then recovered and answered quietly, 'If you think I'm not acting in the best interests of the war effort, I think I should offer to resign from all my work and try something else.'

For the first and last time he saw the executive lose his temper. The man shot to his feet, smashed his fist on the desk and shouted 'Mutiny!' Smashed his fist down again with another 'Mutiny!' And again with a third explosive 'Mutiny!' He subsided, red and quivering, and Wallis walked out of the room. He had lunch somewhere but does not remember where, and afterwards went and told the whole story to Sir Thomas Merton, one of the Supply Ministry's inventions tribunal. Merton promised support, but Wallis came away still depressed, knowing of nothing more he could do; it seemed too late now to organize things for the coming May, and after a couple of days he was resigned to it.

That was the day, 26 February, he got a summons to the office of one of the cautious ones, and there he also found the senior executive who had shouted 'Mutiny!' Proceedings opened by the cautious one saying, a little stiffly:

'Mr Wallis, orders have been received that your dams project is to go ahead immediately with a view to an operation at all costs no later than May.'

It took some time for Wallis to take it in.

(The Chief of the Air Staff, as it happened, had sanctioned the project a week before, and Churchill and Merton were enthusiastic about it.)

CHAPTER 4

A SQUADRON IS BORN

After battling for so long, Wallis, in the weeks that followed, sometimes ruefully thought he had got more action than he could stand. Life was work from dawn till midnight, planning, draughting, thinking and discussing, grabbing a sandwich with one hand while the work went on.

He told his workers briefly what he wanted them to do, but not what the bombs were to do, or when, or where. Only he, Harris and a selected few others knew that, and apart from them a curtain of secrecy came down. Each craftsman worked on one part and knew nothing of the others.

The shape of the large bombs, known by the code name of 'Upkeep', took a lot of devising. The central core holding the explosive was to be in the form of a cylindrical steel barrel nearly 7 feet long. To fit around that Wallis had squads of men carving thick staves like the outside of a barrel which were to be clamped around the cylinder with very strong bands of high tensile steel to form his required elongated barrel shape, and then each bomb as it was completed had to be 'balanced' so that no single arc was heavier than the others, rather like balancing a motor car wheel, so that its rotation sets up no vibrations. If one of the bombs had a little 'throw' on one segment the whole cumbersome weapon revolving at nearly 500 rpm would tear it out of its cradle and possibly tear the aircraft apart too.

Apart from these demanding details, one of the first things Wallis himself had to do was calculate as closely as possible the speed, height and distance from the dam that the bomb should be released. No good having them bounce over the top or hit the dam wall so hard that the bomb broke open and de-fused itself or, worse, blew up and wrecked the aircraft without denting the dam. A horrible thought. It was a complex three-way equation, made more difficult by his awareness that pilots were not going to find it easy to fly to precise limits, especially at night. (He already knew it had to be by night. No Lancaster would even reach the low level targets by day, but cover of darkness should protect them well.)

The pilot precision problem was beginning to bother him, and it bothered him still more when he worked out the equation – a speed of 240 miles an hour at 150 feet above the water and 800 yards from the dam wall. The speed was no trouble, but the height, at night, was perilously low and the range of 800 yards might be awkward too. He had an uncomfortable feeling that he had concentrated too much on bomb performance and not enough on the human and flight element.

An urgent call brought Mutt Summers to his office and Mutt was stumped for an answer too.

'If I only had more *time*,' Wallis said. 'I *know* there must be an answer but we've got barely ten weeks to get the whole thing done.'

'On these figures, how much margin of error have we got?' Summers asked.

'Just about none,' Wallis said. 'Not unless we come down lower. A lot lower. And that's too risky for the aircrews.'

After a while, Summers said: 'I think this is more my department. If there's an answer, we'll find it, and we'll find it in time. You concentrate on getting the bomb ready and I'll pester a few people on the flight problem.'

Wallis had no other choice. He still worried, but getting the five-tonners produced and aircraft modifications perfected in the short time allotted kept him busy over 16 hours a day. He was beginning to feel the strain and getting little sleep. Luckily, the teamwork was excellent. By normal standards the task was impossible in the time but people ignored inconvenient regulations and cut whatever corners they safely could. The bombs were on time coming off the production line. Shaped like portly barrels, Wallis had been able to keep the girth at the fattest point well under seven feet in diameter. That was slim enough to fit under the aircraft connected by a drive with an electric motor mounted to one side in the belly of the aircraft.

Roy Chadwick, chief Avro designer, fairly soon got the first modified Lancaster converted with the two heavy caliper struts sticking down outside each side of the fuselage like legs and part of the fuselage above cut away to allow for rotation. He had this aircraft test flown with one of the first bombs rotating at nearly 500 rpm for five minutes and there was no hint of trouble. When the time came the bombs would not have to be rotated for more than a couple of minutes before release.

Explosives experts, tactical authorities, secret service men and hundreds of others had a part in it, and over Germany every day a fast Mosquito flew 25,000 feet over the dams taking photographs. Deep in the underground vaults of Bomber Command men studied the photographs through thick magnifying glasses to check the level of the rising water and the defences. If the secret leaked out they would see the extra flak and the raid would have to be called off. It was going to be suicidal enough as it was. There seemed to be at least six gun positions around the Moehne alone, and that was no matter for comfort because the bombs would have to be dropped from very low level, so low that a pilot could lean out and almost dangle his fingers in the water. They would have to fly between two towers on top of the dam, and some of the guns were in these towers.

The Mosquitoes flew a devious way and crossed the dams as though by accident so the Germans would not be suspicious. An ugly sign appeared in the first few days: photographs showed the anti-torpedo boom in front of the Moehne was being repaired; it had been loose and untidy, and now it was being tightened. Nothing else appeared to be happening though, and after a while it was reasonable to assume that it was only a periodical check. While the work pressed on in England, it seemed that the Germans were doing nothing significant. And therein lies a story! Barnes Wallis was not the only patriot to find that officialdom can be an immovable object to anything but irresistible force.

On 29 August 1939, a certain *Oberbürgermeister* Dillgardt had written from his office in the Ruhr to the Wehrmacht chiefs in Muenster. 'In view of the present military situation,' he said delicately, he wanted to raise the question of the defence of large dams like the Moehne and the Eder. Dillgardt was an unusually perspicacious man and it is uncanny how his layman's mind worked along the same path as Wallis's.

Dillgardt said he was worried because he thought that a large bomb exploded deep in the water some 20 metres from the dam might conceivably blow a large hole in it owing to the compressive effects of the water. He admitted humbly that his experts did not agree with him, but he painted an ugly picture of what would happen if the dams were breached – almost identical with Wallis's conclusions. He submitted, with respect, that the dam defences be strengthened.

The military authorities wrote back politely. Dillgardt could 'rest assured that the matter will receive the most careful and immediate consideration', and Dillgardt, presumably aware of the real meaning of this fatal phrase, wrote again, drawing their attention to a book called *The Curse of Bombing*, in which the author, Camille Rougeron, spoke of the danger of bombing attacks on dams. The authorities thanked him again but the matter stayed 'under consideration'.

Over the next three years the files between Dillgardt and the Wehrmacht grew to imposing fatness, a series of harrowing appeals sandwiched between dignified and adroit evasions. In a peacetime paper battle civilian officials can usually vanquish military officials, but in wartime the boot is on the other foot, and the military men in Muenster were impregnable.

Dillgardt even predicted that any attack would be made in May, when the dams were full. He pointed out the increasing size and power of British bombs, asked for heavier torpedo nets, for smoke screens, balloon barrages, searchlights and heavy flak, and every time he was fobbed off returned tenaciously to the attack. Now and then he tasted victory; early in 1940 the Wehrmacht posted some heavy flak and searchlights around the Moehne, perhaps to keep Dillgardt quiet, and a few weeks later took them away again.

Twice more, when his persistence exasperated them into some concession, the Wehrmacht posted a little light flak there and then took them away again. And as Dillgardt pestered them anew a note of asperity crept into the answering letters; the formal politeness deteriorated more and more. Sarcastically the generals expressed their gratitude for having their duty so generously explained to them by a civilian. Uncrushed, the dogged Dillgardt sent fresh reminders until one day a tormented general wrote tersely:

'*Sir,*

> *There is no further need for regular reports to be sent in to this office regarding storage level of these dams.*
> HEIL HITLER!'

Later on they threw him a last crumb by sending some 20 mm guns.

At his headquarters in the wood Sir Arthur Harris ('Bert' to his friends and 'Bomber' to the public) had been pondering how the attack should be made – and who should make it. On 15 March he sent for Air Vice-Marshal the Honourable Ralph Cochrane, who two days before had become Air Officer Commanding No. 5 (Bomber) Group.

'I've got a job for you, Cocky,' Harris said and told him about Wallis's weird bomb and what he proposed to do with it. At the end he said: 'I know it sounds far-fetched, but I think it has a good chance.'

Cochrane said: 'Well, sir, I've known Wallis for twenty-five years. He's a wonderful engineer and I've never known him not to produce what he says he will.'

'I hope he does it again now,' Harris said. 'You know how he works. I want you to organize the raid. Ask for anything you want, as long as it's reasonable.'

Cochrane thought for a moment.

'It's going to need some good aircrews,' he said. 'I think I'd better screen one of my squadrons right away and start them on intensive training.'

'I don't want to do that,' Harris said. 'I don't want to take a single squadron out of the line if I can help it, or interfere with any of the main force. What I have in mind is a new squadron, say, of experienced people who're just finishing a tour. Some of the keen chaps won't mind doing another trip. Can you find enough in your group?'

'Yes, sir.' Cochrane asked Harris if he wanted anyone in particular to command the new squadron, and Harris said: 'Yes, Gibson.'

Cochrane nodded in satisfaction, and ten minutes later, deep in thought, he was driving back to the old Victorian mansion outside Grantham that was 5 Group Headquarters. There could probably have been no better choice than Cochrane for planning the raid. A spare man with a lean face, his manner was crisp and decisive, perfectly reflecting his mind. The third son of a noble Scottish family, he was climbing to the top on his own ability;

he had perhaps the most incisive brain in the RAF – and that is no diplomatic exaggeration. His god was efficiency and he sought it so uncompromisingly – almost ruthlessly according to some of his men, who were afraid of him, but his aircrews would do anything he asked, knowing that it would be meticulously planned.

Moreover, Cochrane knew Wallis well; had worked with him in the Royal Naval Air Service in World War I, flying his experimental airships and testing the world's first airship mooring mast, which Wallis had designed. Ever since then Cochrane had had a quick sympathy for the scientific approach.

That night a nuggetty little man with a square, handsome face, named Guy Gibson, took off on the last trip of his third tour. If he got back he was due for leave and a rest, having been on ops almost constantly since the war started. The target was Stuttgart and his Lancaster was laden with one of the new 8,000-lb 'blockbusters' (not the penetrating 'earthquake' type that Wallis envisaged, but bombs had made startling strides in the past year).

An engine failed on the way to Stuttgart and the aircraft would not hold her height. Gibson eased her out of the stream, dropping towards the ground, but headed on. The last trip of a tour is an ordeal with its hopes of a six-months' reprieve. Before take-off the reprieve seems so near and yet so far, and waiting to get it over is not pleasant. Gibson took a chance rather than turn back and go through the waiting again.

Over Stuttgart he had the other three engines shaking the aircraft at full power and managed to drag up to a safe enough height to drop his bomb, then dived to the dark anonymity of earth and hugged the ground all the way back. That was Gibson's 173rd trip. He was a wing commander with the DSO and DFC. Aged twenty-five.

He woke late, head still ringing with the engine noise, and lay curled up, half thinking, half dreaming of leave in Cornwall. That morning his leave was cancelled and, to his dismay, he was posted to 5 Group Headquarters.

A day or so later he was shown into Cochrane's office and saluted smartly.

'Ah, Gibson,' Cochrane said. 'First, my congratulations to the bar to your DSO.'

'Thank you, sir.'

'Would you like to do one more trip?'

Gibson gulped and said, a little warily:

'What kind of trip, sir?'

'An important one. I can't tell you any more about it now except that you would command the operation.'

Gibson said slowly, 'Yes, I – I think so, sir,' thinking of the flak and the fighters he hoped he had finished with for a time.

'Good; that's fine. I'll let you know more as soon as I can,' and a moment later Gibson was outside the door, wondering what it was all about. He waited two days before Cochrane sent for him again, and this time another man was with him, Group Captain Charles Whitworth, who commanded the bomber base at Scampton, a stocky, curly-haired man of about thirty, with a long list of operations behind him and a DSO and DFC on his tunic. Gibson knew him and liked him.

Cochrane was friendly. 'Sit down,' he said and held out a cigarette. 'I asked you the other day if you'd care to do another raid and you said you would, but I want to warn you that this will be no ordinary sortie and it can't be done for at least two months.'

Gibson thought: 'Hell, it's the *Tirpitz*. Why did I say yes!' The 45,000-ton 'unsinkable' battleship was lying in a Norwegian fiord, a permanent menace to the Russia convoys and a lethal target to tackle.

Cochrane was still talking. 'Training for this raid is so important that the Commander-in-Chief wants a special squadron formed. I want you to form it. You'd better use Whitworth's main base at Scampton. As far as aircrews are concerned, you'll want good ones; you'd better pick them yourself. I'm telling all the squadrons they'll have to give up some of their best crews. I'm afraid they won't like it, so try and take men who are near the end of their tours. There's a lot of urgency in this because you haven't got very long and training is going to be very important. Go to it as fast as you can and try and get your aircraft flying in four days.'

'Well, er . . . what sort of training, sir?' Gibson asked. 'And . . . what sort of target?'

'Low flying,' Cochrane said. 'You've got to be able to low-fly at night till it's second nature. No, I can't tell you the target yet. That's secret, but you've all got to be perfect at low flying. At night. It's going to be the only way, and I think you can do it. You're going to a place where it'd be wrong to send a single squadron at the normal height by itself.'

Gibson knew what that meant. Germany! A single squadron at 15,000 feet would get all the night fighters. It was not so bad for the main force, the streams of hundreds of bombers; they confused the enemy radar, dispersed the fighters, and there was protection in numbers. Not so with a lone squadron. But low level, 'on the deck', yes. Well, maybe! Well, it was going to be low level anyway. Over Germany! He knew a man named Martin who knew all about low flying over Germany. Gibson had met him when Martin was being decorated for it. Cochrane was still talking:

'I'm sorry I can't tell you any more for the moment, Gibson. The immediate problem is to get your crews and get them flying.'

'How about aircraft, sir?'

'The equipment staff have that in hand. The first will be flown in tomorrow.' The interview was clearly over and Cochrane was already frowning at some papers on his desk. Gibson saluted, and as he turned the door handle Cochrane looked up again.

'One thing more,' he said. 'You'll have to watch security. As far as others are concerned this is just an ordinary new squadron. We'll think up a cover plan later.'

Outside the door Whitworth said, 'See you at Scampton in a couple of days. I'll get things fixed up for you. I imagine you'll be having about seven hundred men.'

Somewhat bewildered, Gibson went off to the SOA to see how one went about forming a new squadron, and half an hour later he was looking at a long list of things he had to do and people he had to see.

A staff officer helped him pick aircrew from the group lists. Gibson knew most of the pilots – he got the staff man to promise him Martin and help him pick the navigators, engineers, bomb aimers, wireless operators and gunners; when they had finished they had 147 names – twenty-one complete crews, seven to a crew. Gibson had his own crew; they were just finishing their tour too, but they all wanted to come with him.

The Staff Officer Personnel told him how many men of different trades he wanted for his ground crews and promised to siphon off picked men from other squadrons and post them to Scampton in forty-eight hours.

The equipment officer promised to deliver ten Lancasters to Scampton within two days. Just for a start. More would follow. With them would come the spare spark plugs and tools, starter motors and drip trays, bomb dollies and winches, dope and paint and chocks and thermos flasks. Gibson was startled by the unending list. Another man promised the thousand and one items for the men: blankets and lorries and bootlaces, beer and socks, toilet paper and so on. He was two days on these details, helped by Cochrane's deputy, the SASO, Group Captain Harry Satterly, a big, smooth-faced man who was excellent at detail; and then it was all done – except for one thing.

'What squadron are you?' Satterly asked.

'What d'you mean, sir?'

'What number? You've got to have a number.'

'Oh,' said Gibson, 'where d'you get that?'

'Somewhere in Air Ministry,' Satterly said, 'but they probably don't work so fast there. I'll get on to them and fix it up. Meantime you'd better call yourselves "X Squadron".'

Just before dinner on 21 March, Wing Commander Guy Gibson, DSO, DFC, commander of 'X', the paper squadron, arrived at Scampton to take formal command. In the officers' mess he found some of his crews already

arrived and the mess waiters looked curiously at them as they stood around
with pints of beer in their fists. It was obvious they were not to be an
ordinary squadron; the average age was about twenty-two but they were
clearly veterans. DFC ribbons were everywhere; they had all done at least
one tour, and some had done two.

Gibson moved among them, followed by the faithful Nigger, his big
black Labrador dog, who rarely left his heels. Someone laid a half pint of
beer on the floor for Nigger, who stuck his muzzle noisily into it and did not
look up till he had licked it dry.

From his old 106 Squadron, Gibson had brought three crews as well as
his own – those of Hopgood, Shannon and Burpee. Hopgood was English,
fair and good looking except for a long front tooth that stuck out at an
angle. Dave Shannon, DFC, was a baby-faced twenty-year-old from
Australia, but did not look any more than sixteen, so he was growing a
large moustache to look older. He was slender, with long fingers and thick,
fair hair, and moved gracefully.

Gibson spotted Micky Martin with satisfaction. They had met at
Buckingham Palace when Gibson was getting his DSO and the King was
pinning on the first of Martin's DFCs. Though he came from Sydney, Martin
was in the RAF, slight but good looking, with a mild glint in his eyes and a
monstrous moustache that ended raggedly out by his ears. At the Palace they
had talked shop and Martin had explained his low-flying system.

He had worked it out that if you flew lower than most bombers you
would avoid the fighters; lower still and the heavy flak would all burst well
above. And if you got right down to tree-top height you would be gone
before the light flak could draw a bead on you. There was still the risk of
balloons, but Martin reasoned there would not be any balloons along main
roads or railways, so he followed those. He had had the same two gunners
for two years, Toby Foxlee and Tammy Simpson, both fellow-Australians,
and on their low-level junkets they had become expert at picking off
searchlights. Simpson and Foxlee had both come with him; he'd also
brought an experienced navigator, a lean, long-chinned Australian called
Jack Leggo, and his bomb aimer, Bob Hay, also Australian, had been a
bombing expert at Group. Leggo was to be navigation officer of the new
squadron, and Hay was to be bombing leader. It is unlikely that there was
a finer crew in Bomber Command; hence Gibson's pleasure.

He had chosen 'Dinghy' Young as his senior flight commander. Young
had already ditched twice in his two tours, and both times got back home in
his rubber dinghy. Bred in California, educated at Cambridge, he was a
large, calm man whose favourite trick was to swallow a pint of beer without
drawing breath.

Les Munro was a New Zealander, tall, blue-chinned and solemn, a little

older than the others. He was standing by the bar looking into space when
Gibson located him. 'Glad to see you, Les,' Gibson said. 'I see you're setting
a good example already, drinking a little and thinking a lot.' Munro up-
ended his pint and drained it. 'No, sir,' he said, 'thinking a little and
drinking a lot.'

The other flight commander was Henry Maudslay, ex-50 Squadron, ex-
Eton, an athlete, polished and quiet, not a heavy drinker. Towering above
the rest was the blond head of a man who weighed nearly 15 stone, with a
pink face and pale blue eyes; good looking in a rugged way. Joe McCarthy,
from Brooklyn, USA, former life-guard at Coney Island, had joined the
RAF before America came into the war.

No one knew what they were there for but, looking at the men around
them, realized something special was in the wind. Someone finally asked
Gibson what 'the form' was and Gibson simply said: 'I know less than you,
old boy, but I'll see you all in the morning to give you what gen I can.'

The party broke up late and some of the crews were merry, though none
so much as Nigger. Gibson's crew had been shoving cans of beer under
Nigger's nose all the time, and Nigger, who had never been known to refuse
one, staggered cheerfully out after Gibson, leaving a zigzag liquid trail
down the corridor.

In the morning Gibson called all the crews to the long briefing room on
top of station headquarters and said:

'I know you're wondering why you're here. Well, you're here as a crack
squadron to do a special job which I'm told will have startling results and
may shorten the war. I can't tell you what the target is or where it is. All I
can tell you is you'll have to practise low flying day and night until you can
do it with your eyes shut . . .'

There was a little murmuring as they heard 'low flying' and they started
making rough guesses. A voice said distinctly, 'Christ! The *Tirpitz!*' Gibson
said, 'Don't jump to conclusions. Maybe it's the *Tirpitz*, maybe not.
Whatever it is I want you to be ready. If I tell you to fly to a tree in the
middle of England I want you to be able to do it. If I tell you to fly through
a hangar that isn't wide enough for your wingtips I want you to have a go
at that too. You've got to be able to do anything you're told without
question.' And there was a breathless silence.

'Discipline is going to be essential. So is security. You're going to be
talked about. It's unusual to have a crowd like you forming a squadron.
Rumours are flying around already, but' – and punching his fist at the air
in emphasis – 'you've got to keep your mouths shut. If you get stuck in a
pub on the hops and someone asks you what it's all about, tell him to mind
his own business. Your lives really depend on secrecy. If we can surprise
them everything'll be fine. If they're ready for us . . .' He looked at them in
silence.

He went on to talk about training and organization, and when it was over the crews trooped out with little flutters in their stomachs, the sort of feeling you get before a raid. It goes once you get into the air.

Dinghy Young and Maudslay were busy dividing the crews into flights and Gibson walked over to No. 2 hangar, the great steel shed that was to be squadron headquarters. Along the sides were the little office rooms and outside one a queue of 'erks'.[1] Inside, a dapper little man with a toothbrush moustache broke off his interviewing and saluted smartly; Flight Sergeant 'Chiefy' Powell had just arrived to be the squadron's disciplinary NCO. The ground crews were arriving in scores and Powell already had half of them organized in their billets and sections. Discip. NCOs run a close second to service police for unpopularity, but Chiefy Powell was to become a sort of godfather to the squadron. He knew far more than Gibson about the detail that makes a squadron tick; Gibson had been too busy flying. He gave Powell and Heveron, the orderly room sergeant, a free hand and 'X' squadron rapidly took shape but was still only a paper squadron, their entire equipment consisting of one trestle desk, one chair and one phone.

Cochrane rang Gibson: 'I'm sending you over a list of lakes in England and Wales that I want photographed. Get someone on to it as soon as you can.'

Gibson, who had learned not to ask questions, said, 'Yes, sir,' wondering when the fog of secrecy was going to lift. Lorries were rolling in with maps and Mae Wests, boots and more 'erks' and envelopes and paper clips and spanners and all the other things.

Then the first crisis. A conscientious service policeman considered that the 'erks' arriving from 'X' Squadron were inexcusably scruffy and went eagle-eyed round the huts 'lumbering' scores of men for dirty boots, tarnished buttons and crooked collars. Zealously he typed all the names on the regulation forms and dumped the wad in front of Chiefy Powell.

'I'm putting seventy-five of your men on a charge, Flight,' he said primly. The snorting Powell took the charges in to Gibson, and Gibson riffled through them.

'God,' he said, 'the men didn't look too bad to me.'

'They've been travelling to get here and some of them need new uniforms.' Powell was like a hen guarding her chicks.

'Fair enough.' Gibson ripped the charge forms into shreds and looked round the room. 'We need a wastepaper basket.'

He told Powell to arrange with the station equipment officer for a clothing parade in the morning, and Powell, holding the phone in his hand, called back through the door a couple of minutes later that the equipment officer said it could not be done.

'Give me that bloody phone,' Gibson said, and five seconds later on the

[1] Ground crews.

other end of the line a pilot officer (equipment) jumped with fright as the earphone seemed to erupt against his head. The squadron was re-outfitted next morning.

Gibson spent hours interviewing his aircrews, sizing up the ones he didn't know, and found that some of the squadron commanders, told to send their best men, had played the age-old service game and got rid of a couple they did not want. Gibson told them to pack and go back.

Chiefy Powell found the same thing in the 'erks' who were still arriving, among them being two outrageous duds from Gibson's old squadron, 106. A week before Gibson had been trying to get rid of them from 106. Now, with pleasure, he sent them back to 106. Some WAAF drivers and clerks had arrived and two of them were pregnant; Gibson, more interested in the birth of a squadron, returned them too.

He walked into the mess bar just before dinner, tired but feeling they were getting somewhere, and Charles Whitworth buttonholed him:

'Well, Gibby,' he said, 'you're going to command 617 Squadron now.'

The little man looked thunderstruck. 'What the hell!' he exploded. '617? I thought . . . I . . . Who and where the hell are they?'

'Here,' said Whitworth peaceably. 'You. Your new number. Someone in Air House has moved off his bottom. Your squadron marking letters are AJ.'

He called for a pint each and they drank to 617 Squadron.

CHAPTER 5

OVER THE HURDLES

Humphries, the new adjutant, arrived next afternoon; a little fair-haired man, only twenty-eight, he was keen on flying but his eyes had stopped him. Gibson told Humphries as much as he knew himself and as Humphries was leaving his office Gibson said:

'I don't know yet what it's all about, but I gather this squadron will either make history or be wiped out.'

Humphries looked at him, not knowing whether he was joking.

'I beg your pardon, sir,' he said, but Gibson was looking at maps on his desk and didn't answer.

In the morning the curtain lifted a little. Gibson got a call from Satterly, who told him to catch a certain train to Weybridge, where he would be met at the station.

'May I know whom I'm meeting, sir?'

'He'll know you,' Satterly said.

Gibson walked out of Weybridge Station at half-past two and a big man squeezed behind the wheel of a tiny Fiat said, 'Hello, Guy!'

'Mutt,' Gibson said, surprised. 'God, are you the man I'm looking for?'

'If you're the man I'm waiting for, I am,' Summers said. 'Jump in.' They drove down the winding tree-lined road that leads to Vickers and went past the main gates without turning in. 'What's all this about, Mutt?' Gibson said, unable to hold back any longer.

'You'll find out.' He turned off up a side road to the left. 'You wanted to be a test pilot for me once. D'you remember?'

'I remember.' That was when he had first met Summers. It must have been eight years ago now, back in 1935, when he was eighteen. He had wanted to fly, so he had got an introduction to Summers at Vickers and asked about becoming a Vickers test pilot. 'Go and join the Air Force and learn to fly first,' Summers had advised.

'You'll be doing some testing soon,' Summers said. 'Not for me exactly, but quite a test.' He turned in some double gates and they pulled up outside the house at Burhill. Summers led the way into a room with windows looking over the golf course, and a white-haired man got up from a desk.

'I'm glad you've come,' Wallis said. 'Now we can get down to it. There isn't a great deal of time left. I don't suppose you know much about the weapon?'

'Weapon?' Gibson said. 'I don't know anything about anything. Group Captain Satterly said you'd tell me everything.'

Wallis blinked. 'Don't you even know the target?'

'Not the faintest idea.'

'My dear boy,' Wallis said in a sighing and faintly horrified voice. 'My dear boy.' He wandered over to the window and looked out, pondering. 'That makes it very awkward.'

'Well,' Gibson said, 'The SASO said . . .'

'I know,' said Wallis, 'but this is dreadfully secret and I can't tell anyone whose name isn't on this list.' He waved a bit of paper in Gibson's direction and Gibson could see there were only about half a dozen names on it.

Summers said, 'This is damn silly.'

'I know,' Wallis said gloomily. 'Well, my dear boy . . . I'll tell you as much as I dare and hope the AOC will tell you the rest when you get back.' Gibson waited curiously, and finally Wallis went on: 'There are certain objects in enemy territory which are very big and quite vital to the war effort. They're so big that ordinary bombs won't hurt them, but I got an idea for a special type of big bomb.'

He told Gibson about the shock waves and his weird idea for dropping bombs exactly in the right spot. Gibson was looking baffled trying to follow the shock wave theory.

'You've seen it working in pubs, Guy,' Summers said. 'A dozen times. The shove-ha'penny board. Remember how you get two or three discs lying touching and flick another one in behind them? The shock waves go right through them but they all stay where they are except the front one, and that goes skidding off. That's the shock wave.'

'Ah, now I get it.'

'I thought you would.'

'Come and I'll show you,' Wallis said and led Gibson into a tiny projection room. Wallis thumbed the switches and a flickering screen lit up with the title 'Most Secret Trial No. 1.' A Wellington dived into view over water and what looked like a black barrel fell from it, seemed to drop slowly and then was hidden in spray as it hit. Gibson started in amazement as out of the spray the black thing shot, bounced a hundred yards, bounced again in a cloud of spray and went on bouncing for what seemed an incredibly long time before it vanished. He was still staring at the screen when the lights went up again and he heard Wallis's voice.

'Well, that's my secret bomb,' Wallis said. 'That's how we . . . how *you're* going to put it in the right place.'

'Over water?' Gibson said, fishing for a clue.

'Yes,' but Wallis avoided the subject of the target. 'Over water at night or in the early morning when it's very flat, and maybe there will be fog. Now, can you fly to the limits I want, roughly a speed of two hundred and forty miles per hour, at 150 feet over smooth water, and be able to bomb accurately?'

'It's terribly hard to judge height over water,' Gibson said, 'especially at night. Not too bad in moonlight if there's a chop on the water. You know, a few white horses. But smooth water?' He wrinkled his brow. 'A bit dicey. It's like a mirror. How much margin of error?'

'Very little, I'm afraid. Almost none. Otherwise . . .' Wallis hesitated, frustrated by security. 'It's got to reach the right spot at the right speed and the right height – 150 feet. If one of the factors is wrong, the sum doesn't add up.'

'Well . . .' Gibson was thinking about echo altimeters – bouncing an electric signal down and back off the water again – but decided (correctly) that they wouldn't be fast or sensitive enough. He said hopefully: 'We can try a couple of things. I suppose we can find some way.' He sounded a little dubious and Wallis sighed.

'Oh, I hope so. There isn't much time and there's an awful lot to do.'

On the way back to Scampton, Gibson puzzled over the target. The only likely ones, he decided, were either the *Tirpitz* or the U-boat pens, and he

shuddered a little at the thought. They would be smothered in guns. At
Scampton he found some Lancasters had arrived and ground crews were
checking them over. In the morning he told his senior men what height
they would have to bomb at but nothing about the bomb itself.

Dinghy Young said: 'We'll have to do all the training we can by
moonlight, and you don't get much reliable moonlight in this country.'

'Could we fly around with dark glasses on?' Maudslay asked.

'No, that's no good. You can't see your instruments properly.'

Gibson said he'd heard of a new type of synthetic night training. They
put transparent amber screens round the perspex and the pilot wore blue
glasses; it was like looking out on moonlight but you could still see your
instruments. He would see if Satterly could get them some.

Leggo was worried about navigation. Low-flying navigation is different.
You don't see much of the area when you're low, so they were going to need
large-scale maps with plenty of detail. Large-scale maps meant constant
changing and awkward unfolding. He suggested they use strip maps
wound on rollers; navigators could prepare their own. And if they were
flying low, radio was not going to be much use for navigation. It would be
mostly map reading.

Bill Astell, deputy A Flight commander, took off the first Lancaster and
was away five hours, coming back with photographs of lakes all over the
north country. Gibson laid out ten separate routes for the crews to practise
over, and in the days that followed the Lancasters were nosing thunderously into the air all day and cruising at 100 feet over the flat fens of
Lincolnshire, Suffolk and Norfolk.

Flying low seems faster and is more exciting, also more dangerous. There
is the temptation to slip between chimneys or lift a wingtip just over a tree,
and the RAF was losing a lot of aircraft every month from fatal low-flying
accidents. It was (naturally) strictly forbidden, and the pilots were
delighted to be ordered to do it. Across several counties outraged service
police reached for notebooks and took the big AJ aircraft letters as they
roared over their heads; the complaints came flooding into Gibson's office,
and with smug rectitude he tore them up.

After a few days they came down to 50 feet and flew longer routes,
stretching out to the north country, threading through the valleys of the
Pennines, climbing and diving over the Welsh mountains, then down to
Cornwall and up to Scotland, eventually as far as the Hebrides, winging
low over the white horses while the pilots flew steady courses and the rest of
the crews gave a hand with the map reading.

Gibson took his own Lancaster, G for George, and flew over to a lake in
the Pennines to test the business of flying accurately at 150 feet over water.
Diving over the hills he throttled back and flattened out over the lake, but

it took him time, busily juggling control column, trimmers and throttles, to get the needle fairly steady within a few feet of the 150 ft. mark. He just had time to note that the speed was still too high when the hills at the far end loomed ahead and he had to ease the stick back quickly and slam on throttle. G George lifted noisily and cleared the crest with an adequate margin but not a generous one. Gibson's chunky bomb-aimer, Spam Spafford, had a front-row view in the nose and said conversationally over the intercom: 'That was interesting, Skipper. About 50 feet I'd say.'

Gibson didn't answer at first. He was thinking how much difference the weight of a heavy bomb load on board would have had. Then he said: 'Keep interested, Spam. I'm doing a one-armed fiddler act up here. Next time, *you* watch the hills in front and say "When", loud and clear.' Spafford agreed to give it his urgent and immediate consideration.

Gibson made another run, but slower this time. He had both height and speed needles closer to the mark by the time Spafford yelled in his ear. They tried it several times more and Gibson was getting his approach drill into a fairly consistent groove, not spot on but not far off, apart from one run when he hit a thermal over the approach crest and had to abort early. It was promising, but only in a limited way. Over Germany, barometric pressures would be unpredictable, and altimeters work off (adjustable) barometric pressure. Gibson knew he still had to be able to do it at night, without relying too much on the altimeter, unless Intelligence could find some kind and courageous soul in the target area who could radio target area pressure at the right time.

His limited hope did not last long. They tried it again at dusk that evening, with fog drifting over the lake. Spafford couldn't see the hills and Gibson couldn't see the water until, on the second run, cutting the corners a bit, he hit a slight down-draft, presumably from the last ridge on the run-in. Gibson reacted fast but they near as dammit went in. He heard a grunt over the intercom as Trevor-Roper, in the rear turret, saw ripples on the water from the slipstream. Even Spafford was shaken. He had had a brief close-up of the looming water from the nose perspex, and as Gibson hauled her up, Spafford muttered, for all to hear: 'Christ! This is bloody dangerous!' (The only one not perturbed was Nigger, dozing by the G-box. Nigger often flew with Gibson – though not on ops – and went everywhere with him on the ground.)

Gibson flew back and told Cochrane that if he could not find some way of judging height accurately there would be no chance of doing the raid.

'There's still time to worry about that,' Cochrane said. 'Just now I want you to have a look at models of your targets.' He waved a hand at three packing cases in a corner of his office and Gibson eyed them curiously. 'You can't train your men properly unless you know what they are, so I'm letting you know now, but you'll be the only man in the squadron to know. Keep it that way.'

A corporal brought in a hammer, and Cochrane sent him out of the room while Gibson gently prised the lids loose and lifted the battens. He stood looking down at the models, and his first reaction was a feeling of tremendous relief. Thank God, it wasn't the *Tirpitz*! It took him a couple of seconds after that to realize they were dams. One was the Moehne, and the other two the Eder and the Sorpe, handsome models that showed not only the dams but the countryside in detail for miles around, as though photographs had taken on a third dimension. There were the flat surfaces of the lakes, the hills, winding rivers and the mosaic of fields and hedges. And in the middle the dams. Gibson stood looking for a long time and then Cochrane laid the lids back over them.

'Now you've seen what you've got to attack,' he said. 'Go and see Wallis again and come and see me when you get back.'

The first thing Wallis said, eagerly, was:

'How did you get on?'

'Only fair by day,' Gibson said, 'but pretty awful at night. In fact, flying level at night over water 150 feet seems plain impossible.'

Wallis sighed and looked anxious – then his stubborn lips compressed. 'We still have some time to work out some way of doing it. We have to. Now I'll tell you more about this Downwood business.'

'Downwood?'

'The code name for the raid.' Wallis explained how the bombs were to explode deep against the dam walls.

'I've calculated that the first one ought at least to crack them, and then more bombs in the same place should shift the cracked wall back till it topples over . . . helped, of course, by the water pressure. The best times, of course, are when the dams are full. That will be in May. You'll need moonlight, and there's a full moon from the thirteenth to the nineteenth of May.'

'About six weeks.'

'Yes. You've *got* to be accurate or you might overshoot and the bomb will hit the parapet and go off there. That won't hurt the dam.'

'Hurt us though,' Gibson said as it dawned on him. 'The aircraft would be just above it.'

'Yes it would.'

'Oh,' Gibson said and went back thoughtfully to Scampton.

The synthetic night-flying gear arrived, transparent amber screens and blue glasses; 'two-stage amber,' it was called. The screens were fitted in the cockpits, pilots donned their glasses and flying by day was exactly like flying in moonlight. They flew thousands of miles with them, first at 150

feet and then, as Gibson decided they were good enough, at 50 feet, the
bomb aimers looking through the nose to warn of trees and hills.

Micky Martin lectured them on night low flying and there was little he
had not learned about the pitfalls. One night he had hit a balloon cable low
over Kassel, flying a Hampden, and should have crashed, but the cable
carried away and they saw it in the moonlight dangling from the wing; not
a comforting sight, because when they had to come in slow to land at base
with flaps and wheels down the cable would drag on the ground and almost
surely catch in a hedge or fence and spin the Hampden in. On the way back
Martin was wondering what to do about it when, to make things worse, a
fighter jumped them. He dived to 50 feet to lose it and the cable caught on a
tree and at diving speed it pulled itself free and they were all right – even
lost the fighter.

Gibson took the screens and blue lenses away and sent the crews on low-
level night cross-countries, first aircraft singly, and then, when the moon
was right, in loose formations. Two crews were too keen and came back
with branches and leaves in their radiators.

So far only Gibson knew what it was all about, but the rest of the people
at Scampton were mighty curious. A pretty little WAAF driver called
Doris Leeman summed up the general feeling when she entered in her
diary: 'Everyone speculating on the reason for the new gen squadron. So
far nothing but training – most unusual as the crews have already done a
tremendous amount of ops. They're evidently specially chosen.' And a day
or so later: 'Have never seen Lancs fly so low as these boys fly them!'

The squadron did not know it, but security men were in the district to
make sure that nothing leaked out. Phones were tapped and all mail
censored. Security, as it happened, was good, though an 'erk' said in a
letter home: 'The aircraft have been flying low with special night aids for
some special op,' and the letter was intercepted.

'Who is this fool?' Gibson asked Chiefy Powell. He always asked Powell
about any ground crew up on a charge. Powell knew them all, and Gibson
knew Powell and trusted his opinions. 'He's a good type, sir,' Powell said,
'and a good fitter.'

Gibson had him brought to his office and tore a ferocious 'strip' off him.
All the ruthless side of his manner came out and the fitter broke down and
cried. Gibson let him go with a reprimand.

One of the aircrews rang his girl friend and told her he could not see her
that night because he was flying on special training. The phone had been
tapped. Gibson called the whole squadron together and ordered the
offender up on a table in the middle of them. He stood there miserable and
pale.

'Look at him!' Gibson bawled. 'Look at the fool. Hundreds of men's lives in danger because one bloody fool can't keep his trap shut.' And more in the same strain.

There were no more lapses.

Gibson was on the move from dawn to midnight every day, usually careering about on a little auto-bike from flights to armoury, to orderly room and so on. When he flew he kept his auto-bike in the hangar, apparently against some fiddling regulation because Scampton's zealous service policeman told Chiefy Powell the auto-bike would have to be moved.

Powell eyed him flintily. 'You'd better see the owner,' he said. 'I don't think he'll move it.'

'I'll see him all right,' said the sergeant, 'and he'll move it too.'

So Chiefy took him to see Gibson and shut the door behind him. There was a violent roaring behind the door and a white-faced sergeant came out.

The bike stayed where it was.

The crews were getting good at low night cross-countries and extended their trips out over the North Sea. Two of them were coming back in formation over Grimsby when the gunners of a couple of naval ships (who have itchy trigger fingers at sea) opened up on them, and as they darted in over the land the shore-based flak had a go too. They landed with little holes punched in the fuselage, complained to Martin and the wiry and diabolical Martin grinned and said, 'Bloody good training. Make you flak-happy!'

They practised low-level bombing on the range at Wainfleet, diving over the sand dropping 11-lb practice bombs with the low-level bombsight. The drops were not nearly accurate enough and Bob Hay said so disgustedly. Gibson took the problem to Cochrane.

Two days later a Wing Commander Dann, from the Ministry of Aircraft Production, called on Gibson.

'I hear you're having bombsight trouble for the dams raid.'

'How the hell do you know about this?' Gibson said.

'I've been let into it because I'm supposed to be a sighting expert,' Dann explained. 'I think I can solve your troubles. You may have noticed there are a couple of towers on top of each dam wall. We've measured them from the air and they're sixteen hundred feet apart. Now this' – and he produced some drawings of a very elementary gadget – 'is how we do it.'

It was laughably simple; a carpenter ran up one of the gadgets in five minutes out of bits of spare wood. The base was a small triangle of plywood with a peephole at one angle and two nails stuck in the other corners. 'You look through the peephole,' Dann said, 'and when the two towers on the dams are in line with the nails, you press the tit. You'll find it'll drop in the right spot but you'll have to stick right on the speed.'

Gibson shook his head in wonder. Workmen put two dummy towers on the dam across the neck of a midland lake, the bomb aimers knocked up their own sights and on his first try one of them dropped eight practice bombs with an average error of only 4 yards.

Still the problem of the height. Gibson tried repeatedly to see if practice made perfect, but it didn't. After his fifth try Dinghy Young landed and said, 'It's no use. I can't see how we're going to do it. Why can't we use radio altimeters?'

Gibson said he had thought of them a long time ago but they were not sensitive enough.

Time was getting short. Gibson got a call from Satterly. 'They've finished the first two prototypes of the new bomb,' Satterly said. 'Fly down to Herne Bay tomorrow and watch the test drops. Take your bombing leader with you.' That was 15 April.

Wallis met them and next morning they drove out to a bare beach near Reculver. Half a mile back from the sea MI5 had cordoned the area off.

'I'm sorry to get you up so early,' said the ever-courteous Wallis, 'but the tide is up and that is the right time. We want to walk out at low tide and see how the bomb stands up to the shock of dropping.'

He pointed to two white buoys bobbing on the water about 100 yards apart. 'The idea is to drop the thing about half a mile short of those markers and if it works all right it should bounce the rest of the way and go right between them.'

'Like goal posts,' Gibson said, and Wallis smiled.

'Yes, but there won't be any goalkeeper.'

In the east came two specks which grew into Lancasters, heading low over the shallows towards the two white buoys bobbing on the water. 'The other one's the camera aircraft,' Wallis said as they watched them, and as the noise of engines filled the air Wallis was shouting above the roar, 'He's high. He's too high.' He sounded agitated. They swept up side by side and a great black thing dropped slowly away under the nearer one. It hit and vanished in a sheet of spray that hissed up towards the plane. For a moment there was nothing but the spray, and then out of it the fragments came flying.

'Broken,' Wallis said and stood there very still. He took a deep breath. 'They said it wouldn't work. Too big and heavy and the case too light. We've got another in the hangars. We'll try it this afternoon. The aircraft was too high.'

Men worked hard that afternoon to strengthen the case of the second bomb while Wallis stripped to his underpants and waded to his neck in the freezing water, feeling with his feet for the fragments of the broken one. A launch took the broken bits on board and Wallis climbed in shivering, oblivious to everything but the ragged edges where the metal had burst.

They were on the dunes again as the sun was going down and the two aircraft came in sight, lower this time. Mutt Summers in the bomb plane was holding her steady at 50 feet. The suspense was painful. The black monster dropped away below, and again the water gushed skywards as it hit and out of the foaming cloud came the flying fragments as it broke.

Wallis said, 'Oh, my God!' and then out of the spray the twisted bulk of the main body of the bomb lurched spinning into the air and skipped erratically for 100 yards or so before it rolled under the water. Wallis stared in silence for a few seconds with the look of a man who had lost 1/- and found 3d. He sighed and said, 'Well, it's a bit better than this morning.'

(In the Lancaster, Summers was not happy. A lump of the casing had hit the elevators and one of them had jammed. The plane could just hold its height while Summers was holding his breath. He did a wide gentle turn and made a heart-stopping landing on the long runway at Manston with the trimmers.)

Wallis told Gibson: 'We've still got a lot of work to do on the bomb; but don't worry, it's going to be all right.' Gibson and Hay took off in a little plane for Scampton and a few hundred feet up the engine coughed and died. There was only one way to go and that was down, but all the good fields were still covered with poles so the Germans could not land troops in an invasion. Gibson did his best to steer between them but a wingtip hit a pole, and as the aircraft slewed the other wing hit and they finished up sitting in a ball of crumpled duralumin, but were able to climb out and stand up, slightly bloody but unbowed.

A man came haring across the field, and when he saw they were not badly hurt he said severely, 'I think they teach you young fellows to fly too early;' and then a policeman arrived and said unemotionally, 'I'm glad to see our landing devices work.'

Gibson and Hay went back to Scampton by train, and on the way Gibson thought up a scheme to overcome the height problem: to dangle a long wire under the aircraft with a weight on it so it would skim the water when the aircraft was exactly at 150 feet. Full of hope, he tried it in G for George, but it didn't work. At speed the line trailed out almost straight behind.

Cochrane set the 'back-room boys' to work on the problem and a day later Ben Lockspeiser, of the Ministry of Aircraft Production, arrived at Grantham with an idea. It was absurd to think how simple it was – and how effective. 'Put a spotlight under the nose,' he said, 'and another under the belly, both pointing down and inwards so they converge at 150 feet. When the two spots come together on the water, there you are!'

Gibson cheerfully told the crews, and when he had finished Spafford said casually, 'I could have told you that. Last night Terry Taerum and I went to see the Ensa show, and when the girl there was doing her striptease there were these two spotlights shining on her. The idea crossed my mind then and I was going to tell you.'

Gibson just looked at him.

Maudslay flew a Lancaster down to Farnborough and they fitted two spotlights on it the same day. Coming back he made test runs across the airfield and it worked beautifully. Maudslay said it was easy to get the circles of light together and keep them there. The idea was that their circumferences should touch each other, forming a figure '8'. He had Urquhart, his navigator, leaning his head out of the perspex observation blister behind the pilot, looking down at the ground and saying, 'Down, down, down . . . up a bit . . . OK,' and that was the procedure they adopted. They all tried it over Derwent Water using the same drill, and could fly to within 2 feet of the prescribed height with wonderful consistency. Everyone got a tremendous kick out of it. That was a very major problem solved.

Down at Weybridge, Wallis was still trying to strengthen the bomb and things were not going well. One of his experiments was to get his technicians working overtime to put a hard steel skin flush around the barrel shape without upsetting the balance.

On 22 April, Wallis and Gibson, plus the usual gaggle of Air Ministry officials, watched as his first new model was dropped over Reculver. It hit and rose briefly from the water and then again fragments flew off it and it didn't work, or skip. The tormented scientist groaned in his anguish. He had been getting little sleep for weeks. Three weeks now to the time for the raid and if they couldn't make it then it would have to be put off for another year; probably, in view of official scepticism, forever. The water in the dams was rising.

Wallis became aware of the Air Ministry officials wandering wordlessly away to their cars and it was not hard to guess what they were thinking.

He became aware of Gibson beside him. 'They left you a bit short of time.'

Wallis turned wryly: 'Not really I suppose. I got my sums wrong. Tried to put in enough RDX to make sure.' He looked at the water where the bomb had sunk. It was smooth and unruffled again. 'Time and tide for nae man bide' he quoted. 'It's the first impact that does the damage. I'd allowed for the extra weight that quadruples the blow but a five-tonner drops just that much faster.'

Gibson said, 'You didn't miss by much.' More of a question than an observation.

'Marginal, but enough.' Wallis sighed 'A bit slower, a bit lower – say 60 feet – and I'd bet my life on it.'

A silence fell between the two and Gibson could feel his scalp crawling a little. He had an unpleasant feeling that he was going to break the first rule of the service – 'Never volunteer for anything!' He said quietly, 'You really think 60 feet would do it, sir?'

Wallis said absently, 'Yes, I'm certain. The initial impact would be so much less.'

Gibson said hesitantly, 'Maybe we could have a crack at that, sir.'

Wallis put his mental slide-rule away and smiled his wan appreciation. 'It's good of you to suggest it, Gibbie, but I said *my* life, not yours. Sixty feet against a defended target – and it *is* defended – wouldn't give you much chance would it!'

Gibson was thinking of his 173 missions and he still had a whole skin. Just one more to do. Did he have the guts to do it and did he have the right to ask the others. He said to Wallis: 'Maybe we'd have a little more chance now than you realize, sir. I didn't have time to tell you before but we have solved the height problem. I mean *really* solved it. Down to inches. Foolproof.'

Wallis looked at him in mild surprise, changing to excitement as Gibson explained about the fore and aft lights. At the end, all Wallis could say for a while was 'Good heavens', in an astonished sort of way. The two stood in silence while Wallis creased his brow in thought. Gibson thought he could practically hear the computer mind ticking over. Wallis started spelling it out so to speak, talking half to himself . . . 'Yes, you could alter the angle of the lights for 60 feet . . . I can calculate a new speed and range – from target to bomb release . . .'

He broke off and looked directly at Gibson:

'You know you and your chaps would not only have to fly much lower into the defences . . . you'd have to delay the drop until you were much nearer the dams, all of you. Isn't that too risky?'

'No, sir,' Gibson lied, and added, more truthfully or more hopefully, 'They won't be expecting us.'

'Oh heavens, I hope not,' Wallis said. 'I've been working on that hypothesis.'

(Gibson thought privately, 'Hell! Me too!')

Wallis looked at him thoughtfully before he spoke again, rather gently. 'Look Gibbie, would you and your boys really be game to have a go from 60 feet. I'm not going to pretend it's not going to be more dangerous but we don't seem to have much alternative.'

Gibson said simply, 'Yes. We'll have a go if it will work.'

Wallis said, his voice a little unsteady with emotion, 'Thanks Gibbie, and to all your boys. I don't know what else to say. I wish it were my life in the balance and not yours.'

Gibson said with forced cheerfulness, 'I wouldn't worry too much about it, sir. They won't be expecting us at 60 feet at night.'

'Not even showing your height lights,' said Wallis painfully.

Gibson said, 'If the bomb works at 60 feet we'll give it a go and that's that, sir.' Wallis seemed to find it a little difficult to speak for a moment and then he said cautiously, 'Well, we're not there yet – first we have to make sure. Test another strengthened bomb from 60 feet and we haven't got much time.'

They turned towards the waiting cars. Wallis went back to Weybridge and Gibson arrived a few hours later at Scampton. He called the pilots, bomb-aimers and navigators together and told them that the arrival of the modified Lancasters might be delayed a day or two as technicians from Farnborough and Avro would be adjusting the height lights to converge at 60 feet. That was the new height for dropping the bomb! He said it calmly without histrionics and there was hardly even a gasp. (As one of them said, years later, 'You have to be breathing to gasp'.)

Gibson finished on a lighter note. 'You had better sharpen your night low-flying reflexes. We can't afford to waste a single bomb.'

No one complained. Likewise no one cried 'Hurrah!'

On 29 April, Wallis finished another strengthened bomb and Vickers test pilot, Shorty Longbottom (a name he never lived down) flew it to Reculver for the drop. Only two Air Ministry officials were there this time. Rain was pouring down but Wallis, out on the dunes, did not even notice it as he watched the Lancaster charging out of the east towards the markers. Shorty had her tucked down neatly to 60 feet at just under 250 indicated air speed, squinting through the rain squalls to hold his height and see the markers. The bomb fell slowly, hit cleanly – and worked. From the first creamy splash of impact the bomb soared up and away, splashed down again without any distortion a couple of hundred yards further on and then on and on till she slid through the marker buoys.

Banking round after the drop, Longbottom saw a white haired figure bobbing about down on the dunes. Wallis had taken his hat off and was waving it in the air, dancing and shouting while the rain ran down his face.

CHAPTER 6

TAKE-OFF

Early in May a strange-looking aircraft flew over Scampton. 'God,' Martin said, squinting up at it, 'is that a Lanc, or isn't it? What a monstrosity!'

The aircraft dropped its wheels, landed and taxied to a hardstanding by 617's hangar, the first of the modified aircraft. It looked like a designer's nightmare; the bomb doors were gone and the mid-upper turret and some of the armour, and there was a lot of queer junk sticking out underneath. It looked better for walking than flying. Avro's had done an unusually difficult and complicated job very quickly and quite brilliantly and the rest of the modified aircraft arrived in the next few days. 'Capable' Caple, 617's 'plumber', or engineering officer, checked them and the pilots found they flew all right, though they had lost a little performance.

A couple of days later, on 8 May, Gibson, Martin and Hopgood flew three of them down to Manston and Martin and Hopgood watched goggle-eyed while a bomb was loaded into each. Two larger dummy towers had been anchored in the water at Reculver. Wallis had already worked out a new drop-range and the quaint, plywood bombsights had been adjusted accordingly for a risky range of 600 yards and a lowered air speed of 230 mph. (The fore and aft height lights on all the squadron aircraft incidentally had been adjusted to converge at 60 feet.) All three aircraft and crews had a run at the towers and it was beautiful to watch. Three enchanting direct hits. Three times in a row the great black barrels skipped and skipped over the water until they ploughed between the dummy towers. Micky Martin came in a little low on his run and the spouting water hit his elevators and tore one of them loose. The big plane dipped towards the grey water but he had just enough control to get the nose up again and landed safely at Manston, where they fitted a new elevator.

'Good thing to check on,' he said, unruffled. 'Now we know what we *can't* do.'

The worry and rush were telling on Gibson now; he was irritable and a carbuncle was forming painfully on his face so that he could not get his oxygen mask on. Not that he was going to need oxygen on a low-level raid, but his microphone was in the mask. He went to the doctor, and in his detached professional way the doctor said, 'This means you're overworked. I'm afraid you'll have to take a couple of weeks off'; and Gibson stared at him ludicrously and laughed in his face.

He planned to control the raid by plain-language radio, and Cochrane got them VHF fighter sets. Hutchison, squadron signals leader, wanted to set them up first in the crew room so they could have dummy practices on R/T procedure, and he and Chiefy Powell went to work on the sergeant carpenter to make screened benches for this, but the carpenter said he could not find any wood and was adamant till Gibson delivered him one of his blistering monologues over the phone, and the benches arrived that afternoon.

The stage was nearly set, but at Bomber Command and at Grantham there was secret dismay. For three days the Mosquito had been bringing back photographs that showed mysterious activity on top of the Moehne Dam. The dark shapes of some new structures had been appearing, growing from day to day. There were about five sets of them, visible as short black rectangles. The interpretive experts puzzled over them for hours, blowing up the photos as large as the grain would take, examining them under strong light and through magnifying glasses nearly as strong as microscopes. The structures threw shadows across the dam top, and they measured the shadows but still were baffled. There seemed to be only one answer – new gun positions. There must have been a security leak somewhere.

At midnight on 13 May a convoy of covered lorries rolled round the perimeter track to the bomb dump at Scampton; a cordon of guards gathered round and the bombs were trollied into the dump and hidden under tarpaulins. They had only just been filled and were still warm to the touch.

Gibson drove off to see Satterly and plan the routes for the raid, taking with him Group Captain Pickard (of 'F for Freddy') because he was a 'gen' man on German flak positions, and on a low-level raid there is nothing more important than plotting a track between the known flak. They spread their maps out on the floor and carefully pencilled in two separate tracks that wound in and out of the red blotches of the known flak.

The first one sneaked in between Walcheren and Schouwen, cut across Holland, delicately threaded between the night-fighter aerodromes at Gilze-Rijen and Eindhoven, snaked round the crimson blotches of the Ruhr, round Hamm, and south to the Moehne. The second one cut in up north over Vlieland, came in over the flak-free Zuyder Zee and joined route one north-west of Wesel. They plotted two more widely differing routes for the trip home so that any flak aroused on the way in would watch out in vain for the return.

The attack would be in three waves, Gibson leading nine aircraft on the southern route, Munro leading others on the northern, and five aircraft taking off a couple of hours later to act as a reserve. If the Moehne, Eder and Sorpe were not smashed by the first two waves, Gibson would call up the reserves. If they *were* smashed the reserves would bomb three smaller dams in the same area, the Schwelm, Ennerpe and Dieml.

Accurate navigation was going to be vital or there were going to be sudden deaths. The pencilled tracks had to go perilously near some of the red flak areas.

'Doc' Watson and his armourers were loading the bombs into the Lancasters. Martin watched Watson winching the bomb up into his aircraft, 'P for Peter' (or, as Martin always insisted with a leer, 'P for Popsie'). 'Just exactly how *do* these bombs work, Doc?' he asked.

'I know as much as you do, Micky,' Watson said busily. 'Sweet Fanny Adams.'

'Ar, what do they pay you for?' Half an hour later the bomb was in position and he and Bob Hay, Leggo, Foxlee, Simpson and Whittaker were crawling about inside the aircraft seeing that everything was in order when a fault developed in the bomb release circuit, the release snapped back and there was a crunch as the giant black thing fell and crashed through the concrete hardstanding, embedding itself 4 inches into the earth below. Relieved of the weight, 'P for Popsie' kicked a little from the expanding oleo legs of the under-carriage.

Martin said, 'What's that?' There was a startled yell from an armourer outside and Martin yelled, 'Hey, the bloody thing's fallen off!'

'Release wiring must be faulty,' Hay said professionally, and then it dawned on him and he said in a shocked voice, 'It might have fused itself.' He ran, yelling madly, out of the nose. 'Get out of here. She'll go off in less than a minute.' Bodies came tumbling out of the escape hatches, saw the tails of the armourers vanishing in the distance and set off after them. Martin jumped into the flight van near by and, with a grinding of gears, roared off to get Doc Watson. He had his foot hard down on the accelerator and swears that a terrified armourer passed him on a push-bike. He ran into Watson's office and panted out the news and Watson said philosophically, 'Well, if she was going off she'd have gone off by now.'

He got into the flight van and drove over to the deserted plane. Pale faces peeped out, watching him from the deep shelters round the perimeter track hundreds of yards away, and Watson turned and bellowed, 'OK. Flap's over. It's not fused.'

The squadron was fused though; painfully aware that something tremendous was about to happen. The aircraft were there, the bombs were there, both had been put together and crews were trained to the last gasp. Now was the time, Gibson knew, nerves would be tautening as they wondered whether there was going to be a reasonable chance of coming back or whether they would be dead in forty-eight hours. (And it was not only the aircrews who were tensed. Anne Fowler was too; she was a dark, slim WAAF officer at Scampton, and in the past few weeks she and the boyish David Shannon had become a most noticeable twosome.)

Perhaps the least affected was the wiry and rambunctious Martin. Aged twenty-four, he had already decided that he was going to die, if not on this raid then on some other. Before the war was over anyway. During his first few 'ops' he had often had sleepless nights or dreamed of burning aircraft. He saw all his friends on his squadron get 'the chop' one after the other till they were all gone and knew it would only be a question of time before he would probably join them. So finally he had accepted the fact that in a fairly short time, barring miracles, he was going to die, not pleasantly. That was his strength and largely why he was so boisterous. Having accepted that, the next step was automatic: to fill every day with as many of the fruits of life as possible. He did so with vigour.

It was corollary, more than a paradox, that he was not suicidal in the air but audacious in a calculating way, measuring every risk and if it were worth while, taking it, spinning it out as long as he could, but making every bomb tell. He did not believe in miracles.

One of the New Zealanders, painfully aware he might well be dead in forty-eight hours had been getting his mind off it in the bar during the past few evenings, and after a few cans he always got a little homesick. He was only about twenty and home for him was about as far away as it was possible to get round the globe. He'd got into the habit, when the bar closed, of weaving over to the phone and saying gravely:

'Get me New Zealand.'

The switch girl got to know the form well and she would answer, equally gravely:

'I'm sorry, sir, but the line to New Zealand is out of order. You'd better go to bed and I'll try in the morning.'

'Oh! Where's bed? Give me a course to steer to bed.'

'You'd better get your batman to give you a course, sir. He'll show you where bed is.'

'Oh, thank you very much.' He was very young and always polite.

On the morning of 15 May, you could clearly sense the tension, more so when word spread that the AOC had arrived. Cochrane saw Gibson and Whitworth alone and was brief and businesslike.

'If the weather's right you go tomorrow night. Start briefing your crews this afternoon and see that your security is foolproof.'

After lunch a little aeroplane landed and Wallis and Mutt Summers climbed out; ten minutes later they were with Gibson and Whitworth with a guard on the door. Gibson could not take his beloved Nigger on the raid but could not bear to leave him out altogether, so he gave him the greatest honour he could think of . . . when (or if) the Moehne Dam was breached he would radio back the one code word 'Nigger'.

In the hangars, messes and barracks the Tannoy came loudly and dramatically to life: 'All pilots, navigators and bomb aimers of 617 report to the briefing room immediately.' At three o'clock there were some sixty of them in the briefing room on the upper floor of the grey-and-black camouflaged station headquarters. They sat silently on the benches, eyeing the familiar maps, aircraft identification and air-sea rescue posters on the walls, waiting. Whitworth, Gibson and Wallis filed down the centre to the dais and Whitworth nodded to Gibson: 'Go ahead, Guy.' The room was still.

Gibson faced them, feet braced apart, flushed a little. He had a ruler in one hand and the other in his pocket, and his eyes were bright. He cleared his throat and said:

'You're going to have a chance to clobber the Hun harder than a small force has ever done before.' Outside his voice, no sound. 'Very soon we are going to attack the major dams in Western Germany.' A rustle and murmuring broke the silence – and some deep breaths. They were going to have a sporting chance. Gibson turned to the map and pointed with his ruler.

'Here they are,' he said. 'Here is the Moehne, here the Eder and here is the Sorpe. As you can see, they are all just east of the Ruhr.' He went on to explain the tactics, told each crew what wave they would be on and what dam they were to attack.

Wallis took over and described the dams and what the queer bombs were supposed to do, how success would cripple the Ruhr steel industry, how other factories would be affected and bridges and roads washed away.

Gibson stood up. 'Any questions?'

Hopgood said: 'I notice, sir, that our route takes us pretty near a synthetic rubber factory at Huls. It's a hot spot. I nearly got the hammer there three months ago. If we go over there low I think it might . . . er . . . upset things.'

Gibson looked thoughtfully at the map. Huls was a few miles north of the Ruhr. Satterly and he had known about the Huls flak when they were planning the route but had taken the track as far away from the Ruhr as they could. Better the flak at Huls than the Ruhr.

'If you think it's a bit too close to Huls we'll bring it down a bit,' and he pencilled in a wider curve round the little dot. 'You'd better all be bloody careful here. The gap isn't too wide. Err on the Huls side if you have to, but watch it, you navigators.'

Maltby got up. 'What are the dams' defences like, sir?'

'We've had extensive photo-recce over them for some time now,' Gibson said, 'and the defences seem to be confined to light flak. You'll be shown their position.' He was uneasily wondering about those mysterious new structures on the top of the Moehne.

'Any balloons, sir?' That was Maudslay.

'Up till yesterday the nearest ones were round a small factory twelve miles away. We don't expect any.'

Someone asked if there were any nets on the lake and Gibson described the torpedo booms in front of the dam walls.

Leggo wanted to know how effective they would be against the bomb, and Gibson, with a sidelong glance at Wallis and a fierce grin, said:

'Not a sausage!'

He crossed the room to a couple of trestle tables where three dust covers were hiding something, pulled the covers off, and there were the models of the dams.

'All of you come over and have a look at these,' he commanded, and there was a scraping of forms as sixty young men got up and crowded round.

'Look at these till your eyes stick out and you've got every detail photographed on your minds, then go away and draw them from memory, come back and check your drawings, correct them, then go away and draw them again till you're perfect.'

They were two hours doing that; each crew concentrated on its own target, working out the best ways in and the best ways out. The known flak guns were marked and they took *very* special note of them. Martin's crew were down for the Moehne with Gibson and Hopgood, and they stood gazing down at the model.

'What d'you reckon's the best way in?' Leggo asked.

'First thing is to get the final line of attack,' Martin said. 'There's the spot!' He put his finger on the tip of a spit of land running out into the Moehne Lake and ran his fingertip in a straight line to the middle of the dam wall, right between the two towers. It met the wall at right angles. 'A low wide circuit,' he said; 'come in over the spit and we're jake.'

It was eight o'clock before Gibson was satisfied they knew it all and said, 'Now buzz off and get some grub. But keep your mouths shut. Not even a whisper to your crews. They'll find out tomorrow. If there's one slip and the Hun gets an inkling you won't be coming back tomorrow night.'

Back at the mess the gunners, engineers and wireless operators, who'd been waiting in a fever of speculation for five hours, were a little hard to convince.

'Well,' demanded Toby Foxlee, Martin's gunner, his eager nose sniffing at the prospect. 'What is it?'

'Nothing,' Martin said airily. 'More training. That's all. You'll hear about it tomorrow.'

'Training?' Foxlee almost wailed. 'I don't believe it. It can't be.'

'It's true.'

'Will you swear it?'

'I swear it,' Martin lied piously.

'Christ!' Foxlee said. 'I need a drink. What're you having?'

'Shandy,' said Martin, who drank little before a raid, and Foxlee gave him a long, cold look.

'Martin,' he said, 'you're a horrible bloody liar.'

They all drank shandy and went to bed, taking little white pills that the doctor had doled out so they would sleep well. As Gibson was going along to his room Charles Whitworth came in looking worried and buttonholed him quietly.

'Guy,' he said, 'I'm awfully sorry, but Nigger's just been run over by a car outside the camp. He was killed instantaneously.'

The car had not even bothered to stop.

Gibson sat a long time on his bed looking at the scratch marks that Nigger used to make on his door. Nigger and he had been together since before the war; it seemed to be an omen.

The morning of May 16 was sunny. Considering the scurry that went on all day it was remarkable that so few people at Scampton realized what was happening. Even after the aircraft took off hours later the people watching nearly all thought it was a special training flight.

It was just after 9 am that Gibson bounced into his office and told Humphries to draw up the flying programme.

'Training, sir?' – more of a statement than a question.

'No. That is yes – to everyone else,' and as Humphries looked bewildered he said quietly: 'We're going to war tonight, but I don't want the world to know. Mark the list "Night flying programme," and don't mention the words "battle order".'

Watson, the armament chief, was dashing around busily, and so was Caple. The pilots were swinging their compasses. Trevor-Roper was seeing that all guns were loaded with full tracer that shot out of the guns at night like angry meteors and to people on the receiving end looked like cannon shells. That was the idea, to frighten the flak gunners and put them off their aim. Each aircraft had two .303 Brownings in the front turret, and four in the tail turret. Each gun fired something like twelve rounds a *second*; each rear turret alone could pump out what looked like forty-eight flaming cannon shells a second; 96,000 rounds lay in the ammunition trays.

Towards noon a Mosquito touched down with the last photos of the dams. The water in the Moehne was 4 feet from the top. After lunch 'Gremlin' Matthews, meteorological officer at Grantham, spoke to all the other group met. officers on a locked circuit of trunk lines for half an hour. Such conferences rarely found agreement but this time they did. The lively bespectacled figure of 'The Gremlin' walked into Cochrane's office as soon as he had put the receiver down.

'It's all right for tonight, sir.' He gave a definite prediction of clear weather over Germany.

'What?' said Cochrane. 'No ifs, buts and probablies?' and 'The Gremlin' looked mildly cautious just for a moment and took the plunge. 'No, sir. It's going to be all right.'

Cochrane went out to his car and drove off towards Scampton.

The Tannoy sounded about four o'clock, ordering *all* 617 crews to the briefing room, and soon there were 133 hushed young men sitting on the benches (two crews were out because of illness).

Gibson repeated what he had told the others the previous night, and Wallis, in his earnest, slightly pedantic way, told them about the dams and what their destruction would do. Cochrane finished with a short, crisp talk.

The final line-up was:

Formation 1: Nine aircraft in three waves, taking off with ten minutes between waves:

> Gibson
> Hopgood
> Martin
> Young
> Astell
> Maltby
> Maudslay
> Knight
> Shannon

They were to attack the Moehne, and after the Moehne was breached those who had not bombed would go on to the Eder.

Formation 2: One wave in loose formation:

> McCarthy
> Byers
> Barlow
> Rice
> Munro

They were to attack the Sorpe, crossing the coast by the northern route as a diversion to split the German defences.

Formation 3:
    Townsend
    Brown
    Anderson
    Ottley
    Burpee

They would take off later as the mobile reserve.

Supper in the mess was quiet, the calm before the storm. No one said much. The non-flying people thought it was to be a training flight, but the crews, who knew it was going to be business – probably sticky – could not say so and there was a faint atmosphere of strain.

With a woman's wit Anne Fowler realized it was to be the real thing. She noticed the crews were having eggs. They often had an egg before a raid, and always after they landed. Most of the others did not notice it, but she started worrying about Shannon.

Dinghy Young said to Gibson, 'Can I have your next egg if you don't come back?' But that was the usual chestnut before an 'op' and Gibson brushed it aside with a few amiably insulting remarks.

In twos and threes they drifted down to the hangar and started to change. It was not eight o'clock yet; still an hour to take-off and still broad daylight. Martin stuffed his little koala bear into a pocket of his battle-dress jacket and buttoned the flap. It was a grey furry thing about 4 inches high with black button eyes, given to him by his mother as a mascot when the war started. It had as many operational hours as he had.

They drifted over to the grass by the apron and lay in the sun, smoking and quietly talking, waiting. Anne was with Shannon. Fay, the other WAAF officer, was talking to Martin's crew. Dinghy Young was tidying up his office, just as a matter of course. He had no premonition. Munro seemed half asleep in a deck chair.

Gibson drove up and walked over to Powell.

'Chiefy, I want you to bury Nigger outside my office at midnight. Will you do that?'

'Of course, sir.' Powell was startled at the gesture from the hard-bitten Gibson. Gibson did not tell him that he would be about 50 feet over Germany then, not far from the Ruhr. He had it in his mind that he and Nigger might be going into the ground about the same time. He said to Hopgood: 'Tomorrow we get drunk, Hoppy.'

Gibson found himself wishing to God it were time to go and knew they were all wishing the same. It would be all right once they were in the air. It always was. At ten to nine he said clearly, 'Well, chaps, my watch says time to go.' Bodies stirred on the grass with elaborate casualness, tossed their parachutes into the flight trucks, climbed in after them, and the trucks moved off round the perimeter track to the hardstandings. Shannon had gone back to the locker room for a moment and when he came out his crew, the only ones left, were waiting impatiently.

The bald-headed Yorkshireman, Jack Buckley, said like a father to his small son, 'Have you cleaned your teeth, David?' Shannon grinned, hoisted himself elegantly into the flight truck and then they had all gone. Shannon had one of the best crews. Buckley, older than most, of a wealthy family, was his rear gunner and a wild Yorkshireman. Danny Walker was an infallible navigator, a Canadian, dark, quiet and intensely likeable. Sumpter, the bomb aimer, had been a guardsman and was tougher than a prize-fighter. Brian Goodale, the wireless op, was so tall and thin and bent he was known universally as 'Concave'. And in the air the babyish Shannon was the absolute master, with a scorching tongue when he felt like it.

At exactly ten past nine a red Véry light curled up from Gibson's aircraft, the signal for McCarthy's five aircraft to start; the northern route was longer and they were taking off ten minutes early. Seconds later there was a spurt of blue smoke behind Munro's aircraft as his port inner engine started. One by one the engines came to life. Geoff Rice's engines were turning; Barlow's, then Byers'. The knot of people by the hangar saw a truck rushing at them across the field, and before it came to a stop big McCarthy jumped out and ran at them, roaring like a bull, his red face sweaty, the sandy hair falling over his forehead. In a murderous rage he yelled:

'Those sons of bitches. My aircraft's u/s and there's no deviation card in the spare. Where are those useless bloody instrument jerks!'

The 15-stone Yank had found his own Lancaster, 'Q for Queenie', out of action with leaking hydraulics, rushed his crew over to the spare plane, 'T for Tom', and found the little card giving the compass deviations missing from it. No hope of accurate flying without it. If McCarthy had met one of the instrument people then he would probably have strangled him.

Chiefy Powell had gone running into the instrument section and found the missing card. He dashed up to McCarthy shouting, 'Here it is, sir,' and McCarthy grabbed it, well behind schedule now, and, turning to run back to the truck, scooped up his parachute from the tarmac where he'd thrown it, but his hand missed the canvas loop handle and he yanked it up by the D-ring of the rip-cord. The pack flaps sprang back in a white blossom as the silk billowed out and trailed after him, and he let out a roar of unbearable fury.

Powell was running for the crew room, but McCarthy snarled, 'Goddamit, I'll go without one.' He jumped into the truck but before the driver could move off Powell came running up with another parachute, and McCarthy grabbed it through the cabin and shot off across the field. There was a swelling roar from the south side; Munro's Lancaster was rolling, picking up speed, and then it was low in the air, sliding over the north boundary, tucking its wheels up into the big inboard nacelles. Less than a minute later, as McCarthy got to his aircraft, Rice was rolling too, followed by Barlow and Byers.

At precisely 9.25, Gibson in 'G for George', Martin, in 'P for Popsie', and Hopgood, in 'M for Mother', punched the buttons of the booster coils and the wisps of blue smoke spurted as the engines whined and spun explosively, first the port inners, the starboard inners, the port outers and the starboard outers. They were going through their cockpit drill while the crews settled at take-off stations, running the engines up to zero boost and testing the magnetos. A photographer's flash-bulb went off by Gibson's aircraft; Cochrane was there too, standing clear of the slipstream. Fay stood by 'P Popsie', waggling her fingers encouragingly at the crew.

'G for George' waddled forward with the shapeless bulk under its belly ('like a pregnant duck', Gibson had said), taxied to the south fence, swung its long snout to the north and waited, engines turning quietly. 'P Popsie' turned slowly in on the left, and 'M Mother' on the right. Gibson rattled out the monotonous orders of his final check.

'Flaps thirty.'

Pulford, the engineer, pumped down 30 degrees of flap and repeated, 'Flaps thirty.'

'Radiators open.'

'Radiators open.'

'Throttles firm?'

Pulford checked the nut on the throttle unit.

'Throttles firm.'

'Prepare to take off,' Gibson said and checked through to all the crew on the intercom. 'OK, rear gunner?' 'OK.' And then all the others. He leaned forward with his thumb up, looking to left and then to right, and Martin and Hopgood raised their thumbs back. Pulford closed his hand over the four throttles and pushed till the engines deepened their note and the aircraft was throbbing . . . straining; then Gibson flicked his brakes off, there was the hiss of compressed air and they were rolling, all three of them, engineers sliding the throttles right forward.

The blare of twelve engines slammed over the field and echoed in the hangar, the tails came up as they picked up speed in a loose vic, ungainly with nearly 5 tons of bomb and over 5 tons of petrol each. Gibson held her down for a long time and the a.s.i. was flicking on 110 mph before he tightened back on the wheel and let her come unstuck after a long, slow bounce. At 200 feet they turned slowly on course with the sun low behind.

McCarthy eased 'T for Tom' off the runway twenty minutes late and set course on his own. At 9.47 Dinghy Young led Astell and Maltby off. Eight minutes after that Maudslay, Shannon and Knight were in the air. Anne waved them off. The final five, the reserve aircraft, did not take off till two hours later. By the time they arrived in the target area Gibson, if still alive, would know where to send them.

CHAPTER 7

ATTACK

Gibson slid over the Wash at a hundred feet. The cockpit was hot and he was flying in his shirtsleeves with Mae West over the top; after a while he yelled, 'Hey, Hutch, turn the heat off.'

'Thank God for that,' the wireless operator said, screwing the valve shut. The heat in a Lancaster runs down the fuselage but comes out round the wireless operator's seat, so he is always too hot, while the rear gunner is always too cold.

The sun astern on the quarter threw long shadows on fields peaceful and fresh with spring crops; dead ahead the moon was swimming out of the ground haze like a bullseye. Gibson flew automatically, eyes flicking from the horizon to the a.s.i., to the repeater compass in its rubber suspension.

The haze of Norfolk passed a few miles to port. In the nose, Spafford said, 'There's the sea,' and a minute later they were low over Southwold, the shingle was beneath them, and then they were over the water, flat and grey in the evening light. England faded behind. 'G George' dropped down to 50 feet, and on each side Martin and Hopgood came down too, putting off the evil moment when German radar would pick them up. You couldn't put it off indefinitely; about twenty miles from the Dutch coast the blips would be flicking on the radar screens and the orders would be going out to the flak batteries and fighter fields.

Martin ranged up alongside and there was a light winking as he flashed his Aldis lamp at them.

'What's he saying, Hutch?' Gibson asked.

'We're going to get screechers tomorrow night.' Hutchison picked up his own Aldis and winked back: 'You're damn right. Biggest binge of all time.' Hutchinson didn't drink.

Taerum spoke: 'Our ground speed is exactly 203 miles an hour. We will be there in exactly one hour, ten minutes and thirty seconds. We ought to cross the coast dead on track. Incidentally, you're one degree off course.' The last part was the standing joke. The pilot who can fly without sometimes yawing a degree or so off course has yet to be born.

In the ops. room of 5 Group HQ at Grantham, Cochrane was walking Barnes Wallis up and down, trying to comfort him. Wallis was like an expectant father, fidgety and jittery, and Cochrane was talking of anything but the bomb, trying to get Wallis's mind off it, but Wallis could think of nothing else.

'Just think what a wonderful job you made of the Wellington,' Cochrane said encouragingly. 'It's a magnificent machine; been our mainstay for over three years.'

'Oh dear, no,' lamented the disconcerted scientist. 'Do you know, every time I pass one I wonder how I could ever have designed anything so crude.'

A black Bentley rushed up the gravelled drive outside, pulled up by the door and the sentries snapped rigidly to attention as Harris himself jumped briskly out. He came into the ops. room. 'How's it going, Cocky?'

'All right so far, sir,' Cochrane said. 'Nothing to report yet.' They walked up and down the long room between the wall where the aircraft blackboards were and the long desks that ran down the other side, where men were sitting. Satterly was there, 'The Gremlin', the intelligence man and Dunn, chief signals officer, sitting by a telephone plugged in to the radio in the signals cabin outside. He would get all the morse from the aircraft there; it was too far for low-flying planes to get through by ordinary speech.

Harris and Cochrane talked quietly, and Wallis was walking miserably with them but not talking, breaking away every now and then to look at the big operations map on the end wall. The track lines had been pencilled in and he was counting off the miles they should be travelling. It was 10.35 when Cochrane looked at his watch and said, 'They ought to be coming up to the Dutch coast now.'

The sun had gone and the moon was inching higher into the dusk, lighting a road ahead across the water; outside the dancing road the water was hardly visible, a dark mass with a couple of little flecks.

Taerum said, 'Five minutes to the Dutch coast,' and the crew snapped out of the wordless lull of the past half hour. 'Good,' Gibson said. Martin and Hopgood eased their aircraft forward till the black snouts nosed alongside Gibson and veered out to make a wider target, their engines snarling thinly in gusts above the monotonous roar in 'G George'. Flying so low, just off the water, they seemed to be sliding very fast along the moonpath towards the waiting flak.

Spafford said, 'There's the coast.' It was a black line lying dim and low on the water, and then from a couple of miles out on the port side a chain of glowing balls was climbing into the sky. 'Flak ship,' said Martin laconically. The shells were way off and he ignored them. The sparkling moonpath ended abruptly, they tore across the white line of surf and were over enemy territory. 'New course 105 magnetic,' Taerum called, and the three aircraft swung gently to the left as they started the game of threading their way through the flak.

The northern wave made landfall about the same time, sighting Vlieland and turning south-east to cut across the narrow part and down over the Zuyder Zee. Munro led them across the dark spit; it was so narrow they would see the water again in about thirty seconds and have another seventy miles of comparatively safe water, but without warning there were flashes below and up came the fiery little balls. Munro felt the shock as they hit the aircraft, and then they were past and over the water again. Munro called on the intercom, to see if the crew were all right, but the earphones were dead.

Pigeon, the wireless op., was standing by his shoulder shouting into his ear, 'No radio. No intercom. Flak's smashed it. I think everyone's OK.' Munro flew on several miles, trying to fool himself they could still carry on, but it was no good and he knew it. Without radio he could not direct the attack on the Sorpe; could not even direct his own crew or get bombing instructions. Swearing, he turned for home.

Inside the Zuyder the water was dark and quite flat, treacherously deceptive for judging height. Geoff Rice slipped down a little to level at 60 feet by his belly lights, but the lights were not working properly and lured him lower as he tried to get a fix. A hammer seemed to hit the aircraft like a bolt and there was a tearing roar above the engines. Rice dragged her off the water, but the belly was torn out of her and the bomb had gone with it. The gutted fuselage had scooped up a couple of tons of water; it was pouring out of her and the rear gunner was nearly drowning in his turret. Marvellously she still flew but was dropping back, and when they found the bomb was gone Rice turned her heavily back towards England.

The remaining two, Barlow and Byers, skirted their pin-point on the cape at Stavoren and ten minutes later crossed to the enemy land again at Harderwijk. No one else knows exactly how soon it was that the flak came curling up at them again, but there is a report that as Barlow's aircraft hit the ground the bomb went off with a blinding flash, lighting the countryside like a rising sun for ten seconds before it died and left nothing. It was either then or soon after that Byers and his crew died too. Nothing more was heard from him. Only McCarthy was left of the Sorpe team, flying sixty miles behind, and perhaps that is what saved him.

Over Holland, Gibson, Martin and Hopgood were down as low as 40 feet, playing hide-and-seek with the ground, the bomb aimers calling terse warnings as houses and trees loomed up, and the aircraft skimmed over them. They were cruising fast and under the cowlings the exhaust manifolds were glowing. Once the three pulled up fast as the pylons of a power line rushed at them, and they just cleared the wires.

Four miles to port they saw the flare-path of Gilze-Rijen, German night-fighter field, and a few miles farther on they passed just to the left of the night-fighter aerodrome at Eindhoven. They could expect night fighters now; the ops. rooms for miles around must be buzzing. Martin and Hopgood closed in on each side of Gibson for mutual protection. They should be able to see any fighter coming in because he would be higher, while they, low against the dark ground, would be hard to see, and that was their strength. Also their weakness where the flak was concerned. Their aircraft were higher, outlined. Just past Eindhoven, Gibson led them in a gentle turn to the north-east on the new course that would take them round the bristling guns of the Ruhr.

A few miles back the other two vics of three were on course too. Dinghy Young pin-pointed over the canal at Rosendaal and turned delicately to take them between the fighter fields, but Bill Astell did not seem sure this was the exact turn point. He bore off a little to the south for a minute and then turned back, but had fallen half a mile behind and was a fraction off track. They did not see him again, and it must have been quite soon after that the flak or fighter, whatever it was, got him.

Fourteen left.

The leading three slid across the border into Germany and saw no light or movement anywhere, only darkness filled with the beat of engines. Taerum thought they were south of track, so they edged to the north, a little nervily because this was the treacherous leg; they were coming up to the Rhine to sneak between the forewarned guns of Huls and the Ruhr. Just short of the river some twelve light flak guns opened up without warning; the aircraft gunners squirted back at the roots of the tracer and then they were out of range. No one badly hit. The Rhine was rushing at them and up from a barge spat a thin line of tracer, but they were past before the bullets found them.

Two minutes later more guns opened up, and this time three searchlights lit on Gibson. Foxlee and Deering were shooting at the searchlights. One of them popped out but the two others held, and the air was full of tracer. The rear gunners came into action, and the searchlights switched to Martin, blinding him, and Gibson could read the big P on the side of the Lancaster. Every gun was firing, the aircraft juddering with the recoil, and then they were through with throttles wide.

Ahead and just to the left another searchlight sprang to life and caught Gibson. Foxlee was firing instantly, holding his triggers in a long burst, his tracer whipping into the light. It flicked out, and as they went over in the dying glow they saw the gunners scattering. Tammy Simpson opened up from the rear turret till they were out of range. You can't take prisoners in an aircraft.

They were past and shook themselves back into formation. Hutchison tapped out a flak warning, giving the exact position, and way back in Grantham, Dunn picked it up and the powerful group radio re-broadcast it at full strength to all other aircraft.

Gibson swung them north around Hamm, whose marshalling yards will for years be notorious. Taerum said, 'New course, skipper, 165 magnetic,' and then they were hugging the ground on the last leg, slicing between Soest and Werl. Now the moon was high enough to light the ground and ahead loomed the dark hills that cradled the water. They climbed to the ridge that rimmed the horizon, crossed into the valley, and down below lay the flat sheet of Moehne Lake.

It was like looking down on the model; the same saucer of water, the same dim fields and across the neck of the lake the squat rampart hugging the water, crowned by the towers. In the half-light it looked like a battleship, but more impregnable. Reinforced concrete a hundred feet thick.

'God,' Bob Hay said, 'can *we* break that?'

The dam came suddenly to life, prickling with sharp flashes, and the lines of angry red meteors were streaming into the sky and moving about blindly as the gunners hosed the area.

'Bit aggressive, aren't they?' said Trevor-Roper. The pilots swung the aircraft away and headed in wide circles round the lake, keeping out of range and waiting for the others. There seemed to be about ten guns, some in the fields on each side of the lake near the dam, and some – a lot – in the towers on the dam.

Gibson started calling the other aircraft, and one by one they reported, except Astell. He called Astell again at the end, but Astell had been dead for an hour. After a while Gibson gave up and said soberly over the intercom., 'Well, boys, I suppose we'd better start the ball rolling.' It was the end of the waiting and the start of action, when thought is submerged. He flicked his transmitter switch:

'Hello all Cooler aircraft, I am going in to attack. Stand by to come in in your order when I tell you. Hello "M Mother". Stand by to take over if anything happens.'

'OK Leader. Good luck.' Hopgood's voice was a careful monotone.

Gibson turned wide, hugging the hills at the eastern end of the lake. Pulford had eased the throttles on and she was roaring harshly, picking up speed and quivering, the nose slowly coming round till three miles ahead they saw the towers and the rampart of the dam, and in between the flat dark water. Spafford said, 'Good show. This is wizard. I can see everything.' They came out of the hills and slammed across the water, touching 240 now, and Gibson rattled off the last orders:

'Check height, Terry! Speed control, Pulford! Gunners ready! Coming up, Spam!' Taerum flicked the belly lights on and, peering down from the blister, started droning: 'Down . . . down . . . down . . . up a bit . . . steady, stead-y-y.' The lights were touching each other, 'G George' was exactly at 60 feet and the flak gunners had seen the lights. The streams of glowing shells were swivelling and lowering, and then the shells were whipping towards them, seeming to move slowly at first like all flak, and then rushing madly at their eyes as the aircraft plunged into them.

Gibson said tersely: 'Bomb on!'

Spafford flicked the switch and heard the whine of the electric motor starting back in the fuselage. He could hear it winding up speed and a vibration grew through the aircraft as the black barrel underneath stirred out of its inertia and started revolving backwards, faster and faster, building up to optimum revs., until G George was thrumming like a live thing.

Gibson held her steady, pointing between the towers. Taerum was watching out of the blister, Pulford had a hand on the throttles and his eyes on the asi, Spafford held the plywood sight to his eye and the towers were closing on the nails. Gibson shouted to Pulford, 'Stand by to pull me out of the seat if I get hit!' There was a sudden snarling clatter up in the nose; Deering had opened up, his tracer spitting at the towers.

The dam was a rushing giant, darkness split with flashes, the cockpit stank of cordite and thought was nothing but a cold alarm shouting, 'In another minute we shall be dead,' and then Spafford screamed, 'Bomb gone!' loud and sharp, and they rocketed over the dam between the towers. A red Véry light soared up as Hutchison pulled the trigger to let the others know, and then the deeper snarling chatter as Trevor-Roper opened up on the towers from the rear.

It was over and memory was confusion as they cork-screwed down the valley, hugging the dark earth sightless to the flak. They were out of range and Gibson lifted her out of the hills, turning steeply, and looked back. A voice in his earphones said, 'Good show, Leader. Nice work.'

The black water between the towers suddenly rose and split and a huge white core erupted through the middle and climbed towards the sky. The lake was writhing, and as the white column reached its peak and hung a thousand feet high, like a ghost against the moon, the heavy explosion reached the aircraft. They looked in awe as they flew back to one side and saw sheets of water spilling over the dam and thought for a wild moment it had burst. The fury of the water passed and the dam was still there, the white column slowly dying.

Round the lake they flew while Hutchison tapped out in code to base. In a few minutes Gibson thought the lake was calm enough for the next bomb and called:

'Hello "M Mother". You may attack now. Good luck.'

'OK Leader. Attacking.' Hopgood was still carefully laconic. He was lost in the darkness over the hills at the end of the lake while the others waited. They saw his belly lights flick on and the two little yellow pools sliding over the water closing and joining as he found his height. He was straight and level on his run; the flak saw him and the venomous fireflies were darting at him. He plunged on; the gap was closing fast when the shells found him and someone said, 'Hell, he's been hit!'

A red glow was blossoming round the inner port wing tank, and then a long, long ribbon of flame trailed behind 'M Mother'. The bomb aimer must have been hit, because the bomb overshot the parapet on to the power house below.

'M Mother' was past the dam, nose up, straining for height so the crew could bale out, when the tanks blew up with an orange flare, a wing ripped away and the bomber spun to the ground in burning, bouncing pieces. The bomb went off near the power house like a brilliant sun. It was all over in seconds.

A voice said over the R/T, 'Poor old Hoppy.'

Gibson called up: 'Hello "P Popsie". Are you ready?'

'OK Leader. Going in.'

'I'll fly across the dam as you make your run and try and draw the flak off you.'

'OK. Thanks, Leader.'

Martin was turning in from the hills and Gibson headed across the lake, parallel to the dam and just out of effective range of the guns. As Martin's spotlights merged and sped across the water Gibson back-tracked and Deering and Trevor-Roper opened up; six lines of tracer converged on the towers, drawing their attention, so that for some seconds most of the guns did not notice Martin rocketing over the water. He held his height and Whittaker had the speed right. They were tracking straight for the middle of the dam between the moonbathed towers when the gunners spotted them and threw a curtain of fire between the towers, spreading like a fan so they would have to fly through it. Martin drove straight ahead. Two guns swung at them, and as the shells whipped across the water sharp-eyed little Foxlee was yelling as he squirted back, his tracer lacing and tangling with the flak.

A sharp 'Bomb gone!' from Bob Hay, and in the same instant a shudder as two shells smacked into the starboard wing, one of them exploding in the inner petrol tank. A split second of flashes as they shot through the barrage. Tammy Simpson opened up from the rear turret, Chambers shot the Véry light and they were down the valley. Whittaker was looking fearfully at the hole in the starboard wing, but no fire was coming. He suddenly realised why and nudged Martin yelling in his ear, 'Thank Christ, the bloody starboard tank was empty!'

Martin shouted, 'Bomb gone, Leader.'

'OK "P Popsie". Let me know when you're out of the flak. Hello "A Apple". Are you ready?'

'OK Leader.'

'Right. Go ahead. Let me know when you're in position and I'll draw the flak for you.'

Martin called again, '"P Popsie" clear now, Leader.'

'OK. Are you hit?'

'Yeah. Starboard wing, but we're all right. We can make it.'

The lake suddenly boiled again by the dam and spewed out the great white column that climbed again to a thousand feet. More water was cascading over the dam, but it cleared soon and the dam was still there.

Dinghy Young was on the air again. '"A Apple" making bombing run.'

Gibson headed back over the lake where his gunners could play with fire, and this time Martin did the same. As Young came plunging across the lake Gibson and Martin came in on each side, higher up, and the flak did not know where to shoot. Young swept past the dam and reported he was all right. The great explosion was up against the dam wall again, beautifully accurate, but the dam was still there, and again Gibson waited till the plume of spray had cleared and the water was calm.

He called Maltby and ordered him in, and as Maltby came across the water Gibson and Martin came in with him, firing with every gun that could bear and flicking their navigation lights on this time to help the flak gunners shoot at the wrong target. The red cartridge soared up from Maltby's aircraft to signal 'Attack successful.'

In a few moments the mountain of water erupted skyward again under the dam wall. It was uncanny how accurate the bomb was. The spray from the explosion was misting up the whole valley now and it was hard to see what was happening by the dam. Gibson called Shannon to make his attack, and the words were barely out of his mouth when a sharp voice filled his earphones:

'Hell, it's gone! It's gone! Look at it for Christ's sake!' Wheeling round the valley side Martin had seen the concrete face abruptly split and crumble under the weight of water. Gibson swung in close and was staggered. A ragged hole 100 yards across and 100 feet deep split the dam and the lake was pouring out of it, 134 million tons of water crashing into the valley in a jet 200 feet long, smooth on top, foaming at the sides where it tore at the rough edges of the breach and boiling over the scarred earth where the power house had been.

Gibson told Shannon to 'skip it'.

The others flew over and were awed into silence. In the moonglow they watched a wall of water rolling down the valley, 25 feet high, moving 20 feet a second. A gunner still on his feet in one of the towers opened up at them until lines of tracer converged on the root of the flak and it stopped abruptly. The awed silence was broken by a babble of intercom. chatter as they went mad with excitement; the only man not looking being Hutchison, sitting at his keyboard tapping out 'Nigger'.

Soon the hissing stream and spray blurred the valley. Gibson called Martin and Maltby to set course for home, and told Young, Shannon, Maudslay and Knight to follow him east to the Eder. Young was to control if Gibson was shot down.

CHAPTER 8

THE WRITHING LAKE

At Grantham a long silence had followed the flak warning at Huls, and then Dunn's phone rang sharply, and in the dead silence they all heard the Morse crackling in the receiver. It was quite slow and Cochrane, bending near, could read it. 'Goner,' he said. 'From G George.' 'Goner' was the code word that meant Gibson had exploded his bomb in the right place.

'I'd hoped one bomb might do it,' Wallis said gloomily.

'It's probably weakened it,' Cochrane soothed him. Harris looked non-committal. There was no more from 'G George', and they went on walking. A long silence. Nothing came through when Hopgood crashed. The phone rang, 'Goner' from 'P Popsie'. Another dragging silence. 'Goner' from 'A Apple'. Wallis swears even today that there was half an hour between each signal, but the log shows only about five minutes. 'Goner' from 'J Johnny'. That was Maltby, and the aura of gloom settled deeper over Wallis.

A minute later the phone rang again and the Morse crackled so fast the others could not read it. Dunn printed it letter by letter on a signals pad and let out a cry, 'Nigger. It's Nigger. It's gone.'

Wallis threw his arms over his head and went dancing round the room. The austere face of Cochrane cracked into a grin, he grabbed one of Wallis's hands and started congratulating him. Harris, with the first grin on his face that Wallis had ever seen, grabbed the other hand and said:

'Wallis, I didn't believe a word you said about this damn bomb, but you could sell me a pink elephant now.'

He said, a little later when some of the excitement had died down: 'I must tell Portal immediately.' Sir Charles Portal, Chief of the RAF, was in Washington that night on a mission, actually at that moment dining with Roosevelt. Harris picked up the nearest phone and said, 'Get me the White House.'

The little WAAF on the switchboard knew nothing of the highly secret raid. Even at Grantham, Cochrane's security had been perfect. She did not realize the importance of it all, or the identity of the great man who was speaking, and was caught off guard. 'Yes, sir,' she said automatically and, so they say, dialled the only White House she knew, a jolly little roadhouse a few miles out of Grantham.

Harris must have thought she was a very smart operator when the White House answered so quickly, and there are reported to have been moments of incredible and indescribable comedy as Harris asked for Portal, and the drowsy landlord, testy at being hauled out of bed after midnight, told him in well-chosen words he didn't have anyone called Portal staying at the place; in fact, he didn't have anyone staying at all, because he didn't have room, and if he did have room he would not have anyone staying there who had people who called him up at that time of night. Not for long anyway.

Harris went red, and there were some explosive exchanges before one of them slammed the receiver down. Someone slipped down and had a word with the little WAAF, and she tried in terror for the next hour to raise Washington, but without success.

Three kilometres down the valley from the Moehne lay the sleeping village of Himmelpforten, which means Gates of Heaven. The explosions had wakened the village priest, Father Berkenkopf, and he guessed instantly what was happening; he had been afraid of it for three years. He ran to his small stone church, Porta Coeli (which also means Gates of Heaven – in Latin) and began tugging grimly on the bell-rope, the signal he had arranged with his villagers. It was not certain how many were warned in time. In the darkness the clanging of the bell rolled ominously round the valley and then it was muffled in the thunder moving nearer. Berkenkopf must have heard it and known what it meant, but it seems that he was still pulling at the bell when the flood crushed the church and the village of the Gates of Heaven and rolled them down the valley.

It went for many miles and took more villages, a tumbling maelstrom of water and splintered houses, beds and frying-pans, the chalice from Porta Coeli and the bell, the bodies of cattle and horses, pigs and dogs, and the bodies of Father Berkenkopf and other human beings.

War, as someone said, is a great leveller, but he did not mean it quite as literally or as bitterly as this.

The Eder was hard to find because fog was filling the valley. Gibson circled it for some time before he was certain he was there. One by one the others found it and soon they were all in a left-hand circuit round the lake. There was no flak; probably the Germans thought the Eder did not need it. It lay deep in a fold of the hills; the ridges around were a thousand feet high and it was no place to dive a heavy aircraft at night.

Gibson said, 'OK Dave. Start your attack.'

Shannon flew a wide circuit over the ridges and then put his nose right down, but the dive was not steep enough and he overshot. Sergeant Henderson slammed on full throttle, and Shannon hauled back on the stick and they just cleared the mountain on the far side.

'Sorry, Leader,' Shannon said a little breathlessly. 'Made a mess of that. I'll try it again.'

Five times more he dived into the dark valley but he failed every time to get into position and nearly stood the Lancaster on her tail to get out of the hills again. He called up finally, 'I think I'd better circle and try to get to know this place.'

'OK Dave. You hang around a bit and let someone else have a crack. Hullo "Z Zebra". You have a go now.'

Maudslay acknowledged and a minute later was diving down the contour of the hills, only to overshoot and go rocketing up again like Shannon. He tried again but the same thing happened. Maudslay said he was going to try once more. He came slowly over the ridges, turned in the last moment and the nose dropped sharply into the gloom as he forced her down into the valley. They saw him level out very fast, and then the spotlights flicked on to the water and closed quickly and he was tracking for the dam.

His red Véry light curled up as Fuller called 'Bombs gone!' but they must have been going too fast. The bomb hit the parapet of the dam and blew up on impact with a tremendous flash; in the glare they saw 'Zebra' for a moment just above the explosion. Then only blackness.

Gibson said painfully, knowing it was useless:

'Henry, Henry – hullo "Z Zebra", are you all right?' There was no answer. He called again and, incredibly, out of the darkness a very faint voice said, 'I think so . . . stand by.' They all heard it, Gibson and Shannon and Knight, and wondered that it was possible. After a while Gibson called again but there was no answer. Maudslay never came back.

Gibson called, 'OK, David, will you attack now?'

Shannon tried and missed again; came round once more, plunged into the darkness and this time made it, curling out of the dive at the foot of the lake and tracking for the dam. He found his height quickly, the bomb dropped clear and Shannon roughly pulled his plane up over the shoulder of the mountain. Under the parapet the bomb spewed up the familiar plume of white water and as it drifted down Gibson, diving over the lake, saw that the dam was still there. There was only Knight left. He had the last bomb. Gibson ordered him in.

Knight tried once and couldn't make it. He tried again. Failed. 'Come in down moon and dive for the point, Les,' Shannon said. He gave more advice over the R/T, and Knight listened quietly. He was a young Australian who did not drink, his idea of a riotous evening being to write letters home and go to the pictures. He dived to try again, made a perfect run and they saw the splash as his bomb dropped in the right spot. Seconds later the water erupted, and as Gibson slanted down to have a look he saw the wall of the dam burst open and the torrent come crashing out.

Knight, more excited than he had ever been, was yelling over the R/T, and when he stopped he left his transmitter on for a few seconds by mistake; the crew's remarks on the intercom were broadcast, and they were very spectacular remarks indeed.

This was even more fantastic than the Moehne. The breach in the dam was as big and there were over 200 million tons of water pouring through. The Eder Valley was steeper and they watched speechlessly as the flood foamed and tossed down the valley, lengthening like a snake. It must have been rolling at 30 feet a second. They saw a car in front racing to get clear; only the lights they saw, like two frightened eyes spearing the dark, and the car was not fast enough. The foam crawled up on it, the headlights turned opalescent green as the water rolled over, and suddenly they flicked out.

Hutchison was tapping 'Dinghy' in Morse; that was the code to say that the Eder was destroyed. When he had finished Gibson called, 'OK all Cooler aircraft. You've had your look. Let's go home,' and the sound of their engines died over the hills as they flew west to fight their way back.

McCarthy had fought a lone way through to the Sorpe, tucked down in rolling hills south of the Moehne. The valleys were full of mist, so it was a long time before he pin-pointed himself over the lake, dimly seeing through the haze a shape he recognized from the model.

He tried a dummy run and found, as the others found before at the Eder, that there was a hill at each end so that he would have to dive steeply, find his aiming point quickly and pull up in a hurry. He tried twice more but was not satisfied and came in a third time, plunging through the mist trying to see through the suffused moonlight. He nearly hit the water and levelled out very low. Johnson picked up the aiming point and seconds later yelled, 'Bomb gone!' and they were climbing up over the far hills when the bomb exploded by the dam wall. McCarthy dived back over the dam and they saw that the crest had crumbled for 50 yards. As they turned on course for England, Eaton tapped out the code word that told of their successful drop.

Wallis's joy was complete. Cochrane radioed 'G George', asking if he had any aircraft left to divert to the Sorpe, and Hutchison answered, 'None'. Satterly, who had been plotting the path of the reserve force by dead reckoning, radioed orders to them.

Burpee, in 'S Sugar', was directed to the Sorpe, but he did not answer. They called again and again, but there was only silence. He was dead.

Brown, in 'F Freddy', was sent to the Sorpe and reached it after McCarthy had left; the mist was swirling thicker and, though he dived low over the dam, Oancia, the bomb aimer, could not pick it up in time.

Brown dived back on a second run but Oancia still found the mist foiled him. They tried eight times, and then Brown pulled up and they had a conference over the intercom. On the next run Oancia dropped a cluster of incendiaries in the woods to the side of the dam. They burned dazzlingly and the trees caught too, so that on the tenth run Oancia picked up the glare a long way back, knew exactly where the target was and dropped his load accurately.

They pulled round in a climbing turn and a jet of water and rubble climbed out of the mist and hung against the moon; down in the mist itself they saw a shock wave of air like a giant smoke ring circling the base of the spout.

Anderson, in 'Y Yorker', was also sent to the Sorpe, but he was still later than Brown, and now the valley was completely under mist so that the lake and the dam were hidden and he had to turn back with his bomb.

Ottley, in 'C Charlie', was ordered to the Lister Dam, one of the secondary targets. He acknowledged 'Message received', but that was the last anyone ever heard from him.

The last man was Townsend, in 'O Orange', and his target was the Ennerpe. He searched a long time before he found it in the mist, and made three runs before he was satisfied and dropped the bomb. It was accurate.

Ten out of the nineteen were coming home, hugging the ground, 8 tons lighter now in bomb and petrol load and travelling at maximum cruising, about 245, not worrying about petrol; only about getting home. The coast was an hour away and the sun less than that. They knew the fighters were overhead waiting for a lightening sky in the east.

Harris had driven Cochrane and Wallis to Scampton to meet the survivors, and in the ops. room at Scampton he picked up the phone to try and get Portal again. This time he prepared the ground for smart service by telling the girl that the speaker was Air Chief Marshal Sir Arthur Harris, Commander-in-Chief of Bomber Command.

'Yes, of course,' said the indulgent girl, who knew the absurd things that plastered New Zealand flight lieutenants were liable to say, 'you've been on it again, sir. Now you go and get your batman to put you to bed. He'll give you your course to steer.'

There was an explosion in the ops room and an unusually intelligent intelligence officer hared down the stairs and told the girl the frightful thing she had done. Someone soothed the irate man in the ops. room while the girl beseeched the GPO to get Washington faster than ever before. This time the lines were clear and before long a mollified Harris had the pleasure of telling Portal, 'Operation Downwood successful . . . yes, successful!'

Gibson saw the dark blotch of Hamm ahead and swung to the east. To the left he saw another aircraft; it was going too near Hamm, he thought, whoever it was, and then the flak came up and something was burning in the sky where the aircraft had been. It was falling, hit like a shooting star and blew up. It may have been Burpee. Or Ottley.

Townsend was the last away from the dams area. He flew back over the Moehne and could not recognize it at first; the lake had changed shape. Already there were mudbanks with little boats stranded on them, and bridges stood long-legged out of the shrinking water. The torpedo net had vanished, and below the dam the country was different. There was a new lake where no lake had been; a strange lake, writhing down the valley.

Miraculously most of them dodged the flak on the way back; lucky this, because dawn was coming, the sky was paler in the east and at 50 feet the aircraft were sitting ducks. In Gibson's aircraft Trevor-Roper called on the intercom., 'Unidentified enemy aircraft behind.'

'OK, Trev.' 'G George' sank till it was scraping the fields and they could see the startled cattle running in panic. Trevor-Roper said, 'OK, we've lost him,' but Gibson still kept down on the deck.

Over Holland he called Dinghy Young, but there was no answer and he wondered what had happened to him. (Group knew! They had got a brief message from Young. He had come over the coast a little high and the last squirts of flak had hit him. He had struggled on a few more miles, losing height, and then ditched in the water.)

Coming to the West Wall, Gibson climbed to about 300 feet, Pulford slid the throttles right forward and they dived to the ground again, picking up speed, and at 270 mph they roared over the tank traps and the naked sand and then they were over the grey morning water and beyond the flak.

Ten minutes later it was daylight over Holland, and Townsend was still picking his way out. He was lucky and went between the guns.

Maltby was first back, landing in the dawn and finding the whole station had been waiting up since dusk. Harris, Cochrane and Wallis met him at the hardstanding and he told them what he had seen. Martin landed. Mutt Summers went out to meet him and found Martin under the aircraft looking at a ragged hole in his wing. 'Hullo, Mutt,' he said. 'Look what some bastard's done to Popsie.'

One by one they landed and were driven to the ops. room, where Harris, Cochrane and Wallis listened intently. Gibson came in, his hair pressed flat from eight hours under his helmet. 'It was a wizard party, sir,' he said. 'Went like a bomb, but we couldn't quieten some of the flak. I'm afraid some of the boys got the hammer. Don't know how many yet. Hopgood and Maudslay for certain.'

They had bacon and egg and stood round the bar with pints, drinking and waiting for the others. It was an hour since the last aircraft had landed. Shannon said Dinghy Young had ditched, and someone said. 'What, is the old soak going to paddle back again? That's the third time he's done it. He'll do it once too often.' Young *had* done it once too often. He was not in his dinghy this time.

Wallis was asking anxiously, 'Where are they? Where are all the others?'

Summers said, 'Oh, they'll be along. Give 'em time. They've probably landed somewhere else'; but after a while it was impossible to cover up any longer and Wallis knew they were all standing round getting drunk for the ones who were not coming back. Except himself; he didn't drink. Martin made him take a half pint but he only held it and stood there blinking back tears and said, 'Oh, if I'd only known, I'd never have started this!' Mutt and Charles Whitworth tried to take his mind off it.

The party was getting wound up. Someone said, 'This shouldn't be only a stag show,' and a couple of minutes later an Australian and three others were invading the sacrosanct WAAF officers' room. One girl sat up in bed and pulled the clothes high over her.

'You can't come in here!' she shrieked.

'Yes I can,' one of them said, grabbing up two tennis balls from the dressing-table and stowing them in his tunic. He strutted round showing off his new bust line. 'All girls together,' he yelled. 'Come and join the party.'

The girl said she never went to parties before breakfast, so they grabbed the bed and started tossing it up towards the ceiling until she squealed, 'All right, but get out while I dress.'

Gibson left the party early, but not for bed; he went over to the hangar to give Humphries and Chiefy Powell a hand with the casualty telegrams to the next of kin. Fifty-six beardless men out of 133 were missing, and only three had got out by parachute at a perilously low height to spend the rest of the war miserably in prison camp. Gibson had expected to lose several over the Moehne, where those sinister installations had been spotted by the recce aircraft, but they had lost only one there. (It was not till after the war that they discovered that those dark shapes on top of the Moehne had been – trees . . . ornamental pine trees. In the middle of the war the Germans would not send extra guns but had gone to the trouble of decorating it.)

Around lunchtime the party survivors transferred to Whitworth's house and Whitworth's best port. Wallis came tiredly downstairs in a dressing-gown, distressed about the losses, and after a while he left to fly back to Weybridge with Summers. Martin gave him a sleeping-pill as he was leaving so he would sleep that night. He slept all right. The weary scientist swallowed the pill sitting up in bed at home and went out like a light.

About two o'clock even the durable Martin and Whittaker were ready for bed, but they were all up again at five o'clock and drove over in buses to a party at Woodhall Spa. On the way back David Shannon and Anne were sitting close together, and Shannon leaned closer so the others couldn't hear and asked her to marry him.

'Oh, David,' she said, and there was a pause, 'n-n-not with that moustache.'

Shannon fingered the growth defensively. It was a dear possession; made him look years older – at least twenty-two. He groaned. 'What is it?' he said. 'My moustache or you?' There was only silence and he sighed, 'All right, I'll whip it off.'

In the morning 617 Squadron went on leave, three days for the ground crew, seven days for the aircrew survivors – except Gibson, who stayed on two days to write to the mothers of the dead. He refused to let Heveron type the usual form letter but wrote them all out in his own hand, different ones each time, fifty-six of them.

In London and in their homes the crews found they were famous, though the headlines in Germany were not so flattering. A recce Mosquito arrived back from over Germany with the first pictures of the damage, and they were breathtaking. The Moehne and Eder lakes were empty and 330 million tons of water were spreading like a cancer through the western Ruhr valleys, the bones of towns and villages showing lifeless in the wilderness.

The Ruhr, which had been enduring its ordeal by fire, was having it now by water. For fifty miles from the Moehne and fifty miles from the Eder coal mines were flooded and factories collapsed. At Firtzlar one of Hitler's largest military aerodromes was under water, the aircraft, the landing ground, hangars, barracks and bomb dump. Roads, railways and bridges had disappeared. The Unterneustadt industrial suburb of Kassel, forty miles from the Eder, was under water, and the flood ran miles on down the Fulda Valley. Canal banks were washed away, power stations had disappeared, the Ruhr foundries were without water for making steel. A dozen waterworks were destroyed as far away as Gelsenkirchen, Dortmund, Hamm and Bochum. The communications system feeding raw materials to the Ruhr and taking away the finished weapons was disrupted. Some factories were not swept away but still could not work because there was no electricity. Or no water.

In the small town of Neheim alone 2,000 men, including 1,250 soldiers, were diverted to repair damage. Another 2,000 men were trying to repair the dams. And in the months ahead, in the Battle of the Ruhr, there was not enough water to put the fires out.

The official German report said it was 'a dark picture of destruction'. By the next autumn they might know how much industrial production would be ultimately affected, but estimated it was going to mean the equivalent of the loss of production of 100,000 men for several months.

A hundred and twenty-five factories were either destroyed or badly damaged, nearly 3,000 hectares of arable land were ruined, 25 bridges had vanished, and 21 more were badly damaged. The livestock losses were 6,500 cattle and pigs.

There was a moral price to pay too; there always is. 1,294 people drowned in the floods, and most were civilians. Most were not Germans – there were 749 slaves and prisoners among the dead. There had been a Russian POW camp in the valley below the Eder.

After the rain the Germans diverted hundreds of soldiers with flak guns to guard all the other dams in Germany. While they were working like beavers to repair the Moehne they also built two tall pylons 2,000 yards back from the dam wall and strung between them a heavy cable across the lake. From this other cables dangled to the water, and lashed to them were contact grenades to catch low-flying aircraft. They strung two heavy anti-torpedo nets near the dam wall, and another one a thousand yards away. On the dry side of the dam they strung a steel mesh curtain on posts sunk into the sloping wall.

Oberburgermeister Dillgardt was vindicated, but it was too late. The stable door was shut, but the horse had gone.

Gibson spent his leave quietly with his wife, Eve, who had had a shock when she had opened the papers and found Guy's name and photographs splashed over the front pages. All the time he had been at 617 he had told her he was having a rest at a flying training school.

Micky Martin was summoned to Australian Air Force Headquarters, where a dark, pretty girl called Wendy tried her damnedest to get him to talk about the raid for a story for Australia, but all the incorrigible Martin would say was, 'Come and have lunch with me,' and kept it up until she did.

Back at Scampton, Gibson found a letter for him addressed from a country vicarage. It enclosed, for his information, a copy of a letter which the writer had sent to *The Times*:

'*Sir*,

In international bird-watching circles, the bombing of the Moehne Dam has caused grave concern. For three years previous to the outbreak of war a pair of ring-necked whooper swans nested regularly on the lake. They are almost the rarest of Europe's great birds. The only other pair known to have raised a brood during recent years were a pair of the Arctic sub-species which were photographed by the aunt of the late Professor Olssen, of Reykjavik, on their nest on the shore of Lake Thongvallavatn, Iceland, in 1927.

Has anything been heard of the fate of the Moehne pair, probably the last in Europe? And, in view of the rarity of these beautiful birds, why was the bombing of their home permitted? Furthermore, assuming that this operation was necessary, could it not have been deferred until the cygnets (if any) were full grown?

Yours faithfully, etc., etc.'

The Times must have smelt a rat and did not publish it, which was just as well because Gibson found later it had been written by two intelligence officers at Scampton.

Micky Martin got a letter too. The Australians wrote saying they were collecting souvenirs for a war museum, and could he send them a souvenir of the dams raid. Martin, irreverent where headquarters were concerned, wrote back:

'*Sir*,

I am very interested in your museum and am sending you, enclosed, the Moehne Dam.

Yours faithfully.'

And under his signature he got Toby Foxlee to scrawl in red ink: '*Opened by censors and contents confiscated by the Metropolitan Water Board.*'

Then the decorations came through – thirty-three of them. Gibson was awarded the Victoria Cross. Martin, McCarthy, Maltby, Shannon and Knight got DSOs, Bob Hay, Hutchison, Leggo and Danny Walker got bars to their DFCs. There were ten DFCs, among them Trevor-Roper, Buckley, Deering, Spafford and Taerum. Brown and Townsend got the Conspicuous Gallantry Medal, and there were twelve DFMs, among them being Tammy Simpson, Sumpter, Oancia and Pulford.

When he heard the news Gibson rang for Flight Sergeant Powell.

'Chiefy,' he said quietly, 'if I ever change, tell me.'

On 27 May the King and Queen visited the newly famous squadron, and the crews pressed their uniforms and stood in front of their aircraft to be presented, though one noted pilot overlooked one point and was standing there smartly to attention with an orange sticking out of his pocket. That day was Shannon's twenty-first birthday, and Gibson had primed the King beforehand, so that when Shannon was presented the King shook him warmly by the hand and said jokingly, 'You seem to be a very well preserved twenty-one, Shannon. You must have a party tonight.'

Gibson had had a competition for a design for a squadron badge, and after the parade he showed the King the roughs and asked if he would choose one. The King called the Queen, and unanimously they picked a drawing showing a dam breached in the middle with water flowing out and bolts of lightning above. Underneath, the motto was '*Après nous le déluge*'; most apt, particularly as it had a royal background – Marie Antoinette had used it.

That night, when the royal party had left, Shannon had his party. Towards the end an apparition came leaping into the mess. Charles Whitworth had robed himself in hunting kit, red coat and white breeches, and pranced around tootling on a hunting horn, hurdling the furniture till there was a bellow from the doorway: 'What the devil's going on here!' In the frame of the door stood an obviously senior officer, rows of braid up his sleeve, gold oak leaves on his cap and ribbons plastered across his chest. A hush fell, and then slightly glazed eyes focused and a chorus of catcalls burst the silence.

'Shannon!'

Shannon had slipped away and put Whitworth's tunic and hat on. He stalked in, stopped in front of Whitworth and boomed, 'Who is this wretched fellow in fancy dress?'

Whitworth blew him a raspberry on his hunting horn.

'Whip him-off to the guard-room!' Shannon shouted. 'Clap him in irons!'

He turned to his wireless operator, the lanky Concave Goodale, and roared, 'Stand to attention when you look at me!'

'You're not standing so well yourself,' Goodale said rudely.

Buckley padded forward, eyeing his skipper indulgently, and said, 'Let's have his pants.'

Bodies closed in menacingly, but Gibson said, 'No. Give him grace. It's his twenty-first birthday.'

Someone, patently insober, said, 'Shannon, I think you're drunk,' and Shannon said with hauteur:

'Sir, if so, it is by Royal Command.'

CHAPTER 9

THE BLACKEST HOUR

Weeks passed placidly. Gibson wrote and asked the Chester Herald to approve the chosen badge. The squadron got new aircraft and did a lot of training flying, both high and low level, finding it boring, and to give them something to think about Gibson laid on compulsory PT for all aircrew. On the second morning three men did not turn up for it, so Gibson made them run round the perimeter track, four and a half miles, and to make sure they ran the whole way he sent the dismayed Chiefy Powell with them. Powell came in a reluctant fourth. A few days later a couple more decided to chance it and stay in bed; Gibson made them do an extra half hour PT in gas masks and there were no more absentees.

All those decorated were to attend an investiture at Buckingham Palace on June 22, and on the 21st they went up to London in two special carriages. The staider ones and those with wives were mostly in one carriage, and the bloods gathered in the other, pockets bulging with bottles, and settled down to pontoon and poker.

An hour later Humphries was chatting in the respectable carriage to a few of the wives and WAAF officers when a wireless operator appeared in the doorway, immaculately dressed except that he had no pants. Long shirt tails kept him technically decent.

'Losht my pantsh,' he mumbled. 'Very awkward. Can't see King without pantsh.'

Humphries jumped up and screened him from the giggling WAAFs, pushed him into a toilet and walked along to the compartment where Trevor-Roper and Maltby were noisily playing cards. He tried the casual approach:

'I say, have any of you chaps by any chance seen Brian's pants?'

Screams of mirth.

'Why, Adj., has he lost them?'

'You know he has,' Humphries said severely. 'It's not really so funny. He walked into a compartment where there were a couple of ladies.'

Louder screams of mirth. They were crying with laughter.

'Quite well made, isn't he?' gasped Jack Fort and the compartment rocked with laughter again.

Trevor-Roper was eyeing Humphries' pants sinisterly, but Humphries held his ground. 'You wouldn't think it was funny if it had been your girl friends.'

'Ah well,' Maltby said, 'I suppose not.' He pulled a crumpled pair of pants from under the seat and tossed them over.

'Have a Scotch before you go, Adj.', Trevor-Roper said. He whipped the cap off a bottle and poured till the top of the vacuum flask was nearly full. He was grinning; it was clearly a case of sinking the neat spirit or losing his own pants, and Humphries chose the spirit, downing it in one gulp, so that for a fearful instant, through the tears, he thought the top of his head was coming off.

'I'm proud of you, Adj.', Trevor-Roper said. 'Have another.' But Humphries had retreated with the pants.

They got safely to London, a tribute to Humphries' tireless and tactful shepherding, but that evening he fell into bad company again, finding himself in a suite at the Savoy with the mountain of man from Brooklyn, Joe McCarthy, and Toby Foxlee. He does not remember where he went that night but at some hour in the morning he found himself back at the Savoy. Trevor-Roper walked in and said, 'Let's have a drink. The party hasn't started yet.'

In the morning when he tried to open his eyes, Humphries thought the ceiling had fallen on him, but the investiture was at 10.15 am and he just *had* to get up. They were nearly all in the same boat but they all made it, pale and heavy-eyed.

617 Squadron was decorated *en masse* first, taking precedence over the other VCs and high orders, a historical precedent that may never be repeated. And when the band struck up the Anthem it was not the King who emerged but the Queen; the first time a queen had taken an investiture since the days of Victoria.

Gibson went up first to get his VC, and one by one the others. The Queen took Joe McCarthy's great paw and stood chatting with him for a long time, asking him questions about America, while the big blond tough from Brooklyn turned pink and stammered out answers.

That night A. V. Roe's gave them a celebration dinner. The only mistake all night tickled everyone; the printers had labelled the menu 'The Damn Busters'.

More weeks of training, high and low level, and the crews, who were supposed to be the pick of Bomber Command, became 'browned off'. Men of other squadrons who were doing several ops. a week took to ragging them as the 'One op. squadron', and one of the 617 bomb aimers, Jimmy Watson, a droll little Yorkshireman, composed a lament on the subject. Sung to the tune of 'Come and join us', the first verse ran:

> *'The Moehne and the Eder dams were standing in the Ruhr,*
> *But six one seven Squadron went and knocked them to the floor.*
> *Now since that operation six one seven's been a flop*
> *And we've got the reputation of the squadron with one op.'*

Cochrane told Gibson he had done enough operations and would not let him fly again. Squadron Leader George Holden, DSO, DFC, arrived to take over, but Gibson stayed on for a few days. Holden was slight and youthful with fair wavy hair but a brusque manner. Before the war he had worn a bowler and carried a rolled umbrella, but was a very tough young man. He had felt very sick once but kept flying on ops. for over a week till he nearly collapsed after landing one night and went to the doctor, who examined him and said, a little startled, 'Well, I think you've had pleurisy, but you seem to be nearly all right now.'

617 went to war again on 15 July, against power stations in Northern Italy, at San Polo D'Enza, near Bologna, and Aquata Scrivia, near Genoa. Mussolini was toppling, the battle of Sicily was raging, and supplies for the Germans were streaming down Italy on the electrified railways. They hoped to cripple the railways by striking at the power. It was a long way, the aircraft would arrive with tanks two-thirds empty and there was no hope of flying back to England. Yells of joy when they were told they would fly on to Blida, an airfield in North Africa, near Algiers. The only glum one was Gibson, categorically forbidden to go. Holden was to lead six aircraft to Aquata Scrivia, and Maltby to lead the other six to San Polo D'Enza. Gibson sadly waved them off from the end of the runway.

It was a 'cissy' trip; no opposition on the way, but they found the targets cloaked in haze and bombed largely by guesswork. Several aircraft were hit and Allsebrook lost an engine, but they all landed safely at Blida. At the debriefing McCarthy threw his parachute down disgustedly and said, 'You know, if we'd only carried flares tonight we could've seen what we were doing.' No one took much notice just then, but it was that remark, remembered later, that was partly responsible for the history they made.

North Africa was a novelty for about two days. The airfield was a plain of baked earth, and the crews, sweating in wooden barracks, lay about sipping red wine and sunbathing. The weather closed in and they were stranded for ten days, getting browned off by boredom instead.

On the flight home they called at Leghorn to deliver some bombs over the docks, but again there was haze and they were not pleased with the bombing.

Martin flew back over the Alps at 19,000 feet, to the dismay of Tammy Simpson in the rear turret, who had thought they were returning low over France and had worn only his light tropical kit. Back at Scampton they thawed him out with rum.

The squadron greeted them most warmly as they clambered out of the aircraft with bottles of benedictine and wine, and dragging crates of oranges, figs and dates. Martin jumped out wearing a fez.

Gibson was not there to meet them. He had gone. Harris and Cochrane had put a definite stop to his flying by asking Winston Churchill to take him with him to America for a 'show the flag' tour, and Gibson had had no option. He'd been so upset he had not been able to face the farewells.

On 29 July the squadron dropped leaflets on Milan to persuade the wavering Italians that the war was profitless. It was singularly unstimulating, and McCarthy summed up the feeling by grumbling, 'It's not better than selling goddam newspapers.' The only bright feature was that they went to Blida again and re-stocked with benedictine and oranges.

One aircraft had been commissioned to bring back a keg of wine for a senior group captain. They brought it back all right, but it vanished from the aircraft after landing and there was a great deal of care-free laughter in the ground-crew barracks that night; also an explosion from the group captain. Chiefy Powell was told to catch the culprits, but after a decent interval of about three days he reported it was a complete mystery, feeling somewhat disgruntled because he was the only man who had been noble enough to refuse a beaker.

In August they were back to boredom. No ops., but training all and every day.

It was about this time that disturbing reports were coming out of Germany about a mysterious new weapon. Apparently Hitler's notorious 'secret weapon'. Agents could not say what it was but sensed it was something special. A couple of escaped prisoners of war reached England with information that hinted at rockets and indicated an area north-east of Luebeck. In the Pas de Calais area thousands of workmen were swarming about monstrous new concrete works. A recce aircraft brought back a photograph of a strange new factory at Peenemunde, north-east of Luebeck. Lying on the ground were pencil-shaped objects that baffled the interpretive men, but little by little they began to connect the rocket reports with the pencil-shaped objects and the concrete structures, which would obviously be

*impervious to any RAF bombs. The 12,000-pounder thin-case bomb was
nearly ready, but it was purely a blast bomb, to explode on the ground and
knock over buildings. It would not dent masses of concrete half embedded in
the earth.*

*The spies were right. Sixty miles from London, just behind Calais, Hitler
was building his secret-weapon blockhouses, fantastic structures which
would bombard London and the invasion ports non-stop in spite of anything
we could do. They were all of reinforced concrete, walls of 16 feet thick and
roofs 20 feet thick! No known bomb would affect them. The Todt
Organization promised Hitler that.*

*At Watton, Wizernes and Siracourt the blockhouses were to be
assembly, storage and launching sites for rockets and flying bombs. Twelve
thousand slaves were working on them, and deep under the concrete they
were carving tunnels and chambers in the chalk and rock where Germans
could live and fire their rockets without interruption.*

*But greatest nightmare of all was the grotesque underworld being
burrowed under a 20-foot thick slab of ferro-concrete near Mimoyecques.
Here Hitler was preparing his V.3. Little has ever been told about V.3,
probably because we never found out much about it. V.3 was the most secret
and sinister of all – long range guns with barrels 500 feet long!*

*The muzzles would never appear above earth; the entire barrels would
be sunk in shafts that dived at 50 degrees 500 feet into the ground. Hitler
was putting fifteen of these guns in at Mimoyecques, five guns, side by side,
in each of three shafts. They were smooth-bore barrels, and a huge slow-
burning charge would fire a 10-inch shell with a long, steady acceleration,
so there would be no destructive heat and pressure in the barrel. In that way
the barrels would not quickly wear out as Big Bertha did in World War I.
These were more monstrous in every way than Big Bertha; they fired a
bigger shell, could go on firing for a long time and, more important than
that, they had a rapid rate of fire. Thick armour-plate doors in the concrete
would slide back when they were ready, and then the nest of nightmare guns
would pour out six shells a minute on London, 600 tons of explosives a day.
They would keep that up accurately day after day, so that in a fortnight
London would receive as much high explosive as Berlin received during the
whole war. But that fortnight would be only the start of it.*

The War Cabinet did not know this, but they *did* know enough to be
extremely worried. There were anxious (and very secret) conferences
(which coincided with the fact that Cochrane was strongly pressing for
renewed interest in Wallis's shock-wave bomb – he wanted to use it on the
Rothensee ship-lift). Soon the Chief Executive of the Ministry of Aircraft

Production, Air Chief Marshall Sir Wilfred Freeman, sent for Barnes Wallis, who was now held in esteem and some awe. Freeman said:

'Wallis, do you remember that crazy idea of yours back in 1940 about a bomb?'

'I seem to have had a lot of crazy ideas then,' Wallis said wryly.

'I mean about a *big* bomb, a ten-tonner and a six-tonner. You wrote a paper about it. To penetrate deep into the earth and cause an earthquake.'

'Ah, yes,' said Wallis, his eyes lighting up.

'How soon can you let me have some?'

It was so sudden that Wallis was staggered. He thought a while.

'About four or five months,' and he added quickly, 'that is, if I get facilities. There's a lot of work to it, you know.'

'Right. Will you go and see Craven right away, please. I'll ring him and tell him you're coming over.'

Sir Charles Craven, head of Vickers, was also a controller of the Ministry of Aircraft Production. Wallis was shown into his office near Whitehall ten minutes later, and before he could say a word Craven was booming at him:

'What the hell d'you want the services of twenty thousand men in Sheffield for?' Apparently Freeman had already been on the phone.

Wallis explained and got a promise of full support. He had little time to relax in the next few weeks. First he held a 'Dutch auction' with Roy Chadwick the Avro designer.

'Roy,' he said, 'can your Lancs carry seventeen thousand pounds for two hundred and fifty miles?'

'Oh yes,' Chadwick said. 'Easily.'

'Could they carry nineteen thousand?'

'Oh . . . er . . . I think so.'

'Well now, Roy,' Wallis said persuasively, 'how about going to the full ten tons?'

'Oh good Lord, I don't know about that.'

'Now come on . . . if you tried more powerful engines and strengthened the undercarts.'

'Well . . . Oh, I suppose it *could* be done.'

'Thanks,' said Wallis and went off to Sheffield to iron out more of the problems that seemed endless. The bomb had to be made from a *very* special steel; there were only two foundries in the country capable of casting the casings, and both were fully occupied on other vital work.

New methods of casting had to be evolved, new forms of heat treatment for hardening so the bombs could plough into hard ground faster than sound and not break up. The fuses had to stand up to the same shock. There were not enough firms capable of machining the finished bombs. It was a question of finding firms throughout England who might be able to machine one each a month. There had to be special machines designed and built to fill them with explosive, and new methods of testing. The Lancasters would have to be extensively modified to carry them; special trucks and dollies designed and built to handle them, and special winches to get them into the aircraft.

On 30 August, 617 Squadron moved to Coningsby, another bomber airfield in Lincolnshire. Scampton had been a grass field, but Coningsby had long bitumen runways, more suitable for aircraft carrying very heavy loads. Flying was still confined to training, high and low level, aimlessly it seemed, and suddenly they were switched to low level. Cochrane told Holden that they had to be as good as they had been for the dams raid, and there were some new crews to train.

Cochrane and Satterly had long conferences with Holden and Group Captain Sam Patch, the station commander at Coningsby. There was a new verve about the squadron, a feeling of expectancy. At nights the aircraft hurtled low over the flat country and heavy lorries drove in to the bomb dump, their loads hidden under heavy tarpaulins. But it was not to be quite like the dams raid: that was obvious because they were still using the orthodox Lancasters. A flight of Mosquito night fighters arrived at Coningsby, and stayed. Apparently they were going to have fighter escort.

On September 14, Holden drew up a battle order for that night; a short one, eight crews, the pilots being Holden, Maltby, Knight, Shannon, Wilson, Allesbrook, Rice and Divall. Target was the Dortmund Ems Canal, the freight link between the Ruhr and central and eastern Germany, including the North Sea. At that time 33 million tons a year passed along it, of which only a small fraction could be diverted to the railways. Near Ladbergen the fields fell away below the level of the canal and earth banks guided the water across the lowlands. One bomb breaching the bank would flood the countryside and there would be no canal. At least, no water in it; and that would starve the Ruhr of coal – and do many other things. Pre-fabricated U-boats were made in the Ruhr, for instance, and they could only be taken to the sea along the canal.

It was to be another very low-level raid, partly for bombing accuracy and partly because they thought the flak low down was less of a risk than fighters high up, concentrating on eight lonely aircraft. Cochrane saw that it was one of the most carefully planned raids of the war. As in the dams raid, the route curled delicately between the known flak. A specially designed beacon would be dropped near the canal as a pinpoint and night fighters would engage the flak which guarded the most vulnerable points on the canal, although not the point chosen for the attack, which was some two miles from the nearest guns. A weather recce plane would check the visibility in the canal area before the Lancasters arrived. Most important of all they were going to drop the new 12,000-lb light-case bombs for the first time. (Not to be confused with Wallis's developing earthquake bomb.)

They took off at dusk with no illusions; memories of the dams losses were too fresh and they had a human yearning for the placid if less stimulating days of the Italian trips.

They were an hour out, low over the North Sea, when the weather Mosquito found the target hidden under fog and radioed back. Group recalled the Lancasters and as the big aircraft turned for home weighed down by nearly 6 tons of bomb David Maltby seemed to hit someone's slipstream; a wing flicked down, the nose dipped and before Maltby could correct it the wing-tip had caught the water and the Lancaster cart-wheeled, dug her nose in and vanished in spray. Shannon swung out of formation and circled the spot, sending out radio fixes and staying till an air sea rescue flying boat touched down beneath. They waited up at Coningsby till the flying boat radioed that it had found nothing but oil slicks.

Maltby's wife lived near the airfield, and in the morning Holden went over to break the news, dreading it because it had been an ideally happy marriage. Maltby was only twenty-one. The girl met him at the door and guessed his news from his face.

'It was quick,' said Holden, who did not know it was his own last day on earth. 'He wouldn't have known a thing.'

Too stunned to cry, the girl said, 'I think we both expected it. He's been waking up in the night shouting something about the bomb not coming off.'

Holden came back looking tired and got out another battle order. If the weather was right the raid was on again. Martin came back from leave that morning and demanded to take Maltby's place. Tammy Simpson, who had been flying with Martin for two years now, noted philosophically and a little querulously in his diary: 'Micky's a bloody fool volunteering. This is going to be dangerous.' Shannon was hoping the weather would be right this time. Moustacheless, he was to marry Anne in a week and was supposed to have left for London that morning to arrange the wedding. Anne had already wangled a posting for herself to Dunholme Lodge, an airfield near Coningsby.

At dusk in the control tower McCarthy watched the heavy aircraft lift off the runway and head east. Also watching was a languid WAAF who said as the aircraft merged with the darkness. 'My God, I only hope they get there tonight! The trouble the AOC's gone to over this . . .'

McCarthy turned on her and snarled, 'The hell with you and all the AOCs. What about the seven lives in every kite!' The building vibrated as the door slammed behind him.

Over the North Sea the Lancasters kept loose formation in two boxes of four. It felt like the dams raid all over again; they were down to 50 feet to fox the radar and on strict radio silence. The faster Mosquitoes would be taking off now to pass them somewhere on the way in and set about the flak as the bombers arrived. Over the canal itself the weather Mosquito radioed back that it was perfectly clear.

The bombers crossed the Dutch coast and there was no sign of flak. Holden seemed to be flying a perfect course, which was just as well because the moon was up and it was full, throwing soft light over the fields as they moved towards Germany and Ladbergen.

Ahead of them a small town loomed up and high chimneys and a church steeple seemed to be rushing at them. Martin waited for Holden to swing to one side, but Holden elected to bore straight across and climbed to clear the steeple till he was about 300 feet. The more low-flying-wise Martin dropped right down to roof-top height and, on the other side of Holden, Knight and Wilson did the same, till even from the ground they were nearly invisible against the horizon. Holden was limned against the moonlight.

There was one light gun in Nordhoorn and its crew had been alerted. Holden was halfway across when a procession of glowing red balls streamed up, and in a shaven fraction of a second Toby Foxlee was firing back, so that only about five shells pumped up before Foxlee's tracer was squirting down and the gun abruptly stopped.

One of the five shells punched into Holden's inner starboard wing tank. There was a long streamer of flame trailing back beyond the tailplane; the aircraft showed clearly in the glow and they could see it was going down. The port wing was dropping and then the nose; she was falling faster, slewing to the left, right under Wilson and Knight with a 12,000-pounder on board! Martin yelled sharply over the R/T: 'Break outwards!'

Wilson was just turning away when Holden's aircraft hit on the edge of the town almost under him; the 12,000-pounder went off and the town and sky were like day.

Martin called the other two anxiously. Knight came right back and said he was all right, but it was twenty seconds before Wilson answered, a little shakily, saying they were jarred by the explosion but he thought nothing serious was broken. A little later they were back in formation, Martin leading. They swept into Germany, grimmer now. Gibson's crew had been in Holden's aircraft. Spafford, Taerum, Pulford, Hutchison; they were all gone.

One by one they picked up pin-points and the canal was only five minutes away when a blanket seemed to come down in front and they found themselves in mist. It was unbelievable. The area had been clear and moonlit half an hour before, no trace of trouble, and now the ground was a smudge, and they edged up to over a hundred feet to be clear of obstacles. The fog had moved in from the east without warning, almost without precedent. Some of the experts said later that Allesbrook, the deputy controller, should have called it off then, told everyone to go home and forget it till next time, but that is debatable. As it was they pushed on.

There were locks along the canal and every one was armed with flak. The trouble was that the Lancasters could not see the canal until they were right on it, and then it was too late to bomb. They would have to bomb from 150 feet – because they could not see the canal if they went any higher – and hope the flak would miss, which at that height was unlikely.

All of them tried flying across the canal to pick it up, hoping they could swing sharply on to it, but found it was nearly impossible. Split up now, they searched the area but kept blundering into the flak, and then they turned away and tried again, refusing to bomb till they were certain they were in position. The Mosquitoes had arrived and, with their greater speed and smaller size, were charging back and forth trying to silence the gunners, but could not pick them up in the fog.

Allesbrook is believed to have bombed eventually but where his bomb went is not known. They never found the wreckage of his aircraft either. Wilson was heard briefly over the R/T saying something about going in to attack. The bomb was still aboard when the aircraft hit the ground about 200 yards beyond the canal and made a crater 200 feet across. Divall was heard briefly over the R/T, but that was the last anyone ever heard from him.

The gentle little Les Knight shouted over the intercom. that he could see the water, and then flak was coming at them and they were weaving. Johnson, the bomb aimer, yelled that he could see trees looming ahead and *above* them, and as Knight pulled up hard the bomber shuddered as she hit the tree-tops, and then they were clear with branches stuffed in the radiators, both port engines stopped and the tailplane damaged.

With the two starboard engines roaring at full power the Lancaster, with the bomb still aboard, was just able to hold her height. No chance of bombing in that condition, and Knight called up Martin: 'Two port engines gone. May I have permission to jettison bomb, sir?' It was the 'sir' that got Martin. Quiet little Knight was following the copy-book procedure, asking respectful permission to do the only thing that might get him home.

Martin said, 'For God's sake, Les, yes,' and as the bomb was not fused Knight told Johnson to let it go. Relieved of the weight they started to climb very slowly.

After the gunners had thrown out all the guns and fittings they could, Knight got her up to about 14,000 feet and headed towards England, the aircraft waffling soggily at 110 mph. The controls were getting worse all the time, until, though he had full opposite rudder and aileron on, Knight could not stop her turning to port and it was obvious he could never fly her home. He ordered his crew to bale out and held the plane steady while they did. When the last man had gone he must have tried to do the same himself, and must have known all the time what would happen when he slipped out of his seat. There was perhaps a slight chance of getting clear in time, but as soon as he took pressure off stick and rudder the aircraft flicked on her back and plunged to the ground. Knight did not get to the hatch in time.

Geoff Rice tried for an hour to find the canal, was badly holed by flak and finally had to swing his winged aircraft out of the area, jettison the bomb and head for home. Shannon was seventy minutes before he got a quick sight of the high banks of the canal, wheeled the Lancaster along the water and Sumpter called, 'Bomb gone!' There was an eleven-second delay on the fuse, so they only dimly saw the explosion. The bomb hit the tow-path. If it had been a few feet to one side, in the water, it would have breached the canal wall.

Martin spent an hour and a half plunging at 150 feet in the fog around the canal trying to give Bob Hay a good enough sight on the few spots where the high earth bank was vulnerable. Now and then he caught a brief glimpse of the water, but it was either at a spot where the banks were low and solid or the flak was too murderous to give them a chance. It squirted at them when they were right on top of it and they had to wheel away into the fog. The aircraft jolted twice as shells punched into it, and once a sudden burst of tracer ripped through under the cockpit so that Martin jumped with shock, one foot slipped off the rudder bar and the big Lancaster swung so crazily he thought it was all over.

The gunners had been firing whenever they got a chance and Tammy Simpson reported his ammunition was getting low. Martin told him to forget the flak and save what he had left in case they had got a chance to fight their way home.

Once or twice he was able to come up to the canal diagonally so that it was easier to turn along it, but each time the glimpse of water came too late or the flak was coming point blank at them and they had to pull away.

On the thirteenth run Hay got a glimpse of water in the swirling fog and called, 'There it is!' Martin turned away in a slow and regular 360 degrees circle, opening his bomb doors and calculating the exact moment he should come over the water again so the straighten-up would be gentle. It was a beautifully timed turn; they were low over the sliver of water with no flak, just long enough for Hay to call, 'Left, left, a shade right . . . bomb gone!'

and then Whittaker slammed the throttles hard on and Martin pulled her steeply round in a 'splitarse' turn as the flak opened up.

A little later they hurtled back across the canal and saw the water boiling where the bomb had exploded, a few feet from the bank, just a few feet too far, because the bank was still there.

They were still over Germany and dawn was breaking as they came out of the fog. On full throttle, 'P Popsie' was shaking at 267 mph, the fastest she had ever travelled at low level. As they slid round the end of Sylt two last guns sent shells after them and then they were over the sea.

They landed two hours overdue and found Cochrane still waiting. He had heard of the losses from Shannon, who was first back, and his face was leaner and grimmer than ever. Martin was the third back, out of eight. Cochrane knew there would not be any more. He said:

'How was it?'

'I'm terribly sorry, sir,' Martin said. 'It didn't breach. The mist beat us, and the flak.' He told what had happened. Cochrane listened keenly and at the end he was staggered when Martin said, 'I'm very disappointed, sir, but if the weather's clear tomorrow – I mean, that is, tonight now – I think we can get it, if you'll let us have another crack.'

'How many crews have you got left?'

Martin thought for a while and said, 'Well, there are three of us in my flight, and three more in Shannon's flight. That ought to be enough, sir.'

'Six!' Cochrane said. 'Out of your original twenty-one!'

'It ought to be enough, sir. I'm just sorry about last night.'

Cochrane said gently, 'I don't think you have to apologize for anything, Martin. I'll let you know later about tonight. Meantime you'd better go and get some sleep.' He took Sam Patch by the arm and led him over to the corner and Patch for the first time sensed that Cochrane had let slip the mask of his reserve. There was no mistaking it, and almost no defining it, an intensity about his eyes, his whole face and his voice as he said:

'Patch, I'd like to make Martin a wing commander on the spot and put him in command of the squadron. You know the boy better than I do. Would you recommend him?'

Patch thought for a moment before he made the answer for which he has been kicking himself ever since: 'It's two jumps up the ladder, sir; I'm not sure he's ready for it. He's had no experience in administration.'

'Well, I'll at least get him made a squadron leader and give him temporary command.' Cochrane caught Martin as he finished stowing his kit away and said in his sudden-death way, 'You're a squadron leader now, Martin, and for the time being you're in command of the squadron.'

Martin looked after the retreating back and said, 'Christ!' A moment before he hadn't even been a flight commander. Patch said, 'Well, you've got responsibilities now, Mick. Come and have a walk and talk till you relax.' Martin was too exhilarated to sleep. They paced slowly across the airfield, right to the blast walls of the bomb dump, lonely in its isolation on the far side of the field.

'I didn't think anything could have gone wrong,' Patch was saying. 'I thought we had the perfect plan this time.'

'Oh, we should've pranged the thing,' Martin said disgustedly. 'That bloody mist. You couldn't see a thing.'

There was a long silence; the air was fresh, the grass soft and springy under their feet, and Martin, after eight hours in the air, was far from sleepy with the light-headed exhilaration you get after you're so tired you can hardly stand and then get your second wind. He had been awake over twenty-four hours. He said suddenly: 'Well, there it is, sir. Two real ops. and six crews left. Maybe this is the end. They'll make us an ordinary line squadron . . . or disband us altogether.'

'Probably *will* be the end if you try that canal again tonight,' Patch said dryly. 'You were silly to volunteer again. You're not immortal.'

'No, sir.'

'D'you think you'd get away with it again tonight?'

'Couldn't be any worse.'

'I suppose it occurs to you the flak will be expecting you.'

Martin said soberly, 'I suppose so.'

'Forget it a while, Mick,' Patch said. 'I don't think the AOC'll let you try again for a while anyway. He doesn't like losing crews, and you lost five out of eight last night . . . six including Maltby the night before. You'll lose the rest if you go again tonight. We've got to think out a cleverer way of doing it.'

There was another silence and Patch broke it by saying tentatively:

'What d'you think about 617 taking a rest for a while? You've taken an awful beating and you've got to fill up with new crews and train them. What d'you think?'

Martin said, 'No. Let's do another one right away and get the taste out of our mouths. Otherwise we're going to get scared of going back.'

'The AOC'll decide that anyway,' Patch said. 'Maybe you've had your day on special duty.'

They called at the office on the way to see about the casualty reports, but Chiefy Powell and Heveron were already attending to them. Patch took Martin over to the mess for breakfast and sat and talked to him. Patch had not been to sleep for nearly thirty hours himself, but he never changed his routine when a raid was on. He never failed to visit every aircraft before it took off; always waited up till the last crew had landed and then went over to the mess with them for bacon and eggs and yarned as long as they wanted him to. He never went to bed himself till he'd seen the last of the boys off to bed. He was a round-faced, heavy-set, youngish man, direct and honest. If you did a good job, Patch would go to tremendous trouble to let you know. If you did a bad job he would tell you how and why, so you would do better next time. If you failed to mend your ways he would crack down hard, and then in the mess that night he would be normal and friendly to the punished one.

As Martin was finishing breakfast McCarthy and the laconic Munro came in, clicked their heels and peeled off sizzling salutes. 'Good morning, *sir*,' they chorused, and Martin had the grace to blush. They congratulated him and, in grimmer mood, paid their respects to the dead. Martin gave his first orders. 'Will you get cracking on making what aircraft we've got left ready for tonight. I'm thinking we'll be on again. Let me know when the target comes through.' He added, almost as an after-thought, 'May be the same target tonight.'

'All right,' said McCarthy. 'Push off to bed and grab some shuteye.'

Shannon had only got to bed himself about half an hour before. He had written a little note to Anne, apologising for not being able to go up to London. Anne got it over at Dunholme Lodge that afternoon. Quite a short note: 'Sorry, darling. Couldn't make it. Been up two nights. Lost six out of nine. Please forgive. I'm rather tired.' For the first time she saw the writing was shaky.

She had been up all night herself in the ops. room at Dunholme Lodge. About dawn they got a report that five out of the eight were shot down and she was crying when someone ran over and said, 'David's all right. He's back.' But the tears only fell faster.

Martin got nearly five hours' sleep. McCarthy regretfully woke him at two o'clock, shaking his shoulder and saying, 'Target's through, Mick,' until the tired boy shook the sleep out of his head and said, 'Where?'

'Somewhere in the south of France. Bridge or something.'

Martin pulled some clothes on and saw Patch over in the planning room. Patch said, 'You're not going back to the canal yet. You're going with 619 Squadron to have a go at the Antheor Viaduct. It's on the Riviera, near the Eytie border, and carries the only good railway into Italy from France. If you prang it you'll stop half the Hun reinforcements of Sicily.'

Martin said, 'I'm sorry it isn't the canal,' and he so obviously meant it that Patch just looked at him.

They found the viaduct without trouble fifteen miles west of Cannes, seeing in the moonlight the 90-foot stone arches curving across the beach at the foot of a ravine. The idea was to dive to 300 feet and stab 1,000-lb bombs into the stone with delayed fuses. It was like a cocoa-nut shy; bang on the cocoa-nut is yours, miss by an inch and lose your money. They missed by inches. The bombs went through the arches and exploded on the ground all around; the viaduct was pitted by splinters but that was all. The only real result was that it woke the Germans up to the vulnerability of the railway, and soon after that the flak batteries moved in.

Shannon scrounged a few days' leave, went up to London and married Anne. They spent part of their honeymoon in a hotel, and when they walked into the bar one night Anne heard someone say, 'Good God, that boy looks too young to be in the Air Force.' Shannon turned round and the man saw he was wearing a DSO and DFC and his eyes stuck out like organ stops.

The Chester Herald answered Gibson's letter about the squadron badge, questioning the motto. It was true Marie Antoinette had said, '*Après nous le déluge,*' but she had used it in an irresponsible connection. Martin chewed it over with Patch, and Patch said, 'Well, change it to 'Après *moi* le déluge'. That ought to fix it.' Martin wrote back accordingly.

A day or so later Cochrane sent for him. 'I think we might be able to use this dams bomb of Wallis's against the *Tirpitz*,' the AOC said. The *Tirpitz* was still sheltering in Alten Fiord. 'You can't fly up the fiord to get her; that'd be death, but she's moored only about half a mile from the shore where the land rises steeply. You might do it by surprise, hurdle the hill, dive and bomb before they wake up.' There was a hill near Bangor, he said, about the same height and gradient. Martin was to go and practise over it to see if he could level out soon enough on the water at the right height and speed.

Martin flew 'P Popsie' over to North Wales and spent an afternoon diving over the coast, climbing and trying again. It called for most delicate judgment, but towards the end he found he could do it with 40 degrees of flap down. It meant diving 60 mph faster than permitted with 40 degrees of flap and that meant the flap was likely to collapse on one side. If that happened at low level the aircraft would spin straight in. He reported to Cochrane that he was willing to chance that. He knew what the *Tirpitz* defences would be like at low level but thought the raid would be possible.

'We wouldn't need too many aircraft, sir. Myself, McCarthy and Shannon would go. I don't imagine there will be much chance of a second run, but we know the form of attack well and we could practise over the Bangor hills so we get it right the first time.' He suggested they do the raid by moonlight or at dusk or dawn, so there would be some gloom for cover but enough light to see the ship. Matter-of-factly he added: 'I think you should be prepared to lose the three aircraft, sir, but we'll have a go and probably get her.'

Cochrane, who had not met anyone quite like Martin before, looked at him for some time and finally said, 'Well, I'll let you know about it. Meantime start building up the squadron again with new crews. I'll have some picked ones sent to you.'

(Actually it was not the *Tirpitz* that Cochrane was after at this time. 'Tirpitz' was the 'cover plan' to camouflage the real plan. He was, in fact, scheming to smash the big dam at Modane, in Italy, and the hills round Bangor resembled the hill around Modane Dam. Martin discovered that seven years later.)

Martin was interviewing new pilots and crews for the next week, and it was not easy. 617's fame – or notoriety – had spread and it was known as a suicide squadron. Some quite brave men were posted to it but told Martin openly they did not want to stay. Martin did not argue. They were quite willing to fly with their own squadrons, where perhaps one crew in ten finished a tour; in 617 it seemed that no crew had a chance. He did not press anyone who was not willing – they would be no good to him – but sent them back to their old squadrons, and after a week had found only four crews willing to join him: O'Shaughnessy, Willsher, Weedon and Bull. He was doubtful about accepting Willsher because Willsher looked younger even than Shannon, only nineteen, a thin, fair boy a year out of school.

Willsher had trouble finding a crew until a red-faced, broken-nosed, tough-looking Londoner called Gerry Witherick insisted on being his rear gunner. Witherick was unkillable. He had flown nearly a hundred missions and was a hard case with a soft heart and a riotous wit.

A letter came for Martin from the Chester Herald regretting that 'Après *moi* le déluge' was questionable too. An aged Greek had used it to show selfishness.

'Why couldn't the damn Greek stick to his own language?' Martin growled to Sam Patch. 'What d'we do now?'

'Write back politely and explain that the badge had already been chosen by the King,' Patch said. 'Just say how sorry you are that the King's prerogative should be overlooked.'

CHAPTER 10

SNIPER SQUADRON

The fate of 617 was decided at high level. 'We'll make 'em a special duties squadron,' said Sir Arthur Harris. 'They needn't do ordinary ops, but whenever the Army or Navy want a dam or a ship or something clouted we'll put 617 on to it. They'll like that – keep the Army and Navy happy too. And we'll put all the old lags in 617. That's just the thing for them. Make 'em the old lags' squadron.'

'The old lags' was Harris's affectionate and respectful name for the really hard-bitten aircrews who only wanted to do operations. Every now and then there would be a crew who, after finishing their tour, would stubbornly boggle at taking their six months' rest training new aircrews. They insisted on staying on operations and were dearest of all to Harris, probably because they had the same volcanic temperament as himself.

Harris said 617 could stay in 5 Group with Cochrane, and Cochrane had it in his mind to make them a 'sniper' squadron for super-accurate bombing with Wallis's 10-tonner. Ordinary bombing, he knew, would waste most of the 10-tonners, and there would be none to waste. He was well aware (it is no great secret now) that bombing had sometimes been almost primitively inaccurate.

They had started the war bombing by moonlight, but as German night fighters multiplied they had had to use dark nights because of losses, and now they were even having to stick to 'dirty' dark nights when heavy cloud gave added cover (and obscured targets).

British people who had endured the Blitz read with understandable satisfaction of RAF bombers over Cologne or Essen or Hamburg, or of the Hamm sidings being pounded. They did not know (they would have been shaken to know, and the propaganda people did not dare tell them) that many of these raids did little damage. Some did none at all, and many people still do not know that. Harris, people like Cochrane, 'Pathfinder' Bennett and the 'back room boys' were trying to find how to hit targets in blind weather and it was about this time that the main force was starting to produce really good results.

Up to this time a little more than one out of three raids were really effective. The Germans built dummy targets outside cities, spread camouflage nets over tell-tale lakes and rivers in the towns, decoyed the bombers in every way they could, and even lit fires in fields so the bombers would think they were hitting their target. Often the crews bombed open fields instead. A pilot came back from Mannheim and said he was the only aircraft that had found the city. They barked at him for getting lost himself until he produced his aiming point photograph, which showed he was right. The other bombers had dropped their loads on fields or some other town. By 1943 there had been over a hundred attacks on Essen, anything from eighteen to a thousand aircraft dropping a huge weight of bombs against Krupps, but most bombs fell elsewhere and significant damage was quite limited.

That was why the Pathfinder Force had been formed, and now that they were in action bombing was becoming more effective. PFF found and marked the target areas with coloured flares, and the main force bombed these markers. It stopped them bombing open fields, but it was still 'carpet bombing', hateful, and yet, it seemed, necessary.

And losses still mounted. Now they were about 4 per cent; one bomber in twenty-five failed to return. Or average it another way – a squadron of twenty aircraft would lose every one in twenty-five raids. A tour of operations was thirty raids; then, if you were still alive, you had six months' rest and went back for another tour. In lives and labour and for the minor damage done, bombing was not economical enough for Harris.

At Farnborough, in 1941, a man named Richardson had invented a piece of intricate mechanism he called the Stabilizing Automatic Bomb Sight. It incorporated a gyro; in perfect conditions it could aim a bomb uncannily, but Harris thought it was too complicated for the hellish conditions of actual bombing. For one thing, a bomber using it had to run perfectly straight and level up to the target for ten miles, a perfect mark for flak, searchlights and fighters. Harris said it would mean death for too many of his boys, who had little enough chance as it was, and Bomber Command could not take much heavier losses.

Another school of thought said the SABS *could* be used economically by a small force. Cochrane was one of them. He argued that from high level the SABS could hit a well-marked target so accurately that they would not have to send the squadrons back to the same place again and again. In the long run they would lose less. He wanted to train 617 till they could use the SABS in battle and deliver Wallis's 10-tonners, when they arrived, in the right spots.

There were many conferences and then Harris agreed.

Patch called Martin to his office. 'The *Tirpitz* is off for the time being,' he said and Martin sighed gently with relief. 'The AOC has something new for you. From now on your squadron role is changed to ultra-accurate high-level bombing and you're going to be practising till your eyes drop out. You've got to get down to an *average* of *under* a hundred yards from twenty thousand feet.' Martin's eyes almost dropped out on the spot. 'The reasons,' Patch went on, 'are that there's a new bomb coming up . . . a big one. You'll only be able to carry one and they're so expensive every one will have to be spot on.' He said they were getting a new bomb sight at once.

A day later a tall, thin man with lively eyes walked into Martin's office carrying a bundle wrapped in oilskin and announced that he was Squadron Leader Richardson come to help 617 convert to the SABS.

'This is it,' he said, carefully unwrapping the bundle. 'It's the loveliest thing in the world.' The SABS looked like an ordinary bomb sight except that a bulky gyro was encased in it. Richardson handled it lovingly, and in the next few days the squadron found out why. He was not a bomb-aiming enthusiast, he was a fanatic who started talking bomb-aiming at breakfast and was still on the subject at bedtime. If he talked in his sleep no one doubted what the subject would be. He lectured the crews, flew with them, experimented with them and after a time no one had any chance of not knowing everything about the SABS. Bob Hay, haunted now by his own profession, christened him 'Talking Bomb'. Much of the credit for what happened belongs to 'Talking Bomb', who had been a pilot in World War I and managed in due course to fly on fifteen raids with 617 to watch his beloved bomb sight in action.

617 did no ops. for weeks, but night and day the aircraft were 20,000 feet over the bombing range at Wainfleet aiming practice bombs at the white dots on the sands with the SABS. It needed far more than a hawkeyed bomb aimer; it called for teamwork. The gunners took drifts to help the navigator work out precise wind direction and speed, and navigator and bomb aimer calculated obscure instrument corrections. An error of a few feet at 20,000 feet would throw a bomb hopelessly off. Altimeters work off barometric pressure, but that is always changing, so they used a complicated system of getting ground-level pressures over target and correcting altimeters by pressure lapse rates (with temperature complications). A small speed error will also throw a bomb off, and air speed indicators read falsely according to height and the attitude of the aircraft. They had to compute and correct this, and when it was all set on the SABS the pilot had to hold his exact course and height for miles while the engineer juggled the throttles to keep the speed precise. That, oversimplified, expresses about a tenth of the complications. When the bomb aimer had the cross-wires on the target he clicked a switch and the SABS kept itself tracking on the aiming point by its gyros, transmitting corrections to the pilot by flicking an indicator in the cockpit. The bomb aimer did not have to press the bomb button; when it was ready the SABS did that, and even told the pilot by switching off a red light in the cockpit.

First results were only fair, average errors being about 180 yards, but the crews soon started to get the hang of it. 'Talking Bomb' flew with them all, the only way of checking. A good bomb aimer might get poor results because of pilot inaccuracy, so 'Talking Bomb' switched pilots and bomb aimers and coached the weak ones. There was plenty of scope for error. At 20,000 feet the bombs left the aircraft two miles short of the target and dropped for forty-five seconds before they hit, throwing up the little puffs that were plotted from the sandbagged quadrant stations. Results were phoned to Coningsby and the crews got them as soon as they landed so they could see what had gone wrong.

'Talking Bomb' himself was very accurate with the SABS, and before long a couple of crews could emulate him. Martin's was one. Within three weeks Hay set an example with an average of 64 yards. Some of the others, however, were still well over a hundred yards and Cochrane drove over to look into it, got 'Talking Bomb' to give him an hour's instruction on the SABS and took off as bomb aimer in 'P Popsie' to try it. On the ground one or two people indulged in a little anticipatory lip-smacking.

Martin flew sedately and when Cochrane had called his last 'Bombs gone!' brought him straight back. 'Talking Bomb' met them with the results and an expression of great respect. Cochrane had achieved the extraordinary average of 38 yards. For a moment the AOC's face loosened into a faint grin but he froze it off and said crisply, 'Well, if I can do it you people ought to be able to.'

Someone muttered in the background 'If we could we'd all be AOCs,' and that time Cochrane had to laugh.

After he went Hay said darkly to the other bomb aimers, 'Well, you're going to have to pull your fingers out now.' He turned to Martin: 'Hell, Mick, why didn't you kick the rudder as he was going to bomb?'

A letter came to Martin from the Chester Herald, gracefully yielding in the matter of the squadron badge. He had not realized it had been chosen by the King and by no means would he interfere with His Majesty's prerogative. The badge was therefore approved, with the motto 'Après *moi* le déluge'. He enclosed an imposing piece of prose with the official description:

> '*On a roundel, a wall in fesse, fracted by three flashes of lightning in pile and issuant from the breach, water proper.*'

There was a session in the mess that night to celebrate it. Concave Goodale had a bad smoker's cough and had been sitting in a chair coughing to clear his throat for a couple of hours when someone said, 'Poor old Concave. He's nearly dead. He's got a foot in the grave.' Ivan

Whittaker said, 'Oh, he *is* dead. Let's bury him.' He and Martin slipped away and got a sheet from someone's bed, but Concave saw them come in with it and retreated into the lavatory. There was another door on the other side of it, and Whittaker slipped round and caught Concave coming out, throwing the sheet over his head. They carried him back kicking, wrapped him like a cocoon in the sheet and laid him on a trestle table in the kitchen. Someone brought in the padre, a cheerful grey-haired man with a broad Irish brogue who gazed, startled, on the shrouded victim and said, 'What's all this about?'

'Goodale's coughed himself to death,' Whittaker said lugubriously. 'We're going to bury him.' Concave raised his head with a sickly grin. Eight volunteer pall-bearers lifted the table to their shoulders and set off in a wavering slow march, followed by an entourage banging on tin plates, singing 'Abide with him' and moaning the 'Volga Boatman'. In the ante-room they set the table on its trestles again and Concave lay in state in front of the fireplace, the others standing around in a solemn circle. The padre grinned but declined to read the burial service, so someone grabbed a paper-backed novel and chanted an improvised service.

As he intoned 'Dust to dust and ashes to ashes' the elderly local defence officer sprinkled ash from the fireplace on Concave and bawled, 'Slack away.' He nudged one of the trestles, the table-end lurched and Concave rolled off and landed in a half-sitting position on his bottom vertebrae. He let out a groan, his head dropped back with a bump and his eyes rolled up so the whites were visible. He lay still and everyone saluted him. They unwrapped him and said, 'OK Concave, you're in hell now,' but Goodale did not move and the laughter became uncertain and died. Someone said, 'He's really out.' They carried him away and laid him on his bed; the doctor arrived and found a lump on Concave's spine as big as an egg.

The elderly defence officer ran contritely in with one of his dearest possessions, a bottle of very old brandy, pulled the cork, put the bottle to Concave's lips and up-ended it. Concave spluttered and coughed, brandy running down his chin; his eyes opened, he licked his lips and a soft smile dawned. He closed his eyes again, opened his mouth and the defence officer poured in more brandy.

'He'll be all right,' said the doctor. They stayed a while encouraging him to absorb more medicine and then softly retreated, all happy (particularly Concave) except the defence officer, who could not find his bottle of brandy.

There are some who solemnly lament that wartime flying men were known on occasion to drink more than was seemly. That not-always-tactful man Arthur Harris called the worst examples of disapproval 'unctuous rectitude'. Perhaps the rigidly virtuous might acquire a more flexible understanding if they followed the young pilot to the airfield and watched his face in its hood when the chocks were pulled away. Better still, follow him into the air, strapped to a seat and deafened by noise, held precariously aloft by wings relying on inconstant engines and petrol tanks, highly vulnerable to the assaults of flak and fighters, fog and ice-cloud. Follow him up there not once but sixty times till violent death is a threefold statistical certainty.

They played hard because they had little time to play and more often than not it was high rather than potent spirits which affected them.

Higher circles were satisfied now that in Peenemunde lay the heart of Germany's secret weapon, rockets or whatever they were, and Harris sent 600 heavy bombers to dissect the spot. Pathfinders lobbed their markers in the middle, and for the first time the main force used the 'master bomber' technique that Gibson had started over the Moehne Dam; a 'master of ceremonies' circled low directing the bombers by radiophone on to the choicest markers, and Peenemunde rocket centre was almost wiped off the map, putting the advent of rockets over England back by six months. Having failed to protect it, Hans Jeschonnek, Hitler's night-fighter chief, suicided. The Germans learnt anew the virtues of dispersal.

617's bombing kept slowly improving. Three more crews arrived: Bill Suggitt, a Canadian squadron leader, to take over A Flight, Clayton and Ted Youseman, an Englishman, who never stopped talking flying. There were the usual incidents – two aircraft hit trees low flying and were written off (though no one was killed), Martin had an engine catch fire in the air but doused it with the extinguishers. Shannon's aileron cables snapped over the North Sea, but he made an emergency landing, using trimmers to keep his wing-tips level and making a wide, flat turn on rudder alone. He claimed it was better than his usual landing, which, Sumpter said rudely, was nothing to boast about.

Spurred on by Cochrane, Sam Patch and Martin tried to find a way of minimizing the danger of the ten-mile-run-up to the target using SABS. 'Talking Bomb' was a fertile source of ideas.

'This is what you ought to do,' he said. 'You all fly round the target in a great big circle like Red Indians, see? And then someone gives the word and you all turn inwards and come in like the spokes of a wheel. The Hun won't know who to shoot at.'

'That's OK, Talking Bomb,' Martin said, 'but what happens when they all get into the middle?'

'Oh, put 'em at different heights.'

'What about the bombs falling on the lower aircraft?'

'There must be a way over that,' 'Talking Bomb' muttered.

It was a somewhat similar idea that they adopted, and it depended on immaculate timing and navigation. The aircraft, at different heights, would circle a spot in sight of the target but outside the defences, and when the markers were down the leader would assess their accuracy, give the order to bomb and they would all come in, converging slightly. If there were twenty guns below, for instance, and only one aircraft coming in, the twenty guns would all be firing at it, but with twenty planes coming in at the same time, too widely scattered for a box barrage, there would be only one gun against each aircraft – twenty times less chance of being hit.

New troubles kept cropping up with the SABS. For instance, the thermometers (necessary in getting outside temperatures for computing precise height from the altimeters) were showing errors up to 5 degrees, enough to throw a bomb over a hundred feet the wrong way. Farnborough put in new type thermometers, but two more corrections were still necessary. Airflow against the bulb caused friction and heat, and this had to be corrected by a table based on the indicated air speed at the time. Then cockpit heating affected part of the thermometer which was inside the aircraft and that, too, had to be calculated and allowed for, but by early November the squadron had an average bombing error of only 90 yards.

Good enough, Cochrane thought, and at dusk on 12 November, Martin led the squadron off to try out the SABS in battle. The target was the Antheor Viaduct again, an easy one so that they could give the SABS fair trial. In the bomb bays hung 12,000-lb light-case 'blast' bombs.

They found the viaduct in half-moonlight, but this time it was different . . . four searchlights and half a dozen guns round it. Running up, the viaduct was hard to pick up in the glare of the searchlights; the next little bay looked exactly the same and several crews bombed the wrong bay. Some of them got the right bay in their graticules but could not distinguish the viaduct. Rice, O'Shaughnessy and one other got near misses, 50 yards away, but the blast was not enough to damage the viaduct.

They flew disgustedly on to Blida again and it was then that Martin recalled what McCarthy had said about flares after San Polo. Everyone agreed that if they had had flares to mark the viaduct they could have hit it. Two days later they flew back to England, but Youseman never arrived. No one ever found out what happened to him and his crew, but a German fighter probably got them over the sea.

Martin reported to Cochrane the need for target marking, and Cochrane sent him and Patch to Pathfinder Headquarters to talk it over with the experts. Pathfinders promised to mark their next target, and Martin put the crews back on training to perfect their SABS technique.

Martin's time as temporary commander was up. Cochrane would not replace him with any ordinary squadron commander (none of whom, in any case, was eager to take on the suicide squadron), but he had found the man he wanted. Leonard Cheshire, at twenty-five, was the youngest group captain in the RAF, and was not only willing to return to operations but actually asked Cochrane to drop him back to wing commander so he could take over the squadron. He did not look the part at all. Gibson had looked the part; Gibson and glamour were indivisible, but Cheshire looked more like a theological student thinly disguised as a senior officer; yet he had done two tours and won a DSO and bar and DFC. He was tall, thin and dark, a strange blend of brilliance (sometimes erratic), self-consciousness, confidence and charm. Highly sensitive and introspective, he yet lacked, quite illogically, the foreboding imagination that makes some sensitive men sweat with fear before a raid. Once he had walked from Oxford to Paris with a penny in his pocket to win half a pint of beer. He liked a suite at the Ritz on leave and to bask in a Mayfair cocktail bar. At twenty he had an Honours degree in Law at Oxford (where his father was Vinerian Professor of Law – England's highest such appointment), and at twenty-four, in a few weeks' joyous leave in New York, he had met and married Constance Binney, who had been America's top film star, successor to Mary Pickford, in 1922. She was a bride of forty-one.

He had a gentle consideration for other people and a Puckish sense of humour, but in the air he was cool, efficient and calculating. In a way he had a mind like Barnes Wallis, liable to get ideas that horrified people but turned out to be right. He had been flying a certain type of heavy bomber at a time when losses of that type were inexplicably heavy. They had acquired too much extra equipment, so that fully loaded, at operational height, they were slow, flew soggily and were inclined to yaw and drop into a fatal spiral with the rudders locked over. Then they added kidney cowls to blanket the exhaust flames from night fighters, and that, for Cheshire, was the last straw. He considered it made the aircraft more dangerous than the enemy and asked permission to take the cowls off his squadron's aircraft.

Everyone flatly disagreed except his AOC, Air Vice-Marshal Carr, who let Cheshire do so, with the result that his losses fell. It was the first step to taking off a lot more: front-turret, mid-upper turret and armour-plate; freed of the excessive drag and weight the plane flew more comfortably, the engines were not overworked and losses fell further.

For two days after Cheshire joined 617 little Doris Leeman, his WAAF driver, sat in the shooting brake outside his office with nothing to do. She watched Cheshire walk away several times, and at last she could stand it no longer and went in to Chiefy Powell. 'Doesn't he *know* I'm waiting for him?' she asked, with the anger of a woman kept waiting inexcusably. 'You'd better tell him,' Powell said, so she knocked at his office door and told him, and was staggered when he confessed he didn't know he had a car at his disposal. It was fairly typical of the man; never taking for granted what lesser men demanded.

The destruction at Peenemunde had put Germany's rocket programme back six months, and they stopped work on the monster rocket blockhouses to go ahead with the more dispersed flying-bomb sites. Recce aircraft were bringing back to England photographs showing mysterious new activity in the same areas, the erection of many low, curved buildings in clearings in woods, and next to them short sets of rails that seemed to start and end in nothingness. Intelligence men christened them 'ski sites' because the low buildings were the same shape as skis, and bit by bit they connected them more definitely with secret-weapon reports.

It was clear that these and other satellite launching sites could be put up very quickly and were more or less mobile. They were springing up all over the place and ordinary blast bombs could smash them, but after Peenemunde, Hitler seemed to be relying for protection on dispersal – numbers, camouflage and mobility – instead of three or four centralized targets.

In Whitehall, Churchill, the Air Council, Harris, Sir Stafford Cripps (now Minister for Aircraft Production) and Sir Wilfred Freeman discussed the situation uncomfortably, and one day Freeman sent for Wallis.

'We're stopping work on the ten-ton bomb,' he said. 'The big targets we had for them aren't so important now, and Sir Stafford doesn't think the ten-tonner justifies all that work.'

Wallis could not dispute the logic of it. The biggest bombers would have a very short range with a ten-tonner – little more than across the Channel, and in that area there seemed no other targets important enough. There were plenty in Germany, of course, but the Lancasters could not carry the 10-tonner as far as that.

Wallis pleaded with Freeman to let him go ahead with the 12,000-lb scaled-down version of the 10-tonner, to penetrate deeply in the same way and cause an earthquake shock. The Lancasters could drop them deep inside Germany on the kind of targets he had originally had in mind. Freeman thought for a long time, and in the end he said yes – a bold decision to make on his own. He knew that neither the Air Council nor the Ministry of Supply liked the idea of either the 10-tonner or the scaled-down version, because they were designed to be dropped at 40,000 feet for proper penetration. The Lancaster could not drop them from higher than 20,000, and the Council and Ministry considered they would not thus penetrate deeply enough for the proper earthquake effect.

Freeman made the decision so much on his own initiative that no Requirement Order was issued for the bombs, which meant that the Air Force did not have to accept them – or pay for them. He gave the scaled-down bomb the code name of 'Tallboy', and Wallis hoped to have one ready for trial by March.

Cochrane had his eye on the mobile launching sites as targets for 617 but left them in peace while Cheshire kept his crews perfecting the SABS technique, and for some weeks the squadron did no operations until, on December 10, Cheshire got a call from Tempsford for the loan of four crews. Tempsford was the hush-hush airfield where the planes took off to land agents in occupied countries and drop arms to Resistance fighters. Cheshire chose McCarthy, Clayton, Bull and Weedon, and they flew their aircraft to Tempsford.

McCarthy landed back at Coningsby two days later, walked into Humphries' office and dumped two kitbags on the floor. 'Bull and Weedon's kit,' he said. 'They've had it.'

'Oh God! When?'

'Last night. We did a special low-level thing, dropping arms and ammunition. They must have hit trouble.' He added disgustedly, 'I didn't even find the damn target area.'

He went back to Tempsford that afternoon, and he and Clayton tried again that night – successfully.

Cheshire, meantime, had had one of his more spectacular ideas. His brother had recently been shot down and captured and Cheshire had been thinking a lot about prisoners of war. He sent for Martin, and Martin found him in the planning room huddled over maps spread out on the table. Cheshire greeted him with bright eyes and a pleased grin. 'Mick,' he said, 'we're going to drop Christmas parcels to the prisoners of war on Christmas Day.'

'Oh,' Martin said. 'Sounds interesting, sir. Whereabouts?'

'Stalag Luft III. Here.' Cheshire stabbed his pencil at a spot on the map, and Martin leaned over and saw the point was resting on a small town called Sagan, between Berlin and Breslau, up near the Polish border. They had never flown so far as that over Germany and Martin said cautiously, 'It's a long way.'

'We've got the range all right.'

'How're we going to find a little thing like that at night?'

'Won't have to, old boy. Going by day. Christmas morning.'

'By day!'

'Yes.'

'By *DAY*!'

'Don't worry. We can do it. Nip in over the Baltic low level and surprise 'em. We'll get away with it.'

'How many aircraft?'

'Three ought to be enough.'

'Who?' Martin felt that his ears were laid back and the whites of his eyes showing.

'Me, you and either Shannon or Munro.'

'Uh!' Martin looked at the map silently. 'What sort of food were you thinking of taking, sir?'

'Oh, things like chickens and raisins and chocolate. It ought to give them a hell of a lift.'

Martin said, trying to keep the edge out of his voice, 'D'you think we could drop some parcels addressed to ourselves? We'll still be there on Boxing Day, you know, either on the ground or under it.'

'Oh, I don't think it'll be that bad, Mick. We'll paint the aircraft white, put red crosses over them and take the guns out.'

'Oh! No guns!'

'We can do the trip by night,' Cheshire said, 'arrive about dawn so we'll have no trouble pin-pointing it, drop the stuff about a hundred feet to make sure it gets into the compounds and nip out across the Baltic. That's the shortest way out, and I'll get Pickard to meet us with his Mossies and take us home.'

Martin said: 'If there's any cloud we could try and make our retreat in them, if there's any retreat.'

'OK,' Cheshire said cheerfully. 'That sounds good enough.'

He called the others to the briefing room and told them: they listened in startled silence, but had acquired such faith in him that he soon had them planning a fund to buy chickens and hams and volunteering to give up their sweet and cigarette rations. They went round surrounding farms, bargaining for chickens, cheeses and bacon; and Cheshire, Martin and Shannon practised low-level formation. Cheshire had warned everyone to keep quiet about it because if Cochrane got to hear there would be no chickens for the prisoners, but probably bread and water for Cheshire.

CHAPTER 11

DIRECT HIT

Harris had been sending bombers by day to smash at the mysterious 'ski sites' in the Pas de Calais, but too many German fighters swarmed up to protect them. It left him with a pretty problem . . . the targets were so small and well hidden that the squadrons would not be able to pin-point and bomb them accurately by night; what was good enough for a big industrial area was not precise enough now. Cochrane asked permission for 617 to try their precision bombing with PFF (Pathfinder Force) to mark the pin-point with incendiaries and Harris agreed.

Night after night 617 was briefed, but the target was smothered under low stratus cloud until, on 16 December, Cheshire led nine Lancasters off. A Pathfinder 'oboe' Mosquito flew with them to mark the target. 'Oboe' was a new way of radar pin-pointing; two beams went out from England and crossed exactly over the target to let the pilot know when he was there. This night the 'oboe' plane dropped a casket of incendiaries, and they cascaded into the wood that hid the 'ski site'. At 10,000 feet 617 saw them winking among the trees like tiny glow-worms, swung in together according to the drill, nicely scattered so that the flak was ineffective, and all the 12,000-pounder 'blast' bombs went down within a couple of minutes. Around the incendiaries the wood erupted in flame.

Back at Coningsby they developed the aiming-point photos (taken by photo-flash) and a groan went up. The markers had been 350 yards from the target; the bombs were all round the markers with an average error of only 94 yards, but that meant that the bombing was so good that the ski site was untouched. It was the most accurate high-level night bombing of the war, but that made it all the more bitter.

It confirmed a suspicion both Cheshire and Cochrane had had . . . Pathfinders were fine for area marking but not precise enough for pin-point targets. Martin suggested they drop parachute flares over the target, lighting up the area so that a couple of aircraft could dive to low level and drop incendiary markers 'spot on' the target. Cheshire agreed, but Cochrane, with the memory of the Dortmund Ems painfully fresh in his mind, would not hear of more low-level work.

Cheshire and Martin went off quietly and tried low-level marking on the ranges in the hope that they could get Cochrane to change his mind. They dropped practice bombs from about 200 feet using the low-level bomb sight and were only mildly satisfied with the results. They found they could land a bomb accurately but the trajectory was so flat that the bomb tended to bounce and skid 200 yards beyond the target. And at night-time they found in the Lancasters that they were shooting past the range target before they saw it.

On 20 December they tried PFF 'oboe' marking again on an armament factory near Liège but found the town hopelessly cloaked under low cloud. On the way back (with their bombs) Martin saw a Lancaster going down in flames with one of the gunners still firing at the fighter. Back at Coningsby they waited up, more out of conscience than hope, but Geoff Rice, one of the five survivors of the original squadron, did not return.

They tried again with the 'oboe' Mosquito on a ski site, but again cloud defeated them.

Cheshire called on an intelligence officer in London for a final check on his POW 'chicken run'. The intelligence man listened to the plan with horror and said, 'My God, you can't do that! If you drop things in the compounds the Germans'll think you're dropping them arms, and as the prisoners rush out to pick them up they'll be mown down.'

Cheshire said, 'I didn't think of that,' went back and told Martin and Shannon sadly that they would have to call it off, but it didn't sadden the other two at all.

The weather closed in until the night of 30 December, when they went with an 'oboe' plane to another ski site. Three bombs were direct hits on the 'oboe' markers, but the markers were again a couple of hundred yards off the target and the ski site escaped.

Cheshire pleaded with Cochrane for permission to mark at low level. His idea was that PFF should drop flares by 'oboe' to illuminate the area, and he and Martin should fly low enough to put a marker right on the spot.

Cochrane replied with a flat no, and added, 'Try and find another way. Try marking with the SABS from about five thousand feet. If you can light the area enough with flares to get a sight, you ought to be able to do it accurately.'

Cheshire suggested in that case that 617 might as well carry their own flares and dispense with the Pathfinders. Cochrane agreed and on 4 January they flew back to the Pas de Calais without the 'oboe' plane. From 12,000 feet the squadron dropped floating flares, but cloud foiled Cheshire and Martin at 5,000 feet, so they both dived to 400 feet (pre-arranged and strictly off the record) and skimmed over the dim clearing from different directions. The markers landed in the clearing but both sets bounced and skidded 100 yards into the woods, so that the clearing was straddled by them.

The squadron managed to put most of their bombs between the markers, badly damaging the ski site; Cheshire thought it was fairly successful but was not exactly delighted . . . skidding markers were too uncertain to rely on. In the next few days he, Martin and 'Talking Bomb' kept experimenting to find a permissible way of marking.

Between 3,000 and 6,000 feet on a clear aiming point by day they found they could put down a marker within 40 yards of a target – near enough for Cochrane – but could not do it on a hazy target, and there was little chance of getting a clear enough aiming point at night. Moonlight and flares would help, but any important target was going to be camouflaged.

That was the week the squadron moved from Coningsby to Woodhall Spa, about ten miles away. Woodhall was a one-squadron station and that was the reason for the move. As a 'special duties' squadron on new and rather hush-hush projects, Cochrane wanted them to go on working in somewhat exclusive isolation.

Snowstorms had mantled the field and the runways were under a 6-inch carpet. Everyone on the squadron, officers and aircrew too, turned out to shovel the snow off the runways so the planes could get off the ground. They worked from dawn till midnight for two days, long lines of men shovelling at the white acres while WAAF's brought them coffee and sandwiches and rewarded them with a rum ration when they finished work at night.

About this time a Military Brain conceived that, if a large dam just north of Rome could be breached, the flood would tangle German communications in Italy and help the imminent break-out from the Anzio beach-head. 617 was the logical squadron for the job, and Cochrane – a little reluctantly – put them on to intensive dams-type training . . . low flying. It would have to be Wallis's dams bombs again, dropped from 60 feet, but the Italian dam lay in a lake surrounded by high hills, a worse proposition even than the Éder. It meant sliding over a hill and losing 1,800 feet in 3,000 yards to be at 60 feet over the water in time to bomb, a frighteningly steep dive in a heavy aircraft at night. It was going to need a lot of skill. They measured 3,000 yards out over the air field, marked the extremities, and Martin stood off from one mark with a theodolite to measure height while each pilot came over the far mark at 1,900 feet and tried to cross the next mark at 60 feet. Pilots who could not do it after a couple of trial runs got the benefit of Martin's salty vocabulary and were spurred on to achieve success next time.

One other complication was that they would have to take off for it from North Africa because all-up weight would be too great from England; and if the Germans got an inkling that the Dam Busters' Squadron was flying to Africa for a raid they would very likely put two and two together, put balloons and guns by the dam and save their dam as well as kill most of the crews.

Cochrane and Cheshire hit on the solution. Cochrane sent in lorry loads of enough arctic equipment and clothing to outfit the whole squadron, and Cheshire stored it under guard in a locked hangar, then dropped a hint that they were going to North Africa. From that moment the whole squadron was convinced they were going to Russia. The more they were told it was to be Africa the surer they were that it was Russia.

The pilots practised low flying constantly over Lincolnshire and Norfolk. On 20 January, O'Shaughnessy was practising diving over the sea by the Wash and levelling out at 60 feet, but he was concentrating so hard on his altimeter that he did not notice the land looming up. The Lancaster smacked her belly on a hill rising off the beach, bounced, charged into another rise in the ground and rolled into a flaming ball, cremating the crew except for Arthur Ward, the wireless operator, who was thrown clear with a broken leg. That was the day the Authorities decided that if the dam were breached it might kill many civilians and perhaps disrupt the Allied advance more than the Germans, and so they called it off. Such is war.

In between low flying Cheshire and Martin had kept experimenting to find a way of marking, and one day, flying back from the range, Martin saw a patch of seaweed in the water that took his fancy. Always ready to spice his flying with a little variety he peeled off in one of his usual spectacular turns, dived steeply and dropped a bomb. It was a direct hit.

When he landed he jumped out of 'P Popsie' quivering with excitement. 'That's it, sir,' he said jauntily to Cheshire. 'We've got it. I didn't use the bomb sight when I dropped that thing over the seaweed and it was a piece of cake. If we can dive-bomb markers point-blank over a target we can put 'em right on the button without the bomb sight and they won't skid off. What's more, we could see the target much better from above than coming up to it down low.'

Cheshire went out and tried it that afternoon and it worked like a charm, almost without practice.

Next night they went back to the Pas de Calais. Munro dropped flares and Martin, turning a blandly blind eye to orders, tried his new method, peeling off, sticking his nose steeply down and aiming his whole aircraft at the ski site. He found that dive-bombing low at night in a four-engined plane was a slightly hair-raising businesss but dropped his markers in the dive and pulled out at about 400 feet. They were a new type of marker, red and green flares known as 'spot fires', and as he pulled up and levelled off Martin saw the two lights like red and green eyes winking in the middle of the clearing. It was a clear night; from 12,000 feet they were plainly visible, and the rest of the squadron plastered the rocket site out of existence.

A couple of nights later they went to another flying-bomb site; Martin dived low again, laid his spot fires accurately and a few minutes later the target was littered about a few smoking craters.

Cheshire went to Cochrane and told him of the new method (that is, told him of the seaweed and the trials over the range, not of Martin's actual dives over the targets). Knowing that Cochrane approved of low-level marking on every count except the risk, Cheshire assured him that the diving attack, straight down, up and away, with only a few fleeting seconds near the ground, was reasonably safe. He added earnestly: 'Sir, if we're going to mark accurately we *must* be low enough to see exactly what we're doing, and I'm sure that Martin is right when he says that right low down we're actually safer. I can't find any way of marking accurately from medium level. Will you let us try this new way on some lightly defended target?'

Cochrane considered for a moment, looked up and said, 'All right, we'll give it a trial.'

The target he chose was the Gnome-Rhone aero-engine factory at Limoges, 200 miles south-west of Paris. The Germans had taken it over but there was hardly any flak for miles.

There was an immediate complication. War Cabinet vetoed the target because the Germans had 300 French girls working at the factory on night shift and there were French homes nearby. Churchill would not have French people killed if he could possibly avoid it, particularly as this was not a vital target.

Cheshire replied that as far as the homes were concerned he would guarantee they would put all bombs on the target itself. To protect the girls in the factory he offered to make several dummy runs over the factory to give everyone plenty of time to get clear. Cochrane backed him up and, after a silence from Whitehall, permission came through for the raid, on the understanding that if one Frenchman was killed there would be no more. Cochrane told Cheshire: 'Our future stands or falls on this one. If anyone slips you won't get another chance. Not in France or Belgium anyway, and I won't let you make guinea-pigs of yourselves over Germany.' Cheshire, at briefing, told the crews the same thing. Cochrane and he planned it with fanatical care.

Twelve aircraft took off into bright moonlight and reached Limoges just before midnight. The town was evidently not expecting bombs because the blackout was bad. Lights showed all over the place and in the factory itself all the workshop lights were on and it was obvious that the Germans had them working hard. Pat Kelly, Cheshire's gay, chunky little navigator, looked down on the lighted streets, making wistful comments about the bistros and French girls he imagined he could see.

Cheshire dived low and hurtled over the factory at a hundred feet, and as he climbed and turned he saw all the lights vanish. He dived back over it again, and Astbury, his bomb aimer, could see people running below and throwing themselves flat. A third time he dived in warning, and on his fourth run held her down to 50 feet till he was practically scraping the workshop roofs. Astbury called 'Bombs gone!' and a cluster of brilliantly glowing incendiaries cascaded into the exact centre of the workshops. In the Lancaster the cameraman filmed it.

Martin dived in the same way and two red spot fires joined the incendiaries. Cheshire called, 'Markers dead centre. Bomb as ordered.'

At 'Zero plus 1' (one minute past midnight) Shannon dropped the first 12,000-pounder from 10,000 feet. It exploded in the middle of the incendiaries and blew them to smithereens but started a big fire that was just as good. In the next eight minutes nine more bombs fell right on the factory, and one fell just outside in the river. The last man, Nicky Ross, had a 'hang-up'; his bomb did not release, so he went away and came in on another run. At 'Zero plus 18' his 12,000-pounder lobbed in the crater that Shannon's bomb had made.

Cheshire cruised overhead for a while, but there was nothing to see but flames and smoke and soon he turned for home. Apart from two machine guns there was no opposition and none of the Lancasters was holed, not even Cheshire's.

In the morning a recce aircraft brought back pictures which showed that of the factory's forty-eight bays half were scars on the ground and the rest were only shells. A target had never been more completely expunged, and Cheshire knew that, on undefended targets at least, he had proved his point. Cochrane was delighted.

(A message reached England from Limoges not long after. The girls of the Gnome-Rhone factory wished to thank the RAF for their considerate warning and would be pleased to welcome the people concerned after the war.)

Bob Hay also deserved credit for the bombing at Limoges. He and 'Talking Bomb' had the bomb aimers so well trained in the SABS that from 15,000 feet *at night* they could guarantee two direct hits on any target, 15 per cent of bombs within 25 yards of the centre and 75 per cent within 80 yards, a remarkable feat when it is considered that the crack Pathfinders were never called upon to mark with more than 150 yards accuracy.

CHAPTER 12

GALLANT FAILURE

In Italy the Allies were preparing to break out from Anzio and the Germans were preparing to stop them. Trains carrying 15,000 tons of supplies a day were passing over the Antheor Viaduct, and for the third time 617 was ordered to smash it.

Cochrane thought a 12,000-lb 'Blockbuster' within 10 yards of the viaduct might knock a span down but this time he warned Cheshire that he must not try 'deck-level' marking unless it were absolutely necessary. There were twelve heavy guns and several lighter guns around the viaduct, plus searchlights.

With heavy bombs the range was dangerously far from Woodhall Spa, so they refuelled at Ford in the south, Cheshire flying McCarthy's 'Q Queenie' as his own aeroplane was being overhauled and McCarthy was on leave.

They found the bay at midnight but it was so dark they could not see the viaduct from above 3,000 feet, and as soon as Cheshire and Martin slipped down to that height the flak opened up terrifyingly, nearly twenty guns predicting and concentrating on the two of them. Cheshire made a run to drop his markers, but the searchlights caught him long before he was in position and shells were bursting all round him, so that he had to turn away. Martin tried a run but the same thing happened. Cheshire came in again and Martin flew parallel, higher and about a mile out, to draw the flak. It took some of the flak off Cheshire, but not enough; his aircraft shuddered in the blast of near misses and jagged lumps of flak ripped holes in his wings and fuselage. He slid out to sea and swung in again, but as he straightened up for the run Martin's voice sounded in his earphones: 'Hold off a minute, Leader. I think I'm in a position for a low run. I can see everything.'

He had dived over the hills inland, was hugging the ridges so that the flak could not see him against the dark mass, and turning down the long ravine that cut down to the viaduct across the bay. When they had looked at the maps at briefing it did not seem possible that an aircraft could get down that way but Martin, who could land a Lancaster out of a steep turn, had his nose dipping into the ravine and could see the viaduct ahead, limned against the phosphorescence of the surf on the beach.

Cheshire called back, 'OK Mick, go ahead.'

'Try and draw the flak as long as you can,' Martin said. He was deep into the ravine; the viaduct was about a mile in front and some 1,500 feet lower; he throttled his engines back to keep the sound from the guns and at 230 mph opened his bomb doors and knew he was making the best bombing run he ever had. The guns down by the viaduct were all firing, but their target was Cheshire weaving in towards them from the other side at 4,000 feet.

In the nose of 'P Popsie' Bob Hay said over the intercom., 'Target markers selected and fused.'

'Right,' said Martin. 'I'm going to level out in the last second.'

'OK.' The bomb sight was no use in a dive. Hay relied on Martin for the signal.

The ravine ridges were towering on each side and the viaduct was rushing at them, growing hugely. One gun on the eastern end suddenly swung and out of its muzzle-flashes a chain of shells was swirling at them. Hay called, 'Now?' and Martin yelled, 'No! No!' He eased the nose up, a second dragged into eternity, he shouted, 'Now!' And as he shouted a shell smashed through the nose and exploded in the ammunition trays under the front turret. The aircraft rocked in the crashing din and jagged steel and exploding bullets shot back into the fuselage, hitting flesh and ploughing through hydraulic and pneumatic pipes, control rods and fuse boxes.

Hay must have pressed the button as the bomb release contacts parted, and then they shot a bare couple of feet over the viaduct and dipped towards the water as half a dozen more guns swivelled and spat at them. Foxlee was still alive; for the first time in months he was in the mid-upper turret instead of the nose, and now he was cursing and shooting back, and so was Simpson in the rear. Martin pulled the nose off the water and Whittaker rammed the throttles forward but there was almost no response from the engines.

'P Popsie' was bathed in glare but Simpson and Foxlee put three of the searchlights out with long bursts. They were practically in the water now, and in the glow of the last light Simpson saw the spray hissing up from the prop-wash and thought for a moment it was smoke from a burning engine. Then they were out of range and Martin lifted 'P Popsie' a few feet off the water, praying with thankfulness as he found she still had flying speed.

Whittaker leaned over and yelled in his ear, 'Port inner and starb'd outer throttles gone and pitch controls for the other two gone.' That meant two engines would stay throttled back as they had been for the run down the ravine, and the other two, in fully fine pitch, were straining themselves at maximum revs on extreme power to keep the aircraft flying.

Martin became conscious of Cheshire's voice: 'Are you all right, "P Popsie"? Are you all right? Can you hear me?' Nearly a mile above he had seen the Lancaster rocket over the viaduct, caught by the searchlights and with all the guns pounding her.

Martin called back: 'Still airborne, Leader. Hit badly I think. Two engines gone and crew hurt.' He had felt the sting in his own leg as the shell went off in the nose and knew he had been hit. Whittaker was doubled up now, holding his legs.

Cheshire's voice came back: 'Can you make it back home, Mick?'

'Not a hope, sir. We'll try and make for the nearest friendly land.'

'All right, boy. Good luck!'

Martin was calling the roll round his crew. The tough little Foxlee was all right. Bob Hay did not answer. Whittaker gave him a twisted grin, swearing and hunched, holding his legs. The rest were all right. He called Hay twice more but there was only silence, so he said, 'Toby, see if Bob's all right. His intercom. must be busted.' Foxlee swung out of his turret and wormed down towards the nose. He lifted his head towards Martin. 'He's lying on the floor. Not moving.'

Over the viaduct Cheshire was trying to drop his markers but again was coned by searchlights and hit by flak, so he had to stand the Lancaster on a wing-tip and pull her round to the safe darkness at sea. It meant several miles for another run. He came in again about 3,000 but again he was battered and had to pull away. He climbed to 5,000 but the flak caught him once more, and now there was another worry on his mind. Out to sea the squadron had been circling for half an hour waiting for the markers and he knew they were getting short of petrol. Met. had radioed that England was under fog and only two fields were suitable for landing. They would need plenty of petrol to search and land through the fog . . . or risk losing the whole squadron.

On his sixth run he dived to upset the predicted flak and was able to drop flares that lit the viaduct. He turned back for another run and this time the searchlights did not find him. The guns predicted on him but he threaded through them and soon his markers sprang to glowing life as they hit; he saw in the light of the flares that they were on the beach about a hundred yards from the viaduct.

He swung in again with his last two markers, but four seconds short of release point two shells hit 'Q Queenie' and she almost stood on her head in the blast. It threw Astbury off his bombing aim, but Cheshire got her back under control and found she would still fly and there was no fire.

The squadron headed in, unable at 10,000 feet to pick up the viaduct from the flares but trying to allow for the error of the markers. The gap was fiendishly hard to judge in the darkness. One 12,000-pounder went off brilliantly 15 yards from the side of the viaduct, but that was 5 yards too far and the viaduct shook but was not damaged beyond chipping from fragments. Six more exploded a few yards further on and pitted the great stone piers a little more. It was good bombing, but not quite good enough. Long after they were supposed to, they turned for home.

Whittaker had taken off his tie and wrapped it round his thigh as a tourniquet. There were a dozen pieces of flak in his legs but the pain was passing into numbness now. He grabbed one of the roof longerons, pulled himself up and found he could stand. Foxlee stuck his head up from the nose and said, 'Bob's unconscious. Get a first-aid kit, will you?' Whittaker pulled one of the little canvas bags out of its stowage and eased himself down into the nose. Hay was lying on his side, his head pillowed on the perspex right up in the nose. 'Give him some morphia,' Foxlee shouted, and Whittaker nodded, unclipped the canvas pack and took out one of the tiny morphia hypodermic tubes. Foxlee unzipped Hay's Irvin jacket sleeve and rolled the battledress sleeve up till Whittaker could see the soft flesh of the forearm, pale in the gloom. He felt the flesh was still warm, jabbed in the needle and squeezed till the tube was empty.

'Let's get him over and see where he's hit,' he shouted. Together in the cramped space they edged him over on to his back and Whittaker crawled up and gently turned the head over. He saw the great hole in the side of the head and felt the stickiness in the same moment. He said, 'Oh, my God!' and felt he was going to be sick, looked up at Foxlee, but Foxlee was looking down. He had lifted his hand off Hay's chest and the blood showed darkly on his fingers. 'He's got it in the chest,' he said, and Whittaker said, 'Yes, the poor devil's had it.'

He crawled back up into the cockpit to his seat beside Martin, leaned over and said, 'Bob's dead.' Martin looked at him a moment, then looked ahead again and gave a little nod.

Whittaker noticed Kenny Stott, the new navigator, standing by Martin's seat. 'Where're we going?' Whittaker said, and Martin gave him a wry little grin. 'Somewhere friendly, I hope,' he said. 'Just been talking it over with Kenny. Got any ideas?'

'Whatever's nearest. How 'bout Gib.? Or Sicily? Or North Africa?'

Stott said, 'What about Sardinia? Or Corsica? Aren't they closer?'

'Is Corsica ours?' Martin asked, and Whittaker cut in, not sensing then the unconscious humour of it: 'Yeah. I saw we got Corsica in the *News of the World* last Sunday.'

'OK. Fair enough. Kenny, give me a course for North Corsica.'

Stott went back to his charts and Whittaker said he would try and assess the damage. Martin found 'Popsie' had just enough power to claim a little more height, very slowly, so he edged the nose up a little, and soggily, not far from stalling speed, the Lancaster started climbing laboriously. In the darkness she was full of noise, the high-pitched screaming of the two good engines battering at the ears in waves because they would not synchronize properly.

He felt his right foot in the flying boot was wet and remembered he had been hit in the calf. He had enough sense not to strip his leg to investigate because the trouser leg and high flying boot would help staunch the blood. The trouble was, if he lost too much blood, he would pass out and they would all die because no one else could fly 'Popsie', particularly the way she was. Against the ragged thrust of the engines the trim would not hold her either straight or level and he was working all the time to keep her flying. With one hand he pulled his tie loose and wrapped it round the calf over the spot where the shrapnel had hit him, knotting it tightly so that it would press the trouser leg against the wound with the effect of half bandage, half tourniquet.

Whittaker came back. 'Not too good,' he said. 'The floor's all smothered in grease. It's from the hydraulics, so you can count them out. Air pressure's gone too.'

'I know,' Martin said. 'I can't get the bomb doors up.'

'The CO_2 bottle seems all right,' Whittaker said, 'so you'll probably be able to get your undercart and flaps down but you won't have any brakes to pull up with.'

'Oh Christ!'

'I've kept the best bit to the last,' Whittaker said morbidly. 'The bomb-release fuses have gone for a Burton and we've still got the bombs on board.'

'I thought so. That's why she's flying like a bloody brick.'

Stott came up with a course for Northern Corsica, and Martin swung on to the new heading. They were about 2,000 feet now.

'We'll have to get rid of the bombs,' Stott said. 'The fusing circuit's bashed in too, so they must still be fused. We can't unfuse 'em. If you can get high enough I might be able to prod the grips through the floor with a ruler and trip them.'

Martin was trying to coax more height out of the stricken plane. He had a 4,000-pounder and several 1,000-pounders in the bomb bays, and the minimum safety height for dropping a 4,000-pounder was 4,000 feet.

Curtis was tapping out a 'Mayday' (SOS) and excitedly reported, after a while, he had made contact with Ajaccio in North Corsica. An advanced RAF fighter unit had just moved in there and the airfield and flarepath were serviceable.

Foxlee came up from the nose and said in a puzzled voice, 'Bob's still warm. His body's quite warm. I think he might be alive.' Whittaker went down to investigate and came back up again, a little excited. 'He *is* warm,' he said. 'He *must* be alive still.' Martin told Curtis to warn Ajaccio to have a doctor meet them. Curtis made contact again and came back to the cockpit. 'They say they haven't got a doctor with any facilities to look after a bad head wound. They say if the kite'll hold together we ought to make for Cagliari. That's in South Sardinia. There's an American bomber base at Elmas Field there, and they've got everything, but it's another one hundred and fifty miles.'

Martin said feelingly, 'Christ, what a party! Give me a new course, Kenny.' The aircraft was still full of numbing noise; a gale was howling through the shell-hole in the nose and the two good engines still screamed in high pitch. Whittaker was watching his gauges nervously, waiting for the engines to crack under the strain.

They were about 2,700 feet when the stars blotted out and they were in heavy rain, followed soon after by hail. Water was sweeping in through the nose, and then darkness swallowed them as they ran into heavy cloud. It was ice cloud. Martin saw supercooled water droplets filming over the leading edge of the wings, forming the dangerous glazed ice that altered the aerodynamic shape and robbed the wings of lift. He had no spare speed to give him lift, and then the propeller of one of the two good engines slipped right back into coarse pitch and could not be budged out of it. The revs. dropped down to about 1,800; the engine was still giving power but the propeller could not use it all. Martin felt the controls getting soggy; he held on to her, correcting the waffling with great coarse movements, trying to coax her to stay up because Stott was shoving a ruler down through the floor into the bomb bay against the bomb grips. He got a 1,000-pounder away and then the aircraft stalled. Martin couldn't hold her; the nose fell, she squashed down and the starboard wing-tip dropped and they were diving and turning, on the verge of a spin. He had hard left rudder on and the rudder caught her, the spin checked and she was diving, picking up speed. He eased her out but they were down to 1,800 feet. That was clear of the cloud, and soon the thin ice cracked and flicked off the wings. He started climbing again. They still needed 4,000 feet to drop the 4,000-pounder.

It took a long time. At 2,500 feet they were in the ice-cloud again, but Stott prodded two more 1,000-pounders free before the ice started to make 'Popsie' soggy again, and this time Martin eased her down out of the cloud before she stalled. He started climbing again and found they were running clear of the worst of the cloud. It was still there, but higher and thinner, and only the barest film of ice seemed to be shining on the wings. 'Popsie' slowly gained height, passed the 3,000 mark, but then progress was terribly slow and when at last they reached 3,200 she could not drag herself any higher. She was still at the climbing angle but moving no higher, like an old man trying to climb a fence and not being able to pull himself up.

'She's only squashing along,' Martin said. 'Can't make the safety height, Kenny. What're our chances if we drop the big one here?'

'Better than trying to land with the bloody thing,' Stott said. 'Let's give it a go.'

He went back to the winch slits in the floor and probed. Martin felt the aircraft jump weakly in the same moment that Stott yelled, 'She's gone!' Martin tried to turn away but knew he could not get far enough for safety. The 4,000-pounder took fourteen seconds to fall and it felt like fourteen minutes. The sea below and a little to one side opened up like a crimson rose and almost in the same moment the shock wave hit the aircraft. She jumped like a startled horse and a wing flicked, but Martin caught her smartly with rudder and they were all right.

Curtis came up a couple of minutes later. 'Elmas Field says the best way in is over the mountains in the middle of Sardinia.'

'How high are they?' Martin asked. Stott said they were 8,000 feet and Martin showed his teeth sardonically.

They got a landfall on Sardinia about 3.30 am and turned to follow the coast all the way round the south tip, and on e.t.a. Martin let down through light cloud and they came out about 1,000 feet and saw the flarepath.

'Thank God for that,' he breathed, and a minute later changed his mind. Elmas was on a narrow spit of land. It had one runway only, a dangerously short one for an emergency landing. Martin steered low over it to see what the overshoot areas were like because they were probably going to need them, and felt a chill as he saw that some genius of an airfield designer had had the fabulous idea of building the runway *across* the spit of land, so that the runway started very abruptly at the beach and stopped just as abruptly and dismayingly quickly at the cliff, where the sea started again. No overshoot.

He still had two 1,000-lb bombs that Stott could not reach and they were almost certainly fused, so a belly landing was out of the question. With the emergency CO_2 bottle the undercarriage might go down, or it might not; the tyres might be all right or they might have been punctured, and if they were the aircraft stood a good chance of ground-looping so that the undercart would collapse on to the fused bombs. If his first approach was not perfect the aircraft, without brakes, would certainly run over the far cliff. There was not enough power to go round for a second approach.

Whittaker yanked down the handle of the CO_2 bottle, and the undercart swung down and seemed to lock. In the gloom they could not see the tyres. There was just enough pressure left to get some flap down. Martin headed in on a long, low approach, dragging in from miles back, while the crew snugged down at emergency stations. Coming up to the runway he was dangerously low, deliberately, and in the last moment he cut all engines and pulled up the nose to clear the dunes. The speed fell and at about 85 mph she squashed on the runway about 30 yards from the end, not even bouncing. The undercart held, and as she rumbled on Martin started fish-tailing his rudders. The far cliff was running towards them and he pushed on full port rudder. 'Popsie' swung and jolted over the grass verge, slowing more appreciably. She started to slew, tyres skidding just short of a ground-loop, and came to a halt 50 yards from the cliff-top.

Foxlee said, 'Well, you old bastard, I'll never bitch about your landings any more.'

An ambulance and fire truck had been chasing them along the runway, and a young doctor swung up into the fuselage and they directed him up to the nose. He was out a minute later and said, 'I'm sorry, but your buddy's gone. He was dead as soon as it happened.'

He went over to Whittaker, lying on the grass, and cut his trouser legs away, exposing the legs messy with blood and torn flesh, and where there was no blood they had a distinct blue tinge. He worked for quarter of an hour on them, dabbing, cleaning and bandaging, while Martin gingerly pulled up his own trouser leg to inspect the damage to himself. The doctor finished bandaging Whittaker and as they loaded him into the ambulance told him, 'That's a close call, boy. You nearly lost a leg.' He turned to Martin. 'Now let's have a look at you,' but Martin said as off-handedly as he could, 'Don't bother about me, Doc. I'm quite all right.'

When he had uncovered his leg he had found one tiny spot of blood on a tiny puncture where a tiny piece of flak, at its last gasp, had just managed to break the skin. It had stung at the time, and imagination had done the rest. The wetness he had felt round his foot was not blood gushing into his flying boot but sweat!

About the same time the rest of the squadron was landing at Ford in thick weather. Tommy Lloyd, Woodhall intelligence officer, had flown to Ford and de-briefed them, and then the weather worsened and it looked as though they were stranded for a while. Suggit thought he could make it to Woodhall Spa all right and offered a seat in his aircraft to Lloyd, a gallant and revered World War I veteran. The immaculate Lloyd accepted but insisted on having a shave before take-off. A little later, spruce and monocled, he climbed into 'J Jug' with Suggit, and five minutes later the aircraft flew into a hill and everyone was killed instantly except Bill Suggit, who lingered a couple of days before he died.

The rest flew back later, and Cheshire's 'erks' found 150 holes in 'Q Queenie'. The port wing had to be scrapped. McCarthy, back from leave, was outraged to find his beloved 'Queenie' so battered and a comic but slightly acid note edged his Brooklyn accent when he said loudly and meaningly in the mess (Cheshire was standing near): 'It's a remarkable coincidence that the wingco had been flying his own aircraft for three months without getting a spot on it, and then sends me on leave and takes mine and does this to it.'

They buried Bob Hay in Sardinia. Whittaker stayed in hospital while the rest made rough repairs, flew 'Popsie' on to Blida, where RAF 'erks' did a thorough overhaul, and then filled her up with benedictine, wine, fruit and eggs and flew back to Woodhall Spa, where Cheshire met them with the news that Cochrane had vetoed any more operations for them. 'It's no use arguing, Mick,' Cheshire said. 'He means it. He says you'll only kill yourself if he lets you go on.' Martin *did* argue, but Cochrane posted him to 100 Group Headquarters, where he immediately wangled himself on to a Mosquito night-fighter squadron doing 'intruder' work over Germany.

[I have a letter which Cheshire wrote to a friend some four years after this, talking about the old days. He said: 'The backbone of the squadron were Martin, Munro, McCarthy and Shannon, and of these by far the greatest was Martin. He was not a man to worry about administration then (though I think he is now), but as an operational pilot I consider him greater than Gibson, and indeed the greatest that the Air Force ever produced. I have seen him do things that I, for one, would never have looked at.']

It is not a bad tribute from a man who has himself often been labelled one of the world's greatest bomber pilots. I have these words of Cheshire's in my notes: 'I learned all I knew of this low-flying game from Mick. He showed me what you could do by coming in straight and hard and low, and I never saw him make a mistake.'

Cheshire himself, in fact, was undoubtedly the most outstanding of the 617 pilots, though if one suggested this he would decry it with a gently and faintly derisive smile. Always he had a talent for self-effacement, a soft-spoken modesty, and many qualities not usual in hearty men of action and courage. His courage could match any man's, and in addition he was always a strange blend of leader, intellectual, man of action and man of ideas and ideals (sometimes eccentric and seldom conformist). Inevitably he had an awareness of this and balanced it by a deprecating introspection. He has never quite rid himself of the idea that he lost his nerve at Antheor, that he should have tried to go in low like Martin, and does himself no justice, because he and his crew would almost surely have died, probably before being able to lay their markers, and that would have destroyed any chance of success for the raid.

As it was, the raid was within 5 yards of success, but that is a sore point with 617. Antheor seemed to have a hoodoo for them.

CHAPTER 13

THE MOSQUITO PLAN

Cheshire reported to Cochrane that the Antheor raid had convinced him of three things:

(a) Accurate marking was essential for accurate bombing of small specific targets.
(b) Accurate marking could only be done reliably at low level.
(c) Low-level marking was *very* dangerous on defended targets with a big aircraft like the Lancaster.

Cochrane was not yet convinced that low-level marking was practicable, but he told Cheshire he would lay on more lightly defended targets so the experiment could go on. He wanted the system perfected by the time Wallis's 'tallboy' was ready; the first one was nearly ready for testing, and after that they would be some time building up stocks. Meantime the squadron needed some re-forming. With Martin and Suggit gone there were no flight commanders.

It was Cochrane's idea to split 617 into three flights for easier organization and training; a happy idea, because it gave Cheshire a chance to promote Shannon, McCarthy and Munro, now the only three of the original squadron left, and all battle-tested, reliable and ideal in temperament and training for 617's unique role. Shannon was an old-young man now, venom-tongued on occasion, highly strung on the ground (though not the slightest neurotic), but calm and detached as an iceberg in the air. McCarthy, strong as an ox and even-tempered, stood no trifling – his way with a young fool who forgot himself was swift and vigorous. Munro, the slow-speaking, taciturn New Zealander, so earnest and dour that he was known as 'Happy', did most of the tedious routine work in the squadron and never even suspected that the WAAFs on the station adored him as a strong, silent man. The Australian, the American and the New Zealander, each in some way typifying their national characters, led by the subtle and audacious Englishman, made a strong combination of leaders in a squadron that ever was an oligarchy, but a respected and revered one.

McCarthy, incidentally, now that he was a squadron leader, let himself take on a little of the colour of his surroundings. With a touch of Brooklyn wit, he bought himself a pipe, a walking stick and a dog, and took the dog for long walks in the countryside, claiming that, as he had to be pretty much of a gentleman officially, he was goddamned if he wasn't going to have a crack at looking the part too.

The squadron had several new pilots now, including another American, Nicky Knilans, a droll youngster from Madison, Wisconsin, with precisely the quality of nervelessness that Cheshire wanted in 617. Knilans had already done about twenty trips with 619 Squadron and been in strife on nearly every one of them. Several times on the way to the target he had had engines shot out, and more shells had ripped chunks out of his aircraft, but he had always pressed on and bombed and had a DSO to commemorate that laudable habit. Once his rear gunner had been cut in two by a night fighter, and it was such a terrible mess that, when they landed back at base, the ambulance driver who met them had had hysterics and largely left it to the nerveless Knilans to get the remains out of the turret.

Knilans had joined the Canadian Air Force before America came into the war and had just recently been transferred. Now a 'lootenant' in the US Air Force, he wanted to stay and finish his tour in the RAF, and had a row with his crew when he had them posted with him (without telling them) to 617. They claimed it was a suicide squadron, but, as Knilans pointed out, few people on 619 had ever finished a tour either, so it didn't make much difference. The crew was even more unhappy when Knilans suddenly seemed to develop into an exceedingly hamfisted pilot. He was given a new aircraft, 'R Roger', when he joined 617 and could not make his usual three-point landings any more; even the take-offs were frightening, as 'R Roger' seemed most reluctant to leave the ground, and when she did leave climbed like a tired duck. 'Give the game away, Nicky,' one of his gunners said. 'You're getting flak-happy. You can't even fly any more.'

'Doggone, it's not me,' said the badgered American. 'It's this bloody-minded aircraft. You don't have to fly it, you have to understand the son of a bitch.'

In the next few weeks 617 was busy training new crews and settling down with the new flight commanders. Cheshire and 'Talking Bomb' kept flying around at 5,000 feet trying medium-level marking, but could find no way of lining-up an indistinct target. Cochrane told them to keep trying.

The first couple of prototype 'tallboys' were finished, and at Ashley Walk range, in the New Forest, the complicated process of testing them started. They were sinister objects, 21 feet long, shining blue-black steel, slim and perfectly streamlined, weighing 12,030-lb. A Lancaster dropped one on test from 20,000 feet, and it sliced through the air like a bullet till it was falling faster than a bomb had ever fallen before. Long before it hit it passed the speed of sound, and as the compressed waves of the sonic barrier piled up round it the bomb vibrated in flight so that it almost toppled and was deflected slightly from its even course, just enough to interfere with the fanatical accuracy that Wallis wanted.

He overcame it with a brilliant idea, offsetting the tail fins so that, as the next bomb dropped and gathered speed, the offset fins began to revolve it. Faster and faster it whirled till by the time it reached the speed of sound it was spinning like a high-speed top, and the gyroscopic action held it perfectly steady as it plunged through the sonic barrier. At Shoeburyness the blind Air Commodore Huskinson put other prototypes through heat and cold and rough-usage tests, dragging them over rough ground on bomb dollies and throwing them against concrete walls. They filled one with RDX, stood it on its nose and exploded it. Instruments scattered for hundreds of yards registered the effects, and in a concrete shelter a very high-speed camera took a slow-motion film of it. It was obviously impossible to point the camera at the bomb; they shielded the camera behind a shelter pointing at a mirror so placed that it reflected the explosion into the lens, and got some extraordinary photographs showing the bomb slowly swelling under the tremendous pressure within, like a balloon blown to bursting point, till it was nearly twice its normal size, and then the casing burst with deeply satisfying results.

At Ashley Walk they dropped a 'tallboy' with dummy filling from 20,000 feet and it sank 90 feet into the earth, almost enough for the maximum camouflet that Wallis had planned from 40,000 feet, and certainly enough to make a respectable earthquake.

Came the day of dropping the first 'live' one, and they buried a movie camera in the earth to film it. There was some discussion as to where the camera should go, and perhaps it was logical (if a little cynical) that they decided to bury it right in the centre of the white circle that was the target, on the assumption that it was the safest spot.

The result was a lesson for anyone who doubted Wallis's genius. Peering over the edge of the sandbagged dug-out half a mile away, they saw the slim shape streak down and hit the centre of the target, right on the camera! The dug-out trembled, and where the camera had been was a smoking, stinking crater eighty feet deep and a hundred feet across.

Cochrane called Cheshire to Group HQ, told him the earthquake bomb had passed its tests with honours and they were now building up stocks for 'a big operation' in the spring and summer. 617 was still the only squadron good enough to drop it with the SABS but they still had not perfected their marking technique.

On 2 March Cheshire led fifteen 617 Lancasters to an aircraft factory at Albert, in France. Over it the Germans had spread enormous camouflage nets painted with dummy roads and buildings. Cheshire identified the

factory from surrounding landmarks, dived low through flak, but his bomb
sight was out of order. Munro dived and planted incendiaries and two red
spot fires, and a few minutes later the blockbusters crashed down. One
toppled and fell outside but the rest, with 617's uncanny accuracy, were
direct hits. No more aircraft were made at Albert for the Germans.

Next night they flew to La Ricamerie needle-bearing works at St
Etienne, near Lyons, smallest and hardest target yet. It lay in a narrow
valley with 4,000-foot hills on each side, and the actual target, in the
middle of a built-up area, was only 40 yards by 70 yards. Cochrane warned
Cheshire again that on no account was a single Frenchman to be hurt.

Met. forecast good weather but the squadron found the target blanketed
under unbroken cloud and brought their bombs back. The attempt,
however, was notable for two incidents that illustrate the remarkable spirit
of the squadron.

Les Munro lost an engine on take-off but got into the air safely and,
instead of turning back, which would have been normal, flew on with three
engines, arriving only a minute late.

The second concerned a Warrant Officer Rushton, a gunner in Duffy's
crew, a hard-boiled bunch of Canadians. Duffy was ill that night and could
not fly, so Rushton begged Cheshire to take him along with him. No
particular reason, except that he did not want to be left out of an operation.
That sort of thing happened often on 617. A navigator broke his collar-
bone in a football game one day and sneaked out of sick quarters next night
to fly with his crew.

Duffy's crew had made themselves notorious the night they had arrived
on the squadron. When they went upstairs to bed they could not find the
toilets but, being resourceful men from the backwoods, had relieved
themselves out of the window. In the morning they were brought before the
group captain, who eyed them coldly and said: 'If you fellows do your job
properly you can get away with almost anything on this squadron, but one
thing you *can't* do is piddle on the group captain.'

He had been walking below at the wrong moment. The rest of the
squadron thought it wonderful that a crowd of new boys should do that to a
senior officer from a great height.

The weather cleared and they tried La Ricamerie again, finding the
valley dark under broken cloud. Cheshire dived low between the hills and
made six risky runs up and down trying to mark but found he could only see
the factory at the last moment. On the sixth run he judged his distance,
shoved his nose down and let go his incendiaries; they lobbed on the main
factory building but had such a low trajectory that they bounced a
hundred yards beyond. Munro dived and undershot. Shannon came in; his
markers hit a workshop roof and bounced. Arthur Knell, a lanky

Australian who had been a champion amateur boxer and taken over Micky Martin's 'P Popsie', came in at roof-top height, and his incendiaries stayed in the middle of the factory.

Cheshire told the bombers above to aim at the last marker, and soon the darkness was lit by flashing explosions and flames. Morning revealed that only the wall round the factory remained; the rest had disappeared and there was no damage outside.

More nights of waiting for the weather; it had been snowing for days and they turned out every day to try and shovel the drifts off the runways and crack the ice off the wings, but as soon as they had finished the snow was coming down again. One night they got off in freezing cold to plaster an aero-engine factory at Woippy, near Metz, but flew through ten-tenths cloud the whole way and found the cloud just as thick over the target. No hope of bombing.

On the way home Duffy's plane was 'jumped' by two JU88s and a FW190. The first burst sent a bullet through the hand of McLean, the rear gunner, but McLean, after a few salty comments, found his hand was still working and more than evened the score by shooting down both 88s, and possibly the FW190 as well.

It was so cold in the rear turrets that the oxygen mask studs on Gerry Witherick's helmet had stuck to his face. He did not know it till he dragged his helmet off and a couple of square inches of skin came away with the studs. The MO consoled him with a rum ration.

Next night to the Michelin rubber factory at Clermont Ferrand, partly sabotaged but still making the Germans 24,000 tyres a month. This was an amazing raid. The factory consisted of four large buildings – three workshops, and the fourth was the workers' canteen, just beside them. War Cabinet was still worried about the risk of killing French people, and from a high level the startling instruction came down that they were to smash the three workshops but on no account damage the canteen. It would be such a fine gesture and such good propaganda! (It would also be, a high officer remarked, 'a bloody miracle'.) To make it more difficult it was a black, moonless night.

Cochrane drew up a most detailed plan and also sent six Lancasters from 106 Squadron with a special new radar navigation aid to drop flares. McLean, his hand swathed in bandages, wanted to fly as usual with Duffy but Cheshire flatly forbade him.

The flares brightly revealed the factory, and Cheshire made three low runs over it at a hundred feet to warn the workers, and on the third run his markers fell short. He called on Munro, Shannon and McCarthy to mark, and they all dive-bombed their spot fires on the workshop buildings.

Seven minutes later the bombing was over and the factory was smothered in flame and smoke. Cheshire radioed back, 'Michelin's complexion seems a trifle red.'

In the morning a Mosquito took a picture of the smoking ruins. Six of the 617 aircraft had been carrying 12,000-lb 'blockbusters' and every one was a direct hit on the workshops, which could work no more. Just beside them the workers' canteen was untouched. Cochrane sent the picture off to War Cabinet.

Cheshire had been pondering some new marking ideas. Remembering Martin's experiences at Antheor and his own and Munro's troubles marking the needle-bearing factory up and down the dark valley, it seemed to him that Lancasters were too big and clumsy for marking; too big a target for the flak and too clumsy for manoeuvring low over rough ground on pin-point targets. He went to Cochrane and suggested that he try marking in a Mosquito, and Cochrane liked the idea. The twin-engined Mosquito was much faster as well as smaller and 'nippier'. Provided Mosquitoes could be used, Cochrane for the first time began to feel more comfortable about the idea of sending crews out to mark at low level.

A new idea was already growing in Cochrane's mind: to have 617 mark for the whole of his 5 Group, about twelve squadrons, instead of the Pathfinders. He did not consider the Pathfinders accurate enough for his purposes and a polite 'cold war' had, in fact, been developing between 5 Group and the Pathfinders, aggravated a little by 617, who were already tending to consider themselves 'Pathfinders to the Pathfinders'. Cochrane had already sounded out Harris on his new idea and Harris had reacted favourably. Cochrane reasoned that if they could show that low marking in Mosquitoes was reasonably safe, Harris would probably give 5 Group its chance. He said to Cheshire:

'Well, I'll see if I can get you a couple of Mosquitoes, and then I'd like you to try them first on easy targets. If it seems all right, you could have a go at a tough one.'

A bond was developing between the two men. Cochrane did not have an easy personality and few of the hundreds who were daunted by him ever realized that underneath the crisp and almost ruthless front he was shy, with rigid control over his emotions. His precise brain dwelt on operational efficiency. He watched his men from close quarters and visited them constantly. He never, for instance, missed attending a squadron dance, so that he could know them and gauge their temper (and so that they could gauge him). Yet the reserve that covered his shyness made him wary of the embarrassments of easy-going familiarity that might lessen his unswerving concentration. Cheshire was brilliant in a more erratic way, and Cochrane's relentless logic was a brake on this occasional waywardness. They were an ideal combination. Cheshire was a natural tactician in personal relationships, gentle and unobtrusive but with a quiet confidence and the charm that comes from treating everyone, high or low, as a real person and not as a Thing.

It was not easy for Cochrane to get hold of Mosquitoes for 617. They were in short supply and great demand; Pathfinders and other squadrons had priorities for them, and the idea of a heavy-bomber squadron using some experimentally evoked sturdy protests in some high places. While Cochrane was working on this, 617 went ahead perfecting their technique with Lancasters on several small French targets. On 18 March they visited the explosives factory at Bergerac, on the banks of the Dordogne, under rigid orders that there was to be *no* low flying. Cochrane would not risk his choice crews before the Mosquitoes arrived.

For once, in the light of flares, Cheshire's bomb aimer, Astbury, got a good sight at 5,000 feet and put his markers on the factory. Munro did the same. Shannon and McCarthy branded the explosives dump nearby, and Bunny Clayton put a 12,000-pounder in the middle of the dump. For fifteen seconds it looked as though the sun was coming up underneath; the ground was one great orange flash that Cheshire described as 'fantastic'. It lit the sky for miles so clearly that Cheshire looked up and saw the remaining ten aircraft of his squadron heading in to bomb, and five minutes later the factory as well as the dump was a sea of flame. Cheshire radioed back, 'The powder works would seem to have out-lived their usefulness.' No bomb fell outside the works.

The Germans had another explosives works in France near a town called Angoulême, in a bend of the Charente. Cheshire led fourteen aircraft there the following night, put his spot fires in the centre and ten minutes later was able to radio back, 'In accordance with tradition.' The factory had ceased to exist. Again no damage outside.

A pleased Cochrane rang Cheshire next day. 'Pack your over-night bag,' he said. 'You're coming down with me to see Air Chief Marshal Harris about a couple of Mosquitoes.'

That night they dined with Harris in his house near High Wycombe, Cheshire for all his urbanity feeling uneasy in the company of the two most terrifying commanders in the RAF. He needn't have worried; the fire-cracker and the meticulous planner chatted nostalgically about their days in Iraq when they were both young flight lieutenants not fanatically addicted to administration.

Over the port Harris suddenly said, 'Cheshire, what makes you think you can mark from nought feet in a Mosquito and get away with it?'

'There's no question that we can mark accurately, sir. The only thing is having a reasonable chance in the face of heavy opposition. Air Vice-Marshal Cochrane thinks a Lancaster is too big and slow. Against heavy opposition I'm inclined to think now he is right, but I believe he agrees with me that the chances in a Mosquito are good. I believe in a Mosquito we can have a go at any target under the sun and mark with under twenty yards accuracy.'

'I've always wanted to bomb Munich properly, and I've never succeeded,' Harris said. 'It's got four hundred guns. 'D'you think you could mark that on the deck and get away with it?'

'Yes, sir. I do.'

Cochrane cut in, saying that they should practise first with the Mosquito on less lethal targets so they would know precisely what was possible.

'All right,' Harris said, 'I'll see if I can get you two Mosquitoes . . . just on loan for a month. If by that time you can mark Munich accurately for me, you can keep them.'

Just behind Calais the Germans had started work again on the bomb-proof rocket and long-range gun bases. Thousands of slaves were crawling over the massive blockhouses and it was obvious that the secret-weapon project was nearing completion again. Whitehall knew now that the weapon was to fall on London and the invasion ports, but kept it very secret. (They still knew nothing of the long-range guns, the 500-ft barrels of which were then being brought up through Belgium.) If the secret weapons started up before the invasion and the RAF could not destroy the blockhouses, London would be destroyed and it was likely that the invasion would also be wrecked.

Churchill was insisting on twice-daily Intelligence reports. Some reports put the weight of the secret-warhead as high as 10 tons of explosive and suggested they might fall at a rate of thousands a week. Churchill ordered the preparation of plans for the evacuation of London and told Sir Arthur Harris that the blockhouses were to be destroyed without fail before they were ready for action.

Wallis's 'tallboy' was the only weapon Harris knew of that might smash them, but the 'tallboys' would not be ready for some time. They would have to be dropped from at least 18,000 feet to get enough speed for penetration, and only one squadron could drop them accurately enough. But the sites would be so well camouflaged in the bomb-pocked earth that a bomb aimer would have trouble getting them in his bomb sight from 18,000 feet even by day. Though the sites were fairly plastered with flak, they would have to be marked clearly and with unprecedented accuracy because there would be no 'tallboys' to waste. It was a pretty problem, and Harris called the Pathfinder chief, Bennett, and Cochrane and Cheshire to a conference at his headquarters.

Bennett said that the Pathfinders were not equipped to mark with such accuracy, and Cochrane suggested that 617 might be able to do the marking as well as the bombing.

Cheshire said: 'I doubt if it could be marked accurately at medium level. You'd have to run-up straight and level, and at that height the searchlights would blind you so you couldn't see the target, and the flak would pretty surely get you anyway. I should think, sir, we could mark it at very low level in a diving attack.'

Cochrane said warningly, 'Not in a Lancaster.'

'No, sir. In a Mosquito, as we discussed before. She's so fast we could be in and out before the defences could nail us.'

Bennett said, 'I don't think you'd find the Mosquito fast enough to dodge the defences . . . you'll have enormous casualties.'

Cheshire held stubbornly to his own viewpoint and added, 'In any case, sir, I can't see that there is any other way.'

The conference was virtually stalemated. Harris said grimly, 'Well, the job's got to be done. If PFF aren't equipped for it, how about your boys, Cochrane?'

Cochrane accepted the challenge. 'We'll get down to it, sir,' he promised.

A day later Cochrane phoned Cheshire: 'I've got two Mosquitoes for you. They're over at Colby Grange. Go and learn to fly them and be quick about it. Let me know as soon as you're ready to use them.'

Cheshire was delighted with the Mosquitoes, and within two days felt at home in them. The only possible fault he could find was that, carrying a load of heavy markers, their range might be a little short for some of the more distant targets. Munich, for instance, would be barely within range, so he asked Group to get him some long-range drop tanks as soon as possible.

A gratifying indication that their bombing success was spreading to the outside world came when the two American Air Force generals, Spaatz and Doolittle, flew over to Woodhall to inspect them and inquire about the marking technique. Cheshire explained it with pride, and Spaatz wanted to know if there was any particular problem they had not solved yet.

'Well,' said Cheshire, straight-faced, 'there is still one problem actually, and that's to find some way of de-calibrating the bomb sights, because damn bomb aimers are lobbing all their bombs in the same hole.'

'Oh, is that so,' Spaatz said with a fierce grin. 'Well, how's about you and us having a bombing contest, and we'll show you how to land a bomb in a pickle barrel?'

Cheshire accepted the challenge, eagerly, but it never came off because there were sterner things to do, which was a pity because it would have settled a lot of arguments. 617 was confident of the result, and probably with justification. With the SABS, the direction of Cochrane and the skill of Cheshire and Martin, they were showing that bombing – and night bombing at that – could be confined almost completely to military targets and that there need be no slaughter of the innocents. 617 was entitled to feel proud of themselves. Morale had climbed far above the grimness of the 'suicide' days, and in the past month they had flown 149 sorties and dropped 473 tons of bombs without, as far as they knew, hurting any civilians.

Significant peaks are seldom seen through the smoke of battle; it is only when time moves the beholder to a clearer perspective that the peaks stand out. No one on 617 at this time realized that they were already a workshop of tradition. Still only a fledgling squadron, they had a spirit probably unequalled by any other unit. Achievement lay behind them already; that was one reason, but only a part of it. More subtle factors invoked the rest.

First, the aircrews were volunteers. They were where they wanted to be; not square pegs in round holes. They could leave whenever they wanted to, and none of them ever wanted to. They had pride in their special competence and purpose and were honoured for it.

Secondly, there was Cochrane, dedicated to his job. His lively little personal assistant, Carol Durrant, deftly warded off all distractions from him and left him free to concentrate on his precise work. Having carefully chosen his squadron commander, he briefed and guided him and then shrewdly left him to choose his own team and run it.

Cheshire had the perception to recognize the peculiar character of a bomber squadron. The Air Force is the only fighting service where one section of the same unit does the most dangerous job of the war and the other the safest. With an expectation of death far higher than the Navy or Army, the aircrews had to face action day after day, week after week, virtually alone, with only their consciences as monitors. The ground crews, on the other hand, were liable to frustrations which could only be soothed if they could be assured of their value, and Cheshire delicately gave them those assurances.

When he landed in the early morning after a raid his driver usually found him under the wing sharing cocoa and sandwiches with his ground crew. As anxiously as they asked him how he had got on he would be asking them if they had managed to get any sleep while he was away, or thanking them for the performance of the aircraft, all with a friendly touch and a few jokes thrown in.

With flying or ground crew he was a leader and never a driver, never bullying, overbearing or petty, though his tongue could be quietly devastating if you merited it. His aircrews almost worshipped him, and the ground crews' feelings were probably deeper because he treated them with warm consideration, and they were not used to it.

Incompetence was never tolerated on the squadron but high spirits were, and the result was what Cochrane had aimed at: a unit of functional quality. He had long thought that one good performer was worth ten bad ones, and with 617 he proved it. The intriguing thing was that, so long as they were completely efficient, the rather punctilious Cochrane never unduly interfered with their somewhat spirited attitude towards life, and so in the intrinsic lunacy of war they found a purposeful comradeship.

Signs of their growing prestige were not lacking. March brought them nine more decorations; popular ones. Among them were a Bar for Martin's DSO, a second Bar for Cheshire's DSO, a Bar for Whittaker's DFC, and the DFC to add to Foxlee's DFM.

Cheshire flew down to Weybridge to see Wallis about tactics for dropping the 'tallboys'.

'I haven't really designed this thing for concrete,' Wallis said, 'so I think, my dear boy, it might not be a good thing to drop them right on the roofs of those wretched concrete affairs; they might bounce out again like corks. However, you needn't worry; just drop them down at the side in the earth and they'll bore down and blow them up from underneath.' He stuck pins in a diagram to show the vulnerable points and added disapprovingly, 'The Germans are very silly not to put twenty feet of concrete *under* these things, not on top.'

Cheshire suggested as tactfully as he could that, though he had enormous faith in his squadron. It was one thing to stick pins in a diagram and another to drop a bomb in that spot from 20,000 feet.

'Oh well,' Wallis said huffily, 'if I'd known you propose to scatter the bombs around the countryside like grass seed I'd never have bothered to design them.'

CHAPTER 14

THE UNAPPEASING OF MUNICH

On 4 April Cheshire reported to Cochrane that he was ready with the Mosquito. Cochrane rang Harris and asked permission for his whole group to operate by themselves, led by 617 to mark the target, which was to be a large aircraft factory just outside Toulouse. Harris agreed, and next night they took off.

Cheshire found his Mosquito handled delightfully. A flare force lit up the factory and Cheshire dived fast and low over it, but, not satisfied with his positioning, pulled up sharply without dropping his markers. Heavy flak opened up on him as he corkscrewed away. He would almost certainly have been hit in a Lancaster, but the shells did not even scratch the Mosquito's paint. He dived again, once more was not satisfied and pulled up in a hail of shells. The third time his markers fell in the centre of the buildings, and again he climbed steeply away, unscathed. At 10,000 feet the squadrons moved in. Munro put an 8,000-pounder right on the markers and the rest of the bombs slathered the spot.

In the morning a recce aircraft found the factory flattened and only an occasional crater in the fields beyond.

Four days later 617 continued the experiment, going alone, led by Cheshire in the Mosquito, to attack the biggest German air park and signals depot in France, at St Cyr, some two miles west of Versailles. Cheshire put his nose nearly straight down from 5,000 feet, let his markers go from 700, and they lobbed on the western corner of the target. He ordered the bombers in and soon rolling coils of smoke hid the target.

Cheshire landed as dawn was breaking and found Cochrane in the de-briefing room; he had been waiting up all night to see how the raid went and took Cheshire aside.

'That's the end of the experiment, Cheshire. I'm satisfied you can do it low in Mosquitoes now, and we're going to start thinking of the big targets. I'm getting you four new Mosquitoes. Train three or four picked pilots to use them and be quick about it.'

The four Mosquitoes arrived that afternoon, and in the next six days McCarthy, Shannon, Kearns and Fawke spent their waking hours flying them. They were to fly Mosquitoes exclusively from now on and their crews were split up. Shannon kept the tough Sumpter as his navigator. Danny Walker stayed as squadron navigation officer, Goodale went off for a well-deserved rest, and Buckley joined another crew. The lanky and good-natured Concave had won a DFC and Bar as a wireless-operator, which is not far short of a miracle, because decorations for good work by a crew usually went first to the pilot, then to the navigator and bomb aimer. Or to a gunner who shot enemy aircraft down, or an engineer who had a chance to keep battered engines going in the air. A wireless operator had little chance.

Decorations were a vexed question because there was no way of equitable distribution. Cheshire had strong views on the subject; as usual, unorthodox views but extraordinarily perceptive. Generally he divided courageous aircrews into two categories: (*a*) men with acute imagination who realized they would probably die and who forced themselves to go on, and (*b*) men who, though intelligent, could shut their minds off from imagination and carry on without acute forebodings of the future. Cheshire puts himself in the second group and, typically, regards the first group as the braver men.

'That's the highest form of courage,' he said once. 'They have a hell of a time but keep going. Usually they're not the spectacular types and they don't win flash awards, but they're the bravest.

'Actually, as far as I could, I tried to get men of the second type, like me. Not thinkers. We didn't have the hard inward struggle and weren't in danger of being deflected by imagination.'

The peculiar thing is that Cheshire *is* a thinker, a highly imaginative one, but with that queer capacity for ignoring the probabilities of personal catastrophe. I don't believe it is escapism either, because he is too coldly perceptive and introspective for that. He examines himself so closely that he would realize in a second if he were trying to delude himself. There is something deeper in it, some sort of fatalism. Most aircrew men had a mental defence mechanism that led them to believe, 'This can't happen to me,' even when they knew it *could* and probably would. Cheshire must have had some of that. Somewhat baffled, I have tried to classify him as a practical mystic, whatever that means.

He told me once: 'Decorations are not particularly a test of courage but a test of success. There aren't many awards for failure; a few, but not many, no matter what bravery was shown.'

It is not a bad comment from a man with his decorations. There is a clash in Cheshire between self-conscious ego and honesty, and the honesty is the stronger.

On 18 April Cheshire reported to Cochrane that the Mosquito crews were all ready, and that night 617 marked for 5 Group against Juvisy marshalling yards, eleven miles south of Paris.

Munro's flares lit the area beautifully; Cheshire, Fawke, Shannon and Kearns dived to 400 feet and lobbed their spot fires into the middle of the web of rails, though one bounced outside. It all went like clockwork. 617 bombed the spot fires accurately, as usual, and then the rest of 5 Group, 200 Lancasters, surged in and excelled themselves. They were used only to area bombing and not precision bombing, but this time, with the bright aiming points of the markers, they put nearly all their bombs in the target area. Some fell outside on the marker that bounced but morning reconnaissance showed the ragged end of rails in acres of erupted earth where a thousand craters overlapped each other. (It was eighteen months after the war before the yard was again in action.)

From the spot fire that bounced, Cheshire learned the importance of releasing the markers before the Mosquitoes started to flatten out of the dive, and that was another step towards perfection of the technique.

Next night they led 5 Group to the other important Paris marshalling yards, La Chappelle, a very ticklish target because these yards lay just outside the Gare du Nord and were fringed by high tenement buildings. Light and heavy flak hosed up at them, but the Mosquitoes plunged through it and laid all their spot fires except one in the centre of the rails; the one that missed fell on the tenements. The bombing that followed was as accurate as ever, but inevitably some of the bombs fell on the inaccurate marker and the whole tenement buildings were flattened. (For a year Cochrane worried about the French people who he thought must have died in them, until he discovered that the tenements had been occupied by a regiment of the Luftwaffe.)

Once again 617 lost no aircraft and the Mosquitoes did not have a single hole among them. To Cheshire and Cochrane – and to Harris too – it was further confirmation of their ideas.

Cochrane flew to Woodhall that morning after the raid, saw Cheshire privately in Cheshire's office and, as usual, wasted no words:

'Now you can have a crack at Germany. Tomorrow you're going to Brunswick . . . One Group as well as Five Group, so you'll be leading about four hundred aircraft. Pathfinders will drop flares and you'll mark with red spots.'

There was one alternative, he said. If cloud hid the target, special radar Pathfinders would mark 'blind' with green spots instead.

The first PFF flares went down over Brunswick, but Cheshire could see no target (rail yards) by their light. More flares went down seven miles north, and over that spot Kearns and Fawke saw the target and dropped their red spots 'on the button'. Cheshire gave the order to bomb, and the first bombs were just exploding when the reserve radar Pathfinders ran into cloud nearby and dropped their green spots on fields three miles away. Most of the main force, according to orders, turned for them.

Cheshire called till he was blue in the face, but the radio was jammed and only a few aircraft picked up his message. Nearly all the bombs fell on the wrong markers out in the fields.

After they landed back at Woodhall, Cochrane flew over in his Proctor and Cheshire started apologizing for the mix-up. Cochrane cut in:

'All right, Cheshire. Don't you worry about that. You did your part perfectly. We've learned a bit more from it and we'll see the trouble doesn't happen again. How do you feel about Munich?'

'As soon as you like, sir. We're ready.'

'I've been on to Air Chief Marshal Harris. If the weather is all right you're going tomorrow night, leading the whole group again. You'll go for the rail yards.'

Together they planned it, and this time it looked as though it could not miss. Bomber Command was to raid Karlsruhe half an hour before to draw the fighters. 617 was to lead 5 Group towards Switzerland as a feint; six Lancasters were to swerve south towards Milan dropping bundles of 'window' (thin strips of metal foil) to delude German radar into thinking 5 Group was heading for Italy. Just before the Group reached Munich, radar Pathfinders were to drop flares, and Cheshire and the Mosquitoes were to mark, the rest of 617 were to drop more markers from medium level with the SABS in case the early markers were blown out, and then the 200 Lancasters were to bomb.

One point worried Cheshire. 'Munich is about as far as a Mosquito can get without overload tanks,' he said. 'I've asked for them but they haven't come yet. We're not going to have enough margin for bad winds or upset timing without them.'

'Give Group a sharp nudge about them,' Cochrane said. 'I'm going down to the C-in-C with the plan.'

Cheshire phoned Group, and they said they would do all they could. He phoned them again next morning and was dismayed when they told him the tanks were in acutely short supply and other Mosquito units had priorities. It seemed that one or two people still tended to regard 617's Mosquitoes as an unorthodox and slightly reprehensible novelty.

Cheshire got hold of Pat Kelly, his navigator, and they worked out a new plan for the Mosquitoes: to fly first to Manston, in Kent, a hundred miles nearer the target, pour in all the petrol they could and fly straight to Munich across all the defences. Kelly plotted the distance, worked out their range from Manston and looked up grimly.

'If everything goes dead to time – which I've seldom seen – and if the winds are all in our favour – which I've never seen – we might just get back, but probably won't.'

Cheshire went to a high officer at base and explained respectfully that, even taking off from Manston, he doubted if the four marking Mosquitoes would get back. It was usual to have a couple of hours' petrol in reserve – at least – to allow for contingencies. With the very best conditions they might arrive back with a few minutes' petrol. Personally he had never had to fly on a raid in such conditions. Nor did he know anyone who did. What should he do?

The answer was not inspiring.

'If you can't do this marking in Mosquitoes,' the high officer said, 'you'll have to do it in a Lancaster. Whatever you do the raid has to go on.'

Cheshire said, 'Yes, sir.'

He went back and collected the four Mosquito crews. They got a preliminary Met. report: heavy cloud – possible ice cloud – over the western half of Germany; perhaps clear over Munich. At 14,000 feet the winds might be reasonably favourable. The four navigators bent over their calculations and looked up grimly.

Kelly said, 'If everything goes perfectly we might get back to Manston.' They all knew that a raid rarely went perfectly.

One of them exploded: 'Hell sir, we don't mind sticking our necks out over the defences. That's just part of the job, but we can't see any point in such a bloody unnecessary risk. What sort of fools are we supposed to be?'

Cheshire said, 'I'm sorry, but we've got to go.' There was a brief silence and one of them said, 'All right.'

The four Mosquitoes flew down to Manston and were refuelled and parked at take-off point so they would waste no fuel taxi-ing. Sitting silently over dinner with the others, Cheshire got a phone call from Cochrane.

'I'm deeply sorry about the overload tanks,' Cochrane said. 'Can you make it?'

'We'll have a go, sir. I think it will be all right.'

'I just want to let you know,' Cochrane said, 'I've had a word with the C-in-C. When you get back he's giving the whole squadron a week's leave.'

Cheshire went and told the others, and Kelly said acidly, 'Fat lot of good that's going to do us.' Cheshire had never seen them like that. They seemed almost on the verge of mutiny, not because they were too scared (they were scared all right, but so is nearly every airman before a raid), but this time it was unnecessary.

Around dusk Cheshire said, 'Well, let's get it over.' They walked out silently; it was clear over England, the sun dipping under the horizon and the sky above flaming orange. Cheshire said, 'What a glorious sunset!' From the others a sullen silence, and then Shannon, without even lifting his eyes towards the west, said, 'Damn the sunset. I'm only interested in the sunrise.'

They took off without warming up, climbed straight on course to 14,000 feet and over the North Sea ran into heavy cloud.

They were coming up to the Rhine. Or hoped they were. Cloud lay on the earth like a deep, drifting ocean, rolling up unbroken to 17,000 feet, and in the hooded glow of the cockpits each pilot found comfort in the dim shape of his navigator beside him, feeling they were outcasts sealed in a small world. Beyond the numbing thunder of engines lay nothing but blackness and they only sensed that somewhere in a few square miles of sky they were together, unseen. Cheshire broke radio silence to ask Shannon how he was finding the weather and felt his scalp prickle as a voice out of the past spoke in his earphones, 'Is that you, sir?' He recognized it instantly, through the static and the careful anonymity . . . Micky Martin.

He called back, 'Is that you, Mick?'

'Yessir.'

'Where on earth *are* you?'

'Oh, I'm around.'

'What the hell are you doing?'

'Sticking my neck out for you types.'

(Martin was a hundred miles away in another Mosquito, a night fighter, his job being to 'beat up' German night-fighter fields, encouraging the fighters to stay on the ground while the bombers plastered Karlsruhe and Munich; another part of Cochrane's planning.)

One wastes no time in radio chatter over enemy soil. Plotting stations, need few seconds for a 'fix'. Cheshire said, 'Good luck to you, Mick,' and Martin answered laconically, 'Good luck to you too. Be seeing you.'

The other Mosquitoes heard it and flew on a little more cheerfully. It seemed an omen somehow, but whether for good or bad they were not quite sure.

Apparently it was for good! The clouds thinned, winds stayed kind and exactly on zero hour they came out over Munich. No mistaking it; the flare force had arrived and massed guns were vomiting upwards. At 14,000 feet the flashes of bursts split the night and lines of red balls were marching up from the lighter guns. There must have been a hundred searchlights; pale fingers probing the dark, lighting now and then on aircraft which glinted like ants and turned to burrow into the crevices of the night. Mostly they vanished, but one was caught in a second beam, and a third. They saw it coned and held as it dived and turned and climbed, a trapped little ant. The flak hunted it; in the glare they saw the brighter flashes all round and then the ribbon of flame as the Lancaster dived again; this time the nose never lifted.

A flare abruptly glowed in the darkness, then another, a third – five . . .

one by one they lit till thirty hung flaming in the sky over the naked city, so that Cheshire recognized from the photographs the kidney-shaped park, the long lake, drilled streets of pygmy houses and the lined acres of the rail yards. He shouted over the R/T, 'Marker Leader going in' and peeled off from 10,000 feet, holding the nose down till the little Mosquito was moving into the flak faster than she had ever travelled. Sliding past 5,000 feet he lined her up on the rail yards, focused his mind on them, still aware in a curiously detached way of shells, balloon cables and searchlight dazzle, hoped he would miss them and coldly shut his mind to them. The little plane was shivering with the headlong surge and the busy fury of the engines; Cheshire barely heard the screaming noise: she was twisting in the rising speed against the trim and he was coaxing her to arrow dead straight in the dive, forcing himself to wait for the dragging seconds till he suddenly jabbed the bomb button and eased back on the stick. He felt her lifting out instantly, the mounting 'g' ramming him hard down into his seat, a phantom load dragging at his lips, his cheeks, his eyeballs and his blood, heavier and heavier, till his vision was greying out as the Mosquito flattened low over the roof-tops, curved up and climbed nimbly away. He let her lift into the darkness over the flares before he rolled her out on one wing, looked over the side and saw his markers, two red eyes glowing in the rail yards.

Shannon dived in the same way and put his markers within a hundred yards of Cheshire's. Kearns did likewise. Cheshire called the 617 Lancasters, told them to back up, and minutes later their clusters of incendiaries splashed into brightness on the rail yards.

It was the spearhead that Bomber Command had never had over Munich; even the giant flashes from the 8,000-pounders and the coils of smoke soon rolling over the rail yards did not hide the pin-points of the markers, and the bomb aimers made the most of it.

The destruction was not all on one side. Cheshire several times saw the trails of flame, like shooting stars, streaking for the ground and the explosions when they hit. It was the flak that caused most of them. Nearly all the fighters had been sent to Karlsruhe or down to Milan, and few had enough petrol to fly back to Munich.

Petrol shortage or not, Cheshire flew full throttle round and round the inner city at 1,000 feet, checking the accuracy and ready to call up with new instructions if the bombing looked like moving off the target area. The gunners below could hear him and the searchlights and flak chased him, but the Mosquito was too fleet. Once a beam held him for a second and destroyed his night vision, but he was too fast to hold low down and passed into darkness again. Light flak exploded around him; he heard the crack of the shells and the aircraft shook from near misses. A dozen lumps of shrapnel gashed it and hit the engines but hurt no vital spot.

Satisfied he could do no more he turned for home; the other Mosquitoes were already on their way. It was not a happy trip back; no flak or fighters to speak of, but Kelly doing intricate petrol calculations, thumbing the fuel gauge, plotting his track and e.t.a., and trying to look philosophical. It seemed the longest trip they had ever made, and then they came in over Manston with ten minutes' petrol on the gauges. Some gauges on low tanks are as reliable as a woman's intuition. They might have petrol for ten minutes, or fifteen minutes, or ten seconds, and were going to need at least five minutes for approach, circuit and landing.

Throttled right back in coarse pitch, Cheshire flicked his navigation lights on and dipped his nose towards the long runway, where the flarepath shone like a stolid but comforting guard of honour. Kelly said: 'What's wrong with their runway? Look at those funny lights down there.' Cheshire looked . . . puzzled. There *were* lights blinking in and out of the flarepath. 'Funny,' he said. It hit him suddenly and he shouted to Kelly, 'Turn those bloody navigation lights off. It's a Jerry fighter.'

The target, they found out later, was Gerry Fawke, just settling down on the runway. The fighter had stalked him round the circuit and gone for the kill when Fawke had his flaps, undercart and speed right down and was helpless, unable to turn sharply – unless he wanted to stall and spin it. Luck, it seemed, stayed with 617 that night. The German fighter, with a 'sitter' in front of his guns, missed completely. Fawke rolled to a stop and the flarepath flicked off. Cheshire made a careful approach, took a quick sight at the last moment with his landing lights and set his aircraft down safely. In the briefing room he found the other Mosquito crews. None had got down with more than fifteen minutes' petrol to spare (a terrifyingly small margin).

Shannon said, 'Wake me at sunrise. I want to see it.'

Back at Woodhall later in the morning, they found the 617 Lancasters all back except Cooper. No one ever found out where Cooper went down. Cochrane flew over, showing what was, for him, extravagant delight, a wide but faintly embarrassed smile, as he congratulated and thanked them. He said to Cheshire, 'You might like to look at this.' It was an aerial photograph of Munich, brought back by recce Mosquito an hour earlier. Round a couple of scars on the outskirts were circles of ink, and Cochrane tapped the spots with his finger. 'That's how it was up to yesterday afternoon after all the other raids.' He put his finger on the cratered rail yards. 'Last night,' Cochrane said. 'It seems to justify us.'

The photograph staggered even Cheshire, who knew what the bombing had been like. There must have been a hundred times more damage in that one raid than the dozen previous ones, especially as the previous damage had been on no significant target. This time they had struck an effective blow.

It proved Cheshire's contention that he could mark a heavily defended target at low level without undue risk, but the photograph also showed that one solitary marker from the high force had fallen outside the target area and drawn some of the bombs, so that a lot of houses were either gutted shells or mounds of rubble. Unfortunate though that was, it led to further improvement in the marking technique. Cochrane and Cheshire had both thought it too dangerous to rely on one marker only, since it might be obscured by smoke or hit by a bomb. Now they realized that dropping too many markers could also be risky, and thereafter they tended to cut the number of markers down to try and eliminate such accidents as the one stray marker at Munich.

Many ordinary people probably died in those crumbled houses, and the post-war domestic moralists, whose virtue increases as the memories of Nazism recede, are likely to point the accusing finger. Most will probably keep pointing it until, Heaven help us, another war starts and their virtue will become tempered by the slightly more powerful instinct of self-survival. A few will continue to point the finger with wistful idealism until one day, perhaps, morals and the practical affairs of man become compatible.

On the strength of Munich, Cochrane drove down to see Harris and asked for four extra Mosquitoes so that another of his squadrons could learn the 617 way of target marking.

Harris, who never did things by halves, said, 'Not four Mosquitoes, Cocky'; and almost before Cochrane could feel his disappointment Harris went on, 'I'm sending you a squadron of Mosquitoes from Pathfinders and two Pathfinder Lancaster squadrons. You can operate as a group by yourselves now. Get 617 to teach the new Mosquitoes low marking, and then they can mark for your group, with the two Lanc. squadrons as flare force. That'll release 617 for some special jobs.'

CHAPTER 15

EARTHQUAKE BOMB

Cochrane sent for Cheshire and took him walking in the grounds of headquarters away from listening ears.

'You'll be doing no more operations for a month,' he said, 'and then you'll be doing a very special one. You'll spend the next month training for it. I warn you now it's going to be dull training, but it may be the most important job you've done. You will have to fly more accurately and carefully than you've ever imagined.'

He would say no more, but next day a scientist, Dr Cockburn, arrived at Woodhall from London and also took Cheshire walking. They lay alone on the grass by the airfield, obviously for privacy, and the imaginative Cheshire was highly intrigued by the 'cloak and dagger' atmosphere. Cockburn said: 'I understand you can be trusted to keep your mouth shut, so I'm going to tell you something a lot of Cabinet Ministers and generals don't know yet. You know by now an invasion is coming off very soon. If the weather is right it will be in about a month, and landings will be made west of Le Havre. We want to fool the Germans we're going in somewhere else.'

Cheshire waited.

'On that night,' Cockburn went on, 'there's going to be a big convoy fourteen miles wide passing across the Channel at seven knots.'

'Sounds a pretty big invasion,' Cheshire said.

'That isn't the invasion. They'll be heading towards Cap d'Antifer, on the other side of Le Havre.'

'A diversion!'

'Yes.'

'I must say,' Cheshire said, 'it sounds a pretty big diversion. Have they got all those ships to spare?'

'No. They won't be ships. They'll be you and your boys.'

Cheshire rolled over and looked at him. 'Us!' he said blankly and then got the glimmerings of an idea. 'Dropping window?'

'That's it,' said Cockburn. 'It's going to need the most precise flying you've ever done. Can you do this . . . can you all fly in a very wide formation, invisible to each other, and do a lot of intricate manoeuvring, keeping within three seconds of all your e.t.a.'s and within twenty feet of your height?'

'My God! I don't know. Doesn't sound very possible.'

'It'll have to go on for hours and hours,' Cockburn said, 'so you'll do it in two waves. Eight aircraft for a few hours and then the second eight taking over from them.' He went on to explain the technique: lines of aircraft a set distance apart, flying precise courses at precise speeds and height, throwing out window at intervals of a precise number of seconds. The planes would fly thirty-five seconds on course, turn evenly, fly a reverse course for thirty-two seconds, a slow turn again back to the first course and start throwing out more window. They would thus start the original course again at a point slightly ahead of where the previous one started and the first of the new lot of window would drop from the aircraft at the moment that the first bundle dropped on the previous leg hit the water, so there would be no interruption of the steady blips on German radar. It would go on like that for eight hours, timed to give an effect of a large convoy several rows of ships deep moving at seven knots towards the French coast.

'We've got the theory worked out,' Cockburn said at the end. 'Are you good enough to do it?

Cheshire said, 'I think my crews are good enough for anything, but I don't think they're going to be happy doing a stooge job on invasion night.'

'It so happens,' Cockburn said, 'that there'll be no flying job more important than this on that night. You might tell them that. The fact that they may not be fired at is beside the point.'

The training never let up except for one day when the weather closed in. Otherwise there was no moment, night or day, in the next month when some 617 aircraft were not flying, particularly by night, cruising at a steady 200 mph on a steady course and height, curving in even turns to reverse courses, turning back on the stop watch, unspectacular, tedious and demanding meticulous care and skill. Understandably the crews, with the uninhibited sap of youth running in them, became restless, and Cheshire, bubbling as ever with ideas, evolved schemes to occupy them. The first was a route march that left them limp and protesting.

Next, from the Commandos, he got the idea of an escape exercise so that, if they were ever shot down and got away with their lives, they would have a few clues about getting back through hostile territory. It was a Sunday afternoon when he lined up all the crews who were not flying, took away their hats and all their money, packed them in covered vans so they could not see outside and drove them to different spots twenty miles from the airfield. He warned them that the Home Guard and police had turned out with orders to nab any airmen without hats, and promised every one who got back safely a bottle of beer. So the game started.

Some cut across the fields to walk, some stole bikes to pedal, some hitched lifts in lorries. The police and Home Guard nailed at least half of them and there were some thrilling chases across country. One man, running from the Home Guard, fell into a canal; another, caught by a policeman, entered a little too warmly into the spirit of the thing and laid the constable out with a sizzling punch. After that the police entered more warmly into the spirit of things too, and locked six of them up for the night.

Nicky Knilans and his team had the best idea; they hitched a lift to the White Horse pub, where they were known to the point of affectionate notoriety, borrowed money from the publican and drank ale till closing time, whereupon they borrowed their bus fare home. Police stopped the bus, so they jumped off the back, took to the woods and straggled home hours later to demand their prize beer.

With only monotonous training instead of ops at night the tension had relaxed and the mess became almost a home from home. Cheshire's ex-film star wife, Constance Binney, was a cheerful influence; she played the piano beautifully, and after dinner the crews clustered round and sang.

Several dogs haunted the mess, and one Scottie used to jump out from dark doorways and snap at passing ankles. It became a favourite trick among the boys to imitate the Scottie. Nicky Knilans saw McCarthy coming up the stairs one day, so he got down on his knees in a dark doorway and waited. He heard the footsteps clumping along the hall and as the legs appeared leapt out with a growl and grabbed the nearest ankle in his teeth, looked up with a grin . . . and the grin faded. McCarthy had turned off into a room and Knilans saw a strange wing commander looking down at him blankly. The wing commander shook his head and walked on, all his views on Americans fully confirmed.

They all sensed the invasion was drawing near; Cheshire had the idea that the Germans might drop paratroops on British airfields on D-day, so he persuaded Doc Watson's armament section to issue as many aircrew as they could with either a revolver, Sten gun, rifle or hand grenade. It was one of his few sad mistakes. For three days life was a precarious possession at Woodhall. First they set dinner plates up on the lawn near the mess and loosed off at them with Sten guns from the second-floor windows. That palled after a while, so they started lobbing hand grenades in the general direction of the sergeants' mess. At night Buckley became a terrible menace, keeping vigil by his bedroom window and loosing off clips from his Sten gun over the heads of late home-comers so that they had to crawl over the back lawn on their bellies.

Even Witherick, who was known to be too durable for death by any of the known methods of war, commented uncomfortably, 'Hell, the only time you're safe on this damn squadron is when you're in the air!' It became obvious that German paratroops were less of a menace than the local aircrew army, so Cheshire collected all the weapons and returned them to the armoury. Peace descended once more on the mess, to the regret of Shannon and McCarthy. Shannon and McCarthy were rarely seen apart; they drank together and dined together and it was logical, therefore, that they should act together to revive the reign of terror, climbing to the roof of squadron headquarters to drop a Véry cartridge down the adjutant's chimney. They knew the innocent Humphries had a fire in the grate.

A Véry cartridge in artful hands is like a semi-lethal firework; exploding in a confined space it resembles a small but concentrated bombing raid, providing a monstrous crash, sheets of coloured flame and clouds of choking smoke. Half the beauty of the thing is that it goes on for about fifteen seconds. They dropped it down the chimney and started laughing as the waves of sound came rocking up from below.

Unfortunately it was not Humphries' chimney, but the commanding officer's. Cheshire scuttled out, pursued by flashes and rolling fumes, ran on to the tarmac and spotted his two flight commanders hiding behind a chimney. With aristocratic dignity he said nothing but for several nights Shannon and McCarthy found themselves doing duty officer together, an irksome task which kept them out of their beds and abstemiously patrolling the station buildings.

Throwing Véry cartridges into the mess fire had long been a favourite sport, so Cheshire thought it time to issue a stern order that no firearms, cartridges or pyrotechnics of any kind be brought into the mess building.

He was woken that night by a scuttling outside his window, threw it wide open and saw a rat running across the roof. Quick as lightning he grabbed his own .38 revolver from his dressing-table and took a pot-shot that bowled the rat over and echoed through the quiet night like a small cannon. Cheshire was still leaning out of his window, revolver in hand, when the next window shot open and the head of Danny Walker poked out. 'Got the dirty rat that time,' Cheshire said triumphantly and became conscious of Walker's eyes staring coldly, focusing on the hand that held the gun. He felt his face going red and ducked inside, laying the pistol down, and heard Walker's voice next door, talking loudly to a mythical room-mate, 'But I tell you, old boy, I distinctly heard the man say that *no* one under *any* circumstances was to have a firearm inside the mess.'

On 1 June Avro experts fitted new automatic pilots in the Lancasters for the D-day operation, and Nicky Knilans at last found out why his much-cursed 'R Roger' flew like a lump of lead. They found it needed longer elevator cables than the others, inspected to find out why and discovered that the elevators had been put on upside down at the factory. Knilans had been flying it for months like that and, as Cheshire said, 'Only you and

God, Nicky, know how you stayed up.'

'Not me, sirrrr,' Knilans said in his American drawl . . . 'Only God. I didn't know.' At any rate he was very relieved, but not so much as his crew. 'R Roger' had so often frightened them.

On 5 June everyone was confined to camp, and at dusk, with guards on the doors of the briefing room, Cheshire told the crews that the invasion was about to start. The first wave of eight planes took off about 11 pm with twelve men in each aircraft, an extra pilot, extra navigator and three men to drop the bundles of window out.

They made absolutely no mistakes that night, though it would have taken an error of only four seconds in timing to make the convoy suspiciously change position on the German radar. Hour after hour they flew in the blackness over the Channel, turning on stop-watches up and down on reversed courses while the window was tossed out at four-second intervals. Around 3 am the second wave of eight aircraft took over, the trickiest part of all because they had to come in directly behind with split-second timing to carry on. They saw nothing of the invasion.

They were to break away just before dawn, before the light was good enough for the Germans to see from the shore that they had been tricked. By that time they should be within seven miles of the French coast, and that is exactly where they were. Farther north another squadron was doing a similar task with at least as much success.

They had their reward as they turned for home; the German coastal batteries opened up . . . not the flak but the big guns, aiming 12-inch shells by radar prediction at the ghost armada. German E-boats came out from Calais and Boulogne but they would have needed aerial torpedoes to do any damage.

It is history now that the Germans really thought that the main invasion was aiming at that area. (In a prison camp in the heart of Germany that day, I heard the German radio announcing two huge armadas heading towards Cap d'Antifer and Calais. It gave us great joy, but we wondered for months what had happened to those convoys.)

Inland from Boulogne and Dieppe the bulk of the German Army, which should have been hurrying to the real invasion area on the other side of Le Havre, waited . . . and waited, poised to swoop on the armadas that were not there. By the time the Germans woke up to it other squadrons had blasted bridges over the Seine between them and the invasion and the Allied troops were consolidating their landings with greater freedom from counter-attack than they had dreamed possible.

Cheshire was driving round the perimeter track with Munro that evening for no particular reason that he can remember, and just past the A Flight hardstandings they passed a huge tarpaulin-covered lorry cruising slowly along.

'What's that doing here?' Munro murmured, not very curiously, and Cheshire, his head still full of D-Day precautions, said, 'Lord knows. Let's find out.

They drove across the lorry's bows; it stopped and they climbed out of their jeep and went back to the lorry driver. 'What have you got in there?' Cheshire asked.

'Boilers for the cookhouse sir,' the driver said.

'Aren't you going the wrong way? The cookhouse is over there,' Cheshire waved a hand to the rear.

'Well I dunno, sir. They told me to deliver them over there.' The driver pointed to the far side of the field.

'The bomb dump! That's the bomb dump. Who told you that?' A suspicious edge had crept into Cheshire's voice.

'That's what they told me, sir.'

Cheshire said, 'Let's have a look at this, Les. Something funny here.' He heaved himself over the tailboard of the lorry. Another tarpaulin covered a shapeless bulk in the back; he tugged a corner clear and, unbidden, a grunt of surprise came out of him. 'My God,' he said, 'look at these!'

Lashed to the floor were two shining steel monsters. They were like sharks, slim, streamlined and with sharp noses. 'Bombs,' Cheshire said, almost in awe. 'Wallis's "tallboys".'

They followed the lorry to the bomb dump and were staggered to find the dump nearly full of 'tallboys', snugged down under tarpaulins. An armament officer said apologetically, 'They've been coming in at night time for the past week, sir. I was told to keep quiet about them.'

Cheshire tore back to his office, got Cochrane at Group on the secret scrambler phone and told him he had just been inspecting 'the new boilers for the cookhouse in the bomb dump.' He heard what sounded like the ghost of muted amusement in Cochrane's voice: 'Just see they're safely in storage, Cheshire. You'll be using them soon.'

The call came without warning forty-eight hours later. Intelligence had reported a German panzer division moving up from Bordeaux by rail to attack the invasion. The trains would have to pass through the Saumur Tunnel, near the Loire, over a hundred miles inland, and in the late afternoon Harris suggested to Cochrane that they might have a chance of blocking the tunnel before the train reached it. They would have to move fast; it would be nightfall before bombers could reach the spot, and a tunnel on a dark night would be an elusive pin-point of a target. Only one squadron could do it; that was obvious. And probably only one type of bomb!

Cheshire got the order about 5 pm to take off as soon as they could, and there was a mad rush to collect everyone (Shannon and Munro, for instance, were playing cricket at Metheringham), trolley the 'tallboys' out of the dump and winch them up into the bomb bays. They were airborne soon after dusk, and shortly after midnight Cheshire, in his Mosquito, dropped flares by a bend of the river and saw where the rails vanished into the tunnel that led under the Saumur hill.

He dived-bombed from 3,000 feet, aimed his red spots point blank, and as he pulled up from about a hundred feet saw them lying beautifully in the tunnel mouth. Ninety seconds later the Lancasters were steady on their bombing runs, and a couple of minutes later the first earthquake bombs ever dropped on business were streaking down.

Ten thousand feet above, the crews felt disappointed. The 'tallboys' did not make a splash of brilliant light like the blockbusters but showed only momentary red pin-points as they speared into the earth and exploded nearly a hundred feet deep. The little flashes they made were all round the markers but the crews turned for home with a feeling of anti-climax, and it was not till the recce Mosquito landed next morning with photographs that the impact of what they had done hit them. With one exception the fantastic craters were round the tunnel mouth, two of them in a line along the rails as though giant bites a hundred feet across and seventy feet deep had been torn out of the track bed.

But what really staggered everyone was the bomb that had fallen on the hill 60 yards from the tunnel mouth. No one ever found out whose bomb it was, which is a pity, because some bomb aimer would have received an instant decoration (though the credit should really go to Barnes Wallis). The hill rose steeply from the tunnel mouth, and under the spot where this bomb hit lay 70 feet of solid earth and chalk down to the tunnel. The bomb had bored straight through it into the tunnel itself and exploded there. Something like 10,000 tons of earth and chalk were blown sky-high and the mountain collapsed into the tunnel. It was one of the most startling direct hits of all time.

The panzer division did not get through. It was several days before dribs and drabs of them started to reach the invasion front on other transport, but by then it was too late for the decisive counter-attack they were supposed to have made. The morning after the raid the Germans collected all the excavation gear in the district and slaved for weeks clearing the tunnel, filling in the craters and laying new rails. They just had it nicely finished when the Allies broke out of their bridgehead and took it over. (They found then that only one 'tallboy' had fallen outside the target area . . . it had exploded among a group of very old Frenchmen and blown them to smithereens, but no one else was upset, because they had been there a long time, lying several feet deep in a cemetery.)

The morning after the Saumur raid a high officer from Bomber

Command burst into Sir Wilfred Freeman's office waving a recce photograph of the smashed tunnel.

'My God,' he yelled, 'why haven't we been able to use this incredible thing before? How many more of them have we got?'

'None for you, I'm afraid,' said a Vicker's executive who happened to be in the room, and the high officer looked at him open-mouthed.

'What'd you mean?'

'Well, we've got some more, but they're all ours. None for you.'

'What *are* you talking about?'

'Your boys have never given us a Requirement Order for them, so we had to make them on spec. They all belong to us.'

'I see,' said the High Bomber Officer. 'We'll fix this Requirement Order business right away.' He crossed to the desk, picked up the phone and the Requirement Order was delivered that afternon.

In the nights that followed the invasion, German E-boats sneaking out of Le Havre caused death and destruction among the convoys ferrying men and guns over to Normandy. The darkness that covered the convoys from the Luftwaffe also hid the speeding E-boats that weaved among the landing craft, loosed their torpedoes and vanished. By day they sheltered in the concrete pens at Le Havre, and around dusk they slid out of the pens and gathered in the harbour, preparing for the night's forays. Cochrane thought that, if the 'tallboys' could make an earthquake on land, they might just as easily make a tidal wave in water. Wallis promised him they would, and so as soon as the weather cleared, on 14 June, 617 flew over at dusk to Le Havre on the second 'tallboy' raid. Some 400 more Lancasters of 1 and 5 Groups followed them, loaded up with 1,000-lb bombs.

Cheshire, in his Mosquito, whipped round the harbour area at 3,000 feet, saw the dozens of E-boats lined up, and as he peeled off in a dive-bombing attack the flak came up in streams. He'd never seen flak like it. In the dusk it looked like green and red bubbles rising in shaken soda-water. The air was full of rushing tracer and he knew that that was not even the half of it . . . only a quarter. One in four of the light flak shells were tracer; the rest were rushing with them, but not visible. Two miles outside the harbour the other Mosquitoes saw him diving into the beaded curtain of red and green and thought he had no chance. At about 700 feet (as he let his markers go) they saw the nose start to come up. The little Mosquito flattened low over the water, holed half a dozen times already, and Cheshire held her straight, heading out to sea, relying on speed alone to beat the guns. A minute later he was back to 3,000 feet and out of range. On the quay, by the lines of E-boats, the red markers were winking clearly.

Shannon, deputy marker, who had seen the flak like a wall of flame, called up: 'Hello, Leader, shall I go in and back up?'

Sitting beside and slightly behind him, Sumpter picked a heavy torch out of its stowage, held it over Shannon's head and muttered, 'God, David, if he says yes, I'll brain you! We can die more peacefully out here.'

A few seconds dragged while Cheshire looked again at his markers and called back, 'No, David; they'll do,' and ordered the Lancasters circling a few miles away, at 12,000 feet, to head in. Fifteen 'tallboys' dropped almost together into the water by the pens and then the 400 other Lancasters moved in and the harbour vanished under smoke.

When the recce photographs came back in the morning even Wallis was staggered. Not one E-boat was left afloat in Le Havre. Two were still visible, thrown bodily up on to the quay, and the rest were swallowed in the maelstrom of water torn apart by the 'tallboys' and then by the smaller bombs. (For a time they thought that some may have slunk out of the harbour that night to a safer port, but weeks after, when the British took Le Havre, they found that none had escaped.) The crashing water had even smashed through the doors of the pens and destroyed any chance of shelter in them. In fact, three of the 'tallboys' had been direct hits on the pens, bored through the concrete and wrecked the neat little quays inside.

Next night the squadron went to repeat the dose at Boulogne, also a troublesome E-boat base. Thick cloud hung over the port with heavy flak bursting through it. Cheshire marked alone (his Mosquito newly patched from last night's damage), but the crews above found it nearly impossible to draw a bead on them. About ten were able to drop their 'tallboys' without being able to see results, and the remaining ten brought their bombs back. (Cochrane had made a strict order that no 'tallboys' were to be wasted. Crews were never to jettison them except in extreme emergency. If they could not see their target reasonably clearly they must bring their 'tallboys' back. Landing an aircraft with a 6-ton bomb on board is not as difficult as it sounds.)

We know now that in these two raids on Le Havre and Boulogne 133 small ships (mostly E-boats) were sunk. As Harris said the morning after Boulogne in his message of thanks to Cheshire and his squadron, 'If the Navy had done what you have done it would have been a major naval victory.'

That was the morning the V1 'buzz-bombs' started to fall on London. The V2 rockets would follow soon. . . . Intelligence was sure of that.

CHAPTER 16

SMASHING THE SECRET WEAPON

Cheshire had only tumbled into bed at 5 am after the Boulogne raid, and was dragged out of sleep at 9 am to find his batman tugging at his shoulder.
'Phone, sir.'
He took up the phone and heard the Base Intelligence Officer's voice: 'Can you please come over to the ops. room right away. It's urgent, sir.'
He was there in ten minutes, and the intelligence officer greeted him with a few words that shook the last of the tiredness out of him: 'The secret weapon has started, sir. They're landing missiles on London and the invasion ports. Don't know how serious it is yet, but you're to stand by to take off as soon as the weather clears. This is your target,' he passed over an aerial photograph, an enlargement that showed an enormous square concrete building. 'We don't know how thick the concrete is,' the intelligence officer was saying, 'but as far as we can gather from agents over there it might be up to twenty feet thick . . . roof as well as the walls. It's near a place called Watten, just behind the Pas de Calais.'
Air Commodore Sharp, the base commander, bustled in. 'You know about these from the AOC,' he said. 'I gather the rest of Bomber Command is cracking at the mobile sites, but they think the worst trouble will come from these four blockhouses, and your "tallboys" are the only things with a hope of touching them. You'll have to go in daylight to see your aiming points properly and mark them with smoke bombs. We'll give you fighter cover.'
Cochrane had a word with him over the phone a little later, brief and to the point: 'We've got to knock these out somehow, and we'll have to go on until we do. Whitehall is all set for the evacuation of London and we don't know yet whether these things might wreck the invasion. You'll have to work hard.'
To lay on the raid, plan it, brief the crew, bomb and fuel the aircraft took at least two hours. This time it was more difficult, because the 'tallboys' needed special handling, but they did it inside two hours that morning. The crews were briefed and they all went down to the flights, pulled on their flying kit and waited. Over the Pas de Calais a sheet of ten-tenths stratus stretched for miles at 2,000 feet, making it impossible to bomb. They could not have seen any aiming point from above, and they would have to bomb from at least 15,000 feet for penetration. The idea was to get near misses as much as direct hits. A direct hit might not pierce the concrete

roof, but near misses would bore into the earth by the foundations and shake the structure with earthquakes. Wallis thought that a near miss up to 40 yards away would do more damage than a direct hit. The concrete monster at Watten was not the great primary source of power that Wallis had at first visualised for his earthquake bomb, but, fortuitously, it was an even more important target.

The crews stood by all day at the flights. Lorries brought food and coffee from the mess for them, and over the radio they heard the grim reports of the flying bombs falling on London. But the cloud stayed over the Pas de Calais, over Watten and the other concrete rocket sites.

At eleven o'clock they were released but no sooner had they climbed into bed than they were called up again, pulled on their clothes and rushed down to the flights. Before they had their kit on the raid was cancelled once more. Back to bed . . . and at 4 am called out again. A cup of tea and down to the flights and then it was cancelled again. They went back to bed and were called at 7 am. Down to the flights once more. Met. thought the cloud might be clearing.

It did not clear but the crews stood by all day, lying on the grass by the tarmac waiting for the call, but the call never came. It went on for three days like that till bed was only a memory. They lived down on the flights while the low cloud lingered over France and the buzz-bombs kept falling, ate cold food brought from the mess and tried to sleep curled up in blankets on the floors.

The eighteen Lancasters bombed-up on the hardstandings brought another complication. Under the load of petrol and bombs the undercarriages began to sink. The bombs would have to come off, at least temporarily. But it would take hours to bomb up again and they could not afford the time if the weather cleared briefly. Cheshire had them de-bombed on a rota system so that at any one time only two or three aircraft were without bombs. As soon as their undercarts had been relieved they winched the bombs up into them again and gave temporary relief to other aircraft.

On the morning of the third day, exhausted, they were stood down and went off to bed, and in the early afternoon the clouds over France rolled away. From Group came the instant call ordering a 'time on target' which gave them a bare ninety minutes to get airborne again.

No one at Woodhall will easily forget that hour and a half of mad rush. In the middle of it Cheshire was in the ops. room settling the hundred and one final details inseparable from a raid – time and place of fighter rendezvous, bomber marshalling points, codes and so on – when a young pilot officer rushed in and said that a headquarters group captain wanted to see him immediately outside. 'Ask him if he'll please excuse me just now. I'm terribly busy,' Cheshire said. The P/O rushed outside and was back again in a few seconds. 'He says he's sorry, sir, but it's most important. You *must* come.'

Cheshire groaned, 'What the hell's happened now?' and dashed out, thinking it was another cancellation.

The group captain was waiting on the grass verge. He had just arrived and had not heard about the raid. Cheshire saluted and the group captain looked a little severely at him. 'Do you realize, Cheshire, that your squadron is last in the Group war savings scheme?' he said. 'I'm very concerned and you've got to do something about it immediately.'

Cheshire looked blankly at him.

'Yes, sir, I'll do something right away,' saluted and was running back to the ops. room before the group captain could stop him. By some sort of miracle the eighteen Lancasters, headed by two Mosquitoes, were climbing away from Woodhall on the scheduled minute.

Cheshire flew over Calais at 8,000 feet and searched the area for several minutes before he was able to pin-point the camouflaged mass of concrete in the ground haze. The earth for a mile around was torn up by the fruitless bombs of other raids, so that nothing stood out clearly. As he flew over it seventy guns opened up and black puffs stained the air all round him. He felt reluctantly that there was only one thing to do: ten miles away he peeled off, held the nose steeply down and came in straight and fast on high power, so the engines were screaming in his ears and the plane shaking like a live thing. He let his smoke bombs go at 2,000 feet (as it was daylight the smoke would show more clearly than red flares), pulled steeply out of the hail of fire, marvellously untouched, looked back and saw no sign of smoke. The markers had failed to ignite.

Shannon dived the other Mosquito in the same way, and as he pulled up smoke puffed on the ground near the target. In the haze it seemed near enough, and there were no markers left anyway, so Cheshire called the Lancasters and saw them wheel in at 18,000 feet, open bomb doors and track stolidly through the flak. Fascinated, he saw the 'tallboys' for the first time falling in daylight, the sun glinting off them as they streaked down, picking up speed till they were moving faster than sound, and then they vanished in a wisp of dust at the moment of impact. They had eleven-second delayed fuses and the seconds dragged till the ground burst in the shadow of the concrete and tens of thousands of tons of earth reared up in a climbing mushroom. Cheshire gaped, and beside him, dumbfounded, Kelly muttered, 'God help the Jerries!' The target was hidden.

Recce photos later showed the bombs had circled Shannon's smoke markers, but also showed the markers had been about 70 yards wide. Some of the 'tallboys' had fallen some 50 yards from the concrete target and, in the hopes that they had done the job, Cochrane sent 617 next day to

Wizernes, where a huge concrete dome, 20 feet thick, lay on the edge of a chalk quarry, protecting rocket stores and launching tunnels that led out of the face of the quarry, pointing towards London.

The squadron reached the spot but found it hidden under cloud and brought their 'tallboys' back. Cheshire landed with a new idea forming in his mind. If a Mosquito was better for marking than a Lancaster, then an even smaller and faster aircraft should be better still. He took his idea to Sharp, and the base commander said: 'The American fighters have got the range you want. How about a Mustang or a P.38?' Cheshire said he thought that either would be ideal, and Sharp promised to try and get one through Air Ministry. He tried for the next two days but Air Ministry did not seem to be able to help, so Sharp said he would fly over to an American base himself and try 'off his own bat'. He had worked with the Americans before and appreciated their methods of direct attack.

Meantime Cheshire took 617 to Wizernes again but once more the cloud hid it. On the 24th they tried again and this time located the camouflaged dome dimly in the ground haze. Cheshire dived through the brisk flak but his smoke bombs 'hung-up', so Fawke dived and laid his markers on the edge of the dome and the bombs fell spectacularly round the markers. Three of them exploded next to the tunnels in the side of the quarry, one sliced deep under the edge of the dome, and Dicky Willsher, who had just had his twentieth birthday, sent one right into the mouth of one of the tunnels. The face of the quarry seemed to burst open.

The flak got Edward's plane on the run-up. A shell exploded in the port wing and the tanks caught fire. The others saw the Lancaster lose height slowly for a few seconds, then the nose dropped into a steep dive and she went over on her back. Two parachutes came out before she hit and the 'tallboy' blew up. It was the first crew the squadron had lost for several weeks. Several men had been wounded in the air and a few aircraft written off, but for some weeks death had taken a holiday, the longest holiday it ever took in the squadron.

Though they were on daylight raids now the squadron did not fly close shoulder-to-shoulder formation as the Americans did. The SABS was one reason; having to fly undeviatingly for ten miles on the run-up would make a close formation a sitting target for the flak. On the run-ups they flew what Cheshire called a 'gaggle' – lines of five aircraft abreast, each 200 yards apart and each rank 300 yards behind the one ahead. Every plane flew at a different height as well, so that, while they were a most dispersed target for the flak, they could converge on the target and bomb almost together.

That had another advantage. Smoke from the first bombs had often obscured the target from later bomb aimers, but with the gaggle formation the last bombs were on the way down before the first bombs hit.

When he landed back at Woodhall, Cheshire found a Mustang waiting. Sharp's American friends had promptly said, 'Sure,' and an American pilot had flown one over. The pilot explained the cockpit to Cheshire, bade him a cheerful farewell and left him inspecting his new toy. It was only then he began to realize fully what he had taken on. He had never flown an American aircraft before; in fact, had not flown a single-engined aircraft since his early training days five years before. He had never flown a single-engined fighter at all, nor had he had to do his own navigation for years. The ground crews had their problems too. For a long time they could not even find where to fill the petrol tanks.

Cheshire decided that before he took it for a practice flip he would try and learn a little more about it, but those prudent hopes crashed in the morning when Cochrane ordered the squadron off for the Siracourt rocket site. They found then that the smoke markers would not fit in the racks under the Mustang's wings, and the armourers worked like furies rigging a makeshift wire contraption to hold the markers on. One of the navigators helped Cheshire work out his courses, and he wrote them on a piece of paper and strapped it to his knee. He took off in the Mustang half an hour early to get the feel of it, but did not try any practice landings; there was too much chance of breaking it on his first landing, and if he was going to do that he preferred it to be after the raid had been done.

It is unlikely that a pilot has ever before or since done an operation – particularly such a specialist one – on his first flight in a new type of plane. The change in his case from multi-engined to single-engined fighter makes the feat all the more remarkable. It bristled with difficulties. His timing had to be within thirty seconds over the target to co-ordinate with the bombers, and the Mustang cruised about 90 mph faster than the Lancasters. He could not very well work out changes of wind as well as map-read and fly. He had to be his own navigator, bomb aimer, gunner and wireless operator as well as learn to fly a new type well enough in an hour to be able to dive-bomb through thick flak.

From the start the Mustang delighted him and inside half an hour he felt he had the 'feel' of it. She was lighter than the Mosquito and there was no comparison at all with a Lancaster. From 7,000 feet he spotted the concrete slab that protected the underground Siracourt rocket dump, and when the bombers reached marshalling point he dived to 500 feet, revelling in the way the Mustang picked up speed, and put his smoke bombs within a few feet of the concrete. Someone put a 'tallboy' through the middle of the slab, and it pierced 16 feet of ferro-concrete before it exploded. Another hit the western wall and blew it in, and another erupted deep under the rim of the slab.

Night had fallen when they got back from Siracourt, and Cheshire's first

Mustang landing had to be a night landing, which makes it about twice as difficult. He remembers little about it (in the same way that a man who bales out never remembers pulling the rip-cord) except that suddenly the little fighter was rolling smoothly on the runway, to his mild surprise and relief.

(If 617's bombing seems monotonously 'dead-eye' remember that they dropped them at nearly 200 mph, 18,000 feet up and several miles back from the little squares of concrete that merged with the earth and were usually unseen by the bomb aimer. From that height and distance even the white square on a bombing range looks the size of a pin-head. Cheshire's smoke-bombs were as good an aiming point as possible, but usually the ground haze veiled the smoke. No other squadron could have done it.)

Grey cloud still hung over the Pas de Calais; it was forming over the North Sea and blowing over the land, and 617 stood by at dawn every day waiting for it to lift while the buzz-bombs fell on London. To the south the invasion was locked in the bridgehead, and even if they broke out the Seine still barred the way to the rocket sites. In London the nation's leaders (though not the unaware people) waited anxiously in case the mystery sites should start up. They guessed they must be nearly ready.

Several times the crews ran to the aircraft, and once actually took off, but the cancellation came instantly. The raids a squadron did never reflected the ordeal behind them, the nerve-fraying sequence of briefing every morning about 5 am, followed by postponement, by stand-by, ready to take off when the order came, never knowing if one would still be alive by nightfall. And then the dusk would come, bringing release till 5 o'clock the next morning. It went on like that day after day, not only at this time but all through the war for every squadron. Often they took off and battled through the flak and fighters only to find the target lost under cloud, so that they had to bring their bombs back, to be ready at dawn next day.

Cheshire had done ninety-eight raids now. At the ruling casualty rate he was living strictly on borrowed time. Statistically he should have been killed for certain four times. Arthur Pollen, the Woodhall intelligence officer, asked him how he felt about it, and Cheshire answered, 'You don't feel the strain, Arthur. You keep on going more or less automatically and don't worry.' Pollen noticed as he was talking that Cheshire's right eye was twitching, but Cheshire was not aware of it.

At last, on 4 July, the weather cleared. Not a moment too soon. London was taking a beating. As the clouds rolled away over France 617 took off to hit back, target this time being the big store of rockets and buzz-bombs hidden in a cave at Creil, near Paris. It ran deep under a hill – at least 25 feet of chalk and clay over it – and the idea was both to collapse it and seal it up. Fawke went ahead in a Mosquito to get weather and wind information in advance. Cheshire flew his now beloved Mustang, and seventeen Lancasters carried the 'tallboys'.

Cheshire dived to 200 feet and aimed his markers so accurately that Fawke did not have to back up. Several 'tallboys' then smashed through the cave roof with great ease; others collapsed the entrance and wrecked the railway that brought the rockets into the cave.

Next afternoon to Mimoyecques, where the Germans were sinking the fantastic gun barrels 500 feet into the ground to fire 600 tons of explosive a day on London. War Cabinet still did not know this; they only knew it was one of Hitler's secret-weapon sites. From above it was nearly invisible, a 30 by 20 yards square of camouflaged concrete shielding the gun tunnels beneath.

An hour before dusk Cheshire, in the Mustang, found the spot in the chalk hills behind Calais, dived and lobbed his markers on it. When the 'tallboys' came down he saw one direct hit, and four were 'very near misses', which were probably more effective.

A message summoning him to Cochrane met him when he landed and he drove straight over to Group. Cochrane said when he walked in: 'I've been looking at the records and I see you've done a hundred trips now. That's enough; it's time you had a rest. I've got hold of Tait to take over.' Cheshire opened his mouth to argue and Cochrane said, 'It's no use arguing. . . . Sorry, but there it is. A hundred is a good number to stop at.' He went on and thanked him, quietly and with no flowery nonsense, and dropped another bombshell: 'Shannon, Munro and McCarthy will come off too. They've been going continuously for about two years and it's time they had a rest as well.'

There were, as Cheshire expected, protests from Shannon, Munro and McCarthy, but from that moment they were changed men, gayer, but in a less violent way, and only then he realized that the strain had been telling on his three durable flight commanders. Munro, known so long as 'Happy' because he never smiled, became like a small boy, running round the mess cracking puns and laughing at anything.

They had earned a rest; all of them had DSOs, DFCs and Bars. The squadron gave them a send-off at which one or two (prodded perhaps by alcohol) were near tears, but before the hangovers had subsided Wing Commander Willie Tait had arrived to take over. He put Fawke up to flight commander and brought two veteran pilots, Cockshott and Iveson, as his other lieutenants. Tait was a Welshman, belonging to no recognizable type but with a unique Celtic streak of his own. Smoothly brown-skinned and slim, with straight black hair, he had his own brand of introspection and dry wit. He had a habit sometimes, when he was with you, of saying nothing at all for long stretches of time, standing with his mouth primly pursed, a half can of beer held in extraordinary fashion under his armpit, his arm curled round and the glass caught between his hand and wrist. If he opened his mouth at all it was to stick a large pipe in it and hold it tightly to his mouth with his whole hand clenched over the stem, as though he were trying to hold thoughts inside himself. He was twenty-six, had two DSOs and a DFC.

The cloud was back over France, so that for ten days there was no bombing; a lucky reprieve for the rocket sites, but at least it gave the squadron a chance to settle down under the new leaders, and Tait a chance to learn the marking technique in the Mustang.

On 17 July Met. reported the clouds rolling away, and a couple of hours later 617 was on the way to Wizernes. For this, his first marking effort, Tait flew one of the Mosquitoes with Danny Walker as navigator. Thick haze lay over the ground and they circled a long time in the flak before they could faintly pick up the great blockhouse merging with the torn earth. Tait dived from 7,000 to 500 feet before he let his smoke marker go accurately, and Fawke backed up. A few minutes later both Knights and Kearns got direct hits with 'tallboys', and several more 'tallboys' sent up awe-inspiring eruptions 40 to 50 yards away, more or less where Wallis preferred them.

More days of waiting for the weather, and on the 20th they went back to Wizernes. Tait, flying the Mustang for the first time on business, found wisps of broken cloud drifting over the area and thick haze on the ground. A lot of flak was coming up, he dived through it and lobbed his smoke markers, pulled steeply up to 4,000 feet, looked down and could only just see the smoke drifts. Obviously the bombers, miles back at 18,000 feet, would never see it, and so he did an unheard-of-thing . . . called up the bombers and said, 'Try and aim at me,' then dived into the bursting flak directly over the blockhouse and circled it at 1,000 feet, hoping the glinting of his wings would draw the eyes of the bomb aimers to the spot.

The Mustang shook in the shell blasts, and little holes were suddenly appearing in the wings and fuselage as machine-gun bullets and shrapnel punched through. Two bullets went through the petrol tank (which was self-sealing) and just missed the glycol coolant tank (which was not), and even then the bomb aimers did not see him.

They called up on their bombing runs and said they could not identify a thing, and Tait at last swung away out of the flak, an extremely lucky young man to be still airborne and personally unpunctured. The squadron turned and brought their 'tallboys' back home.

They waited five more days for the cloud to clear and on the 25th went to Watten, Tait again in the Mustang. Murderous flak came spitting up all round the blockhouse, but this time, for the first time in weeks, there was neither haze nor cloud and in the crystal-clear air the target stood out so clearly that the bomb aimers reported they could see it from miles back, and Tait did not have to mark.

They had half-hour delay fuses on the 'tallboys' that day, so they saw no explosions, but as the bombs sliced into the earth puffs of dust shot into the air from the shadow of the blockhouse.

Fawke lingered half an hour near the spot with a camera in his Mosquito and brought back beautiful photographs of the explosions . . . five direct hits and half a dozen very-*very* near misses. The squadron did not escape scot-free. Three aircraft were badly hit by flak, one gunner died, his throat cut by flak, and one aircraft had to jettison its 'tallboy' to stay in the air. Harris sent them special congratulations.

Again they waited for the weather and on 31 July flew to deal with a flying-bomb storage dump in a railway tunnel near Rilly La Montagne. Once more the air was crystal clear, no marking was needed and they caved in each entrance to the tunnel with their uncanny accuracy. They lost one of their most distinguished crews this day. F/Lt Jock Reid had won a VC on a previous tour; a quiet young man, bashful about the red ribbon under his wings. Flak got his Lancaster as they were driving up to the target and only two parachutes came out.

Next day they tried to go back to Siracourt but once more the cloud beat them and they brought their bombs back. Actually it did not matter. The battle of the rocket sites was over. The liberating armies burst out and reached the Pas de Calais area and, as it happened, there was nothing for them to do about the rocket sites except stare in wonder. 617 had destroyed them.

At Watten they found that 'tallboys' had smashed the roof and wrecked the building inside so badly that the Germans had abandoned it.

The great rocket assembly and launching site at Wizernes was reduced to rubble. The 10,000-ton dome on top was knocked off its foundations, the launching tunnels below had caved in, and so had most of the maze of galleries where men were to have lived and stored and fired their rockets.

At Creil they found that the deep limestone caves which were to have protected their rockets and buzz-bombs had collapsed for hundreds of yards and buried them instead. Much the same at Rilly La Montagne.

A 'tallboy' had gone right through the 16-ft concrete roof at Siracourt site, exploded beneath it and wrecked it. Near misses had shaken two of the four sides of the lower walls to pieces. The Germans had stopped work on the site to dig deep air-raid trenches and then abandoned the lot.

Most spectacular was the wreckage at Mimoyecques, where the fabulous guns of V3 were to have fired on London. One 'tallboy' had ripped a corner off the 20-foot thick concrete roof and completely blocked the left-hand gun shaft. A near miss had collapsed the right-hand shaft and shaken the remaining shaft out of plumb. Five hundred feet down when the bombers came, 300 workers had been sheltering in what they must have thought was complete safety. They are still there, entombed.

Hitler had squandered men and materials to shield his 'impregnable' rocket sites, only to find, too late, that for all the fabulous concrete top his *Festung Europa* had no roof . . . all because a stubborn, white-haired old scientist in 1939 would not believe that the world's experts were right about bombing.

When the first cannon-ball smashed a breach in a castle wall it was not only the stonework that fell; it also burst the bulwarks of the powerful isolationist barons and was the beginning of the end of the feudal system. And when the first 'tallboy' fell on Watten it not only pierced the shield of the secret weapons, but stripped another layer of protection from Germany. Hitler could not, or would not, believe it and tried to build more protection on top. He sent nearly 10,000 workmen to the great U-boat pens at Hamburg, Bremen, Ijmuiden and Bergen to pile more concrete on top. They already had ferro-concrete roofs 16 feet thick, but the Germans wanted to increase this up to 30 feet. After the waste of work on the rocket sites it was an enormous diversion of his war effort.

It was logical that Churchill, Freeman and Harris should send Wallis over to France to see what his 'tallboys' had done, with an eye to what they might do in the future. After Churchill, Wallis was probably the first man to go over there as a civilian. He refused to wear uniform. 'What's the use of uniform to an old man with white hair like me?' he said. 'Good heavens, I couldn't even stand being tortured!' So he went in a dirty old raincoat and grey slacks, and an American major wanted to arrest him in France as a spy.

The Calais area had not yet been properly cleared, but Wallis was so fascinated by the great blockhouses and the damage that he pottered about abstractedly, oblivious of the guns going off all round. When he flew home they took him to Harris's office in the trees near High Wycombe, and Harris silently showed him photographs of the workmen swarming over the U-boat pens at Hamburg, Bremen and Ijmuiden. They were enormous pens, some of them 300 feet square and 70 feet high. It was obvious that they were being further strengthened. Agents' reports confirmed this.

'Looks as though we're going to have some more substantial targets,' Harris said. 'After what you've seen of the rocket sites, do you think a "tallboy" could cope with these?'

'I think one or two "tallboys" broke up on the concrete,' Wallis said. 'If we're going to have something still bigger to deal with, I think we should throw something bigger at them.' He added artlessly, 'Something like a ten-tonner. I've been suggesting a ten-tonner for some time now, and I believe the Lancaster has developed enough to carry it into Germany.'

Harris looked at him. He said after a while, 'Mr Wallis, I said once you could sell me a pink elephant. I think perhaps this time you might at last sell your ten-tonner.'

That was a *very* satisfying day in Wallis's life.

CHAPTER 17

VICTORIA CROSS

617 was a delighted squadron; not because of the coming 10-ton bomb (they were not told about that yet) but because Leonard Cheshire had just been awarded the VC. It was the second VC to the credit of the newest squadron in the RAF, and one of the most remarkable VCs ever awarded.

The citation specified no one act of superb gallantry but listed some of the things he had done: the time a shell had burst inside his aircraft and he had continued on to the target, his volunteering for a second tour as soon as he had finished his first, his third tour, and then his insistence on dropping rank to do a fourth in a 'suicide squadron'. There was a piece on his part in the Munich raid, when he cruised through the flak over the roof-tops, and it noted that he had done a hundred raids.

A VC is often won in a moment of exalted heroism, but there can be no tougher way of winning it than by four years of persistent bravery. It was Cochrane who put Cheshire up for the medal. Higher commanders sometimes lose touch with the men under them, but the brusque Cochrane, who was always round the Group, never did that, and his crews sensed it. He won their utter faith not by geniality but by hard work and clear thinking to avoid tactical blunders that would have wasted their lives.

The perceptive Cheshire probably saw that more clearly than anyone. I quoted a letter of Cheshire's earlier paying tribute to Micky Martin. There is another part of the letter that reads: 'In tracing the evolution of our low-level bombing technique don't under-estimate the contribution of Cochrane. He is the only senior officer with a really clear, unbiased brain that I have met. He followed our course with great attention to detail, was remarkably quick to grasp the fundamentals and was seldom hoodwinked. If I ever asked for anything and he refused, he always gave me clearly his reasons.

'If we ever needed anything we usually got it immediately. I used to think that if I asked him for an elephant I'd get it by return of post. As a matter of fact I once *did* ask him for an elephant because the tractors kept getting bogged in the mud, but the mud dried up and he said we didn't need the elephant then.

'One day I asked him for two Lancasters fitted with nitrogen tanks (a guard against fire) for the leading high-level crews. He hadn't a hope on earth of getting them officially because they were all booked up months in advance by the Pathfinders, who, though they didn't need them as badly as we did, had the highest priority of all. Cochrane merely called up the makers, asked them to let us have the first two that came off the line without letting anyone know, and we got them three days later.

'It was much the same with everything else, and we should have been lost without someone as strong and critical as Cochrane behind us. He is, of course, a strict disciplinarian, ruthless in dealing with inefficiency, and there is no doubt that he was the key figure behind all that 617 achieved.'

617 had lost its priority targets now and Cochrane was busy finding new ones of sufficient importance and diminutiveness to merit the 'tallboys' and 617's specialist attention. Tait had been completely accepted by the squadron. An *élite* corps, they had regarded him a little aloofly (after Cheshire and Martin) until he had gone down to circle Wizernes in his Mustang as a personal aiming point for the bombs as well as the flak; then they went so far as to chide him with fond concern for sticking his neck out so imprudently. Tait, on the other hand, had completely accepted 617, finding in it a rare spirit he had not seen since the first year of the war, before the full impact of it had hit the squadrons. In this fifth year of the war there were few volunteers for rugged ventures. 617 was different. They were all volunteers liable for any dangerous but profitable task.

They bombed a bridge at Etaples with 1,000-pounders (the rocket sites had drawn heavily on 'tallboy' supplies), but though they hit the bridge the bombs did little damage to it.

Cut-off German garrisons were fiercely defending the French Atlantic ports of Brest, Lorient and La Pallice, while the Kriegsmarine used the ports as U-boat bases. Cochrane switched 617 on to the massive concrete U-boat pens in those ports, and on 5 June the squadrons bombed the Brest pens in daylight, battling through the heaviest flak they had met for some time to score six direct 'tallboy' hits before smoke covered the target.

On the bomb run a salvo of three flak shells slammed into Cheney's Lancaster. The last one exploded in the bomb bay, badly wounded the navigator and wireless operator, and fire broke out in the starboard outer engine. Cheney feathered, pulled the extinguisher and got the aircraft back under control. He asked for a new course, and the navigator, unable to speak, crawled up and pointed out the figures in his log book. Both wounded had lost their oxygen masks, and Cheney pushed the nose down to lose height so they could breathe, and then fire broke out all along the starboard wing. The aircraft was riddled with holes and the end was near. Cheney shouted, 'Bale out!' and held the plane steady while all the crew except himself and the wireless operator got out.

The wireless operator could not move and Cheney tried to trim the aircraft in a slow climb while he went back to help him. Several times he had to scramble back to the controls as the Lancaster fell into a dive, but he finally got the wounded man to the escape hatch, saw that he was conscious and able to pull the rip-cord and pushed him clear. The hatch jammed then, and he sweated and tugged at it while the aircraft plunged down till he forced it open and slipped through himself.

He landed in the sea and after a couple of hours a French fishing boat picked up him and two others, and later they got back to the squadron. No one ever found out what happened to the others.

The day after Brest they went to the U-boat pens at Lorient and scored at least two direct 'tallboy' hits and several near misses before smoke blotted them out.

Duffy and his crew of tough Canadians did not go on that trip. Tait had told them the previous night that they had finished their tour and were to go on rest, so Duffy took up his navigator in one of the Mosquitoes for a final local flip. It was the one that Cheshire had flown to mark on the Munich raid and it may have been that he strained the mainspar on that mad dive, because when Duffy was pulling out of a dive over Wainfleet Sands the starboard wing folded and at about 400 mph they went many feet deep into the mud.

Duffy's DFC and promotion to flight lieutenant came through that afternoon.

The weather stayed fine and the squadron worked hard, averaging a 'job' every couple of days. They went back to plaster the pens at Brest a couple of times and made several visits to similar targets at Lorient, Bordeaux and La Pallice.

On most of these raids the bombers took off independently to rendezvous over Hastings and form up into their 'gaggle' at about 18,000 feet. 'Baby-face' Willsher had been living there peacefully a year or so before and used to pick out his mother's house, stand up in the cockpit and wave out of the window, yelling, 'Hi Mum! Hullo Mum!' His mother must have seen them go over a dozen times, blissfully unaware that her favourite young man was on his way to the flak and fighters.

They lost two or three on the raids but morale was high. Some old crews went (or, rather, were sent) on rest; new crews came in, and between raids they all practised hard with the SABS on the bombing range.

Sometimes there were not enough 'tallboys' and they carried 2,000-lb armour-piercing bombs, but these hardly chipped the pens. Sir Arthur Harris was constantly demanding more 'tallboys', sending for his armament staff officer and saying to him: 'Can you scrape up enough "tallboys" by tomorrow for a go at Brest?' (Or Lorient, or La Pallice, or wherever it might happen to be.)

The answer too often was: 'No. I'm afraid not, sir.'

'That's no damn good to me. Go and see Freeman.'

Off the armanent officer would go to Sir Wilfred Freeman, who would usually end up by saying, 'Tell Bert he can't have the moon.' Back he would go and deliver the message in diplomatic language, to which Harris would reply with a ferocious grunt.

For one of the raids on La Pallice they could scrape up only seven 'tallboys', and the squadron lobbed six of them as direct hits on the pens, getting more congratulations from Cochrane, who said, 'You've broken all records.'

Wallis had not designed the 'tallboy' to go through thick ferro-concrete, but it was such an extraordinary weapon that time and again it did so, even though it never had time to reach its prescribed speed. They usually dropped it from around 18,000 feet instead of 40,000 because the Lancasters could not carry it higher.

The Brest pens had concrete roofs 16 feet thick. One or two of the 'tallboys' split on them, but the rest penetrated deep and exploded the rest of the way through, creating chaos in the shelters. After the first raid the Germans tried to repair and strengthen them but a couple more raids taught them that it was no good. The 'impregnable' concrete monsters were vulnerable, and that made their French ports too hot for U-boats. Agents sent word to Britain that the U-boats were fleeing from these ports and were not expected back.

The agents also suspected that the Germans planned to sink the old battleship hulk *Gueydon* in the mouth of Brest Harbour so the Allies could never use the port. 617 flew over and dropped 1,000-pounders on her at her old anchorage from three miles up and by evening the old battleship was many fathoms deep.

Wallis's new 10-tonner was coming along as fast as possible, but that was not very fast because it was a far more complicated job, even, than the 'tallboy'. Freeman had christened it with the code name of 'Grand Slam' and delivery date for the first one was roughly February, 1945. Meantime the Americans were starting to produce 'tallboys' and were evolving a new (and very efficient) method of making 'grand slams'.

CHAPTER 18

TO RUSSIA

It might be said that the fate of the battleship was finally sealed in the bath of Air Vice-Marshal the Honourable Ralph Cochrane. In his waking moments work was rarely absent from his mind; he had been thinking of the *Tirpitz* for a long time, and it was in his bath one morning that he finally made up his mind to get permission for 617 to sink her. He climbed out, dried, dressed and flew down to see Harris, and Harris said yes.

Tirpitz was still in Alten Fiord, in the Arctic Circle, by the northern tip of Norway. Merely lying inside her girdle of torpedo nets she forced the Allies to divert three battleships, badly needed elsewhere, to guard the Russian convoys. The Allies had been trying to 'get' her for over two years. First a Russian submarine damaged her; then British midget submarines put her out of action for six months. Next the Fleet Air Arm hit her, but now she was ready for sea again.

Cochrane flew to Woodhall. 'Tait,' he said (typical of the man), 'you're going to sink the *Tirpitz*.' For a while they discussed ways and means. One problem, Cochrane warned, would be the smoke screen round the ship. The Germans had run a pipeline round the shores of the narrow fiord and could pour out smoke by turning a tap. Also there were scores of smoke pots round the ship, and they could smother the fiord under smoke in eight minutes. There would be no time to waste manoeuvring for a bomb run. Tait went over to the mess to have a glass of beer and think about it.

He spread maps on his office floor and measured the distance there and back. It was formidable; something like 3,000 miles . . . probably beyond range. He loaded three Lancasters with bombs and full petrol and sent off three of the youngest crews (because the maximum range is what the least experienced can do) to fly round England a distance equal to the distance to the target. He sent another plane with half petrol to fly similarly, representing the distance back with a lighter load. When they landed he measured the petrol they had used, and the two ends of the string did not meet. He reported to Cochrane that the *Tirpitz* was just outside their range.

Two days later Cochrane flew over and said, 'You can do it from Russia.' He put a finger on the map . . . 'Here. Yagodnik.' Yagodnik was a Russian airfield on an island in the Dvina River, about twenty miles from Archangel . . . only 600 miles from Alten Fiord. 'Fly to Yagodnik from northern Scotland with your bombs,' Cochrane said. 'Refuel there, do the job, return to Yagodnik to refuel again and come home.'

He said there were enough 'tallboys' now to send 9 Squadron with them; 9 Squadron could not use the SABS but had become nearly as accurate with the Mark XIV bomb sight. Two Liberators would carry ground crews and spares.

The planners worked fast and three days later, on a good weather report, the squadron (carrying their 'tallboys') flew to Lossiemouth, refuelled and in bright sunshine on 10 September took off heavily on the long haul to Russia, laden a ton overweight with petrol and bombs.

At dusk they crossed the Norwegian coast, and as they droned steadily north, nearer the Pole, the magnetic compasses started to play tricks, but luckily the night stayed clear and they were able to pin-point themselves over the fiords and check with the sextants. They crossed the Gulf of Finland and flew on through the night till, in the half-light of an Arctic dawn they turned east for Yagodnik.

Long separated from the others in the night, each plane found itself drifting alone through pale grey cloud. Some Russian had said the cloud had never been below 1,000 feet in twenty-five years, but Tait was at 1,000 feet and could see nothing.

He eased her down gently, but at 500 feet still saw nothing but greyness. They should be over the steppes now; if so the ground would be flat with no treacherous hills rising in their path. He hoped they were over the steppes.

At 400 feet they saw trees like ghosts through the drifts and some of the strain lifted from the little huddle in the cockpit. They had been sitting there ten hours, silent in the glow of the instruments.

On and on they flew over a flat sea of trees, endless, desolate and remote; no roads, no towns, not even a track, here and there a small pool of grey water. Otherwise only trees with mist twisting round their trunks. Drizzle blurred the windscreen; they were flitting in and out of cloud even at 300 feet, and Arthur Ward, the wireless operator, could not raise the Yagodnik radio beacon (none of the others raised it either. It was the wrong kind of beacon).

ETA was up. They should be there now, but still only the trees and less than an hour's petrol. Tait turned south to search. Knowing the compasses and weather might play tricks, they had been relying on that beacon. Worry was hammering at him; not so much on his own account but for all his other aircraft.

Daniels, the bomb aimer, suddenly shouted that he could see a river through a break in the cloud and Tait slanted the nose down; they broke into clear air and below was an airfield with a Lancaster landing and two more circling. Five minutes later they were thankfully on the ground and found that only a handful of aircraft had arrived. Including 9 Squadron, there were over twenty more to account for. They walked over to a ramshackle hut on the field, Tait feeling the dread rising in him. None of the missing planes could have more than half-an-hour's petrol. It looked like disaster.

In the next half-hour seven more Lancasters and the two Liberators arrived, the crews dog-tired after twelve hours in the air and marvelling at having made it safely after the past hours of taut nerves.

The moment came when none of the aircraft could still be in the air, and thirteen were still missing. A Russian interpreter came over and said that a Lancaster had landed on an airfield on another island in the river. Five minutes later he reported that four Lancasters were safely there. Then word started coming in from all over the place of Lancasters in various fields a hundred miles around, and in three hours they knew the location of every aircraft.

It was unbelievable. In the wilderness the Russians had traced the aircraft as fast as could be done in England and dropped parachute medical teams and guides to isolated ones. (One parachute guide reached a stranded crew all right, but it was a case of the blind leading the blind because the guide himself got lost for twenty-four hours!) It was equally incredible that there were no casualties, though two 617 aircraft and four of 9 Squadron were written off because they were irretrievable in marshes.

Knilans had been getting ready to crash-land when he came to a small field, and the petrol gauges were on 'Zero' when he dropped the plane low over a fence and, with brakes hard on, pulled up inches short of the trees. Minutes later Iveson droned into sight and landed safely in the same field. Wyness and Ross crash-landed in marshland. Flak hit Carey's plane badly over Finland, but Gerry Witherick nailed one of the gunners before they were out of range and they reached Yagodnik, where they riveted patches over the holes.

The Russians lodged all the sergeants in underground huts and escorted the officers over a gangplank to a houseboat where a banner flapped, bearing the words, 'Welcome to the glorious flyers of the RAF.' 'Cor,' said Witherick, 'what a line!' Otherwise there were no social distinctions. Both huts and houseboat crawled with bugs and had the same musty smell of drains and lavatories. While the well-warned crews sprayed their quarters with Keatings and tried to prise the windows open, Tait stood by to fly to Iveson and Knilans. A Russian pilot took him to an antique biplane, and Tait flinched when he saw two mongoloid Russians hitting the engine with a hammer; they stopped, he climbed reluctantly in and the cabin lid closed over him like a coffin top.

To his faint surprise, the Thing flew and half an hour later the Russian pilot landed next to the two Lancasters. Tait found his two crews held in a tumbledown wooden house set in a sea of mud. The Russians had fed them well but were not allowing them out. Some Russian girls were there but the crews were behaving impeccably, not even ogling the girls, partly because the girls were not attractive and partly because one of them had entertained them by lifting a burly Russian guard off the floor with one hand. Paddy Blanche, Knilans' gunner, was recovering. He hadn't been injured, but at lunch-time they had set a tumbler of vodka in front of him, and he had thought it was water and drunk it straight off before his face had turned white then crimson and purple as he fought for breath.

Iveson had just enough petrol to get to Yagodnik and took off at full throttle, barely clearing the trees. The Russians brought more petrol for Knilans; he roared over the grass to take-off but his spark plugs were fouled and the engines were sluggish. Feeling the power lacking (she would have lifted easily enough but for the 6-ton bomb) Knilans shoved the throttles through the 'gate', hauled her off the ground and she lunged into the tree-tops and cut a swathe through the foliage for a hundred yards. Boughs shot up all round, twigs and leaves scooped into the radiators, a lopped branch knifed through the nose and shot into the cockpit beside Knilans, and then the engines hauled her clear. Wind howled through the smashed nose into Knilans' face so that he could hardly see and flew with a hand over his face, peeking between two fingers. One engine cut out because of overheating from the blocked radiator, but they made it safely to Yagodnik and the ground crews set about repairs.

Rain poured on Yagodnik and for three days they waited for it to lift. Friendly Russians tried hard to amuse them, but outside the huts lay a sea of mud and the crews relaxed indoors, chasing bugs and eating sour black bread, borshch and half-cooked bacon . . . when the last of the breakfasters rose the head of the lunch queue sat down. They washed it down with vodka, which (said Willie Tait) was the secret of Russian survival in that climate. His opinion was respected because he was the only one the bugs refused to bite. Tait claimed it was because they were capitalist bugs and respected his rank, but Witherick said that even Russian bugs had to draw the line somewhere.

A Russian interpreter, who grinned all the time (showing steel false teeth) and smelled of perfume, took them at night to an underground cellar to see an unnerving film that went on for hours, all about battles . . . mostly Russian tanks, planes and cheering soldiers rushing forward in a con-tinuous pandemonium of crashing explosions . . . dead Germans everywhere.

Next day a team of bullet-headed little men (imported for the occasion) played them at football. Whenever Russian players tired they went off and on came reserves, among them the local Russian commander and the airfield commander, who were fed assiduously with passes by their men until a glancing blow off the senior man's knee went into the goal, whereupon the band struck up triumphantly and the rest of the team, duty done, went back to playing normally. The Russians won easily, 7–0.

On 15 September the sun crawled out of the horizon low to the south and shone in a clear sky. The crews were out in their aircraft, running up the engines hopefully, when the weather plane darted over the airfield like a blue kingfisher and landed with the report that the sky over Alten Fiord was clear. Minutes later twenty-eight Lancasters of the two squadrons were lifting off the bumpy grass and turning west. Tait flew slowly, the rest of his squadron picking up station behind till they were in their gaggle low over the White Sea, and on strict radio silence to delay detection. Grey water close below muffled the thunder of the engines till they crossed the barren shore of Lapland and the echoes came up from the ice-worn rocks. The land was lifeless but for odd stunted trees; it rose a little and the aircraft lifted their noses gently over the contours.

Tait had an engine running rough, shaking the plane like a rolling-mill, but he headed on worrying about having enough power for the bombing climb. Ninety miles from Alten Fiord the mountains reared ahead and, on full throttle and revs, Tait's rough engine cleared and he climbed easily over the last ridge. They were dead on track.

Ahead Alten Fiord lay quietly in the sun like a map; they raced for it at 11,000 feet to beat the smoke screen, but as they picked out the black shape at her anchorage under the cliff, white plumes started vomiting out of the smoke pots and streaming across the water.

The bombers were quivering on full power five minutes from bombing point as the white veils started wreathing her. There must have been a hundred pots pouring smoke. Flak was firing from the heights now; the gaggle ran steadily through the black puffs, and then the *Tirpitz's* guns opened up. Two minutes from release point the drifting veils were fast smothering her. Daniels, in the nose of Tait's aircraft, took a long bead and called, 'Bomb sight on!'

The black hull finally vanished in its shroud but the mast-tops stood clear a few seconds later, and then they too were gone. Daniels tried to hold his graticule on the spot but found no mark in the drifting smoke and guessed as the seconds dragged that he must be wandering off. The Lancaster leapt as the bomb clattered away and Tait swung the wheel hard over, swerving out of the flak.

Behind him the others had all lost their mark in that agonizing last minute. Howard, Watts and Sanders bombed on dim gun flashes through the smoke. Kell and Knilans bombed on the spot last seen, and the others, in frustration, did not bomb at all. Pale flickers in the smoke showed bombs exploding, and after one of them a plume of black smoke spurted through the whiteness. Tait felt a moment of hope but judged it was only a 'tallboy' striking the shore. Some of the Lancasters swung back through the flak for a second run, but the screen was thicker than ever and they turned for Yagodnik.

When they landed, Woods, one of the bomb aimers, said he had seen Daniels' 'tallboy' hit the ship, but no one believed him. The Russians did not try to hide their displeasure at the failure. Some of the bombers still had their 'tallboys' and they wanted to go back and try again, but the weather broke once more, rain drizzled down, winter's cloud hung over the north, and disconsolately they gave up the idea and took off for home. Levy's aircraft never arrived. Somewhere over Norway they wandered off track – probably through a flabby compass – and flew into the mountains. They were an all-Jewish crew, a quiet, unobtrusive team, utterly reliable. With Levy were four of Wyness's crew.

It was the nearness to success that hurt Cochrane most. He said wryly, 'Another minute's sight and you'd have got her. I was afraid those smoke pots might balk you.' He did not tell Tait at the time but he had no intention of leaving the *Tirpitz* in peace.

A couple of nights later the squadron joined 5 Group to bomb the Dortmund Ems Canal, scene, a year earlier, of 617's blackest night. Mosquitoes marked at low level in the way they had learned from Cheshire and the bombs that followed split the canal embankment. The group bombed more accurately now than a year earlier. After his experiment with 617, Cochrane had seen that the rest of his squadrons trained hard in the same direction.

Tait had lost an engine on take-off that night but had feathered and kept going hard on the other three; slower, of course. He came out of cloud over the target and saw the water that was the artery of Germany's northern transport system pouring through the gaps into the countryside. There was a price on it that night; fighters got among the returning bomber stream, and Tait saw the path back littered with burning Lancasters. 617 was lucky and lost only one. Stout's plane went down somewhere; they never found out where.

The canal had a bad time after that. The water drained for miles between lock gates, and scores of barges were stranded on the mud with coal, prefabricated U-boats and other essentials. Hitler drove 4,000 slaves to rebuild the breached walls, and when they had nearly finished, 5 Group knocked them down again. Back to work went the reluctant slaves, and this time they finished it. The Germans opened the lock gates to let the water through again, and two hours later the Lancasters were over and away went the walls again. They never did get the canal working again.

Knilans was told he had 'finished'. After two straight tours without rest he had 'operational fatigue'; his mind still registered mistakes in the air but his muscles would not respond. He had another disappointment too. His DSO medal arrived – in the post. Knilans had set his heart on having it pinned on at an investiture.

Humphries kept it for him in the squadron safe while Knilans miserably waited for his posting, and whenever the inactivity got a little too much for him he used to wander down to the squadron office, moon around bashfully for a while and then say, 'Humph, can I have look at my medal?' Humphries would solemnly take it out of the safe, and Knilans would hold it in his hand and sigh, 'Heck, I guess that King never will get to meet me now.'

He was entitled to several medal ribbons, including some American ones, but for a long time the only one he would wear was the DSO ribbon. (Later he added to it when his DFC came through.)

Recce aircraft reported the *Tirpitz* was missing from Alten Fiord and there was a great 'flap' (particularly among the nautical people) till a message came through from a Mr Egil Lindberg. Lindberg was a Norwegian who operated a secret transmitter from a room above the morgue in Tromso. The *Tirpitz* had arrived in Tromso, he reported, with a great hole in her for'rd deck. She had been hit by a very heavy bomb (Daniels's 'tallboy' *had* hit the ship. He was probably the most 'hawk-eyed' bomb aimer of the war). Lindberg thought the *Tirpitz* had come to Tromso because the repair facilities were better there. Cochrane got the news and did not care a hoot about the repair facilities. The important thing to him was that Tromso was 200 miles south of Alten Fiord – it shortened the return trip by 400 miles . . . and that put the *Tirpitz* just within range of Lossiemouth.

He called Wing Commander Brown, his engineering staff officer, and said, 'Brown, we've got to get three hundred more gallons in 617's Lancasters.'

'Yes sir. We can fit overload tanks in the bomb bays.'

'No, we shall want the "tallboys" there. Come on, come on, you're versatile. Is there anything in the depots that would do? We haven't time to get anything made.'

Brown was miserably without a glimmer of an idea till he remembered some Wellingtons had once carried long pencil-shaped overload tanks. If they could find some of those they could slide them into the Lancaster fuselages. Cochrane grunted approval, and Brown scoured England by telephone, locating tanks one by one and sending trucks to collect them.

A new consideration interrupted Cochrane's *Tirpitz* plans. The right flank of the American dash across France into Germany had been halted at the Belfort Gap; ahead the Rhine barred the way into Germany, and on the Rhine by the Swiss frontier lay the Kembs Dam. It was obvious that when the Americans stormed the river the Germans would blow up the flood-gates, releasing a massive head of water that would sweep the assault forces to destruction in mid-river or isolate those who got across. There was only one way out – smash the flood-gates first, let the water spend itself and then drive at the river. Only a heavy charge, deep in the water and pressed against the sluice gates, would burst them; the ideal target for the freak bomb 617 had used on the Moehne and Eder but the modified aircraft to carry that bomb had long been re-modified to normality. It would take weeks to adapt more aircraft for the bomb and train the crews in the delicate technique; more weeks than they could afford.

It was no good trying to bomb it from high level. The chance of a heavy bomb landing in exactly the right spot, within a foot of the dam wall on the upstream side, was far too slim. A direct hit on the top would do no good. There was only one way . . . Cochrane decided that a 'tallboy' dropped low over the water just short of the flood-gates would slide cleanly into the water till it hit a gate and stuck in the concrete. They would give it a delayed fuse so the low-flying bombers would not be blown up as well.

It would have to be done very accurately; that meant doing it in full daylight, and the dam was circled with guns. The bombers would have to fly very low, straight and level, and run the gauntlet. No question as to who should do it!

Cochrane planned it craftily. They would split into two formations; one would come in and bomb from the west at 8,000 feet, drawing the flak; and in the precise moment their bombs were hitting, six Lancasters would sneak in low from the east for the real assault. At the same instant a Mustang squadron would dive on the flak-pits with guns and rockets so the flak might not notice the low-level force, at least till the bombs were gone. It was going to need split-second timing, and 617 practised every day for a week till their final rehearsal over Wainfleet went perfectly. Tait was insisting on leading the low-level force.

They knew, or sensed, that the Kembs might be a 'shaky do', though that did not much affect their thinking or living. They were used to it and the mind makes its own defences. After battle they always flew home to the island fortress and lived among fields and placid villages, which rather insulated them in the mess from the sharper realities of battle, just enough to take some of the edge off the fear that lived in them like a raw little nerve.

617's mess at Woodhall was in the Petwood Hotel for instance; stockbroker's tudor if you like but a pleasant place, agreeably panelled and set in gardens. The beer was good, WAAFs in white coats served your meals and you slept in a bed with sheets, remote from battle. You lived like a normal human and it fortified that deceitful little thought, 'It can't

happen to me', until the weather cleared and you got a time on target: then
the transition was always brutally swift – four hours later you would be a
few hundred miles away, tight-lipped and sweating it out in the noise, the
ugliness, the fear and the death.

Sometimes, if the time on target were a few hours away, some of the
insulation stayed a while round the little nerve, as on 7 October, the day of
the Kembs raid. Take-off was in the afternoon and after morning briefing
and testing the planes the crews read in the mess or walked in the garden
and two of the flight commanders, Tony Iveson and 'Duke' Wyness, even
went over to a nearby army mess to lunch with their friend the lieutenant-
colonel, commander of the local regiment.

Among the waiters, white linen and conversation the war shrank; it was
not forgotten but you observed it through the wrong end of a telescope and
talked of it as if it were almost abstract. Wyness, for instance, talked during
lunch not of the raid but in philosophical terms of courage and cowardice
in the face of the enemy, saying with the earnest assurance of twenty-three
years that a man's duty lay along the path of the utmost endurance in the
face of the enemy's efforts.

That very neatly expressed the distinctive quality of the squadron and it
was apt enough coming from Wyness because he himself was quite typical
of the new types who made the squadron. He already had a DFC when he
came to 617 and a reputation as a 'press on' type, a handsome young man,
a six-footer, slim, with blue eyes, a somewhat classical nose and really
golden, curly hair.

One of the pilots under him was Kit Howard and the orderly room had a
story that Wyness came from the estate of Howard's family, though neither
Howard nor Wyness seemed to notice it. In both of them, as in Tait, Iveson
and the others, was the continuity of the early, chosen types like Gibson,
Cheshire, Martin and Shannon. They maintained the quality and
buttressed the tradition.

And then, after lunch, they accepted the transition and went to battle.
The colonel drove them to their planes in his jeep, asked them both to dine
with him that evening when they got back, and waved them off.

They all took off into light haze and ran into a pall of cloud over
Manston, where they were to meet the fighters. It is dangerous to break
radio silence on the outward journey but this time it was less of a risk than
missing the fighter escort, so Tait made two short transmissions; the first to
617: 'Four thousand feet. Don't acknowledge.' They recognized his voice,
climbed blind through the cloud and at 4,000 feet came into the sunshine.
Tait called the fighter leader and told him they were overhead; two
minutes later the Mustangs lifted out of the white carpet, shook themselves
into formation and they were on their way.

It was clear over France, and strange to be flying peacefully over the land that had been hostile so soon before. Bomb craters still studded the fields but the scars were already softening as rain and sun mellowed the torn earth and the grass crept in.

The scars vanished over Champagne and they flew over green and yellow meadows and towns by gleaming rivers. Tait, for the first time, felt an intruder, finding it hard, this day, to adjust himself to the sharp transition. Raiding at night they were alone in darkness filled with unknown danger, and inside the cockpit it was tense and appropriate to war, but this peaceful sunshine made it somehow unreal and the task ahead repugnant. He found himself thinking of wine and clear river water, lost in introspection while a separate part of his brain and his arms and feet were part of the aeroplane, flying on undeviatingly.

Patches of cloud brought him back to reality. Cloud over the Rhone would hide the high force and leave him and the 'suicide squad' open to the flak. The cloud thinned again; the high force swung behind Fawke and started climbing; Tait slid to the right and nosed down till he was hugging the ground under the radar waves, and the other five Lancasters trailed after him. They skirted the Swiss frontier, clearly marked with red and white crosses on the ground, but Watts must have swung his plane a shade too close and the Swiss flak opened up on him, smashing his starboard outer engine. He feathered quickly, hauled over to the left and kept going. From a rear turret a voice said, 'It's OK I'm here.' Gerry Witherick was riding with Watts this day, and everyone knew he always got back unscratched.

They slid past Basle on the right and turned down the river, opening bomb doors. Three miles ahead Tait saw flashes round the low parapet of the Kembs, but the guns were aiming high at Fawke's formation. Great flashes and columns of spray rushed up round the dam; the timing of the high-force bombs was perfect. Tait's aeroplane was rock-steady on course and no word was spoken, except once, a terse 'OK' from Daniels. They were committed to it now, sliding over the smooth water with taut nerves and dry mouths. Tait saw Mustangs diving out of the sun over the dam and dared to hope the flak would not see him, but abruptly the white-hot balls came darting at them. He felt the plane jump as the bomb slid away, slammed the throttles on, did not see the bomb knife cleanly into the water 10 yards from the right-hand sluice gate, but heard the vibrant rattle as the rear gunner opened up and they hurtled over the dam.

Behind him Castagnola's plane lurched in Tait's slipstream and threw the bomb wide. Tait hauled hard over to the right for the shelter of the hills, climbing on full power, engines blaring in fine pitch as they dragged her up. He turned abeam and saw a Lancaster rocking over the dam on fire, flame and smoke streaming in her wake. She dropped a wing and plunged into the river bank, rolling over in a ball of fire. When it is quick it is a good way to die.

Tait heard a voice in his earphones – Howard's, he thought – saying, 'Had a hang-up. Going round again.' Howard, of the noble family, was rather a formal boy, but brave. Perhaps foolhardy. This time the gunners were wary, not distracted. Howard came alone down the river and all the guns saw him. They got him a long way back and he blew up in mid-air with the bomb on board.

The surviving bombers turned for home; in five minutes the sound of their engines had died away and the dam lay quietly in the sun as though nothing had happened, except for two columns of greasy smoke pouring from the spots where Howard and Wynes and their crews had died.

There had been half-hour delay fuses on the low-force 'tallboys'. Twenty minutes after the raid a Mosquito droned high over the dam and circled it, the pilot watching till he saw the water beside the right-hand sluice-gate burst and mushroom into the air. A massive torrent plunged through the gate, and in twenty-four hours the banked headwaters of the Rhine had dropped so much that barges far into Switzerland grounded on the mud.

Tait had made a 'dicy' landing with a flak shell in one wing-root and a tyre shot away. Several of the others were badly holed. Iveson, without changing, walked over to the army mess to tell the colonel that his other dinner guest, the boy who had lunched with him, was lying several hundred miles away in another country, cremated in his plane. He found the colonel (who was a Scottish rugby international) in the bar, took him aside and they sat on the stairs while Iveson told him about it. The hurt was gathering in the colonel's face and then, very quietly, he was crying: you could, I suppose, call it crying; no noise, no sobs, no shaking shoulders but the tears starting to glisten in his eyes till they spilled and kept wetting his cheeks.

When he was able to, he said, a little unsteadily and with humility, how futile he felt his own efforts were in comparison to the Air Force. He said he had never had much chance for action but now he felt the impact of the war more than ever before.

So did Iveson when he saw the tears. They had got so used to seeing planes beside them with their friends fall smoking out of the sky that the familiar expression they all used, 'got the chop', had almost a humorous quality about it, but that was just part of the insulation, the old mental defence mechanism.

(Three weeks later, in the landing on Walcheren, the colonel won a DSO for some act of inspired bravery.)

The squadron never knew for certain whether the raid helped the advance, whether their fourteen room-mates died in saving hundreds or whether it was just one of the premiums paid in war, a precaution which, after all, was not needed. So many valiant deeds in war are sterile. The monstrous rocket sites they bombed in the Pas de Calais may never have been finished in time, whether they had bombed them or not. It was a part of war. Tait was well aware that most of the effort of war was spent against an enemy who was not there; that for every shell which hit a target, hundreds were fired that missed, and for every bullet, thousands.

The next days were a fever of activity getting ready for the *Tirpitz*. The brunt of it fell on Cochrane, Tait, Brown and the ground crews. With tests and graphs Tait worked it out that from Lossiemouth they could just reach the *Tirpitz* in Tromso with a bare – a very bare – safety margin in case of adverse winds, but it meant loading in so much petrol they would be taking off nearly 2 tons over the maximum permissible weight. He agreed to try that if they could have Merlin 24 engines . . . they were more powerful than the engines in the 617 Lancasters. There were some of these engines in 5 Group, scattered among odd aircraft in various squadrons at other airfields. For three days and nights the ground crews worked non-stop in shifts, taking the Merlin 24's out of aircraft all over Lincolnshire, bringing them back to Woodhall, taking out the 617 engines, putting in the new ones and taking the 617 engines to be put in the other aircraft they had 'robbed'. It would have been so simple if they could merely have exchanged planes, but only the 617 Lancasters had the specially big bomb bays to carry the 'tallboys'. The weather was dense fog continuously, and at night the bright hangar lights gleamed like will-o'-the-wisps across the streaming tarmac.

Brown had collected the long, thin overload tanks from all over England. The erks had to take the rear turrets off every plane to slide the tanks in, then put the turrets back on again. They took the mid-upper turrets off completely, also the pilot's armour plate and any equipment not vitally necessary, so as to save weight.

(The same things were done on 9 Squadron aircraft too. Cochrane was sending them as well.)

That done they waited on the weather, and that was the worst time of all. In October and November a prevailing westerly blows continuous stratus cloud from the sea over Tromso . . . except for perhaps three days a month, when the wind briefly changes to the east and the sky is clear for a few hours. They would have to be in position at Lossiemouth to take off when one of these clear periods existed, and hope it would last till they got there. But neither Harris nor Cochrane could let them stay at Lossiemouth indefinitely 'on spec'. They needed them down south in case of emergency targets. The only way was for the squadron to fly to Lossiemouth when a break seemed possible. At the most they had six weeks left for the attack. After 26 November the sun does not rise above the horizon at Tromso, though for a few days after that there would be just enough twilight at midday for bombing. After that no light till spring. A nice problem in long-range weather forecasting.

The word came on 28 October, and thirty-six Lancasters of 617 and 9 Squadrons flew north to a bleak field near Lossiemouth. At midnight a Mosquito over Tromso radioed that the wind was veering to the east, and in drizzling rain, at the deathly hour of 1 am, the Merlin 24's straining on emergency power, dragged the overburdened Lancasters off the ground.

They flew low as usual, in sight of the caps on the dark water; hours later crossed the Norwegian coast and turned inland towards Sweden to keep the mountains between them and the Tromso radar. They wheeled left in a long climb, topped the ridges and saw Tromso Fiord and the ship . . . and saw in the same moment, moving in from the sea, towering drifts of cloud. The wind had changed.

It was a race again, like those sickening moments over Alten Fiord, but this time the white screens were higher and thicker. At 230 mph the bombers charged towards the ship and the cloud. A minute from release point they still saw the ship, but with thirty seconds to go the cloud slid between them!

They couldn't dive under it to bomb; lower down the 'tallboys' would not have penetrated the armoured decks. Daniels tried to keep his bomb sight on the spot where he last saw the ship. Flak was bursting through the cloud among them now. Daniels called 'Bombs gone!' and Tait dived into the cloud to try and see where it fell. Fawke, Iveson, Knights and one or two more bombed on vague glimpses and dived too. Others swung away to try another run. Through gaps in the cloud at about 13,000 feet Tait saw flashes as bombs exploded in the water round the ship. One or two others said they thought they saw a direct hit or near miss. Martin (a different Martin) made two more runs, got a glimpse on the third run and bombed half blindly. Gumbley made four runs but got no sight at all.

Carey's Lancaster had been hit by flak on the first run; the starboard outer engine stopped and petrol streamed out of a riven tank, luckily without catching fire. He turned back on three engines for another run and the cloud foiled him. He tried again and again, ploughing steadfastly through the flak till, on the sixth run, an almost desperate bomb aimer let his 'tallboy' go with faint hope.

Tait had ordered everyone to dive to 1,000 feet to pick up speed and steer for home. As Carey screamed down he passed over a small island; a single gun on it pumped a shell into another engine, which died instantly; petrol was streaming out of another burst tank (miraculously no fire again), and then the hydraulics burst and the bomb doors and undercarriage flopped down. The two good engines on full power just held her in the air against the drag; the engineer thumbed his gauges, scribbled a few calculations and said, 'Sorry, Skip, not enough gas to get home.'

From the rear turret came a protesting, grimly flippant voice: 'Hell, this can't happen to me.' Witherick was flying with Carey this time. He had a habit of switching crews.

'Christ!' said Carey. 'Can't it? You watch!'

He turned the winged plane back towards the land and, staggering through the air a few hundred feet up, they threaded through a mountain pass and slowly crossed the barren country. Half an hour later the navigator said they were over Sweden. The two engines were dangerously hot and Carey crash-landed in a bog near Porjus. The Lancaster tilted frighteningly on her nose, poised a moment and settled back, and they climbed out.

The rest of the squadron landed at Lossiemouth and heard that a recce plane radioed that the *Tirpitz* was untouched. They flew down to Woodhall, where Tait found a message from Cochrane: 'Congratulations on your splendid flight and perseverance. The luck won't always favour the *Tirpitz*. One day you'll get her.'

On 4 November they flew up to Lossiemouth again. A gale warning came through that night and in the morning the weather was dreadful. It stayed dreadful; they flew back to Woodhall and waited, practising bombing whenever they could. Five days later they were still getting gale and frost warnings and time was getting short.

Arthur Kell's bomb aimer tripped on the stairs and fractured his skull, and Tait told Kell he would have to miss the next *Tirpitz* trip unless he could find a SABS-experienced bomb aimer. Kell rang Astbury, now twice tour-experienced, waiting at Brighton for a ship home to Australia. Astbury went AWL from his draft and turned up at Woodhall, a misdemeanour to which Tait turned a blandly Nelsonian blind eye.

CHAPTER 19

THE NAKED BATTLESHIP

A new complication jolted Cochrane. Intelligence reported that twenty to thirty German fighters had moved in to Bardufoss airfield, thirty miles from Tromso. No doubting why! Two strong attacks had been made on the *Tirpitz*; the Germans would give the next one a lethal reception. For accuracy the squadron would have to bomb by day spread out in the gaggle so they could not give each other protection, and the RAF's .303 guns were no match for the cannon of fighters. If the fighters fell on them – and that seemed likely – there was every chance of slaughter. Few bombers, if any, would return.

Cochrane found himself in the old position of the commander forced to stay at his desk and decide whether to send his men into an ambush. Some commanders grow too detached to be particularly conscious of it. There had been two unlucky failures, and he spent troubled hours trying to equate the chance of a 'third time lucky' success with the probable losses. For all his coldness there was a personal factor this time that he tried to eliminate. 617 never knew (and would never have guessed) that they were the apple of his eye; he had a respect for them amounting to affection.

But it was an operational war. That was the clinching factor. He decided they would have to go if the cloud let them.

Next day the weather was improving. Tait was playing football with his crews on the airfield, surrounded by the circle of silent cloaked Lancasters, when he was summoned to the operations room, and there, still in striped jersey and studded boots, he got his orders. In a few hours they were flying up to Northern Scotland.

That was about the afternoon a paper was dumped in an 'In' tray in Whitehall, and a senior officer with a lot of braid round his sleeve picked it out and groaned when he read the rather peremptory suggestion from High Circles that instead of 'tallboys' on the *Tirpitz* raid they should drop 2,000-lb armour-piercing bombs. In the room at the time was an airman who had done a lot of work in developing the 'tallboy'. 'Oh God,' he said, 'the two-thousand-pounders'll never do it! What do we do now?' The high officer pondered, his fingers relaxed and the slip of paper floated back into the 'In' tray. 'Have lunch,' he said, and added a moment later, piously, 'I'll look into this tomorrow. I *do* hope I'm in time.'

Some time after midnight the weather Mosquito, sliding through darkness on the way back from Tromso, reported fog, in the fiords and cloud half-way up Norway. There was a possibility Tromso might be clear by dawn, but there were distinct icing conditions (a real bogy for heavy-laden aircraft). It was not encouraging. Tait discussed it with the Met. men, and at the end he said, 'All right. We'll give it a go.'

Over Lossiemouth stars were glinting in a clear sky and the air was frosty. Tait drove out to his aeroplane and found the dangerous rime ice already forming on his wings in spite of the glycol the ground crew had poured on the leading edge. One by one round the field the engines were whining and coughing explosively, bringing the big bombers to quivering life. When Tait started his starboard inner it let out a high-pitched scream as the starter stuck in engagement. He hoped it would clear before the engine seized – in much the same way as he hoped the rime ice would clear. With 7 tons of fuel and 6 tons of bomb, each plane was grossly overweight at 32 tons. No margin for any trouble on take-off.

At 3 am the straining engines dragged them into the air, the great wheels slowly retracted and locked, the engines relaxed and they turned slowly on course at 1,000 feet. (Tait's engine chewed the gears off the starter motor and was all right. He was flying his own aircraft again, 'D Dog', for the first time since she was crippled over the Kembs Dam. He always had luck in her.)

They flew slowly to save petrol, flame floats bobbing on the water in their wake as they checked for drift. Tait had slipped in the automatic pilot and tried to doze, as he always did on outward trips over water; he believed in taking sleep when he could get it, but seldom got it.

The sky was paling in the east as they reached the Norwegian coast, turned right, climbed over the mountains and dipped into the inland valleys. The sun lifted over the horizon and the valleys lay soft under snow, flecked with pink like vast wedding cakes, except to the south, where the sun splintered on the ice-peaks and sparkled with the colours of the spectrum like a diamond necklace, radiantly lovely. Fog-filled lakes passed slowly below but there was no cloud. Rendezvous was a narrow lake cradled between steep hills a hundred miles south-east of Tromso, and Tait flew slowly towards it, saw no water but recognized it as a long pool of fog in the trough and over it saw aircraft circling like black flies.

He flew across it firing Véry lights to draw them, and they turned in behind and started the climb towards Tromso. That was the moment the radar picked them up, and within a minute the fighter operations room at Bardufoss knew that enemy bombers were closing on the *Tirpitz*. At 14,000 feet the bombers were all at battle stations. One last mountain shouldered up, and as they lifted over the peak it lowered like a screen and there again, folded in the cliffs, lay Tromso Fiord and the black ship, squat in the distance, like a spider in her web of torpedo nets. It was like looking down from the 'gods' on a Wagnerian stage, a beetle in green water cupped in the snowy hills, all coral and flame. There was no cloud. And no smoke screen. *Tirpitz* lay naked to the bomb sights.

Even the air was still. On the flanks of the gaggle Tait saw the front rank riding steadily. They seemed suspended; motionless but for the sublime hills falling slowly behind, immaculate and glowing with the beauty of sunrise and the indifference of a million years to the ugliness of the intrusion. So must many an Arctic coast burn unseen.

Far below the basin seemed to sleep in the shadow, but *Tirpitz* broke the spell with a salvo, sparkling from stem to stern with flashes as billows of smoke from the guns wreathed her and drifted up. Her captain had just radioed urgently to Bardufoss to hurry the fighters.

Tait opened the bomb doors and slid the pitch levers up to high revs; the engines bellowed and the exhausts glowed even in that cold light. Black puffs stained the sky among the gaggle as the flak reached them, and then the guns round the fiord opened fire. Tait watched anxiously for the smoke pots, but the smoke never came (the pots were there all right, just brought down from Alten, but the Germans had not yet primed them). The bomb sight was on the ship drawing nearer while the gunners in the rear turrets watched the ridges anxiously for the first fighters. It was all up to the rear gunners when the fighters came; there were no mid-upper gunners.

Now it was water, far below, sliding under the nose. Tait felt his hands on the wheel were clammy, and Daniels' breathing rasped over the intercom. The bomber was unswerving, shaking in the engines' thunder, and out of the cockpit Tait could see the bomb doors quivering as the airflow battered at them. The red light came on – ten seconds to go . . . seconds that dragged till 'D Dog' leapt as the grips snapped back and the bomb lurched away. Tait hauled hard over to the left and on either side saw others of the front rank doing likewise.

One by one the gaggle wheeled as the bombs went. They watched, wordless, through the perspex for thirty seconds till a great yellow flash burst on the battleship's foredeck. From 14,000 feet they saw her tremble. Another bomb hit the shore; two more in close succession hit the ship, one on the starboard side, by the bridge, and another abaft the funnel (one of them was Astbury's). Another one split the sea 5 feet from her bows, and then the smoke pall covered her and only dimly through it they saw the other bursts all inside the crinoline of nets.

One constant glare shone through the smoke. She was burning. There came another flash and a plume of steam jetted 500 feet into the air through the smoke as a magazine went up.

Three minutes later 9 Squadron bombed the dark shroud over her, and then the black flies crawling in the sky turned south-west and curved down towards the sea, picking up speed for the run home. They never saw a fighter. The last thing they saw as the smoke lifted was the *Tirpitz* starting to list.

The cloud they had feared closed in on the long slog home, and Tait was driving blindly through it when his artificial horizon collapsed in a mess of ball bearings and mechanism. After eleven hours in the air his eyes felt like hot coals as he focused rigidly on the other instruments; then the aerial iced up and they could not get a homing for a long time, and when they did it was a diversion. Lossiemouth was cloaked in rain, and Tait turned east and found a small Coastal Command field, where he touched down smoothly.

At the control tower a young pilot officer asked if they had been on a cross-country, and Tait primly pursed his mouth, looked in aloof shyness at the ground and said, 'Yes.' A torpedo-bomber squadron lived on the field, and later he told the CO where they had been.

'Did you get her?' the CO asked.

'I think so! Gave her a hell of a nudge anyway.'

'Thanks,' the CO said. '*We* might have had to do it. Low level. I shouldn't have liked it.'

They drove over to Lossiemouth, where they met the rest of the squadron, and were drinking in the bar when the rcccc plane radioed that *Tirpitz* was upside down in Tromso Fiord, her bottom humped over the water like a stranded whale.

In his room in Tromso, Lindberg, the Norwegian agent, was tapping out the Morse signals that confirmed it. Under his floor, in the morgue, the Germans were laying out their dead.

Not all of the dead. A thousand men were trapped below when she rolled over. The Germans tried to cut holes in the hull to reach them but did not get any out. They had spent the war miserably, lying in the bleak fiords of Norway, never venturing out. They fought the ship to the last, died without honour when the war was nearly over, and after the war still lay rotting in her hull.

The fighter commander at Bardufoss was facing court martial. Radar had warned him forty-five minutes before the bombers reached the ship, and all that time the *Tirpitz's* captain had been sending him urgent messages. He was still asking for the fighters when the bombs blotted out his radio, but the fighters never came.

Just after *Tirpitz* saw the bombers come over the mountain, a message came from Bardufoss that an enemy formation was over the airfield and the fighters could not take-off, but there were no Allied fighters for a thousand miles. No one seems to know quite what happened. Some of the fighters are said to have taken off, but by some miracle they did not intercept.

The squadron flew back to Woodhall and were greeted outside the

control by an Army band playing 'See the conquering heroes come'. In the
mess they found messages from the King, War Cabinet, Harris, Cochrane,
Wallis, the Navy, Prince Olav of Norway, and even one from the Russians,
congratulating them.

(It was not till after the war they found it had all been unnecessary. The
bomb Tait and Daniels had dropped six weeks earlier at Alten Fiord had
damaged *Tirpitz* beyond repair.) The Germans towed her to Tromso, not
to repair her but to moor her in shallow water as an unsinkable fortress.
Powerful German forces in Northern Norway meant to hold out there.
They blundered and moored her in 50 feet of water and tried to repair the
mistake by filling in the sea-bed beneath her with dredges, but did not have
time. There was still enough water below to let her down.

Someone at the Admiralty apparently did not *quite* agree and said (a
little huffily, according to the story) that they could not mark her as
definitely sunk because her bottom was still showing; but that did not deter
a certain dynamic personality at Bomber Command from grunting with
deep satisfaction to one of his subordinates when he heard the *Tirpitz* was
sunk, 'That's one in the eye for the Nautics!'

The incredible Cochrane took it all in his stride. At least on the surface.
They held a conference every morning at 5 Group to discuss the previous
night's operations, and the coming night's plans. Cochrane presided over
them, looking flintily over his half-moon glasses like Harris and the
morning after the raid, when he sat down, his staff officers thought that this
time they would see a break in the iron exterior. Cochrane glanced at his
minutes and said, 'Er . . . last night's raid. . . . Successful! *Tirpitz* sunk!
Now, about tonight's operations . . .'

CHAPTER 20

BACK FROM THE DEAD

After the excitement of the *Tirpitz* came anti-climax. Unbroken cloud lay over Europe for weeks, making high precision bombing impossible. 617 stood by constantly, were briefed hopefully a dozen times and then the cancellations came. Once they got into the air but were recalled.

Carey, Witherick and company arrived back, gloating over their taste of peacetime flesh-pots in Sweden but furious at missing the end of the *Tirpitz*. 'You might have waited for us, sir,' Witherick said aggrievedly to Tait. 'You *know* I always come back.'

Increasing sea losses testified to the fact that Germany's fleet of 'schnorkel' U-boats was increasing. For all the main force bombing, the U-boats found shelter in the massive pens and Cochrane switched 617 on to them again. They battered the pens at Ijmuiden (the port of Amsterdam) with six direct hits. Calder's Lancaster was badly hit by flak and he made an emergency landing at a nearer base. A fair-haired, keen-faced young Englishman, Calder was making a name for himself as a determined pilot. Joplin was hit in Knilan's old 'R Roger', struggled back to England but crashed near Woodhall, killing two of the crew. Calder led them on the next trip and they slammed some more 'tallboys' on top of the Ijmuiden pens, leaving a huge hole in the massive concrete roof.

Cochrane decided that Tait had done enough. Tait had four DSOs now and two DFCs – a record – and Cochrane did not want him to strain his luck too far. Shopping round for a new commander, he found no one with all the qualities he wanted till an air commodore heard the position was vacant and asked to be dropped in rank and given the job – a laudable request, as it meant stepping down from a highly-prized rank. This was Johnnie Fauquier, a Canadian, and a tough one, a thick-set, ex-bush pilot, who did not smile much (nor say much. With his curt voice he did not have to say much). Ten years older than most of them, he was as forceful as a steam-roller. The night he arrived there was a party to say farewell to the revered Tait and welcome the new man.

To put it mildly, 617's welcome to a new commander was exacting. They were, perhaps, a little above themselves, conscious of their lustre and jealous of trespass on it. It is a trait common to an elect corps, an inseparable if less tractable facet of the unique ardour that leads men to the corps and drives them on to the heights. It is the hand-maiden of achievement and often the mainspring of it. You find it among commandoes, business tycoons, geniuses, and sometimes in child delinquents. It is invaluable in a soldier and sometimes indecorous in a civilian. 617 had it. That was the first thing Fauquier found out.

Someone said, 'Sing a song or take your pants off' . . . their favourite way of puncturing the dignity of a high officer. Fauquier unhitched his pants imperturbably, and Witherick, secure in the legend of his immortality, cooled him off with a can of beer strategically aimed from the rear. Fauquier philosophically hitched up his pants and thus passed the test.

He had his revenge. Cochrane had told him when he took over, 'You've got to see 617 is kept up to the mark and stays as good as ever.' Fauquier saw to that. Feeling that the war was almost over, the crews had been in a mood to relax and were scandalized when Fauquier got them out of bed in the frosty early mornings for PT. Storms were sweeping over Europe and the runways were snowed up, so there was no flying. Fauquier gave them lectures instead, and then made them shovel snow off the runways.

On the last day of the year the weather eased and he led them on more serious work. Convoys had been streaming out of Oslo under cover of night as the Germans tried to move troops back from Norway to reinforce the crumbling fronts. Cochrane told them to unmask a convoy with flares and set about it. It was a bleak, black night, but they found the convoy and, lit by the floating flares, the convoy fanned out and scattered. The bombers chased them, but the ships zig-zagged all over the sea. 617 had never dealt with mobile targets before and cursed eloquently as they found they had not mastered the technique of positioning the flares. Fauquier and a couple of others found a cruiser and hunted her, only to see their bombs fall just too wide to be effective. The others all missed too and flew home in chastened mood, but cheered up considerably when they heard that the cruiser in her efforts to dodge the bombs had run on the rocks.

More days waiting for weather; more briefings, more cancellations, till 12 January, when they went to Bergen, in Norway, on the old campaign against U-boats. For the first time Fauquier flew a Mosquito to direct them and for the first time in months German fighters fell on them like a swarm of hornets. They got Pryor on their first strike and he went straight into the sea. Three of them lunged at Nicky Ross on the flank of the gaggle. Watts, next to him, saw the tracer flicking into the Lancaster and lumps flying off her. He wheeled to help him, but Ross was going down, slewing into a spiral with three engines smashed. Near the water he seemed to recover; the spiral stopped, the mad dive eased and the plane had almost flattened out when it abruptly vanished in a sheet of spray.

The fighters hammered Iveson too, set his port inner on fire and riddled his tailplane and rudder so that he had almost no fore-and-aft control. He was fighting to keep her flying, while his two gunners and the wireless operator baled out, and suddenly the fighters broke off the attack and vanished. They were not very resolute.

Heavy flak over Bergen crippled Castagnola and he had to jettison and turn for home. The rest took vengeance. Someone put a 'tallboy' squarely on the stern of a large ship and in two minutes she had blown up, rolled over and sunk. The rest got several direct hits on the pens.

Next morning Chiefy Powell was sadly typing out the casualty report on Nicky Ross (who had been on the squadron nearly a year – longer than any other pilot) when the door swung open and in walked Ross himself.

Powell gaped.

'Wotcher, Chiefy,' quoth the ghost. 'Home again!'

'Good God, sir! Where've you come from?'

'Air sea rescue picked us up. Bloody cold in that dinghy.' He sat on a corner of the desk and rattled on amiably about the details.

After some splutters Powell found speech. 'D'you know what I was doing when you walked in, sir? Typing your death notice!'

'Ar, hold it for a while, Chiefy,' said the cheerful Ross. 'You're a bit premature.'

Bad weather again. Weeks of it, with stand-by, briefings, cancellations, training and more training – and PT.

Meantime the first 'grand slam' was nearly ready. A thousand craftsmen had been working for months on the top-secret project and only a bare dozen of them knew what it was all about. In Sheffield the English Steel Corporation had spent weeks trying to find a steel that would stand up to the shock. They forged shells from all the steels they knew and fired them into concrete and steel till they found one that stood up to it, a secret formula of their own. Two firms in the country could cast the complicated casing, and for each bomb they had to build an individual concrete covered core to the most precise ten-thousandth of an inch, position it meticulously inside a sand-surfaced mould, pour the molten steel in and wait for two days for it to cool before they could chip the core away. The 10-ton casting then travelled a hundred miles for machining.

It puzzled the workmen. One man watching the shining brute said he thought it was a midget submarine. The executives labelled it officially as a 'boiler', but that fooled no one. Around the Sheffield pubs the men sometimes referred to it surreptitiously as 'the big bastard'. It was a devil to handle. The Army had nearly all the cranes, and the firms had to make special trailers for it because the railways did not have the facilities to handle it. At the filling factory they built a special cradle for it, stood it inside on its nose and built a high platform so they could pour in the tons of explosive a bucketful at a time. They tried thirty different types of fuse before they picked one they thought would stand up to the shock of impact.

Like the 'tallboy', 'grand slam's' tail had offset aerodynamic fins to make it spin so fast in falling that the gyroscopic effect would stop it toppling as it shuddered through the sonic barrier. When the tail was put on 'grand slam' would be 25 feet 6 inches long. At its thickest part it was 3 feet 10 inches in diameter, and the finished bomb was to weigh just over 22,000 lb. It was such a difficult undertaking that they could produce no dummies for normal tests; they hoped to have one prototype to drop before they used it on business.

But that was a few weeks ahead yet.

The German fighter force was nearly spent now, making it possible for 617's inadequately armed Lancasters to penetrate deeper and deeper against the enemy by day. They carried on with 'tallboys' against the U-boat pens, slathering the concrete strongholds at Poortershaven, Ijmuiden, Hamburg and the monster at Farge, near Bremen, losing two or three crews but getting literally dozens of direct hits on the massive roofs.

Designed for earth penetration and dropped from less than half the prescribed height, the 'tallboys' never did quite penetrate the thickest of the concrete before exploding, but did almost as well. As on the Brest pens, they knifed deeply in and then blew right through the ceiling.

At Hamburg they brought down a thousand tons of concrete that crushed two U-boats inside and crippled six others. They smashed servicing gear, killed dozens of men and created panic.

At Ijmuiden they brought down 13,000 tons of concrete over hundreds of feet of roof and wall (near misses did a lot of that by shock wave). Much the same things happened at Bergen and Poortershaven. At Bergen a near miss sank two U-boats and lofted another one on to the dock wall.

Congestion in these ports and pens had been growing steadily worse as the Allies overran Germany's other bases. Now, after the bombing, it was lapsing into chaos, U-boat raids were dwindling and the morale of the men who built, serviced and sailed them was decaying.

His armies poised for the jump over the Rhine, Eisenhower asked the Air Forces for an all-out assault on German communications to sever the front from the rest of Germany. Now that the Dortmund Ems Canal was permanently drained the vulnerable points were the railway bridges, and most vital of these was the Bielefeld Viaduct, not far from Bremen, main link between the Wehrmacht defending the arsenal of the Ruhr and the great centres of north-west Germany. The idea was to starve the front of men and materials and split the country into 'islands' that could be taken one by one.

Three thousand tons of bombs had already been aimed at the Bielefeld Viaduct; the earth for a mile around it was torn into overlapping craters, but the 75-foot arches of the viaduct still firmly bridged the marshes for the trains running south. The light-case bombs of the main bomber forces were not powerful enough to do more than chip it. Cochrane turned 617 on to it, and so began the battle of Bielefeld.

They took off with their 'tallboys' one morning, but found the viaduct under ten-tenths cloud and brought them back. Next day they tried once more but again found unbroken cloud. Days later the cloud had cleared; they flew back to Bielefeld, found it reasonably clear and a few minutes later the viaduct was hidden under smoke as the 'tallboys' crashed round it. Half an hour later, when the smoke lifted, a recce aircraft found the viaduct still there. 'Tallboy' craters lay in its shadow, but the viaduct was no rotund target like a bull's-eye or a U-boat pen. From 18,000 feet it was almost indistinguishably threadlike. It was like trying to stick a dart in a line.

They waited on the weather and tried again a few days later, but once more found it under cloud. Doggedly they went back a fifth time and turned away in fuming frustration once more. There seemed to be something diabolical about the persistence of the cloud that shielded it.

That night two heavy trailers rolled round the perimeter track to the bomb dump carrying the first two 'grand slams'. In the morning armourers trollied them out and slowly winched them up into Fauquier's and Calder's Lancasters, specially modified in readiness for this day. They had the most powerful Merlin engines, the fuselages, undercarriages and main beams of the bomb bays had been strengthened and the bomb doors taken off (they could not have closed round the great girth of 'Grand Slam').

'Grand slam' had never been tested. There had not been time. Only one other 'grand slam' existed, and that very morning a Lancaster was going to drop it over the range in the New Forest. Group was waiting for that, and also for the cloud to clear.

Just before noon Met. reported the cloud over Germany rolling away. As Fauquier was briefing his crews a phone message reached Group from the New Forest: 'The beast went off all right!'

CHAPTER 21

'GRAND SLAM'

At one o'clock 617's engines were bursting into life round the field. Fauquier was running up his engines, testing his magnetos, when there was a crash from the starboard inner and the propeller jerked to a grinding halt as it seized. Fauquier, muttering with frustration, knew the aircraft would never get off the ground on three engines. There was only one thing to do . . . borrow Calder's aircraft. The fact that he might then be shot down instead of Calder never even occurred to him, and would not have worried him if it had. He scuttled out of his plane and went haring across the field.

Calder saw the running figure, shouting and waving hands in urgent signals, guessed what had happened and cracked his throttles open. The Lancaster lurched forward and, with the small figure sprinting despairingly in the rear, rolled thunderously down the runway, picking up speed till it lifted heavily over the far fence on the way to drop the world's biggest bomb.

The 'tallboy'-armed gaggle fell in behind, watching Calder's wings in wonder and alarm. On the ground a Lancaster has no perceptible dihedral, the wings spread in a flat, straight line, but Calder's wings now were a graceful arc, curving up at the tips as they took the strain of the 10-tonner. Those underneath could see the great missile hanging in the bomb bays where the bomb doors used to be.

The sky was clear of cloud; they skirted the flak at Bremen and ten minutes later picked up the line of the viaduct threading across the marshes. Calder headed in, the laden bomber thrusting smoothly through the bumps till Calder felt her bound up as the 'grand slam' slipped away from the grips.

Wheeling away, they watched it drop like a silver shark, slowly starting to spin as its nose dipped lower and it picked up speed, lunging towards the viaduct. It fell for some thirty-five seconds and from far above the sharpest eyes picked up the squirt of mud as it speared into the marsh 30 yards from the foot of one of the arches.

Eleven seconds later the marsh seemed to split and a vast core of mud and smoke vomited up, blotting out 500 feet of the viaduct. In the next seconds 'tallboy' explosions erupted along both sides of the viaduct. Calder peeled off to try and see what had happened; slowly the mud settled, the wind wafted the smoke away, and as the target appeared through the veils Calder saw that the viaduct looked like a Roman ruin. Seven massive arches over a hundred yards were missing.

He could see almost no collapsed masonry underneath and thought for a moment that the bomb had blasted the arches into dust, but could not believe that possible.

Later they found that the one 'grand slam' had completely vindicated Barnes Wallis's theory that a near miss could be more effective than a direct hit. It had penetrated about a hundred feet, and the shock wave had shivered the arches to cracking point; the explosion had produced a near 'camouflet', blasting an enormous subterranean cavity underneath, and robbed of their foundation in the mud, the weakened arches had collapsed into the abyss. It was the perfect trapdoor effect, the 'hangman's drop' that Wallis had planned in 1939.

A recce photograph showed an enormous crater which Wallis described as 'exquisite'. Cochrane wired 617. 'You certainly made a proper mess of it this time and incidentally added another page to your history by being the first squadron to drop the biggest bomb on Germany. Good work. Keep up the training. We can't afford to put them in the wrong place.'

In the next few days trailers delivered several more 'grand slams' to the bomb dump, and on 19 March Fauquier got his delayed chance to drop one. The target was in historic territory for 617, the Arnsberg Bridge, a long masonry viaduct a few miles north of the Moehne Dam. Five Lancasters carried 'grand slams', and the other fourteen had 'tallboys'. The first bomb was a direct hit on the viaduct, and the rest, including Fauquier's 'grand slam', went down into the centre of the smoke that gushed up. When the smoke lifted, the central spans were a pile of rubble in the river bed.

Two days later they went to the Arbergen Bridge, near Bremen. Flak got a direct hit on Gumbley's aircraft on the run-up and he went straight down in flames. Price had to swerve out of the way of the falling aircraft, marring his bombing run, but he straightened up and his bomb aimer, Pilot Officer Chance – by a very good chance indeed – lobbed his 'tallboy' a direct hit on the viaduct. There was one more direct hit and a lot of near misses. Two piers collapsed, another one was thrown 15 feet out of alignment and earthquake shock threw a span off another pier. Target destroyed.

Next day they went to the Nienburg Bridge, near Bremen, over which the Germans were taking oil to the front. It was not heavily defended, so Fauquier evolved a new plan to try and save some of the precious earthquake bombs. On the way up to the target he ordered four aircraft to start their bombing runs and told the others to circle nearby and wait for orders in case the first four missed. It was an unprecedented idea, and the very fact that Fauquier considered it possible speaks eloquently of their phenomenal accuracy. He himself dived low to one side of the target to watch.

The results were fantastic. The four Lancasters made a steady run in loose formation and bombed almost in the same second. Fauquier saw the first two bombs hit simultaneously (one of them a 'grand slam') on each end of the bridge. The bridge span lifted bodily and still intact into the air, seemed to hang there a second, and in that very moment a third bomb hit it fair and square in the middle. When the smoke had cleared there was no visible sign of the bridge whatsoever and the squadron turned for home, taking their fifteen remaining bombs with them.

Fauquier said when he landed, 'Hell, I'd hate to have to do *that* again to prove it'.

The Germans had one last railway bridge still serving the Ruhr; it was also near Bremen, and 617 went there early next morning. The first three bombs (from 16,000 feet) hit almost in the same second, all direct hits (including Fauquier's and Calder's 'grand slams'). The next two were very near misses, followed by what seemed to be one more direct hit before smoke smothered the ruins.

(Kehrl, head of the German planning office, said later that chaotic communications was responsible for 90 per cent of the decline in German war production in the last three months of the war.)

If Wallis's big bombs had been available earlier (with the aircraft to carry them) the Germans would probably not have lasted as long as they did. Their industry and transport would have been disrupted earlier, just as Wallis had forecast in 1939, though the RAF might have suffered sore losses battling through the fighters by day deep into Germany in the earlier stages, as the Americans did.

As there were no worthwhile bridges left, 617 went back on the U-boat pens. At Farge, near Bremen, 7,000 slaves had sweated for two years to build the biggest concrete structure in the world, 1,450 feet long, over 300 feet wide and 75 feet high, a staggering monument to Hitler's ruthless obstinacy. The first design was for a roof 16 feet thick, but after 617 had visited the Brest pens Hitler had put on another thousand slaves, and in March, 1945, the roof was 23 feet of solid reinforced concrete and the pens were just ready for use.

617 paid their call on 27 March and sank two 'grand slams' deep in the roof which exploded right through, making holes 20 feet across and bringing down thousands of tons of concrete. Several 'tallboys', direct hits and near misses, cracked the monster and undermined it and the pens were never used.

It was hard to find good targets now till a recce plane brought a report that Germany's last pocket battleship, the *Lutzow*, was sheltering in Swinemunde, in the Baltic, deep into enemy territory towards the Russian Front, where fighters could be expected. 617 slogged up there on 13 April (not an encouraging date) only to find it smothered under cloud. They went back two days later; ten-tenths cloud again. By this time it was obvious they were after the *Lutzow*. Fauquier guessed the German fighters would be alerted and he asked for, and got, an escort of long-range fighters. Next day they went back with the fighters and found the target clear but the flak waiting for them.

They picked out the *Lutzow* far below, a microbe on the water beside the quay, and as they turned on her the flak burst among them savagely, predicting deadly accurately on the unwavering formation. Clusters of puffs blotched the patch of sky in which they moved, so that nearly every one of the eighteen bombers was hit and holes opened in wings and fuselages as shrapnel ripped through. Gordon and Gavin both lost engines and started to lag. A heavy shell got a direct hit on Powell; his port wing folded up and the big plane spun down dragging a tail of flame like a comet. One parachute came out.

Then the gaggle was peeling off out of the flak as the bombs went down. Three bombs hit close together, straddling the ship, one in the alley between the bows and the quay. Other bombs vanished into the spray and smoke that enveloped her.

They flew back unmolested and next morning were stood down completely. After the flak only two of their aircraft were serviceable, and the ground crews were toiling over the others, riveting on patches. The aircrews were content to relax and await news of the *Lutzow*. The recce aircraft landed with photographs, and such was the squadron's self-confidence that a howl of incredulity went up as they saw the *Lutzow* still by the quay, apparently untouched. The recce pilot swore there was no mistake. He had flown right over her, and there, indubitably, she lay, decks clearly visible.

It was not for another two days they found out that *Lutzow* had sunk as far as the sea-bed would let her. The near miss by the bows had torn out her bottom; the dock was not very deep, but *Lutzow* was finished, lying on the mud.

(Someone in the Navy claimed she was not *really* sunk because her decks were still above water.)

As soon as their aircraft were repaired 617 took some 'grand slams' and 'tallboys' to Heligoland and plastered half the island fortress's big guns. Next day they went back and plastered the other half, ending Germany's mastery of the approaches to the north-west ports.

Cochrane went to take over Transport Command, which, now the shooting was nearly over, was coming into its own. The new 5 Group AOC told Fauquier he was grounded because he did not want him killed in the last moments. The tough Canadian had just finished his third tour and had won three DSOs and a DFC.

The remnants of the Wehrmacht were said to be pulling back into Hitler's 'Southern Redoubt' in Bavaria, where Berchtesgaden lay. It seemed that there was no more work for 617 till someone remembered that Hitler had recently told his Party chiefs, 'I have read these days in the British Press that they intend to destroy my country house. I almost regret that this has not been done, for what I call my own is not more valuable than my compatriots possess.'

Eager to ease his conscience, 617 flew to Berchtesgaden, hoping that if Hitler was there they might bury him in his house. As the world knows, Hitler was in Berlin, but it made no difference because the land was deep under snow and Berchtesgaden merged with the white hills and low cloud so that the squadron could not pick it out. However, they identified the nearby SS barracks, home of Hitler's bodyguard, and flattened them with four 'tallboys' and a selection of 1,000-pounders, and that, with Hitler away, was probably more useful than laying their eggs on the Eagle's Nest.

That was 617's last operation, or perhaps not quite the last. Fauquier went to Germany on his own and by chance received from a beaten enemy a somehow symbolic surrender in the name of the squadron.

The Admiralty, while admitting 617's accuracy on the U-boat pens, would not believe that their big bombs had gone through the concrete roofs. Harris told Fauquier to go over and see, and he flew to a Tactical Air Force base just south of Hamburg. In the morning, with another group captain and an interpreter, he drove off in a jeep for the Hamburg dock area on the understanding that Hamburg was to surrender at ten o'clock that morning.

Driving through Hamburg they wondered why they saw no signs of Allied troops and why German soldiers stared at them, but it never occurred to them that Hamburg had not, in fact, surrendered and no British troops, apart from themselves, had reached the city.

They pulled up in the shadow of the great pens, walked through a side door and stood fascinated by the cavernous ruin inside. Several of the big bombs had punched through the roof, and twisted metal and the rubble of fallen concrete littered the place. They were looking soberly down on two crushed U-boats sunk in one of the docks when they became aware that they were not alone. A Nazi sailor stood behind them. He saluted. Would the officers be good enough to come and see his commanding officer? They followed him to the other side of the pens and stopped in surprise to see 200 German sailors lined up. The commanding officer marched up, clicked his heels and saluted. He would like, he said, to surrender the Hamburg dock area.

Fauquier was most embarrassed. He did not know that Hamburg was still in German hands. Neither, as it happened, did the German officer. The pens were out of touch by phone with Hamburg city, and that is the only reason he was surrendering to Fauquier instead of Fauquier to him.

The interpreter rather tactlessly told the German that Fauquier had led the raid which had smashed the pens, a most disconcerting *gaffe*. Fauquier waited warily for the avenging wrath and was astonished when the German clicked his heels, bowed to him and said cordially 'My congratulations on a very good raid.'

Fauquier, not knowing quite what to do, clicked his own heels, bowed back and said, 'Thank you.'

The German said that he had been in the pens at the time with a lot of his men and everyone had been killed except him. He was the sole survivor because he had happened to be in the steel-enclosed overhead crane. He invited them to lunch in his mess. The mess was a literal 'mess' in a crazily-tilted cabin of a half-sunken cargo ship. They followed him on board and lunched on dry biscuits spread with sausage meat while the German told them their bombs were rocket-propelled to break through the concrete roof of the pens. Fauquier did not enlighten him.

Totally unaware of the protocol of surrender, Fauquier got the Germans to pile all their small arms in the jeep and drove off back through the city.

And then on 8 May it was all over and the 150 pilots, navigators, bomb aimers, wireless operators, engineers and gunners realized they were going to have the same chance as ordinary people of walking down the years to a more natural death.

But no. Not quite. 617 and one other squadron were detailed for 'Tiger Force', to be the RAF's contribution to the strategic bombing of Japan. They were to fly from Okinawa and drop their 'tallboys' and 'grand slams' on the bridges connecting the Kyushu to the main Japanese island of Honshu to cut off reinforcements when the Americans invaded Kyushu, as they planned, in January, 1946. They were all set to go when the two bombs so much deadlier than 'Grand Slam' fell on Hiroshima and Nagasaki and Japan surrendered.

'Hell!' said the thwarted volunteers. 'They must have heard we were coming.'

EPILOGUE

617 is still flying, but all that is left of the old days now is the squadron number and the tradition. The men who won over 150 decorations and made the tradition are scattered, and many of them are dead.

Gibson is dead. When he came back from America he toyed with the idea of going into politics but soon perceived there is a little more to politics than wisdom and sincerity, so he politely declined the prospect of directorships and elected to stay in the RAF.

On 11 July 1944, he was disconsolately flying a desk when Micky Martin flew over in a Mosquito, and Gibson eyed the little plane wistfully. Martin took him up for a couple of circuits and then Gibson flew it himself; he said when he landed, 'I'm fed up with sitting on my tail. I'm going back on ops.' He worried his seniors till they reluctantly agreed, and a few weeks later Gibson took off in a Mosquito for one last raid to act as master bomber of 5 Group on a factory at Rheydt, near the Ruhr. He guided the bombing, and when it was over they heard his voice on the R/T saying, 'O.K., chaps. That's fine. Now beat it home.'

No one knows exactly what happened after that. They think Gibson may have been hit by flak. He crashed into a low hill in Holland sixty miles from Rheydt on the way home, and the Dutch buried him there.

The Moehne Dam has been repaired, the lake refilled, but the valley below is littered with twisted, rusted girders and lumps of concrete and the earth still looks as though a giant's rake had scoured it. Where Himmelpforten stood the foundations still lie round the ruins of the church. Set among them is a rough wooden cross with neither name nor inscription. As far as sixty miles away the surviving villagers found the church's chalice, christening font, crucifix and some of the stones, and less than a mile away stands the new church of Porta Coeli built by the villagers. Around the altar is a Latin inscription, restrained and unmalicious: 'The wreckage of the church of Himmelpforten, destroyed by flood in 1943, served six years later to build this new altar and this new Porta Coeli.'

Martin distinguished himself as a night-fighter pilot, winning another bar to his DFC. After the war he shepherded the squadron of Vampires in the first jet flights across the Atlantic, nursing them skilfully through foul weather that nearly brought them to disaster. Then he broke the London-Capetown and return record in a Mosquito and added an AFC to his two DSOs and three RFCs. That year he was awarded the Britannia Trophy, Britain's premier aviation award.

Cheshire's forecast about Martin and his potential came true. As I revise this in 1969, Micky Martin is now an Air Vice-Marshal in command of the

RAF's biggest Group. But still not far under the brass hat and braid lies the same old blithe and mettlesome spirit. He had married the girl, Wendy, who was so reluctant to lunch with him after the dams raid, and under her tuition has become a very accomplished painter in oils. (At the dawn of 1971 Martin was promoted again and knighted, becoming Air Marshal Sir Harold Martin, KCB, DSO, DFC, AFC.)

Cochrane is now an Air Chief Marshal, three times knighted and second in command of the RAF. Now that the pressure of war is off his austerity has thawed, except when he finds inefficiency, and then he is his old incisive self, still probably the best brain in the Air Force.

Not far from Whitehall, Willie Tait has also been patiently at an RAF desk. Usually he wears mufti and a bowler, and looks deceptively shy and neat until someone blunders; then the lips still tighten into that prim, pursed look that Cochrane once called his 'mule face'.

Fauquier retired with his old rank of air commodore and is now head of a big company in Toronto. His business, oddly enough, is building concrete structures. A change from knocking them down.

Cheshire! Cheshire had a variety of ideas for after the war, most of them as original as himself. One was the 'Modern *Mayflower*', to take picked comrades on a chartered ship and settle on an island. Another was to fly orchids from the Caribbean to New York, and another to grow mushrooms in disused tunnels. He had another scheme for forming a company with Martin, Shannon and Munro for experimental aviation. Cheshire said they might finish up flying to the moon, and they looked sideways at him, though it seems now that he was not looking impossibly far ahead after all.

Then the Prime Minister sent him to the Pacific, and he flew in an American plane as Attlee's personal representative to watch the atom bomb fall on Nagasaki. He came back, resigned from the Air Force and collected a band of unsettled ex-servicemen to form a communal group which he called '*Vade in Pacem*' (May you walk in peace) in an old house in Hampshire left him by an aunt. Cheshire's health broke down; he went to Canada to recover, and for eight months in a forest hamlet in the Rockies the intellectual VC delivered groceries, cut wood and collected corpses for the local undertaker.

He sold his clothes to pay his fare back to England, arriving in Hampshire at Christmas, 1947, to find his settlement breaking up and £18,000 of debts on his head. He sold his furniture to pay his more pressing debts, and was sitting alone in the empty house when he heard of an old man dying of cancer nearby; he had put his age back fifteen years to join the RAF in the war and now had no one to help him. Cheshire borrowed a bed and took him in, nursed him, cooked for him, scrubbed the floors, carried the bedpans, washed the old man's pyjamas and lived off the garden. He heard of a bed-ridden woman of ninety-five with no one to help her, borrowed another bed and took her in.

The man was dying, and Cheshire was sitting with him in the middle of the night when he stopped breathing. There was a religious book on the bed, and Cheshire picked it up and started to read. When he had finished it he went to see the local Roman Catholic priest and four months later joined the Catholic Church.

Meantime, of its own volition, the house had grown into a hospital. Incurables kept knocking on the door and he took them in. The place had a strange spirit about it; bed-ridden patients helped by sewing and darning; a few who could walk put rags under their feet and shuffled over the floors to scrub them. Nurses and students came down to help in their spare time, and several men and women gave up their jobs for the privilege of living and working in the place. They had nearly forty patients and no money but somehow kept going.

Cheshire sold some cottages on the property, and some time about the middle of 1949 found he was free of debt. I've asked him several times how he paid it all off, and he always says, 'I can't really explain it. Things just seemed to work out.' He did, in fact, develop a fatalistic attitude that if he did not worry things would be all right. Peculiarly enough, they were.

A man called Cowie did his books, and one Wednesday he went to Cheshire and said, 'Look, we're ten pounds short for our bills on Friday. We can't meet them.'

'This isn't Friday,' Cheshire said. 'See me about it then. Something will turn up.'

On Friday a letter arrived with £12 in notes from a woman in London. No one had been in touch with her.

Weeks later they were about £10 short again on the Wednesday. On the Friday a letter arrived from the same woman with another £12. Again no one had told her. The same thing happened once more a few weeks later.

Cowie, who has no faith (he is an agnostic) says that sort of thing kept happening. After a while, in spite of himself, he developed some of Cheshire's fatalism, and once, just before Christmas, when they had debts of £40 to pay and no money in the bank, Cowie went nervously to Cheshire and said: 'I've sent off those cheques for the full amount. I only hope something turns up'.

Next morning's post brought a cheque for £41.

The renown of the place spread until regular benefactors shouldered the burden of paying some of the bills. That left Cheshire with time on his hands, and it was Sir Ralph Cochrane who found him a job. A singularly appropriate one – working for Barnes Wallis.

Later Cheshire felt the call to go with his Homes for the Needy and since then he has established them, with the help of the Church, in various quarters of the world. At last he has found his niche – a full and satisfying one.

At Weybridge, Wallis is the white-haired patriarch, pink-faced, gentle and abstracted as ever, an old-fashioned doyen with new-fangled vision browsing over the same old drawing board, still getting outlandish ideas which unaccountably work.

Strange about Wallis. He designed and constructed the only successful British airship during the 'Thirties. Then he designed the Wellesley bomber which captured the world's long distance flight record. Then he designed the Wellington bomber, which was the mainstay of the RAF Bomber Command until 1953 and was still operational into the 'Sixties. When I was researching this book back in 1950, I can remember Barnes Wallis enthusiastically showing me his design for a 'swing-wing' aircraft. It was turned down by the British Government but later taken up by the Americans and French!! At this moment of revision, 1969, he is working on a radical aircraft wing structure that will enable an aircraft to fly at 18,000 miles an hour. But the only official recognition he ever received was a CBE after the dams raid. About as mean as one could get. In early 1969, some twenty-six years too late, the British Government belatedly offered him a knighthood. He accepted without much feeling one way or the other and the now Sir Barnes retains his same kindly and gentle attitude to the world.

After the war his friends urged him to claim a reward for his wartime inventions, but he said that if he did he would never touch such money for himself. I asked him why and he said: 'My dear chap, go and read your Bible, turn up Samuel II, Chapter 23. You probably haven't got a Bible so I'll tell you this story about David.

'He was hiding in the cave of Adullam after the Philistines had seized Bethlehem, and in his anguish he said, "Oh that one would give me drink of the water of the well of Bethlehem, which is by the gate!" Now the three mighty men who were his lieutenants were with him, and I'm dashed if they didn't fight their way through the Philistine lines and draw a goatskin of water out of the well by the gate. They fought their way back and took the water to David in the cave, but when they told him how they had got it he would not drink it. They asked him why, and he said:

'"Is not this the blood of the men that went in jeopardy of their lives?"'

THE END

(Just after this book was first published the Royal Commission on Awards to Inventors granted Barnes Wallis £10,000 for his wartime work. He immediately put it into a fund to help educate the sons and daughters of men who died serving with the Royal Air Force.)